The Good Housekeeping

Illustrated

Microwave

Cookbook

The Good Housekeeping

Illustrated
Microwave
Cookbook

Edited by
Joyce A. Kenneally,
Director, Microwave Cookery
& Food Appliances
Good Housekeeping Institute

Hearst Books   New York

GOOD HOUSEKEEPING

Editor-in-Chief   John Mack Carter

Institute Director   Amy Barr

Microwave Cookery & Food Appliances

Director   Joyce A. Kenneally

Associate   Sharon Franke

Special recipe consultant   Rebecca Marshall

A DORLING KINDERSLEY BOOK

Editorial Director   Amy Carroll

Art Director   Denise Brown

Managing Editor   Jeni Wright

Designers   Sue Storey
Sally Powell
Sally Hibbard

Editors   Elizabeth Wolf-Cohen
Susan Thompson
Jillian Somerscales
Irene Lyford
Marian Broderick
Beverly Le Blanc

Published by The Reader's Digest Association, Inc., with permission of
Hearst Books, an affiliate of William Morrow and Company, Inc.

Library of Congress Catalog Card Number: 89-084254
ISBN: 0-688-08473-7
Printed in the United States of America

Foreword

A new kind of cooking has taken America by storm. In busy households all across the country, and in many other parts of the world as well, the microwave oven is becoming the cooking appliance of choice. That's what this book is all about. Whether you are a beginning microwave cook or an experienced one, The Good Housekeeping Illustrated Microwave Cookbook is the book you can turn to for everything you'll need to know. It's chock-full of delicious recipes, cooking tips, and how to's, plus a wealth of understandable information about microwave ovens, cooking, and techniques, all to guarantee perfectly cooked food.

A beautiful color picture index of all the recipes is found at the beginning of the book, organized according to the time required for preparation and cooking. This makes recipe selection and meal planning even easier since you can see exactly how the food will look and how long it will take before making your selection.

Next, we show you step-by-step how to prepare the recipes. We illustrate the cooking techniques you will use, list the equipment needed and exactly how long the recipe will take from start to finish.

We know you're interested in good nutrition, so each recipe includes not only the calorie count, but a thorough nutritional analysis as well.

Menus are included to show how to combine recipes for everyday and special occasion meals. And a plan of action is included with each menu so you will know exactly what to prepare when, and how much time will be needed.

Many of these recipes were developed by my staff and me for the pages of Good Housekeeping magazine. Others were developed just for this book by our cookbook consultant, Rebecca Marshall. All have been thoroughly tested in a wide variety of 600-, 650-, and 700-watt microwave ovens. Because time is of the essence, we have made them as simple as possible and kept cookware to a minimum.

We hope, through the pages of this first Good Housekeeping microwave cookbook, you will discover, as we have, that microwave cooking is fun and that it is possible to cook almost anything – well!

Joyce Kenneally

Joyce Kenneally
Director, Microwave Cookery & Food Appliances, Good Housekeeping Institute

Contents

How to Use the Book

The Good Housekeeping Illustrated Microwave Cookbook contains everything today's cook needs to know to make eye-catching and delicious meals in the microwave for everyday and special occasions. The book is divided into three major sections – *Microwave Know-How*, *The Color Index*, and *The Recipes* – with problem-solving *Questions and Answers* and an *Index* at the back. The recipe section also contains tips on preparing ingredients and ideas for serving and presentation, plus full-color menus for entertaining.

Even if you are an experienced microwave cook, it is a good idea to read through *Microwave Know-How* first, as the information in this section clearly illustrates Good Housekeeping's tried-and-tested techniques. Then browse through *The Color Index* to choose those dishes that suit your schedule and meal plans. Finally, turn to the listed page in the appropriate chapter of *The Recipes* and follow step-by-step instructions and color photographs for culinary success.

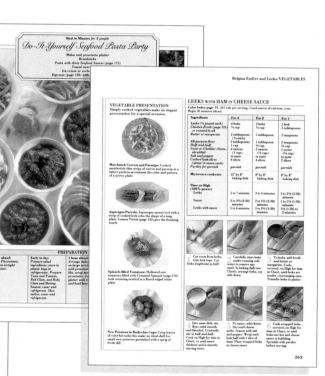

Microwave Know-How
This introductory chapter illustrates the cookware and cooking techniques you'll need to turn out attractive and well-prepared food. Also included are cook's tips for using the microwave in conjunction with conventional cooking appliances, and for entertaining, as well as advice on taking care of your microwave.

The Color Index
In this section you will find photographs of over 500 specially created recipes in menu order, and organized according to the time required for preparation and cooking – under 30 minutes, 30 to 60 minutes, and over 1 hour. Captions describe the dishes in detail, inform you how many servings they make, and direct you to the pages where the recipes appear in the book.

The Recipes
Among over 500 triple-tested step-by-step recipes are more than 170 key recipes. These are fully illustrated and, where applicable, are written for 4, 2, and 1 servings. Each is accompanied by its calorie count and nutritional information. You'll also find explanations and illustrations throughout for preparation and serving techniques, including handling ingredients, types of equipment, and garnishes. There is also a wide selection of menus for such special occasions as dinners, buffets, and parties, each photographed in color and accompanied by a preparation timetable.

Microwave Know-How

All About Microwave Ovens and Microwaving

Microwave ovens offer many choices, so you will be certain to find one just right for you. **Countertop ovens** are the most popular. To save space, some models can be installed under a cabinet, built into, or mounted on, a wall. An **over-the-range microwave oven** with built-in ventilation and light takes the place of a range hood. Another option, a **Hi-low oven**, is an all-in-one unit that features an eye-level microwave oven above a gas or electric range. A **convection microwave oven** can be used as a convection oven, a microwave oven, or with the two methods together. It's like having three ovens in one. There has been some confusion about convection ovens because consumers do not know what they are. It's really quite simple: A convection oven is a thermal oven like a conventional electric oven, but it has a fan to circulate the hot air so it cooks more quickly than a conventional oven. It browns and crisps foods when baking, roasting, and broiling.

Microwave ovens are available in a variety of sizes. **Full-size ovens** (1.1 to 1.6 cubic feet) are ideal for families or anyone who entertains a lot because they are roomy enough for large cookware and bulky foods. **Mid-size ovens** (.8 to 1 cubic foot) are a good compromise when you need a fair amount of cooking space but don't have the room for a full-size model. **Compact ovens** (.6 to .7 cubic foot) and **sub-compact ovens** (.4 to .5 cubic foot) are perfect for cooking for one or two, or to use as a second or backup oven. **Multi-use ovens** are a space-saving type of countertop or under-the-cabinet oven. They perform the functions of several appliances – a microwave oven, a conventional oven, and a toaster oven all in one.

MICROWAVE WATTAGE AND POWER

A microwave oven's output wattage tells you the amount of microwave power available for cooking. Oven wattages range from 400 to 720 watts. Higher-wattage ovens (600 to 720 watts) cook faster than lower-wattage ovens (400 to 500 watts). The most popular oven wattage is 650, and all the microwave recipes in this book have been developed for cooking in 600- to 700-watt ovens. With a lower wattage oven, everything takes longer to cook and it is necessary to make adjustments in cooking times.

Variable power levels let you adjust the cooking power to get better, more even results. This is accomplished by cycling the microwave power on or off at various intervals to achieve different percentages of full power. Models are available with High power only (just for reheating) or with up to 10 power levels. Four or five levels are adequate to cook most foods.

A Defrost setting is an essential feature for defrosting foods.

MICROWAVE FEATURES

Microwaves are distributed in the oven in a variety of ways. An oven may have a stirrer fan, rotating antenna, or turntable, all designed for even cooking of food. Some ovens have both a stirrer and a turntable; others feature a turntable that can be switched off or removed.

Electronic touch controls are more accurate than mechanical dial-type controls. They are easy to use, and greatly expand the oven's functions.

Automatic programs eliminate guesswork and are particularly helpful to cooks new to microwaving. All that is necessary is to enter the food category, desired doneness, and weight or amount. The oven then automatically selects the correct time and power levels to cook or defrost. Some models have sensors to monitor humidity, vapor, or heat given off by food, and the oven uses this information to calculate precise cooking times.

"Push-button magic" can include pads marked with standard food items, a double-quantity key that automatically increases the cooking time for twice the amount of food, and reheat sensors labeled "refrigerator," "freezer," or "room temperature" for no-guess warming up.

A temperature probe is another popular feature; it works like a thermometer. The probe is inserted into the food and the desired temperature is set. When that temperature is reached, the oven turns off automatically.

HOW TO TEST FOR WATTAGE

If you do not know the wattage of your microwave, here is a simple way to determine what it is:

1. Fill a 4-cup microwave-safe glass measure with 4 cups tap water.
2. Record the temperature of the water.
3. Place the water-filled measure in the microwave and heat on High (100% power) 2 minutes.
4. Record the temperature of the heated water.
5. Subtract the first water temperature from the second, then multiply the resulting figure by 19.5. The result will be the approximate wattage output.

Some microwave ovens have turntables that help ensure even cooking of food.

A temperature probe turns the oven off when desired temperature is reached.

HOW MICROWAVE OVENS WORK

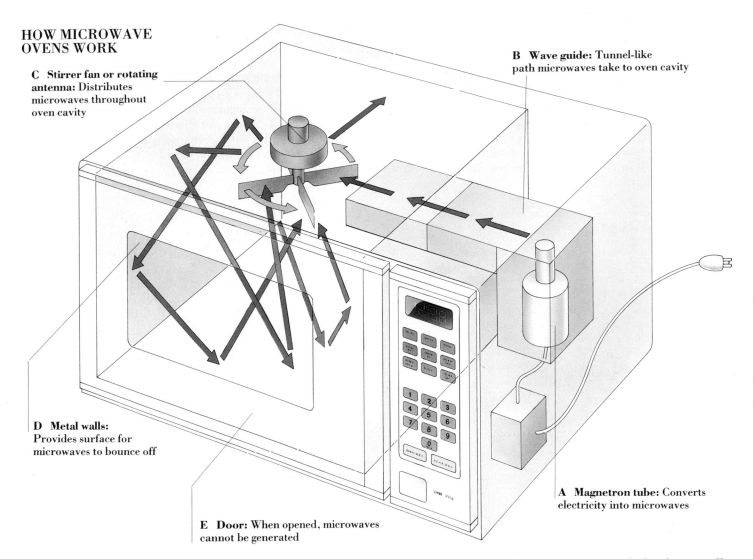

C Stirrer fan or rotating antenna: Distributes microwaves throughout oven cavity

B Wave guide: Tunnel-like path microwaves take to oven cavity

D Metal walls: Provides surface for microwaves to bounce off

A Magnetron tube: Converts electricity into microwaves

E Door: When opened, microwaves cannot be generated

Microwaves are high-frequency, electro-magnetic waves, similar to radio waves. When a microwave oven is turned on, microwaves are generated by the magnetron tube (A), which converts household electricity into microwaves. It's a little like having a miniature broadcasting station in your oven.

Microwaves travel from the magnetron through a tunnel-like wave guide (B) and enter the oven cavity through one or two openings at the top, bottom or sides. A stirrer fan or rotating antenna (C) distributes microwaves throughout the oven's cavity. Never operate an empty microwave; if food isn't present to absorb the microwaves, the oven may be damaged.

Because microwaves cannot penetrate metal; they bounce off the oven's metal walls (D) and penetrate the food from all directions to a depth of up to 1½ inches. They don't cause any structural or chemical change in food molecules; they simply cause water, fat, and sugar molecules in food to vibrate about 2½ billion times per second, producing heat from friction. The center of the food is cooked by transference of heat (conduction), as in conventional cooking.

When the oven is turned off, or the door (E) is opened, microwaves cannot be generated and none remain inside, just as when you turn off your radio the sound stops.

MICROWAVE TIMINGS

Most of our recipes give a range of microwave-cooking times, for instance, "3 to 4 minutes," because we develop them for ovens of 600 to 700 watts. The longer time is for 600-watt ovens and the shorter time is for 700-watt ovens. To avoid overcooking, choose the shorter time, then check for doneness (page 26). Continue cooking for the longer cooking time, if necessary, then check again for doneness.

POWER LEVELS

High	100% power
Medium-High	70% power
Medium	50% power
Medium-Low	30% power
Low	10% power.

Among manufacturers there is no standard language for power levels. The recipes in this book, however, all use the scale on the left:

If your microwave has different power settings, i.e. 100%, 80%, 60%, 40%, 20%, you will have to experiment.

Cookware and Utensils

Cookware and utensils specifically designed for use in the microwave are widely available; a selection is featured below. For the most part this special equipment is made from materials that allow microwave energy to pass through their surfaces to heat the food within. However, they can still become hot to the touch if the food within gives off a lot of heat.

Browning dishes and microwave grills are examples of cookware specifically designed to make the finished appearance of microwaved food more closely resemble conventionally cooked food. They are therefore good only for microwave use.

Many items already in your kitchen can be used in the microwave; these include casseroles, bowls, and dishes made of heat-safe glass, glass-ceramic, china, and pottery free of metal. Plastic containers marked "Microwave-safe" or "Suitable for the microwave" are extremely useful. Paper goods can be used for short-term heating. Do not use recycled paper towels as they may contain metal fragments.

Divided dish for heating or cooking different foods at the same time. It sits on a collapsible trivet used for elevating casseroles and baked goods

Plastic colander for cooking and draining ground meat

Bent-handled plastic ladle that can be used for stirring and serving

Microwave-safe saucepan

Small glass-covered dish for oven-to-table serving of individual portions or leftovers. It sits on a spring-operated turntable accessory, which rotates food so it cooks evenly

Bent-handled plastic spoon that can be left in bowl for stirring

Bundt cake pan for
prettily shaped cakes

Muffin pan. Also can be
used for cupcakes and
poached eggs

Loaf pan for cakes,
meat loaves, or
terrines

Plastic mold for
cakes or custards

Individual custard cups can be
used for poached eggs, muffins,
and cakecups.

Tube pan for cakes
or meat loaves

Roasting dish with nonstick
finish. Also can be used for
casseroles

Browning dish with
nonstick insert for
searing and coloring

Roasting pan with rack
for roasts. Also can be
used for whole chicken
or chicken pieces

Browning dish
to brown and
crisp meats,
fish, and
poultry

Bacon rack with
ridges for fat to
run off

13

Suitable Kitchenware

Testing for microwave safety: To determine the suitability of a piece of cookware, pour cold water into a 1-cup glass measure and place it in the microwave alongside the dish or utensil to be tested. Heat on High (100% power) 1 minute. The water should be warm, the dish or utensil cool. If the dish is warm, don't use it in the microwave – it may overheat and break.

Oven glass
Any containers of heat-safe glass can be used for cooking and heating as long as they are free of metal trimming or content. Such containers are readily available from supermarkets and hardware and department stores.

Glass-ceramic
Containers made of this material can be used for cooking and heating, and make attractive oven-to-table serving dishes. Do not use any plastic storage lids that may accompany the casserole dishes in your microwave oven unless marked "Microwave-safe."

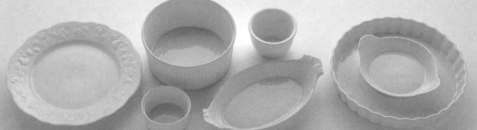

Plastics and paper
Use only plastic containers marked for general microwave use, microwave plastic wrap, and cooking bags. Dishwasher-safe rigid plastic containers can be used for short-term reheating. Waxed paper is a useful covering, and paper towels can be used for short-term heating.

Porcelain and china
Sturdy porcelain and china without metal content or trim can be used successfully in the microwave, and make attractive oven-to-table containers. Plates are especially handy when cooking for one, and can also be used in place of a cover.

Stoneware and pottery
Sturdy glazed stoneware and pottery without metal content or trim can be used for cooking and heating. Avoid pieces that have glazes with a metallic sheen. Other "natural" materials such as wicker can also be used for short heating times.

Unsuitable Equipment

While much equipment normally found in the kitchen can be used in your microwave oven, certain items should definitely be avoided; not only will they interfere with the normal microwave cooking processes, but they may also cause damage to your oven. The main materials to avoid are metal – it can cause arcing (blue sparks), which can pit oven walls or cause fires – unglazed pottery, certain plastics (see below), and recycled paper. If in doubt, carry out the simple suitability test shown on page 14.

Metals and foils
Do not use any metal item unless it is marked "Microwave-safe" or your owner's manual gives guidelines for its use. Avoid metal or part-metal pots, pans, thermometers, skewers, baking trays, and utensils. Make sure containers do not have metal in their handles or around their rims, or any metal screws. Do not use paper bags and boxes, large sheets of foil, or metal ties for roasting bags. Small pieces of foil used for shielding food should not come into contact with the oven's walls; keep at least 1 inch away. Carefully follow recipe directions, and any other guidelines on using foil in the microwave.

Melamine and polystyrene
Some hard and soft plastics, like Melamine dinnerware and polystyrene (foam) cups and boxes, may overheat and break or melt if used for microwaving. Foods high in fat or sugar can also cause plastic containers to distort or melt.

Decorated china and glass
Many dinner sets contain gold or silver decorative trims. These pieces are not suitable for the microwave – they can cause arcing, and a broken dish or damaged oven can result. Do not use lead crystal, glass, or china that has been repaired with glue.

Unglazed pottery
Do not use pottery or earthenware, either handmade or commercially produced, if it is not covered with a glaze on the outside as well as inside; it may absorb moisture and become hot. Pottery with a metallic glaze is also unacceptable for use in the microwave.

Food Facts

Microwave energy cooks food quickly but not always evenly. Microwaves penetrate food up to a depth of 1½ inches, and heat is conducted from the outer edges toward the center (much as it is in conventional cooking); it is therefore possible to overcook or burn the outside edges of foods while the centers remain underdone. Special techniques have been developed to ensure that food is cooked evenly throughout; these are shown on the following pages. But the makeup of the foods themselves can also affect the way they react to microwaves. Composition, size, shape, density, temperature, thickness, fat and bone content, the

presence of a membrane, casing, or hard skin all affect the cooking process and the final result. Knowing how and why food reacts the way it does will mean there will be fewer surprises for you when it is cooked, and will make clear why our recipes recommend that you cook food in a particular way. Moreover, the "starting" temperature of foods can make a big difference in cooking results. Our recipes assume that meat, fish, poultry, eggs, and most vegetables will be at refrigerator temperature, and canned and dry goods at room temperature.

THE COMPOSITION OF FOOD

Water attracts microwaves, so food high in water like tomatoes as well as food low in moisture like popcorn, can be microwaved without added liquid or fat.

Fat attracts microwaves, too. Cheese cooks quickly but does not brown. Bacon cooks and browns quickly. Large roasts brown only with prolonged cooking.

Sugar also attracts microwaves. The sugary fillings of foods such as pastries and turnovers reach a high temperature faster than the outsides.

Moisture content of food
Foods that have a high moisture content cook better and more quickly in the microwave oven than those with a low moisture content.

Size of food
Large, bulky pieces take longer to cook than smaller or thinner pieces. The more exposed the surface area, the faster the item will cook. Here, the sliced and matchstick-thin strips will cook more quickly than the larger pieces and whole carrot.

Shape of food
The thinner parts of unevenly shaped food will cook more quickly than the thicker parts. Here, the salmon steak and monkfish pieces will cook more evenly than the fillet; thinner edges must be placed in the center of the dish or folded under.

Bone content
Bones conduct heat, so cuts that contain bone, or the part of the meat that does, will cook more quickly than the boneless parts. Such meat may cook unevenly.

Fat content
Since fat attracts microwaves, meat high in fat will cook more quickly than lean meat. Lean, boneless meat cuts cook more slowly but more evenly than those with a higher fat and bone content. Both bone and fat attract microwaves, resulting in quicker, less even cooking.

Membranes
Egg yolks, oysters, and chicken livers have membranes that need piercing to stop steam from building up and causing bursting.

Casings
Sausages and other foods with casings should also be pierced to prevent steam from building up and causing bursting.

Outer skins
Vegetables such as acorn squash, potatoes, sweet potatoes, peppers, and tomatoes should be pierced to prevent steam buildup.

Density of food
Dense, heavy foods like potatoes take longer to cook than porous, airy ones like breads and cakes.

Temperature of foods
Recipe timings are influenced by the "starting" temperature of foods used: Microwave cooking is so fast that this can make a big difference. Room-temperature foods, whether fresh, packaged, or canned, normally cook faster than chilled or frozen foods.

Height of food in the oven
Areas closest to the source of energy cook fastest. Therefore, the breast of a whole chicken, which is closer to the top of the oven and receives more energy in some microwave ovens, is likely to be cooked before the center part. Chicken pieces in a casserole, however, are more likely to cook evenly.

Arranging Food for Better Cooking

For an even result throughout, food should be cooked in dishes of the appropriate shape and size. Ring-shaped dishes are best as microwave energy penetrates the food from the center, sides, and bottom. Round dishes also permit fairly even cooking. With square and oblong dishes, corners cook faster than the centers. When cooking more than two dishes at a time, arrange them in a circle if possible.

The center of a dish heats more slowly than its edges, so place foods that take longer to cook toward outer edges of dish, quicker-cooking ones toward center. If possible, arrange pieces of food in a circle, and leave space between the pieces. This allows microwave energy to penetrate the food quickly and evenly. Smaller amounts of food cook more quickly than larger ones, and so do the thin ends of meat, fish, and poultry, and meat near the bone. These must be shielded – covered with smooth strips of foil to prevent overcooking. If the strips of foil are applied at the beginning of cooking time, be sure to remove them in time in order to allow the shielded portions of the food to cook thoroughly.

Always be sure to use the exact size and shape of dish specified in the recipe, or the timing and the finished results may be different from those expected.

Food composition
Delicate, quicker-cooking parts should be placed toward the center, the more fibrous, less tender parts closer to the edges.

Unevenly-shaped foods
Alternate the ends of food such as corn-on-the-cob, and rearrange halfway through cooking to produce an overall uniformity in the finished dish.

Foods of uniform size
Place food in a circle with space between pieces. This enables micro-wave energy to reach all sides of food so it cooks evenly.

Foods of different densities
Place denser, slower-cooking ingredients near edge of dish, more delicate, quicker-cooking ones in center to ensure even cooking.

Pieces, slices, or whole items
Slices or pieces cook more quickly than whole items. The thinner parts should be placed toward the center of a dish while the thicker ends should face outward.

Large or small quantities
Small amounts cook faster than large ones. Cooking time in the microwave is always directly related to the amount of food and increases with the quantity; the more food, the longer the cooking time. Individual portions cook faster than large casseroles or roasts.

Individual portions
Placing custard cups or ramekins in a circle with space in between the dishes will result in more even cooking, particularly in ovens without turntables. However, individual dishes may need to be rearranged during cooking due to uneven heat patterns in the oven.

Shielding vulnerable parts of food
Shield thin ends of meat, bone tips, meat near the bone, and the cut edges of roasts and poultry with smooth strips of foil to prevent them from overcooking.

ARRANGING FOOD FOR REHEATING

Platefuls of leftovers can be reheated easily in the microwave oven. Make certain all the food is of the same temperature, either chilled or at room temperature. Arrange thick and dense pieces of food such as chicken pieces on the outside of the plate, with quicker-to-heat foods such as rice on the inside. If possible, arrange foods in a ring shape, and spread them so they are low and even in the dish. You can do this with mashed potato, for instance, by making a depression in the center. Delicate foods like stuffing should be placed underneath denser meat slices to prevent overcooking. Cover plates with plastic wrap.

Covering Techniques

By covering food to be cooked in the microwave, moisture is retained and steam is produced. Steam heat, added to the molecule-vibrating action of microwaves, results in a speeded-up cooking time, and more even cooking of certain foods. Steam also tenderizes foods. Those that especially benefit from covering are vegetables, casseroles, less tender cuts of meat, thicker pieces of fish, and soups.

Microwave-safe casserole lids, roasting bags, and plastic wrap are all equally effective in retaining heat and moisture. However, when cooking foods that require frequent stirring, rearranging, and/or checking such as custards, sauces, stews, and casseroles, it is easiest to use a lid. Use waxed paper to hold in some steam and to prevent spatters with food that does not need much steam to tenderize, such as a roast. Waxed paper is often blown off the food by the action of the microwave's fan; crumpling the paper slightly helps keep it in place.

Microwave-safe paper towels are good for foods that can be cooked uncovered but tend to spatter, such as bacon and butter or margarine. They are also useful in absorbing extra fat or moisture and for keeping bread surfaces dry. Where a drier cooking surface or less moisture is desired, as with cakes, cook in the microwave without covering.

Lids and covers
Casserole and dish lids made of microwave-safe material, are perfectly adequate as coverings, if recipe does not specify any other.

Plastic wrap
Use microwave-safe plastic wrap to cover dishes without lids. Build-up of steam can cause wrap to split, so vent when using (page 21).

Waxed paper
This forms a looser covering than plastic wrap and is particularly good for preventing spatters. Use it with foods that might become soggy if tightly covered.

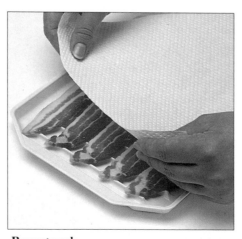

Paper towels
White microwave-safe paper towels allow steam to escape and prevent spatters. They also absorb moisture between food and oven surface to keep food dry.

Plates as covers
If no other suitable cover is available, a plain, untrimmed, and undecorated plate can be used. Select one large enough to completely cover the cooking bowl.

Venting plastic wrap
Cover casserole or dish with plastic wrap, then turn back a corner to form a narrow vent; this allows excess steam to escape.

Removing plastic wrap
Carefully peel back the plastic away from you to avoid any escaping steam, which can cause burns.

Removing lids
Use a pot holder to lift the cover as it will be hot from rising steam, and open it away from you to avoid escaping steam.

Paper towels
Wrap them around food or place them underneath to soak up excess moisture and prevent certain foods from becoming soggy.

Cooking and roasting bags
These handy kitchen items can be used to reheat leftovers or to steam and tenderize food. If steaming larger, uncooked items, use a roasting bag loosely fastened with string or plastic ties. Pierce if directed in recipe or as manufacturer directs.

LINING DISHES

Plastic wrap
This can be used under meat loaves, pâtés, and terrines to prevent sticking and in order to remove them easily.

Paper towels and waxed paper
Cut to fit, these can be used to line cake pans and dishes for baking; they will prevent contents from sticking when removed. The paper is not affected by microwaves and can easily be peeled off bottom of cake after standing time.

Browning Techniques

Most food cooked in the microwave is done so quickly that fat rarely has a chance to rise to the surface and brown. That is why microwaved meat, for instance, usually looks different from meat that has been cooked conventionally. Some foods, such as roasts with a good fat covering, bacon, whole chickens, and turkey breasts, will brown because they have a high fat content. Except for bacon, however, they will not crisp.

Specially designed cookware, called browning dishes or grills, sear and brown foods the way a conventional skillet does. They have a special coating that absorbs microwave energy and reaches temperatures of 500° to 600°F. They have feet or ridges to keep countertops safe from scorching. (Even so, be careful not to place them directly on surfaces that are not heat-safe.) Before placing any food on a browning dish or grill, it should be preheated in the microwave as the manufacturer directs.

You can also use a wide variety of readily available sauces and coatings that are brushed or sprinkled on, or rubbed into the food to produce a more attractive finished appearance.

Browning dish or grill
Both dishes and grills contain a special substance that causes them to become extremely hot. Often there is a well to catch drippings, and feet to protect countertops.

Using a browning dish or grill
Preheat the dish or grill as the manufacturer directs. Add meat, pressing down so that it is seared on the hot surface, and put back in the oven. Do not cover dish. Turn meat over to brown other side – if possible, on an unused part of the dish. If food is cooked in batches, the dish may need to be reheated. Always follow the manufacturer's directions.

Using a browning agent
Chicken cooked in the microwave without a browning agent is pale, such as the leg above. However, if it is coated with a browning sauce, as on the whole bird (right), it looks brown and crisp.

BROWNING AGENTS

Soy and teriyaki sauces and diluted browning sauces are highly seasoned coatings for meat and poultry.

Barbecue sauce can be brushed on meat and poultry occasionally during cooking to add flavor and color.

Steak or Worcestershire sauces can be brushed onto beef, pork, or lamb cuts, or hamburgers.

Paprika is a delicious coating for poultry. Brush on some melted butter first, then sprinkle it on the surface.

Bread crumbs, seasoned or unseasoned, can be used on top of uncovered foods or casseroles before microwaving.

Coating mixes, if added to poultry pieces and hamburgers before cooking, enhance their cooked appearance.

Microwave browning agents should be sprinkled on meats and poultry before cooking as an appearance enhancer.

Onion soup or gravy mix can be sprinkled on hamburgers and other beef or lamb cuts before cooking.

Brown sugar can be sprinkled on cakes and quick breads at the end of their cooking time.

Marmalade or preserves can be brushed on ham after microwaving, and on poultry halfway through.

Cinnamon sugar or toasted coconut can be sprinkled on muffins, quick breads, and cakes before or after cooking.

Toasted chopped nuts make an attractive topping for cakes and quick breads. Sprinkle on before cooking.

Brushing on browning and seasoning sauces or marinades gives meat and poultry a darker, richer color.

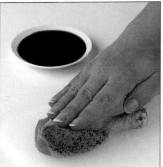

Rubbing soy or barbecue sauce on poultry skin before cooking can improve its normally light appearance.

Glazing with marmalade or a specially prepared fruit glaze improves both the appearance and flavor of ham slices.

Sprinkling on a microwave browning agent or other seasoning can make hamburgers look more tempting.

Cooking Techniques

Because microwaves penetrate food only to a certain depth, it may be necessary to stir, turn over, rearrange, or rotate the food to guarantee even cooking. Various techniques have evolved to enable microwaves to reach every part of the food. Some of the techniques involve the food directly; others consist of moving the dishes.

Some microwave ovens have areas with a concentration of microwaves ("hot spots") and consequently cook food more quickly. To identify these spots, place some water-filled microwave-safe dishes in the oven and heat on High (100% power); check to see which one or ones start to bubble first. Food in these areas will cook most quickly.

As a reminder to stir or rotate foods as the recipe directs, set the oven to that time, rather than the total recipe time, then reset as necessary.

Stirring foods
Casseroles, soups, and stews should be stirred from the outer edge (where the food cooks first) toward the center; the cooler food at the center should be pushed toward the edge of the dish.

Whisking sauces
During the cooking process, whisking keeps sauces smooth and ensures more even cooking. Microwave-safe whisk has bent handle angled to rest in cookware while microwave is in operation.

Turning foods
Dense pieces such as fish cakes should be turned over, as should food cooked in liquid. Hot liquid in the bottom of a dish can transfer additional heat to one side of food and result in uneven cooking.

ROTATING A DISH IN THE MICROWAVE

Casseroles or baked dishes may need to be rotated for even cooking. Make certain to always rotate a dish in one direction only.

For a quarter turn, rotate the casserole or dish so that the side that faced the back faces the side of the oven.

For a half turn, rotate the casserole or dish until the side facing the back of the oven is to the front.

Elevating foods
Raise foods like cobblers, cakes, and quiches off oven floor to allow microwave energy to cook center bottom. Special microwave-safe racks or trivets can be used underneath dishes; meat racks in roasting pans keep roasts from stewing in their own juices.

In addition to special microwave equipment, you can elevate loaf pan, bowl, or casserole on an inverted microwave-safe plate or ramekin.

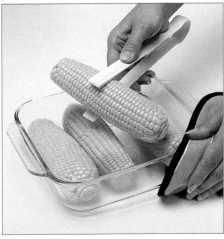

Rearranging dishes
For individual portions to cook evenly, it may be necessary to rearrange them at least once during cooking. Turn each dish so that outside edges move to the inside.

Rearranging foods
With delicate foods that can be damaged through handling, such as baked apples, you can rearrange the food by turning the entire dish. Pieces of food such as corn-on-the-cob have to be turned over or rotated during microwaving for even cooking. Take pieces of food from the center of the dish and move to the outside and vice versa.

Testing for Doneness

When removed from the oven, microwave-cooked food may look different from conventionally cooked food, so there are a number of tests to tell whether it is done.

In assessing the doneness of food, you must take into account the standing time. This is part of the cooking process and allows uneven heat to equalize itself. The food is removed from the oven and normally left covered for several minutes while it finishes cooking. That is why it can look underdone when it is first removed from the oven, but will be done after standing for the time given in the recipe. For this reason, many tests for doneness are carried out after standing time.

Most of our recipes give a range of cooking times for 600- to 700- watt microwave ovens. But it is also important to recognize that your microwave may have a "personality" and cooking pattern of its own, which you should get to know, that can also influence cooking time. To avoid overcooking, choose the lesser amount of time, check for doneness, then cook longer if necessary. Always undercook rather than overcook, and allow the food to stand exactly as directed in the recipe; if it is underdone, it can be cooked further. When cooking individual portions, test each one separately for doneness.

THERMOMETERS

  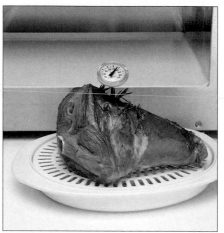

Microwave-safe thermometer: For meats such as lamb and pork, the most reliable test is a thermometer. This can be used inside a microwave oven.

Probe: Certain ovens contain probes that monitor food temperatures throughout the cooking process and turn off the oven when the pre-set temperature is reached.

Instant-read thermometer: This is used to test food outside the microwave. It should be inserted in food immediately after it is taken out of the oven.

Testing reheated food
Feel the center of the bottom of the dish with your hand; if it is hot, the food is heated through; if it is cool, so is the food.

Testing cakes
After standing time in recipe, moist spots on top of cake will have dried out and cake will begin to pull away from side of pan. The cake is done when a toothpick inserted in the center comes out clean.

Testing custards
These are done when a knife inserted halfway between the center and edge comes out clean. The center will look soft but sets during standing time.

Testing fish
Fish is cooked when flesh is opaque; it should flake easily when tested with a fork.

Testing meat
Meat reaches its final desired temperature outside the oven. Small pieces or cubes are done when a fork easily penetrates the surface through to the bottom.

Testing a whole chicken
Chicken is done when thickest part of leg feels soft when pressed with fingers and juices run clear if this part is pierced.

Standing time
Microwaved foods continue to cook by internal heat after they are removed from the oven. For instance, eggs should be just past the runny stage when removed from the oven. After standing 1 to 2 minutes, they will be set, and will look similar to conventionally cooked eggs.

TENTING
Standing time is important for roasts. The internal temperature of the meat rises significantly during standing time, and this extra time is necessary for it to reach the final, desired temperature. Letting roasts stand also allows their juices to settle while the meat firms up for easier carving. Most roasts should be left to stand covered with a loose tent of foil and checked with a thermometer to see if they have reached the final temperature specified in the recipe.

Cook's Tips

Use your microwave for a variety of cooking techniques. Soften cream cheese or butter for cakes and cookies, melt chocolate without fuss, and toast seeds or nuts for many dishes. You can even make caramel in the microwave: follow our directions, watching carefully since caramel continues to cook and darken when removed from the oven. Do not stir unless recipe directs.

Melt chocolate
In small microwave-safe bowl, place one 1-ounce chocolate square. Heat on High (100% power) 1 to 2 minutes, just until shiny. Stir until melted and smooth.

Soften butter
On microwave-safe plate, place butter in non-foil wrapper. Heat on Medium-Low (30% power) 30 to 40 seconds for 1 stick, until spreadable.

Soften cream cheese
On microwave-safe plate, place 8 ounces cream cheese. Heat on Medium-Low (30% power) 1½ (1:30) to 2 minutes, until spreadable.

Toast coconut
On microwave-safe plate, place contents of 7-ounce bag shredded coconut. Heat on High (100% power) 5 to 6 minutes, until toasted, stirring occasionally.

Toast sesame seeds
In 1-cup microwave-safe glass measure, place ½ cup sesame seeds. Heat on High (100% power) 3 to 5 minutes, until golden, stirring occasionally.

Toast nuts
In 1-cup microwave-safe glass measure, place ½ cup shelled nuts. Heat on High (100% power) 2½ (2:30) to 4 minutes, until lightly browned, stirring occasionally.

Scald milk
Into 2-cup microwave-safe glass measure, pour 1 cup milk. Heat on High (100% power) 2 to 2¾ (2:45) minutes, until milk bubbles around edge.

Caramelize sugar
In 4-cup microwave-safe glass measure, place 1 cup sugar; add 3 tablespoons water. Cook on High (100% power) 5 to 7 minutes, without stirring, until mixture is golden.

Clarify butter
In 2-cup microwave-safe glass measure, place 8 tablespoons butter (1 stick), cubed. Heat on High (100% power) 1½ (1:30) to 2 minutes, until melted. Skim foam from top.

Soften peanut butter
Remove lid from jar of peanut butter. Heat on High (100% power) 1½ (1:30) minutes per 8 ounces. If softening more than 8 ounces, stir halfway through.

Soften crystallized honey
Remove lid from jar of hardened and crystallized honey. Heat on High (100% power) 30 seconds; stir until honey loses its granular texture and is smooth. Repeat if necessary.

Soften brown sugar
Place brown sugar in microwave-safe glass dish. Add 1 apple wedge or 1 slice white bread. Heat, covered, on High (100% power) 30 to 40 seconds. Let stand 30 seconds; remove apple and stir sugar once.

Raising yeast bread dough
In microwave-safe bowl alongside 4-cup microwave-safe glass measure containing 3 cups very hot tap water, place dough. Heat, covered with paper towel, on Low (10% power) 20 to 25 minutes.

Flavor candied fruit
Into small microwave-safe bowl, pour ¼ cup liqueur. Heat on High (100% power) 30 seconds. Add 1 cup candied fruit; stir to mix. Heat on High 2 minutes. Let fruit stand until liquid is absorbed.

Blanch almonds
In 1-quart microwave-safe bowl, heat 1 cup water on High (100% power) 3 to 4 minutes, until boiling. Add 1 cup whole shelled almonds. Heat on High 1 minute; drain. Cool, slip off skins; dry on paper towels.

Dissolve gelatin
In small microwave-safe bowl, sprinkle gelatin over measured liquid. Let stand 1 minute. Heat on High (100% power) 1 to 2 minutes, stirring until gelatin is dissolved.

Soften dried fruit
In 4-cup microwave-safe glass measure, place 1 cup dried fruit and ¼ cup water. Heat, covered, on High (100% power) 45 seconds. Let stand 1 minute.

Shell nuts
In medium microwave-safe bowl, place 2 cups nuts and ¼ cup water. Heat, covered, 2 to 3 minutes on High (100% power) until boiling. Let stand 1 minute. Drain; shell.

Cook's Tips

Your microwave oven can also be used to prepare fruit and vegetables, even hard acorn squash, and unripened avocados. It can have crisp- or soft-skin baked potatoes ready for filling or eating plain in a matter of minutes; make it easier to squeeze lemons, limes, and oranges; and substantially reduce the time involved in peeling tomatoes and other fruits with skins, garlic cloves, and onions.

Soften acorn squash for easier cutting
With fork, pierce whole squash in several places. Heat, covered, on High (100% power) 1 to 1½ (1:30) minutes, until softened. Cut lengthwise in half or quarters.

Soften underripe avocado
On oven floor, place unpeeled avocado. Heat on High (100% power) 1 minute, or until slightly softened. Cool completely before peeling and slicing or mashing.

Tear-free onions
Trim ends of large onion. Place on paper towel on oven floor. Heat on High (100% power) 1 minute. Remove skin, then chop or slice as desired.

Squeeze citrus fruit more easily
On oven floor, place 1 orange, lemon, or lime. Heat on High (100% power) 30 seconds, or just until warm. Cut in half and squeeze to get fresh juice.

Bake potatoes
With fork, pierce skin of one 8-ounce potato in several places. Place on paper towel. Cook on High (100% power) 4 to 6 minutes, until tender, turning over halfway through.

Crisp- or soft-skin baked potatoes
After removal from oven, for crisp skin, wrap baked potato in paper towel; for soft skin, wrap in foil. Let stand 5 minutes.

Peel tomatoes
To 2 cups boiling water in 4-cup microwave-safe glass measure, add 2 tomatoes. Heat on High (100% power) 45 to 60 seconds, until skins split. Plunge into cold water; peel.

Peel small onions
In small microwave-safe glass bowl, place ½ cup small trimmed onions. Heat on High (100% power) 45 seconds. Squeeze from stem end until onions pop out of skins.

Peel garlic
On oven floor, place 3 garlic cloves. Heat on High (100% power) 15 to 30 seconds, just until warm. Squeeze at one end until clove pops out of skin.

Use your microwave to get foods ready just before you bring them to the table. It's easier to spread jams, dish out ice creams, and pour syrups if they are heated for a short time. Crackers and chips can be crisped; pies and cookies can be warmed for a just-baked taste. Cheese and other refrigerated foods benefit from being brought to room temperature by heating for a few minutes in the microwave.

Soften jams and jellies
Remove lid from jar of jam or jelly that has become difficult to spread. Heat on High (100% power) 1½ (1:30) to 2 minutes per 8 ounces.

Heat pancake syrup
Remove lid from syrup bottle or transfer to microwave-safe serving pitcher. Heat on High (100% power) 1½ (1:30) to 2 minutes per 1 to 2 cups syrup, until warm.

Refresh potato chips
On paper towel laid on microwave-safe plate, place 2 to 3 cups potato chips in thin layer. Heat on High (100% power) 15 to 60 seconds. Let stand 5 minutes to crisp.

Soften ice cream
On oven floor, place 1-quart carton ice cream. Heat on Medium-Low (30% power) 30 to 40 seconds, until slightly softened for easy serving.

Heat tacos
On paper towel, place 8 to 10 precooked, crisp taco shells. Heat on High (100% power) 1 to 3 minutes, until warm. Spoon in filling of your choice.

Warm cookies
In paper towel, wrap 2 to 4 cookies. Heat on High (100% power) 30 to 40 seconds, until cookies are warm and slightly softened.

Bring cheese to room temperature
On microwave-safe plate, place 8 ounces unwrapped cheese. Just before serving, heat on Medium (50% power) 45 seconds to 1 minute.

Warm pie slice
Place slice of pie on microwave-safe plate. Heat on High (100% power) 30 to 45 seconds, until warm.

Take chill off refrigerated foods
To bring out flavors of fruit and prepared dishes such as pasta salads, place on microwave-safe plate. Heat on High (100% power) 1 to 2 minutes, until no longer cold.

Converting Conventional Recipes

It is possible to convert many recipes for quick cooking in the microwave oven – for instance, a family favorite like a long-simmering beef stew – but not all. For example, don't try to duplicate crisply fried items.

The following guidelines will help you choose recipes suitable for microwaving; the recipe on this page and those on page 33 should help with the conversions.

First: Look for a microwave recipe that is similar to the conventional one you're trying to convert and use it as a guide. Recipes that serve up to eight people – no more – work best; small quantities cook more quickly and evenly in the microwave.

Second: Reduce or omit fats, liquids, and seasonings.

Third: Use microwave-safe cookware and suitable utensils (page 12).

Fourth: Cut back cooking time to a quarter to a half of the conventional recipe time. Remember, microwave ovens do not need any preheating, which also saves time.

Fifth: Remember, most microwave-cooked food usually needs standing time to finish cooking and even out the internal temperature after being removed from the oven. Be sure to let foods stand on a heat-safe surface.

A Reduce to 1 tablespoon

B Reduce to 1 clove

C Omit

D Reduce slightly

E Reduce slightly

F Use microwave-safe baking dish

G Cook vegetables, covered, on High (100% power) 6 minutes until softened, stirring twice.

JOYCE'S SPAGHETTI SAUCE

8 servings

3 tablespoons olive oil *A*
1 carrot, finely chopped
1 celery stalk, finely chopped
1 onion, finely chopped
2 garlic cloves, finely chopped *B*
1 pound ground beef
1 6-ounce can tomato paste *F*

1 28-ounce can tomatoes in puree
⅓ cup water *C*
¼ cup dry red wine
1½ teaspoons oregano *D*
1½ teaspoons salt *E*

G

1. In 4-quart saucepan over medium-high heat, in hot oil, cook carrot, celery, onion, and garlic about 15 minutes, until tender. *H*
2. Add ground beef; cook until well browned, stirring frequently. Add remaining ingredients; heat to boiling.
3. Reduce heat to low; cover and simmer 30 minutes or until sauce thickens. *I*

H In microwave-safe colander set over microwave-safe pie plate, cook ground beef on High 4 minutes, until no longer pink, stirring twice; discard drippings. Add meat to vegetables with remaining ingredients.

I Cook sauce, covered, on High 10 minutes, or until thickened, stirring twice.

If all vegetables are chopped to equal size, they will cook quickly and evenly.

Replace saucepans with microwave-safe cookware that can be used for serving; this saves dishwashing.

Stir from outer edge toward center, pushing cooler food to edge. Re-cover after stirring.

Cooking ground meat in a microwave-safe colander greatly reduces fat content of finished dish.

FAVORITE RECIPES IN THE MICROWAVE

Here are two more recipes ideal for converting to microwave cooking; potatoes cook faster; quick breads take less time and are moist and light when cooked in the microwave. Underneath the conventional recipes, we explain how easy it is to make the changes for successful microwaving.

TWICE-BAKED POTATOES

6 servings

6 medium potatoes, scrubbed
  and unpeeled
3 tablespoons butter or
  margarine
1 teaspoon salt
Dash white pepper

⅓ cup milk
Toppings:
Minced onion, chopped
  chives, diced Cheddar
  cheese, crumbled crisp
  bacon

1. Preheat conventional oven to 450°F. Pierce potatoes in several places, then put potatoes in oven and bake for 45 minutes or until fork-tender.
2. With sharp knife, and holding potato with clean pot holder, slice each potato lengthwise, to remove top fourth.
3. With spoon, carefully scoop out potatoes to form 6 shells. Scrape potato from top quarters; discard tops.
4. In large bowl with mixer at low speed, beat scooped-out potato, butter or margarine, salt and pepper until well combined and fluffy.
5. Slowly add milk, beating constantly until smooth. With spoon, pile mashed-potato mixture back into reserved potato shells.
6. Sprinkle generously with topping of your choice (above). Place filled potatoes on cookie sheet; return to oven and bake 10 minutes or until tops are golden.

To microwave: Pierce potatoes in several places; place on paper-towel-lined oven floor. Cook on High (100% power) 16 to 20 minutes, turning potatoes over and rearranging halfway through cooking. Prepare potato mixture as above. After filling, reheat 5 to 7 minutes, until hot. *Saves about 30 minutes.*

BANANA-PECAN BREAD

Makes 1 loaf

1¾ cups all-purpose flour
⅔ cup sugar
1 teaspoon ground
  cinnamon
1 teaspoon baking powder
¼ teaspoon baking soda
½ teaspoon salt

8 tablespoons butter or
  margarine (1 stick)
1 cup mashed bananas (about
  2 very ripe medium bananas)
1 teaspoon grated lemon peel
2 eggs, beaten
½ cup pecans, chopped

1. Preheat conventional oven to 350°F. Grease 9″ by 5″ loaf pan.
2. In bowl, combine flour and next 5 ingredients. With pastry blender or 2 knives used scissors fashion, cut in butter or margarine until mixture resembles coarse crumbs. Stir in bananas, lemon peel, eggs, and pecans, reserving 1½ tablespoons for garnish, just until flour is moistened. Spoon into prepared loaf pan, smoothing surface. Sprinkle reserved pecans on top.
3. Bake 55 minutes or until toothpick inserted in center of bread comes out clean. Cool bread in pan on rack 10 minutes; remove from pan and finish cooling on rack.

To microwave: Line 9″ by 5″ microwave-safe loaf pan with paper towel. Omit salt. Spoon batter into prepared loaf pan and top with reserved nuts. Cook, covered loosely with waxed paper, on Medium (50% power) 15 minutes, or until top of bread is moist and springs back when lightly touched, rotating a quarter turn every 2 minutes. Let stand in pan 10 minutes. Invert onto rack; remove paper towel; cool. *Saves about 40 minutes.*

Caring For Your Microwave

Microwave ovens are simple to care for and easy to clean. Because they stay cool, spills don't cook on. Yet, it is best to wipe spills off while they are still warm; if left in the oven, they can absorb microwave energy during cooking. Don't worry if some moisture forms on oven walls or door; it is normal for foods to give off moisture and steam during cooking. Just wipe moisture away after cooking.

CLEANING THE OVEN

It's easy to wipe the inside of a microwave after every use, so cleaning isn't hard work at all. To clean the touch-control panel, be sure to open the door first to prevent the oven from starting accidentally.

For convection ovens, follow the manufacturer's recommended cleaning methods in the use-and-care manual. If your oven has a removable turntable, check the manual to see if it can be put in the dishwasher.

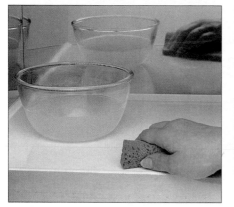  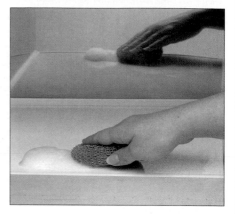

1. Use a clean cloth or sponge dipped in a mild all-purpose cleaner or a solution of liquid dishwashing detergent dissolved in warm water. Rinse well with clear, warm water and dry with a soft cloth or paper towel.

2. Pay special attention to thoroughly cleaning the area around the door seal; this is where small pieces of food often get trapped.

3. If there are areas of cooked-on food, clean them by rubbing gently with a plastic scrubbing pad. An alternative method of removing stubborn food is to soften it with steam by boiling some water in the oven. Do not use steel-wool scrubbing pads.

CLEANING MICROWAVE DISHES

To clean plastic microwave-safe dishes stained by tomatoes, blueberries, or other foods, make a solution of 1 tablespoon chlorine bleach per 1 cup water. Soak dishes about 1 hour, then wash, rinse, and dry. For everyday cleaning, use a mild dishwashing liquid. Rub gently with a plastic scrubbing pad to remove stuck-on food.

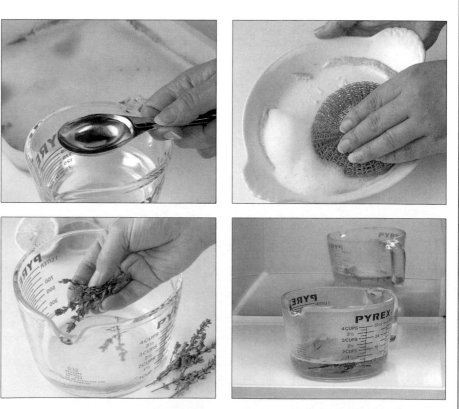

DEODORIZING THE OVEN

Your microwave oven may pick up odors from cooking. Air the oven occasionally by leaving the door ajar, and wipe the inside with baking soda dissolved in warm water. Or, you can use our secret formula: In 4-cup microwave-safe glass measure, combine *1 cup warm water* and *a few thyme sprigs* or *2 lemon slices* or *2 teaspoons pumpkin-pie spice*. Heat on High (100% power) 3 minutes, or until boiling. As a bonus, not only will the inside of your oven smell fresh, but the whole kitchen will smell as if you've been cooking up a storm.

BEFORE YOU CALL FOR SERVICE

Are you using your microwave oven correctly? Before you call for service, make these checks:

Oven not turning on?
Make sure the oven door is securely closed. The oven will not switch on if it is not; this is a safety measure built into microwave ovens. Check that your oven is properly plugged in, that no circuit breakers are open, and that no fuses are blown. Also check that the oven's master switch is in the operating position.

Food isn't cooking?
Check that the oven is not set on "timer" or "hold."

In recipes where you are directed to microwave the food in its own packaging, such as store-bought frozen vegetables, be sure the packaging is not foil, through which microwaves cannot pass. Check that your cookware is microwave-safe (page 12); some materials, such as glazed pottery, block microwave energy.

Food cooking too slowly?
Your oven may not be operating at full power if it is sharing a circuit with another appliance. Also your microwave may be a lower wattage than the microwave used in the recipe you are following; all our recipes are developed in 600- to 700-watt ovens but if your oven has a lower wattage, cooking is slower.

Check to see if power level is set correctly.

Also, make sure food is at the correct temperature. Meat, fish, poultry and most vegetables should be at refrigerator temperature, and canned and dry goods at room temperature.

If standing time is included in the recipe, make sure you let the dish stand for the full time specified. The standing time is needed to equalize the temperature through the food, and to complete the cooking process, and shouldn't be ignored. Also, if recipe directs, be sure the food is left covered or tented during standing. You should always check that the food has been cut to the size specified in the recipe; you may have cut it too large.

Food cooking too quickly?
The starting temperature of food going into the microwave affects cooking time. Microwave recipes assume that foods used in the recipe have been stored correctly. Refrigerated food should be cold, not brought to room temperature before use, or it will cook too quickly.

You may have a single-setting oven which cooks certain foods like eggs and cheese too quickly. If this is the case, pour 2 cups water into a microwave-safe glass measure and place in the oven while cooking these foods. The water attracts microwave energy and "slows" down the oven.

Check that the power level is set correctly, and that food is cut to the specified size and not smaller.

Check the wattage of your oven. The higher the wattage, the faster food will cook. Or use our test on page 10.

Food cooking unevenly?
Make sure the air vent in your microwave is not blocked.

There are also several techniques to prevent uneven cooking in the microwave, such as elevating the dish on a trivet, rack, or inverted ramekins; this exposes areas at the bottom of the dish to the microwaves. Other techniques include arranging food with thicker parts toward edges of dish and stirring and rotating during cooking.

In recipes calling for food to be cut into pieces, check that the pieces are of a uniform size to prevent uneven cooking.

Some microwave ovens have "hot spots" where there is a concentration of microwaves. Fans inside the ovens help to distribute the microwaves more evenly, but it is still necessary to use techniques such as rotating the dish and rearranging food during cooking.

Blue sparks (arcing)?
Be sure any foil you use to shield food, or to cover food you don't want cooked, is smooth, and at least 1 inch away from oven walls. Check that the cookware is microwave-safe (even metal rims on dishes can cause arcing), and that any ties used to seal roasting bags are made of nylon or string, not metal.

MICROWAVE SAFETY
Microwave ovens are made in compliance with strict government safety standards: A seal around the door keeps the microwaves inside, and a special system stops the generation of microwaves the instant the door is opened. You should, however, examine a new oven for any signs of shipping damage.

Never operate the oven if the door does not close properly, or if the door, its latch, hinge, or sealing surfaces have been damaged in any way. Never block the vents of your oven because they keep the microwave-producing magnetron tube cool and cut down on moisture build-up, enabling you to get the best results from your oven.

Microwave ovens are cooking appliances, designed to defrost, heat, and cook food. You may have heard of other uses for the oven – don't try them; they can be dangerous, possibly lead to a fire, and, at the very least, damage your oven. Use the microwave oven only as intended. Always use microwave-safe cookware and utensils (page 12), and do not turn the oven on when the cavity is empty. If you have young children, it is a good idea to leave a bowl of water in your microwave when the oven is not in use. This way, if the oven is accidentally turned on, the water attracts the microwaves and prevents damage to the oven.

If you are concerned about the safety of your oven, have it tested by a qualified service person – don't try using "leakage detectors" which are inaccurate and unreliable.

Meal Planning With Your Microwave

Your microwave oven can be a great boon when planning meals for yourself or the whole family and when entertaining. It can help save on preparation and cleanup time, and it preserves the nutrients in the food as well. To plan meals to be cooked entirely or in part in your microwave, keep in mind the following points.

BASIC PRINCIPLES

1. The more food in the oven, the longer it takes to cook. It's best to keep the number of servings down to eight to take advantage of the oven's ability to cook quickly. If serving meat and potatoes to feed 12, for example, cook the roast in the microwave, but plan to bake the potatoes in your regular oven.

2. You can switch power settings in the time it takes to push a button. This means that after you've cooked the roast on a lower power setting, you can cook the vegetables on High (100% power) without waiting for the oven to warm up, as you would when cooking conventionally. There isn't any need to cool the micro-wave down either when going from a higher to a lower power setting.

3. Dense foods such as roasts, whole poultry, and casseroles usually require standing time to complete the cooking process, and they retain heat well after being removed from the oven. While they finish cooking outside the oven, you have time to cook the vegetables, and reheat soups and sauces, rolls, bread, and so on.

4. Use microwave-safe dishes, serving platters, and casseroles so you can heat up food between courses and bring it to the table piping hot. Pretty china and serving pieces for use in the microwave are widely available.

COMBINATION COOKING

A microwave used in combination with one or more other appliances is often the most efficient way to prepare a meal. For example, you can prepare pasta just as quickly on top of the stove, leaving your microwave oven free for making certain your favorite sauce is ready at the same time.

After cooking a casserole in the microwave, you can place it under the broiler for a browned topping, while using the microwave to cook accompanying vegetables. Or you can brown meat on top of the stove before you begin cooking it in the microwave. Look for cookware that can be used on top of the stove and in the microwave as well as in a conventional oven.

FREEZER-TO-TABLE COOKING

It's easy to cook food in advance, freeze it, then pop it in the microwave oven when guests arrive so it's ready in a matter of minutes. For example, some of our appetizer recipes can be frozen for up to a month before serving. For a piping hot, homemade morning treat, breakfast muffins can be cooked ahead and frozen, then quickly defrosted and reheated in the microwave as and when you need them (see our Chart on page 298 for timings).

Holiday pies can be made ahead of time; one-crust favorites, such as pecan, defrost well in the microwave. A 9-inch pie takes only 6 to 8 minutes on High to thaw completely and evenly.

THE QUICK WAY TO COOK INGREDIENTS

It's time-saving to cook poultry, vegetables, and fruit in the microwave before using in salads, casseroles, or other dishes. Chicken is tender and juicy when cooked on Medium (50% power) for 7 to 9 minutes per pound. Four all-purpose potatoes (about 6 ounces each), peeled and cut into 1-inch chunks, for example, cook on High (100% power) in 10 to 12 minutes. See also our vegetable charts (pages 237 to 251) and fruit charts (pages 313 to 315).

CUT DOWN ON GRILLING TIME

Use your microwave to precook vegetables before you finish them on the grill. Grilling time can be reduced to 2 to 5 minutes if you cook your vegetables first in a small amount of water until almost tender (see vegetable charts on pages 237 to 251). Meats and poultry can be partially cooked so the grilling time is cut in half. Avoid spoilage by grilling immediately after precooking in the microwave – never leave precooked food out at room temperature. Barbecue sauces can also be prepared in double-quick time using your microwave.

ENTERTAINING MADE EASY

Throughout *The Good Housekeeping Illustrated Microwave Cookbook* we have included suggestions on serving and garnishing the recipes to make them perfect for that special occasion. We have also included special *Meal in Minutes* menus, complete with preparation timetables and serving suggestions to cover most of your entertaining needs. Not all the dishes and ingredients in these menus are prepared in the microwave; many can be bought commercially prepared, and some are conventionally cooked. In each menu however, the microwave is used as much as possible, to make entertaining easier. The preparation timetables also give advice for advance preparation so there aren't any last-minute panics, and you can enjoy the meal as much as your guests.

The Color Index

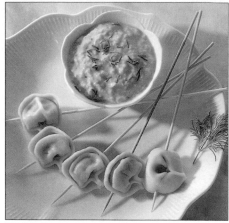

HOT SHRIMP DIP WITH DILL
Shrimp, garlic, green onion, and celery blended with a peppery sauce and served with tortellini on bamboo skewers.
Makes 2 cups. Page 112

BACON-HORSERADISH DIP
Cream-cheese-based dip in Pepper Bowl garnished here with chives. Served with celery, breadsticks, and bagel chips.
Makes 2 cups. Page 111

SPICY CRAB DIP
Crab meat, combined with pimentos, curry powder, and cream cheese, served with a selection of vegetables.
Makes 2 cups. Page 111

BAKED STUFFED TOMATOES
Scooped-out tomatoes filled with a mixture of Parmesan cheese, garlic, and bread crumbs, quickly cooked, then served with uncooked tomato tops and a decorative garnish of parsley sprigs.
4 tomatoes. Page 119

ANGELS ON HORSEBACK
Oysters, flavored with Worcestershire and mustard, wrapped in bacon and garnished with lemon and parsley.
24, 12, 6 oysters. Page 113

TEX-MEX MIXED NUTS *(left) Mixed nuts cooked in spices and left to cool. Makes 2 cups.*
Page 294. **MEXICAN DIP** *(center) Cream cheese mixed with salsa and green onion. Makes*
1 cup. Page 112. **MEDITERRANEAN EGGPLANT DIP** *Cooked eggplant mixed with red onion, green pepper, and tomato, served with pita. Makes 3 cups. Page 111*

BUFFALO CHICKEN WINGS
Chicken wings, cooked in a hot-pepper-and-catchup sauce, and served with celery and a blue-cheese dressing for dipping.
12 pieces. Page 114

EL NACHO GRANDE
Alternate layers of tortilla chips and a spicy mixture of melted peppery cheese, onion, coriander, and ripe olives.
6 servings. Page 114

CHEESE STICKS
Breadsticks, spread with a softened cheese mixture, rolled in poppy and sesame seeds, chives, and paprika, with a chive garnish.
16 sticks. Page 113

OYSTERS ROCKEFELLER
Oysters, topped with a spinach mixture and bacon and cooked on the half-shells. Here garnished with lemon.
12 large oysters. Page 122

CREAMED MUSHROOMS ON TOAST
Mushrooms, cut into quarters and cooked in a sherried cream sauce. Served with toast and garnished with green onion.
4 servings. Page 120

TARTLETS: ASPARAGUS AND BRIE; MUSHROOM; TOMATO-BASIL; AND BLACK BEAN FILLINGS *A variety of tasty fillings with various garnishes, served in an array of tartlet shells. Tartlets can be made ahead, reheated and filled, just before serving.*
Each filling is enough for 16 to 20 tartlets. Page 117

POTATO SKINS WITH CHEDDAR CHEESE *Wedges of scooped-out baked potatoes, topped with a cheese mixture, and served with sour cream or yogurt.* 16, 8, 4 pieces. Page 114

QUESADILLAS
Tortilla "sandwiches" with a chili-cheese filling, here served with taco sauce, sour cream, radish, chili flower, and lettuce. 16 wedges. Page 116

STUFFED ARTICHOKE BOTTOMS
Crispy bacon, mixed with golden raisins, red onion, and bread crumbs, served in cooked artichoke bottoms. 4, 2, 1 servings. Page 118

MIDDLE-EASTERN MEATBALLS
Spicy ground-beef mixture, shaped into bite-sized meatballs, served on skewers, with a lemon and mint garnish. About 26 meatballs. Page 113

ARTICHOKES WITH LEMON AND GARLIC *Artichokes, with slices of lemon and garlic between their leaves, cooked with wine, and served with clarified butter.* 4, 2, 1 servings. Page 120

POACHED APPLES WITH PROSCIUTTO
Apples, cooked in spiced white wine, filled with sour cream and blue cheese, served with salad greens, capers, and thin slices of prosciutto. Accompanied by creamy scrambled eggs and chives. 6 servings. Page 119

CRAB-FILLED MUSHROOMS
Mushroom caps filled with a mixture of crab meat and hot-pepper sauce. Garnished here with parsley and Lemon Twists.
12 mushrooms. Page 118

COUNTRY-STYLE PORK PÂTÉ
Ground beef and pork, combined with diced baked ham, ground chicken livers, herbs, and spices, set into a bacon-lined pan to cook, then served chilled. Garnished with gherkins, salad greens, and olives.
16 first-course servings. Page 115

ELEGANT SEAFOOD SALAD
Chilled cooked shrimp, scallops, and mussels, served on salad greens, with Lemon-basil Sauce and cocktail sauce.
6 servings. Page 122

SEAFOOD PÂTÉ
Shrimp and scallops, blended with fresh tarragon, tomato, and cream, served chilled, with tarragon and tomato garnish.
16 first-course servings. Page 115

CHICKEN LIVER PÂTÉ
Chicken liver, brandy, and bouillon mixture, served on Radish Flowers, Pear Slices, and crackers, with assorted garnishes.
Makes 1 cup. Page 116

CLAMS CASINO
Cherrystone clams, mixed with bacon, green pepper, Parmesan, oregano, and bread crumbs and cooked in their shells.
12 clams. Page 122

SAVORY SAUSAGE PARCELS
Italian sausage, onion, cheese, and bread-crumb mixture rolled in grape leaves and "tied" with pimento strips.
12 parcels. Page 118

CELEBRATION SHRIMP
Large shrimp stuffed with a savory cheese-and-pepper mixture; here garnished with salad greens and peach slices.
4, 2, 1 servings. Page 119

SOUPS

FRESH TOMATO SOUP
Tomatoes and vegetables blended until smooth, then cooked in a seasoned broth; garnished with sour cream and chives.
Makes 6 cups. Page 127

LIGHT AND CREAMY ASPARAGUS SOUP *Blended asparagus, onion, and bouillon, with half-and-half. Served hot or chilled with yogurt or cream and chervil.*
Makes 4 cups. Page 128

VEGETABLE BROTH
Leek, onion, celery, carrots, tomatoes, and mushrooms, cooked with tomato juice, seasonings, and water, then strained.
Makes 3 cups. Page 125

CARROT SOUP WITH ORANGE
Thinly sliced carrots cooked with onion and grated orange peel in Chicken Broth, then blended with butter until smooth, reheated, and served with a decorative garnish of feathered cream and parsley.
Makes 4 cups. Page 128

CHICKEN BROTH
Chicken bones, cooked in water containing herbs and peppercorns, with added leek, carrot, and celery, then strained.
Makes 3 cups. Page 125

FISH BROTH
White-fish bones, cooked in dry white wine and water, with leek, carrot, celery, thyme, and peppercorns, then strained.
Makes 3 cups. Page 125

42

FOUR BEAN SOUP
Black, pinto, and red and white kidney beans cooked with vegetables and bacon in broth. Garnished with celery leaves.
Makes 7 cups. Page 129

FRENCH ONION SOUP GRATINÉ
Sliced onions, simmered in condensed beef broth, flavored with sherry or Madeira and tomato paste, served piping hot with the classic topping of toasted French bread slices covered with melted Swiss cheese.
Makes 6 cups. Page 131

WINTER VEGETABLE SOUP
Carrot, turnip, celery, cabbage, acorn squash, and onion cut into delicate pieces and cooked in a seasoned broth.
Makes 6 cups. Page 128

CURRIED ACORN SQUASH SOUP
Acorn squash blended with onion, apple, and curry powder, with broth and half-and-half added.
Makes 4 cups. Page 129

LOUISIANA GUMBO
Shrimp, oysters, and okra in a thick, spicy tomato base with celery, onions, and garlic. Served here with hot cooked rice.
Makes 8 cups. Page 132

NEW ENGLAND CLAM CHOWDER
Traditional soup made with diced clams, salt pork, onions, milk, and diced potatoes. Here garnished with cherrystone clam shells and parsley and accompanied with oyster crackers.
Makes 6 cups. Page 133

MANHATTAN CLAM CHOWDER
Onions, carrots, celery, bacon, potato, and herbs are cooked with clams and tomatoes in this popular soup. Garnished with parsley.
Makes 6½ cups. Page 133

SOUPS

CREAM OF SPINACH SOUP *(left) Blended spinach, potatoes, and broth, enriched with half-and-half and garnished with cream. Makes 4 cups.* **VICHYSSOISE** *Classic creamy leek and potato soup, served chilled with apple and parsley for garnish. Makes 8 cups. Page 127*

CHICKEN NOODLE SOUP
Tender pieces of chicken and vegetables in Chicken Broth with fine egg noodles added. Serve with saltines if you like. Makes 4 cups. Page 131

MINESTRONE
Fresh vegetables cooked with prosciutto, beans, pasta, and tomatoes, topped with grated Parmesan cheese. Makes 8 cups. Page 130

BEEF BROTH
Beef bones, onion, and tomato roasted in a conventional oven, then cooked with water, leek, herbs, and peppercorns, and strained. Makes 3 cups. Page 125

SPLIT PEA AND HAM SOUP
Ham hock cooked in Chicken Broth with split peas and vegetables, garnished with parsley, and served with French bread. Makes 8 cups. Page 129

CORN CHOWDER WITH CRAB CAKES
Frozen corn, cooked in a creamy potato mixture, here served with Cocktail Crab Cakes, oyster, and shrimp. Makes 6 cups. Page 133

SOUTHERN PEACH SOUP *(left) Fresh peaches cooked with dry white wine and minced gingerroot, then flavored with yogurt and bourbon, and served chilled. Makes 3 cups.* **RED PLUM SOUP** *Red plums cooked in spiced red wine, chilled, and topped with sour cream or yogurt. Makes 3 cups. Page 134.*

EGGS BAKED IN HAM NESTS
Shredded ham and green onions, and egg,
baked in individual dishes, here served with
toast points.
4, 2, 1 servings. Page 137

POACHED EGGS
Eggs simply cooked in water and vinegar;
here served on toast with herb-flavored
sausage patties and a parsley garnish.
4, 2, 1 servings. Page 138

SCRAMBLED EGGS
Seasoned eggs cooked until light and fluffy;
here served with toast points, cherry
tomatoes, and a parsley garnish.
4, 2, 1 servings. Page 139

PIPERADE
Red peppers and chopped onion, cooked,
then mixed with eggs and scrambled. Here
served with French bread and basil garnish.
6 servings. Page 139

BACON AND EGGS
Crisply "fried" bacon and an egg sunny-
side up; here served with a warm roll and a
tomato half sprinkled with chives.
4 servings. Page 140

EGGS IN BRIOCHES
Hollowed-out individual brioches, lined with Muenster or Swiss cheese,
are used as cases for baking eggs. We serve them here with smoked
salmon, fresh asparagus with Hollandaise Sauce, and a chive garnish.
6 servings. Page 137

EGGS AND CHEESE

UNDER 30 MINUTES

30-60 MINUTES

WELSH RABBIT
Well-seasoned thick cheese topping served over toast or muffins; garnished with gherkins, olives, onions, and parsley.
6 servings. Page 142

SWISS CHEESE FONDUE
Microwave version of traditional cheese-wine mixture, served hot with bread cubes, tomatoes, and green pepper for dipping.
4 servings. Page 142

POACHED EGGS FLORENTINE
Classic combination of eggs and spinach, on English muffin halves. Served with Hollandaise Sauce and asparagus.
4 servings. Page 138

SPANISH OMELET (*left*) *Onion, green pepper, and tomato fill our version of this favorite. 2 servings.* **FRENCH DESSERT OMELET**
Moist omelet with filling of strawberries, garnished here with confectioners' sugar and a whole strawberry. 2 servings.
Page 141

MACARONI AND CHEESE
Elbow macaroni, covered in a thick, onion-flavored cheese sauce, with crunchy bread-crumb topping and parsley garnish.
4 servings. Page 142

CAMEMBERT IN GRAPE LEAVES
Camembert, with a layer of apple slices, wrapped in grape leaves. Served with apple wedges and garnished here with parsley.
2 servings. Page 144

SOUFFLÉED CHEESE OMELET
Egg yolks folded into beaten whites give a light, fluffy omelet. Garnished with cucumber, tomato, and parsley.
2 servings. Page 141

SOPA SECA
Creamy onion-tomato mixture, flavored with herbs and hot-pepper sauce, layered with tortilla chips and melted cheese.
6 servings. Page 143

TOMATOES WITH GOAT CHEESE AND BASIL SOUFFLÉ *Hollowed-out tomatoes filled with goat cheese soufflé; served here with salad and garnished with basil.* 8 servings. Page 145

SMOKED SALMON AND CHIVE ROULADE (*top*) *A light soufflé roll with filling of smoked salmon and cream cheese.* 4 servings.
MUSHROOM-CHEESE ROULADE *Rolled soufflé filled with onion, tomatoes, and mushrooms cooked in wine, and Swiss cheese.*
4 servings. Page 146

CHEESE SOUFFLÉ
Shredded Swiss cheese and grated Parmesan in a white sauce form the basis of this microwave version of an old favorite.
6 servings. Page 145

ASPARAGUS TIMBALES
Asparagus, onion, eggs, and cheese cooked in ramekins, served with smoked salmon; garnished with asparagus and lemon.
4 servings. Page 143

CRUSTLESS BROCCOLI AND SWISS CHEESE QUICHE (*left*) *Lightly cooked broccoli and onion in creamy egg and cheese mixture.* 6 servings.
BACON AND POTATO QUICHE *Potato cubes, peas, green onions, and crisp bacon in a mixture of Cheddar cheese and eggs.* 8 servings.
Page 144

SAVORY SALMON STEAKS
Salmon steaks topped with green onion and mayonnaise, and garnished with Radish Flowers, green onions, and cucumber. 2 servings. Page 152

FLOUNDER FILLETS WITH SAVORY SAUCE (*left*) *Flounder fillets in crumb coating; here served with two sauces. 4 servings. Page 157.*
ROLLED FLOUNDER WITH CUCUMBER, TOMATO, AND BASIL SAUCE *Flounder fillets with cucumber stuffing, served with a cucumber, tomato, basil, and wine sauce. 4 servings. Page 156*

SOLE WITH GRAPES
Sole fillets, seasoned with tarragon and lemon juice, are served with a creamy, white-wine sauce and grapes. 4, 2, 1 servings. Page 155

SWORDFISH STEAKS AMANDINE
Tender swordfish steaks served with a buttery toasted almond and parsley sauce. Garnished with parsley. 4 servings. Page 155

FISH STEAKS WITH SALSA
Salmon, cod, or halibut steaks with chili-flavored mayonnaise; served here with tomatoes, green pepper, onion, and olives. 2 servings. Page 151

SEA BASS WITH SUMMER VEGETABLES
Whole sea bass, brushed with butter, sherry, and lime juice before cooking; served with colorful assortment of carrot, yellow squash, and zucchini ribbons. Garnished here with salad greens, lemon, and lime. 6 servings. Page 161

FISH FILLETS FLORENTINE
Fish fillets with spinach, mushrooms, bread cubes, and shredded cheese. Served with cooked tomato wedges. 4 servings. Page 157

SOLE AND ASPARAGUS WITH CHEESE SAUCE *Tender sole fillets, wrapped around asparagus spears, in a creamy cheese sauce.*
4 servings. Page 159

SWORDFISH STIR-FRY (*left*) *Swordfish strips cooked with Chinese-style flavorings; served with Chinese pea pods, mushrooms, onions, tomatoes, and baby corn.* 4 servings. Page 155. **MONKFISH SATAY WITH CHUNKY PEANUT SAUCE** *Skewered monkfish, red pepper, and green onions, served with oriental-style sauce.* 4 servings. Page 154

RED SNAPPER PIQUANTE
Whole fish, cooked with matchstick-thin vegetables in Chinese-style sauce of sherry, soy sauce, garlic, and ginger; here garnished with kiwifruit and toasted almonds.
4 servings. Page 161

SCALLOPS IN CHIVE CREAM
Sea scallops cooked in a blend of Chicken Broth, cream, and wine, flavored with chives. Here served in scallop shells.
4 servings. Page 168

LETTUCE SALMON
Salmon steaks, lightly cooked on a bed of lettuce and thinly sliced red pepper, seasoned with soy sauce.
2 servings. Page 152

BABY CLAM AND SHRIMP SAUCE (*left*) *Tomato-based sauce, served here with tagliatelle.* 4 servings. **RED CLAM SAUCE** (*center*) *Bacon-clam sauce, served here with linguine.* 4 servings. **TUNA AND TOMATO SAUCE** *Rich tuna sauce, served here with pasta bows.* 4 servings. Page 173

UNDER 30 MINUTES

"BOILED" SHRIMP CAJUN-STYLE *(left) Shrimp tossed in herbs and cooked in beer with a dash of Worcestershire; garnished here with lime. 4, 2, 1 servings. Page 164.* **SHRIMP CREOLE** *Fiery mixture of shrimp with green pepper, onions, Worcestershire, tomatoes, and hot-pepper sauce. Served with rice and a thyme garnish. 4 servings. Page 165*

PARTY SHELLFISH
Scallops, shrimp, and crab claws, cooked in a creamy sauce with roasted sweet red peppers, sherry, and parsley.
6 servings. Page 172

CURRIED BAY SCALLOPS
Bay scallops cooked in a curry-butter mixture with onion, celery, and carrots, and garnished with coriander.
4 servings. Page 168.

OYSTER STEW *(left) Shucked oysters cooked in rich half-and-half mixture and garnished with a sprinkling of paprika. 4 servings.* **SCALLOPED OYSTERS** *Shucked oysters in cream sauce, with Melba-toast topping; garnished here with lemon and parsley. 4 servings. Page 169*

CREAMED OYSTERS WITH BISCUITS
Shucked oysters cooked in a creamy onion-celery mixture, served in split baking-powder biscuits, and topped with bacon.
4 servings. Page 169

CRAB CAKES *(top) Tasty patties, here garnished with lemon and coriander. 12 crab cakes.* **DEVILED CRAB** *Crabmeat in piquant cream-based sauce. 4 servings.*
Page 170

CRAB CLAWS WITH HERB BUTTER
Crab claws served with warm, herb-flavored butter and garnished with lemon wedges and parsley sprigs.
4 servings. Page 170

TUNA-SPINACH LOAF
Satisfying dish of chopped spinach and flaked tuna, mixed with bread, sour cream, and eggs, and seasoned with lemon juice and hot-pepper sauce. Cooked in a loaf pan, it is garnished with lemon and parsley.
6 servings. Page 162

COD MEDITERRANEAN
Cod steaks seasoned with oregano and served with a rich tomato-vegetable sauce; garnished here with oregano.
2 servings. Page 153

PEPPERY COD STEAKS
Chili-flavored red-pepper sauce spooned over lightly cooked cod steaks; served here with green beans.
6 servings. Page 153

TUNA PATTIES FLORENTINE
Flaked tuna and spinach patties, here served with tomato-cucumber salad and garnished with lemon wedges and parsley.
6 servings. Page 163

STUFFED TROUT (top) *Trout stuffed with a well-seasoned mixture of onion, carrot, celery, and chopped walnuts.* 4, 2, 1 servings. **CAJUN TROUT** *Whole trout coated in seasoned cornmeal and served with a herbed sauce of onion, green pepper, and tomatoes.* 2 servings.
Page 160

30-60 MINUTES

SHRIMP-STUFFED SOLE
Sole fillets with a shrimp, vegetable, and bread-crumb stuffing; here served with Hollandaise Sauce and garnished with dill.
4, 2, 1 servings. Page 156

RED SNAPPER WITH OYSTER STUFFING
Whole red snapper with a rich stuffing of coarsely chopped oysters, onion, celery, and bread crumbs, seasoned with tarragon. Here garnished with lemon and lime slices and Lemon Julienne.
4 servings. Page 162

FLOUNDER IN PAPER PARCELS
Flounder fillets cooked in parchment paper with orange-flavored vegetables, garnished with orange and basil.
4, 2, 1 servings. Page 157

ORIENTAL FISH IN LETTUCE LEAVES
Flounder fillets wrapped in lettuce leaves, served with vegetables in Chicken Broth, and garnished with coriander.
4, 2, 1 servings. Page 158

LOBSTER AND SHRIMP STEW WITH CHICKEN *Tasty stew in a rich broth with corn kernels, onion, and tomatoes. Here served with chive-topped potatoes.*
4 servings. Page 173

COUNTRY-STYLE BLUEFISH AND POTATOES
Hearty dish of whole bluefish cooked on bed of browned, chopped bacon, thickly sliced onions, and potato chunks. Here delicately garnished with a thyme sprig.
6 servings. Page 161

CIOPPINO
A traditional San Francisco dish with a selection of clams, shrimp, scallops, and crab; here served with French bread.
8 servings. Page 173

"STIR-FRIED" SHRIMP AND BROCCOLI
Shrimp, flavored with sherry and ginger, tossed with broccoli, red pepper, and mushrooms, and served with rice.
4, 2, 1 servings. Page 166

STUFFED SHRIMP SUPREME
Shrimp with zucchini and red-pepper stuffing, cooked in a sherry-lemon sauce; served with pecan-coated goat cheese.
4 servings. Page 165

LOBSTER THERMIDOR (*top*) *Chunks of lobster meat in a creamy mushroom and sherry sauce, served in the shell. 4, 2, 1 servings.*
SZECHUAN LOBSTER *Lobster meat, served with tender vegetables cooked in blend of garlic, cashews, soy, and sesame oil. 4 servings.*
Page 167

SEAFOOD BAKE
Littleneck clams, shrimp, and sea scallops cooked in a mixture of sliced leeks, garlic, sliced red pepper, lemon, and clam juice, spinach leaves, and chunky pieces of corn-on-the-cob.
8 servings. Page 172

SHRIMP IN SAFFRON CREAM
Shrimp tossed in a creamy saffron-flavored sauce, served with tender-crisp Chinese pea pods and matchstick-thin carrots.
6 servings. Page 164

MUSSELS IN WHITE WINE
Mussels cooked in a tomato and white-wine broth, seasoned with garlic and basil. Traditionally served with French bread.
4, 2, 1 servings. Page 168

SAVORY FISH KABOBS
Chunks of swordfish, green pepper, mushrooms, and tomatoes marinated in mixture of green onions, curry powder, marmalade, and Worcestershire, cooked on skewers and served on herbed rice.
4, 2, 1 servings. Page 154

BAKED CLAMS WITH PESTO
Cherrystone clams on the half-shell, topped with pesto-mayonnaise sauce and bread crumbs, and garnished with basil.
4 appetizer servings. Page 166

CALIFORNIA-STYLE MARINATED SALMON STEAKS *Salmon marinated in chili, lime juice, oil, and honey before cooking, then served with lime and parsley.*
4, 2, 1 servings. Page 152

SALMON STEAKS WITH MARINATED CUCUMBER *Salmon steaks, served with sliced cucumber in vinegar, sugar, and onion, and Green Mayonnaise Dressing.*
4, 2, 1 servings. Page 151

STEAMED CLAMS MEXICAN
Cherrystone or littleneck clams cooked in taco sauce, seasoned and garnished with coriander sprigs.
4 servings. Page 166

PAELLA
Classic party dish of shellfish, sausage, chicken, green pepper, and tomatoes, cooked with rice. Garnished with parsley.
8 servings. Page 171

BOUILLABAISSE
Well-seasoned Mediterranean fish stew mussels, lobster, red snapper, and cod, served with French bread.
8 servings. Page 172

CAJUN CRUMB CHICKEN
*Cut-up chicken with coating of mustard,
honey, corn-flake crumbs, and spices.
Garnished with salad, cucumber, and lime.
4 servings. Page 183*

CREAMY CHICKEN BREASTS
*Chicken breasts in a curried asparagus,
green-onion, and cream sauce. Here served
with rice garnished with green onion.
4 servings. Page 187*

CHICKEN À LA KING
*Warmed patty shells with a colorful filling
of chicken, onion, mushrooms, green
pepper, and pimento in a rich sauce.
4 servings. Page 189*

DEVILED CHICKEN
*Chicken drumsticks and thighs coated in a
mustardy mayonnaise and corn-flake crumb
mixture. Garnished with lemon and parsley.
4 servings. Page 188*

**CHICKEN LIVERS WITH TOMATO
SAUCE** *Livers in a tomato sauce seasoned
with steak sauce, oregano, and thyme; here
garnished with parsley and served with rice.
4 servings. Page 189*

"BARBECUED" CHICKEN *(bottom) Chicken thighs cooked until
tender in a piquant onion and green-pepper sauce. 4 servings. Page 188.*
HONEY-SOY CHICKEN *Chicken pieces with an oriental-style glaze,
served with a medley of Chinese pea pods, carrot, and mushrooms.
Here accompanied by rice with green-onion garnish. 4 servings. Page 184.*

COQ AU VIN
Microwave version of the classic French dish of chicken pieces cooked in a red-wine sauce with salt pork, carrots, mushrooms, pearl onions, and tomatoes. Garnished here with chopped parsley.
4, 2, 1 servings. Page 182

CHICKEN PAPRIKASH
Chicken pieces cooked in tomato sauce with paprika; served with sour cream and garnished with chives.
4 servings. Page 182

LEMON CHICKEN
Chicken pieces in a piquant lemon-pimento sauce, topped with crumbs and garnished with Lemon Twists and parsley.
4 servings. Page 182

CHICKEN CACCIATORE
Chicken pieces in spaghetti sauce with olives, green pepper, pesto, and onions. Served with spaghetti and a basil garnish.
4 servings. Page 183

CHICKEN MARENGO
Classic dish of chicken pieces, shrimp, onions, and mushrooms in a wine-tomato sauce, seasoned with rosemary.
4 servings. Page 183

QUICK CHICKEN STEW
A hearty stew of chicken pieces, potatoes, carrots, green beans, and onion cooked in broth and garnished here with thyme.
4 servings. Page 184

CHICKEN KIEV
Boned, skinned chicken breasts, rolled around a butter filling, dipped in egg-yolk mixture, then cooked in a garlic and bread-crumb coating. Garnished here with mixed salad and lemon.
4 servings. Page 186

CHICKEN FRICASSEE
Chunks of boneless chicken breasts with peas, carrots, and green beans in a rich sauce; served here with tagliatelle.
4 servings. Page 185

BROCCOLI-STUFFED CHICKEN BREASTS *Breaded chicken breasts stuffed with ham, broccoli, and cheese, and served with cheese sauce and a parsley garnish.*
6 servings. Page 186

POACHED CHICKEN WITH VEGETABLES *Chicken breasts, leeks, mushrooms, and artichoke hearts served here with a basil garnish.*
4, 2, 1 servings. Page 185

CHICKEN BREASTS PARMESAN
Crumb and cheese coated chicken breasts with a zesty olive-basil-tomato sauce. Accompanied with tagliatelle.
4 servings. Page 187

HERB-AND-CHEESE CHICKEN BREASTS *Breaded chicken breasts with herbed cheese filling, served with chicory, asparagus, and cherry tomatoes.*
8 servings. Page 185

SAVORY STUFFED CORNISH HENS *(left) Crumb-coated Cornish hens with savory stuffing of mushrooms, zucchini, cheese, and rice.* 2 servings.
SPLIT CORNISH HENS *Cornish-hen halves with garlic-herb stuffing; garnished with basil and served with cherry tomatoes.* 4, 2, 1 servings.
Page 191

30-60 MINUTES

CHICKEN CREPES FLORENTINE
Crepes with a spinach and chicken filling, topped with Parmesan-flavored Basic White Sauce, garnished with chives.
4, 2, 1 servings. Page 190

CHICKEN RATATOUILLE
Hearty mixture of chicken, green pepper, yellow squash, zucchini, and tomatoes, topped with melted mozzarella cheese.
4 servings. Page 190

TURKEY TORTILLA ROLL-UPS
A turkey, onion, green pepper, tomato, and corn filling rolled up in tortillas; topped with enchilada sauce and cheese.
4 servings. Page 194

DUCK BREASTS WITH APPLE AND GREEN PEPPERCORNS
(top) Sliced duck-breast halves and apple served with a green-peppercorn-flavored sauce. 4 servings. Page 193. **HONEY-PECAN CHICKEN** *Chicken breasts with a honey and pecan-crumb coating, served sliced with a cranberry-wine sauce.* 6 servings. Page 187

TURKEY ROLLS WITH CHEESE FILLING *Breaded cutlets filled with Boursin, mozzarella, and sun-dried tomatoes; here sliced with basil and salad garnish.*
4, 2, 1 servings. Page 196

TURKEY-NOODLE CASSEROLE
Chunks of turkey breast, peas, and noodles in a creamy sauce, topped with Melba-toast crumbs and here garnished with parsley.
4 servings. Page 196

TURKEY BREAST WITH CHESTNUT STUFFING *Quickly cooked turkey breast, served with a delicious stuffing of whole chestnuts, celery, and golden raisins.* 16 servings. Page 195

CURRIED CHICKEN THIGHS *Marinated chicken thighs coated in crumbs before cooking; served with a curried yogurt sauce.* 4 servings. Page 189

DUCKLING WITH ORANGE SAUCE *Tender duckling quarters in a rich, savory orange sauce, with added brandy and fine orange-peel strips; served here with Chinese pea pods and a garnish of orange slices and parsley.* 4 servings. Page 192

APRICOT-GLAZED DUCKLING *Duckling quarters with glaze of mustard, apricot preserves, soy sauce, and ginger; served with sliced carrots and zucchini.* 4 servings. Page 192

DUCKLING WITH CHERRY SAUCE *Duckling quarters cooked until tender, then served with a rich, cherry and red-wine sauce; garnished with watercress.* 4 servings. Page 193

DUCKLING WITH OLIVES AND ALMONDS *Duckling quarters served in a seasoned sauce of almond-stuffed olives, onions, and sherry.* 4 servings. Page 193

MEAT

STEAK AU POIVRE
Succulent beef tenderloin steaks with crushed peppercorn coating served with a tasty brandy and sour cream sauce, and accompanied here with sautéed julienned leeks.
4, 2, 1 servings. Page 204

BEEF AND ASPARAGUS AMANDINE
Parsley-topped beef and asparagus spears accompanied with sliced almonds in a zesty soy-lemon sauce.
4 servings. Page 205

STEAK FORESTIÈRE
Juicy beef tenderloin steaks served with a Madeira, mushroom, and tomato sauce. Accompanied here with green beans.
4 servings. Page 204

STEAK WITH MUSHROOMS AND ARTICHOKES *Medium-rare steaks, seasoned with marjoram and served with a variety of vegetables in a red-wine sauce.*
4 servings. Page 204

BEST-EVER BURGERS
Medium-rare beef burgers topped with onion rings in a wine sauce. Accompanied with carrot and zucchini ribbons.
2 servings. Page 210

SURPRISE BURGERS
Pimento-, olive-, and chili-sauce-filled burgers; here garnished with baby corn, salad greens, and sliced tomato.
4, 2, 1 servings. Page 209

CHEESEBURGERS
Ground-beef and shredded-cheese patties in a seasoned coating, topped with a lightly spiced mixture of onion rings and sliced mushrooms. Here served with toast triangles and garnished with parsley.
4 servings. Page 209

CHILI CON CARNE
A classic, spicy chili topped with sour cream, shredded cheese, and coriander. Here with tortilla chips and a bowl of salsa.
6 servings. Page 211

MEXICAN BEEF CASSEROLE
Layers of spicy ground beef, enchilada sauce, tortillas, and cheese. Garnished with olives and coriander.
6 servings. Page 210

COME-ON-OVER CHILI
Spiced beef, red kidney beans, zucchini, corn, and onions make a quick and easy chili. Here with regular long-grain rice.
8 servings. Page 211

INDIVIDUAL MEAT LOAVES
Seasoned beef and cucumber loaves, filled and topped with cheese; garnished with salad and parsley.
4, 2, 1 servings. Page 211

MEXICALI PORK BURRITOS
Tortillas with beans, pork, and cheese, topped with Creamy Avocado Sauce and taco sauce. Garnished with lemon and parsley.
4, 2, 1 servings. Page 219

STIR-FRY WITH PORK
A traditional dish of pork-tenderloin slices, soaked in an oriental-style marinade before cooking, then served with a selection of tender-crisp vegetables in a butter-lemon sauce.
4 servings. Page 217

PORK WITH VEGETABLES
Juicy pork cutlets are cooked until tender in bouillon and arranged with lightly cooked asparagus, baby carrots, and Belgian endive. A green-onion sauce, flavored with mustard, is spooned over.
4 servings. Page 217

HAM AND BEAN CASSEROLE
A substantial casserole of smoked-ham cubes, white kidney beans, and vegetables, cooked in an herby chicken broth.
6 servings. Page 221

VEAL MARSALA
Crumbed veal cutlets with butter-Marsala mixture; sprinkled with parsley and here accompanied with asparagus.
4, 2, 1 servings. Page 224

VEAL WITH SPINACH
Veal cutlets in a seasoned crumb coating; served with lemon-flavored wilted spinach and cherry tomatoes.
4 servings. Page 224

ROAST PORK HASH
Cubes of cooked roast pork, onion-flavored cooked potatoes, eggs, and cream. Served with thyme-sprinkled carrots.
4 servings. Page 216

LAMB MEDALLIONS WITH ORANGE
Boneless lamb chops on parslied toast with orange and herby mayonnaise. Served with Chinese pea pods and rosemary garnish.
8 servings. Page 229

BACON-WRAPPED LAMB CHOPS
Juicy boneless lamb loin chops with a fruity bread filling, wrapped in bacon, and cooked. Here accompanied with green beans, small potatoes sprinkled with chopped chives, and Currant-orange Sauce.
4 servings. Page 228

SAUSAGE AND VEGETABLE CASSEROLE *A ratatouille-style casserole with eggplant, zucchini, yellow pepper, slices of kielbasa, and garbanzo beans.* 6 servings. Page 234

REUBEN MEAT LOAF
Sauerkraut and Swiss cheese in a meat loaf, topped with Thousand Island dressing. Garnished with Radish Flowers and parsley. 6 servings. Page 212

MEAT LOAF MILANESE
Meat loaf with red potatoes and beans, and a tomato-basil sauce. Garnished with parsley and Lemon Julienne. 6 servings. Page 212

KIELBASA AND RED CABBAGE
Kielbasa, apples, and shredded red cabbage cooked with apple juice, sugar, and vinegar. Garnished with watercress. 4 servings. Page 232

SAUSAGE AND BISCUIT SUPPER
A creamy sausage meat, red pepper, and parsley gravy, served with hot buttermilk biscuits. Garnished with parsley. 4 servings. Page 232

ROAST BEEF WITH HERBS
A tender beef rib eye roast, coated with an herby mayonnaise, black-pepper and bread-crumb mixture and cooked medium-rare. Here cut into thin slices and garnished with whole radishes and basil leaves. 10 servings. Page 202

MACARONI AND BEEF BOLOGNESE
Pasta shells and chopped vegetables in a hearty meat sauce. Here sprinkled with Parmesan and garnished with parsley.
6 servings. Page 213

STUFFED CABBAGE
A traditional dish of cabbage leaves with a beef-onion-raisin filling and served with a delicately spiced tomato sauce.
4 servings. Page 213

VERMONT PORK AND BEANS
Smoked boneless pork loin chops and beans are cooked in a sweet-and-sour sauce and garnished with a parsley sprig.
6 servings. Page 220

SAVORY RIBS
Pork loin country-style ribs cooked in a tangy tomato sauce with sauerkraut and green pepper. Here with salad greens.
4 servings. Page 220

HAM LOAF
A seasoned, molded loaf of smoked ham and ground veal with pimentos and olives. Garnished with lemon and parsley.
8 servings. Page 221

GLAZED HAM
Fully cooked ham coated with a zesty apple-mustard glaze. Here served with thin carrot strips and baby corn.
8 servings. Page 221

LAMB PILAF
Vegetables, rice, and cubes of roast lamb cooked in curried broth. Served with a cooling yogurt sauce and mint garnish.
8 servings. Page 227

ZESTY LEG OF LAMB
Leg of lamb, brushed with a flavorsome glaze of chutney, mustard, garlic, vinegar, and Worcestershire during cooking. Here served with small potatoes and peas, and garnished with a sprig of mint.
8 servings. Page 227

APRICOT-GLAZED RACK OF LAMB
*A delicious glaze of apricot preserves, lemon juice, and mustard gives
this lamb rib roast its beautiful color. Here garnished with watercress
sprigs and accompanied with glazed carrots.*
4 servings. Page 227

FREEZER-TO-TABLE POT ROAST
*A convenient pot roast cooked with carrots
and rutabaga in a seasoned orange sauce;
with parsley garnish.*
12 servings. Page 203

CORNED BEEF AND CABBAGE
*A traditional, hearty dish of spicy corned
beef and cabbage with sliced carrot, onions,
and celery.*
6 servings. Page 208

SAUSAGE AND PEPPERS
*A colorful combination of Italian sausage,
onions, and green, yellow, and red peppers,
in a fennel-flavored tomato sauce.*
6 servings. Page 234

KNACKWURST AND POTATO SUPPER
*Knackwurst and potatoes in a piquant
onion sauce on a bed of chicory; sprinkled
with bacon and here garnished with beets.*
4 servings. Page 232

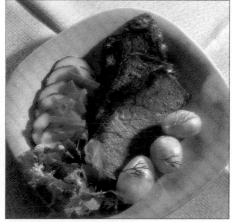

BARBECUE BRISKET
*Lean beef brisket, cooked in a tangy
barbecue sauce. Served here with dill-
topped potatoes and salad garnish.*
6 servings. Page 208

OLD-FASHIONED POT ROAST
A classic combination of beef and vegetables cooked in a rich wine broth until tender. Garnished with sprigs of parsley.
6 servings. Page 203

STEAK AND MUSHROOM PIE
A hearty pie filled with tender beef, mushrooms, and onions cooked in a wine sauce, and topped with a golden conventionally cooked pastry crust. Here accompanied with lightly cooked carrots.
8 servings. Page 205

BEEF BOURGUIGNON
Beef chunks with mushrooms, pearl onions, carrots, and celery in a red-wine sauce; garnished with parsley.
4 servings. Page 206

RIB ROAST
A traditional succulent beef rib roast, seasoned with spices and herbs and cooked to medium-rare. Here accompanied with steamed broccoli flowerets, carrots, and roast potatoes.
6 servings. Page 202

BEEF STROGANOFF
Tender beef and mushrooms in a creamy sauce with buttered noodles as an accompaniment; garnished with parsley.
6 servings. Page 206

BEEF CARBONNADE
A casserole of beef, bacon, and onions, cooked in beer. Here served with potatoes sprinkled with chopped parsley.
8 servings. Page 207

OLD-FASHIONED BEEF STEW
A traditional dish of vegetables and beef cooked in tomato-flavored Beef Broth with thyme and bay leaves.
6 servings. Page 207

BEEF GOULASH
A hearty blend of beef, onions, and green peppers in a tomato-paprika sauce. Delicious alone or with buttered noodles.
6 servings. Page 206

PARTY BURGERS
Medium-rare sirloin-steak burgers, arranged on herb-dipped toast rounds with a variety of decorative party toppings.
12 servings. Page 210

PORK LOIN ROAST WITH GARLIC SAUCE
A succulent dish of pork loin roast cooked in a garlic broth; broth is then processed and seasoned with salt, pepper, and lemon juice and passed separately. Garnished with sprigs of watercress.
10 servings. Page 216

PORK LOIN WITH APRICOT STUFFING
A boneless pork loin roast, seasoned with pepper to taste and cooked until tender. Here cut into thin slices and complemented with a fruity stuffing of apricots, apple, onion, and celery, and parsley garnish.
16 servings. Page 216

PORK JAMBALAYA
A hearty casserole of pork cubes, rice, and a variety of vegetables, cooked in Beef Broth with Creole flavorings.
6 servings. Page 219

67

PORK EMPANADAS
Spicy pork filling in cheesy cornmeal pastry packages; here with taco sauce, sour cream, and coriander garnish.
4 servings. Page 218

ROAST LOIN OF VEAL WITH ACORN SQUASH *A tender veal roast with a garlicky squash sauce. Here garnished with watercress and served with zucchini.*
8 servings. Page 223

HOLIDAY VEAL ROAST (*top*) *Lean veal breast stuffed with spinach, cheeses, and roasted pimentos. Here served with Sweet-pepper Medley.*
12 servings. Page 222. **STUFFED SHOULDER OF VEAL** *Veal shoulder roast with filling of Italian ravioli, ham, and cheese; cooked in dry white wine and broth.* 10 servings. Page 223

OSSO BUCO
Veal shank, vegetables, and orzo in a tomato-wine sauce with dried mushrooms and herbs; here with parsley.
4 servings. Page 224

VEAL STEW PROVENÇALE
Seasoned veal, onions, green and red peppers, and olives in an herby sauce; here served with bow ties tossed with parsley.
4 servings. Page 226

VEAL RAGOUT
Veal chunks, pearl onions, mushrooms, celery, and carrot in cream sauce; served with herbed rice and parsley garnish.
4 servings. Page 226

LAMB CURRY
Indian-style dish of tender lamb chunks cooked in a spicy fruit and vegetable sauce, with a traditional garnish of toasted almonds and coriander leaves. Accompanied with rice and mango chutney.
4 servings. Page 230

MOROCCAN LAMB WITH COUSCOUS
Savory couscous topped with a mixture of lamb chunks and selected vegetables cooked in a richly spiced tomato sauce.
6 servings. Page 230

LAMB STEW WITH FETA
Traditional mixture of lamb, zucchini, and olives cooked in tomatoes and wine served over cheesy macaroni with dill.
6 servings. Page 231

MARINATED LAMB CHOPS WITH
HERBED PEAS *Rib lamb chops marinated in mustard, mint, and apple jelly; served with minted peas and mint garnish.*
4, 2, 1 servings. Page 228

LAMB STEW WITH LEEKS
A hearty stew of lamb cubes, leeks, carrots, and unpeeled small potatoes, seasoned and cooked in own juices.
6 servings. Page 231

LAMB AND EGGPLANT CHARLOTTE
Molded lamb and eggplant, seasoned with oregano and nutmeg and served with our Tomato Sauce; garnished with parsley.
8 servings. Page 231

LEMON-LIME THAI KABOBS
Chunks of lamb soaked in a spicy lemon-lime marinade, cooked with chunks of papaya and green pepper, on wooden skewers. Served on a bed of Hot Cooked Rice.
4 servings. Page 229

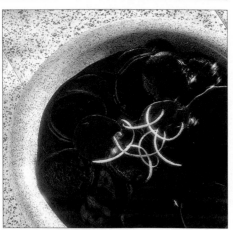

HARVARD BEETS
An easy dish of canned sliced beets in a tangy sweet-and-sour sauce and garnished with Orange Julienne.
4, 2, 1 servings. Page 254

CALIFORNIA ASPARAGUS WITH CELERY AND PECANS *(top)*
Tender-crisp asparagus and celery tossed with toasted pecans. 4 servings. **ASPARAGUS BUNDLES** *Asparagus spears with a green-onion tie in a buttery pimento and green-onion sauce. 4, 2, 1 servings.* Page 252

NEAPOLITAN BROCCOLI
Broccoli flowerets cooked in a mixture of ripe olives, capers, peppers, garlic, and green onions. Garnished with almonds.
4 servings. Page 255

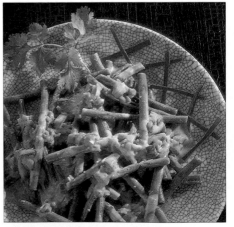

CHINESE GREEN BEANS WITH PEANUT SAUCE *Green beans cooked until tender-crisp, tossed in a spicy oriental-style sauce with peanut butter and red pepper.*
4, 2, 1 servings. Page 253

LIMA BEANS WITH BUTTERED BREAD CRUMBS *A quick and easy dish of lima beans with added Parmesan cheese, sprinkled with crispy bread crumbs.*
4, 2, 1 servings. Page 253

BRUSSELS SPROUTS WITH CHESTNUTS *A hearty side dish of tender Brussels sprouts cooked in broth with butter and whole chestnuts.*
4, 2, 1 servings. Page 256

PARTY BRUSSELS SPROUTS
Brussels sprouts cooked with small white onions in seasoned liquid until tender-crisp, then tossed with crisp diced bacon.
6 servings. Page 256

CREAMED CORN WITH PEPPERS *(left) Corn kernels with green pepper, onions, and tomato in a creamy sauce flavored with oregano.*
4 servings. Page 260. **SUCCOTASH** *A traditional and substantial combination of corn kernels, baby lima beans, diced potatoes, and diced bacon. 4 servings. Page 261*

GINGER-ORANGE CARROTS
Strips of carrot cooked with orange juice, soy, ginger, and green onions. Garnished here with Orange Julienne.
4 servings. Page 257

GLAZED CARROTS
Sliced carrots cooked in broth and sugar until tender-crisp, then glazed with butter and garnished with parsley.
4 servings. Page 258

THREE-PEPPER BUTTER *(top) Green, cracked, and ground red pepper in melted butter* **FRESH-SNIPPED-HERB BUTTER** *(center) Snipped fresh herbs in melted butter and lemon juice.* **GOLDEN SPICED BUTTER** *Curry powder and Dijon mustard in melted butter.*
Each enough for 4 ears of corn. Page 260

71

VEGETABLES

CAULIFLOWER WITH MINT-FLAVORED SPINACH *(left)*
Cauliflower flowerets cooked in a spiced spinach mixture with yogurt added. 6 servings. Page 259. **CAULIFLOWER WITH LEMON AND DILL SAUCE** *A whole cauliflower served with a creamy sauce delicately flavored with lemon and dill. 8 servings. Page 258*

SOUTHERN-STYLE CORN PUDDING
A favorite combination of corn, bread crumbs, eggs, and half-and-half cooked until set, and sprinkled with paprika.
4 servings. Page 260

SZECHUAN EGGPLANT
An oriental-style dish of eggplant in a spicy ginger-soy sauce with green onion added; garnished with Green-onion Pompom.
4 servings. Page 261

OKRA, HAM, AND TOMATOES
Diced ham and onion combined with whole okra and cooked in a spicy tomato sauce. Here served over rice, garnished with lemon slices, and accompanied with corn bread.
4 main-dish servings. Page 265

HERBY MUSHROOMS WITH TOMATOES AND GARLIC *Whole button mushrooms with herbed vinegar, tomatoes, and onion. Here with parsley garnish.*
6 servings. Page 264

CREAMED ONIONS
Pearl onions cooked in an onion- and nutmeg-flavored white sauce, here garnished with chives.
8 servings. Page 266

GREEN PEAS WITH BACON AND ONIONS *Cooked in bacon drippings for extra flavor, our peas and pearl onions are then sprinkled with diced bacon.*
4 servings. Page 267

LEMON PEAS
A simple dish of tender peas lightly cooked with grated lemon peel and butter, then garnished with lemon and mint.
4, 2, 1 servings. Page 267

MASHED POTATOES
Fluffy potatoes beaten with butter and half-and-half then topped with chives. Here shown with Almost Instant Gravy.
4 servings. Page 269

SPRING VEGETABLES WITH LEMON-CHIVE BUTTER *(left) Zesty butter is spooned over this seasonal selection of tender-crisp vegetables.*
6 servings. Page 275. **NEW POTATOES WITH BUTTER AND CHIVES**
An elegant dish of new potatoes with chive butter; garnished here with chives. 4, 2, 1 servings. Page 268

HOME-STYLE POTATOES WITH BACON AND ONIONS *Diced potatoes cooked with sliced onion, with diced bacon added. Garnished with parsley.*
4 servings. Page 269

STEWED FRESH TOMATOES
Peeled tomato wedges and green onions flavored with garlic salt; here decoratively garnished with Green-onion Pompoms.
6 servings. Page 272

GREEN TOMATO CURRY
An Indian-style dish of green tomatoes, apple slices, and diced onion seasoned with curry and chili powders.
4 servings. Page 273

73

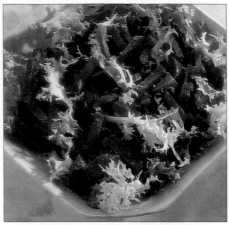

BRAISED GREEN BEANS WITH TOMATOES AND ONIONS *A flavorful mixture of green beans, tomatoes, and red onion slices, sprinkled with Parmesan.* 4 servings. Page 252

FRESH BEETS WITH CHICORY *Chicory with tender strips of beet coated in a tangy dressing of olive oil, red-wine vinegar, mustard, and oregano.* 6 servings. Page 254

BROCCOLI MORNAY *Tender-crisp broccoli coated in a cheese sauce with a hint of mustard, sprinkled with an onion-crumb topping.* 4 servings. Page 255

SCALLOPED CABBAGE *Shredded cabbage and sliced onions cooked until tender, with cream added, and topped with bread crumbs; here with dill garnish.* 8 servings. Page 256

BELGIAN ENDIVE AU GRATIN *(top) Halved endive with a rich cheese sauce.* 4 servings. **"BRAISED" BELGIAN ENDIVE** *(bottom) Endive cooked until tender in an herby broth.* 4, 2, 1 servings. Page 262. **CARROT AND POTATO PANCAKES** *Variation on a favorite recipe; here served with applesauce and sour cream.* 4 servings. Page 257

SWEET-AND-SOUR SHREDDED RED CABBAGE *Brown sugar and red-wine vinegar give shredded red cabbage a distinctive flavor.* 8 servings. Page 257

74

CELERIAC PUREE
Pureed cooked celeriac-potato mixture with butter, cream, and seasonings; garnished here with parsley.
6 servings. Page 259

STUFFED ONIONS
Cooked, hollowed-out onions filled with celery, red pepper, onion, and bread crumbs; here with parsley garnish.
4, 2, 1 servings. Page 265

SWEET-AND-SOUR ONIONS
Sliced onions cooked in broth, red wine, and vinegar until glazed. Here garnished with parsley.
8 servings. Page 266

LEEKS WITH HAM IN CHEESE SAUCE
Leeks cooked in broth, then wrapped with ham, and served in cheese sauce. Here with parsley and chicory garnish.
4, 2, 1 servings. Page 263

CREAMY ONIONS AND RICE
Sliced onions and rice cooked in broth until tender, with added cream and shredded cheese. With parsley garnish.
4 servings. Page 267

POTATOES AU GRATIN
Classic dish of sliced potatoes topped with melted cheese, onion, and seasoned bread crumbs; here with parsley garnish.
8 servings. Page 268

STUFFED POTATOES ORIENTALE (left) *Baked potatoes with a Japanese-style filling. Garnished here with Green-onion Pompoms.*
4, 2, 1 servings. Page 269. **ORIENTAL-STYLE MUSHROOMS**
Marinated pork with mushrooms, Chinese pea pods, and tomato strips in a ginger-soy sauce. 4 servings. Page 264

CREAMED SPINACH
Cooked spinach in a seasoned white sauce. Here shown drizzled with sauce and garnished with lemon.
8 servings. Page 270

75

HONEY-ORANGE-GLAZED ACORN SQUASH *(tòp) Squash halves with a sweet filling.* **MAPLE BUTTERNUT SQUASH** *(center) Tender squash with apple, onion, and syrup.* **SPAGHETTI SQUASH WITH MEAT SAUCE** *Pork-sausage-meat sauce tops tender squash strands.* 4 servings. Page 271

MASHED HARVEST VEGETABLES
Mashed winter squash and rutabaga are combined with orange-flavor liqueur, orange peel, and cinnamon.
8 servings. Page 274

RATATOUILLE
A French-style oregano-seasoned vegetable mixture of red pepper, eggplant, zucchini, and tomatoes; garnished with basil.
8 servings. Page 275

GARDEN MEDLEY
A colorful combination of zucchini, red peppers, eggplant, potatoes, onions, and tomato, garnished here with basil.
6 servings. Page 274

MIXED COMPANY VEGETABLES
An attractive selection of sliced carrots, broccoli flowerets, and whole mushrooms cooked until tender, then combined with strips of red pepper and a soy and green-onion sauce.
8 servings. Page 274

TWICE-BAKED SWEET POTATOES
A mixture of cooked sweet potato, yogurt, and chili powder served hot in sweet-potato shells; garnished here with parsley.
4, 2, 1 servings. Page 272

SWEET POTATO PUDDING
Sweet potatoes mashed with half-and-half, nutmeg, cinnamon, vanilla, and sugar, then cooked with a crumb-pecan topping.
10 servings. Page 272

MARINATED OKRA
Lightly cooked okra marinated in a mixture of oil, vinegar, mustard, sugar, thyme leaves, and crushed red pepper.
4 servings. Page 265

ZUCCHINI LINGUINE WITH SUN-DRIED TOMATOES AND PINE NUTS *An imaginative dish of zucchini strips cooked with pine nuts and sun-dried tomatoes.*
4 servings. Page 273

STUFFED ZUCCHINI
Hollowed-out zucchini filled with diced zucchini, red pepper, tomato, bread crumbs, and Parmesan cheese.
2 servings. Page 273

EGGPLANT STUFFED WITH TABBOULEH (top) *Eggplant halves filled with a refreshing minted bulgur mixture.* 4 main-dish servings.
Page 261. **SPINACH GNOCCHI WITH BUTTER AND PARMESAN**
Italian-style dish of spinach-ricotta ovals with melted butter and Parmesan; here garnished with parsley. 8 servings. Page 270

SALADS

UNDER 30 MINUTES

30-60 MINUTES

SPINACH SALAD WITH HOT BACON DRESSING *A popular salad of spinach and red onion tossed in a tangy mustard dressing and sprinkled with diced bacon.* 4, 2, 1 servings. Page 278

WARM SALAD OF ARUGULA, CORN, BLACK BEANS, AND AVOCADO *Wilted arugula with hot corn, black beans, and onion. Topped with avocado and bacon.* 8 servings. Page 279

OLD-FASHIONED CHICKEN SALAD *Chicken-breast chunks in mayonnaise dressing with celery, onion, and pimento. Here with red-tipped oak leaf lettuce.* 4, 2, 1 main-dish servings. Page 276

CHICKEN CLUB SALAD *Thyme-flavored chicken-breast halves, sliced and served with crisp bacon, tomato slices, lettuce, and toast points.* 2 main-dish servings. Page 276

ANTIPASTO SALAD DINNER *(top) Vegetables, salami, and cheese in Vinaigrette Dressing.* 6 main-dish servings. Page 277. **PEPPER SALAD** *(bottom) Peppers, onion, and olives with feta and dressing.* 6 servings. Page 279. **CLASSIC POTATO SALAD** *Potatoes, celery, and egg in mayonnaise; here with parsley garnish.* 6 servings. Page 281

POTATO DELI DINNER *Potatoes, bacon, celery, and onion in a tangy dressing, served with salad greens, deli-sliced meats, and cheese strips.* 6 main-dish servings. Page 277

WARM SALAD OF ARTICHOKE HEARTS AND CHERRY TOMATOES *Artichoke hearts and tomatoes in a buttery onion, tarragon, and wine sauce.* 6 servings. Page 279

GARDEN VEGETABLES AND PASTA SALAD *A hearty combination of fresh vegetables, cheese cubes, and bow-tie macaroni in a flavorful dressing.* 6 main-dish servings. Page 280

SUPREME SHRIMP SALAD *Shrimp, small potatoes, green and garbanzo beans, red pepper, and olives. Tossed with Zesty Mayonnaise Dressing.* 6 servings. Page 282

THAI-STYLE BEEF AND NOODLE SALAD *(left) An imaginative dish of beef with red pepper, noodles, and cashews in Thai-style dressing.* 4 main-dish servings. Page 277. **SHRIMP SALAD WITH CHINESE PEA PODS** *Shrimp, pea pods, green onions, red pepper, and baby corn cooked in wine, then seasoned with lemon and dill.* 4 servings. Page 282

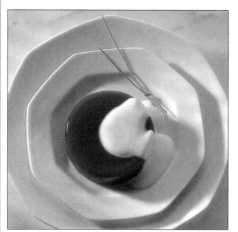

TOMATO ASPIC *A simple, chilled tomato mold spiced with hot-pepper sauce and garnished with plain low-fat yogurt and chives.* 4, 2, 1 servings. Page 281

CHICKEN AND POTATO SALAD WITH ZESTY DRESSING *Chicken, potatoes, red onion, yellow pepper, and olives in dressing. Here with basil garnish.* 6 main-dish servings. Page 276

THREE BEAN SALAD *(left) Colorful dish of beans in an oil-vinegar dressing.* 8 servings. Page 280. **LENTILS VINAIGRETTE** *(center) Lentils and vegetables in a fresh-herb dressing.* 8 servings. Page 280. **WILD RICE SALAD** *Wild rice and long-grain rice with green onions, apple, celery, pine nuts, and raisins.* 8 servings. Page 281

SPAGHETTI WITH MEAT AND TOMATO SAUCE *An herby tomato-based meat sauce with chopped vegetables served over cooked spaghetti in this ever-popular dish.* 4, 2, 1 servings. Page 286

PENNE WITH DOUBLE-CHEESE SAUCE *Onions, red peppers, and pitted ripe olives tossed with mozzarella and fontina cheeses, parsley or basil, and tender penne.* 4 servings. Page 286

CHEESE TORTELLINI WITH BROCCOLI AND PINE NUTS *A hearty dish of cheese-filled tortellini and broccoli flowerets and stalks cooked with crushed red pepper, garlic, and pine nuts for added flavor, then tossed with grated Parmesan cheese.* 8 servings. Page 287

TAGLIATELLE WITH BACON, MUSH-ROOMS, AND PEAS *Pasta tossed with a creamy green-onion, mushroom, and pea sauce, sprinkled with bacon and Parmesan.* 4 servings. Page 286

MADE-IN-MINUTES SPAGHETTI SAUCE *(left) A favorite pasta sauce, seasoned with basil and thyme; here garnished with basil. 6 cups.* Page 289. **CREAMY TOMATO SAUCE** *A creamy tomato-based sauce with herbs and garlic; garnished with parsley. 2 cups. Page 288*

CHEESE-FILLED JUMBO SHELLS
*Jumbo shell macaroni filled with three cheeses, egg, and parsley,
then cooked in spaghetti sauce and garnished with chopped parsley
and grated Romano cheese.*
4 servings. Page 289

**BOW TIES WITH CHICKEN AND
VEGETABLES** *Pasta bow ties combined
with chicken-breast strips and vegetables
cooked in an oriental-style sauce.*
4 servings. Page 287

SAVORY RICE
*Rice cooked in Chicken Broth with onion
and green pepper, combined with Cheddar or fontina cheese and sour cream.*
4, 2, 1 servings. Page 291

MILANESE-STYLE RISOTTO
*Arborio rice, garlic, and onion cooked in
saffron-flavored broth, then mixed with
peas and grated Parmesan cheese.*
4 servings. Page 291

FETTUCCINE PRIMAVERA
*A colorful mixture of springtime vegetables, including leeks, broccoli,
mushrooms, zucchini, peppers, carrots, and tomatoes, mixed with a
creamy white sauce with Monterey Jack cheese, and fettuccine.*
4 servings. Page 287

RED BEANS AND RICE
A filling dish of rice topped with red kidney beans, celery, and onion in a spicy sauce, and sprinkled with crisp diced bacon.
4 servings. Page 291

CHINESE-STYLE RICE WITH PORK
Cubes of tender boneless pork loin cutlets are cooked with onion, celery, red pepper, and rice, then flavored with a soy and ginger oriental-style sauce; here accompanied with soy sauce.
4 servings. Page 290

INDIAN PILAF
An authentic dish of tender spiced rice, chopped coriander or parsley, and raisins, topped with golden-brown sliced almonds.
4 servings. Page 292

ARROZ CON POLLO
Chicken pieces are coated in flour, browned, and cooked with turmeric-flavored rice, smoked ham, onion, celery, and green pepper. Here garnished with sliced pimento and parsley.
4, 2, 1 servings. Page 290

BULGUR PILAF WITH PEPPERS
Cracked wheat softened in broth, then mixed with peppers, mushrooms, and basil; here with basil garnish.
8 servings. Page 293

BARLEY WITH WILD MUSHROOMS
A savory combination of pearl barley and wild-mushroom pieces cooked until tender in Beef Broth, then garnished with parsley.
4 servings. Page 293

ITALIAN SAUSAGE, RICE, AND BEANS
A hearty dish of sweet Italian-sausage links, cooked rice, kidney beans, onions, and tomatoes, with oregano and garlic.
4 servings. Page 290

MEAT-FILLED MANICOTTI *(top) Meat with herbs, currants, and nuts in manicotti shells; here with white sauce and Parmesan.* 4 servings. Page 289. **WILD RICE AND MUSHROOM PILAF** *Wild rice cooked with bouillon; combined with onion, mushrooms, and seasoning. Garnished with coriander.* 4 servings. Page 292

POLENTA WITH MEAT SAUCE
A decorative dish of seasoned cornmeal and mozzarella, cut into shapes and cooked with Made-in-minutes Spaghetti Sauce.
4 servings. Page 293

LASAGNA
Layers of rich meat sauce, pasta, and cheese, finishing with mozzarella and Parmesan. Here accompanied with salad.
10 servings. Page 288

LASAGNA ROLLS WITH SPINACH AND MUSHROOMS *Lasagna noodles with a cheese, spinach, and mushroom filling; here with Creamy Tomato Sauce.*
4 servings. Page 288

SOUTH-OF-THE-BORDER CORN MUFFINS *Bacon, green onions, and cheese in corn muffins; with srambled eggs, tomato, bacon, coriander, and green onions.* Makes 12. Page 299

BANANA MUFFINS *A sugar-cinnamon-nutmeg topping complements the fruity flavor of these banana muffins with added grated orange peel.* Makes 12. Page 299

GINGERBREAD MUFFINS *Spicy muffins made with ground ginger, cinnamon, cloves, nutmeg, sour cream, and molasses. Here served with butter.* Makes 12. Page 299

WARM VEGETABLE SALAD WITH CHEESE IN PITA *(top) Tender-crisp vegetables with melted cheese in pitas; garnished with parsley.* 4, 2, 1 servings. **PITA POCKETS WITH SOUVLAKI** *Sliced lamb with piquant vegetables and feta cheese in toasted pitas.* 4 servings. Page 305

SMOKED TURKEY AND SWISS ON CROISSANTS *Croissants with mustard, smoked turkey, tomato, and Swiss cheese; garnished with salad greens.* 4 servings. Page 300

ROAST BEEF AND BRIE SIZZLER *Tarragon- and mustard-flavored butter on French bread with hot roast beef and Brie; here with cherry tomatoes and tarragon.* 4 servings. Page 301

SLOPPY JOES
Ground beef, onion, green pepper, and celery in chili-catchup sauce in hamburger buns; here with celery-leaf garnish.
4 servings. Page 303

DESIGNER BAGELS *Warmed bagel halves topped with: Orange Julienne with Orange Butter; ripe olives, sun-dried tomatoes, and basil with ricotta cheese; red-pepper strips with Smoked Salmon and Chive Spread.*
Makes 12 bagel halves. Page 309

EASY BEEF TORTILLAS
Ground beef with onion and garlic in spicy tomato sauce on tortillas and here served with traditional accompaniments.
4 servings. Page 302

TUNA MELT
Tuna in piquant cream-cheese mixture in toasted English muffin with melted cheese. Here accompanied with salad greens.
4 servings. Page 308

REUBENS
Corned beef, sauerkraut, and Swiss cheese on rye with Russian dressing. Here garnished with dill pickles and parsley.
4, 2, 1 servings. Page 303

OPEN-FACED HOT TURKEY SAND-WICHES WITH GRAVY *Thinly sliced cooked turkey on whole-wheat toast with piping hot gravy. Garnished with parsley.*
2 servings. Page 300

SAVORY BREADSTICKS *(left) Bacon slices wrapped around breadsticks make an irresistible canapé, served here with a decorative chive-tomato garnish. Makes 12. Page 306.* **GARLIC-CHEESE BREAD**
A popular accompaniment to Italian food with added mozzarella; served here with salad. 6 pieces. Page 308

30-60 MINUTES

MOZZARELLA FRENCH BREAD
Hollowed-out French bread filled with cheese, pimento-stuffed green olives, green onions, and prosciutto.
8 servings. Page 309

NUTTY GOAT CHEESE TOASTS
Pecan-coated goat cheese on toasted French bread with sun-dried tomatoes and olive oil. Accompanied with salad greens.
Makes 24. Page 306

PIZZA TARTLETS
Warmed tartlet shells filled with pizza sauce, mozzarella, anchovies, and olives. Garnished with basil.
Makes 16. Page 306

CRANBERRY-NUT BREAD
Graham-cracker crumbs add texture to this quick bread with cranberries, walnuts, and orange peel. Here served with butter.
12 servings. Page 297

POLENTA BREAD TOASTS
Toasted slices of Italian-style bread made with cornmeal, golden raisins, Parmesan cheese, and pine nuts. Served with butter.
12 servings. Page 297

ZUCCHINI BREAD
In this traditional favorite, walnuts, poppy seeds, and lemon peel are added for extra flavor. Served here with Orange Butter.
12 servings. Page 297

MEATBALL SUBS
Garlic- and mushroom-flavored meatballs in spaghetti sauce in toasted hero rolls with parsley garnish and extra sauce.
4 servings. Page 303

CHICKEN FAJITAS
Chicken, onion, and green pepper wrapped in tortillas with Guacamole, sour cream, and cheese. Served with Pico de Gallo.
4 servings. Page 306

STEAK HEROES
Thin slices of steak with green pepper, red onion, and melted cheese in toasted French bread. Garnished here with parsley.
4, 2, 1 servings. Page 301

CHICKEN CLUB SANDWICHES
A filling sandwich of chicken coated with stuffing mix, bacon, lettuce, and tomatoes on whole-wheat toast.
4 servings. Page 300

CALZONE
Italian-style folded pizzas with hearty fillings of your choice; here served with radicchio leaves and parsley garnish.
2 servings. Page 310

PORK CUTLET SUPPER SANDWICHES
Bread-crumbed pork cutlet topped with barbecue sauce and coleslaw in a hamburger bun; here served with watercress.
4 servings. Page 301

FOUR SEASONS PIZZA
Artichoke hearts, prosciutto, tomatoes, and roasted sweet red peppers top pesto sauce or basil on a pizza base.
4 servings. Page 310

MEDITERRANEAN PIZZA
Sliced red onion and assorted herbs with tangy crumbled goat cheese or feta create an original pizza topping.
4 servings. Page 310

TOASTED SANDWICHES WITH CAMEMBERT AND PEARS *(top)*
Unusual combination of Camembert and pear in white bread, browned and cut into quarters; with pear and mint garnish. 4 servings. Page 309
CROQUE MONSIEUR *A classic ham and Swiss cheese toasted sandwich; served here with salad.* 4, 2, 1 servings. Page 308

SPICED APPLE SLICES
Fluted apple rings gently poached in apple juice with brown sugar, spices, and lemon peel. Garnished here with mint.
4 servings. Page 317

GLAZED BANANAS WITH ORANGE
Bananas and oranges in a cinnamon-flavored, brown-sugar and butter glaze with pecans and Orange Julienne.
4 servings. Page 319

CHERRIES IN RED WINE
Fresh cherries cooked in a wine sauce with red-currant jelly and cinnamon; here served with ice cream and mint garnish.
6 servings. Page 319

PASTRY CREAM
Different-flavored Pastry Creams in tartlet shells with pretty garnishes: Almond Pastry Cream and Mocha Pastry Cream (left); plain Pastry Cream; Orange Pastry Cream (right).
Makes 3 cups. Page 324

RED FRUIT COMPOTE
Colorful dish of mixed berries and cherries in sauce flavored with orange-flavor liqueur; garnished with kiwifruit slices.
8 servings. Page 323

SPICED PINEAPPLE
Ground ginger or cinnamon flavor these sugar-glazed pineapple slices; garnished with Lime Julienne and mint leaves.
4 servings. Page 321

APPLE CARAMEL DESSERT
Lightly spiced pastry base topped with decoratively arranged apple slices in caramel; serve warm or chilled.
6 servings. Page 318

NEW ENGLAND BAKED APPLES
Seedless raisins, chopped walnuts, and ground cinnamon mixed with butter or margarine fill hollowed-out cooking apples, that are then cooked and basted with apple juice and maple syrup.
4, 2, 1 servings. Page 317

APPLE BETTY PUDDING
Whole-wheat bread crumbs and apple-sauce in a spiced pudding; served here with cream and orange garnish.
6 servings. Page 318

APPLE-WALNUT CRISP
A spiced walnut, flour, and sugar topping over apple slices; here with whipped cream, and apple and mint garnish.
8 servings. Page 318

DRIED FRUIT COMPOTE
Dried apricots, prunes, and figs with candied cherries in a spiced sauce, garnished with Orange Julienne.
8 servings. Page 323

CARAMEL PEARS IN STRAWBERRY SAUCE
Peeled poached whole pears are served on individual dessert dishes with smooth strawberry puree; creamy caramel sauce is spooned over just before serving. Here with mint garnish.
4, 2, 1 servings. Page 321

POACHED PEARS WITH CHOCOLATE SAUCE *Poached pear "fans" served with rich chocolate sauce; here feathered with extra cream.*
4 servings. Page 321

ZABAGLIONE WITH CHERRIES
A rich Italian-style dessert of egg yolks beaten with sugar and kirsch or Marsala, served over sweet cherries.
4 servings. Page 319

PLUM KUCHEN
Pitted plum quarters arranged in baking dish on top of slightly sweetened buttermilk biscuits and topped with brown sugar and Melba-toast Crumbs.
6 servings. Page 322

WHITE-CHOCOLATE MOUSSE
A rich, chilled dessert made with melted white chocolate, beaten eggs, vanilla extract, and softly whipped cream.
8 servings. Page 329

CHOCOLATE-DIPPED FRUIT
A selection of fruit dipped in melted semisweet and white chocolate makes an impressive end to any meal.
14 to 30 pieces. Page 327

CHOCOLATE-COCONUT DESSERT CUPS *Ice cream served in chocolate-coconut cups; here served with Chocolate-dipped Fruit and mint garnish.*
6 servings. Page 331

CREAMY RICE PUDDING
A filling family favorite made with cream, vanilla, ground spices, and raisins. Can be served warm or chilled.
6 servings. Page 332

OLD-FASHIONED BREAD AND BUTTER PUDDING *Cinnamon, nutmeg, cloves, and vanilla add flavor to this microwave version of a classic pudding.*
10 servings. Page 334

CHOCOLATE-CINNAMON BREAD PUDDING *Give a new look to a favorite dish by combining cinnamon bread with half-and-half, eggs, sugar, and chocolate.*
10 Servings. Page 335

BROWNIE PUDDING
A warm dessert made from a brownie-type mixture with cocoa and walnuts, then dusted with confectioners' sugar.
8 servings. Page 332

"NOUVELLES" STRAWBERRIES
Here, strawberries are cut in half and attractively arranged on chilled orange- and chocolate-flavored custard sauces.
6 servings. Page 322

RASPBERRY-POACHED PEARS WITH CHOCOLATE-RASPBERRY SAUCE *An elegant dessert with a sumptuous sauce; here feathered with sweetened cream.*
6 servings. Page 320

ORANGE CHALLAH PUDDING
A new version of a favorite pudding with traditional Jewish egg-enriched bread, orange juice, and ground nutmeg.
10 servings. Page 334

RICH NOODLE PUDDING
Conventionally cooked egg noodles with cottage cheese, sour cream, dried apricots, golden raisins, and browned bread crumbs.
8 servings. Page 335

LIGHT CHEESE RING WITH FRUIT (top) *Molded cottage cheese and Neufchâtel cheese with orange peel; served with a selection of fruit and mint garnish.* 8 servings. Page 323. **STRAWBERRY CHARLOTTE**
A rich mousse encased in ladyfingers, garnished with cream and strawberries, and tied with ribbon. 12 servings. Page 324

CHOCOLATE MOUSSE TORTE
A creamy chocolate mousse with a crunchy chocolate-nut base; garnished with cream, chopped nuts, and Chocolate Rounds.
16 servings. Page 328

ELEGANT POACHED PEACHES
Peaches cut in half and cooked in a grenadine-based syrup, then filled with moistened amaretti-cookie crumbs; served on a pureed raspberry sauce flavored with almond extract.
4 servings. Page 320

CRÈME CARAMEL
A velvety smooth set custard flavored with vanilla; served chilled with a rich, golden-brown caramel sauce.
4 servings. Page 325

RASPBERRY CREAM PARFAITS *(top) Layers of luscious raspberry mousse and whipped cream; here garnished with Chocolate Curls.*
6 servings. **FROSTY LEMON SOUFFLÉS** *Delicately flavored lemon custard with cream and egg whites; served frozen.* 8 servings. Page 326

CRÈME BRÛLÉE
Melted brown sugar forms a crisp topping over a chilled, rich custard base; garnished here with a Strawberry Fan.
4 servings. Page 325

RHUBARB TAPIOCA WITH CREAM
Two favorite family desserts combined in one, made richer with topping of whipped cream. Garnished here with mint.
8 servings. Page 326

CHOCOLATE-CHESTNUT CREAM
Chestnut puree and chocolate are set with gelatin in this soufflé-like dessert. Here garnished with cream and Chocolate Curls.
12 servings. Page 327

NUTTY CHOCOLATE PUDDING
Chopped pecans add crunch to this rich pudding topped with whipped cream and sprinkled with cinnamon.
6 servings. Page 332

POTS DE CRÈME ÉLÉGANTS
A simple mousse of semisweet chocolate and eggs, flavored with vanilla and topped here with whipped cream.
4 servings. Page 328

TINY CHOCOLATE CONES
A chocolate-cream mixture here piped into colorful foil cones and sprinkled with finely chopped macadamia nuts.
Makes 25 cones. Page 329

TIRAMISÚ
Layers of almond-flavored cake and cream-cheese sauce with rum or coffee, lightly dusted with cocoa, and served chilled.
16 servings. Page 327

CHOCOLATE-CREAM LOAF
Finely chopped pistachio nuts top this chilled dessert "loaf" of semisweet chocolate and whipped cream; here shown sliced and served with raspberry sauce and Chocolate Leaves.
16 servings. Page 328

CHOCOLATE-ALMOND DESSERT
Raisins plumped in almond-flavor liqueur and combined with amaretti cookies in a frosted cake-like dessert.
8 servings. Page 329

INDIVIDUAL RASPBERRY CHEESECAKES *Pureed raspberries in cheesecake on vanilla-wafer crumb crusts; garnished with raspberry and mint.* 8 servings. Page 336

CREAMY CHEESECAKE
A classic cheesecake on a crumb crust, here topped with sour cream; garnished with strawberries, raspberries, and mint. 12 servings. Page 335

CHOCOLATE-AMARETTI CHEESECAKE *(top) Chocolate mousse-like cake with amaretti crust, garnished with cream and Chocolate Curls.* 12 servings. Page 336. **CHOCOLATE CREAM PUFFS** *Choux-paste puffs, here filled with Pastry Cream, with Chocolate Glaze, dusted with confectioners' sugar.* 12 cream puffs. Page 331

VANILLA ICE CREAM
Classic vanilla-flavored ice cream, served here with sliced orange, strawberries, and kiwifruit, and a mint sprig for garnish. 8 servings. Page 330

MANGO SORBET
Mango, lime juice, and dark rum are pureed together and then frozen to make this exotic frosted dessert. 4 servings. Page 330

KIWIFRUIT SORBET
A frozen tangy puree of kiwifruit and lemon juice, served here with kiwifruit slices and mint leaves for garnish. 4 servings. Page 330

WHITE CHOCOLATE AND STRAW-BERRY GÂTEAU *Sumptuous layer cake with strawberries; filled and frosted with White-chocolate Mousse.*
12 servings. Page 342

SUNNY ORANGE LAYER CAKE
Mandarin orange sections garnish this cake filled with Lemon-curd Filling and frosted with Orange Whipped Cream.
10 servings. Page 340

BLACK FOREST CAKE
Kirsch flavors this extra-rich cake made from devil's-food-cake mix and decorated with cream, cherries, and chocolate.
12 servings. Page 343

BOSTON CREAM PIE
Creamy vanilla pudding sandwiched between cake layers, frosted with Chocolate Glaze and feathered icing.
12 servings. Page 344

STRAWBERRY SHORTCAKE
A whipped-cream mixture flavored with vanilla is combined with cut-up straw-berries to fill a luscious three-layer cake.
8 servings. Page 342

BÛCHE DE NOËL
A traditional French Christmas "log" of chocolate-fudge jelly roll with chilled chocolate pudding filling; generously covered with Chocolate-cream Frosting and marked to resemble bark.
14 servings. Page 345

CAKES

PINEAPPLE UPSIDE-DOWN CAKE
A popular dessert or after-school treat, canned pineapple rings and maraschino cherries in a sugar-butter glaze top this yellow-cake layer which can be served warm or chilled.
12 servings. Page 339

PEANUT-BUTTER CUPCAKES
A creamy chocolate and peanut-butter frosting tops these light cupcakes of yellow-cake mix and peanut butter.
12 cupcakes. Page 340

TWO-TONED LAYER CAKE
Chocolate mousse is spread between four cake layers, the whole cake then lavishly frosted with Chocolate-cream Frosting.
12 servings. Page 341

APPLESAUCE SPICE CAKE
A spicy yellow-cake batter with apple slices and walnut-crumb topping, and drizzled with Confectioners' Icing.
6 servings. Page 339

CARROT CAKE
Ground cinnamon, allspice, and nutmeg are combined with yogurt, golden raisins, walnuts, and shredded carrots in a yellow-cake mix. Decoratively finished with Cream-cheese Frosting and walnuts.
10 servings. Page 341

APRICOT PARTY ROULADE
Light-as-a-feather jelly roll filled with apricot preserves and coated with almond-flavored whipped cream.
14 servings. Page 346

CHOCOLATE SWIRL BUNDT CAKE
Devil's-food-cake mix with surprise filling of sweetened cream cheese and drizzled with Chocolate Glaze.
16 servings. Page 347

CHOCOLATE FUDGE BOMBE
A rich, chocolate-fudge-cake bombe lavishly filled with a creamy chocolate-mousse mix, and beautifully decorated with piped whipped cream rosettes and a dusting of cocoa.
10 servings. Page 347

FUDGE BROWNIES
Moist brownies enriched with eggs, topped with extra chocolate and chopped walnuts, and chilled, after cooking, until firm.
24 brownies. Page 348

BUTTERSCOTCH BROWNIES
Pecans, flaked coconut, and semisweet-chocolate pieces are added to these flavor-packed brownies.
24 brownies. Page 348

NO-BAKE MINT BROWNIES
Graham-cracker crumbs combined with chopped walnuts add texture and flavor to these quick and easy cookies.
24 brownies. Page 348

COOKIES

CREAM-CHEESE BROWNIES *(left) Almond-flavored softened cream cheese creates a marbled design in fudge-brownie mix. 16 brownies.*
ROCKY ROAD BROWNIES *Miniature marshmallows, chocolate pieces, and chopped walnuts top a rich fudge-brownie mix. 16 brownies.*
Page 349

ALMOND SHORTBREAD
Vanilla and almond extracts flavor this classic shortbread which is attractively topped with toasted sliced almonds.
8 wedges. Page 349

COCONUT ROUNDS
Delicate toasted-coconut cookies with added orange peel, attractively decorated with melted semisweet chocolate.
30 cookies. Page 350

LEMON TUILES
Light-as-a-feather cookies flavored with lemon peel and almond extract and sprinkled liberally with sliced almonds.
30 tuiles. Page 350

FRUIT AND NUT BARS
Dried apricots, raisins, prunes, almonds, and walnuts covered with a semisweet-chocolate topping.
16 bars. Page 354

MEXICAN WEDDING COOKIES
Traditional crescent-shaped walnut cookies dusted with a thick layer of confectioners' sugar until completely coated.
24 cookies. Page 351

FLORENTINES
Authentic thin, chewy cookies made with sugar, cream, honey, butter or margarine, chopped candied fruit, and sliced almonds. Cooled then coated on one side with melted chocolate.
24 pieces. Page 351

MAPLE SNAPS
Buttery walnut cookies with maple- and corn-syrup base, flavored with maple extract and cooked until lightly browned.
24 cookies. Page 351

CHOCOLATE-CHIP CRISPS
Sweetened and lightly spiced ground-walnut cookies topped with chopped walnuts and miniature chocolate pieces.
30 cookies. Page 354

VIENNESE MELTAWAYS *(top) Melt-in-the-mouth almond cookies, here dusted with confectioners' sugar and cocoa. Makes 36. Page 350.*
CARAMEL-PECAN BARS *Cookie base topped with pecans and creamy caramel then drizzled with melted chocolate. 24 cookies. Page 354*

CHOCOLATE-MALLOW FUDGE
Squares of fudge created from two types of chocolate, chopped walnuts, and melted marshmallows.
36 pieces. Page 357

HOLIDAY MINTS
White, green, and pink mint candies here shown half-dipped into melted chocolate for an extra-festive look.
36 candies. Page 355

PEANUT BRITTLE
A classic candy of roasted peanuts combined with caramel made from light corn syrup, sugar, and butter or margarine.
Makes 1 pound. Page 356

MAPLE-WALNUT DROPS
Candies based on the ever-popular combination of walnut and maple, sweetened with brown sugar.
42 candies. Page 355

PISTACHIO BITES
Vanilla and pistachio flavor layers of creamy white chocolate in this melt-in-the-mouth candy.
32 pieces. Page 358

FUDGE SLICES
A feast of plump maraschino cherries in a fudge roll, coated with melted caramel and chopped walnuts.
36 slices. Page 357

BUTTER CARAMELS
Individually wrapped chewy candies made from heavy cream, sugar, corn syrup, butter, and vanilla.
64 caramels. Page 356

CHOCOLATE-CHERRY CUPS *(top) Tiny chocolate cups with orange-flavor filling and each topped with a maraschino cherry. 36 candies.*
Page 356. **SUPER-EASY TRUFFLES** *Melted semisweet chocolate with added butter, cream, and almond extract; attractively piped into bonbon cups. 30 truffles. Page 357*

COCONUT HAYSTACKS
Lightly toasted coconut is mixed with melted bittersweet chocolate, then shaped to resemble haystacks.
20 candies. Page 358

ORANGE CHIFFON PIE
Orange peel and orange and lemon juice make refreshing additions to this classic chiffon pie.
10 servings. Page 368

BANANA-COCONUT PIE
Sliced banana covered with a creamy vanilla-flavored filling in a Baked Piecrust; topped with toasted coconut.
10 servings. Page 366

GRASSHOPPER PIE
Inspired by the Grasshopper cocktail, the filling in this Chocolate-wafer Crumb Crust is a luscious combination of creamy custard, coffee, and crème de menthe liqueur, with a Chocolate Curl garnish.
10 servings. Page 367

GRAHAM-CRACKER CRUMB CRUST
Our versatile crumb crust is shown here with a chiffon-style filling and decorated with piped cream and mandarin oranges.
Makes 9″ crumb crust. Page 361

PASTRY FOR TART SHELL
A conventionally baked, classic shell for tarts of all types; here filled with glazed, fresh strawberries.
Makes 9″ to 10″ tart shell. Page 361

BAKED PIECRUST
A traditionally baked pastry piecrust, here shown with a Leaf Edge, filled with custard, and topped with fresh blueberries.
Makes 9″ piecrust. Page 361

LEMON MERINGUE PIE
*A classic, all-time favorite of lemon-flavored custard in a Baked
Piecrust with attractively swirled meringue topping, conventionally
baked until golden.*
10 servings. Page 365

DELUXE APPLE PIE
*An old-fashioned pie filled with tender
apples, lightly spiced, with a
complementary oat-crumb topping.*
10 servings. Page 363

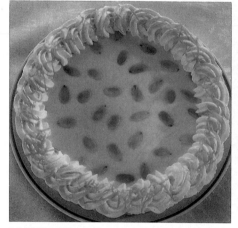

LIGHT LEMON AND ALMOND TART
*A creamy lemon and almond filling in a
conventionally baked Tart Shell, topped
with cream, almonds, and Lemon Julienne.*
10 servings. Page 370

PEACHES AND CREAM PIE
*Instant vanilla pudding combined with
cream and peach preserves in a crumb
crust and topped with cooked peach slices.*
10 servings. Page 365

SUMMER FRUIT TART
*Creamy custard in a wafer crumb crust
topped with glazed strawberries,
raspberries, blueberries, and kiwifruit.*
10 servings. Page 364

PILGRIM PUMPKIN PIE
*A pumpkin custard flavored with cinnamon,
ginger, and nutmeg, in a Baked Piecrust;
served chilled and garnished with cream.*
10 servings. Page 365

BLACK-BOTTOM PIE
*These slices elegantly reveal a Gingersnap-crumb Crust filled with a
layer of rich chocolate custard and another layer of delicate rum-
flavored custard. Here garnished with piped cream.*
10 servings. Page 367

MINCE AND APPLE TARTLETS
A store-bought mincemeat filling with added apple, chopped walnuts, and lemon juice in tartlet shells topped with pastry holly leaves, hearts, and stars. If you like, serve with Hard Sauce.
10 servings. Page 371

AMARETTO PIE
Amaretto-flavored chiffon in an amaretti-cookie-crumb crust; garnished with piped whipped cream and sliced almonds.
10 servings. Page 370

CHOCOLATE-BROWNIE PIE
A chocolate and walnut filling cooked until lightly set in a Baked Piecrust; with cream and walnut garnish.
10 servings. Page 371

PECAN PIE
A traditional Thanksgiving favorite topped with pecan halves; here shown with a Braided Edge on piecrust.
10 servings. Page 371

STRAWBERRY CHIFFON PIE
Attractively arranged strawberry slices top a light and creamy mousse-like mixture set in a Graham-cracker Crumb Crust; garnished with a whole strawberry, glazed, and served chilled.
10 servings. Page 368

COCONUT BAVARIAN-CREAM PIE
A toasted-coconut crust holds a chiffon filling flavored with coconut and almond; whipped cream and coconut garnish.
10 servings. Page 369

APPLE, PEAR, AND CRANBERRY TART
A popular combination of fruits, in a baked tart shell, topped with decorative pastry cut-outs glazed with egg yolk.
10 servings. Page 363

BAVARIAN CREAM PIE
A rich vanilla filling with whipped cream and egg whites in a Baked Piecrust, here with Leaf Edge.
10 servings. Page 369

RASPBERRY CHESS PIE
A Southern favorite, flavored with vanilla and nutmeg, lightly broiled and topped with fresh raspberries.
10 servings. Page 364

CHOCOLATE-CREAM PIE
A generous layer of cream tops a luscious chocolate filling in a Vanilla-wafer Crumb Crust; with piped cream garnish.
10 servings. Page 366

APRICOT-CUSTARD TART
Classic Tart Shell filled with canned apricot halves lightly set in an almond-flavored creamy custard; garnished with toasted sliced almonds and served well chilled.
10 servings. Page 364

PEACH SAUCE
*Simple and elegant puree of peaches,
flavored with almond extract and nutmeg;
served here with raspberries and mint.*
Makes 1 cup. Page 382

BRANDIED STRAWBERRY SAUCE
*Strawberries and brandy added to melted
red-currant jelly; here served chilled over
ice cream and garnished with mint.*
Makes 2½ cups. Page 382

FUDGE SAUCE
*Luscious sauce of cocoa and sugar with
added cream; here poured over sautéed
bananas and sprinkled with almonds.*
Makes 1¼ cups. Page 383

CUSTARD SAUCE
*A popular dessert sauce of half-and-half,
sugar, egg yolks, and vanilla; here served
over a colorful variety of sliced fruits.*
Makes about 1¼ cups. Page 382

ORANGE SAUCE
*Orange-flavor liqueur and grated orange
peel in sugar syrup; served here with
orange slices and whole strawberries.*
Makes 2½ cups. Page 383

MELBA SAUCE
*A sieved, thickened sauce of raspberries
and red-currant jelly; here with poached
pear halves and mint garnish.*
Makes about 1 cup. Page 383

CHOCOLATE SAUCE
*Unsweetened chocolate melted with sugar,
cream, and butter, and flavored with
vanilla; here poured over a banana split.*
Makes 3 cups. Page 382

HOT FRUIT SAUCE
*Chopped nectarines and plums cooked with
sugar and orange juice; served here with
ice cream and mint garnish.*
Makes 4 cups. Page 382

BLUEBERRY SAUCE
*Delicately spiced blueberries with sugar,
lemon juice, and lemon peel; here with a
poached whole peach garnished with mint.*
Makes about 1 cup. Page 383

BUTTERSCOTCH SAUCE
A warm sauce of brown sugar, half-and-half, corn syrup, and butter; served here over ice cream with wafer fans.
Makes 1 cup. Page 382

CHERRY SAUCE
Sweet pitted cherries cooked with sugar and water, flavored with almond extract, and served warm; here poured over blintzes.
Makes 2 cups. Page 383

HARD SAUCE
A butter-based sauce with confectioners' sugar and vanilla; here served with warm Mince and Apple Tartlets.
Makes about ⅔ cup. Page 383

BÉARNAISE SAUCE
White-wine vinegar, green onion, tarragon, and parsley in classic French sauce; served here with filet mignon and salad greens.
Makes about 1 cup. Page 381

HOLLANDAISE SAUCE
A seasoned sauce of egg yolks, lemon juice, and melted butter, served here over asparagus with herb garnish.
Makes about 1 cup. Page 381

BARBECUE SAUCE
A jalapeño pepper, onion, and catchup mixture shown here with cooked chicken, parsley-garnished potatoes, and salad.
Makes about 1 cup. Page 379

BROWN GRAVY
A broth- and vegetable-based gravy; here with lamb chops, broccoli, carrots, mashed potatoes, and parsley garnish.
Makes about 2 cups. Page 380

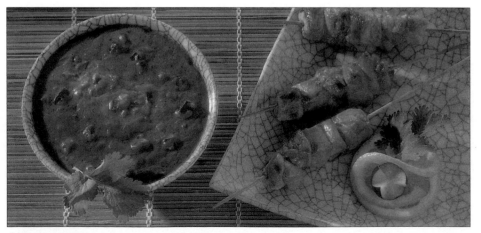

SATAY SAUCE
A peanut-butter sauce with garlic, diced red pepper, ginger, vinegar, and soy. Here shown with chicken kabobs, and garnished with lemon, radish, and coriander.
Makes about ⅓ cup. Page 379

CRANBERRY SAUCE *A classic accompaniment to turkey, given extra zest by orange juice and red-port wine. Makes 1¾ cups. Page 379.* GIBLET GRAVY *Strained, thickened broth and vegetable stock, with added giblet meat. Makes 4 cups. Page 380. Both shown here with roast turkey, potatoes, carrots, and chive garnish.*

CORN RELISH
A spicy mixture of corn, green and red peppers, tomato, onion, and vinegar; served here with garnished, glazed chicken. Makes about 4 half-pints. Page 377

MINT JELLY
A set jelly of mint, apple-juice, and vinegar; served here with lamb chops, new potatoes, and green beans.
Makes 4 half-pints. Page 376

TOMATO SAUCE
Strained, thickened sauce flavored with green onion, garlic, parsley, and basil; shown here with garnished jumbo shrimp.
Makes about 2½ cups. Page 380

APRICOT-PINEAPPLE BUTTER
A delicious spread of dried apricots and crushed pineapple; here with a toasted split English muffin with butter curls.
Makes about 2 half-pints. Page 375

TOMATO CATCHUP
A piquant relish flavored with vinegar and mixed spices; here shown with a garnished burger and French fries.
Makes 3 half-pints. Page 377

CANTALOUPE CHUTNEY
Curried mixture of melon, tomatoes, onions, and raisins, seasoned with mustard; served here with phyllo pastries. Makes about 4 half-pints. Page 378

HOT-PEPPER JELLY
A sweetened, set mixture of red-pepper juice and white vinegar; here served with ham, tomato, and mixed salad. Makes 2 half-pints. Page 376

CRANBERRY-CHESTNUT RELISH
Spicy mixture of cranberries, marrons, golden raisins, and pearl onions; here with cold roast turkey and mixed salad. Makes 4 half-pints. Page 377

HEIRLOOM CHUTNEY
Ginger- and mustard-spiced apples, onions, pepper, and prunes; here with cheese, bread, crackers, and salad. Makes about 4 half-pints. Page 378

PICCALILLI
Spiced green tomatoes, peppers, and onion mixture; here served with cheese, crackers, and salad garnish. Makes 4 half-pints. Page 378

BLACKBERRY SPREAD *(left) Zesty blackberry-apple mix.* Makes 4 half-pints. Page 376. **FRESH STRAWBERRY JAM** *(center) Preserve of crushed fresh strawberries.* Makes about 4 half-pints. Page 375. **PEACH PRESERVES** *Sliced peaches in sugar-lemon syrup.* Makes 4 half-pints. Page 375. *All shown here with croissants, breakfast rolls, and butter.*

Appetizers

DIPS · NIBBLES · PÂTÉS · FILLED APPETIZERS
VEGETABLE APPETIZERS · SEAFOOD APPETIZERS

Appetizers

A microwave makes entertaining easier and far less time consuming. Many of our appetizers can be made and frozen up to a month before serving. When you are ready to serve, they can be popped into a microwave oven to be ready in no time. If you arrange hors d'oeuvres on microwave-safe trays when cooking, they can be served straight from the microwave, saving on extra dishwashing. Also, they can be quickly popped back into the microwave for reheating during the course of the occasion. You even can add your toothpicks before cooking. Wooden or plastic picks, including those with frills, may be used in your microwave oven, as can bamboo skewers. However, do not use colored picks that can leave dye on your food.

When unexpected guests drop in, you can have something hot and delicious to welcome them with in only a few minutes. Variously shaped tartlet shells can be kept in the freezer and, when needed, defrosted in the microwave and quickly filled.

In addition to the delicious assortment of appetizer recipes included here, many of the sandwiches in our Breads and Sandwiches chapter (pages 295-310) can be adapted for buffets and other special occasions. Your microwave oven can also be used for a wide variety of commercially available packaged and frozen appetizers; just follow the directions provided with the product.

The microwave can be used to soften cheeses for use in dips or for making into cheese balls, and it is wonderful for bringing cheese from the refrigerator to perfect eating temperature. Place ½ pound unwrapped cheese in the microwave and heat on Medium (50% power), 45 seconds to 1 minute, until the chill is gone. To bring chilled dips to room temperature, heat 2 cups of dip on Medium 2 to 3 minutes just before serving. Use your microwave as well to refresh stale snacks such as pretzels, popcorn, potato chips, and mixed assortments that have lost their crispness. Heat them in 2- or 3-cup batches on High (100% power) 15 to 60 seconds.

QUICK AND EASY APPETIZERS

When unexpected guests drop in, use the microwave as an extra helper in the kitchen to create quick and easy appetizers from ingredients on hand. In a matter of minutes, you'll have an attractive appetizer that looks like it took a great deal of time and effort to prepare.

Sliced tomato and avocado (left), *drizzled with Italian salad dressing and sprinkled with microwave-crisp bacon. Garnished with basil leaves.*

Well-drained canned pineapple rings (right) topped with cream cheese and chives, sprinkled with paprika. Garnished with celery leaves, chives, and Lime Twists (page 132).

Dips

SPICY CRAB DIP

Color Index page 38. Makes 2 cups. 37 cals per tablespoon. Low in cholesterol, sodium. Begin 15 minutes ahead.

1 tablespoon butter or margarine
2 teaspoons curry powder
1 small onion, minced
1 celery stalk, minced
½ 2-ounce jar diced pimentos, drained
1 8-ounce package cream cheese

1 tablespoon milk
1 teaspoon lemon juice
¾ teaspoon salt
½ 16-ounce container lump crab meat
2 tablespoons chopped parsley
Crudités

1. In medium microwave-safe bowl, place butter or margarine, curry powder, onion, celery, and pimentos. Cook on High (100% power) 2½ (2:30) minutes, stirring twice.
2. To mixture, add cream cheese. Cook on High 1 minute, until softened. Stir until well mixed.
3. Into cream-cheese mixture, gently stir milk, lemon juice, salt, crab meat, and parsley.
4. *To serve:* Spoon dip into serving bowl. Accompany with crudités.

BACON-HORSERADISH DIP

Color Index page 38. Makes 2 cups. 38 cals per tablespoon. Low in cholesterol, sodium. Begin 25 minutes ahead.

4 slices bacon, diced
1 8-ounce package cream cheese
½ cup sour cream
2 tablespoons prepared horseradish

¼ teaspoon pepper
Pepper Bowl (optional, below)
Celery sticks, potato chips, breadsticks, and bagel chips

1. In 12″ by 8″ microwave-safe baking dish, place diced bacon. Cook on High (100% power) 4 minutes, or until browned, stirring occasionally. Remove bacon to paper towels to drain.
2. Discard all but 1 teaspoon drippings. To drippings, add cheese. Soften on High 1 minute.
3. Into mixture, stir sour cream, horseradish, and pepper. Crumble bacon; add to dip. Cover and refrigerate 20 minutes.
4. Spoon dip into dish or Pepper Bowl; serve with celery sticks, potato chips, breadsticks, and bagel chips.

Making the Pepper Bowl

With sharp knife, cut off top of pepper and a thin slice from the bottom so pepper sits flat.

From top of pepper (stem end) scrape out seeds and white membrane; discard.

Dips are popular appetizers as they are easy to prepare and can be served at any time. We offer a selection that will suit all occasions. Freshly cut raw vegetables, or crudités, are low-calorie accompaniments, while potato or corn chips are more substantial.

MEDITERRANEAN EGGPLANT DIP

Color Index page 38. 16 cals per tablespoon. Low in cholesterol, fat, sodium. Begin 25 minutes ahead.

Ingredients for 3 cups		Microwave cookware
1 medium eggplant (about 1½ pounds) *1 small red onion* *1 medium green pepper* *4 garlic cloves* *2 celery stalks with leaves* *¼ cup olive or salad oil* *1 medium tomato, chopped* *2 tablespoons red-wine vinegar*	*1 tablespoon sugar* *1 teaspoon oregano* *½ teaspoon thyme leaves* *1½ teaspoons salt* *6 green olives, chopped* *1 tablespoon capers, drained* *Pepper to taste* *Parsley sprigs for garnish* *Pita bread, toasted and cut into triangles*	12″ by 8″ baking dish or tray Medium bowl

1 Line baking dish or tray with paper towels. Pierce skin of eggplant in several places. Place eggplant in baking dish or tray. Cook on High (100% power) 7 minutes, turning over halfway through cooking.

2 Meanwhile, chop red onion, green pepper, garlic, and celery.

3 In bowl, mix chopped vegetables, oil, tomato, vinegar, sugar, oregano, thyme, and salt. Cook, covered, on High 3 minutes. Set aside.

4 Cut eggplant lengthwise in half. With spoon, scoop out flesh. In food processor with knife blade attached or in blender, process flesh until smooth. Spoon into bowl with vegetable mixture.

5 Stir vegetable mixture and pureed eggplant together. Add olives, capers, and pepper. Chill.

6 *To serve:* Spoon dip onto individual plates or into serving bowl; garnish. Accompany with toasted pita triangles.

Meal in Minutes *for 4 people*

Fast Light Lunch

Artichokes with Lemon and Garlic, page 120
Piperade, page 139, with
Heart-shaped Croutons (below)
Fresh fruit plate

PREPARATION TIMETABLE

1½ hours ahead:	*Prepare a selection of fresh seasonal fruit. Sprinkle cut fruit with lemon juice to prevent discoloration; cover and refrigerate.*
1 hour ahead:	*Prepare and cook Artichokes with Lemon and Garlic; do not garnish. Set on serving plates and keep warm.*
30 minutes ahead:	*Make Croutons, and Piperade through step 2.*
Just before serving:	*For artichokes, reheat butter in microwave; garnish. Continue cooking Piperade from step 3. Garnish with basil and Croutons.*

HEART-SHAPED CROUTONS

1 Remove crusts from **4 slices bread.** Cut bread diagonally into quarters.

2 Round off top 2 corners of each triangle; cut a "V" from top center to form heart shape. Bake conventionally as for Croûtons (page 127).

3 Dip tops of croutons into **2 tablespoons melted butter**, then into **4 tablespoons chopped parsley**.

Dips

MEXICAN DIP

Color Index page 38. Makes 1 cup. 45 cals per tablespoon. Low in cholesterol, sodium. Begin 15 minutes ahead.

1 green onion, minced
1 tablespoon butter or margarine
2 3-ounce packages cream cheese

¼ cup salsa (or to taste)
1 to 2 tablespoons milk
Chopped green onion for garnish

1. In medium microwave-safe bowl, place minced green onion and butter or margarine. Cook on High (100% power) 1 minute.
2. To green-onion mixture, add cream cheese. Heat on Medium (50% power) 1 to 1½ (1:30) minutes, until softened. Stir until smooth.
3. Into cream-cheese mixture, stir salsa; add enough milk to thin dip to desired consistency. Spoon dip into small serving bowl and garnish with green onion.

HOT SHRIMP DIP WITH DILL

Color Index page 38. Makes 2 cups. 25 cals per tablespoon. Low in cholesterol, fat, sodium. Begin 20 minutes ahead.

2 tablespoons olive or salad oil
3 garlic cloves
1 green onion, thinly sliced
1 celery stalk with leaves, cut into 2-inch pieces
½ pound medium shrimp, shelled and deveined

3 tablespoons all-purpose flour
1¼ cups milk
1½ teaspoons tomato paste
½ teaspoon salt
⅛ teaspoon ground red pepper (or to taste)
2 teaspoons lemon juice
Fresh dill for garnish
Cooked tortellini

1. In medium microwave-safe bowl, combine olive or salad oil, garlic, green onion, celery, and shrimp. Cook, covered, on High (100% power) 3 minutes, stirring halfway through cooking.
2. With slotted spoon, remove shrimp mixture from bowl, reserving liquid. In food processor with knife blade attached or on chopping board, finely chop shrimp mixture; set aside.
3. To liquid remaining in bowl, add flour; stir until blended and smooth. Cook on High 1 minute. Remove from microwave.
4. Into flour mixture, gradually stir milk and tomato paste. Add salt and ground red pepper. Cook on High 4 minutes, stirring twice during cooking.
5. Into mixture, stir lemon juice and reserved shrimp mixture. Cook on High 2 minutes.
6. *To serve:* Transfer dip to serving bowl and garnish with fresh dill. Serve immediately with tortellini.

Nibbles

MIDDLE-EASTERN MEATBALLS

Color Index page 40. Makes about 26. 33 cals each. Low in cholesterol, sodium. Begin 35 minutes ahead.

1 egg	*¼ teaspoon pepper*
¾ pound ground beef	*¼ teaspoon ground*
3 garlic cloves, minced	*cinnamon*
1 medium onion, grated	*⅛ teaspoon ground*
2 tablespoons raisins,	*cloves*
minced	*⅛ teaspoon ground*
2 tablespoons chopped	*nutmeg*
mint leaves	*Lemon slices and mint*
1 tablespoon lemon juice	*leaves for garnish*
2 teaspoons ground	
cumin	
1 teaspoon salt	

1. In medium bowl, beat egg. Add ground beef, garlic, onion, raisins, mint, lemon juice, cumin, salt, pepper, cinnamon, cloves, and nutmeg; mix until well combined.

2. Shape mixture into 1-inch meatballs. Place on microwave-safe rack set in 12″ by 8″ microwave-safe baking dish.

3. Cook meatballs on High (100% power) 4 to 5 minutes. Rearrange meatballs halfway through cooking. Let meatballs stand, covered with paper towel, 3 minutes before serving.

4. *To serve:* Thread each meatball on a long wooden skewer; arrange on plate and garnish with lemon slices and mint leaves.

CHEESE STICKS

Color Index page 39. Makes 16. 90 cals each. Low in cholesterol, sodium. Good source of vitamin A. Begin 20 minutes ahead.

½ 8-ounce package	*4 drops hot-pepper*
cream cheese	*sauce*
2 tablespoons butter or	*16 breadsticks*
margarine (¼ stick)	*¼ cup each: poppy*
2 tablespoons grated	*seeds; chopped chives;*
Parmesan cheese	*sesame seeds; paprika*
½ teaspoon Dijon	
mustard	

1. In medium microwave-safe bowl, place cream cheese and butter or margarine. Heat on High (100% power) 1½ (1:30) minutes. Stir until smooth.

2. Into cream-cheese mixture, stir Parmesan, mustard, and hot-pepper sauce; mix well.

3. With knife, spread an equal amount of cheese mixture onto half of each breadstick.

4. Place the poppy seeds, chives, sesame seeds, and paprika on separate pieces of waxed paper. Lightly roll 4 breadsticks in each of the coatings. Serve immediately.

All of our nibbles can be prepared in advance and reheated as necessary. For an alternative to Angels on Horseback (below), make Devils on Horseback by replacing the oysters with prunes.

ANGELS ON HORSEBACK

Color Index page 38. 29 cals per oyster. Low in cholesterol, fat, sodium. Begin 25 minutes ahead.

Ingredients	For 24 oysters	For 12 oysters	For 6 oysters
Bacon slices	*12 slices*	*6 slices*	*3 slices*
Worcestershire	*4 teaspoons*	*2 teaspoons*	*1 teaspoon*
Dijon mustard	*1 teaspoon*	*½ teaspoon*	*¼ teaspoon*
Oysters, shucked	*24 oysters*	*12 oysters*	*6 oysters*
Parsley sprigs and lemon slices for garnish	*garnish*	*garnish*	*garnish*
Microwave cookware	12″ by 8″ baking dish	12″ by 8″ baking dish	8″ by 8″ baking dish
Time on High (100% power)			
Bacon	4 minutes	2 minutes	1½ (1:30) minutes
Oysters	3 minutes	1½ (1:30) minutes	1 minute
Standing time	2 minutes	1 to 2 minutes	1 minute

1 With sharp knife, cut each bacon slice crosswise in half.

2 Line baking dish with double thickness of paper towels. Arrange bacon on paper towels, in batches if necessary; cover with paper towel. Cook on High for time in Chart. Remove bacon to paper towels to drain.

3 Meanwhile, in bowl, combine Worcestershire and mustard. Add shucked oysters; stir to coat.

4 Wrap each bacon slice around an oyster, securing it with a wooden toothpick.

5 Arrange bacon-wrapped oysters in same baking dish. Cover dish with paper towel. Cook on High for time in Chart, turning once.

6 Let oysters stand for time in Chart. Garnish with parsley sprigs and lemon slices. Serve immediately.

Nibbles

POTATO SKINS WITH CHEDDAR CHEESE

Color Index page 40. 72 cals per piece (without dip). Low in cholesterol, sodium. Begin 40 minutes ahead.

Ingredients	For 16 pieces	For 8 pieces	For 4 pieces
Baking potatoes, unpeeled	4 medium	2 medium	1 medium
Cheddar cheese, shredded	6 ounces (1½ cups)	3 ounces (¾ cup)	1 ounce (¼ cup)
Green onions, minced	2 green onions	1 green onion	½ green onion
Salt	½ teaspoon	¼ teaspoon	to taste
Pepper	to taste	to taste	to taste
Green onions for garnish	4 green onions	2 green onions	1 green onion
Sour cream or yogurt	dip	dip	dip
Microwave cookware	12″ platter	12″ platter	8″ platter
Time on High (100% power)			
Potatoes	16 to 18 minutes	10 to 12 minutes	6 to 7 minutes
With cheese topping	4 to 5 minutes	2 to 3 minutes	1 minute
Standing time			
Potatoes	5 minutes	5 minutes	5 minutes
With cheese topping	2 minutes	1 to 2 minutes	1 minute

1 Wash and dry each potato; pierce 3 times. Place on paper towels.

2 Cook potatoes on High for time in Chart, turning over once.

3 Wrap potatoes in clean cloth towel. Let stand for time in Chart.

4 Meanwhile, in bowl, combine cheese and minced green onions.

5 Cut each potato lengthwise into quarters.

6 Scoop out potatoes, leaving ¼-inch potato layer on skins.

9 Cook potato skins on High for time in Chart. Let stand for time in Chart, to allow cheese to cool slightly. Garnish platter with green onions and serve with sour cream or yogurt.

7 On platter (see Chart), arrange skins spoke-fashion.

8 Sprinkle skins with salt, pepper, and cheese mixture.

EL NACHO GRANDE

Color Index page 39. 6 servings. 326 cals per serving. Good source of calcium. Begin 15 minutes ahead.

4 ounces Monterey Jack cheese with jalapeño pepper ("Pepper Jack"), shredded (1 cup)
4 ounces Cheddar cheese, shredded (1 cup)
½ small red onion, diced
⅓ cup pitted ripe olives, sliced
⅓ cup chopped coriander leaves
1 7-ounce bag corn tortilla chips
Sour cream and salsa (optional)

1. In medium bowl, mix cheeses, onion, olives, and coriander; set aside.
2. On 12″ round microwave-safe platter, arrange one third tortilla chips in single layer. Top with one third cheese mixture. Continue alternating tortilla chips and cheese mixture making 2 more layers, finishing with cheese mixture.
3. Cook on High (100% power) 2 to 3 minutes, until cheese melts and bubbles.
4. Serve immediately. If you like, accompany with sour cream and salsa.

BUFFALO CHICKEN WINGS

Color Index page 39. Makes 12. 190 cals each. Low in cholesterol. Begin 25 minutes ahead.

6 chicken wings
1 small onion, minced
¼ cup catchup
2 tablespoons butter or margarine (¼ stick)
2 tablespoons steak sauce
2 tablespoons light-brown sugar
2 tablespoons orange juice
¼ to ½ teaspoon hot-pepper sauce
3 celery stalks, cut into sticks
1 cup creamy blue-cheese salad dressing

1. With sharp knife, remove small tips from each chicken wing. Cut wings in half at joint, making 12 pieces.
2. In medium microwave-safe bowl, combine onion, catchup, butter or margarine, steak sauce, brown sugar, orange juice, and hot-pepper sauce. Cook on High (100% power) 4 minutes, stirring sauce once.
3. In 12″ by 8″ microwave-safe baking dish, arrange chicken pieces in single layer; spoon over half the sauce. Cook chicken pieces on High 6 minutes.
4. Turn wings over and coat with remaining sauce. Cook on High 6 minutes, or until chicken is fork-tender and juices run clear.
5. Transfer chicken pieces to warmed serving dish. Garnish with prepared celery sticks. Pass blue-cheese salad dressing as dip for chicken and celery sticks.

Pâtés

COUNTRY-STYLE PORK PÂTÉ

Color Index page 41. 16 first-course servings. 198 cals per serving. Good source of vitamin A, iron. Begin 1 day ahead.

½ pound baked ham, diced	¼ teaspoon ground nutmeg
½ pound ground chicken livers	8 slices bacon
4 slices bacon, diced	¾ pound ground beef
4 garlic cloves, minced	¾ pound ground pork
1 medium onion, minced	1 teaspoon salt
¼ cup brandy	⅛ teaspoon pepper
1 teaspoon thyme leaves	Sliced gherkins, salad greens, and olives for garnish
½ teaspoon oregano	
¼ teaspoon ground cloves	

1. In large bowl, combine ham, chicken livers, diced bacon, garlic, onion, brandy, thyme, oregano, cloves, and nutmeg; cover bowl and set aside.
2. Meanwhile, line 9″ by 5″ microwave-safe loaf pan with bacon slices, allowing slices to hang over edge of pan; set aside.
3. To ham mixture, add ground beef and pork, salt, and pepper; stir until well mixed. Spoon pâté mixture into bacon-lined pan, smoothing top with back of spoon. On level surface, tap corner of pan several times to disperse any air bubbles. Fold bacon over top of pâté mixture.
4. Elevate loaf pan on microwave-safe trivet, rack, or ramekins turned upside down. Cook, covered loosely with waxed paper, on High (100% power) 20 minutes. Pour off excess fat.
5. Let pâté stand 30 minutes to cool. Cover loaf pan with waxed paper or plastic wrap, then foil-wrapped cardboard and foil-wrapped weight (below). Refrigerate overnight.
6. Remove weight, cardboard, and plastic wrap. Place plate or chopping board upside down on loaf pan and invert to unmold. With knife, scrape off any coagulated cooking juices and excess fat.
7. *To serve:* Garnish pâté and cut into thin slices. If you like, accompany with crackers, mustard, and extra gherkins.

Wrapping and Weighting the Pâté

Cut a piece of cardboard to the size of the top of the loaf pan and wrap completely in foil. Place over pâté mixture.

Wrap a brick in foil or use several cans to weight the pâté. Place weight on the foil-wrapped cardboard.

Pâtés make elegant appetizers that cook quickly in the microwave but need to be chilled to be at their best. Use plastic wrap to line loaf pans for easier removal and elevate to ensure even cooking.

SEAFOOD PÂTÉ

Color Index page 41. 128 cals per serving. Begin early in day.

Ingredients for 16 first-course servings		Microwave cookware
½ pound small shrimp, shelled and deveined	1½ cups chilled heavy or whipping cream	9″ by 5″ loaf pan
1 shallot, minced	1 egg	Small bowl
1 tablespoon butter or margarine	1 teaspoon salt	Trivet, rack, or ramekin
1 small tomato, seeded and chopped	⅛ teaspoon white pepper	
3 tablespoons chopped tarragon leaves	Tarragon leaves and chopped tomato for garnish	
1 pound sea scallops	Mayonnaise (optional)	

1. Line loaf pan with plastic wrap, allowing the plastic wrap to extend 2 inches beyond the edges of the pan.

2. With sharp knife, chop shrimp. In small bowl, mix shrimp, shallot, and butter or margarine. Cook on High (100% power) 1 minute, stirring once. Add tomato and tarragon; stir and set aside.

3. In food processor with knife blade attached or in blender, process scallops until smooth. Gradually pour in cream until well mixed; blend in egg, salt, and pepper. Spoon mixture into medium bowl.

4. Fold in reserved shrimp mixture and gently spoon into loaf pan; smooth with back of spoon. On level surface, tap corner of pan several times to disperse air bubbles. Fold edges of plastic wrap over pâté mixture.

5. Elevate pan on trivet, rack, or ramekin turned upside down. Cook on Medium (50% power) 10 minutes. Cover pâté mixture with cookie sheet or tray to flatten surface. Let stand 20 minutes. Refrigerate at least 3 hours.

6. *To serve:* Unfold edges of plastic wrap. Place chilled platter upside down on loaf pan and invert to unmold. Remove plastic wrap completely and garnish pâté with tarragon and tomato. If you like, serve with mayonnaise.

Pâté and Filled Appetizers

CHICKEN LIVER PÂTÉ

Color Index page 41. Makes 1 cup. 46 cals per tablespoon. Low in sodium. Good source of vitamin A. Begin early in day.

4 tablespoons butter or margarine (½ stick)
1 green onion, minced
1 garlic clove, minced
½ pound chicken livers
1 tablespoon brandy

¼ teaspoon instant chicken-flavor bouillon
Assorted crackers
Radish Flowers and Pear Slices (below)

1. In 1-quart microwave-safe casserole, place butter or margarine, green onion, and garlic. Cook on High (100% power) 3 to 4 minutes, stirring once.
2. Pierce chicken livers with fork; add to butter mixture. Cook, covered loosely with waxed paper, on High 3 to 5 minutes, just until livers are no longer pink, stirring once. Let stand 2 minutes.
3. In food processor with knife blade attached or in blender, process chicken-liver mixture, brandy, and bouillon until well blended and smooth, stopping occasionally and scraping sides with rubber spatula.
4. Spoon chicken liver mixture into freezer-to-microwave container; cover and freeze.
5. About 15 minutes before serving, defrost pâté: Remove container cover. Cook, covered loosely with waxed paper, on Medium (50% power) 4 to 6 minutes, just until thawed but not warm, stirring to break up frozen mixture. Serve pâté on crackers, Radish Flowers, and Pear Slices.

Making the Radish Flowers

With small sharp knife, about ¼ inch from stem end, cut zig-zag pattern through radish.

Twist top from bottom of radish, leaving a flower-shaped cup (which can be filled).

Making the Pear Slices

Cut pear lengthwise into quarters. Core centers and cut remaining pear into thin slices.

Rub each slice with cut lemon to prevent pear surface from discoloring.

QUESADILLAS

Color Index page 40. 84 cals per wedge. Low in cholesterol. Begin 45 minutes ahead.

Ingredients for 16 wedges		Microwave cookware
4 mild green chilies *6 ounces Cheddar cheese* *½ cup chopped coriander leaves* *2 green onions, sliced* *1 5.8-ounce can whole-kernel corn, drained* *2 tablespoons chopped mild green chilies*	*8 6-inch flour or corn tortillas* *Salad leaves and radishes for garnish* *Taco sauce (optional)* *Sour cream (optional)*	Browning dish

1 To make chili flowers, with sharp knife, slit each chili several times, about ½ inch from stem. (If you like, wear rubber gloves for protection.)

2 Place each cut chili in bowl of ice water to separate petals; set aside for garnish.

3 Preheat browning dish as manufacturer directs. Meanwhile, into pie plate or onto flat dish, shred cheese to make 1½ cups.

4 In medium bowl, mix cheese, chopped coriander, green onions, corn, and chopped green chilies. Spoon an equal amount of mixture onto 4 tortillas.

5 Cover each tortilla with one of the 4 remaining tortillas.

6 Place 1 quesadilla on browning dish. Cook on High (100% power) 1½ (1:30) minutes, turning quesadilla over after 1 minute.

7 Remove quesadilla from dish; let stand 2 minutes. Meanwhile, repeat with remaining quesadillas. Reheat browning dish as necessary and keep cooked quesadillas warm.

8 Cut each quesadilla into 4 wedges. Arrange wedges on plates.

9 Garnish each plate. If you like, serve with taco sauce and sour cream.

Tartlets

Filled tartlets make attractive appetizers. Buy the shells or make
them yourself and keep them in the freezer. They can be
heated in the microwave and then filled with our delicious hot fillings.
Each filling is enough for sixteen to twenty 2-inch tartlets.

ASPARAGUS AND BRIE FILLING

Color Index page 39. Makes 16 tablespoons. 28 cals per
tablespoon. Low in cholesterol, fat, sodium.
Begin 15 minutes ahead.

*1 pound thin
asparagus spears
4 ounces Brie cheese
2 green onions, thinly
sliced
1 teaspoon tarragon
1 tablespoon water*

1. Hold base of each asparagus
spear firmly and bend; the end will
break off at the spot where the spear
becomes too tough to eat. Discard
the tough ends.
2. Trim asparagus tips to 2-inch
pieces; set aside for garnish. Thinly
slice remaining asparagus.
3. Cut Brie into ½-inch cubes. In
medium microwave-safe bowl, combine sliced asparagus, Brie, green
onions, and tarragon. Cook, covered, on High (100% power) 2½
(2:30) minutes. Stir until cheese is
melted. Spoon filling into tartlets.
4. On small microwave-safe plate,
place reserved asparagus tips and
water. Cook, covered, on High 1
minute. Use for garnish.

MUSHROOM FILLING

Color Index page 39. Makes 20 tablespoons. 21 cals per
tablespoon. Low in cholesterol, fat, sodium.
Begin 25 minutes ahead.

*½ pound mushrooms
4 green onions,
minced
3 garlic cloves,
minced
3 tablespoons butter
or margarine
¼ cup chopped
parsley
3 tablespoons dry
sherry
¼ teaspoon salt
Pepper to taste
Parsley for garnish*

1. In food processor with knife
blade attached or on chopping
board, finely chop mushrooms.
2. In medium microwave-safe bowl,
place mushrooms, green onions,
garlic, and butter or margarine.
Cook on High (100%) 6 minutes,
stirring occasionally.
3. Into mixture, stir chopped parsley, sherry, salt, and pepper. Cook
on High 6 minutes, stirring once.
Spoon filling into tartlets; garnish.

TOMATO-BASIL FILLING

Color Index page 39. Makes 16 tablespoons. 8 cals per
tablespoon. Low in cholesterol, fat, sodium.
Begin 10 minutes ahead.

*2 medium tomatoes
2 garlic cloves,
minced
1 medium celery
stalk, minced
1 tablespoon grated
Parmesan cheese
2 teaspoons prepared
pesto
¼ teaspoon salt
Ground red pepper to
taste
Small basil leaves for
garnish*

1. Seed and chop tomatoes. In
medium microwave-safe bowl, combine tomatoes, garlic, and celery.
Cook on High (100% power) 4 minutes, stirring once.
2. Into tomato mixture, stir Parmesan, pesto, salt, and ground red
pepper. Spoon filling into tartlets.
Garnish with basil leaves.

BLACK BEAN FILLING

Color Index page 39. Makes 20 tablespoons. 25 cals per
tablespoon. Low in cholesterol, fat, sodium.
Begin 15 minutes ahead.

*½ small red onion,
minced
½ small red pepper,
minced
3 garlic cloves, minced
2 tablespoons salad
oil
1 teaspoon oregano
2 teaspoons chili
powder
½ 16-ounce can black
beans, drained and
rinsed
1½ teaspoons cider
vinegar
½ teaspoon salt
⅛ teaspoon pepper
Sour cream for
garnish*

1. In medium microwave-safe bowl,
combine onion, red pepper, garlic,
oil, oregano, and chili powder. Cook
on High (100% power) 3 minutes.
2. Into onion mixture stir beans,
vinegar, salt, and pepper. Cook on
High 3 minutes, stirring once. Spoon
filling into tartlets. Garnish with
sour cream.

Filled Appetizers

STUFFED ARTICHOKE BOTTOMS

Color Index page 40. 125 cals per artichoke. Low in cholesterol. Begin 55 minutes ahead.

Ingredients	For 4	For 2	For 1
Artichokes	4 medium	2 medium	1 medium
Water	½ cup	¼ cup	2 tablespoons
Bacon slices, diced	4 slices	2 slices	1 slice
Red onion, diced	1 small	½ small	¼ small
Dried bread crumbs	½ cup	¼ cup	2 tablespoons
Golden raisins	2 tablespoons	1 tablespoon	1½ teaspoons
Rosemary	1½ teaspoons	¾ teaspoon	to taste
Pepper	to taste	to taste	to taste
Lemon, green salad, and red onions for garnish	garnish	garnish	garnish
Microwave cookware	3-quart casserole	2-quart casserole	9" pie plate
	9" pie plate	9" pie plate	9" pie plate
Time on High (100% power)			
Artichokes	22 to 24 minutes	14 to 16 minutes	7 to 9 minutes
Bacon	4 to 5 minutes	2 to 3 minutes	1½ (1:30) to 2 minutes
Stuffed artichokes	2 minutes	1 minute	45 seconds

1 Rinse artichokes well. With serrated knife, cut off stem and 1 inch straight across top of each artichoke.

2 With fingers, pull off any small, loose, or discolored leaves from bases. With kitchen shears, carefully trim thorny tips of leaves.

3 In casserole or pie plate, place artichokes, base down. Add water. Cook, covered, on High for time in Chart, rearranging once.

4 In pie plate (see Chart), place double thickness of paper towels. Place bacon on top; cover with paper towel. Cook on High for time in Chart. Remove bacon to paper towels to drain. In bowl, combine bacon and remaining ingredients except garnish.

5 With fingers, pull off all artichoke leaves. (If you like, serve leaves with a dip.) Place artichoke bottoms on pie plate used for bacon. With spoon, scrape out and discard fuzzy centers (the chokes). Trim base and edges of each bottom.

6 Top each artichoke bottom with about 2 tablespoons stuffing. Cook on High for time in Chart. Garnish and serve immediately.

SAVORY SAUSAGE PARCELS

Color Index page 41. Makes 12. 60 cals each. Low in cholesterol, sodium. Begin early in day.

2 tablespoons lemon juice	1 4-ounce jar pimentos, drained
2 cups water	1 ounce mozzarella cheese, shredded (¼ cup)
12 medium grape leaves, fresh or in brine (rinsed and drained)	2 tablespoons dried bread crumbs
¼ pound hot or sweet Italian-sausage links	Salad oil
2 tablespoons minced onion	Lemon slices and basil leaves for garnish
1 garlic clove, minced	

1. In medium microwave-safe bowl, place lemon juice and water. Heat on High (100% power) 5 to 6 minutes, until boiling. To water, add grape leaves. Cook, covered, on High 10 minutes. Drain; cover leaves with cold water.
2. Remove casings from sausage links. Crumble sausage into 1-quart microwave-safe casserole; stir in onion and garlic. Cook on High 2 to 3 minutes, until sausage loses its pink color, stirring to break up meat. Drain well.
3. From pimentos, cut 24 matchstick-thin 2-inch strips; set aside. Chop remaining pimento; add to sausage with cheese and bread crumbs.
4. Pat grape leaves dry. Place 1 tablespoon sausage mixture in center of each leaf; fold sides over mixture, then roll up. With parcel seam side down, decorate with pimento strips. On waxed-paper-lined cookie sheet, freeze until firm. Place in freezer container; cover and freeze.
5. About 5 minutes before serving, place each frozen parcel, seam side down, on microwave-safe rack set in 12" by 8" baking dish; brush lightly with oil. Cook, covered, on High 1½ (1:30) to 2 minutes, until hot. Garnish.

CRAB-FILLED MUSHROOMS

Color Index page 41. Makes 12. 90 cals each. Begin early in day.

¾ cup lump crab meat, drained	2 tablespoons dried bread crumbs
⅓ cup mayonnaise	¼ teaspoon salt
2 tablespoons minced celery	⅛ teaspoon hot-pepper sauce
2 tablespoons minced onion	12 mushroom caps
1 tablespoon lemon juice	2 tablespoons salad oil
1 tablespoon dry sherry	Lemon slices and parsley sprigs for garnish

1. In medium bowl, mix first 9 ingredients.
2. Brush mushrooms with oil. Spoon an equal amount of crab mixture into each. On waxed-paper-lined cookie sheet, freeze until firm. Place in freezer container; cover and freeze.
3. About 10 minutes before serving, on microwave-safe rack set in 12" by 8" baking dish, place frozen mushrooms. Cook on High (100% power) 5 to 6 minutes, until hot. Garnish.

POACHED APPLES WITH PROSCIUTTO

Color Index page 40. 6 servings. 236 cals per serving. Begin 40 minutes ahead.

6 small apples	3 tablespoons coarsely
1 cup dry white wine	crumbled blue cheese
1 teaspoon whole	4 eggs
allspice	3 tablespoons heavy
Salad greens	cream
6 ounces thinly sliced	2 teaspoons chopped
prosciutto or smoked	chives
salmon	1 teaspoon salt
Capers	Pepper to taste
1/3 cup sour cream	

1. Cut off top quarter of each apple; set aside. Core each apple, but do not cut all the way through base of apple.
2. In 2-quart microwave-safe casserole, arrange apples; replace apple tops. Add wine and allspice. Cook, covered, on High (100% power) 5 minutes, rearranging once. Drain apples and tops on paper towels.
3. Line 6 plates with greens; arrange apples and prosciutto or salmon on greens; garnish with capers.
4. In small bowl, combine sour cream and blue cheese. Spoon mixture into apples. Arrange apple tops over filled apples.
5. In 1-quart microwave-safe casserole, beat remaining ingredients. Cook on High 1½ (1:30) minutes, or until softly set, stirring twice. Spoon onto plates. Let stand 2 to 3 minutes before serving.

BAKED STUFFED TOMATOES

Color Index page 38. Makes 4. 121 cals each. Low in cholesterol. Good source of vitamin A. Begin 20 minutes ahead.

4 medium tomatoes	Pepper to taste
1/4 teaspoon salt	1 tablespoon chopped
1/4 cup grated Parmesan	parsley
cheese	2 tablespoons olive or
2 tablespoons dried	salad oil
bread crumbs	Parsley sprigs for
2 garlic cloves, minced	garnish
1 teaspoon oregano	

1. Cut thin slice from bottom of each tomato so tomatoes sit flat. Cut slice from each stem end and reserve.
2. With spoon, scoop out flesh and seeds from each tomato; discard. Sprinkle the inside of each tomato with salt.
3. In small bowl, combine Parmesan, bread crumbs, garlic, oregano, pepper, and parsley.
4. In 12″ by 8″ microwave-safe baking dish, arrange tomatoes about 1 inch apart. Spoon stuffing into tomatoes; pack in firmly. Drizzle olive or salad oil over tomatoes. Cook on High (100% power) 6 minutes, rearranging once.
5. Let tomatoes stand 2 minutes before serving. Replace tomato slices on top; garnish.

CELEBRATION SHRIMP

Color Index page 41. 113 cals per shrimp. Good source of calcium. Begin early in day.

Ingredients	For 4	For 2	For 1
Fresh large shrimp, shelled and deveined	12 large shrimp	6 large shrimp	3 large shrimp
Lemon juice	1 tablespoon	2 teaspoons	1 teaspoon
Dry sherry	2 tablespoons	1 tablespoon	1½ teaspoons
Dried bread crumbs	1/4 cup	2 tablespoons	1 tablespoon
Gruyère or Edam cheese, shredded	3 tablespoons	1½ table- spoons	2 teaspoons
Red, green or yellow pepper, minced	3 tablespoons	1½ table- spoons	2 teaspoons
Parmesan cheese, grated	2 tablespoons	1 tablespoon	1½ teaspoons
Salt	1/4 teaspoon	1/8 teaspoon	to taste
Hot-pepper sauce	to taste	to taste	to taste
Peach slices and salad greens for garnish	garnish	garnish	garnish
Microwave cookware	12″ round baking dish	10″ round baking dish	9″ pie plate
Time on Medium-Low (30% power)	6 to 8 minutes	4 to 6 minutes	2 to 3 minutes

1 In bowl, combine shrimp, lemon juice, and half the sherry. Toss to coat; set aside. In another bowl, combine next 6 ingredients and remaining sherry.

2 With sharp knife, cut each shrimp three quarters of the way through along center back; spread open. Pound shrimp lightly to flatten.

3 Divide cheese mixture into same number of balls as shrimp; roll into log shapes. Place 1 log along center back of each shrimp. Reshape shrimp firmly around filling.

4 On waxed-paper-lined cookie sheet, freeze shrimp until firm. Place in freezer container; cover and freeze until ready to use.

5 About 15 minutes before serving, in baking dish or pie plate (see Chart) arrange shrimp in circle with tails pointing toward center of dish.

6 Cook shrimp, covered loosely with waxed paper, on Medium-Low for time in Chart, until shrimp turn pink. Turn each shrimp over and rotate dish halfway through cooking. Garnish; serve immediately.

Vegetable Appetizers

ARTICHOKES WITH LEMON AND GARLIC

Color Index page 40. 260 cals per artichoke. Good source of vitamin C, iron. Begin 55 minutes ahead.

Ingredients	For 4	For 2	For 1
Artichokes	4 medium	2 medium	1 medium
Lemon, thinly sliced and cut into quarters	1 lemon	½ lemon	¼ lemon
Garlic cloves, thinly sliced	4 garlic cloves	2 garlic cloves	1 garlic clove
Dry white wine	½ cup	¼ cup	2 tablespoons
Butter	8 tablespoons (1 stick)	4 tablespoons (½ stick)	2 tablespoons (¼ stick)
Lemon and parsley for garnish	garnish	garnish	garnish
Microwave cookware	3-quart casserole	2-quart casserole	9″ pie plate
	Medium bowl	Medium bowl	Small bowl
Time on High (100% power)			
Artichokes	22 to 24 minutes	14 to 16 minutes	7 to 9 minutes
Butter	1½ (1:30) to 2 minutes	45 seconds to 1 minute	45 seconds

1 Rinse artichokes well. With serrated knife, cut off stem and 1 inch straight across top of artichoke. Pull off any small, loose, or discolored leaves from base. With kitchen shears, carefully trim thorny tips of artichoke leaves.

2 Push lemon quarters and garlic slices between artichoke leaves. In casserole or pie plate (see Chart), place artichokes, base down. Drizzle with wine.

3 Cook artichokes, covered, on High for time in Chart, until a leaf can be pulled off easily; rearranging artichokes halfway through cooking.

4 In bowl (see Chart) place butter. Heat, covered with paper towel, on High for time in Chart. Skim off white foam; discard. Pour clarified butter into ramekin or small bowl.

5 Gently push artichoke leaves out from the middle; remove center leaves to expose fuzzy centers (the chokes). With spoon, scrape out and discard the chokes.

6 To serve: Place each artichoke on plate; drizzle with cooking liquid. Garnish with lemon and parsley. Pass clarified butter for dipping.

CREAMED MUSHROOMS ON TOAST

Color Index page 39. 4 servings. 245 cals per serving. Low in cholesterol. Good source of riboflavin, niacin, iron. Begin 25 minutes ahead.

1 pound mushrooms
2 tablespoons butter or margarine (¼ stick)
4 green onions, sliced
3 garlic cloves, minced
¾ cup Chicken Broth (page 125), or canned broth
2 tablespoons dry sherry
2 tablespoons heavy or whipping cream

¼ teaspoon salt
Pepper to taste
1 tablespoon cornstarch dissolved in 2 tablespoons cold water
8 slices white bread, toasted and cut in half

1. Trim mushrooms and cut into quarters.
2. In 12″ by 8″ microwave-safe baking dish, place mushrooms and next 3 ingredients. Cook on High (100% power) 5 minutes, stirring twice.
3. Into mushroom mixture, stir broth, sherry, cream, salt, and pepper. Cook on High 3 minutes. Stir in dissolved cornstarch. Cook on High 3 minutes, or until slightly thickened, stirring once.
4. To serve: Arrange 4 pieces of toast on each plate. Ladle mushroom mixture over toast.

MUSHROOMS

Nowadays, there are many kinds of mushrooms available across the country, both homegrown and imported varieties. They are a delicious and low-calorie ingredient. Try mixing two or three types together in dishes like our Creamed Mushrooms on Toast (above).

Shiitake Mushrooms

Oyster Mushrooms

Cultivated Mushrooms

Button Mushrooms

Cocktails For A Crowd

Cocktails with Tex-Mex Mixed Nuts, page 294, olives, and breadsticks
Bacon-horseradish Dip, page 111 (double quantity), with crudités and bagel chips
Buffalo Chicken Wings, page 114 (double quantity)
Celebration Shrimp, page 119
Country-style Pork Pâté, page 115, with gherkins and crackers
Cheese and fresh fruit

PREPARATION TIMETABLE

Up to 1 week ahead:	**Up to 2 days ahead:**	**1 day ahead:**	**2 hours ahead:**	**About 15 minutes ahead:**
Prepare Celebration Shrimp through step 4. Prepare Tex-Mex Mixed Nuts and store in airtight container.	*Prepare Country-style Pork Pâté; wrap well and refrigerate without unmolding. Check all bar supplies: liquors, wines, mixers, soft drinks, and mineral water; if necessary, buy ice or make extra ice and keep in plastic bags in the freezer.*	*Prepare Buffalo Chicken Wings; cover and refrigerate. Select cheeses and fruit; keep chilled. Make Bacon-horseradish Dip; cover and refrigerate. Prepare vegetables for crudités; store in plastic bags in refrigerator.*	*Arrange crudités and bagel chips on platter. Spoon Bacon-horseradish Dip into serving bowl. Unmold pâté and accompany with gherkins and crackers. Arrange cheese and fruit on board or tray; keep covered until guests arrive. Arrange seasonal fresh fruit in bowl.*	*Fill serving bowls with olives and Tex-Mex Mixed Nuts. Arrange breadsticks for serving. Place glasses, cocktail ingredients, and ice bucket on trays. Reheat chicken wings and cook shrimp in microwave just before you are ready to serve.*

Seafood Appetizers

ELEGANT SEAFOOD SALAD

Color Index page 41. 214 cals per serving. Good source of iron.
Begin 2¼ hours ahead or early in day.

Ingredients for 6 servings		Microwave cookware
½ pound medium shrimp, shelled and deveined	1 dozen mussels, cleaned Lemon-basil Sauce (below)	12" by 8" baking dish 9" quiche dish or pie plate
½ pound sea scallops, sliced	Salad greens ½ cup seafood-cocktail sauce	
3 green onions, sliced or cut into very thin strips	Green grapes, Pear Slices (page 116), and red currants for garnish	
2 tablespoons lemon juice		
1 tablespoon salad oil		
½ teaspoon salt		

1 In baking dish, place shrimp, scallops, green onions, lemon juice, salad oil, and salt. Cook, covered, on High (100% power) 3 to 5 minutes, until shrimp turn pink and scallops are opaque.

2 Stir seafood mixture. Cover and refrigerate until chilled. Meanwhile, in quiche dish or pie plate, arrange mussels. Discard any that are open.

3 Cook mussels, covered, on High 2 to 2½ (2:30) minutes, just until shells open; discard any that remain closed. Remove mussels from shells; reserve 12 half-shells.

4 Make Lemon-basil Sauce: In food processor with knife blade attached or in blender, place *1 cup loosely packed basil leaves, 2 tablespoons lemon juice, 1 garlic clove, 1 tablespoon water, ¼ teaspoon salt, ¼ teaspoon pepper,* and *¼ cup olive or salad oil*; process.

5 Line 6 plates with salad greens. Arrange shrimp, scallops, and mussels on greens. Fill 6 reserved mussel half-shells with Lemon-basil Sauce and 6 with seafood-cocktail sauce; arrange 1 of each on each plate.

6 *To serve:* Garnish each plate with green grapes, Pear Slices, and red currants.

OYSTERS ROCKEFELLER

Color Index page 39. Makes 12. 51 cals each. Low in cholesterol, sodium. Good source of vitamin A, iron.
Begin 25 minutes ahead.

2 slices bacon, diced
½ 10-ounce package frozen chopped spinach, slightly thawed
2 green onions, sliced
1 garlic clove
2 tablespoons chopped parsley
2 tablespoons butter or margarine (¼ stick)
2 tablespoons grated Parmesan cheese
⅛ teaspoon ground red pepper
2 tablespoons anise-flavor liqueur
12 large oysters on the half-shell
Rock or coarse salt (optional)

1. In 9" microwave-safe pie plate, place bacon. Cook, covered with paper towels, on High (100% power) 2 to 3 minutes, until browned, stirring once. Remove to paper towels to drain.

2. In medium microwave-safe bowl, combine next 5 ingredients. Cook on High 4 minutes, stirring occasionally.

3. In food processor with knife blade attached or in blender, process spinach mixture until smooth. In bowl, mix spinach with Parmesan, ground red pepper, and liqueur; set aside.

4. Arrange oysters on 12" microwave-safe platter or plate. (If you like, press oysters in shell into ¼-inch-deep layer of rock or coarse salt to keep from tipping over.) Spoon spinach mixture onto oysters; sprinkle with bacon.

5. Cook oysters on High 3 to 4 minutes, until hot.

CLAMS CASINO

Color Index page 41. Makes 12. 55 cals each. Low in cholesterol, sodium. Good source of iron.
Begin early in day.

4 slices bacon, diced
12 cherrystone clams, shucked, reserving 12 bottom shells
½ cup fresh bread crumbs (1 slice bread)
3 tablespoons grated Parmesan cheese
2 tablespoons minced green pepper
1 garlic clove, minced
½ teaspoon oregano
Lemon slices, cut in half, and red pepper, cut into matchstick-thin strips, for garnish

1. In 12" by 8" microwave-safe baking dish, place bacon. Cook, covered with paper towels, on High (100% power) 4 to 5 minutes, until browned, stirring once. Remove to paper towels to drain. Reserve 2 tablespoons bacon drippings in dish.

2. Coarsely chop clams. To bacon drippings, add clams and next 5 ingredients; mix well.

3. Spoon an equal amount of clam mixture into each clam shell. On waxed-paper-lined cookie sheet, freeze filled shells until firm. Place in freezer container; cover and freeze.

4. About 10 minutes before serving, place clams in 10" round microwave-safe dish. Cook, covered loosely with waxed paper, on Medium (50% power) 6 to 7 minutes. Garnish.

Soups

BROTHS · QUICK AND EASY SOUPS · VEGETABLE SOUPS
HEARTY SOUPS · SOUP GARNISHES · CHOWDERS
FRUIT SOUPS

Soups

Our recipes range from simple basic broths that can be used as soup bases, to more substantial soups such as our Four Bean Soup (page 129) and Minestrone (page 130) that are main dishes. Some are warm and welcoming on a cold winter's day; others such as chilled Vichyssoise and Cream of Spinach Soup (page 127) and our fruit soups (page 134), are a refreshing treat on a warm day.

The microwave oven can be used to cook soups made from fresh ingredients that would take much longer to cook if prepared conventionally. Other time-saving uses for the microwave include reconstituting dried soups, cooking ingredients from frozen, and heating canned soups (always remove the soup from the can first). Soups should be stirred during cooking in the microwave and especially just before serving in order to equalize the temperature. Bear in mind that the edges of the soup may bubble long before the center is hot.

A microwave can also make broth – an essential base for soups and other recipes – in a fraction of normal cooking time. On page 126 we show how, with only a few added ingredients, broths can be transformed into elegant, delicious dishes. Our homemade broths (page 125) are superior in flavor and contain less salt than bouillon cubes or envelopes or canned broth but equal quantities of any of these products can be successfully substituted in our recipes where we call for broth.

Most of our broths and soups can be frozen and then defrosted and reheated in the microwave. Soups are best frozen in 1- or 2-cup quantities, but make sure containers are only two-thirds full, otherwise they may overflow when reheating. If you freeze the soup in a non-microwave-safe container, remove it as a block by placing the container under running hot water, then place the block in a microwave-safe bowl or casserole to defrost in the microwave. Using a fork, break the block apart as it thaws to hasten the process. (For more information, see Chart, page 130.) If you are going to freeze soup, season lightly when making, then adjust seasoning after reheating.

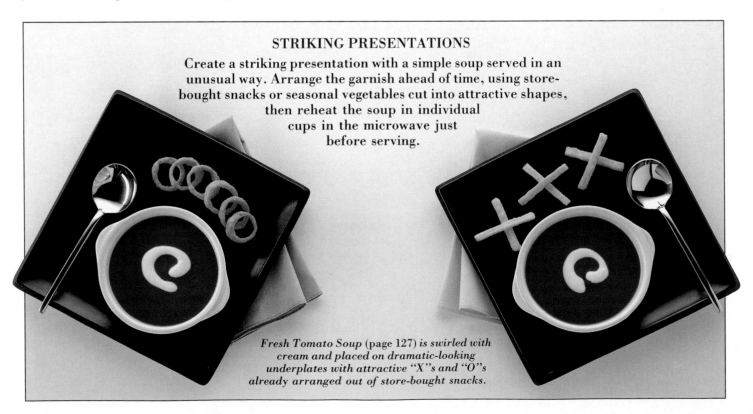

STRIKING PRESENTATIONS

Create a striking presentation with a simple soup served in an unusual way. Arrange the garnish ahead of time, using store-bought snacks or seasonal vegetables cut into attractive shapes, then reheat the soup in individual cups in the microwave just before serving.

Fresh Tomato Soup (page 127) is swirled with cream and placed on dramatic-looking underplates with attractive "X"s and "O"s already arranged out of store-bought snacks.

The microwave shortens the time for making broths at home, and an added advantage is that you can make a relatively small quantity quickly, as and when you need it. Alternatively, you can make a larger quantity and freeze it in 1- or 2-cup containers.

VEGETABLE BROTH

Color Index page 42. Makes 3 cups. 37 cals per cup. Low in cholesterol, fat, sodium. Good source of vitamin A. Begin 40 minutes ahead.

1 medium leek
1 medium onion with skin
3 medium carrots
2 medium tomatoes
1 garlic clove
6 mushrooms, cut in half
4 large celery stalks, cut into thirds
1 parsley sprig
1 bay leaf
6 whole peppercorns
½ cup tomato juice
3½ cups cold water

1. Cut leek lengthwise in half; carefully wash under running cold water until all sand is removed. Cut onion, carrots, tomatoes, and garlic into quarters.
2. In deep 2-quart microwave-safe bowl, combine all ingredients. Cook, covered, on High (100% power) 20 minutes, stirring occasionally. Let stand 5 minutes.
3. Line strainer with double layer of cheesecloth. Into medium bowl, strain liquid through cheesecloth. Discard vegetables.

FISH BROTH

Color Index page 42. Makes 3 cups. 41 cals per cup. Low in cholesterol, fat. Begin 40 minutes ahead.

1½ pounds white-fish bones (except bones from flat fish such as flounder, fluke, and sole)
½ medium leek
½ medium carrot
½ medium celery stalk
6 whole peppercorns
½ teaspoon thyme leaves
1 cup dry white wine
3 cups cold water

1. Under running cold water, wash fish bones to remove any blood or scales. With kitchen shears, cut into 4-inch pieces.
2. Cut leek lengthwise in half; carefully wash under running cold water until all sand is removed.
3. In deep 2-quart microwave-safe bowl, combine all ingredients. Cook, covered, on High (100% power) 15 minutes, stirring occasionally. Let stand 5 minutes.
4. Line strainer with double layer of cheesecloth. Into medium bowl, strain liquid through cheesecloth. Discard bones and vegetables.

BEEF BROTH

Color Index page 44. Makes 3 cups. 31 cals per cup. Low in cholesterol, fat, sodium. Begin 1½ hours ahead.

3 pounds beef or veal bones
1 medium onion with skin, cut into quarters
1 medium tomato, cut into quarters
1 small leek
2 garlic cloves, cut into quarters
1 bay leaf
1 parsley sprig
6 whole peppercorns
4 cups cold water

1. Preheat conventional oven to 450°F. In foil-lined roasting pan, cook bones, onion, and tomato about 1 hour to brown bones.
2. Cut leek lengthwise in half; carefully wash under running cold water until all sand is removed.
3. In deep 2-quart microwave-safe bowl, combine all ingredients. Cook, covered, on High (100% power) 20 minutes, stirring occasionally. Let stand 5 minutes. Skim off any fat.
4. Line strainer with double layer of cheesecloth. Into medium bowl, strain liquid through cheesecloth. Discard bones and vegetables.

CHICKEN BROTH

Color Index page 42. Makes 3 cups. 47 cals per cup. Low in cholesterol, fat, sodium. Begin 40 minutes ahead.

1½ pounds chicken bones
1 medium leek
1 medium carrot
1 medium celery stalk
1 parsley sprig
1 thyme sprig or ½ teaspoon thyme leaves
1 bay leaf
6 whole peppercorns
4 cups cold water

1. With cleaver or kitchen shears, chop or cut chicken bones into 4-inch pieces.
2. Cut leek lengthwise in half; carefully wash under running cold water until all sand is removed.
3. In deep 2-quart microwave-safe bowl, combine all ingredients. Cook, covered, on High (100% power) 20 minutes, stirring occasionally. Let stand 5 minutes. Skim off any fat.
4. Line strainer with double layer of cheesecloth. Into medium bowl, strain liquid through cheesecloth. Discard bones and vegetables.

Quick & Easy Soups

Use our homemade broths (page 125) as a base for these instant soups that are suitable for a first course, light meal, or after-school snack. Or create your own recipes by adding different combinations of ingredients according to personal taste.

Oriental-style Soup (*right*): To *2 cups Fish Broth*, add ¼ *cup chopped, cooked shrimp, 3 sliced green onions*, and ½ *teaspoon slivered peeled gingerroot.* Cook, covered, on High (100% power) 5 minutes, or until boiling. Garnish with *coriander leaves.*

Double Vegetable Soup (*below*): To *2 cups Vegetable Broth*, add ¼ *cup* each *thinly sliced celery, carrot*, and *leek*, and ¼ *cup asparagus tips.* Cook, covered, on High (100% power) 3 minutes. Add ¼ *cup shredded spinach.* Cook, covered, on High 2 minutes.

Beefy Italian Broth (*above*): To *2 cups Beef Broth*, add ¼ *cup* each *sliced mushrooms, fennel*, and *carrots*, and *1 tablespoon shredded basil leaves.* Cook, covered, on High (100% power) 5 minutes, or until boiling. Add ¼ *cup Gruyère* or *provolone cheese cubes.* Garnish with *rosemary* and *basil leaves.*

Chicken and Pasta Soup (*left*): To *2 cups Chicken Broth*, add ¼ *cup small pasta shapes* (such as animals, alphabets, or bow ties) and ¼ *cup diced carrots.* Cook, covered, on High (100% power) 5 minutes, or until boiling. Add ¼ *cup cooked, shredded chicken.* Cook on High 2 to 3 minutes, until hot. Serve with *saltine* or *oyster crackers.*

Vegetable Soups

VICHYSSOISE

Color Index page 44. Makes 8 cups. 133 cals per cup. Low in cholesterol. Begin early in day.

2 medium leeks (about
   ¾ pound)
3 medium potatoes
   (1 pound), sliced
2 tablespoons butter or
   margarine (¼ stick)
½ teaspoon salt
⅛ teaspoon white
   pepper
1 cup water

1 cup Chicken Broth
   (page 125) or canned
   broth
1 small tart apple,
   peeled, cored, and
   sliced
1 cup half-and-half
Unpeeled apple slices
   and parsley sprigs for
   garnish

1. Cut off roots and green tops from leeks; discard. Cut the white part of the leeks into 1-inch pieces; carefully wash under running cold water until all sand is removed.
2. In deep 3-quart microwave-safe bowl, place leeks, potatoes, butter or margarine, salt, and pepper. Cook, covered, on High (100% power) 7 minutes, stirring once.
3. To vegetables, add water, broth, and apple slices. Cook, covered, on High 6 to 8 minutes, until potatoes are tender, stirring once.
4. In food processor with knife blade attached or in blender, process mixture until smooth (in 2 batches if necessary). Return to bowl and stir in half-and-half; cover and refrigerate until chilled.
5. *To serve:* Garnish with apple slices and parsley sprigs.

CREAM OF SPINACH SOUP

Color Index page 44. Makes 4 cups. 174 cals per cup. Low in cholesterol. Good source of vitamin A, vitamin C, calcium, iron. Begin early in day.

2 tablespoons butter or
   margarine (¼ stick)
1 medium onion, chopped
2 small potatoes, diced
   (about 1 cup)
1¼ cups Chicken Broth
   (page 125) or canned
   broth
¾ pound torn spinach
   leaves

½ cup half-and-half or
   milk
1 tablespoon cornstarch
   dissolved in 2 table-
   spoons cold water
1 teaspoon salt
¼ teaspoon pepper
Ground nutmeg to taste
Whipping cream or plain
   yogurt for garnish

1. In deep 3-quart microwave-safe bowl, combine butter or margarine, onion, potatoes, and ¼ cup broth. Cook, covered, on High (100% power) 8 minutes, stirring twice.
2. To vegetable mixture, add spinach. Cook, covered, on High 5 minutes. In food processor with knife blade attached or in blender, process spinach mixture until smooth; return to bowl.
3. To spinach mixture, add remaining broth, half-and-half or milk, dissolved cornstarch, salt, pepper, and nutmeg; stir until smooth. Cook on High 5 minutes, stirring once. Serve hot or refrigerate to serve chilled later. Garnish with whipping cream or plain yogurt.

FRESH TOMATO SOUP

Color Index page 42. 55 cals per cup. Low in cholesterol, fat. Good source of vitamin A, vitamin C. Begin 25 minutes ahead.

Ingredients for 6 cups		Microwave cookware
7 medium, ripe tomatoes (about 2½ pounds)	1 tablespoon tomato paste	Deep 3-quart bowl
1 medium onion, chopped	1½ teaspoons salt	
1 medium celery stalk, chopped	¼ teaspoon pepper	
2 garlic cloves, minced	Hot-pepper sauce to taste	
½ bay leaf	Sour cream and chopped chives for garnish	
¼ teaspoon ground cloves		
1 cup Chicken Broth (page 125) or canned broth		

1 With small sharp knife, remove stem ends from tomatoes; cut tomatoes into bite-sized chunks.

2 In bowl, combine tomatoes, onion, celery, garlic, bay leaf, and cloves. Cook, covered, on High (100% power) 15 minutes, stirring often.

3 Discard bay leaf. In food processor with knife blade attached or in blender, process tomato mixture until smooth.

4 In same bowl, mix tomato mixture and remaining ingredients except garnish. Cook, covered, on High 5 minutes, stirring once.

5 Serve hot or refrigerate to serve chilled later. Garnish.

CROUTONS

To **1 tablespoon melted butter or margarine** and **2 tablespoons salad oil**, add **4 slices bread** cut into different shapes; turn to coat. Bake in conventional oven at 450°F 8 to 10 minutes until golden, turning halfway through cooking.

Vegetable and Hearty Soups

WINTER VEGETABLE SOUP

Color Index page 43. 108 cals per cup. Low in cholesterol. Good source of vitamin A, vitamin C. Begin 35 minutes ahead.

Traditionally, vegetable soups are thick, substantial dishes. For a lighter version, try our Winter Vegetable Soup, which can be cooked in much less time than if prepared conventionally. If you like, vary our recipe by using other seasonal vegetables.

Ingredients for 6 cups		Microwave cookware
1 large carrot	*½ teaspoon thyme*	Deep 3-quart bowl
1 large turnip (about	* leaves*	
* ½ pound)*	*1 bay leaf*	
1 large celery stalk	*¼ teaspoon rosemary*	
½ small head green	*3 cups Chicken Broth*	
* cabbage (about*	* (page 125) or canned*	
* ¾ pound)*	* broth*	
1 medium onion	*1 teaspoon salt*	
½ acorn squash (about	*Pepper to taste*	
* ½ pound)*		
2 tablespoons butter or		
* margarine (¼ stick)*		

1 With sharp knife, cut carrot, turnip, and celery into matchstick-thin strips.

2 With sharp knife, thinly slice green cabbage and onion. Peel and dice acorn squash.

3 In deep bowl place butter or margarine. Heat, covered with paper towel, on High (100% power) 45 seconds, or until melted.

4 To same bowl, add carrot, turnip, celery, cabbage, onion, squash, thyme, bay leaf, and rosemary. Stir in ½ cup broth, mix well.

5 Cook vegetable mixture, covered, on High 12 minutes, or until vegetables are tender, stirring occasionally.

6 To soup mixture, add remaining broth, salt, and pepper. Cook, covered, on High 3 minutes, or until hot, stirring once. Remove bay leaf. Serve immediately.

CARROT SOUP WITH ORANGE

Color Index page 42. Makes 4 cups. 137 cals per cup. Low in cholesterol. Good source of vitamin A. Begin 25 minutes ahead.

4 to 6 medium carrots
* (about 1 pound), thinly*
* sliced*
1 medium onion,
* chopped*
1 teaspoon grated
* orange peel*
2½ cups Chicken Broth
* (page 125) or canned*
* broth*

2 tablespoons butter or
* margarine (¼ stick)*
¾ teaspoon salt
⅛ teaspoon pepper
Whipping cream and
* parsley for garnish*

1. In deep 2-quart microwave-safe bowl, combine carrots, onion, orange peel, and ½ cup broth. Cook, covered, on High (100% power) 12 minutes.
2. In food processor with knife blade attached or in blender, process carrot mixture with butter or margarine until smooth.
3. Return carrot mixture to bowl. Stir in remaining broth, salt, and pepper. Cook, covered, on High 4 minutes or until hot, stirring once.
4. Serve hot or refrigerate to serve chilled later. Garnish with cream and parsley.

LIGHT AND CREAMY ASPARAGUS SOUP

Color Index page 42. Makes 4 cups. 157 cals per cup. Begin 25 minutes ahead.

2 tablespoons butter or
* margarine (¼ stick)*
1 medium onion, sliced
1 pound asparagus,
* trimmed and cut into*
* 2-inch pieces*
1 cup water

2 chicken-flavor bouillon
* cubes or envelopes*
1 cup half-and-half
Plain yogurt or
* whipping cream and*
* chervil sprigs for*
* garnish*

1. In deep 2-quart microwave-safe bowl, place butter or margarine and onion. Cook on High (100% power) 45 seconds, or until melted.
2. To onion mixture, add asparagus, water, and bouillon. Cook, covered, on High 10 to 12 minutes, until asparagus is tender.
3. In food processor with knife blade attached or in blender, process asparagus mixture until smooth. Return to bowl. Stir in half-and-half. Cook on High 2 to 3 minutes, until hot, stirring once.
4. Serve hot or refrigerate to serve chilled later. Garnish with a swirl of yogurt or whipping cream and a sprig of chervil.

CURRIED ACORN SQUASH SOUP

Color Index page 43. Makes 4 cups. 277 cals per cup. Good source of vitamin A, calcium, iron. Begin 35 minutes ahead.

2 medium acorn squash (about 1½ pounds each)	*1 tablespoon curry powder*
4 tablespoons butter or margarine (½ stick)	*1½ cups Chicken Broth (page 125) or canned broth*
1 medium onion, chopped	*½ cup half-and-half or milk*
1 medium tart apple (about 6 ounces), peeled, cored, and diced	*Toasted, sliced almonds and chopped parsley for garnish*

1. Cut squash lengthwise in half; discard seeds. In 13″ by 9″ microwave-safe baking dish, place squash. Cook, covered, on High (100% power) 8 minutes, or until flesh is fork-tender, rearranging squash halfway through cooking. Let cool slightly.
2. Meanwhile, in deep 2-quart microwave-safe bowl, combine butter or margarine, onion, apple, and curry powder. Cook on High 5 minutes, stirring twice.
3. With spoon, scoop out flesh from squash; discard skin. In food processor with knife blade attached or in blender, process flesh until smooth. To squash, add onion-apple mixture; process until smooth.
4. Return squash mixture to same bowl. Add broth and half-and-half or milk; stir until blended. Cook on High 3 to 5 minutes, until hot.
5. Serve hot or refrigerate to serve chilled later. Garnish with almonds and chopped parsley.

FOUR BEAN SOUP

Color Index page 43. Makes 7 cups. 301 cals per cup. Low in cholesterol. Good source of iron. Begin 35 minutes ahead.

4 slices bacon, diced	*1 teaspoon oregano*
1 medium onion, chopped	*1 16-ounce can each pinto, white kidney, red kidney, and black beans, drained*
1 large celery stalk, chopped	
2 garlic cloves, minced	*2 cups Chicken Broth (page 125) or canned broth*
1½ teaspoons ground cumin	
1 teaspoon chili powder	*Celery leaves for garnish*

1. In deep 3-quart microwave-safe bowl, place bacon. Cook, covered with paper towel, on High (100% power) 4 to 5 minutes, stirring once.
2. To bacon, add onion, celery, garlic, cumin, chili powder, and oregano; mix well. Cook on High 5 minutes, stirring once.
3. To bacon mixture, add beans and broth; mix well. Cook on High 10 minutes, stirring twice.
4. In food processor with knife blade attached or in blender, process 2 cups of soup. Return to unblended soup; stir. Serve immediately, garnished with celery leaves.

Small portions of our hearty soups can be served as first courses before light main dishes. Larger bowls of soup can make a filling, informal lunch or supper, especially when accompanied with garlic bread or rolls warmed briefly in the microwave.

SPLIT PEA AND HAM SOUP

Color Index page 44. 282 cals per cup. Low in cholesterol. Good source of vitamin A, thiamine, iron. Begin 1½ hours ahead.

Ingredients for 8 cups		Microwave cookware
1 16-ounce package split peas	*1 bay leaf*	Deep 3-quart bowl
½ smoked ham hock, or 1 ham bone with about 2 cups meat left on	*1 teaspoon thyme leaves*	
	½ teaspoon rosemary	
	3 cups water	
1 medium onion, chopped	*3 cups Chicken Broth (page 125) or canned broth*	
1 medium carrot, thinly sliced	*Salt and pepper to taste*	
1 large celery stalk, thinly sliced	*Chopped parsley for garnish*	

1 In strainer under running cold water, rinse split peas.

2 In bowl, combine split peas, ham hock or ham bone, onion, carrot, celery, bay leaf, thyme, and rosemary. Add water to cover.

3 Cook split pea-ham mixture, covered, on High (100% power) 20 minutes, stirring halfway through cooking. Add broth. Cook, covered, on High 20 minutes, stirring halfway through cooking. Let stand on heat-safe surface, covered, 30 minutes. Remove bay leaf.

4 Remove ham hock or ham bone to cutting board. With sharp knife, cut off meat; discard bone. Cut meat into bite-sized pieces and return to soup mixture, reserving some for garnish if you like.

5 In food processor with knife blade attached or in blender, process soup mixture until smooth (in several batches if necessary). Return to bowl.

6 Stir any reserved ham into soup. Cook, covered, on High 6 minutes, or until hot. Stir in salt and pepper to taste; garnish with parsley.

Easy Italian Supper

Italian-style cold cuts platter with breadsticks
Minestrone (right)
Creamy Cheesecake, page 335 (or bakery cheesecake)
Espresso (below) with amaretti cookies

PREPARATION TIMETABLE

1 day ahead:	*If making cheesecake, prepare, cover and refrigerate overnight.*
2 hours ahead:	*Arrange a selection of Italian-style meats, such as salami, ham, mortadella, and prosciutto-wrapped melon, on a platter. Decorate with ripe olives, sliced fennel, and strips of red and yellow peppers. Cover until ready to serve.*
1½ hours ahead:	*Prepare Minestrone. Remove cheesecake from refrigerator; place on serving plate.*
Just before serving:	*If necessary, reheat soup on High (100% power) until bubbling. Prepare espresso.*

ESPRESSO

Espresso is the perfect coffee to round off an Italian-style meal. Use dark roast, from Italian delicatessens, specialty stores, and some supermarkets.

For espresso coffee, brew **12 tablespoons Italian-roast coffee** with **2¼ cups water** in a drip pot or macchinetta. Serve in demitasse cups with **lemon peel**. Add **sugar** if you like. **Amaretti cookies** are a traditional accompaniment.

Hearty Soups

MINESTRONE

Color Index page 44. Makes 8 cups. 151 cals per cup. Low in cholesterol. Good source of vitamin A, vitamin C, calcium, iron. Begin 1¼ hours ahead.

2 tablespoons olive or salad oil	½ small head green cabbage, cut into 2-inch pieces
1 ounce prosciutto, thinly sliced, or cooked ham, diced	¼ pound green beans, cut into 1-inch pieces
1 medium onion, diced	1 28-ounce can tomatoes
1 large celery stalk, diced	1 10½-ounce can white kidney beans, drained
1 medium carrot, diced	½ cup shredded basil leaves
2 garlic cloves, minced	Grated Parmesan cheese for garnish
½ teaspoon oregano	
2 cups water	
½ cup elbow macaroni	

1. In deep 3-quart microwave-safe bowl, place oil. Heat on High (100% power) 3 minutes. Stir in prosciutto or ham, onion, celery, carrot, garlic, and oregano. Cook on High 4 minutes, stirring twice.

2. To mixture, add water, macaroni, cabbage, green beans, and tomatoes with their liquid. Cook, covered, on High 20 minutes, or until vegetables and macaroni are tender.

3. Into mixture, stir white kidney beans and basil. Let soup stand, covered, 10 minutes.

4. Ladle soup into individual bowls and sprinkle with Parmesan. Serve hot.

REHEATING FROZEN SOUP

For 4	For 2	For 1
4 cups	2 cups	1 cup
Microwave cookware		
2-quart bowl	1-quart bowl	Deep bowl
Time on Medium-Low (30% power)		
12 to 15 minutes	6 to 8 minutes	3 to 4 minutes
Time on Medium-High (70% power)		
10 to 12 minutes	9 to 11 minutes	6 to 8 minutes

1. Defrost soup in microwave-safe bowl (see Chart) on Medium-Low for time in Chart, breaking soup apart with fork as it thaws.

2. Increase power level to Medium-High and heat soup for time in Chart, until bubbling, stirring twice.

FRENCH ONION SOUP GRATINÉ

Color Index page 43. Makes 6 cups. 221 cals per cup. Good source of calcium.
Begin 45 minutes ahead.

3 tablespoons butter or margarine	2 cups water
3 large onions, sliced (about 4 cups)	1 tablespoon tomato paste
1 10½-ounce can condensed beef broth	½ loaf French bread, cut into 6 slices and toasted
2 tablespoons dry sherry or Madeira wine	6 ounces Swiss cheese shredded (1½ cups)

1. In deep 3-quart microwave-safe bowl, place butter or margarine. Heat, covered with paper towel, on High (100% power) 45 seconds to 1 minute, until melted. Add onions; stir to coat. Cook, covered, on High 15 minutes, stirring twice.
2. To onion mixture, add undiluted beef broth, sherry or Madeira, water, and tomato paste; stir until blended. Cook, covered, on High 8 minutes, stirring twice. If not serving soup immediately, refrigerate until cold, then freeze in 1- or 2-cup quantities (below).
3. Ladle soup into 6 microwave-safe bowls or mugs. Place 1 slice toast in each bowl of soup and sprinkle generously with Swiss shredded cheese.
4. Arrange soup bowls in ring on 12" round microwave-safe platter (in 2 batches if necessary). Cook on High 3 minutes, or until cheese melts. Serve immediately.

Serving the Soup

Top each serving with slice of toasted French bread. Sprinkle toast generously with shredded Swiss cheese.

Heat soup in microwave as directed above, until cheese begins to melt and bubble.

Freezing the Soup

Ladle chilled soup into freezer containers in 1- or 2-cup quantities.

For a complete meal, serve one of our hearty soups with a vegetable side dish or a tossed salad and hot crusty bread. Quick and easy to prepare in the microwave, they also make substantial first courses.

CHICKEN NOODLE SOUP

Color Index page 44. 202 cals per cup. Low in sodium. Good source of vitamin A, niacin, iron. Begin 1¼ hours ahead.

Ingredients for 4 cups		Microwave cookware
4 chicken legs or 1 pound chicken pieces, bone-in (3 thighs or 2 breast halves)	3 cups Chicken Broth (page 125) or canned broth	Deep 2-quart bowl
2 tablespoons butter or margarine (¼ stick)	1 cup fine egg noodles Salt and pepper to taste	
1 medium onion, thinly sliced	Chopped parsley for garnish	
1 large celery stalk, thinly sliced	Saltine or oyster crackers (optional)	
1 large carrot, thinly sliced		

1 Remove skin from chicken; discard. In bowl, heat butter or margarine, covered with paper towel, on High (100% power) 45 seconds, or until melted.

2 Into same bowl, stir onion, celery, and carrot. Cook on High 3 minutes, stirring once.

3 Add 1 cup broth. Place chicken on top of vegetables. Cook, covered, on High 10 minutes, turning chicken over halfway through cooking.

4 Remove chicken to board or plate. Add remaining broth and noodles to vegetable mixture. Cook, covered, on High 7 minutes, stirring once.

5 Meanwhile, remove chicken from bones; discard bones. Coarsely chop chicken, then stir into soup.

6 Let soup stand 3 to 5 minutes. Before serving, skim any fat from surface. Add salt and pepper; garnish with chopped parsley. If you like, serve with saltine or oyster crackers.

Hearty Soups

Our hearty soups, containing vegetables combined with meat, chicken, fish or shellfish, make meals in themselves. Serve Louisiana Gumbo (below), in true Creole style with corn bread or corn muffins.

LOUISIANA GUMBO

Color Index page 43. 157 cals per cup. Good source of calcium, iron. Begin 50 minutes ahead.

Ingredients for 8 cups		Microwave cookware
¾ pound medium shrimp 2 tablespoons butter or margarine (¼ stick) 3 tablespoons all-purpose flour 3 medium celery stalks with leaves, sliced 2 large onions, chopped 2 garlic cloves, minced 1 tablespoon Worcestershire	1 28-ounce can tomatoes ½ pint oysters with their liquid 1 10-ounce package frozen okra, thawed and cut crosswise into ½-inch pieces Salt and hot-pepper sauce to taste Hot cooked rice (optional)	Deep 3-quart bowl

1 Insert tip of kitchen shears under shell of each shrimp and snip along back to expose vein. Peel back sides and lift shrimp out, holding the tail. Rinse shrimp with running cold water to remove vein. Refrigerate until needed.

2 In bowl, place butter or margarine. Heat, covered with paper towel, on High (100% power) 45 seconds, or until melted. Stir in flour until smooth.

3 Cook on High 7 minutes, or until flour is rich golden-brown in color, stirring often. Remove bowl from oven.

4 Stir in celery, onions, and garlic. Cook on High 4 minutes, stirring once. Add Worcestershire and tomatoes. Cook, covered, on High 5 minutes, stirring once.

5 To gumbo, add shrimp, oysters, and okra. Season with salt and hot-pepper sauce.

6 Cook gumbo, covered, on High 7 minutes, or until shrimp turn pink and oysters curl. If you like, serve with hot cooked rice.

SOUP GARNISHES

Even the most simple soup can be made to look elegant just by adding a garnish. Some garnishes need a little preparation time but others can be ready in no time at all.

Green-onion Pompom: Trim top of green onion. Slit top down to bulb 3 or 4 times; place in bowl of ice water so top will curl.

Lemon/Lime Twist: Cut a thin slice from lemon or lime. Make 1 cut from center to edge of slice; twist into spiral shape.

Carrot Curl: With swivel-vegetable peeler, shave lengthwise strips from carrot. Roll up and secure each strip with toothpick. Place in bowl of ice water, about 1 hour. Drain; remove toothpick and use immediately.

Leek/Carrot Julienne: Cut leek and carrot lengthwise into matchstick-thin strips. Sprinkle on individual servings.

Mushroom Pinwheel: Holding blade of paring knife against mushroom cap and pressing gently, twist blade edge clockwise from center to edge of mushroom. Repeat evenly around mushroom cap.

Fresh Herbs: Chop fresh herbs with knife on cutting board, or use whole leaves or sprigs.

Chowders

MANHATTAN CLAM CHOWDER

Color Index page 43. Makes 6½ cups. 189 cals per cup. Low in cholesterol. Good source of vitamin A, iron. Begin 35 minutes ahead.

5 slices bacon, diced	1 cup water
3 small onions, minced	1 14½- to 16-ounce can
2 large carrots, chopped	tomatoes
2 large celery stalks, chopped	½ pint shucked clams with their liquid, chopped, or 1 10-ounce can diced clams
1 medium potato (about 6 ounces), peeled and chopped	¼ teaspoon pepper
1 bay leaf	Chopped parsley for garnish
¼ teaspoon thyme leaves	

1. In deep 3-quart microwave-safe bowl, place bacon. Cook, covered with paper towel, on High (100% power) 5 minutes, stirring twice.
2. To bacon, add onions, carrots, celery, potato, bay leaf, and thyme; stir. Cook, covered, on High 7 minutes, or until vegetables are tender, stirring twice.
3. To vegetable mixture, add water, tomatoes, clams, and pepper; mix well. Cook, covered, on High 5 minutes, or until hot. Discard bay leaf and garnish soup with chopped parsley.

CORN CHOWDER WITH CRAB CAKES

Color Index page 44. Makes 6 cups. 220 cals per cup (without Crab Cakes). Low in cholesterol. Good source of vitamin A. Begin 1¼ hours ahead.

Cocktail Crab Cakes (page 170)	1 teaspoon salt
2 tablespoons butter or margarine (¼ stick)	½ cup water
1 tablespoon all-purpose flour	2 cups half-and-half
1 tablespoon paprika	1 10-ounce package frozen whole-kernel corn
1 medium potato (about 8 ounces), peeled and chopped	Chopped parsley for garnish
1 celery stalk, minced	6 oysters on the half-shell (optional)
½ onion, chopped	6 large shrimp, shelled, deveined, and cooked (optional)
1 chicken-flavor bouillon cube or envelope	

1. Prepare Cocktail Crab Cakes. Keep warm while making chowder.
2. In deep 3-quart microwave-safe bowl, place butter or margarine. Heat, covered with paper towel, on High (100% power) 45 seconds, or until butter or margarine melts. Stir in flour and paprika; mix well. Add potato, celery, onion, bouillon, salt, and water. Cook, covered, on High 10 to 12 minutes, until vegetables are tender, stirring twice.
3. To vegetable mixture, add half-and-half and corn. Cook on High 6 to 8 minutes, until corn is tender (do not boil).
4. *To serve*: Ladle into soup bowls and sprinkle with parsley; accompany with Cocktail Crab Cakes and, if you like, oysters and shrimp.

Our microwave New England Clam, Manhattan Clam, and Corn Chowders contain the same delicious ingredients as chowders cooked traditionally, but they are ready to eat much sooner.

NEW ENGLAND CLAM CHOWDER

Color Index page 43. 312 cals per cup. Good source of calcium, iron. Begin 45 minutes ahead.

Ingredients for 6 cups		Microwave cookware
½ pint shucked clams with their liquid, or 1 10-ounce jar diced clams	3 tablespoons all-purpose flour	Deep 3-quart casserole
¼ pound salt pork or bacon, diced	3 cups milk	2½-quart bowl
2 medium onions, sliced	¼ teaspoon pepper	
2 medium baking potatoes (about 1 pound), peeled and diced	¼ teaspoon celery salt	
	Cherrystone clam shells (optional)	
	Chopped parsley for garnish	
	Oyster crackers	

1 Drain clams. If using shucked clams, cook, covered, in casserole on High (100% power) 5 minutes, stirring once. Cut clams into dice-sized pieces. Refrigerate until needed.

2 In bowl, place salt pork or bacon. Cook on High 4 to 5 minutes, until browned, stirring twice. Stir in onions and cook on High 2 minutes, stirring once.

To salt-pork mixture, add potatoes; stir to coat with fat. Cook, covered, on High 5 minutes, stirring occasionally, or until potatoes are tender.

4 Into mixture, stir flour to coat potatoes; cook on High 3 minutes, stirring halfway through cooking. Gradually stir in milk until smooth.

5 To bowl, add chilled clams, pepper, and celery salt. Cook on High 5 minutes, or until hot, stirring twice.

6 *To serve*: Ladle chowder into individual soup bowls. If you like, place 1 cherrystone clam shell in each bowl. Sprinkle with parsley and serve with oyster crackers.

Fruit Soups

RED PLUM SOUP

Color Index page 44. Makes 3 cups. 99 cals per cup. Low in cholesterol, fat, sodium. Begin early in day.

1½ pounds red plums
1½ cups Zinfandel or
  other red wine
1 teaspoon vanilla
  extract

1 3-inch-long cinnamon
  stick
¼ cup sugar
Sour cream or yogurt for
  garnish (optional)

1. Pit plums and cut into quarters. In deep 2½-quart microwave-safe bowl, combine plums, wine, vanilla extract, cinnamon stick, and sugar. Cook, covered, on High (100% power) 8 to 10 minutes, until plums are tender, stirring twice. Discard cinnamon stick.

2. In food processor with knife blade attached or in blender, process plum mixture until smooth. If you like, strain soup to remove plum skins.

3. Refrigerate soup until chilled. If you like, garnish each serving with a dollop of sour cream or yogurt.

GARNISHES FOR FRUIT SOUPS

A pretty garnish can add greatly to the decorative appeal of a refreshing summer soup. Edible flowers make a particularly attractive garnish, or try one of the other garnishes suggested below.

Rose Petals

Nasturtiums

Toasted, Slivered Almonds

Chopped Hazelnuts

Slivered Gingerroot

Star Fruit (Carambola)

Blueberries

Pomegranate Seeds

Sliced Kiwifruit

Passion-fruit Pulp

Fruit soups are best known as desserts but also make an unusual, refreshing first course, especially for a summer meal. They look particularly attractive served in white china bowls or dessert goblets. Most fruit soups are purees, sweetened and diluted with wine, fruit juice, or water. Some do not require cooking while others take only a few minutes in the microwave. Once you have tried our Red Plum Soup and Southern Peach Soup, experiment with other fruit such as cherries, blueberries, raspberries, strawberries, and tropical fruits.

SOUTHERN PEACH SOUP

Color Index page 44. 77 cals per cup. Low in cholesterol, fat, sodium. Begin early in day.

Ingredients for 3 cups		Microwave cookware
1½ pounds ripe peaches or 2 16-ounce cans peaches, drained *1 cup dry white wine* *½ cup water* *¼ cup sugar*	*1 teaspoon minced peeled gingerroot* *2 tablespoons bourbon* *¼ cup plain yogurt* *Plain yogurt and mint leaves for garnish*	Deep 2½-quart bowl

1 Cut peaches in half; twist apart. Remove pits and cut peach halves lengthwise into halves or quarters.

2 In bowl, combine peaches, wine, water, and sugar. Cook, covered, on High (100% power) 10 minutes, stirring twice.

3 In food processor with knife blade attached or in blender, process peach mixture until smooth.

4 Over bowl, set strainer. Pour peach mixture through to remove skin.

5 Into peach mixture, stir gingerroot. Cook, covered with paper towel, on High 5 minutes, stirring twice. Stir in bourbon and yogurt. Refrigerate until chilled.

6 *To serve:* Ladle soup into bowls. If you like, garnish with additional yogurt and mint leaves, and surround bowl with cracked ice.

Eggs and Cheese

BAKED EGGS · POACHED EGGS · SCRAMBLED EGGS
FRIED EGGS · OMELETS · MELTED CHEESE
BAKED CHEESE · SOUFFLÉS · ROULADES

Eggs and Cheese

Eggs and cheese are delicate ingredients that need some special handling when cooked in the microwave. Cooked conventionally, the white of an egg sets before the yolk. However, the opposite is true in microwave cooking. Because egg yolks contain a high proportion of fat, they attract more microwave energy. Therefore, our recipes include standing times in which the white sets without the yolk overcooking. Even when yolks and whites are mixed together, as in scrambled eggs, they still require standing time. Expect eggs to look very soft when removed from the microwave. Mixing in a little cream or milk before standing slows the cooking process, making the eggs creamier.

Most importantly, never put an egg in its shell into the microwave oven whether to cook or reheat it. Steam builds up in the shell and the egg will burst. Even out of the shell, you should pierce the yolk with a toothpick before it is fried, baked, or poached. The yolk has an outer membrane and an unpierced egg can burst.

Melted cheese is a quick and easy topping for hamburgers, sandwich fillings, and snack crackers, and is easily produced in the microwave oven. Most cheeses melt rapidly because of their high fat content, but do not all soften at the same rate. In general, drier cheeses such as Cheddar, Parmesan, and Gruyère take more time to soften than soft, moist ones such as cream cheese, Camembert, and Bel Paese. However, cheese can quickly overcook and become stringy, so that processed cheese often produces more acceptable results. Warming unwrapped chilled cheese on Medium (50% power) 45 seconds to 1 minute in the microwave oven will make it easier to slice.

Soufflés can be cooked in the microwave oven but be sure to follow our directions. Soufflés cook very rapidly in a microwave; they do rise very high, but fall quickly when removed from the oven, and they do not form a crust. Egg- and cheese-based quiches and casseroles reheat successfully in the microwave, but most other egg and cheese dishes toughen.

CREATIVE CHEESE TOPPINGS

Decorate soft cheese – either slices of Brie or smaller whole cheeses – by pressing the edge of a sharp knife into the top to create patterns and then adding your choice of flavorings.

Press nuts, seeds, spices, or herbs onto surface. Refrigerate, then bring to room temperature in microwave on Medium (50% power) when ready to serve.

EGGS IN BRIOCHES

Color Index page 45. 6 servings. 311 cals per
serving. Good source of calcium, iron.
Begin 25 minutes ahead.

6 individual brioches
6 slices Muenster or
  Swiss cheese
6 eggs
Salt and pepper to taste

Smoked salmon
Fresh chives for garnish
Asparagus (page 237)
  with Hollandaise Sauce
  (page 381)

1. With serrated knife, cut top from each
brioche; set aside. Hollow out each brioche,
leaving a ¼-inch-thick shell.
2. Line each brioche with slice of cheese. In 12″
round microwave-safe baking dish, arrange
brioches in a ring, 1 inch apart.
3. Break 1 egg into each brioche. With toothpick, pierce egg yolk. Cook, covered, on High
(100% power) 4 to 5 minutes, until almost set.
4. Let brioches stand, covered loosely with
waxed paper, 2 to 3 minutes, until white is
opaque. If eggs are not of desired doneness, cook
on High 15 seconds at a time, until done. Season.
5. On serving plate, arrange each brioche with
its top. Serve with smoked salmon garnished with
chives and Asparagus with Hollandaise Sauce.

Preparing the Brioches

Using a small, serrated
knife or a spoon, scoop
out inside of brioche.

Line each brioche with
slice of cheese, pushing
cheese into hollow.

Baked Eggs

Timing is crucial when cooking eggs in the microwave. Do not
return eggs to the oven without letting them stand for the time
specified; this allows the whites to continue cooking until just set
without overcooking the yolks. Eggs Baked in Ham Nests (below)
makes a change from baking eggs in custard cups or ramekins.

EGGS BAKED IN HAM NESTS

Color Index page 45. 200 cals per serving. Good source of thiamine.
Begin 15 minutes ahead.

Ingredients	For 4	For 2	For 1
Ham slices	8 slices	4 slices	2 slices
Green onions	2 onions	1 onion	½ onion
Butter or margarine, softened	2 teaspoons	1 teaspoon	½ teaspoon
Eggs	4 eggs	2 eggs	1 egg
Salt and pepper	to taste	to taste	to taste
Microwave cookware	4 5″ baking dishes	2 5″ baking dishes	1 5″ baking dish
Time on High (100% power)	4 to 5 minutes	2 to 2½ (2:30) minutes	45 seconds to 1 minute
Standing time	2 minutes	2 minutes	1 minute

1   Stack ham slices. Roll up or fold, and thinly slice.

2   Thinly slice green onions. Place in bowl with ham; toss.

3   In baking dishes (see Chart), brush softened butter or margarine. For each serving, arrange ham-onion mixture around edge of dish.

4   Break each egg onto saucer. Gently slip eggs into middle of ham nests. With toothpick, pierce yolk of each egg to prevent bursting during cooking.

5   Cook eggs, covered, on High for time in Chart, until white is opaque but not set.

6   Let eggs stand, covered loosely, for time in Chart. If eggs are not of desired doneness after standing time, cook on High 15 seconds at a time, until done to your liking. Sprinkle with salt and pepper before serving.

Poached Eggs

POACHED EGGS *

Color Index page 45. 80 cals per serving. Low in sodium.
Begin 15 minutes ahead.

Ingredients	For 4	For 2	For 1
Water	½ cup	¼ cup	2 tablespoons
White vinegar	2 teaspoons	1 teaspoon	½ teaspoon
Eggs	4 eggs	2 eggs	1 egg
Salt and pepper	to taste	to taste	to taste
Parsley sprigs for garnish	garnish	garnish	garnish
Microwave cookware	1-cup glass measure	1-cup glass measure	1-cup glass measure
	4 custard cups	2 custard cups	1 custard cup
Time on High (100% power) Water and vinegar	3 minutes	1½ (1:30) minutes	45 seconds
Time on Medium (50% power) Eggs	3 to 3½ (3:30) minutes	1½ (1:30) to 2 minutes	45 seconds to 1 minute
Standing time	2 to 3 minutes	2 minutes	1 minute

1 In glass measure (see Chart), heat water and vinegar on High for time in Chart, or until boiling. Meanwhile, into each custard cup (see Chart), break 1 egg.

2 With toothpick, pierce yolk of each egg to prevent bursting during cooking.

3 Carefully pour water and vinegar over eggs. Place custard cups on floor of oven.

4 Cook eggs, covered, on Medium for time in Chart, until white is opaque but not set.

5 Let eggs stand, loosely covered, for time in Chart. If eggs are not of desired doneness after standing time, cook on High 15 seconds at a time, until done to your liking.

6 With slotted spoon, remove each egg from custard cup and drain over paper towel. Transfer to serving dish and sprinkle with salt and pepper. Garnish with parsley sprigs.

POACHED EGGS FLORENTINE *

Color Index page 46. 4 servings. 397 cals per serving. Good source of vitamin A, calcium, iron. Begin 40 minutes ahead.

Hollandaise Sauce (page 381)
½ cup water
2 teaspoons white vinegar
4 eggs
Ground nutmeg, salt, and pepper to taste
1 10-ounce package frozen spinach, thawed
2 English muffins, split and toasted

½ pound asparagus, cooked and drained (optional)
Fresh chives and bacon bits for garnish

1. Prepare Hollandaise Sauce. Cover and set aside, keeping warm and stirring occasionally.
2. In 1-cup microwave-safe glass measure, heat water and vinegar on High (100% power) 3 minutes, or until boiling. Meanwhile, break eggs into 4 custard cups. With toothpick, pierce yolk of each egg to prevent bursting.
3. Carefully pour water and vinegar over eggs. On 12″ microwave-safe platter, arrange custard cups. Cook eggs, covered, on Medium (50% power) 3 to 4 minutes, until white is opaque but not set. Let stand, loosely covered, 2 to 3 minutes. Season with nutmeg, salt, and pepper.
4. Meanwhile, in 9″ microwave-safe pie plate, place thawed spinach. Cook on High 3 minutes, stirring once.
5. *To serve*: Place 1 toasted muffin half on each plate. Top with an equal amount of hot spinach. With slotted spoon, drain each egg over paper towel; arrange on spinach. If you like, accompany with cooked asparagus. Spoon over Hollandaise Sauce. Sprinkle with chives and bacon bits. Serve immediately.

Assembling the Eggs Florentine

Using a slotted spoon, drain each egg over paper towel before placing on spinach-covered muffin.

Spoon warm Hollandaise Sauce over each egg and garnish as above.

Scrambled Eggs

PIPERADE

Color Index page 45. 6 servings. 195 cals per serving. Good source of vitamin A, vitamin C, iron. Begin 20 minutes ahead.

2 tablespoons olive or salad oil	¼ teaspoon basil
2 medium red or green peppers, cut into thin strips	1 teaspoon salt
	¼ teaspoon pepper
1 medium onion, chopped	Basil leaves for garnish
6 eggs	

1. Into 9″ round microwave-safe quiche dish, pour oil. Heat on High (100% power) 3 minutes. Stir in pepper strips and onion. Cook on High 4 minutes, stirring twice.

2. In medium bowl, with whisk or fork, beat eggs, basil, salt, and pepper.

3. Pour beaten egg mixture over pepper-onion mixture. Cook on High 2½ (2:30) minutes, or until eggs are softly set but still very moist, stirring cooked edge into center of dish during cooking. Let stand, loosely covered, on heat-safe surface 2 to 3 minutes.

4. If eggs are not of desired doneness after standing time, cook on High 15 seconds at a time, until done to your liking. Garnish with basil leaves. Serve immediately.

SCRAMBLED EGGS AND BACON BREAKFAST

It's easy to cook eggs and bacon for 4 people in a matter of minutes. Begin with steps 1 and 2 of the **Scrambled Eggs** recipe (right). Then separate **8 slices bacon** and arrange on a paper-towel-lined microwave-safe platter. Cover with another paper towel and place on microwave-oven shelf. Cook on High (100% power) 2 to 3 minutes. Turn bacon slices over and return to microwave. Continue with steps 3, 4, and 5 of Scrambled Eggs recipe, cooking eggs and bacon together on High for time in Chart, until eggs are softly set but still very moist, stirring twice, and bacon is browned. Remove bacon to another paper towel to drain. Remove eggs and let stand, loosely covered, for time in Chart.

To prevent overcooking, scrambled eggs should be removed from the microwave before they are completely cooked; they set during the standing time. If you like, mix a little milk or cream into scrambled eggs after they are removed from the oven to slow down the cooking process; this will also make them creamier.

SCRAMBLED EGGS

Color Index page 45. 104 cals per serving. Begin 10 minutes ahead.

Ingredients	For 4	For 2	For 1
Butter or margarine	1 tablespoon	1½ teaspoons	1 teaspoon
Eggs	4 eggs	2 eggs	1 egg
Water	2 tablespoons	1 tablespoon	1½ teaspoons
Salt	⅛ teaspoon	to taste	to taste
Pepper	to taste	to taste	to taste
Microwave cookware	2-quart casserole	1-quart casserole	Individual soup bowl
Time on High (100% power)			
Butter	30 seconds	15 seconds	10 seconds
Eggs	1½ (1:30) to 2½ (2:30) minutes	1 to 1½ (1:30) minutes	45 seconds to 1 minute
Standing time	2 to 3 minutes	2 minutes	1 minute

1 In casserole or soup bowl (see Chart), heat butter or margarine, covered with paper towel, on High for time in Chart, or until melted.

2 In mixing bowl, with whisk or fork, beat eggs, water, salt, and pepper. Pour into casserole or soup bowl with melted butter or margarine.

3 Cook egg mixture on High for time in Chart, stirring cooked edge into center of dish halfway through cooking. If cooking for 4 or 2, stir twice during cooking.

4 Remove eggs from oven. Eggs will be softly set and very moist.

5 Loosely cover dish or soup bowl. Let eggs stand for time in Chart.

6 Eggs will finish cooking during standing. If eggs are not of desired doneness after standing, cook on High 15 seconds at a time, until done to your liking.

Bon Voyage Brunch

Mimosas
Eggs in Brioches, page 137, with extra smoked salmon
Asparagus (page 237) with Hollandaise Sauce, page 381
Muffins and coffeecakes (bakery)
Citrus fruit salad
Chocolate-dipped Fruit, page 327
Coffee

PREPARATION TIMETABLE

1 day ahead:	*Prepare a fruit salad of grapefruit, orange, and tangerine sections. Cover and refrigerate. Prepare Chocolate-dipped Fruit. Arrange on serving plate; cover loosely. Store in a cool, dry place; do not refrigerate. Chill Champagne and orange juice for Mimosas.*
2 hours ahead:	*Make Hollandaise Sauce; keep warm and stir occasionally. Prepare asparagus, but do not cook.*
30 minutes before serving:	*Prepare Eggs in Brioches through step 2. Cook asparagus according to directions in Chart on page 237; arrange on warmed serving platter with Hollandaise Sauce.*
Just before serving:	*Complete Eggs in Brioches; arrange on platter with smoked salmon. Arrange muffins and coffeecakes on serving platter; if you like, heat briefly in microwave. Mix Champagne with orange juice for Mimosas.*

Fried Eggs

BACON AND EGGS *

Color Index page 45. 4 servings. 270 cals per serving. Begin 15 minutes ahead.

8 slices bacon	Chopped chives for
4 eggs	garnish
Salt and pepper to taste	Rolls (optional)
2 tomatoes, cut in half	

1. Preheat browning dish as manufacturer directs. Arrange bacon slices in single layer on browning dish. Cook on High (100% power) 2 minutes. With spatula, turn bacon over. Cook on High 2 to 3 minutes, depending on desired doneness. Remove to paper towels to drain; set aside and keep warm. Discard half the bacon drippings.

2. Break eggs, one at a time, into saucer. Gently slip each egg onto browning dish, placing them evenly around dish. With toothpick, pierce yolk of each egg to prevent yolks from bursting.

3. Cook eggs on High 1 to 2 minutes, until cooked to required doneness. If you like, with spatula turn eggs over for eggs "over easy." Season with salt and pepper.

4. *To serve:* Arrange eggs and bacon on warmed serving platter or dinner plates. Garnish with tomato halves sprinkled with chopped chives. If you like, accompany with warm rolls.

FRIED EGGS *

Fried eggs are quick and easy to make in the microwave. Preheat browning dish as manufacturer directs. For each *egg*, melt *1 tablespoon butter* or *margarine* in browning dish. Break each egg, one at a time, into saucer, then gently slide egg onto browning dish; space eggs evenly, or if frying only 1, place in center of dish. With toothpick, pierce each yolk.

For eggs sunny-side up: Cook on High (100% power) 1½ (1:30) to 2 minutes for 4 eggs; 45 seconds to 1¼ (1:15) minutes for 2 eggs; and 30 seconds to 1 minute for 1 egg.

For eggs "over easy": Cook as above, turning eggs over with spatula after 1¼ (1:15) minutes for 4 eggs; 45 seconds for 2 eggs; and 30 seconds for 1 egg.

Quick bacon and eggs for one: Preheat browning dish as manufacturer directs. Cut 2 bacon slices crosswise in half and arrange against edge of dish. Cook on High (100% power) 45 seconds to 1 minute, then turn bacon over. Break 1 egg into saucer, gently slide onto browning dish; pierce yolk. Baste egg with bacon drippings, cook on High 45 seconds to 1 minute. Let stand, covered, 1 minute.

Omelets

SOUFFLÉED CHEESE OMELET

Color Index page 46. 2 servings. 261 cals per serving. Good source of vitamin A, calcium. Begin 15 minutes ahead.

2 tablespoons butter or margarine (¼ stick)	⅛ teaspoon pepper
3 eggs, separated	2 ounces Cheddar cheese, shredded (½ cup)
1 teaspoon milk	
½ teaspoon tarragon	Cucumber, tomato, and parsley for garnish
½ teaspoon salt	

1. In 9″ microwave-safe pie plate, place butter or margarine. Heat, covered with paper towel, on High (100% power) 45 seconds, or until butter or margarine has melted.
2. In small bowl, with fork, beat egg yolks with milk, tarragon, salt, and pepper until well mixed.
3. In large bowl, with mixer at high speed, beat egg whites until stiff peaks form. With rubber spatula, gently fold egg-yolk mixture into beaten egg whites.
4. Spoon egg mixture into pie plate. With spatula, smooth top. Cook on High 1½ (1:30) to 2½ (2:30) minutes, until top is almost dry.
5. With spatula, mark a line through center of omelet. Sprinkle cheese over half the omelet. With spatula, gently fold omelet over cheese.
6. Slide omelet onto warmed serving platter. Garnish with cucumber, tomato, and parsley. Serve immediately.

USING LEFTOVER CHEESE: Small pieces of one or more hard cheeses can be shredded and used as an alternative filling.

FRENCH DESSERT OMELET

Color Index page 46. 2 servings. 209 cals per serving. Good source of vitamin A, iron. Begin 15 minutes ahead.

½ cup strawberries, sliced	4 eggs
½ teaspoon sugar	1 teaspoon milk
2 teaspoons butter or margarine	Confectioners' sugar
	Strawberry for garnish
	Plain yogurt (optional)

1. In small bowl, combine strawberries and sugar.
2. In 9″ microwave-safe pie plate, place butter or margarine. Heat on High (100% power) 30 seconds, or until butter or margarine has melted.
3. In small bowl, with fork, beat eggs and milk until well mixed. Pour into pie plate. Cook on High 1 minute. With spoon or spatula, move cooked edge to center of plate. Cook, covered with paper towel, on High 1 to 1½ (1:30) minutes, until omelet is set but still moist in center.
4. Spoon strawberries over half the omelet. With spatula, fold omelet over strawberries.
5. Slide omelet onto warmed serving platter. Sift confectioners' sugar over omelet. Top with whole strawberry. If you like, serve with yogurt.

Omelets should be cooked in pie plates in order to have smooth and shapely edges. To ensure a flat surface, be gentle when stirring, and move the cooked edge to the center, so that uncooked egg mixture flows under omelet. A properly cooked omelet will be set throughout but the center top will appear moist. If the omelet is too moist in the center when checked with a knife, cover, return to the oven, and cook on High (100% power) 15 seconds at a time.

SPANISH OMELET

Color Index page 46. 253 cals per serving. Good source of vitamin A, vitamin C, iron. Begin 15 minutes ahead.

Ingredients for 2 servings		Microwave cookware
1 tablespoon olive or salad oil	1 tablespoon milk	9″ glass pie plate
1 medium onion, thinly sliced	Salt, pepper, and hot-pepper sauce to taste	
1 small green pepper, coarsely chopped	Parsley for garnish	
1 small tomato, chopped	Chorizo sausages or ham (optional)	
4 eggs		

1 In pie plate, combine oil, onion, green pepper, and tomato. Cook, covered, on High (100% power) 4 minutes, stirring twice.

2 Meanwhile, in medium bowl, with fork, mix eggs, milk, salt, pepper, and hot-pepper sauce.

3 With spoon, transfer vegetable mixture to another bowl. Season to taste. Pour egg mixture into pie plate. Cook on High 1 minute.

4 With spoon or spatula, move cooked edge to center of plate. Cook, covered with paper towel, on High 1 to 1½ (1:30) minutes, until omelet is set but still moist in center.

5 Spoon vegetable mixture over half the omelet. With spatula, gently fold omelet over vegetables.

6 *To serve:* Slide omelet onto warmed serving platter. Garnish with parsley and, if you like, serve with chorizo sausages or ham.

Melted Cheese

Cheese is a delicate ingredient and needs careful handling in the microwave to avoid becoming tough and stringy. Our recipes call for shredded or grated cheese because in these forms it will melt rapidly in a hot mixture. It is important to stir shredded or grated cheese after it has been added to any hot mixture, to make sure that it melts completely and blends evenly.

MACARONI AND CHEESE

Color Index page 46. 581 cals per serving. Good source of thiamine, riboflavin, calcium, iron. Begin 35 minutes ahead.

Ingredients for 4 servings		Microwave cookware
1 8-ounce package elbow macaroni	1/8 teaspoon pepper	2-quart soufflé dish or casserole
3 tablespoons butter or margarine	1 1/2 cups milk	
1 small onion, minced	8 ounces Cheddar cheese, shredded (2 cups)	
1 tablespoon all-purpose flour	1/4 cup dried whole-wheat or seasoned bread crumbs	
1/2 teaspoon salt	Extra cheese (optional)	
1/4 teaspoon dry mustard	Parsley for garnish	

1 Prepare macaroni conventionally as label directs; drain in colander.

2 Meanwhile, in soufflé dish or casserole, place butter or margarine. Heat, covered with paper towel, on High (100% power) 45 seconds, or until melted. Add onion; stir to coat. Cook on High 2 minutes, or until softened.

3 Into onion mixture, with whisk or spoon, stir flour, salt, mustard, and pepper until smooth and blended. Cook on High 1 minute, stirring once.

4 Into mixture, gradually stir milk. Cook on High 3 to 4 minutes, until mixture thickens and is smooth, stirring twice. Remove dish from oven and add cheese. Stir sauce until cheese melts.

5 Into cheese sauce, stir drained macaroni. Cook on High 5 to 7 minutes, rotating dish twice during cooking. Let stand on heat-safe surface 5 minutes.

6 Onto casserole, sprinkle dried whole-wheat or seasoned bread crumbs and, if you like, extra shredded cheese. Cook on High 30 seconds, or if you like and dish is broiler-safe, brown under preheated broiler. Garnish.

WELSH RABBIT

Color Index page 46. 6 servings. 347 cals per serving. Good source of vitamin A. Begin 15 minutes ahead.

4 tablespoons butter or margarine (1/2 stick)
1/4 cup all-purpose flour
1/2 teaspoon salt
1/8 teaspoon ground red pepper
1/8 teaspoon dry mustard
1/2 cup beer
1 1/2 cups milk
1 teaspoon Worcestershire

8 ounces Cheddar cheese, shredded (2 cups)
6 slices white or rye bread, toasted, or 6 English muffin halves
Gherkins, stuffed olives, pickled onions, and parsley for garnish

1. In 2-quart microwave-safe casserole, place butter or margarine. Heat, covered with paper towel, on High (100% power) 45 seconds to 1 minute, until butter or margarine has melted.
2. Into melted butter or margarine, with whisk or spoon, stir flour, salt, ground red pepper, and dry mustard until smooth and blended. Cook on High 1 minute, stirring once.
3. Into mixture, gradually stir beer, milk, and Worcestershire until smooth. Cook on High 5 minutes, stirring twice. Add shredded cheese, stirring until melted.
4. Serve hot cheese mixture over toast or English muffin halves. Garnish with gherkins, stuffed olives, pickled onions, and parsley.

SWISS CHEESE FONDUE

Color Index page 46. 4 servings. 825 cals per serving. Good source of vitamin A, thiamine, iron. Begin 10 minutes ahead.

1 garlic clove, cut in half
1 1/2 cups dry white wine
16 ounces Gruyère cheese, shredded (4 cups)
3 tablespoons all-purpose flour
1/8 teaspoon pepper

1/8 teaspoon ground nutmeg
Paprika (optional)
1 loaf French bread, about 18 inches long, cut into 1-inch cubes
16 cherry tomatoes
1 green pepper, cut into cubes

1. In 2-quart microwave-safe casserole or ceramic fondue dish, place garlic and wine. Cook on High (100% power) 4 minutes, or until wine is boiling.
2. Meanwhile in medium bowl, toss shredded Gruyère cheese with flour until well mixed.
3. Remove garlic from wine; discard. To wine, add shredded cheese a handful at a time, stirring constantly until cheese melts. Season with pepper and nutmeg. If you like, sprinkle with paprika.
4. *To serve*: Place fondue in center of table. With long-handled fondue forks or skewers, let each person spear chunks of French bread, cherry tomatoes, and green pepper cubes to dip into fondue.

ASPARAGUS TIMBALES

Color Index page 47. Makes 4 timbales. 314 cals each. Good source of vitamin A, thiamine, vitamin C, iron. Begin 40 minutes ahead.

3 tablespoons butter or margarine	1/8 teaspoon ground nutmeg
2 tablespoons dried bread crumbs	Salt and pepper to taste
1/2 pound asparagus	1/2 cup half-and-half
1 small onion, minced	6 ounces thinly sliced smoked salmon or prosciutto
4 egg yolks	
1/4 cup grated Parmesan cheese	Lemon for garnish

1. In medium microwave-safe bowl, place butter or margarine. Heat, covered with paper towel, on High (100% power) 45 seconds to 1 minute, until melted. Brush inside of four 4-ounce ramekins with some melted butter or margarine. Sprinkle bread crumbs around the inside of each ramekin to coat. Set aside.

2. Hold base of each asparagus spear firmly and bend; the end will break off where the spear becomes too tough to eat. Discard ends.

3. Trim 4 asparagus tips to 2 inches long; reserve. Coarsely chop remaining asparagus. In bowl with melted butter or margarine, combine chopped asparagus and onion. Cook, covered, on High 4 to 5 minutes, until asparagus is tender, stirring once.

4. On cutting board, finely chop asparagus mixture; return to bowl. With fork or whisk, beat in egg yolks, cheese, nutmeg, salt, and pepper.

5. In 2-cup microwave-safe glass measure, cook half-and-half on Medium (50% power) 1 1/2 (1:30) to 2 minutes until half-and-half forms small bubbles around edge.

6. Into asparagus mixture, gradually stir half-and-half. Ladle a quarter of mixture into each ramekin. Arrange in a ring on 12" microwave-safe platter. Elevate platter on microwave-safe trivet, rack, or ramekins turned upside down. Cook on Medium 5 to 7 minutes, until knife inserted 1/2 inch from center comes out clean, rotating platter twice. Let timbales stand, covered, on heat-safe surface, 5 minutes.

7. *To serve:* Unmold timbales onto individual plates. Serve with smoked salmon or prosciutto. Garnish with reserved asparagus and lemon.

Preparing the Ramekins

Using a pastry brush, brush the ramekins with some melted butter.

Coat each ramekin with bread crumbs; tilt to cover bottom and sides.

When microwaving cheese casseroles or quiches, elevate the dish on a microwave-safe trivet, rack, or ramekin turned upside down, to ensure even cooking on the underside. Ramekins arranged in a ring should be rearranged and rotated during cooking.

SOPA SECA

Color Index page 46. 390 cals per serving. Good source of vitamin A. Begin 45 minutes ahead.

Ingredients for 6 servings		Microwave cookware
1 tablespoon salad oil	1/2 teaspoon salt	12" by 8" baking dish
1 medium onion, chopped	Hot-pepper sauce to taste	Trivet, rack, or ramekins
2 green onions, sliced	4 ounces Monterey Jack cheese, shredded (1 cup)	
1 garlic clove, minced		
1/2 teaspoon oregano	1/4 cup coriander leaves, chopped	
1/2 teaspoon ground cumin	6 ounces tortilla chips	
1 16-ounce can crushed tomatoes	Coriander leaves for garnish	
1 cup heavy or whipping cream		

1 In baking dish, place oil, onion, green onions, garlic, oregano, and cumin. Elevate dish on trivet, rack, or ramekins turned upside down.

2 Cook onion mixture, covered, on High (100% power) 3 minutes, or until onion has softened slightly, stirring once.

3 To onion mixture, add tomatoes and cream. Cook on High 7 to 8 minutes, until cream has thickened, stirring twice. Add salt and hot-pepper sauce to taste.

4 Remove half the tomato sauce to small bowl. In another bowl, toss shredded cheese with coriander until well mixed.

5 Cover remaining tomato sauce with half the tortilla chips, half the cheese mixture, and the remaining sauce. Add another layer of tortilla chips and cheese mixture. Cook on High 4 to 5 minutes, until cheese melts and tomato sauce is bubbling, rotating dish once.

6 Let casserole stand 5 minutes on heat-safe surface before serving. Garnish with coriander leaves.

Baked Cheese

Traditional quiches cannot be cooked successfully in the microwave, but our crustless varieties are delicious and less caloric. Medium heat is necessary to prevent cheese's delicate texture from becoming tough and rubbery. For a perfect result, a quiche that is light and tender, preheat the liquid ingredients first, then combine with eggs. This way, the eggs won't overcook, as they might if heated with a cold liquid.

CRUSTLESS BROCCOLI AND SWISS CHEESE QUICHE

Color Index page 47. 244 cals per serving. Good source of vitamin A, vitamin C, calcium. Begin 45 minutes ahead.

Ingredients for 6 servings		Microwave cookware
1 bunch broccoli (about 1 pound), chopped 1 small onion, minced ½ cup half-and-half 4 eggs	8 ounces Swiss cheese, shredded (2 cups) ¼ teaspoon ground red pepper Tomato Rose (page 236) and basil leaves for garnish	9″ quiche dish 2-cup glass measure Trivet, rack, or ramekin

1 In quiche dish, place broccoli and onion. Cook, covered, on High (100% power) 5 minutes, stirring once. Set aside, covered.

2 In glass measure, heat half-and-half on Medium (50% power) 1½ (1:30) to 2 minutes, until small bubbles form around edge.

3 In medium bowl, with fork or whisk, beat half-and-half and eggs until blended. Stir in cheese and ground red pepper.

4 Slowly pour egg mixture over broccoli and onion; stir gently to distribute vegetables evenly.

5 Elevate dish on trivet, rack, or ramekin turned upside down. Cook on Medium 12 to 14 minutes, until knife inserted in center comes out clean, rotating dish twice.

6 On heat-safe surface, let quiche stand, covered, 10 minutes. Garnish. Serve warm, or refrigerate to serve chilled later.

BACON AND POTATO QUICHE

Color Index page 47. 8 servings. 241 cals per serving. Good source of vitamin A. Begin 45 minutes ahead.

6 slices bacon, cut into 2-inch pieces
½ pound potatoes, cut into ¾-inch cubes
½ pound fresh peas, shelled
¾ cup milk
6 eggs

6 ounces Cheddar cheese, cut into ½-inch cubes
2 green onions, thinly sliced
½ teaspoon salt
Chives for garnish (optional)

1. In 10″ microwave-safe quiche dish, place bacon. Cook, covered with paper towel, on High (100% power) 5 to 6 minutes, until bacon is browned, stirring once. Remove to paper towels to drain. Discard all but 2 tablespoons drippings. Stir in potatoes and peas. Cook, covered, 4 to 6 minutes, until tender, stirring once.
2. Into medium microwave-safe bowl, pour milk. Cook on High 2 to 2½ (2:30) minutes, until milk forms small bubbles around edge. Add eggs; beat until blended. To beaten eggs, add cheese, green onions, salt, and bacon; mix well. Carefully pour mixture over vegetables in dish.
3. Elevate dish on microwave-safe trivet, rack, or ramekin turned upside down. Cook on Medium (50% power) 10 to 12 minutes, until egg mixture is slightly set but still moist, stirring cooked edge toward center twice. On heat-safe surface, let quiche stand, covered, 5 minutes. If you like, garnish with chives.

CAMEMBERT IN GRAPE LEAVES

Color Index page 46. 2 servings. 250 cals per serving. Good source of vitamin A. Begin 20 minutes ahead.

1 Red Delicious or other dessert apple
2 teaspoons brandy
1 4½-ounce Camembert cheese

2 grape leaves, fresh or in brine (rinsed and drained), or fresh lettuce leaves
Parsley for garnish

1. Core apple. Thinly slice one-quarter of apple; cut remainder into wedges. In small bowl, toss apple slices and wedges in brandy. Set aside.
2. Cut Camembert in half horizontally. Arrange apple slices on cut side of half the cheese; cover with remaining half of cheese, cut side down.
3. Place cheese in center of 1 grape or lettuce leaf. Cover with remaining leaf. Fold edges of leaves around cheese to completely enclose it; secure with string. Place wrapped cheese in center of small microwave-safe plate. Cook on Medium (50% power) 2 minutes. Remove string.
4. To serve: Arrange apple wedges around wrapped cheese. Garnish with parsley sprigs. Cut and spread cheese on apple wedges.

Soufflés

TOMATOES WITH GOAT CHEESE AND BASIL SOUFFLÉ

Color Index page 47. 8 servings. 106 cals per serving. Low in sodium. Good source of vitamin A. Begin 35 minutes ahead.

8 medium tomatoes	2 ounces soft goat
Salt and pepper to taste	cheese, such as
2 tablespoons butter or	Montrachet
margarine (¼ stick)	1 tablespoon minced
2 tablespoons all-	basil leaves
purpose flour	2 eggs
½ cup milk	Basil leaves for garnish

1. Cut a slice from the top of each tomato. With spoon, scoop out pulp from each tomato to leave a ¼-inch shell. If necessary, cut a small slice from the bottom of each tomato so that it will stay level. On 12″ microwave-safe platter, arrange tomato shells in a ring. Season each tomato; set aside.
2. In medium microwave-safe bowl, place butter or margarine. Heat, covered with paper towel, on High (100% power) 45 seconds, or until melted. With whisk or spoon, stir in flour until smooth and blended. Cook on High 1 minute, stirring once. Gradually stir in milk. Cook on High 2 to 3 minutes, until mixture thickens and is smooth, stirring twice.
3. To sauce, add cheese. Stir sauce until cheese melts, then add minced basil and salt and pepper.
4. Separate eggs. Blend yolks into cheese sauce. In large bowl, with mixer at high speed, beat egg whites until stiff peaks form. With spatula, gently fold cheese mixture, a third at a time, into beaten egg whites, just until blended.
5. Spoon an equal amount of mixture into tomato shells. Cook on Medium-Low (30% power) 6 minutes. Increase power level to Medium (50% power) and cook 5 minutes longer. Increase power level to High and cook 2 minutes more.
6. *To serve:* Place each stuffed tomato on a warmed dinner plate. Garnish with basil leaves.

COOKING WITH CHEESE
The quality of the cheese used in cooking makes a great difference in the finished microwave recipes. Always add cheese toward the end of cooking time so it does not overcook and become stringy or tough. For melted cheese dishes, well-aged, high-quality cheeses will result in smooth, tasty dishes. If a sauce separates or curdles, pour sauce into blender or food processor and blend 1 to 2 minutes. To reheat cheese sauces, heat on Medium (50% power) and stir frequently.

CHEESE SOUFFLÉ

Color Index page 47. 335 cals per serving. Good source of calcium. Begin 35 minutes ahead.

Ingredients for 6 servings		Microwave cookware
4 tablespoons butter or margarine (½ stick)	8 ounces Swiss cheese, shredded (2 cups)	4-cup glass measure
¼ cup all-purpose flour	⅛ teaspoon ground nutmeg	2-quart soufflé dish
1 cup milk	½ teaspoon salt	
5 eggs, separated	Tomato Sauce	
¼ cup grated Parmesan cheese	(page 380, optional)	

1 In glass measure, place butter or margarine. Heat, covered with paper towel, on High (100% power) 45 seconds to 1 minute, until melted. With whisk or spoon, stir in flour until blended. Cook on High 1 minute, stirring once.

2 Into mixture, gradually stir milk until smooth. Cook on High 2 to 3 minutes, until sauce is very thick, stirring twice.

3 In small bowl, lightly beat egg yolks. Stir small amount of hot sauce into egg yolks. Slowly pour egg-yolk mixture into remaining hot sauce, beating rapidly to prevent lumping. Stir in Parmesan and ¼ cup Swiss cheese. Add nutmeg and salt.

4 In large bowl, with mixer at high speed, beat egg whites until stiff peaks form.

5 With spatula, gently fold remaining cheese and egg whites alternately, a third at a time, into cheese mixture, just until blended. Pour mixture into ungreased soufflé dish. Gently smooth top.

6 Cook on Medium-Low (30% power) 8 minutes. Increase power level to Medium (50% power) and cook 7 to 9 minutes longer, until top is dry but soufflé still moves when dish is shaken gently. If you like, serve with Tomato Sauce.

Roulades

Soufflé-based dishes like our Smoked Salmon and Chive Roulade or Mushroom-Cheese Roulade make pretty food for a buffet party. If you follow our instructions for rolling the roulades from a long rather than a narrow end, you will find they are easier to cut into neat, thin slices – just perfect for dainty presentation on a large plate, serving platter, or tray.

SMOKED SALMON AND CHIVE ROULADE

Color Index page 47. 233 cals per serving. Good source of vitamin A.
Begin 45 minutes ahead.

Ingredients for 4 servings		Microwave cookware

6 eggs
Salt and pepper to taste
3 ounces thinly sliced
  smoked salmon
1 4-ounce package
  whipped cream cheese
  with chives, softened
	1/3 cup chopped chives
	Chives for garnish
		13" by 9" baking tray or
		  dish
		Trivet, rack, or
		  ramekin

1 Line tray or dish with waxed paper. Set aside. Separate 4 eggs. In small bowl, with fork or whisk, lightly beat egg yolks and 2 remaining whole eggs. Season with salt and pepper.

2 In large bowl, with mixer at high speed, beat egg whites until stiff peaks form. With rubber spatula or whisk, gently fold egg-yolk mixture into egg whites, just until blended.

3 Pour soufflé mixture into waxed-paper-lined tray or dish. With knife or spatula, smooth top. Elevate tray or dish on trivet, rack, or ramekin turned upside down. Cook on High (100% power) 3 to 4 minutes, until knife inserted in center comes out clean.

4 Invert roulade onto clean cloth towel lined with waxed paper. Peel paper off top of roulade. Starting at a long end, roll roulade with waxed paper, jelly-roll fashion. Let stand, seam side down, 5 minutes.

5 Carefully unroll roulade. Arrange smoked salmon to within 2 inches of edges. Spread cream cheese over salmon; sprinkle with chopped chives. Starting from same long end, roll up roulade without waxed paper.

6 To serve: Lift roulade with long spatula onto serving platter. Refrigerate 15 minutes. Cut into slices and garnish with chives.

MUSHROOM-CHEESE ROULADE

Color Index page 47. 4 servings. 242 cals per serving. Good source of vitamin A, riboflavin, iron. Begin 45 minutes ahead.

2 tablespoons butter or margarine (1/4 stick)
1 small onion, chopped
2 tomatoes, diced
1/2 pound mushrooms, coarsely chopped
1/4 cup dry white wine
1 tablespoon chopped basil leaves

2 ounces Swiss cheese, shredded (1/2 cup)
6 eggs
Salt and pepper to taste
Basil leaves for garnish

1. Line 13" by 9" microwave-safe baking tray or dish with waxed paper; set aside.
2. In 8" by 8" microwave-safe baking dish, place butter or margarine. Heat, covered with paper towel, on High (100% power) 45 seconds, or until melted. Add onion, tomatoes, and mushrooms. Cook on High 5 minutes, stirring twice.
3. To vegetable mixture, add wine. Cook on High 5 minutes, or until most of the wine has evaporated; add chopped basil. Strain liquid from vegetable mixture and discard. Stir in cheese.
4. Separate 4 eggs. In small bowl, with fork or whisk, lightly beat egg yolks and 2 remaining whole eggs. Season with salt and pepper.
5. In large bowl, with mixer at high speed, beat egg whites until stiff peaks form.
6. With rubber spatula or whisk, gently fold egg-yolk mixture into egg whites, just until blended.
7. Pour soufflé mixture into waxed-paper-lined tray or dish. With knife or spatula, smooth top. Elevate tray or dish on microwave-safe trivet, rack, or ramekins turned upside down. Cook on High 3 to 4 minutes, until knife inserted in center comes out clean.
8. Invert roulade onto clean cloth towel lined with waxed paper. Peel paper off top of roulade. Starting from a long end, roll roulade with waxed paper, jelly-roll fashion.
9. Let stand, seam side down, 5 minutes, then carefully unroll. Spread mushroom mixture over roulade to within 2 inches of edges. Starting from same long end, roll up roulade, without waxed paper.
10. To serve: Lift roulade with long spatula onto serving platter. Refrigerate 15 minutes. Cut into slices. Garnish with basil leaves.

SPINACH AND RICOTTA CHEESE ROULADE: Prepare roulade (above), substituting 1 10-ounce package frozen chopped spinach, thawed and squeezed dry, for the mushrooms. Cook with tomatoes for 3 minutes only. Omit wine. Stir in basil and 3/4 cup ricotta cheese. If you like, serve with our Tomato Sauce (page 380).

Fish and Shellfish

DEFROSTING AND COOKING FISH AND SHELLFISH · FISH STEAKS

FISH FILLETS · WHOLE FISH

CANNED FISH · SHRIMP · CLAMS · LOBSTER

MUSSELS · SCALLOPS · OYSTERS · CRAB

MIXED SEAFOOD DISHES

Fish and Shellfish

The microwave is ideal for cooking both fish and shellfish, as they are naturally delicate foods and require minimal cooking to preserve their flavors and textures. They dry out, toughen, or break apart easily, so the quick, moist cooking of the microwave, combined with careful handling, can produce excellent results. Microwaved fish can be made to look broiled by cooking it in a browning dish or by brushing it with browning, teriyaki, or soy sauce. Breaded fish, such as frozen fish fillets and sticks, can be cooked quickly and successfully in a browning dish; some brands are now available in their own special crisping packages.

To test fish for doneness, the flesh should be opaque; it should also flake easily when tested with a fork. Fish that turns dark and dry when removed from the microwave has been overcooked. To prevent this, place thicker areas towards the edge of the dish and overlap thin ends of fillets, or tuck thin ends under. Cook in the microwave for the minimum suggested time only, then check for doneness.

Shielding will prevent delicate or thin areas from overcooking. Recipes for large whole fish usually call for standing time, in which case, test for doneness afterward, as the fish continues to cook during that time. Shellfish cooks quickly in the microwave, so be careful not to let it overcook because it will become tough and rubbery. Shrimp should be just pink, oysters should just curl at the edges, and scallops should be opaque. Clams and mussels cooked in the shell should be removed from the microwave when shells have opened; any that remain closed should be discarded.

Thick fish steaks or pieces cooked in liquid should be turned over once halfway through cooking. To avoid uneven cooking, the dishes in which whole fish, lobster tails, and fillets are cooked should be rotated in the microwave; this prevents the buildup of heat in any one part of the fish. To avoid unwanted cooking juices in the bottom of the dish, line it with paper towels or elevate the fish on a microwave-safe trivet or rack in the dish.

"CANDY-CANE" SHRIMP
Large shrimp are always a popular choice for elegant appetizers and salads. Shrimp can be made even more appetizing by wrapping them in thin strips of bacon or vegetables, creating a pretty "candy-cane" effect.

Pre-cooked bacon strips (left) wrap large shrimp and crisp while shrimp cooks. Serve with mixed salad leaves.

Quickly cooked strips of leek or spring onion (right) wrap jumbo shrimp and create an elegant look. Garnish with Green-onion Pompom (page 132), and salad greens.

148

Defrosting Fish and Shellfish

Frozen fish and shellfish defrost rapidly in the microwave but be careful not to let them start cooking during the defrosting process. When defrosted, they should feel cold but pliable.

Most fish fillets, and blocks of shellfish such as crab meat and scallops, can be defrosted in their packages. If you carefully separate fish and shellfish pieces as soon as possible during defrosting and spread them in a single layer, they will defrost more quickly.

During defrosting, thin areas of whole fish may become warm and start to cook; protect these spots by shielding them with smooth pieces of foil.

Whole fish and large shellfish should be left to stand, covered, after defrosting in the microwave to let the temperature equalize throughout the food. Whole fish must be completely defrosted before cooking. There must be no ice crystals in the cavity, so rinse whole fish under running cold water if cavity is still icy.

As with all frozen foods, it is best to cook fish and shellfish as soon as possible after defrosting, to prevent the growth of harmful bacteria in the defrosted food, as well as for maximum freshness and flavor. Many ovens have a special defrosting facility, in which case follow the manufacturer's directions.

DEFROSTING A 16-OUNCE PACKAGE OF FISH FILLETS

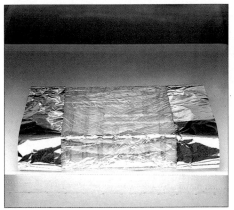

Heat fish in package on Medium (50% power) 1½ (1:30) minutes. Turn package over, then shield ends of package with smooth pieces of foil.

Heat on Medium-Low (30% power) 1½ (1:30) minutes. Turn package over and rotate a half turn. Heat on Medium-Low 1½ (1:30) minutes.

On heat-safe surface, let stand 10 minutes. Carefully separate fillets; rinse under running cold water if some areas are still icy or stiff.

DEFROSTING WHOLE FISH AND STEAKS

Place fish in a microwave-safe dish and turn over halfway through defrosting time. Shield vulnerable areas with foil after turning.

DEFROSTING SHELLFISH

Shellfish can be defrosted in package, but large quantities are best defrosted in shallow, microwave-safe dish. Separate pieces halfway through defrosting.

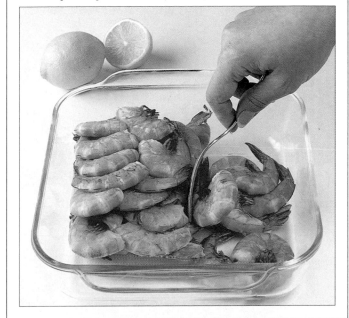

149

Cooking Fish and Shellfish

Quick-cooking method
To "steam" fish portions quickly and easily, place them in the center of lightly moistened paper towels. Bring all corners to the center and twist to close; place on microwave-safe platter. Cook 1 8-ounce fish steak on High (100% power) 2½ (2:30) to 3 minutes; 2 8-ounce fish steaks on High 4½ (4:30) to 5 minutes, rotating once.

Improving appearance
Microwaved fish can be made to look broiled by cooking in a browning dish (right) or by coating with browning, teriyaki, or soy sauce.

Absorbing excess moisture Absorb unwanted juices in bottom of dish by using paper towels as liners; separate ends of fish with plastic wrap. Or, elevate fish on a microwave-safe trivet or rack in the dish.

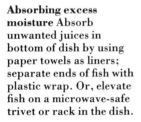

Even cooking
Roll fillets jelly-roll fashion; secure with wooden toothpicks, and arrange around edge of round dish. Leave space between each portion and leave center open for more even cooking.

Shielding
Cover delicate parts of a whole fish, like the tail or eyes, with smooth strips of foil.

ROTATING AND TURNING FISH AND SHELLFISH

Whole fish, lobster tails, and fillet dishes should be rotated to avoid the buildup of heat in any one spot during cooking.

Shrimp arranged in a circle with tails pointing toward center should be turned over with tongs and dish rotated halfway through cooking.

Thick fish pieces or steaks cooked in liquid should be turned over halfway through cooking to ensure even distribution of heat.

"Stir-frying" shrimp
Because shrimp cook rapidly, stir-frying in a browning dish is an ideal way to prepare them. The frequent turning and stirring ensures even distribution of heat.

Fish Steaks

FISH STEAKS WITH SALSA

Color Index page 48. 2 servings. 371 cals per serving. Good source of vitamin A, vitamin C, iron. Begin 20 minutes ahead.

1 8- to 8¼-ounce can tomatoes	¼ teaspoon salt
1 small green pepper, thinly sliced	2 tablespoons lime or lemon juice
1 small onion, chopped	2 salmon, cod, or halibut steaks (6 ounces each)
½ 3½-ounce can pitted ripe olives, drained and cut in half	1 tablespoon dry sherry
2 tablespoons coarsely chopped coriander or parsley	2 tablespoons mayonnaise
1 tablespoon salad oil	½ teaspoon cider vinegar
1 garlic clove, crushed	¼ teaspoon chili powder
	Coriander sprigs for garnish

1. Prepare salsa: Drain tomatoes, reserving 2 tablespoons tomato liquid. In medium microwave-safe bowl, combine tomatoes and reserved liquid, green pepper, onion, olives, coriander or parsley, oil, garlic, salt, and 1 tablespoon lime or lemon juice; stir, breaking up tomatoes. Cook on High (100% power) 5 to 6 minutes, until green pepper is tender-crisp, stirring halfway through cooking. Cover and set aside.
2. Lightly moisten 2 paper towels; place 1 fish steak on each. In small bowl, combine sherry and remaining lime or lemon juice; pour half the mixture over each steak.
3. Twist corners of each paper towel together. Place fish steaks on microwave-safe platter. Cook on High 2 to 2½ (2:30) minutes, just until outer edges of fish are opaque, rotating steaks once.
4. Meanwhile, in same cleaned bowl, combine mayonnaise, vinegar, and chili powder.
5. *To serve*: Remove fish steaks from paper towels. Place fish on warmed dinner plates. Spoon mayonnaise mixture over each fish steak and accompany with salsa. Garnish.

Preparing the Salsa

In colander set over bowl, drain canned tomatoes. Reserve 2 tablespoons tomato liquid. Cook drained tomatoes on High 5 to 6 minutes with reserved liquid, thinly sliced green pepper, chopped onion, halved ripe olives, chopped coriander or parsley, oil, garlic, salt, and lime or lemon juice.

SALMON STEAKS WITH MARINATED CUCUMBER

Color Index page 54. 320 cals per serving (without dressing). Low in fat (without dressing). Good source of vitamin A, thiamine, riboflavin, niacin, iron. Begin early in day.

Ingredients	For 4	For 2	For 1
Salmon steaks (8 ounces each)	4 steaks	2 steaks	1 steak
Lemon juice	2 tablespoons	1 tablespoon	1½ teaspoons
Cucumbers (6 ounces each), thinly sliced	2 cucumbers	1 cucumber	½ cucumber
Salt	2 teaspoons	1 teaspoon	½ teaspoon
White vinegar	⅓ cup	3 tablespoons	1 tablespoon
Sugar	1 tablespoon	2 teaspoons	1 teaspoon
Pepper	¼ teaspoon	⅛ teaspoon	to taste
Onion, thinly sliced	1 small onion garnish	½ small onion garnish	¼ small onion garnish
Salad leaves and lemon wedges			
Green Mayonnaise Dressing (page 159)	4 tablespoons dressing	2 tablespoons dressing	1 tablespoon dressing
Microwave cookware	8″ by 8″ baking dish	8″ by 8″ baking dish	8″ by 8″ baking dish
Time on High (100% power)	4 to 5 minutes	3 to 4 minutes	2 to 3 minutes

1 In baking dish (see Chart), arrange salmon steaks. Sprinkle with lemon juice.

2 Cook, covered, on High for time in Chart, just until outer edges of fish are opaque, rotating dish once.

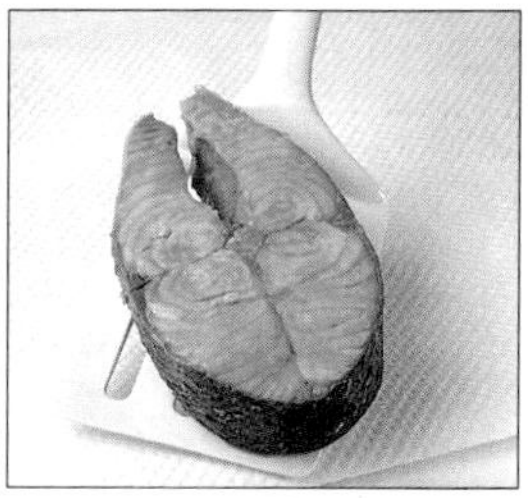

3 Drain each steak over paper towels. Place steaks in same cleaned dish; cover and refrigerate.

4 Meanwhile, in medium bowl, toss cucumber and salt. Let stand 30 minutes. Over small bowl, set strainer. Place cucumber mixture in strainer. Press to extract excess liquid; discard liquid.

5 Return cucumber to medium bowl. Add vinegar, sugar, pepper, and onion; mix well. Cover and refrigerate 3 hours or until well chilled.

6 Place salmon steaks on individual plates with salad leaves, marinated cucumber, and lemon wedges. Pass Green Mayonnaise Dressing separately.

Fish Steaks

For best results when microwaving, fish steaks should be arranged in the dish so that the thickest parts are at the edges. With delicate fish, it is best to rotate the dish halfway through cooking rather than to turn fish over. Thicker fish steaks can be turned over, however, to help prevent juices in the bottom of the dish transferring additional heat to only one side.

CALIFORNIA-STYLE MARINATED SALMON STEAKS

Color Index page 54. 292 cals per serving. Good source of vitamin A, riboflavin, niacin. Begin 2¼ hours ahead.

Ingredients	For 4	For 2	For 1
Canned whole green chilies, drained	2 medium chilies	1 medium chili	1 small chili
Lime juice	⅓ cup	3 tablespoons	1 tablespoon
Salad oil	2 tablespoons	1 tablespoon	1½ teaspoons
Salt	1 teaspoon	½ teaspoon	¼ teaspoon
Honey	1 teaspoon	½ teaspoon	¼ teaspoon
Oregano	½ teaspoon	¼ teaspoon	⅛ teaspoon
Ground red pepper	⅛ teaspoon	to taste	to taste
Salmon steaks (6 ounces each)	4 steaks	2 steaks	1 steak
Lime wedges and parsley for garnish	garnish	garnish	garnish
Microwave cookware	Browning dish	Browning dish	Browning dish
Time on High (100% power)	3 to 4 minutes each batch	3 to 4 minutes	2 to 2½ (2:30) minutes

1 Wearing rubber glove for protection, slit chilies lengthwise. With tip of sharp knife, remove seeds and discard. Finely chop chilies.

2 In baking dish, combine lime juice, oil, salt, honey, oregano, ground red pepper, and chopped chilies.

3 To mixture, add salmon steaks. Cover and refrigerate 2 hours to blend flavors, turning steaks often.

4 Just before serving, preheat browning dish as manufacturer directs. On browning dish, place salmon steaks; press with spatula to sear.

5 Cook on High for time in Chart, just until outer edges of fish are opaque, turning once. If cooking for 4, cook in 2 batches, reheating dish between batches.

6 To serve: Arrange salmon steaks on warmed dinner plates. Garnish with lime wedges and parsley.

SAVORY SALMON STEAKS

Color Index page 48. 2 servings. 316 cals per serving. Good source of vitamin A, riboflavin, niacin. Begin 10 minutes ahead.

2 salmon, cod, or halibut steaks (6 ounces each)
4½ teaspoons lemon juice
1 teaspoon prepared mustard
2 tablespoons mayonnaise

1 teaspoon finely chopped green onion
Radish Flowers (page 116), green onions, and cucumber slices for garnish

1. In 12″ by 8″ microwave-safe baking dish, arrange salmon steaks. Sprinkle each steak with 2 teaspoons lemon juice. Cook, covered, on High (100% power) 2 minutes.
2. Meanwhile, in small bowl, combine mustard, mayonnaise, green onion, and remaining lemon juice.
3. Turn steaks over in baking dish. Onto each steak, spoon half the mayonnaise mixture. Cook on High 30 seconds, or just until outer edges of fish are opaque.
4. To serve: Place fish steaks on warmed serving platter. Garnish with Radish Flowers, green onions, and cucumber slices.

LETTUCE SALMON

Color Index page 49. 2 servings. 361 cals per serving. Good source of vitamin A, thiamine, riboflavin, niacin, vitamin C, iron. Begin 15 minutes ahead.

1 large red pepper, thinly sliced
2 tablespoons butter or margarine (¼ stick)
1 small head romaine lettuce or escarole (12 ounces), cut into 3-inch pieces
1 tablespoon soy sauce

¼ teaspoon cracked pepper
2 salmon, cod, or halibut steaks (6 ounces each)
1 tablespoon lemon or lime juice

1. In 12″ by 8″ microwave-safe baking dish, place red pepper, butter or margarine, and lettuce. Cook, covered, on High (100% power) 2 to 3 minutes, until lettuce is slightly wilted. Add soy sauce and pepper; stir.
2. Arrange fish steaks on vegetables; sprinkle fish with lemon or lime juice. Cook, covered, on High 2 to 3 minutes, just until outer edges of fish are opaque, rotating dish once.
3. To serve: Place each fish steak on a warmed dinner plate, on a bed of wilted lettuce and red pepper.

COD MEDITERRANEAN

Color Index page 51. 2 servings. 318 cals per serving. Good source of vitamin A, riboflavin, niacin, vitamin C, iron. Begin 35 minutes ahead.

1 small onion, chopped	½ cup pitted ripe olives, cut in half
1 garlic clove, minced	
1 tablespoon salad oil	2 cod or halibut steaks
1 medium zucchini	(6 ounces each)
1 8- to 8¼-ounce can tomatoes	¼ teaspoon oregano
	Oregano or parsley
¼ pound mushrooms, sliced	sprigs for garnish
2 tablespoons tomato paste	

1. In 1½-quart microwave-safe casserole, place onion, garlic, and oil. Cook, covered, on High (100% power) 4 to 4½ (4:30) minutes, until onion is softened, stirring halfway through cooking.
2. Cut zucchini into ¼-inch-thick slices. To onion mixture, add zucchini, tomatoes with their juice, mushrooms, and tomato paste. Cook, covered, on High 10 minutes, stirring once.
3. To vegetables, add olives. Cook, covered, on High 5 to 7 minutes, stirring once. Set aside.
4. Lightly moisten 2 paper towels; place 1 fish steak on each. Sprinkle fish steaks with oregano. Twist corners of each paper towel together. Place fish steaks on microwave-safe platter. Cook on High 2 to 2½ (2:30) minutes, just until outer edges of fish are opaque, rotating steaks once.
5. *To serve:* Remove fish steaks from paper towels. Place fish on warmed dinner plates; spoon vegetable mixture around fish. Garnish.

PEPPERY COD STEAKS

Color Index page 51. 6 servings. 163 cals per serving. Begin 35 minutes ahead.

1 small onion, chopped	¼ teaspoon salt
1 small red pepper, chopped	⅛ teaspoon garlic powder
1 celery stalk, chopped	6 small cod steaks, each
½ cup chili sauce	½ inch thick
2 tablespoons salad oil	Basil leaves for garnish
¼ teaspoon crushed red pepper	

1. In 1-quart microwave-safe bowl or casserole, combine onion, red pepper, celery, chili sauce, oil, crushed red pepper, salt, and garlic powder. Cook, covered, on High (100% power) 6 to 8 minutes, stirring occasionally. Reduce power level to Medium (50% power) and cook 3 minutes longer, until vegetables are tender.
2. In 13″ by 9″ microwave-safe baking dish, arrange cod steaks. Cook, covered, on Medium-High (70% power) 9 to 10 minutes, just until edges of fish are opaque, rotating dish once.
3. *To serve:* Place cod steaks on warmed dinner plates. Spoon sauce over and around cod. Garnish with basil leaves.

Elegant Summer Supper

Hot Peanut Dip (below) with crudités
Salmon Steaks with Marinated Cucumber, page 151
Fresh mangoes with strawberry sauce
feathered with cream

PREPARATION TIMETABLE

Early in day:	*Cook salmon; cover and refrigerate. Prepare marinated cucumber and dressing; cover and refrigerate.*
30 minutes ahead:	*Prepare crudités and arrange on small plates; cover. Prepare dip; spoon into small bowls. Slice mangoes; cover and refrigerate.*
10 minutes ahead:	*Arrange salmon steaks on dinner plates with marinated cucumber and salad. Assemble mangoes and sauce on individual plates. Heat dip in small bowls; place on plates with crudités.*
Just before serving:	*Feather strawberry sauce with cream and decorate with strawberries.*

HOT PEANUT DIP
Served with crisp vegetables, this dip makes a tasty appetizer.

In 4-cup microwave-safe glass measure, combine ½ **cup water,** ¼ **cup soy sauce,** ⅓ **cup sugar,** **1 tablespoon chili powder,** and **1 crushed garlic clove.** Cook, covered, on High (100% power) 3 minutes. Let stand 5 minutes.

Into chili-soy mixture, whisk ⅓ **cup smooth peanut butter** and **2 tablespoons lime juice.** Spoon into 4 small microwave-safe bowls. Heat on High 1 minute, or until hot.

Fish Steaks and Fillets

SAVORY FISH KABOBS

Color Index page 54. 187 cals per serving. Low in sodium. Good source of vitamin A, niacin, vitamin C. Begin 1¼ hours ahead.

Ingredients	For 4	For 2	For 1
Salad oil	1 tablespoon	1½ teaspoons	¾ teaspoon
Green onions, sliced	6 green onions	4 green onions	2 green onions
Mild curry powder	1 teaspoon	½ teaspoon	to taste
Marmalade	1 tablespoon	1½ teaspoons	¾ teaspoon
Worcestershire	2 teaspoons	1 teaspoon	½ teaspoon
Swordfish steak, 1 to 1½ inch thick	1 pound	½ pound	¼ pound
Green pepper	1 pepper	½ pepper	¼ pepper
Mushrooms	4 mushrooms	2 mushrooms	1 mushroom
Cherry tomatoes	8 tomatoes	4 tomatoes	2 tomatoes
Hot cooked herbed rice	2 cups	1 cup	½ cup
Parsley sprigs and lemon slices for garnish	garnish	garnish	garnish
Microwave cookware	12″ by 8″ baking dish	12″ by 8″ baking dish	12″ by 8″ baking dish
Time on High (100% power) Onion mixture	2 to 3 minutes	2 minutes	1½ (1:30) minutes
Kabobs	2 to 2½ (2:30) minutes	1½ (1:30) minutes	30 seconds to 1 minute

1 In baking dish (see Chart), combine oil, green onions, and curry powder. Cook, covered, on High for time in Chart, or until green onions are softened. Stir in marmalade and Worcestershire.

2 With sharp knife, cut swordfish steak into 1½-inch chunks. Cut green pepper into 1½-inch pieces. Cut each mushroom in half.

3 Into green-onion mixture, stir swordfish chunks, green pepper, mushrooms, and tomatoes. Let stand 45 minutes until flavors blend.

4 Onto 10″ wooden skewers, thread swordfish chunks and vegetables, alternating the fish and vegetables.

5 Arrange skewers in same baking dish. Cook on High for time in Chart, or until fish is opaque, turning kabobs over halfway through cooking.

6 *To serve*: Spoon herbed rice into warmed serving dish. Arrange kabobs on top; garnish with parsley sprigs and lemon slices.

MONKFISH SATAY WITH CHUNKY PEANUT SAUCE

Color Index page 49. 4 servings. 305 cals per serving. Low in cholesterol. Good source of vitamin A, vitamin C. Begin 25 minutes ahead.

1 red pepper	¼ cup chunky-style peanut butter
4 green onions	3 tablespoons lemon juice
3 tablespoons peanut or salad oil	1 pound monkfish fillet or swordfish steak
1 garlic clove, minced	Lemon slices and Green-onion Pompoms (page 132) for garnish
3 tablespoons soy sauce	Hot Cooked Rice (page 293, optional)
1 tablespoon rice-wine vinegar or cider vinegar	
½ teaspoon ground ginger	
1 tablespoon apricot jam	

1. Finely dice a quarter of the red pepper; reserve. Cut remaining pepper into 1½-inch chunks; set aside. Thinly slice 1 green onion.

2. In 1½-quart microwave-safe casserole, combine reserved diced red pepper, sliced green onion, 1 tablespoon oil, garlic, 2 tablespoons soy sauce, vinegar, and ginger. Cook on High (100% power) 2 minutes, or until vegetables are softened.

3. Into vegetables, stir apricot jam, peanut butter, and 1½ tablespoons lemon juice until blended. Set sauce aside.

4. In 2-cup microwave-safe glass measure, combine remaining oil, soy sauce, and lemon juice. Cook on High 1 minute.

5. Cut fish into 1½-inch cubes. Cut remaining 3 green onions into 2-inch lengths. On four 10″ wooden skewers, thread red-pepper pieces, fish cubes, and green-onion pieces. Brush each kabob with lemon-soy mixture. Arrange skewers on 12″ round microwave-safe platter. Cook on High 2½ (2:30) to 3½ (3:30) minutes, until fish is opaque, turning kabobs over once.

6. *To serve*: Place small dish of peanut sauce on each plate. Garnish plates with lemon slices and Green-onion Pompoms; if you like, serve with rice.

PREPARING KABOBS

Kabob recipes can be prepared quickly and easily in the microwave with little clean-up afterward. For easier handling, you can marinate, skewer and arrange kabobs all in the same microwave-safe baking dish, tray, or platter. When cooking kabobs in the microwave, be sure to use wooden or other microwave-safe skewers, and leave a small space between each piece of food for even cooking, as shown above.

SWORDFISH STIR-FRY

Color Index page 49. 4 servings. 211 cals per serving. Good source of vitamin A, niacin, vitamin C, iron. Begin 25 minutes ahead.

2 tablespoons soy sauce	2 tablespoons water
2 tablespoons rice wine or sherry	1/4 pound fresh shiitake mushrooms, sliced
1 tablespoon honey	2 green onions, thinly sliced
2 tablespoons salad oil	
1/2 teaspoon Chinese five-spice powder	1/2 pint cherry tomatoes
1 pound swordfish, cut into 1/2-inch strips	1 15-ounce can baby corn, drained and rinsed
1/4 pound Chinese pea pods	

1. In medium bowl, combine soy sauce, rice wine or sherry, honey, 1 tablespoon oil, and Chinese five-spice powder. Add swordfish; stir to coat.

2. Preheat browning dish as manufacturer directs. Place swordfish strips on browning dish in single layer. Cook on High (100% power) 1 minute. With spatula, turn swordfish strips over. Cook on High 30 seconds longer. Set aside.

3. In 13″ by 9″ microwave-safe baking dish, place Chinese pea pods and water. Cook on High 3 to 3½ (3:30) minutes, until crisp. Rinse under running cold water; drain.

4. In same dish, combine remaining oil, mushrooms, and green onions. Cook on High 2 minutes, or until softened, stirring once.

5. To mixture, add Chinese pea pods, tomatoes, baby corn, and 1 tablespoon marinade from swordfish. Cook, covered, on High 3 to 4 minutes, until vegetables are tender-crisp, stirring once.

6. *To serve:* Arrange vegetables on microwave-safe serving platter. Arrange fish strips on top of vegetables. Reheat on High 1 minute.

SWORDFISH STEAKS AMANDINE

Color Index page 48. 4 servings. 220 cals per serving. Good source of vitamin A. Begin 20 minutes ahead.

1/3 cup sliced almonds	1 tablespoon dry white wine
2 tablespoons butter or margarine (1/4 stick)	1 tablespoon chopped parsley
1/8 teaspoon paprika	Parsley for garnish
1 swordfish steak, 1/2 inch thick (1 pound)	

1. In small microwave-safe bowl, combine almonds, butter or margarine, and paprika. Cook on High (100% power) 4 to 5 minutes, until almonds are golden brown, stirring after 2 minutes, then at 1-minute intervals; set aside.

2. In 8″ by 8″ microwave-safe baking dish, place swordfish; sprinkle with wine. Cook, covered, on High 4½ (4:30) to 6½ (6:30) minutes, until swordfish turns opaque and flakes easily, rotating dish twice.

3. Divide swordfish into 4 or 8 pieces. Remove pieces to warmed dinner plates. Into almond mixture, stir parsley. Spoon over fish. Garnish.

SOLE WITH GRAPES

Color Index page 48. 282 cals per serving. Good source of vitamin A. Begin 25 minutes ahead.

Ingredients	For 4	For 2	For 1
Sole or flounder fillets (6 ounces each)	4 fillets	2 fillets	1 fillet
Lemon juice	1 tablespoon	1½ teaspoons	3/4 teaspoon
Tarragon, crushed	1/2 teaspoon	1/4 teaspoon	1/8 teaspoon
Salt and white pepper	to taste	to taste	to taste
Green or red seedless grapes	1 cup grapes	1/2 cup grapes	1/4 cup grapes
Dry white wine	3 tablespoons	2 tablespoons	1 tablespoon
Butter or margarine	2 tablespoons	1 tablespoon	1½ teaspoons
All-purpose flour	1 tablespoon	1½ teaspoons	3/4 teaspoon
Half-and-half	1/2 cup	1/4 cup	2 tablespoons
Lemon slices, parsley sprigs, and grapes for garnish	garnish	garnish	garnish
Microwave cookware	8″ by 8″ baking dish	8″ by 8″ baking dish	9″ pie plate
	Small bowl	2-cup glass measure	1-cup glass measure
Time on High (100% power)			
Butter mixture	1 minute	1 minute	45 seconds
With half-and-half	3 minutes	2 minutes	1 minute
Fish	5 to 6 minutes	3 to 3½ (3:30) minutes	1½ (1:30) to 2 minutes

1 Rinse fillets and pat dry with paper towels. Place on cutting board. Brush fillets with lemon juice. In small bowl, combine tarragon, salt, and white pepper; sprinkle evenly over fillets.

2 Fold fish fillets into thirds. In baking dish or pie plate (see Chart), arrange folded fillets. Add grapes and sprinkle with a third of wine. Cover dish with waxed paper; set aside while preparing sauce.

3 In bowl or glass measure (see Chart), place butter or margarine, flour, and salt and pepper. Cook, covered, on High for time in Chart, or until butter or margarine has melted. With whisk, stir until smooth. Gradually stir in half-and-half until blended. Cook on High for time in Chart, or until mixture thickens. Into sauce, stir remaining wine. Cover and keep warm.

4 Cook fish, covered, on High for time in Chart, or until flesh flakes easily. If cooking for 4, rotate dish after 4 minutes.

5 On warmed plates, arrange fish, sauce, and grapes; garnish.

Fish Fillets

SHRIMP-STUFFED SOLE

Color Index page 52. 344 cals per serving. Good source of iron.
Begin 45 minutes ahead.

Ingredients	For 4	For 2	For 1
Hollandaise Sauce (page 381)	½ cup	¼ cup	2 tablespoons
Salad oil	2 tablespoons	1 tablespoon	1½ teaspoons
Onion, minced	1 small	½ small	¼ small
Garlic clove, minced	1 garlic clove	½ garlic clove	to taste
Green pepper, minced	¼ cup	2 tablespoons	1 tablespoon
Shrimp, shelled, deveined, and diced	1 pound shrimp	½ pound shrimp	¼ pound shrimp
Dried bread crumbs	¼ cup	2 tablespoons	1 tablespoon
Fresh dill, chopped	1 tablespoon	1½ teaspoons	¾ teaspoon
Salt and pepper	to taste	to taste	to taste
Sole or flounder fillets (6 ounces each)	4 fillets	2 fillets	1 fillet
Dill sprigs for garnish	garnish	garnish	garnish
Microwave cookware	2-quart casserole	1-quart casserole	9″ pie plate
	12″ by 8″ baking dish	8″ by 8″ baking dish	9″ pie plate
Time on High (100% power) Vegetables	2 to 2½ (2:30) minutes	1½ (1:30) minutes	1 minute
With shrimp	3 minutes	2 minutes	1½ (1:30) minutes
Stuffed sole	5 to 6 minutes	3 to 3½ (3:30) minutes	1½ (1:30) to 2 minutes

1   Make Hollandaise Sauce; keep warm. In casserole or pie plate (see Chart), place oil, onion, garlic, and green pepper. Cook on High for time in Chart.

2   To vegetable mixture, add shrimp; stir to coat with oil. Cook on High for time in Chart, or until shrimp are pink, stirring halfway through cooking.

3   Into shrimp mixture, stir bread crumbs and chopped dill; mix well. Season with salt and pepper.

4   On cutting board, lay fillets, boned side down. Place an equal amount of stuffing in center of each fillet.

5   Starting at narrow end, roll up each fillet. In baking dish or pie plate, place fillets seam side down.

6   Cook shrimp-stuffed fillets on High for time in Chart, or until flesh flakes easily when tested with a fork and stuffing is hot. If making for 4, rotate dish after 4 minutes. Arrange each stuffed fillet on warmed serving plate. Pour Hollandaise Sauce over fish. Garnish with dill sprigs. Serve immediately.

ROLLED FLOUNDER WITH CUCUMBER, TOMATO, AND BASIL SAUCE

Color Index page 48. 4 servings. 144 cals per serving. Good source of vitamin A.
Begin 25 minutes ahead.

1 tablespoon butter or margarine
2 green onions, cut into matchstick-thin strips
2 teaspoons fresh basil leaves, minced
1 small cucumber (6 ounces), cut into matchstick-thin strips
1 pound fresh or frozen (thawed) flounder fillets

½ teaspoon salt
½ cup dry white wine
2 tomatoes, seeded and diced
1 teaspoon cornstarch dissolved in 1 tablespoon cold water
Basil leaves for garnish (optional)

1. In 9″ microwave-safe pie plate, place butter or margarine. Heat on High (100% power) 30 to 45 seconds, until melted.
2. Into melted butter or margarine, stir green onions, half the basil, and half the cucumber. Cook on High 2 to 2½ (2:30) minutes, until cucumber is slightly softened.
3. Cut each flounder fillet lengthwise in half, removing all bones and any cartilage. On cutting board, lay fillet halves, boned side down; sprinkle with half the salt. Arrange a quarter of the cooked cucumber pieces at wide end of each piece of fish. Starting at wide end, roll up each fillet and secure with wooden toothpick.
4. In same pie plate, arrange filled fish bundles in a ring. Pour in white wine. Cook, covered, on High 3 to 4 minutes, just until flesh flakes easily when tested with a fork, rotating dish halfway through cooking. Meanwhile, dice remaining cucumber.
5. With slotted spatula, remove fish bundles to platter. Into wine mixture, stir tomatoes, dissolved cornstarch, and remaining cucumber, basil, and salt. Cook on High 2 to 3 minutes, until sauce thickens, stirring twice. Add fish bundles. Cook on High 1 minute.
6. *To serve:* Place fish bundles on warmed dinner plates. Spoon sauce around fish bundles. If you like, garnish with basil leaves.

Rolling and Arranging the Fish Fillets

At wide end of fish fillet, place cucumber pieces. Roll up fillet jelly-roll fashion and secure with wooden toothpick.

Stand fish bundles filled with cucumber mixture upright in pie plate, leaving space between each one.

FISH FILLETS FLORENTINE

Color Index page 48. 4 servings. 396 cals per serving. Good source of vitamin A, riboflavin, niacin, vitamin C, calcium, iron. Begin 25 minutes ahead.

2 medium tomatoes, each cut into 8 wedges	¼ teaspoon pepper
½ teaspoon salt	1 10-ounce package frozen chopped spinach, thawed and drained
2 tablespoons salad oil	
¾ teaspoon oregano	
½ pound mushrooms, sliced	4 ounces fontina or Swiss cheese, shredded (1 cup)
1 onion, chopped	4 fish fillets (6 ounces each)
1 cup fresh bread cubes	

1. In 1½-quart microwave-safe casserole, place tomatoes, salt, 1 tablespoon salad oil, and ¼ teaspoon oregano. Cook, covered, on High (100% power) 2 to 3 minutes, until tomatoes are softened. Set aside.

2. In 12″ by 8″ microwave-safe baking dish, place mushrooms, onion, and remaining oil. Cook, covered, on High 5 to 6 minutes, stirring halfway through cooking. With slotted spoon, transfer half the mushroom mixture to small bowl; set aside. Into mushroom mixture remaining in baking dish, stir bread cubes, pepper, spinach, remaining oregano, and ¾ cup cheese.

3. Onto each fillet, spoon a quarter of the spinach mixture to cover half the fillet. Fold over other half to cover mixture. Arrange fillets in same baking dish; sprinkle with remaining cheese and reserved mushroom mixture. Cook on High 5 to 6 minutes, until flesh flakes easily, rotating dish once. Reheat tomatoes on High 30 seconds.

4. *To serve:* Place fillets on warmed serving platter. Accompany with cooked tomato wedges.

FLOUNDER FILLETS WITH SAVORY SAUCE

Color Index page 48. 4 servings. 235 cals per serving (without sauce). Good source of vitamin A, thiamine, riboflavin, iron (without sauce). Begin 20 minutes ahead.

Spicy Cocktail Sauce or Zesty Cucumber Sauce (page 159)	¾ teaspoon paprika
	4 flounder fillets (4 ounces each)
1 cup corn-flake crumbs	1 egg, slightly beaten
2 tablespoons chopped parsley	Lettuce leaves
1 teaspoon grated lemon peel	Radishes and cucumber slices for garnish

1. Prepare sauce of your choice.

2. On waxed paper, combine corn-flake crumbs, parsley, lemon peel, and paprika. Dip fillets in beaten egg, then coat with crumb mixture.

3. On microwave-safe rack set in 13″ by 9″ microwave-safe baking dish, place fillets. Cook on High (100% power) 5 to 6 minutes, just until flesh flakes easily when tested with a fork, rotating dish once. Arrange fish with lettuce leaves. Garnish and serve with sauce.

FLOUNDER IN PAPER PARCELS

Color Index page 52. 51 cals per serving. Low in cholesterol, sodium. Good source of vitamin A, vitamin C. Begin 35 minutes ahead.

Ingredients	For 4	For 2	For 1
Green peppers, cut into thin strips	2 small green peppers	1 small green pepper	½ small green pepper
Cherry tomatoes, cut into quarters	8 tomatoes	4 tomatoes	2 tomatoes
Green onions, sliced	2 green onions	1 green onion	½ green onion
Mushrooms, sliced	4 mushrooms	2 mushrooms	1 mushroom
Fresh basil leaves	8 leaves	4 leaves	2 leaves
Orange peel, minced	1 tablespoon	2 teaspoons	1 teaspoon
Flounder fillets (6 to 8 ounces each)	4 fillets	2 fillets	1 fillet
Salt	to taste	to taste	to taste
Butter or margarine	4 teaspoons	2 teaspoons	1 teaspoon
Orange slices and basil leaves for garnish	garnish	garnish	garnish
Microwave cookware	12″ platter	12″ platter	9″ plate
Time on High (100% power)	3 to 3½ (3:30) minutes each batch	3 to 3½ (3:30) minutes	1½ (1:30) to 2 minutes

1 In small bowl, place green-pepper strips, cherry tomatoes, green onions, mushrooms, basil leaves, and orange peel; toss to mix.

2 For each fillet, fold a 14″ by 8″ sheet of parchment paper lengthwise in half. Cut a large heart shape. Place open sheets on work surface. Using half the green-pepper mixture, place an even amount on right-hand side of each heart, near the fold line.

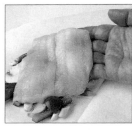

3 Place 1 fish fillet, with thin end folded under, on top of each layer of green-pepper mixture. Season with salt. Place remaining mixture evenly over fillets. Dot with butter or margarine.

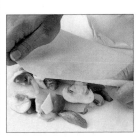

4 Fold left side of parchment paper over fish. Double-fold edges to seal.

5 On platter or plate (see Chart), place packages with double-folded side toward edge. Cook on High for time in Chart, rotating dish once. If cooking for 4, cook packages in 2 batches.

6 *To serve:* Place each package on plate. With small, sharp knife, cut a cross in the center of each package, to allow the steam to escape. Fold back package edges; garnish and serve.

157

Fish Fillets

ORIENTAL FISH IN LETTUCE LEAVES

Color Index page 52. 167 cals per serving. Good source of vitamin A.
Begin 35 minutes ahead.

Ingredients	For 4	For 2	For 1
Soy sauce	1 tablespoon	1½ teaspoons	¾ teaspoon
Rice-wine vinegar or cider vinegar	1 tablespoon	1½ teaspoons	¾ teaspoon
Garlic cloves, minced	2 garlic cloves	1 garlic clove	½ garlic clove
Minced peeled gingerroot	½ teaspoon	¼ teaspoon	to taste
Coriander leaves, chopped	1 tablespoon coriander	1½ teaspoons coriander	¾ teaspoon coriander
Flounder fillets (4 to 6 ounces each), cut into 2-inch pieces	4 fillets	2 fillets	1 fillet
Lettuce leaves (Bibb or Boston)	4 large leaves	2 large leaves	1 large leaf
Carrots, cut into matchstick-thin strips	2 medium carrots	1 medium carrot	½ medium carrot
Green onions, thinly sliced	2 green onions	1 green onion	½ green onion
Celery stalks, cut into matchstick-thin strips	1 celery stalk	½ celery stalk	1 2-inch piece celery stalk
Chicken Broth (page 125) or canned broth	1 cup broth	½ cup broth	¼ cup broth
Salt	to taste	to taste	to taste
Coriander leaves for garnish	garnish	garnish	garnish
Microwave cookware	13" by 9" baking dish 1-quart soufflé dish	13" by 9" baking dish Medium bowl	8" soup bowl Small bowl
Time on High (100% power)			
Lettuce leaves	1 to 1½ (1:30) minutes	1 minute	30 to 45 seconds
Vegetables in broth	4 to 5 minutes	3 to 4 minutes	2 to 2½ (2:30) minutes
Fish bundles	3 to 5 minutes	2 to 3 minutes	1 to 2 minutes
Standing time	3 minutes	2 minutes	2 minutes

USING LEAVES TO MAKE PARCELS

Lettuce, cabbage, spinach, and grape leaves make ideal wrappers. Our Stuffed Cabbage (page 213) and Camembert in Grape Leaves (page 144) also use leaves to protect the fillings and flavor.

Arrange leaves on cutting board, vein side up. With sharp knife, remove any tough ribs or stems from leaves.

After cooking leaves, fold sides around fillings as if you were wrapping a package, making sure fillings are completely enclosed.

1 In bowl, combine soy sauce, vinegar, garlic, gingerroot, and coriander. Into mixture, stir flounder pieces; set aside.

2 In baking dish or soup bowl (see Chart), place lettuce leaves. Cook, covered, on High for time in Chart, or just until wilted. Uncover and let cool; leaves may darken on standing.

3 In soufflé dish or bowl (see Chart), combine carrots, green onions, celery, and broth. Cook, covered, on High for time in Chart, or until vegetables are tender-crisp.

4 On cutting board, place lettuce leaves, vein side up. Place an equal amount of marinated fish in center of each leaf. Fold to enclose fish completely (see Box, above right).

5 In baking dish or soup bowl used for lettuce, carefully place fish bundles seam side down, leaving 1-inch space between each.

6 Ladle hot vegetable broth mixture over fish bundles. Cook, covered, on High for time in Chart. Let stand on heat-safe surface for time in Chart. Season with salt.

7 *To serve:* Transfer lettuce-wrapped fish bundles to warmed soup plates. Ladle an equal amount of vegetables and broth over each bundle; garnish with coriander.

SAUCES FOR FISH

Because fish and shellfish generally have a delicate flavor, they can be enhanced if served with a sauce. If making ahead, cover and refrigerate until ready to use.

Zesty Cucumber Sauce: Finely shred *1 small cucumber;* pat dry with paper towels. Combine cucumber with *¼ cup mayonnaise, 1 teaspoon chopped parsley, 1 teaspoon cider vinegar,* and *1 teaspoon prepared mustard.* Makes ½ cup. 53 cals per tablespoon.

Spicy Cocktail Sauce: Combine *¼ cup chili sauce, 3 tablespoons catchup, 1 tablespoon drained sweet-pickle relish,* and *1 teaspoon prepared horseradish.* Makes ½ cup. 19 cals per tablespoon.

Green Mayonnaise Dressing: In blender process *2 cups mayonnaise, ⅓ cup chopped parsley, 4 teaspoons tarragon vinegar, ½ teaspoon tarragon,* and *2 chopped green onions,* until smooth, and evenly blended. Makes 2 cups. 93 cals per tablespoon.

SOLE AND ASPARAGUS WITH CHEESE SAUCE

Color Index page 49. 249 cals per serving. Good source of calcium. Begin 25 minutes ahead.

Few things are tastier than the classic combination of cheese-wine sauce poured over delicate white fish, as in our Sole and Asparagus with Cheese Sauce. Try any one of the many types of sole available on the market, such as Dover, lemon, and grey. Flounder makes a superb and convenient alternative – and the asparagus gives that extra special touch.

Ingredients for 4 servings		Microwave cookware
1 10-ounce package frozen asparagus spears *4 sole or flounder fillets (4 ounces each)* *1 tablespoon butter or margarine* *½ cup half-and-half or milk* *2 tablespoons dry white wine*	*1 tablespoon all-purpose flour* *½ teaspoon salt* *⅛ teaspoon ground red pepper* *2 ounces Cheddar cheese, shredded (½ cup)* *Lemon Twists (page 132, optional) for garnish*	8″ by 8″ baking dish

1 Unwrap frozen asparagus package. On oven floor, place asparagus in package. Heat on Medium-Low (30% power) 2 minutes, or until spears separate easily.

2 On cutting board, place fish fillets, boned side down. On narrow end of each fish fillet, place an equal amount of asparagus spears.

3 Starting at narrow end, roll up each fish fillet around asparagus spears.

4 In baking dish, arrange fish fillets, seam side down; dot with butter or margarine. Cook, covered, on High (100% power) 4 to 6 minutes, just until flesh flakes easily when tested with a fork, rearranging fillets once. Remove fillets to platter; keep warm.

5 Into cooking liquid in baking dish, whisk half-and-half, wine, flour, salt, and pepper. Cook on High 3 to 4 minutes, until sauce thickens slightly, stirring twice.

6 Into sauce, stir cheese. Cook on High 1 minute; stir until smooth. Spoon over fillets. If you like, garnish with Lemon Twists.

Whole Fish

STUFFED TROUT

Color Index page 51. 345 cals per serving. Good source of vitamin A, thiamine, iron. Begin 35 minutes ahead.

Ingredients	For 4	For 2	For 1
Butter or margarine	4 tablespoons	2 tablespoons	1 tablespoon
Onion, chopped	1 medium onion	1 small onion	½ small onion
Carrot, chopped	1 small	½ small	2 tablespoons
Celery stalks, chopped	2 small	1 small	½ small
Garlic cloves, minced	2 garlic cloves	1 garlic clove	½ garlic clove
Walnuts, chopped	¼ cup	2 tablespoons	1 tablespoon
Thyme leaves	1½ teaspoons	¾ teaspoon	½ teaspoon
Salt	to taste	to taste	to taste
Dry sherry or white wine	3 tablespoons	1½ tablespoons	2½ teaspoons
Dried bread crumbs	¼ cup	2 tablespoons	1 tablespoon
Trout (8 to 10 ounces each), dressed, with tail left on	4 trout	2 trout	1 trout
Lemon slices and walnut halves for garnish	garnish	garnish	garnish
Microwave cookware	Large bowl 13″ by 9″ baking dish	Medium bowl 13″ by 9″ baking dish	9″ pie plate 12″ by 8″ baking dish
Time on High (100% power)			
Butter or margarine	45 seconds to 1 minute	45 seconds	30 seconds
With vegetables	5 minutes	3 minutes	2 minutes
With seasonings	2 minutes	1½ (1:30) minutes	1 minute
Stuffed trout	4 to 5 minutes each batch	4 to 5 minutes	2½ (2:30) to 3 minutes
Standing time	5 minutes	3 minutes	2 minutes

1 In bowl or pie plate (see Chart), place butter. Heat, covered with paper towel, on High for time in Chart.

2 Into melted butter, stir onion, carrot, celery, garlic and walnuts. Cook on High for time in Chart, stirring twice.

3 Add thyme, salt, and a third of the sherry or wine. Cook on High for time in Chart, stirring once. Add bread crumbs.

4 Season trout cavities. Place an even amount of stuffing in each.

5 In baking dish (see Chart), arrange trout. Sprinkle remaining sherry or wine over trout. Cook, covered, on High for time in Chart, or until flesh is opaque, rotating dish halfway through cooking. If cooking for 4, cook trout in 2 batches. Let stand, covered, on heat-safe surface for time in Chart.

6 *To serve*: Remove trout to warmed dinner plates. Garnish.

CAJUN TROUT

Color Index page 51. 2 servings. 457 cals per serving. Good source of vitamin A, vitamin C, iron. Begin 35 minutes ahead.

3 tablespoons butter or margarine	¼ cup yellow cornmeal
1 large onion, chopped	¼ teaspoon sugar
1 green pepper, chopped	2 8- to 10-ounce brook or rainbow trout, dressed, with tails left on
1 garlic clove, minced	
1 8-ounce can crushed tomatoes	1 tablespoon salad oil
Salt to taste	Lime Twists (page 132) for garnish
¼ teaspoon ground red pepper	Hot Cooked Rice (page 293, optional)
½ teaspoon thyme leaves	
½ teaspoon oregano	

1. In 2-quart microwave-safe casserole, place 2 tablespoons butter or margarine. Heat, covered with paper towel, on High (100% power) 45 seconds, or until melted.

2. Into melted butter or margarine, stir onion, green pepper, and garlic. Cook on High 5 minutes, or until softened, stirring twice.

3. Into onion mixture, stir tomatoes, salt, and half each of the ground red pepper, thyme, and oregano. Cook on High 5 minutes. Set aside.

4. On waxed paper, mix cornmeal, sugar, remaining ground red pepper, thyme, and oregano. Season each trout lightly with salt. Dip each trout in cornmeal mixture, using hand to pat cornmeal onto trout to coat well.

5. Meanwhile, preheat browning dish as manufacturer directs. On browning dish, place butter or margarine and oil; add trout. Cook on High 4 to 5 minutes, until flesh flakes easily when tested with a fork, carefully turning fish over once.

6. *To serve*: Transfer trout to warmed dinner plates. Spoon sauce around trout. Garnish and, if you like, accompany with rice.

SERVING A WHOLE FISH
With a sharp knife, break skin along backbone. Divide top side of fish into serving portions, cutting down to the bone and removing each portion as shown below.

Ease fish from bone; with server or spatula, lift each portion of fish and place on warmed dinner plate.

Slide spatula or server under bone and lift to separate it from lower section. Continue portioning in the same way.

COUNTRY-STYLE BLUEFISH AND POTATOES

Color Index page 52. 6 servings. 335 cals per serving. Good source of vitamin A. Begin 45 minutes ahead.

6 slices bacon, chopped	Salt and pepper to taste
2 large onions, thickly sliced	1 3-pound bluefish, dressed, with tail left on
1½ pounds small red (new) potatoes, scrubbed and cut into quarters	Rosemary sprigs for garnish

1. In 13" by 9" microwave-safe baking dish, place bacon. Cook, covered with paper towels, on High (100% power) 5 to 7 minutes, until browned, stirring halfway through cooking. Discard all but 3 tablespoons drippings.
2. To bacon, add onions and potatoes. Cook, covered, on High 8 to 10 minutes, until potatoes are almost tender, stirring twice. Season.
3. Brush fish and fish cavity with cooking liquid from vegetables. Shield tail of fish with smooth strip of foil.
4. Place fish on potatoes. Cook, covered, on High 6 to 8 minutes, just until outer edges of fish are opaque, removing foil and rotating dish halfway through cooking. Let stand, covered, on heat-safe surface 5 minutes.
5. *To serve:* On warmed serving platter, place fish. Spoon onion-potato mixture around fish and garnish with rosemary sprigs.

RED SNAPPER PIQUANTE

Color Index page 49. 4 servings. 246 cals per serving. Good source of vitamin A, vitamin C, iron. Begin 25 minutes ahead.

1 2½-pound red snapper, dressed, with tail left on	4 large carrots, cut into matchstick-thin strips
2 tablespoons butter or margarine (¼ stick), melted	2 celery stalks, sliced
	1 garlic clove, sliced
6 green onions, cut into 2-inch pieces	1 tablespoon salad oil
	2 tablespoons dry sherry
2 large red peppers, cut into matchstick-thin strips	2 tablespoons soy sauce
	¼ teaspoon ground ginger

1. Shield tail of fish with smooth strip of foil. In 13" by 9" microwave-safe baking dish, place fish. Brush with melted butter or margarine. Arrange green onions and next 3 ingredients around fish.
2. In medium microwave-safe bowl, place garlic and oil. Cook on High (100% power) 1½ (1:30) to 2 minutes, until garlic is golden. Discard garlic. Into oil, stir sherry, soy sauce, and ginger. Pour over fish and vegetables.
3. Cook, covered, on High 12 to 14 minutes, just until outer edges of fish are opaque, removing foil, rotating dish, and stirring vegetables halfway through cooking. Let stand, covered, on heat-safe surface 5 minutes before serving.

The microwave is ideal for cooking larger whole fish such as sea bass, red snapper, salmon, bluefish, or trout; it seals in their delicate flavors. Use smooth strips of foil to shield the tail of any whole fish that would otherwise overcook (page 19) but be sure to keep foil at least 1 inch away from oven walls.

SEA BASS WITH SUMMER VEGETABLES

Color Index page 48. 138 cals per serving. Good source of vitamin A. Begin 25 minutes ahead.

Ingredients for 6 servings		Microwave cookware
1 3-pound sea bass or bluefish, dressed, with tail left on	⅛ teaspoon pepper	13" by 9" baking dish
2 tablespoons butter or margarine (¼ stick)	1 garlic clove, minced	Small bowl
2 tablespoons dry sherry	1 large carrot	Large bowl
1 tablespoon lime or lemon juice	1 medium yellow straightneck squash	
¼ teaspoon salt	1 medium zucchini	
	Salad leaves, and orange and lemon slices for garnish	

1 With smooth strip of foil, wrap tail of sea bass to prevent it from overcooking. In baking dish, place fish.

2 In small bowl, place butter or margarine, sherry, lime or lemon juice, salt, pepper, and garlic. Cook on High (100% power) 1 minute, or until melted. Lightly brush fish and fish cavity with some butter mixture. Reserve remainder.

3 Cook fish, covered, on High 6 to 8 minutes, just until outer edges are opaque, removing foil and rotating dish halfway through cooking. Carefully transfer fish to warmed serving platter; let stand, covered, 5 minutes.

4 Meanwhile, with vegetable peeler, shred carrot, yellow squash, and zucchini into long ribbons about 1 inch wide, pressing lightly with peeler so ribbons will be very thin.

5 In large bowl, gently toss vegetable ribbons and reserved butter mixture. Cook, covered, on High 30 seconds.

6 *To serve:* Arrange vegetables around fish. Garnish with salad leaves and orange and lemon slices. Serve immediately.

Whole and Canned Fish

RED SNAPPER WITH OYSTER STUFFING

Color Index page 52. 227 cals per serving. Good source of vitamin A, iron. Begin 35 minutes ahead.

Ingredients for 4 servings		Microwave cookware
2 tablespoons butter or margarine (¼ stick)	1 teaspoon minced tarragon leaves	9″ pie plate
1 small onion, diced	2 tablespoons dried bread crumbs	13″ by 9″ baking dish
1 medium celery stalk, diced	Salt and pepper to taste	
1 garlic clove, minced	1 2½-pound red snapper, dressed, with tail left on	
6 oysters, shucked, with their liquid		
2 tablespoons dry white wine	Lemon and lime slices for garnish	
¼ cup heavy or whipping cream		

1 In pie plate, place butter or margarine. Heat, covered with paper towel, on High (100% power) 45 seconds, or until melted.

2 Into melted butter or margarine, stir onion, celery, and garlic. Cook on High 2 to 2½ (2:30) minutes, until vegetables are softened.

3 Drain oysters, reserving liquid. Strain oyster liquid through cheesecloth or filter paper; reserve 2 tablespoons. Coarsely chop oysters.

4 Into onion mixture, stir reserved oyster liquid, white wine, cream, and tarragon. Cook on High 4 to 5 minutes, until sauce thickens, stirring occasionally. Stir in oysters and bread crumbs; season.

5 Shield tail of fish with smooth strip of foil; place in baking dish. Fill cavity with stuffing; spread any extra stuffing around fish. Cook, covered, on High 10 to 12 minutes, just until outer edges of fish are opaque, removing foil and rotating dish halfway through cooking. Carefully transfer fish to warmed serving platter; let stand, covered, 5 minutes.

6 *To serve:* Garnish fish with lemon and lime slices. Cut top side of fish into serving-sized portions just down to bone. Remove with a fish server. Serve each portion with some of the oyster stuffing. Remove backbone and repeat with other side of fish.

TUNA-SPINACH LOAF

Color Index page 51. 6 servings. 242 cals per serving. Good source of vitamin A, calcium, iron. Begin 40 minutes ahead.

2 tablespoons salad oil
1 medium onion, minced
1 lemon
1 10-ounce package frozen chopped spinach
1 12½- to 13-ounce can tuna
4 slices white bread

½ 8-ounce container sour cream (½ cup)
2 eggs
¼ teaspoon salt
¼ teaspoon hot-pepper sauce
Parsley for garnish

1. Lightly grease 9″ by 5″ microwave-safe loaf pan.

2. In medium microwave-safe bowl, combine oil and onion. Cook, covered, on High (100% power) 2 to 3 minutes, until onion softens.

3. Meanwhile, thinly slice half the lemon for garnish; cover and refrigerate. Squeeze juice from remaining lemon half.

4. Remove frozen spinach from package and place on microwave-safe plate. Cook on Medium-Low (30% power) 5 to 6 minutes, until thawed, turning spinach over once. Drain well.

5. Drain tuna. In large bowl, finely flake tuna. With hands, finely tear bread; add to tuna. Add onion mixture, lemon juice, spinach, sour cream, eggs, salt, and hot-pepper sauce; mix well. Spoon tuna mixture into prepared loaf pan.

6. Cook, covered with waxed paper, on Medium-High (70% power) 11 to 13 minutes, until knife inserted 1 inch from center comes out clean, rotating pan halfway through cooking. (If ends of loaf begin to overcook, shield with 3-inch-wide strips of smooth foil.) Let loaf stand, covered, on heat-safe surface 5 minutes.

7. Unmold loaf onto warmed serving platter (below). Garnish with reserved lemon slices and parsley sprigs. Cut loaf into slices.

Unmolding the Loaf

With knife, loosen loaf from side of pan. Place serving platter upside down on pan and invert. Place on work surface; carefully remove pan to unmold loaf.

TUNA PATTIES FLORENTINE

Color Index page 51. 6 servings. 190 cals per serving. Good source of vitamin A, iron. Begin 35 minutes ahead.

2 tablespoons butter or margarine (¼ stick)
1 10-ounce package frozen chopped spinach
1 12½- to 13-ounce can tuna, drained and flaked
½ cup fresh bread crumbs (1 slice)
2 eggs

1 tablespoon chopped capers
1 tablespoon grated onion
1 tablespoon lemon juice
½ teaspoon salt
Lemon wedges and parsley for garnish

1. In large microwave-safe bowl, place butter or margarine. Heat, covered with paper towel, on High (100% power) 45 seconds, or until butter or margarine is melted. Set aside.
2. Remove frozen spinach from package and place on microwave-safe plate. Cook on Medium-Low (30% power) 5 to 6 minutes, until thawed, turning spinach over once.
3. Squeeze spinach to remove as much liquid as possible. To melted butter or margarine, add spinach, tuna, bread crumbs, eggs, capers, grated onion, lemon juice, and salt; mix well.
4. Shape tuna mixture into six 3-inch patties. Place patties in 13" by 9" microwave-safe baking dish. Cook, covered with waxed paper, on Medium (50% power) 12 minutes, or until firm, rearranging patties halfway through cooking. Let stand, covered, on heat-safe surface 5 minutes before serving. Garnish.

LEMON AND LIME GARNISHES

Lemon is the traditional garnish for fish, and lime adds an extra touch of color. The acidity of these fruits balances the oil content of bluefish, salmon, and tuna, and brings out the flavor of more delicate white fish.

Lemon or lime loops: Cut *1 lemon* or *lime* lengthwise in half, then cut each half into ¼-inch-thick slices. Cut peel from fruit, leaving ¾ inch attached. Curl peel under to form loop.

Lemon or lime bundles: Place *lemon or lime half*, cut side down, in center of small piece of cheesecloth. Gather edges of cloth together; place *1 parsley sprig* at gathered edge and tie tightly with string.

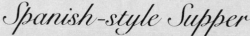
Meal in Minutes *for 8 people*
Spanish-style Supper
Olives and tortilla chips
Paella, page 171, with sourdough bread
Crème Caramel, page 325 (double quantity), with strawberries
Sangria (below)

PREPARATION TIMETABLE

Early in day:	Prepare Crème Caramel through step 5, in 2 batches.
1½ hours ahead:	Prepare and cook Paella.
Just before serving:	Fill serving bowls with olives and tortilla chips. Unmold Crème Caramel and garnish. Make Sangria.

SANGRIA

Sangria makes a delightful accompaniment to a Spanish-style meal. Use a dry, fruity, Spanish wine and a pitcher large enough to hold the cut-up fruit. Be sure to serve the Sangria in large glasses so each guest receives some wine-soaked fruit.

Into large pitcher, pour *1 cup each lemon juice, orange juice,* and *sugar*; stir to dissolve sugar. Stir in *6½ cups red wine, ½ cup brandy, 2 7-ounce bottles chilled club soda, 2 cups sliced fruit (orange, lemon, apple, peach, banana, strawberry),* and *2 trays ice cubes*.

163

Shrimp

"BOILED" SHRIMP CAJUN-STYLE

Color Index page 50. 222 cals per serving. Good source of niacin, calcium, iron. Begin 25 minutes ahead.

Ingredients	For 4	For 2	For 1
Medium shrimp in their shells	*2 pounds shrimp*	*1 pound shrimp*	*½ pound shrimp*
Basil	*1½ teaspoons*	*¾ teaspoon*	*½ teaspoon*
Celery salt	*1½ teaspoons*	*¾ teaspoon*	*½ teaspoon*
Rosemary	*1½ teaspoons*	*¾ teaspoon*	*½ teaspoon*
Thyme leaves	*1½ teaspoons*	*¾ teaspoon*	*½ teaspoon*
Dry mustard	*1 teaspoon*	*½ teaspoon*	*¼ teaspoon*
Fennel seed	*1 teaspoon*	*½ teaspoon*	*¼ teaspoon*
Ground red pepper	*to taste*	*to taste*	*to taste*
Beer	*½ cup*	*¼ cup*	*2 tablespoons*
Worcestershire	*1 teaspoon*	*½ teaspoon*	*¼ teaspoon*
Lemon slices (optional)	*4 lemon slices*	*2 lemon slices*	*1 lemon slice*
Hot cooked herbed rice (optional)	*2 cups rice*	*1 cup rice*	*½ cup rice*
Parsley sprigs for garnish	*garnish*	*garnish*	*garnish*
Microwave cookware	2-quart soufflé dish	2-quart soufflé dish	1-quart soufflé dish
Time on High (100% power)	8 to 10 minutes	4 to 6 minutes	2 to 3½ (3:30) minutes
Standing time	3 to 4 minutes	3 minutes	2 minutes

1 In colander, place shrimp. Rinse under running cold water to clean; drain well.

2 In soufflé dish (see Chart), combine basil, celery salt, rosemary, thyme leaves, mustard, fennel seed, and ground red pepper until well mixed.

3 To mixture, add shrimp; toss to coat shrimp in seasonings. Add beer and Worcestershire; mix well.

4 Cook shrimp, covered, on High for time in Chart, or just until shrimp turn pink, stirring twice. Let stand, covered, on heat-safe surface for time in Chart.

5 Meanwhile, if you like, for each serving, prepare finger bowl by filling soup or dessert bowl with warm water and floating lemon slice on top.

6 *To serve:* Arrange shrimp in warmed soup plates. If you like, accompany with herbed rice; garnish. If using finger bowls, place by each setting.

SHRIMP IN SAFFRON CREAM

Color Index page 53. 6 servings. 205 cals per serving. Good source of vitamin A, vitamin C, iron. Begin 35 minutes ahead.

⅛ teaspoon saffron threads
Water
4 medium carrots, cut into matchstick-thin strips
1½ pounds medium shrimp, shelled and deveined (below)
¼ cup lemon juice
¼ cup dry vermouth or dry white wine
2 tablespoons minced green onion or onion
1 teaspoon salt
1 cup half-and-half
2 teaspoons cornstarch
¾ pound Chinese pea pods

1. In 4-cup glass measure, soak saffron threads in 1 tablespoon boiling water.

2. In 12″ by 8″ microwave-safe baking dish, place carrots and ¼ cup water. Cook, covered, on High (100% power) 4 to 6 minutes, until tender. Transfer to plate; cover and keep warm. Reserve cooking liquid in baking dish.

3. In 13″ by 9″ microwave-safe baking dish, place shrimp, half each of the lemon juice, vermouth or wine, onion, and salt. Cook, covered, on High 5 to 6 minutes, just until shrimp turn pink, stirring once. Over small bowl, strain shrimp; discard liquid; keep shrimp warm.

4. To saffron mixture, add half-and-half, cornstarch, and remaining lemon juice, vermouth or wine, onion, and salt. With spoon, stir until well blended. Cook, covered, on High 4 to 6 minutes, until saffron cream boils and thickens slightly, stirring once. Set aside; keep warm.

5. To reserved carrot liquid in baking dish, add Chinese pea pods. Cook, covered, on High 4 to 5 minutes, until tender-crisp, stirring once. Add carrots to one side of dish, keeping vegetables separate. Cook, covered, on High 1 minute.

6. Gently toss shrimp in saffron cream. Spoon an equal amount onto each warmed dinner plate. Arrange vegetables around shrimp mixture.

SHELLING AND DEVEINING SHRIMP
Shrimp may be shelled and deveined before or after cooking. Shrimp cooked in their shells are easier to handle once they cool.

Snip shrimp along back, exposing vein. Peel back shell; pull shrimp free.

Scrape away black or green vein; rinse shrimp under running cold water.

SHRIMP CREOLE

Color Index page 50. 4 servings. 463 cals per serving. Good source of vitamin A, niacin, vitamin C, calcium, iron. Begin 20 minutes ahead.

4 tablespoons butter or margarine (½ stick)	1 teaspoon thyme leaves
3 small onions, cut into ½-inch wedges	2 teaspoons Worcestershire
1 small green pepper, cut into ½-inch pieces	1 teaspoon prepared horseradish
3 garlic cloves, minced	1 28-ounce can pureed tomatoes
1½ pounds large shrimp, shelled and deveined (see Box, page 164)	Salt, pepper, and hot-pepper sauce to taste
¼ teaspoon ground cloves	2 cups Hot Cooked Rice (page 293)
	Thyme sprigs for garnish

1. In 2½-quart microwave-safe casserole, place butter or margarine. Heat, covered with paper towel, on High (100% power) 45 seconds to 1 minute, until melted.
2. Into melted butter or margarine, stir onions, green pepper, garlic, shrimp, cloves, and thyme leaves. Cook, covered, on High 6 minutes, or just until shrimp turn pink, stirring twice.
3. Into shrimp mixture, stir Worcestershire, horseradish, and pureed tomatoes. Cook on High 4 minutes, or until flavors blend, stirring halfway through cooking. Season.
4. *To serve*: Ladle shrimp over hot rice. Garnish with thyme sprigs.

BUYING SHRIMP

Shrimp are sold in their shells or shelled. One pound of uncooked shrimp in their shells yields slightly more than ½ pound after shelling and deveining. The shrimp "count" gives the approximate number of shrimp to the pound. Medium shrimp count 24 to 30 shrimp per pound, large shrimp 12 to 18 per pound, and jumbo or extra large 10 to 14 per pound.

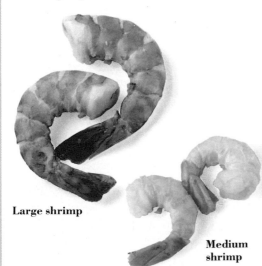

Large shrimp

Medium shrimp

Filled shrimp dishes such as our Stuffed Shrimp Supreme (below) make an impressive addition to any dinner or buffet table. To assure a neat and attractive finished result, it is essential to use large shrimp and to shred or mince the stuffing ingredients.

STUFFED SHRIMP SUPREME

Color Index page 53. 349 cals per serving. Good source of iron. Begin 45 minutes ahead.

Ingredients for 4 servings		Microwave cookware
1 pound large shrimp, shelled and deveined (see Box, page 164)	1 egg, beaten	13″ by 9″ baking dish
1 cup shredded zucchini	2 tablespoons butter or margarine (¼ stick), melted	12″ dinner plate
⅓ cup minced red pepper	2 tablespoons sherry	
¼ cup dried bread crumbs	1 tablespoon lemon juice	
½ teaspoon salt	2 tablespoons minced pecans	
Ground red pepper to taste	1 6-ounce package goat cheese	
	Lettuce leaves for garnish	

1 With sharp knife, cut each shrimp along back, three quarters through. Spread open and pound lightly to flatten.

2 Squeeze zucchini to remove excess moisture. In bowl, combine zucchini, red pepper, bread crumbs, salt, ground red pepper, and beaten egg.

3 Spoon an equal amount of zucchini mixture along center of each shrimp. Fold shrimp over filling. Arrange stuffed shrimp in single layer in baking dish.

4 In ramekin or small bowl, combine melted butter or margarine, sherry, and lemon juice; pour over stuffed shrimp. Cook, covered with waxed paper, on Medium-High (70% power) 6 to 8 minutes, until shrimp turn pink, rotating dish once. Set aside, covered.

5 Place minced pecans in shallow dish. With small, sharp knife, cut goat cheese into 8 slices. Press cheese slices into pecans to coat. Place on plate. Heat on Medium (50% power) 1 to 2 minutes, until cheese softens slightly.

6 *To serve*: Garnish serving platter with lettuce leaves. Arrange stuffed shrimp and pecan-coated cheese slices on platter; pour any remaining butter mixture over shrimp.

Shrimp, Clams, and Lobster

"STIR-FRIED" SHRIMP AND BROCCOLI

Color Index page 53. 222 cals per serving. Good source of vitamin A, vitamin C, iron. Begin 40 minutes ahead.

Ingredients	For 4	For 2	For 1
Cornstarch	*2 teaspoons*	*1 teaspoon*	*½ teaspoon*
Dry sherry	*2 tablespoons*	*1 tablespoon*	*1½ teaspoons*
Minced peeled gingerroot	*½ teaspoon*	*¼ teaspoon*	*to taste*
Medium shrimp, shelled and deveined (see Box, page 164)	*24 shrimp (1 pound)*	*12 shrimp (½ pound)*	*6 shrimp (¼ pound)*
Broccoli, flowerets and stalks, sliced	*1 bunch*	*½ bunch*	*¼ bunch*
Water	*¼ cup*	*2 tablespoons*	*1 tablespoon*
Red pepper, sliced	*1 large*	*1 medium*	*1 small*
1 15-ounce can straw mushrooms, drained	*1 can straw mushrooms*	*½ can straw mushrooms*	*¼ can straw mushrooms*
Butter or margarine	*1 tablespoon*	*1½ teaspoons*	*¾ teaspoon*
Salad oil	*1 tablespoon*	*1½ teaspoons*	*¾ teaspoon*
Garlic cloves, minced	*2 garlic cloves*	*1 garlic clove*	*½ garlic clove*
Hot Cooked Rice (page 293, optional)	*2 cups rice*	*1 cup rice*	*½ cup rice*
Soy sauce (optional)	*to taste*	*to taste*	*to taste*
Microwave cookware	2-quart casserole	1-quart casserole	Small bowl
	Browning dish	Browning dish	Browning dish
Time on High (100% power)			
Broccoli	4 to 5 minutes	3 to 3½ (3:30) minutes	2½ (2:30) minutes
Butter mixture	1 minute	45 seconds	30 seconds
Shrimp	2 to 3 minutes	1½ (1:30) to 2 minutes	1 minute
Vegetables	2 to 3 minutes	1½ (1:30) to 1¾ (1:45) minutes	1 minute

1 In small bowl, combine cornstarch, sherry, and gingerroot until blended. Add shrimp. Cover and refrigerate 15 minutes, stirring twice.

2 In casserole or bowl (see Chart), place broccoli and water. Cook, covered, on High for time in Chart; rinse. Stir in red pepper and mushrooms; set aside.

3 Preheat browning dish as manufacturer directs. On browning dish, place butter or margarine, oil, and garlic. Cook on High for time in Chart, stirring halfway through cooking. Add shrimp to browning dish in single layer. Cook on High for time in Chart or just until shrimp turn pink, stirring halfway through cooking. Transfer shrimp to bowl; cover. Reheat browning dish.

4 On browning dish, place vegetables. Cook on High for time in Chart, stirring once.

5 Add shrimp to vegetables; gently toss to mix. If you like, serve with rice and soy sauce.

BAKED CLAMS WITH PESTO

Color Index page 54. 4 appetizer servings; 2 main-dish servings. 205 cals per appetizer serving. Good source of calcium, iron.
Begin 35 minutes ahead.

2 dozen cherrystone or littleneck clams
¼ cup mayonnaise
2 tablespoons prepared pesto
Rock or coarse salt

2 tablespoons Italian-style dried bread crumbs
Fresh basil leaves for garnish

1. With stiff brush, scrub clams under running cold water to remove any sand.
2. In 2-quart microwave-safe casserole, arrange clams, hinge end down. Cook, covered, on High (100% power) 7 to 10 minutes, just until they open. Uncover and let cool.
3. Meanwhile, in small bowl, combine mayonnaise and pesto.
4. Remove top shell from each clam. Rinse clams in own liquid from shell to remove sand. Onto 10″ flat microwave-safe dinner plates, pour rock or coarse salt to make layer ½ inch thick. Into salt, press clams in shell to keep upright.
5. Top each clam with an equal amount of pesto-mayonnaise mixture; sprinkle evenly with bread crumbs.
6. Cook clams, in batches if necessary, on High 1½ (1:30) to 2 minutes, until hot. Garnish with basil leaves and serve immediately.

STEAMED CLAMS MEXICAN

Color Index page 54. 4 servings. 163 cals per serving. Low in fat. Good source of iron.
Begin 35 minutes ahead.

4 dozen cherrystone or littleneck clams
1 12-ounce bottle taco sauce

⅓ cup fresh coriander or parsley sprigs

1. With stiff brush, scrub clams under running cold water to remove any sand.
2. In 2-quart microwave-safe casserole, arrange half the clams, hinge end down. Pour half the taco sauce over clams. Reserve 8 sprigs coriander or parsley for garnish, then add half the remaining sprigs to the casserole. Cook, covered, on High (100% power) 7 to 10 minutes, until clams open (see Box, page 167); keep warm. Repeat with remaining clams, sauce, and coriander or parsley sprigs.
3. Serve steamed clams immediately, garnished with reserved coriander or parsley sprigs.

SZECHUAN LOBSTER

Color Index page 53. 4 servings. 292 cals per serving. Good source of vitamin A, vitamin C, calcium, iron. Begin 50 minutes ahead.

4 cooked lobsters	2 teaspoons soy sauce
1 tablespoon peanut or salad oil	1 teaspoon sesame oil
	½ pound green beans
2 teaspoons rice-wine vinegar or cider vinegar	3 green onions, cut into 2-inch pieces
3 garlic cloves, minced	1 green pepper, cut into matchstick-thin strips
½ cup dry-roasted cashews	Hot Cooked Rice (page 293, optional)
1 teaspoon chili powder	

1. Remove meat from lobsters (below right, steps 1 to 3). Cut lobster meat into 2-inch pieces.

2 In 12″ by 8″ microwave-safe baking dish, combine oil, vinegar, garlic, cashews, chili powder, soy sauce, and sesame oil. Cook on High (100% power) 2 minutes.

3. To cashew mixture, add green beans, green onions, and green pepper. Stir to coat with cashew mixture. Cook, covered, on High 6 to 8 minutes, until beans are tender.

4. Add lobster meat to vegetables. Cook, covered, on High 2 to 3 minutes, until lobster is hot.

5. *To serve:* Spoon lobster and vegetables onto warmed dinner plates. If you like, accompany with rice.

COOKING CLAMS

Cooking clams in the microwave is quick, simple, and clean. All clams should be thoroughly scrubbed with a wire brush or stiff plastic brush under running cold water to remove sand and surface dirt and any other deposits clinging to their shells. Discard any clams that are open or partially open. Arrange clams hinge end down in a casserole. Cook, covered, on High (100% power) for time in recipe. If some clams do not open, first remove the opened clams and reserve, then cover dish again and cook on High 1 to 2 minutes longer. Remove the opened clams and place them with the others. Discard any that still have not opened.

LOBSTER THERMIDOR

Color Index page 53. 322 cals per serving. Good source of calcium. Begin 45 minutes ahead.

Ingredients	For 4	For 2	For 1
Cooked lobsters (1¼ pounds each)	4 lobsters	2 lobsters	1 lobster
Butter or margarine	4 tablespoons (½ stick)	2 tablespoons (¼ stick)	1 tablespoon
Mushrooms, cut into quarters	4 ounces	2 ounces	1 ounce
1 10¾-ounce can cream of mushroom soup	1 can soup	½ can soup	¼ can soup
Milk	¼ cup	2 tablespoons	1 tablespoon
Sherry	2 tablespoons	1 tablespoon	1½ teaspoons
Parsley for garnish	garnish	garnish	garnish
Microwave cookware	Large bowl	Medium bowl	Medium bowl
Time on High (100% power)			
Butter and mushrooms	4 minutes	3 minutes	2 minutes
With soup and milk	4 minutes	2 minutes	1½ (1:30) minutes
With lobster	4 minutes	2½ (2:30) minutes	1½ (1:30) minutes

1 To prepare lobsters, break off claws and legs but leave lobsters whole for presentation. With lobster or nutcracker, crack the large claws. Remove meat to medium bowl.

2 With kitchen shears, cut thin underside shell from tail of each lobster; gently pull meat from shell. Devein the tail. Reserve any red roe (coral) or green meat (tomalley) in large bowl. Cut tail meat into chunks and add to bowl.

3 Lift out bony portion from head shell; add roe or green meat to bowl. Discard sac and spongy gray gills from top of head. Break bony portion apart. Pick out any meat; add to bowl. Rinse whole lobster shells; set aside.

4 In bowl (see Chart), place butter or margarine and mushrooms. Cook on High for time in Chart. Stir in soup and milk. Cook on High for time in Chart.

5 Into mushroom mixture, stir sherry and lobster meat. Cook on High for time in Chart, until lobster is hot.

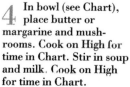

6 *To serve:* Spoon an equal amount of lobster mixture into cleaned shells. Garnish with parsley.

Mussels and Scallops

When cooking mussels, it is essential to scrub the shells well with a wire brush or stiff plastic brush and to scrape any calcium and salt deposits from their surfaces. It is also necessary to remove the "beards," the stringlike threads that attach the mussels to their beds, by scraping them away with a sharp knife and rinsing under running cold water. Before cooking, discard any mussels with open shells. After cooking, discard any mussels that remain closed.

MUSSELS IN WHITE WINE

Color Index page 54. 216 cals per serving. Low in cholesterol. Good source of iron. Begin 35 minutes ahead.

Ingredients	For 4	For 2	For 1
Mussels	4 dozen	2 dozen	1 dozen
Olive or salad oil	¼ cup oil	2 tablespoons oil	1 tablespoon oil
Garlic cloves, sliced	4 garlic cloves	2 garlic cloves	1 garlic clove
Tomatoes, diced	4 tomatoes	2 tomatoes	1 tomato
Dry white wine	1 cup wine	½ cup wine	¼ cup wine
Basil	½ teaspoon	¼ teaspoon	⅛ teaspoon
French bread (optional)	French bread	French bread	French bread
Microwave cookware	2-quart soufflé dish	2-quart soufflé dish	1½-quart soufflé dish
Time on High (100% power)	5 to 7 minutes each batch	5 to 7 minutes	4 to 5 minutes

1 With stiff brush, scrub mussels to remove any sand; rinse under running cold water.

2 With small, sharp knife, scrape any barnacles from shells and scrape away stringy "beards." Rinse again.

3 In soufflé dish (see Chart), place mussels. If cooking mussels for 4, prepare in 2 batches.

4 To mussels, add oil, garlic, tomatoes, wine, and basil.

5 Cook mussels, tightly covered with plastic wrap, on High for time in Chart, just until mussels open.

6 *To serve:* Arrange mussels in warmed soup bowls with their broth. If you like, serve with French bread.

SCALLOPS IN CHIVE CREAM

Color Index page 49. 4 servings. 220 cals per serving. Begin 25 minutes ahead.

1 pound sea scallops
2 tablespoons butter or margarine (¼ stick)
1 medium onion, minced
¼ cup heavy or whipping cream
¼ cup Chicken Broth (page 125) or canned broth
¼ cup dry white wine
¼ cup minced fresh chives
1 tablespoon cornstarch dissolved in 2 tablespoons cold water
Salt and pepper to taste
Fresh chives for garnish

1. Rinse scallops under running cold water to remove any sand; pat dry.
2. In 12″ by 8″ microwave-safe baking dish, place butter or margarine and onion. Cook, covered with paper towels, on High (100% power) 3 to 4 minutes, until onion is transparent and softened, stirring halfway through cooking.
3. To onion mixture, add scallops, cream, broth, and wine. Cook, covered, on High 4 to 6 minutes, just until scallops are opaque.
4. Into scallop mixture, stir chives and dissolved cornstarch. Cook on High 2 to 3 minutes, until thickened. Season.
5. *To serve:* Spoon scallop mixture into 4 small dishes or large scallop shells. Garnish with chives and serve immediately.

CURRIED BAY SCALLOPS

Color Index page 50. 4 servings. 185 cals per serving. Good source of vitamin A. Begin 25 minutes ahead.

1 pound bay scallops
2 tablespoons butter or margarine (¼ stick)
1 to 1½ teaspoons curry powder
1 onion, thinly sliced
2 medium celery stalks, cut into matchstick-thin strips
2 large carrots, cut into matchstick-thin strips
2 tablespoons dry white wine
Salt to taste
Fresh coriander or parsley sprigs for garnish

1. Rinse scallops under running cold water to remove any sand; pat dry.
2. In 12″ by 8″ microwave-safe baking dish, place butter or margarine. Heat, covered with paper towels, on High (100% power) 45 seconds, or until melted. Add curry powder according to taste; stir until well blended. To mixture, add onion, celery, and carrots; stir to coat with curry butter. Cook on High 2 to 3 minutes, until carrots are tender-crisp.
3. To curry-butter mixture, add scallops. Drizzle with white wine. Cook, covered, on High 3 to 4 minutes, just until scallops are opaque, stirring twice. Season with salt.
4. *To serve:* Arrange curried scallops on warmed dinner plates. Garnish with coriander or parsley.

Oysters

OYSTER STEW

Color Index page 50. 4 servings. 301 cals per serving. Good source of calcium, iron. Begin 25 minutes ahead.

2 tablespoons butter or margarine (¼ stick)
1 pint shucked standard oysters, with their liquid
1 tablespoon all-purpose flour

2 cups half-and-half
¼ teaspoon celery salt
Salt and pepper to taste
Paprika for garnish
French bread (optional)

1. In 8-cup microwave-safe glass measure, place butter or margarine. Heat, covered with paper towel, on High (100% power) 45 seconds, or until melted.
2. Meanwhile, drain oysters, reserving liquid. To melted butter or margarine, add oysters. Cook on High 1 minute, or just until edges begin to curl. With slotted spoon, remove oysters to bowl.
3. To cooking liquid, gradually add flour; stir until blended. Into mixture, slowly stir half-and-half and oyster liquid. Add celery salt, salt, and pepper. Cook on High 4 to 5 minutes, until slightly thickened, stirring twice.
4. To half-and-half mixture, add oysters. Cook on High 2 to 2½ (2:30) minutes, just until oysters are hot.
5. *To serve:* Ladle oyster stew into soup bowls. Garnish with a sprinkling of paprika. If you like, accompany with French bread.

SCALLOPED OYSTERS

Color Index page 50. 4 servings. 595 cals per serving. Good source of vitamin A, iron. Begin 20 minutes ahead.

8 tablespoons butter or margarine (1 stick)
2 cups Melba-toast Crumbs (page 196)
1 pint shucked standard oysters, with their liquid
½ cup heavy or whipping cream

¾ teaspoon salt
½ teaspoon Worcestershire
2 tablespoons chopped parsley
Lemon slices and parsley sprigs for garnish

1. In 12″ by 8″ microwave-safe baking dish, place butter or margarine. Heat, covered with paper towels, on High (100% power) 1½ (1:30) to 2 minutes, until melted. Stir in Melba-toast Crumbs. Remove half the mixture to small bowl; set aside.
2. In bottom of same baking dish, spread remaining Melba-toast Crumbs in thin layer. Cover with undrained oysters.
3. In another small bowl, combine cream, salt, and Worcestershire. Pour mixture over oysters. Top with reserved Melba-toast Crumbs; sprinkle with chopped parsley.
4. Cook scalloped oysters on High 4 to 5 minutes, until hot. Garnish with lemon slices and parsley sprigs. Serve immediately.

Oysters are sold fresh in the shell, fresh-shucked, shucked and frozen, or canned. Eastern oysters are graded by size: extra-large, "extra-selects" or large, and "selects" or medium. "Standards," or small oysters, are used in soups and stews. Large oysters are delicious for serving raw on the half shell.

CREAMED OYSTERS WITH BISCUITS

Color Index page 50. 365 cals per serving. Good source of calcium, iron. Begin 25 minutes ahead.

Ingredients for 4 servings		Microwave cookware
4 slices bacon, chopped *1 small onion, chopped* *1 celery stalk, chopped* *1 garlic clove, minced* *½ teaspoon thyme leaves* *1 tablespoon all-purpose flour* *1 pint shucked standard oysters, with their liquid*	*½ cup half-and-half* *Salt and pepper to taste* *4 large baking-powder biscuits or 4 cornbread cakes* *Parsley sprigs for garnish*	*12″ by 8″ baking dish* *8″ by 8″ baking dish*

1 In 12″ by 8″ baking dish, place bacon. Cook, covered with paper towels, on High (100% power) 4 to 5 minutes, until browned, stirring twice. With slotted spoon, remove bacon to paper towels to drain; reserve.

2 To drippings in baking dish, add onion, celery, garlic, and thyme leaves. Cook on High 3 to 4 minutes, until onion is softened. Stir in flour until blended.

3 Over small bowl, drain oysters; reserve ¼ cup liquid. Set oysters aside. Into onion mixture, stir reserved oyster liquid and half-and-half. Cook on High 3 to 4 minutes, until mixture thickens, stirring twice.

4 To mixture, add oysters; season. Cook on High 1 to 2 minutes, just until edges of oysters begin to curl and sauce is hot. On heat-safe surface, let oyster mixture stand, covered, 5 minutes.

5 Meanwhile, line 8″ by 8″ baking dish with paper towel. Place biscuits or cornbread cakes in dish. Heat on High 2 minutes.

6 *To serve:* Split biscuits or cornbread cakes in half. Place on warmed dinner plates. Spoon oyster mixture over bottom half of each biscuit or cornbread cake; top with remaining half. Garnish and sprinkle with reserved bacon.

169

Crab

CRAB CAKES

Color Index page 50. 119 cals each. Good source of vitamin A, calcium, iron. Begin 25 minutes ahead.

Our Crab Cakes can be made with fresh, frozen, or canned crab meat or with other shellfish or fish. Popular alternatives, for example, are tuna and salmon cakes made with canned fish. Shaped into tiny patties, Crab Cakes make an attractive cocktail tidbit or an ideal accompaniment to soups and chowders such as our Corn Chowder (page 133).

Ingredients for 12 crab cakes		Microwave cookware
1 16-ounce container lump crab meat or 2 6-ounce packages frozen Alaska King crab meat, thawed and drained *1½ cups fresh bread crumbs* *¼ cup minced red or green pepper* *¼ cup sherry* *2 tablespoons minced onion*	*1 egg, beaten* *½ teaspoon salt* *¼ teaspoon hot-pepper sauce* *½ cup dried whole-wheat bread crumbs* *2 teaspoons paprika* *4 tablespoons butter or margarine (½ stick)* *Spicy Cocktail Sauce (page 159, optional)*	*10″ round baking dish*

1 In medium bowl, place crab meat. Pick over crab meat to remove any remaining pieces of shell or cartilage.

2 To crab meat, add fresh bread crumbs, minced pepper, sherry, onion, egg, salt, and hot-pepper sauce; toss.

3 On waxed paper, combine dried bread crumbs and paprika.

4 Shape crab meat mixture into 12 round patties. For Cocktail Crab Cakes, shape crab mixture into 24 small patties.

5 In baking dish, place butter or margarine. Heat, covered with paper towel, on High (100% power) 45 seconds to 1 minute, until melted. Dip patties into melted butter or margarine, then coat with bread crumbs.

6 In same baking dish, place 6 large or 12 miniature patties. Cook each batch, covered with waxed paper, on High 3 to 5 minutes, until cakes are set, turning once. Repeat with remaining patties. If you like, serve with Spicy Cocktail Sauce.

DEVILED CRAB

Color Index page 50. 4 servings. 308 cals per serving. Good source of calcium. Begin 20 minutes ahead.

1 16-ounce container lump crab meat *4 tablespoons butter or margarine (½ stick)* *¼ cup heavy or whipping cream* *1 egg, beaten* *2 tablespoons chopped parsley*	*1 tablespoon Dijon mustard* *1 tablespoon lemon juice* *1 teaspoon Worcestershire* *2 tablespoons dried bread crumbs* *Lemon for garnish*

1. Pick over crab meat to remove any remaining pieces of shell or cartilage.
2. In 4-cup microwave-safe glass measure, place butter or margarine. Heat, covered with paper towel, on High (100% power) 45 seconds to 1 minute, until melted.
3. To melted butter or margarine, add cream, egg, parsley, mustard, lemon juice, Worcestershire, and bread crumbs; stir until blended.
4. Into cream mixture, gently stir crab meat until just mixed, taking care not to break up the meat.
5. Into each of 4 ceramic microwave-safe scallop shells or ramekins, spoon a quarter of crab mixture. Cook on High 4 to 5 minutes, until hot. Garnish with lemon; serve immediately.

CRAB CLAWS WITH HERB BUTTER

Color Index page 50. 4 servings. 338 cals per serving. Good source of vitamin A, calcium. Begin 25 minutes ahead.

4 green onions, minced *1 garlic clove, minced* *¼ teaspoon oregano* *¼ teaspoon thyme leaves* *¼ teaspoon tarragon* *8 tablespoons butter (1 stick)* *2 tablespoons lemon juice*	*Salt and pepper to taste* *2 tablespoons chopped parsley* *4 large crab claws, cooked* *Lemon wedges and parsley sprigs for garnish*

1. In 4-cup microwave-safe glass measure, place green onions, garlic, oregano, thyme leaves, tarragon, and butter. Cook, covered with paper towel, on High (100% power) 1½ (1:30) to 2 minutes, until butter is melted and foamy. Skim foam from butter; discard.
2. To herb butter, add lemon juice, salt, pepper, and parsley. Set aside and keep warm.
3. In 13″ by 9″ microwave-safe baking dish, arrange crab claws with thicker parts toward edges of dish. Cook, covered, on High 4 to 6 minutes, until hot.
4. *To serve:* Arrange crab claws on warmed serving platter. Garnish with lemon and parsley. Pass herb butter separately.

Mixed Shellfish

PAELLA

Color Index page 54. 297 cals per serving. Good source of niacin, iron.
Begin 1¼ hours ahead.

The paella of Spain has become a classic party dish worldwide. The
ingredients vary from region to region, but usually include large
amounts of shellfish with chicken, sausages, and rice, giving the
paella its contrast of textures and flavors. Traditionally, it is
cooked on a wood fire in a wide, shallow pan. Our microwave
version can be made in any microwave-safe soufflé or gratin dish
and leaves the hostess time to assemble a fruity Sangria (page 163).

Ingredients for 8 servings		Microwave cookware
1 dozen mussels	1 medium green pepper,	3-quart soufflé dish
1 dozen littleneck clams	chopped	1-cup glass measure
¼ cup dry white wine	½ teaspoon crushed	
½ pound hot Italian-	saffron threads	
sausage links	1 cup regular long-grain	
4 chicken-breast halves,	rice	
skinned and boned	1 cup Chicken Broth	
(about 1 pound)	(page 125) or canned	
½ teaspoon salt	broth	
2 garlic cloves, minced	1 8-ounce can	
¼ teaspoon thyme leaves	crushed tomatoes	
1 pound shrimp, shelled	Parsley sprigs for garnish	
and deveined		
1 medium onion,		
chopped		

1 With stiff brush, scrub mussels and clams under running cold water; remove beards from mussels (page 168).

2 In soufflé dish, arrange clams in a ring around edge of dish. Place mussels in center.

3 To shellfish, add white wine. Cook, covered, on High (100% power) 3 to 5 minutes, until shellfish are open (see Box, page 167).

4 Discard top shells of mussels and clams; rinse shellfish in cooking broth. Transfer to plate; cover and refrigerate.

5 Into glass measure, pour cooking broth. Let broth stand until sand settles. Spoon off ¾ cup broth, cover and refrigerate; discard remaining broth.

6 Cut sausages into 1-inch lengths; place in soufflé dish used for shellfish. Cook, covered with paper towel, on High 5 minutes, or until lightly browned. Remove to drain on paper towels. Reserve drippings.

7 Cut chicken into 2-inch strips. In medium bowl, combine chicken, salt, garlic, and thyme leaves.

8 To sausage drippings in soufflé dish, add seasoned chicken. Cook, covered with paper towel, on High 4 to 5 minutes, until chicken is tender, stirring once. Remove chicken; set aside.

9 To same soufflé dish, add shrimp, onion, and green pepper. Cook, covered, on High 2 to 3 minutes, just until shrimp turn pink, stirring once. Remove shrimp and set aside, leaving vegetables in soufflé dish.

10 To vegetables, add saffron and rice. Stir to coat. Cook on High 2 minutes, stirring once.

11 Into rice, stir reserved broth, Chicken Broth, and tomatoes. Cook on High 15 minutes, or until rice is tender, stirring once.

12 Into rice mixture, carefully stir reserved sausage, chicken, and shellfish.

13 Cook paella, covered, on High 2 to 3 minutes, until hot. Be careful not to overcook.

14 To serve: Place paella in warmed serving dish, arranging mussels and clams on top. Garnish.

Mixed Shellfish

BOUILLABAISSE

Color Index page 54. 205 cals per serving. Begin 1¼ hours ahead.

Ingredients for 8 servings		Microwave cookware

1 dozen mussels
3 tablespoons olive or
  salad oil
1 medium onion, diced
3 garlic cloves, minced
3 medium tomatoes,
  chopped
1 bay leaf
1 cup dry white wine
¼ cup tomato paste
1 teaspoon salt
½ teaspoon thyme leaves
2 cups Chicken Broth
  (page 125) or canned
  broth
½ teaspoon crushed
  saffron threads
	1 uncooked lobster
	  (1¼ pounds)
	1 pound red snapper
	  fillets, cut into 2-inch
	  pieces
	1 pound cod steak, cut
	  into 2-inch pieces
	1 tablespoon anise-
	  flavor liqueur
	Hot-pepper sauce to
	  taste
	Chopped parsley for
	  garnish
	French bread (optional)
		Large bowl

1 With stiff brush, scrub mussels to remove any sand; rinse under running cold water. Scrape away any barnacles and "beards." In large bowl, place mussels. Cook, covered, on High (100% power) 2 to 3 minutes, just until open. Remove to another bowl; rinse each mussel in own liquid from shell to remove any sand. Into 4-cup glass measure, pour cooking broth. Let stand until sand settles. Spoon off 1 cup clear broth, cover and refrigerate; discard remaining broth.

2 In same large bowl, combine oil, onion, garlic, tomatoes, and bay leaf. Cook on High 3 to 4 minutes, until onion is softened, stirring twice. Add wine and next 5 ingredients and reserved cooking broth. Cook on High 12 minutes, stirring every 3 minutes.

3 On cutting board, place lobster. Insert point of knife through back shell, where tail and body meet, to sever vein.

4 With knife, cut lobster lengthwise in half through shell. Devein tail. Leave greenish-gray liver (tomalley) and roe (coral), if present.

5 Remove sand sac from head; break off claws. Cut each claw across joints into 3 pieces Crack claws. Cut lobster into chunks.

6 To tomato mixture, add lobster. Cook on High 4 minutes, stirring once. Add fish. Cook on High 2 minutes. Add liqueur, hot-pepper sauce, and mussels; stir to blend. Let stand, covered, 5 minutes. Remove bay leaf. Ladle into soup bowls; garnish. If you like, accompany with French bread.

SEAFOOD BAKE

Color Index page 53. 8 servings. 184 cals per serving. Good source of iron. Begin 45 minutes ahead.

4 ears corn
12 littleneck clams
2 8-ounce bottles clam
  juice
2 leeks, thinly sliced
2 tablespoons butter or
  margarine (¼ stick)
1 pound medium shrimp,
  shelled and deveined
  (see Box, page 164)
	2 garlic cloves, minced
	¾ pound sea scallops,
	  sliced
	1 red pepper, sliced
	2 tablespoons lemon
	  juice
	1 cup loosely packed
	  spinach leaves, well
	  washed and trimmed

1. Remove and reserve husks from corn. Remove silks. Cut ears crosswise into 2-inch pieces; reassemble in reserved husks. Cook on High (100% power) 6 minutes, rearranging once. Remove husks from corn and discard.
2. Scrub and rinse clams. In 2-quart microwave-safe casserole, place microwave-safe steamer or trivet; add ½ cup clam juice. Cook, covered, on High 2 minutes. Add clams. Cook, covered, on High 3 to 4 minutes, just until clams open.
3. In 3-quart microwave-safe casserole, place leeks and butter or margarine. Cook, covered, on High 3 to 4 minutes. Add corn, shrimp, garlic, scallops, pepper, lemon juice, and remaining clam juice. Cook, covered, on High 6 minutes, stirring twice. Add clam mixture. Cook on High 3 to 4 minutes, until hot. Stir in spinach leaves and let stand, covered, 5 minutes before serving.

PARTY SHELLFISH

Color Index page 50. 6 servings. 219 cals per serving. Good source of vitamin A, calcium. Begin 20 minutes ahead.

2 tablespoons butter or
  margarine (¼ stick)
2 tablespoons all-
  purpose flour
½ teaspoon salt
1¼ cups half-and-half
½ pound sea scallops
½ pound medium
  shrimp, shelled and
  deveined (see Box,
  page 164)
	1 tablespoon chopped
	  parsley
	1 4-ounce jar roasted
	  sweet red peppers,
	  drained and chopped
	1 tablespoon sherry
	1 12-ounce package
	  frozen Alaska Snow
	  crab cocktail claws,
	  thawed and drained
	Parsley for garnish

1. In medium microwave-safe bowl, place butter or margarine. Heat, covered with paper towel, on High (100% power) 45 seconds, or until melted. Add flour and salt; stir. Stir in half-and-half. Cook on High 3 to 4 minutes, until sauce thickens, stirring twice.
2. In 10″ round microwave-safe baking dish, place scallops and shrimp. Cook, covered, on High 2½ (2:30) to 3 minutes, stirring once. Add sauce, chopped parsley, chopped sweet peppers, sherry, and crab claws. Cook, covered, on High 1½ (1:30) to 2 minutes, just until scallops turn opaque and shrimp turn pink.
3. Transfer to serving platter; garnish.

CIOPPINO

Color Index page 52. 8 servings. 185 cals per serving. Good source of iron. Begin 45 minutes ahead.

1 dozen cherrystone or littleneck clams	*1 12- to 14-ounce jar spaghetti sauce*
2 tablespoons olive or salad oil	*½ pound medium shrimp, shelled and deveined (see Box, page 164)*
1 large onion, chopped	
1 medium green pepper, chopped	
2 medium celery stalks, chopped	*½ pound sea scallops*
	1 12-ounce package frozen Alaska King crab legs, thawed and cut into 2-inch pieces
2 garlic cloves, minced	
1 cup dry red wine	

1. With stiff brush, scrub clams under running cold water to remove any sand. In deep 3-quart microwave-safe casserole, place clams. Cook, covered, on High (100% power) 4 to 6 minutes, just until clams open (see Box, page 167).
2. Discard top clam shells; rinse clams in own liquid from shell to remove any sand; place on large plate. Into 4-cup glass measure, pour broth. Let stand until sand settles; spoon off ¾ cup broth, cover and refrigerate; discard remainder.
3. In same casserole, combine oil, onion, green pepper, celery, and garlic. Cook on High 3 to 4 minutes, until vegetables have softened. Add red wine, spaghetti sauce, and reserved clam broth. Cook on High 10 minutes, stirring twice.
4. Into mixture, stir shrimp, scallops, and crab legs. Cook, covered, on High 5 to 7 minutes, until shrimp turn pink and scallops are opaque, stirring occasionally. Serve hot.

LOBSTER AND SHRIMP STEW WITH CHICKEN

Color Index page 52. 4 servings. 240 cals per serving. Good source of vitamin A, niacin. Begin 40 minutes ahead.

2 cooked lobsters (about 1¼ pounds each)	*½ 10-ounce package frozen corn kernels, thawed*
2 tablespoons butter or margarine (¼ stick)	*1 tablespoon cornstarch dissolved in ½ cup Chicken Broth (page 125) or canned broth*
1 onion, chopped	
2 tomatoes, chopped	
1 teaspoon basil	
2 chicken-breast halves, skinned, boned, and cut into 2-inch pieces (about ½ pound)	*½ pound cooked shrimp, shelled and deveined (see Box, page 164)*
	Salt and pepper to taste

1. Remove meat from lobsters (page 167). Cut meat into 2-inch pieces.
2. In 13" by 9" microwave-safe baking dish, place butter or margarine, onion, tomatoes, and basil. Cook on High (100% power) 3 to 4 minutes. Add chicken and corn. Cook on High 4 to 6 minutes, until chicken is opaque, stirring twice.
3. Into chicken mixture, stir broth mixture and lobster. Cook on High 2 minutes. Add shrimp. Cook on High 1 to 2 minutes, until sauce thickens and lobster is hot, stirring twice. Season.

TUNA AND TOMATO SAUCE

Color Index page 49. 4 servings. 426 cals per serving. Low in cholesterol. Good source of thiamine, niacin, iron. Begin 15 minutes ahead.

8 ounces any pasta	
1 tablespoon olive or salad oil	
1 small onion, chopped	
2 garlic cloves, minced	
10 pitted ripe olives, chopped	
1 tablespoon capers, drained	
1 6½-ounce can tuna in oil	
¼ teaspoon crushed red pepper	
1 14½- to 16-ounce can crushed tomatoes	
¼ cup chopped parsley	

1. Cook pasta conventionally as label directs.
2. Meanwhile, in 12" by 8" microwave-safe casserole, place oil and next 4 ingredients. Cook, covered with paper towels, on High (100% power) 3 to 4 minutes, until onion is transparent, stirring halfway through cooking.
3. To mixture, add tuna and its oil and crushed red pepper, breaking tuna into bite-sized pieces. Cook, covered with paper towels, on High 2 to 3 minutes, until hot. Add tomatoes and parsley; mix. Cook, covered with paper towels, on High 4 to 5 minutes, until bubbling, stirring twice.
4. *To serve:* Drain pasta and place on warmed dinner plates; spoon sauce over.

RED CLAM SAUCE

Color Index page 49. 4 servings. 445 cals per serving. Good source of thiamine, niacin, iron. Begin 15 minutes ahead.

8 ounces any pasta	
3 slices bacon, diced	
1 small onion, diced	
1 12- to 14-ounce jar spaghetti sauce	
½ teaspoon oregano	
1 10-ounce can whole baby clams, drained	

1. Cook pasta conventionally as label directs.
2. Meanwhile, in 2-quart microwave-safe casserole, place diced bacon. Cook, covered with paper towel, on High (100% power) 2 to 3 minutes, until browned.
3. To bacon, add onion. Cook, covered with paper towel, on High 3 minutes, stirring twice.
4. Into mixture, stir spaghetti sauce and oregano. Cook, covered with paper towel, on High 3 to 4 minutes, until hot. Add clams. Cook, covered with paper towel, on High 2 minutes, or until clams are hot.
5. *To serve:* Drain pasta and place on warmed dinner plates; spoon sauce over.

BABY CLAM AND SHRIMP SAUCE

Color Index page 49. 4 servings. 390 cals per serving. Begin 20 minutes ahead.

8 ounces any pasta	
1 10-ounce can whole baby clams	
2 tablespoons olive or salad oil	
2 garlic cloves	
1 28-ounce can tomatoes	
1 tablespoon sherry	
½ teaspoon ground red pepper	
½ pound medium shrimp, shelled and deveined (see Box, page 164)	
¼ cup chopped parsley for garnish (optional)	

1. Cook pasta conventionally as label directs.
2. Meanwhile, drain baby clams, reserving liquid.
3. In 2½-quart microwave-safe casserole, place oil and garlic. Cook on High (100% power) 2 minutes, stirring once. Discard garlic. Add tomatoes with their liquid, sherry, ground red pepper, and reserved clam liquid. Cook on High 10 minutes, stirring twice.
4. To mixture, add clams and shrimp. Cook on High 2 to 3 minutes, until shrimp turn pink and clams are hot.
5. *To serve:* Drain pasta and place on warmed dinner plates; spoon sauce over. If you like, garnish with parsley.

Meal in Minutes *for 8 people*
Do-It-Yourself Seafood Pasta Party

Melon and prosciutto platter
Breadsticks
Pasta with three Seafood Sauces, page 173
Tossed mixed salad
Ice cream or sorbet of your choice
Espresso, page 130, with Florentines, page 351

PREPARATION TIMETABLE

1 day ahead:	**Early in day:**	**1 hour ahead:**	**30 minutes ahead:**	**Just before serving:**
Make Florentines; store in airtight container.	*Prepare salad ingredients; store in plastic bags in refrigerator. Prepare Tuna and Tomato, Red Clam, and Baby Clam and Shrimp Sauces; cover and refrigerate. Slice melon; cover and refrigerate.*	*Arrange melon slices on large serving platter with prosciutto; if you like, wrap melon with prosciutto. Garnish platter with ripe olives and basil leaves; cover.*	*Cook 3 kinds of pasta conventionally; keep warm. Meanwhile, reheat seafood sauces on microwave-safe shelf. Place salad ingredients in bowl and toss with dressing of your choice.*	*Transfer pasta and seafood sauces to warmed serving bowls; if you like, garnish with fresh basil or parsley. Prepare Espresso.*

Poultry

DEFROSTING, COOKING, AND BROWNING POULTRY
CUT-UP CHICKEN · CHICKEN BREASTS
CHICKEN PIECES · COOKED CHICKEN
CORNISH HENS · DUCKLING · TURKEY

Poultry

Poultry, a naturally tender food, is ideal for the fast, moist cooking of a microwave oven. Chicken, duckling, Cornish hens, and turkey all turn out successfully, although smaller portions rather than whole birds are easiest to cook. A whole chicken requires shielding and turning halfway through cooking. A whole turkey must be cooked conventionally if it is over 12 pounds, but turkey breasts and pieces are delicious cooked in the microwave. Duckling is better microwaved, as excess fat is more easily removed. Cornish hens are excellent cooked whole or split. Microwaved chicken should be very juicy. If the chicken is dry or tough, it has been overcooked.

Because chicken skin is high in calories and cholesterol and rarely browns in the microwave, we remove it when fat is not necessary for the recipe. To look as appetizing as possible, poultry should be glazed, simmered in a sauce, or coated. Plain microwaved chicken, however, is perfectly suited to salads and casseroles.

When cooking whole chickens, if you use a temperature probe, make sure the bird's weight is at least 3 pounds. If chicken is too small, the probe may touch a bone and cause an inaccurate reading. When cooking a whole bird, cover its wing and leg tips and the breastbone with small, smooth pieces of foil to prevent overcooking. Chicken pieces have to be arranged carefully for even cooking: place meatier pieces toward edges of dish and bonier parts toward center, then rearrange pieces halfway through cooking. Prevent uneven cooking of boneless chicken breasts by tucking thin ends under. Because the microwave sometimes renders more fat from foods than conventional methods, use a rack to cook duck pieces and cover loosely with waxed paper.

Poultry is done when flesh is opaque and fork-tender; juices should run clear when flesh is pierced with a fork. Standing time is given in those individual recipes where it is necessary to complete cooking.

DINNER-PARTY PRESENTATIONS

Transform a plain, boneless, microwaved chicken breast (page 178) into impressive dinner-party fare by slicing it evenly, then fanning out the slices on a pool of sauce. This quick presentation works with both hot and chilled cooked chicken.

A hot chicken breast (left) sliced and fanned on a pool of Tomato Sauce (page 380), then garnished with fresh herb sprigs.

A sliced cold chicken breast (right), arranged on Creamy Avocado Sauce (page 219) with avocado, parsley, and Orange Julienne (page 334).

Defrosting Poultry

If possible, remove or loosen poultry wrappings before defrosting. Otherwise, remove wrapping after first few minutes of defrosting. If wrapping is left on during defrosting, it will retain heat and the poultry will begin to cook. After defrosting, rinse poultry under running cold water, then pat dry with paper towels.

DEFROSTING A WHOLE BIRD

Place bird on a microwave rack in baking dish. Defrost on Medium-Low (30% power) 5 to 9 minutes per pound. Elevating prevents bottom portion from cooking in own juices.

Halfway through defrosting time, turn bird breast side down; cover with waxed paper to hold heat around bird as it defrosts.

Toward end of defrosting, uncover bird and turn breast side up. Shield any warm spots with smooth pieces of foil. The legs, wing tips, and highest portion of breast normally defrost soonest.

DEFROSTING PIECES

If poultry has been frozen in a polystyrene tray, remove this and the paper liner provided to absorb juices as soon as they can be separated from the poultry. If left in place, defrosting time will be prolonged.

If not in a solid block, arrange boned breasts with thicker portions toward edge of dish. Break apart partially frozen pieces after half the defrosting time.

Rearrange pieces so that icier ones are toward edge of dish and defrost for remaining time; pieces will be cold to the touch and there will be some ice crystals. Let stand for 5 minutes, then rinse.

DEFROSTING A WHOLE TURKEY BREAST

Place breast, skin side down. Defrost on Medium (50% power) 3 to 6 minutes per pound, or defrost on Medium-Low (30% power) 7 to 9½ (9:30) minutes per pound.

Defrost turkey breast for half the time, then turn breast skin side up and shield any warm areas with smooth pieces of foil. Defrost for remaining time.

When turkey breast is defrosted, rinse under running cold water, place in bowl, and let stand 5 to 10 minutes, until cavity is no longer icy.

Cooking Chicken

EXTRA-QUICK CHICKEN BREASTS

Barbecued

In shallow casserole, place *1 8-ounce chicken-breast half*. Cook, covered with waxed paper, on High (100% power) 2 minutes rotating halfway. Brush with *2 tablespoons barbecue sauce*. Cook, covered, 2 to 3 minutes longer, until juices run clear. Let stand 2 minutes.

Poached

Pound *1 chicken-breast half, boned and skinned (about 6 ounces)* to ½-inch thickness. Place *½ cup thinly sliced peppers, carrots, celery*, and *onion* on 2 connected paper towels, top with chicken. If you like, dot with *butter or margarine*; season. Fold sides of towels over chicken; tuck ends under. Moisten "package" with a sprinkling of water and place on microwave-safe plate. Cook 1 package on High (100% power) 2½ (2:30) to 3 minutes; 2 packages, 4½ (4:30) to 5 minutes. Let stand on heat-safe surface 3 minutes before serving on warmed dinner plate.

COOKING CHICKEN

Amount	Time	Power level
1 6-ounce chicken-breast half (boneless)	3½ (3:30) to 4 minutes	High (100% power)
2 6-ounce chicken-breast halves (boneless)	5½ (5:30) to 6 minutes	High
1 8-ounce chicken leg	5 to 5½ (5:30) minutes	High
2 8-ounce chicken legs	8 to 8½ (8:30) minutes	High
Chicken pieces	6 to 7 minutes per pound	High
Whole chicken	7 to 9 minutes per pound	Medium (50% power)

COOKING SMALL TURKEYS

Use a probe or a microwave thermometer while the bird is cooking or check the temperature with an instant-read thermometer once it is out of the microwave. Turkey-breast meat should register 170°F., and thigh or dark meat 175°F. to 180°F. Choose a light, bread-type stuffing and mix and pack it lightly. Heavy stuffings take too long to cook, so the turkey meat will overcook before the stuffing is ready; cooking stuffing in a separate casserole is recommended.

COOKING WHOLE BIRDS

Choose plump birds weighing at least 3, but no more than 12 pounds. Cover wing and leg tips and breast bone with small, smooth pieces of foil to prevent these areas from overcooking.

As a rule of thumb, cook whole chicken on Medium (50% power) 7 to 9 minutes per pound. Place bird breast side down, covered with waxed paper for half the cooking time, then turn breast side up for remaining time.

Larger birds may brown due to the longer cooking times, otherwise brush your bird with barbecue sauce or another browning agent (see Browning Chicken, pages 180 and 181). Chicken is done when juices run clear if thickest part of thigh is pierced with a fork.

If using a thermometer, remove chicken when it reads 180°F. to 185°F.; on standing, the temperature will rise to 185°F. to 190°F. Always tent bird with foil to help hold in heat.

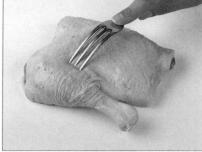

COOKING POULTRY PIECES

Poultry skin is high in calories and cholesterol. Replacing it with melted butter or margarine and a crumb coating is healthier, helps keep poultry moist, and improves its appearance. If you like, use a rack underneath the pieces to keep them free of pan juices.

Loosely cover microwaved crumb-coated poultry with waxed paper, otherwise the crumbs will become soggy. For the best result, cook poultry pieces of about the same size – pieces of different densities cook unevenly.

Arrange meatier portions toward the edges of the dish and bonier parts toward the center, rearranging halfway through cooking. Overcooking of boneless chicken breasts can be prevented by tucking thin ends under so that breasts cook evenly.

COOKING DUCKLINGS

The microwave is ideal for turning out delicious duck. Before microwaving, pierce the skin of the duckling in many places to allow fat to drain and to prevent the skin from splitting during cooking.

Place pieces on a rack in baking dish to allow excess fat to drain off; turn frequently during cooking.

Leg quarters are cooked longer than breast quarters. Baste with a coating during cooking or serve with a sauce when finished.

Browning Chicken

Small poultry pieces do not look the same cooked in the microwave as they do when roasted conventionally. One reason is because microwave cooking times are so quick the bird's fat doesn't have time to get hot enough to caramelize, which is the way conventionally cooked poultry becomes crisp and brown on the surface.

Another reason poultry pieces don't brown is because all the fat is just below the skin's surface, unlike with some meat, which is marbled with fat throughout. Larger birds, however, do brown because of their prolonged cooking time.

Great-tasting microwaved poultry sometimes needs an assist to make it look its best. Here, we show you how to use browning agents and other store-bought products such as sauces and dry coatings to add color to microwaved poultry pieces; we also give instructions on browning chicken under a conventional broiler, and on a microwave browning dish.

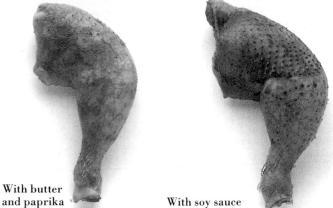

With honey and parsley glaze | With seasoned bread crumbs | With butter and paprika | With soy sauce

---

BROWNING CONVENTIONALLY AND WITH BROWNING DISH

Microwaved chicken pieces can be finished in a conventional oven or under a broiler for a few minutes until the skin browns and crisps.

Using a microwave browning dish to cook small poultry pieces is another way to brown and crisp the surface. The dish is preheated to a high temperature and a small amount of fat melted on it. Uncooked pieces are then placed on the dish, and the combination of high temperature and hot fat gives the food a crisp, brown finish.

Using a browning dish

Microwaved and broiler-finished chicken pieces

These chicken pieces have been cooked in the microwave. Although completely cooked, they still look pale because there was insufficient time for the surfaces to brown.

After microwaving, place chicken pieces on broiler pan and brown under preheated broiler until skin is crisp and colored. Turn pieces over halfway through broiling.

Preheat browning dish as manufacturer directs; this heats up a concealed metal plate. When hot, add butter, margarine, or oil as recipe directs. *Do not touch dish.*

When butter or margarine is melted or oil is hot, add chicken piece, skin side down, pressing lightly with tongs or spatula. Cook as recipe directs, until underneath is browned.

With tongs, carefully turn chicken piece over. Continue cooking as recipe directs, until other side is browned and juices run clear. If cooking in batches, it may be necessary to reheat dish.

SAUCES

Adding extra color to poultry pieces is easy to do by coating the skin with sauces. Thin liquid preparations such as soy, teriyaki, and browning sauces are best diluted with a little water, oil, or melted butter, then they are lightly rubbed into the skin of the chicken with your fingers. Thicker, stickier sauces, such as barbecue sauce and honey-based mixtures, jellies, and glazes are applied with a pastry brush.

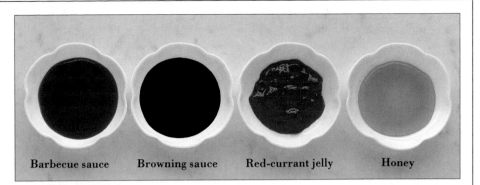

Barbecue sauce   Browning sauce   Red-currant jelly   Honey

Rubbing in sauce

Dilute soy or browning sauce with a little water, oil, or melted butter to make spreading easier and to soften the flavor.

Before cooking, place chicken on plate or board; dip fingers into diluted sauce and gently rub into skin, covering surface completely.

Brushing with honey and lemon

Into honey, stir chopped herbs. Squeeze in lemon juice. Heat on High (100% power) 30 seconds, to make glaze easier to apply.

Begin cooking chicken according to recipe. Shortly before end of cooking, brush with glaze; if applied too early, honey in glaze may burn.

DRY PREPARATIONS

Adding dry preparations before cooking enhances chicken pieces with extra color and texture. The pieces can be brushed with melted butter or margarine, or oil, and then sprinkled with powders or with dry microwave browning mixtures. Prepared coating mixes or bread crumbs are applied after first dipping chicken pieces into beaten egg or milk. If you like, drizzle with melted butter.

Seasoned bread crumbs   Prepared coating mix   Paprika   Microwave browning

Coating with crumbs

With tongs, dip chicken into slightly beaten egg or milk, coating evenly; shake off any excess.

In another dish, place seasoned bread crumbs or prepared coating mix. Pat evenly onto chicken.

Sprinkling on powders

With pastry brush, lightly brush chicken with melted butter or margarine, or oil, to help powder stick to skin.

With chicken on plate, lightly sprinkle with powder. Here we use paprika for a colorful finish.

Cut-up Chicken

COQ AU VIN

Color Index page 56. 404 cals per serving. Good source of vitamin A, riboflavin, niacin, iron. Begin 55 minutes ahead.

Ingredients	For 4	For 2	For 1
Salt pork, diced	4 ounces	2 ounces	1 ounce
Carrots, diced	2 carrots	1 carrot	½ carrot
Mushrooms, cut into quarters	8 ounces	4 ounces	2 ounces
Chicken, cut up and skinned	1 2½-pound broiler-fryer	1 pound chicken	½ pound chicken
Frozen pearl onions, thawed	1 cup	½ cup	¼ cup
Crushed tomatoes, canned	½ cup	¼ cup	2 tablespoons
Dry red wine	1 cup	½ cup	¼ cup
Thyme leaves	¾ teaspoon	½ teaspoon	¼ teaspoon
Pepper	to taste	to taste	to taste
Cold butter, diced	3 tablespoons	2 tablespoons	1 tablespoon
Microwave cookware	13" by 9" baking dish	12" by 8" baking dish	8" by 8" baking dish
Time on High (100% power)			
Salt pork	4 minutes	3 minutes	2 minutes
With vegetables	3 minutes	2 minutes	2 minutes
With chicken	15 to 20 minutes	10 to 12 minutes	8 minutes

1 In baking dish (see Chart), place salt pork. Cook, covered with paper towels, on High for time in Chart, or until crisp, stirring twice.

2 With spoon, discard excess fat from baking dish.

3 To salt pork, add carrots and mushrooms. Cook on High for time in Chart, or until tender, stirring halfway through cooking.

4 To baking dish, add chicken, arranging in a single layer over salt pork and vegetables.

5 To chicken, add pearl onions, tomatoes, wine, and thyme leaves. Cook, covered, on High for time in Chart, or until chicken juices run clear, rearranging pieces halfway through cooking.

6 Remove chicken to warmed dish. Let stand, covered, while finishing sauce. Add pepper to sauce, then gradually whisk in cold butter until well blended. Spoon over chicken.

CHICKEN PAPRIKASH

Color Index page 56. 4 servings. 468 cals per serving. Good source of vitamin A, niacin, vitamin C, iron. Begin 35 minutes ahead.

4 tablespoons butter or margarine (½ stick)	1 tablespoon paprika
2 medium onions, sliced	2 tablespoons tomato paste
1 medium red pepper, thinly sliced	1 chicken-flavor bouillon cube or envelope
2 tablespoons all-purpose flour	¼ cup water
1 14½- to 16-ounce can tomatoes	1 2½-pound broiler-fryer, cut up
	Chives for garnish

1. In shallow 2½-quart microwave-safe casserole, place butter or margarine, onions, and red pepper. Cook, covered, on High (100% power) 6 to 7 minutes, until tender-crisp, stirring twice.

2. Into onion-pepper mixture, stir flour. Add tomatoes with liquid, and next 4 ingredients. Add chicken, arranging thicker, meatier pieces toward edge. Over chicken, spoon tomato sauce. Cook, covered, on High 18 to 20 minutes, until juices run clear, rearranging pieces halfway through cooking. Skim fat. Let stand 5 minutes; garnish.

LEMON CHICKEN

Color Index page 56. 4 servings. 355 cals per serving. Good source of niacin, iron. Begin 45 minutes ahead.

1 large lemon	1 tablespoon cornstarch dissolved in 2 table-spoons cold water
½ 2-ounce jar pimentos	
3 tablespoons olive or salad oil	Salt to taste
1 garlic clove, minced	½ cup Melba-toast Crumbs (page 196) or corn-flake crumbs
1 teaspoon basil	
¼ teaspoon pepper	
1 3-pound broiler-fryer, cut up and skinned	Lemon Twists (page 132) and parsley sprigs for garnish
½ cup Chicken Broth (page 125) or canned broth	

1. With vegetable peeler, remove peel from lemon; chop finely. Squeeze ¼ cup juice from lemon. Thinly dice pimentos.

2. In 2½-quart microwave-safe casserole, combine lemon juice, 2 tablespoons oil, garlic, pimentos, basil, and pepper. Add chicken pieces; stir to coat. Arrange chicken so that thicker, meatier pieces are toward edge of casserole. Add broth. Cook, covered, on High (100% power) 15 to 18 minutes, until juices run clear, rearranging pieces occasionally. Stir in dissolved cornstarch. Cook on High 3 minutes, or until slightly thickened. Season with salt.

3. In small bowl, combine remaining oil, crumbs, and 1 teaspoon lemon peel. (Freeze remaining peel for use in cakes or cookies.) Sprinkle over chicken. Cook on High 2 minutes. Let stand 5 minutes; garnish.

CHICKEN CACCIATORE

Color Index page 56. 4 servings. 560 cals per serving. Good source of thiamine, niacin, vitamin C, calcium, iron. Begin 45 minutes ahead.

2 tablespoons olive or salad oil	½ 15-ounce jar spaghetti sauce
2 medium onions, chopped	½ cup Chicken Broth (page 125) or canned broth
1 medium green pepper, chopped	1 2½-pound broiler-fryer, cut up and skinned
2 garlic cloves, minced	
1 tablespoon prepared pesto or 2 tablespoons dried basil	Salt and pepper to taste
½ teaspoon oregano	1 8-ounce package spaghetti
½ cup pitted green olives, sliced	Basil leaves for garnish

1. In 2½-quart microwave-safe casserole, combine oil, onions, green pepper, garlic, pesto or basil, and oregano. Cook on High (100% power) 3 to 5 minutes, until onions and green pepper are slightly softened, stirring twice. Into onion mixture, stir olives, spaghetti sauce, and broth.
2. To casserole, add chicken, arranging thicker, meatier pieces toward edge. Cook, covered, on High 18 to 20 minutes, until chicken juices run clear, rearranging pieces halfway through cooking.
3. Meanwhile, cook spaghetti conventionally as label directs. Drain.
4. *To serve*: Skim fat from chicken. Season with salt and pepper; let stand 5 minutes. Arrange spaghetti and chicken on warmed dinner plates. Spoon sauce over chicken and garnish.

CAJUN CRUMB CHICKEN

Color Index page 55. 4 servings. 277 cals per serving. Good source of niacin, iron. Begin 25 minutes ahead.

2 tablespoons Dijon mustard	½ teaspoon celery salt
1 tablespoon honey	¼ teaspoon salt
1 tablespoon tomato paste	Ground red pepper to taste
½ cup corn-flake crumbs	1 2½-pound broiler-fryer, cut up and skinned
½ teaspoon poultry seasoning	
½ teaspoon paprika	Cucumber, lime, and salad for garnish

1. In small bowl, combine Dijon mustard, honey, and tomato paste. On waxed paper, combine corn-flake crumbs and next 5 ingredients.
2. Coat chicken pieces, one at a time, in mustard-honey mixture, then roll in seasoned corn-flake crumbs.
3. In 13" by 9" microwave-safe baking dish, arrange chicken so that thicker, meatier pieces are toward edges. Cook, covered loosely with waxed paper, on High (100% power) 11 to 13 minutes, until chicken juices run clear, rearranging pieces once. Let stand on heat-safe surface 5 minutes before serving. Garnish.

Our recipes using cut-up whole chickens are also suitable for pieces of your choice — breasts, drumsticks, or thighs — as long as their weight equals that of the chicken called for in the recipe.

CHICKEN MARENGO

Color Index page 56. 524 cals per serving. Good source of riboflavin, niacin, iron. Begin 45 minutes ahead.

Ingredients for 4 servings		Microwave cookware
3 tablespoons olive or salad oil	1 7½-ounce can crushed tomatoes	13" by 9" baking dish
2 medium onions, chopped	¼ cup chopped parsley	
½ pound mushrooms, sliced	½ 10-ounce package frozen cooked baby shrimp, thawed	
½ teaspoon rosemary	Parsley sprigs for garnish	
1 2¾-pound broiler-fryer, cut up	Hot Cooked Rice (page 293, optional)	
½ cup all-purpose flour		
¼ teaspoon salt		
Pepper to taste		
1 cup dry white wine		

1 In 12" skillet, over medium-high heat, heat 1 tablespoon oil. Add onions, mushrooms, and rosemary. Cook until onions are golden, stirring occasionally. With slotted spoon, remove onion-mushroom mixture to baking dish.

2 Rinse chicken under running cold water. Pat dry with paper towels. On waxed paper, combine flour, salt, and pepper. Coat chicken pieces in seasoned flour.

3 In same skillet, heat remaining oil. Add chicken and cook 5 minutes, or until browned on all sides. On top of onion-mushroom mixture in baking dish, arrange chicken so that thicker, meatier pieces are toward edges.

4 Discard oil from skillet. Pour in white wine. Over medium heat, stir to loosen any browned pieces. Add tomatoes and parsley. Cook until mixture boils, stirring occasionally. Pour mixture over chicken pieces.

5 Cook chicken, covered, on High (100% power) 10 to 12 minutes, until juices run clear, rearranging pieces halfway through cooking. Add shrimp. Spoon over cooking liquid. Cook on High 1 to 2 minutes, just until shrimp are hot.

6 *To serve*: Arrange chicken and shrimp on warmed serving dish or platter. Spoon sauce over and garnish with parsley. If you like, serve with rice.

Meal in Minutes *for 6 people*

French Bistro Dinner

French Onion Soup Gratiné, page 131
Coq au Vin, page 182, for 6
Tossed mixed salad
French bread
Bakery French apple tart
Coffee or Espresso, page 130

PREPARATION TIMETABLE

Early in day or 2 hours ahead:	*Prepare soup through step 2; cover and refrigerate. Prepare salad ingredients; store in plastic bags in refrigerator. Prepare salad dressing of your choice.*
1 hour ahead:	*Prepare Coq au Vin; keep warm. If you like, transfer to warmed casserole dish with cover.*
15 minutes ahead:	*Ladle soup into microwave-safe bowls. Heat on High (100% power) until bubbling; complete recipe. Toss salad ingredients in bowl with dressing.*
Just before serving:	*If you like, heat French bread on High 1 minute. Heat bakery French apple tart on High 2 minutes. Prepare coffee or Espresso to serve with or after French apple tart.*

Cut-up Chicken

HONEY-SOY CHICKEN

Color Index page 55. 4 servings. 530 cals per serving. Good source of vitamin A, niacin, vitamin C, iron. Begin 25 minutes ahead.

1 3-pound broiler-fryer, cut up	*1 large carrot, thinly sliced*
¼ cup honey	*1 15-ounce can straw*
¼ teaspoon ground ginger	*mushrooms or 1 6-ounce can whole*
1 garlic clove, minced	*mushrooms, drained*
2 tablespoons soy sauce	*1 tablespoon sesame or*
2 tablespoons water	*salad oil*
½ pound fresh or 1 6-ounce package frozen Chinese pea pods	*1 tablespoon sesame seeds*
	Coriander for garnish

1. In 12″ by 8″ microwave-safe baking dish, arrange chicken so that thicker, meatier pieces are toward edges. Combine honey, ginger, garlic, and 1 tablespoon soy sauce; brush half over chicken. Cook, covered loosely with waxed paper, on High (100% power) 13 to 15 minutes, until chicken juices run clear, rearranging pieces once. Brush pieces with remaining mixture. Let stand, covered, while preparing vegetables.
2. In large microwave-safe bowl, place water, pea pods, and carrot. Cook, covered, on High 4 minutes; drain. Stir in mushrooms, oil, sesame seeds, and remaining soy sauce. Cook on High 1 to 1½ (1:30) minutes, until hot. Arrange chicken and vegetable mixture on warmed serving platter; garnish with coriander.

QUICK CHICKEN STEW

Color Index page 56. 4 servings. 597 cals per serving. Good source of vitamin A, niacin, vitamin C, iron. Begin 45 minutes ahead.

3 medium potatoes (about 1 pound)	*½ teaspoon thyme leaves*
3 medium carrots	*½ teaspoon salt*
1 10¾-ounce can condensed chicken broth, undiluted	*¼ teaspoon pepper*
	3 tablespoons all-purpose flour
1 small onion, chopped	*1 9-ounce package frozen cut green beans*
1 2½-pound broiler-fryer, cut up	*Chopped thyme or dill sprigs for garnish*

1. Cut potatoes into 1-inch chunks; cut carrots lengthwise into quarters, then crosswise into 2-inch pieces. In 4-quart microwave-safe casserole, combine potatoes, carrots, onion, and broth, reserving ⅓ cup. Place chicken on top so that thicker, meatier pieces are toward edge; sprinkle with thyme, salt, and pepper. Cook, covered, on High (100% power) 18 minutes, stirring occasionally.
2. Into reserved broth, stir flour until well blended; add to chicken mixture with frozen green beans; stir well. Cook, covered, on High 8 to 10 minutes, until chicken and vegetables are tender, stirring once. Let stand on heat-safe surface 5 minutes. Spoon stew into warmed serving plates and garnish.

Chicken Breasts

CHICKEN FRICASSEE *

Color Index page 57. 4 servings. 455 cals per serving. Good source of vitamin A, riboflavin, niacin, calcium, iron. Begin 55 minutes ahead.

4 tablespoons butter or margarine (½ stick)	4 chicken-breast halves, skinned and boned (about 1 pound)
1 medium onion, chopped	½ 10-ounce package each: frozen peas, baby carrots, and French-cut green beans, thawed
½ teaspoon poultry seasoning	
4 tablespoons all-purpose flour	2 egg yolks
3 cups milk	Salt and pepper to taste

1. In 2-quart microwave-safe casserole, place butter or margarine. Heat, covered with paper towel, on High (100% power) 45 seconds to 1 minute, until melted. Add onion and poultry seasoning. Cook on High 2 to 3 minutes, until onion is softened.
2. Into onion, stir flour. Cook on High 1 minute. Gradually stir in milk until smooth. Cook on High 10 to 12 minutes, until thickened, stirring often.
3. Cut chicken into 1½-inch chunks. Add to sauce with vegetables. Cook on High 10 to 12 minutes, until juices run clear, stirring twice.
4. In small bowl, lightly beat egg yolks. Stir in ½ cup cooking liquid until smooth. Return to chicken and vegetables; stir. Cook on Medium (50% power) 3 minutes, or just until thickened, stirring twice; season. Let stand, covered, 5 minutes.

HERB-AND-CHEESE CHICKEN BREASTS

Color Index page 57. 8 servings. 548 cals per serving. Good source of vitamin A, niacin, vitamin C, iron. Begin 35 minutes ahead.

1 8-ounce package cream cheese, softened	1 teaspoon paprika
2 tablespoons milk	2 tablespoons butter or margarine (¼ stick), melted
2 green onions, minced	
2 tablespoons minced parsley	1 head chicory
½ teaspoon thyme leaves	2 10-ounce packages frozen asparagus, cooked
Salt and pepper to taste	
1 garlic clove, crushed	1 pint cherry tomatoes
4 whole chicken breasts, boned and cut in half	½ cup oil-and-vinegar dressing
⅓ cup dried bread crumbs	

1. In bowl, combine first 8 ingredients.
2. Push fingers between skin and meat of each chicken breast to form a pocket. Spread an equal amount of cream-cheese mixture in each pocket.
3. On waxed paper, combine bread crumbs and paprika. Into melted butter, dip chicken breasts, then roll in seasoned bread crumbs to coat.
4. In 13" by 9" microwave-safe baking dish, place chicken. Cook, covered loosely with waxed paper, on High (100% power) 15 minutes, or until fork-tender, rotating dish halfway through cooking.
5. Arrange chicken, chicory, asparagus, and tomatoes on platter. Pass dressing separately.

POACHED CHICKEN with VEGETABLES

Color Index page 57. 324 cals per serving. Good source of niacin, iron. Begin 40 minutes ahead.

Ingredients	For 4	For 2	For 1
Butter or margarine	2 tablespoons	1 tablespoon	1½ teaspoons
Italian salad dressing	¼ cup	2 tablespoons	1 tablespoon
Leeks, sliced	4 small leeks	2 small leeks	1 small leek
Mushrooms, cut in half	4 ounces	2 ounces	1 ounce
1 9-ounce package frozen artichoke hearts, thawed	1 package	½ package	¼ package
Chicken Broth (page 125) or canned broth	1 cup broth	½ cup broth	¼ cup broth
Chicken breasts, skinned and boned	2 whole chicken breasts	1 whole chicken breast	1 chicken-breast half
Cornstarch	1 tablespoon	1½ teaspoons	¾ teaspoon
Cold water	2 tablespoons	1 tablespoon	1 teaspoon
Salt and pepper	to taste	to taste	to taste
Microwave cookware	13" by 9" baking dish	12" by 8" baking dish	8" by 8" baking dish
Time on High (100% power) Vegetable mixture	4 to 5 minutes	3 minutes	2 minutes
With chicken	8 to 10 minutes	5 to 6 minutes	3 to 4 minutes
With cornstarch	3 minutes	2 to 3 minutes	1 to 2 minutes

1 In baking dish (see Chart), place butter or margarine, salad dressing, leeks, mushrooms, and artichoke hearts. Cook on High for time in Chart, or until vegetables are softened, stirring twice.

2 Into vegetable mixture, stir broth. Arrange chicken breasts with thicker, meatier pieces toward edges of dish.

3 Cook chicken, covered, on High for time in Chart, turning chicken over halfway through cooking.

4 To test for doneness, pierce chicken breasts with a fork. Chicken is done when juices run clear.

5 With slotted pancake turner, carefully remove chicken breasts to warmed serving platter. Let stand, covered, while finishing sauce. Dissolve cornstarch in water. Pour into baking dish; stir until well blended. Cook mixture on High for time in Chart, or until thickened. Season to taste with salt and pepper.

6 To serve: Spoon vegetables and sauce over chicken breasts.

Chicken Breasts

Stuffed chicken breasts are extremely versatile, and any number of different fillings are suitable. They can be prepared well in advance and kept refrigerated until ready for cooking. The breasts should be pounded until thin, and then folded over the filling with the thinner ends tucked under. Use wooden toothpicks to hold in the filling if necessary.

BROCCOLI-STUFFED CHICKEN BREASTS

Color Index page 57. 341 cals per serving. Good source of vitamin A, niacin, vitamin C, calcium, iron. Begin 45 minutes ahead.

Ingredients for 6 servings		Microwave cookware
1 10-ounce package frozen chopped broccoli, cooked	1 cup fresh bread crumbs	13″ by 9″ baking dish
2 green onions, minced	1 tablespoon minced parsley	Medium bowl
4 ounces Monterey Jack cheese, shredded (1 cup)	½ teaspoon paprika	
3 whole large chicken breasts, skinned, boned, and cut in half	3 tablespoons butter or margarine, melted	
3 1-ounce slices cooked ham, cut in half	1 tablespoon all-purpose flour	
	¼ teaspoon salt	
	⅛ teaspoon pepper	
	1 cup milk	
	Parsley sprigs for garnish	

1 Drain broccoli well. Place in large bowl. To broccoli, add green onions and half the shredded cheese; mix.

2 Pound each chicken-breast half to ¼-inch thickness. Top each with 1 piece ham and an equal amount of broccoli mixture.

3 Carefully fold chicken in half over broccoli filling; neatly tuck ends under.

4 In pie plate or on waxed paper, combine bread crumbs, parsley, and paprika. Brush chicken with melted butter or margarine, using about 1 tablespoon. Coat chicken with seasoned bread crumbs.

5 In baking dish, place chicken. Cook, covered loosely with waxed paper, on High (100% power) 10 to 12 minutes, until fork-tender, rotating dish once. Arrange chicken on warmed dinner plates or platter. Let stand, covered, while preparing sauce.

6 In bowl, place remaining melted butter or margarine. Add flour, salt, and pepper; mix well. Gradually stir in milk. Cook on High 3½ (3:30) minutes, or until boiling, stirring twice. Add remaining cheese, stirring until melted. Spoon sauce around chicken. Garnish.

CHICKEN KIEV

Color Index page 56. 4 servings. 359 cals per serving. Good source of niacin. Begin 35 minutes ahead.

2 whole large chicken breasts, skinned, boned, and cut in half
Salt and pepper to taste
½ stick chilled butter, cut lengthwise into quarters

2 tablespoons butter or margarine (¼ stick)
1 egg yolk
½ cup dried bread crumbs
2 garlic cloves, minced
2 tablespoons chopped parsley
½ teaspoon paprika

1. On cutting board, with dull edge of French knife or smooth edge of meat mallet, pound each chicken-breast half to ¼-inch thickness. Season with salt and pepper. Place a quarter-piece of butter lengthwise in center of each chicken-breast half. Fold ends over butter; roll up jelly-roll fashion so that butter is enclosed. Secure with toothpicks if necessary. Freeze 30 minutes; remove toothpicks.
2. In small microwave-safe bowl, place 2 tablespoons butter or margarine. Heat, covered with paper towel, on High (100% power) 45 seconds, or until melted. Stir in egg yolk. On waxed paper, combine bread crumbs, garlic, parsley, and paprika. Dip chicken pieces into egg mixture, then coat with bread-crumb mixture.
3. In 12″ by 8″ microwave-safe baking dish, place chicken, at least 1 inch apart. Cook, covered loosely with waxed paper, on High 8 to 9 minutes, until fork-tender, rotating dish once. Let stand 4 minutes before serving.

TO MAKE CHICKEN KIEV FOR TWO, USE:
1 whole chicken breast, ¼ stick chilled butter, 1 tablespoon butter or margarine, 1 egg yolk, ¼ cup bread crumbs, 1 minced garlic clove, 1 tablespoon chopped parsley, and ¼ teaspoon paprika. Prepare as above, melting butter or margarine on High 30 to 45 seconds and cooking chicken, covered loosely with waxed paper, in 8″ by 8″ baking dish on High 6 to 7 minutes. Let chicken stand 5 minutes.

Preparing the Butter and Chicken Breasts

Chill butter thoroughly before use. With sharp knife, cut butter lengthwise into quarters.

With dull edge of French knife or smooth edge of meat mallet, pound chicken-breast halves to ¼-inch thickness.

HONEY-PECAN CHICKEN

Color Index page 58. 6 servings. 335 cals per serving. Good source of niacin. Begin 35 minutes ahead.

1¼ cups cranberries	2 tablespoons grated
½ cup orange juice	orange peel
3 tablespoons sugar	3 whole medium chicken
3 tablespoons red-port	breasts, skinned,
wine	boned, and cut in half
1⅛ teaspoons salt	⅓ cup honey
¾ cup pecans, finely	1 tablespoon Orange
chopped	Julienne (page 334)
¼ cup dried bread	Parsley sprigs for
crumbs	garnish

1. In 4-cup microwave-safe glass measure, place 1 cup cranberries, orange juice, sugar, port wine, and ⅛ teaspoon salt. Cook on High (100% power) 4 to 6 minutes, until cranberries begin to pop, stirring twice. In food processor with knife blade attached or in blender, process cranberry mixture until smooth. Over medium microwave-safe bowl, set sieve. Press mixture through sieve to remove skins and seeds; reserve mixture.

2. On waxed paper, mix pecans, bread crumbs, orange peel, and remaining salt. Brush chicken with honey; coat with pecan mixture. Arrange in 13″ by 9″ microwave-safe baking dish. Cook, covered loosely with waxed paper, on High 10 minutes, or until fork-tender, rotating dish once.

3. To reserved cranberry mixture, add Orange Julienne, and remaining cranberries. Cook on High 2 to 3 minutes; serve with chicken; garnish.

CREAMY CHICKEN BREASTS

Color Index page 55. 4 servings. 442 cals per serving. Good source of vitamin A, niacin. Begin 25 minutes ahead.

2 tablespoons butter or	2 tablespoons all-
margarine (¼ stick)	purpose flour
3 green onions, sliced	¼ teaspoon mild curry
½ pound asparagus,	powder
trimmed and cut into	Salt and pepper to taste
1-inch pieces	1 cup heavy or whipping
2 whole large chicken	cream
breasts, skinned,	
boned, and cut in half	

1. In 12″ by 8″ microwave-safe baking dish, place butter or margarine. Heat, covered with paper towels, on High (100% power) 45 seconds, or until melted. Stir in green onions and asparagus. Place chicken breasts on top, with thicker, meatier parts toward edges of dish. Cook on High 5 to 7 minutes, just until chicken turns opaque. Remove chicken to plate; cover and keep warm.

2. In small bowl, combine flour, curry powder, salt, and pepper. Add to vegetables; stir until blended. Cook on High 1 minute. Gradually stir in cream until smooth. Cook on High 4 to 5 minutes, until sauce thickens.

3. Return chicken to dish; spoon sauce over. Cook on High 1 to 2 minutes, until juices run clear.

A crumbed coating helps keep skinned chicken moist and tender during cooking as well as making it more attractive. Because chicken breasts vary in density, they should be flattened uniformly so that they cook more evenly in the microwave. To help prevent chicken from sticking to the knife or meat mallet when pounding, place it between 2 sheets of waxed paper.

CHICKEN BREASTS PARMESAN

Color Index page 57. 381 cals per serving. Good source of vitamin D, niacin, calcium, iron. Begin 35 minutes ahead.

Ingredients for 4 servings		Microwave cookware
2 whole medium chicken breasts, skinned, boned, and cut in half	1 large onion, chopped	Medium bowl
3 tablespoons butter or margarine	1 garlic clove, minced	13″ by 9″ baking dish
1 egg	1 14½- to 16-ounce can crushed tomatoes	
⅓ cup seasoned dried bread crumbs	½ cup pitted ripe olives, sliced	
½ cup grated Parmesan cheese	⅓ cup packed basil leaves, cut into strips	
½ teaspoon oregano	½ teaspoon salt	
½ teaspoon paprika	Pepper to taste	
	Basil leaves for garnish	

1 Cut each chicken-breast half crosswise in half. With dull edge of French knife or smooth edge of meat mallet, pound each chicken cutlet to ¼-inch thickness.

2 In medium bowl, place 2 tablespoons butter or margarine. Heat, covered with paper towel, on High (100% power) 45 seconds, or until melted. Let cool slightly; beat in egg.

3 On waxed paper, combine bread crumbs, Parmesan cheese, oregano, and paprika. Dip chicken cutlets in butter mixture, then coat in seasoned bread crumbs.

4 In baking dish, place chicken. Cook, covered loosely with waxed paper, on High 6 to 8 minutes, or until fork-tender, rearranging chicken halfway through cooking. Let stand, covered, while preparing sauce.

5 In bowl used to melt butter or margarine, place remaining butter or margarine, onion, and garlic. Cook on High 4 minutes, stirring halfway through cooking. Add tomatoes, olives, basil, salt, and pepper.

6 Cook sauce on High 2 to 3 minutes, until hot, stirring to combine. Serve chicken with sauce. Garnish with basil leaves.

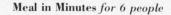

Meal in Minutes *for 6 people*

Tailgate Picnic

Potato chips and pretzels
Corn Chowder, page 133 (omit accompaniments)
Deviled Chicken, right (double quantity)
Garden Vegetables and Pasta Salad, page 280
Bakery muffins, bakery pecan pie
Apples and pears

PREPARATION TIMETABLE

1 day ahead:	*Prepare Deviled Chicken in batches. Cover, let cool, and pack in paper-towel-lined portable container; refrigerate. Prepare Corn Chowder; cover and refrigerate. Cook vegetables for salad; cover and refrigerate. Pack plates, napkins, cutlery, and cups. Wrap fruit, and pack potato chips and pretzels.*
Early in day:	*For salad, cook pasta conventionally as label directs; toss with vegetables and dressing and pack in portable container. Pack pecan pie and muffins in airtight containers.*
Just before leaving:	*Reheat Corn Chowder in microwave on Medium-High (70% power) 5 minutes until bubbling. Pour into wide-mouth thermos and seal tightly.*

Chicken Pieces

DEVILED CHICKEN

Color Index page 55. 4 servings. 293 cals per serving. Good source of riboflavin, niacin, iron. Begin 25 minutes ahead.

2 tablespoons mayonnaise	$\frac{1}{2}$ teaspoon salt
2 tablespoons prepared mustard	$\frac{1}{8}$ teaspoon garlic powder
$\frac{1}{2}$ cup corn-flake crumbs	$2\frac{1}{2}$ pounds chicken drumsticks and/or
1 tablespoon minced parsley	thighs, skinned
$\frac{1}{8}$ teaspoon ground red pepper	Lemon wedges and parsley for garnish

1. In small bowl, combine mayonnaise and mustard. On waxed paper, combine corn-flake crumbs, parsley, ground red pepper, salt, and garlic powder.

2. Brush chicken pieces with mayonnaise mixture, then coat with crumb mixture.

3. In 13″ by 9″ microwave-safe baking dish, place chicken so that thicker, meatier pieces are toward edges. Cook, covered with waxed paper, on High (100% power) 11 to 13 minutes, until chicken juices run clear, rearranging once. Let stand on heat-safe surface 3 minutes.

4. *To serve:* Arrange chicken pieces on warmed serving platter and garnish with lemon wedges and parsley sprigs.

"BARBECUED" CHICKEN

Color Index page 55. 4 servings. 386 cals per serving. Good source of niacin, vitamin C, iron. Begin 25 minutes ahead.

2 medium onions, thinly sliced	2 teaspoons Worcestershire
1 green pepper, cut into matchstick-thin strips	1 teaspoon chili powder
1 garlic clove, minced	$\frac{1}{2}$ teaspoon salt
$\frac{2}{3}$ cup catchup	8 medium chicken thighs
2 tablespoons brown sugar	(about 2 pounds) Parsley sprigs for garnish

1. Prepare barbecue sauce: In medium microwave-safe bowl, place onions, green pepper, garlic, catchup, brown sugar, Worcestershire, chili powder, and salt. Cook, covered, on High (100% power) 8 to 10 minutes, until vegetables are tender, stirring twice; cover and set aside.

2. In 12″ by 8″ microwave-safe baking dish, arrange chicken thighs in single layer so that thicker, meatier pieces are toward edges. Cook, covered, on High 10 minutes, rearranging once. Discard drippings.

3. Over chicken, spoon barbecue sauce. Cook on High 6 to 8 minutes, until chicken juices run clear, rearranging once.

4. *To serve:* Arrange chicken thighs on warmed dinner plates. Garnish with parsley.

Cooked Chicken

CURRIED CHICKEN THIGHS

Color Index page 59. 4 servings. 233 cals per serving. Good source of niacin, calcium. Begin 1 day ahead.

1 cup plain yogurt	*½ cup dried bread*
2 teaspoons curry	*crumbs*
powder	*½ teaspoon salt*
2 garlic cloves, minced	*2 tablespoons salad oil*
1 tablespoon minced	*Salt and pepper to taste*
coriander, basil, or	*Lime wedges and mint*
parsley leaves	*sprigs for garnish*
4 chicken thighs,	
skinned	

1. In large microwave-safe bowl, combine yogurt, curry powder, garlic, and coriander, basil, or parsley. To mixture, add chicken thighs; stir to coat. Cover and refrigerate 12 to 24 hours.
2. Thirty minutes before serving, on waxed paper, mix crumbs and salt. Remove thighs from marinade; set marinade aside. Coat chicken with crumbs.
3. Preheat browning dish as manufacturer directs. Brush with oil. On dish, arrange thighs spoke-fashion. Cook on High (100% power) 5 minutes. With spatula, turn chicken over. Cook on High 5 to 7 minutes, until juices run clear. Let stand on heat-safe surface while preparing sauce.
4. Cook reserved marinade on Medium (50% power) 3 to 4 minutes, until hot, stirring halfway through cooking. Season. Spoon sauce onto warmed dinner plates; arrange chicken on top; garnish.

CHICKEN LIVERS WITH TOMATO SAUCE

Color Index page 55. 4 servings. 219 cals per serving. Good source of vitamin A, riboflavin, niacin, vitamin C, iron. Begin 25 minutes ahead.

2 tablespoons butter or	*1 medium onion, minced*
margarine (¼ stick)	*2 tablespoons steak*
1 pound chicken livers,	*sauce*
cut in half	*½ teaspoon oregano*
½ 7½-ounce can	*½ teaspoon thyme leaves*
crushed tomatoes	*Parsley for garnish*
¼ cup Beef Broth (page	
125) or canned broth	

1. In 12″ by 8″ microwave-safe baking dish, place butter or margarine. Heat, covered with paper towels, on High (100% power) 45 seconds, or until melted. Pierce chicken livers. Add to dish; stir. Cook, covered with paper towels, on High 2 to 4 minutes, until livers lose raw appearance, stirring once. Remove livers; set aside.
2. To drippings in baking dish, add tomatoes, broth, onion, steak sauce, oregano, and thyme. Cook on High 10 minutes, or until flavors are blended and sauce thickens, stirring twice. Return chicken livers to baking dish. Cook on High 1 to 2 minutes, until hot.
3. Spoon livers and sauce onto warmed dinner plates; garnish.

Cooked chicken can be easily combined with other ingredients and ready to serve in a matter of minutes. For our Chicken à la King (below), you can use leftovers from any cooked whole chicken or pieces. Or, if you like, you can use our simple cooking method (page 178) for fresh chicken that adds only a few additional minutes cooking time.

CHICKEN À LA KING ✳

Color Index page 55. 568 cals per serving. Good source of niacin, calcium, iron. Begin 25 minutes ahead.

Ingredients for 4 servings		Microwave cookware
4 tablespoons butter or margarine (½ stick)	*1 cup milk*	4-cup glass measure
1 medium onion, minced	*2 cups cubed cooked chicken*	
1 small green pepper, minced	*1 pimento, diced*	
8 small mushrooms, cut into quarters	*2 egg yolks*	
¼ cup all-purpose flour	*1 tablespoon dry sherry (optional)*	
1 cup Chicken Broth (page 125) or canned broth	*Salt and pepper to taste*	
	4 patty shells, warmed	
	Dill sprigs for garnish	

1 In glass measure, place butter or margarine. Heat, covered with paper towel, on High (100% power) 45 seconds to 1 minute, until melted.

2 To melted butter or margarine, add onion, green pepper, and mushrooms; stir to coat. Cook on High 3 to 4 minutes, until onion softens slightly.

3 Into vegetable mixture, stir flour until blended. Cook on High 1 minute, stirring halfway through cooking. Gradually stir in broth and milk until smooth.

4 Cook sauce on High 4 to 6 minutes, until thickened, stirring twice. To sauce, add chicken and pimento. Cook on High 3 minutes, or until chicken is hot.

5 In small bowl, with whisk, beat egg yolks. Stir ¼ cup sauce from chicken into beaten egg yolks. Pour egg-yolk mixture back into remaining chicken mixture, beating rapidly to prevent lumping.

6 If you like, stir sherry into chicken mixture. Season with salt and pepper. Spoon chicken and sauce into warmed patty shells; garnish.

Cooked Chicken

CHICKEN CREPES FLORENTINE

Color Index page 58. 410 cals per serving. Good source of vitamin A, riboflavin, niacin, calcium, iron. Begin 55 minutes ahead.

Ingredients	For 4	For 2	For 1
Basic White Sauce (page 381)	2 cups sauce	1 cup sauce	½ cup sauce
Grated Parmesan cheese	⅓ cup	3 tablespoons	4 teaspoons
1 10-ounce package frozen chopped spinach, thawed	1 package spinach	½ package spinach	¼ package spinach
Garlic clove, minced	1 garlic clove	½ garlic clove	¼ garlic clove
Butter or margarine	1 tablespoon	1½ teaspoons	¾ teaspoon
Salt and pepper	to taste	to taste	to taste
Cooked chicken or turkey, cubed	2 cups	1 cup	½ cup
7-inch crepes (right)	8 crepes	4 crepes	2 crepes
Microwave cookware	13" by 9" baking dish	12" by 8" baking dish	8" by 8" baking dish
Time on High (100% power)			
Spinach mixture	3 to 5 minutes	3 minutes	2 minutes
Filled crepes with sauce	5 to 7 minutes	5 to 6 minutes	3 to 4 minutes

1 Prepare Basic White Sauce. (If making for 2 or 1, refrigerate leftover sauce to use another day.) Into sauce, stir Parmesan cheese. Onto surface of sauce, lightly press plastic wrap to prevent skin forming. Set aside and keep warm.

2 In baking dish (see Chart), place spinach, garlic, and butter or margarine. Cook, covered with paper towels, on High for time in Chart, or until flavors are blended, stirring twice. Season with salt and pepper.

3 Transfer spinach mixture to bowl. To spinach mixture, add chicken or turkey; stir to combine. Clean baking dish with paper towels.

4 Place 1 crepe at a time on work surface. Spoon an equal amount of spinach-chicken mixture onto each crepe.

5 Roll up each crepe jelly-roll fashion. In cleaned baking dish, place crepes seam side down, at least ¼-inch apart.

6 Pour sauce over filled crepes. Cook on High for time in Chart, or until bubbling. If you like and if dish is broiler-safe, brown under preheated broiler.

CHICKEN RATATOUILLE

Color Index page 58. 4 servings. 346 cals per serving. Good source of vitamin A, niacin, vitamin C, calcium, iron. Begin 40 minutes ahead.

2 tablespoons olive or salad oil	1 7½-ounce can crushed tomatoes, or ½ 15-ounce jar spaghetti sauce
2 garlic cloves, minced	
1 large onion, chopped	
1 medium green pepper, chopped	Salt and pepper to taste
2 yellow squash, cut into 1½-inch chunks	½ 8-ounce package mozzarella cheese, shredded (1 cup)
2 zucchini, cut into 1½-inch chunks	Parsley sprigs for garnish
1 teaspoon basil	
1 teaspoon oregano	
2 cups cubed cooked chicken	

1. In 13" by 9" microwave-safe baking dish, place oil, garlic, onion, green pepper, yellow squash, zucchini, basil, and oregano; stir to combine. Cook, covered, on High (100% power) 5 minutes. Uncover; stir. Cook on High 5 to 10 minutes longer, until vegetables are tender, stirring twice.

2. To vegetable mixture, add chicken and tomatoes or spaghetti sauce; stir to combine. Season with salt and pepper. Sprinkle with cheese. Cook on High 5 to 7 minutes, until cheese is melted and chicken is hot, rotating dish halfway through cooking.

3. If you like and if dish is broiler-safe, brown Chicken Ratatouille under preheated broiler until cheese is golden and bubbly. Serve hot on warmed dinner plates, or cover and refrigerate to serve chilled later. Just before serving, garnish with parsley sprigs.

MAKING AND FREEZING CREPES

In medium bowl, with whisk, beat **⅔ cup all-purpose flour**, **½ teaspoon salt** and **3 eggs** until smooth. Slowly beat in **1½ cups milk** and **1½ tablespoons melted butter or margarine**. Cover and refrigerate batter 2 hours. Brush bottom and side of 7" skillet with **melted butter**.

Over low heat, heat skillet; pour in scant ¼ cup batter. Tip pan to coat bottom. Over low heat, cook batter 3 minutes, or until crepe is set and underside browned. With spatula, turn crepe over and cook other side 1 minute, or until golden. Slip crepe onto waxed paper. Repeat with remaining batter, stacking with waxed paper between crepes.

Crepes can be stored in the freezer for up to 2 months: wrap stacked crepes tightly in foil; label and freeze. To use, preheat conventional oven to 325°F. Place wrapped, frozen crepes on cookie sheet and heat about 30 minutes until hot.

Cornish Hens

SAVORY STUFFED CORNISH HENS

Color Index page 57. 2 servings. 1017 cals per serving. Good source of vitamin A, thiamine, riboflavin, niacin, calcium, iron. Begin 45 minutes ahead.

¼ pound small mushrooms, sliced	1 cup cooked rice
2 tablespoons butter or margarine (¼ stick)	2 1¼-pound Cornish hens
1 small zucchini, shredded	¾ cup herb-seasoned croutons or stuffing mix, finely crushed
2 ounces Swiss cheese, shredded (½ cup)	1½ teaspoons paprika
1 green onion, chopped	Parsley sprigs and matchstick-thin strips of carrot and celery for garnish
¼ teaspoon salt	
⅛ teaspoon pepper	

1. In 1½-quart microwave-safe casserole, place mushrooms and 1 tablespoon butter or margarine. Cook on High (100% power) 2 to 2½ (2:30) minutes, stirring halfway through cooking. Into mushrooms, stir zucchini, cheese, green onion, salt, pepper, and cooked rice. Let cool.

2. Remove giblets and neck from inside each hen. Rinse hens under running cold water. Pat dry with paper towels. Fill each hen cavity with half the stuffing. Tie legs and tail of each hen with string. In small microwave-safe bowl, place remaining butter or margarine. Heat on High 30 to 45 seconds, until melted. Brush onto hens.

3. On waxed paper, combine crushed herb-seasoned croutons or stuffing mix and paprika; use to coat hens. On microwave-safe rack set in 12" by 8" microwave-safe baking dish, place hens. Cook, covered loosely with waxed paper, on High 14 to 16 minutes, until juices run clear when hens are pierced with a fork, rotating dish once. Let stand, covered, 5 minutes.

4. *To serve:* Remove string from hens. Arrange hens on warmed plates; garnish.

Tying and Brushing the Cornish Hens

Using white cotton string, tie legs and tail of each bird. This prevents stuffing from falling out and gives the bird a plump, attractive shape.

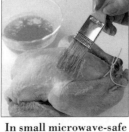

In small microwave-safe bowl, heat butter or margarine until melted. With small pastry brush, apply butter or margarine all over surface of hens. This helps coating to adhere to skin of birds.

SPLIT CORNISH HENS

Color Index page 57. 708 cals per serving. Good source of niacin, iron. Begin 55 minutes ahead.

Ingredients	For 4	For 2	For 1
Cornish hens (1¼ pounds each)	4 Cornish hens	2 Cornish hens	1 Cornish hen
Butter or margarine, softened	4 tablespoons (½ stick)	2 tablespoons (¼ stick)	1 tablespoon
Garlic cloves, minced	2 garlic cloves	1 garlic clove	1 small garlic clove
Basil	1 teaspoon	½ teaspoon	¼ teaspoon
Thyme leaves	1 teaspoon	½ teaspoon	¼ teaspoon
Oregano	1 teaspoon	½ teaspoon	¼ teaspoon
Worcestershire	1 tablespoon	1½ teaspoons	¾ teaspoon
Salt and pepper	to taste	to taste	to taste
Basil leaves for garnish	garnish	garnish	garnish
Sautéed cherry tomatoes (optional)	Cherry tomatoes	Cherry tomatoes	Cherry tomatoes
Microwave cookware	13" by 9" baking dish with rack	13" by 9" baking dish with rack	8" by 8" baking dish with rack
Time on High (100% power)	12 to 14 minutes each batch	12 to 14 minutes	7 to 10 minutes
Standing time	3 to 4 minutes	3 to 4 minutes	2 to 3 minutes

1 Remove giblets and neck from inside of each hen. Rinse hens under running cold water. Pat dry with paper towels. Using kitchen scissors or sharp knife, cut each hen lengthwise in half.

2 In small bowl, combine butter or margarine, garlic, basil, thyme leaves, and oregano; mix well.

3 One at a time, place half a hen on work surface with breast bone facing toward you. Work finger under skin at top of breast to make a pocket. Be careful not to tear skin of hen.

4 Stuff an equal amount of garlic-herb mixture into each pocket.

5 On rack in baking dish (see Chart), arrange hens, breasts toward center. If cooking for 4, cook hens in 2 batches.

6 Brush hens with Worcestershire. Cook, covered loosely with waxed paper, on High for time in Chart, or until juices run clear when hens are pierced with a fork, rotating dish once. Season with salt and pepper. Let stand for time in Chart. Arrange Cornish-hen halves on warmed serving platter; garnish with basil leaves. If you like, accompany with sautéed cherry tomatoes.

Duckling

DUCKLING WITH ORANGE SAUCE

Color Index page 59. 810 cals per serving. Good source of thiamine, riboflavin, niacin, iron. Begin 1½ hours ahead.

Ingredients for 4 servings		Microwave cookware
1 5-pound fresh or frozen (thawed) Long Island duckling, cut into quarters 1 orange 3 tablespoons cider vinegar 2 tablespoons sugar 1½ cups Chicken Broth (page 125) or canned broth	2 teaspoons cornstarch dissolved in 1 tablespoon cold water 2 tablespoons lemon juice 2 tablespoons brandy or cognac Salt and pepper to taste Parsley and orange slices for garnish	13″ by 9″ baking dish with rack 4-cup glass measure

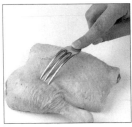

1 Trim excess skin and fat from duckling pieces. Rinse pieces under running cold water. Pat dry with paper towels. With fork, pierce skin of each piece about 10 times to allow fat to drain and prevent skin from splitting during cooking.

2 In baking dish with rack, arrange leg quarters, skin side down, in opposite corners, with bones toward center. Cook, covered, on Medium (50% power) 20 minutes, turning pieces over once. Prick skin with fork. Turn pieces over again, placing skin side down.

3 Add breast quarters, skin side down. Cook, covered loosely with waxed paper, on Medium-High (70% power) 20 minutes, turning pieces over and pricking skin once. Uncover and cook on High (100% power) 5 minutes, or until juices run clear. Cover and let stand.

4 Prepare sauce: With vegetable peeler, remove peel from orange, leaving bitter white pith behind. Stack peel and cut into fine strips. Into small bowl, squeeze juice from orange.

5 In glass measure, combine vinegar and sugar. Cook, covered, on High 3 to 5 minutes, just until mixture turns light golden, watching carefully since mixture burns easily and continues to cook and darken when removed from the oven. Into mixture, stir orange peel and juice, and broth. Cook, covered, on High 5 minutes.

6 Into orange mixture, stir dissolved cornstarch. Cook on High 2 to 4 minutes, until sauce thickens. Add lemon juice and brandy or cognac. Season. Arrange duckling pieces on warmed dinner plates; pour sauce over duckling. Garnish with parsley and orange slices.

APRICOT-GLAZED DUCKLING

Color Index page 59. 4 servings. 847 cals per serving. Good source of thiamine, riboflavin, niacin, iron. Begin 1¼ hours ahead.

2 tablespoons prepared mustard
½ cup apricot preserves
2 tablespoons soy sauce
1 garlic clove, minced
⅛ teaspoon ground ginger

1 5-pound fresh or frozen (thawed) Long Island duckling, cut into quarters
Parsley sprigs for garnish

1. In 4-cup microwave-safe glass measure, combine mustard and next 4 ingredients. Cook on High (100% power) 2 minutes, stirring twice.
2. Prepare and cook duckling as directed for Duckling with Orange Sauce (left) through step 3, brushing duckling pieces with apricot glaze before cooking and every time microwave is opened. Let stand 5 minutes. If you like and if dish is broiler-safe, brown duckling under preheated broiler until skin is crisp. Garnish.

Glazing the Duckling

In 4-cup glass measure, combine mustard, apricot preserves, soy sauce, garlic, and ginger. Cook on High (100% power) 2 minutes.

With small pastry brush, brush the apricot glaze over duckling pieces every time microwave is opened.

POULTRY GLAZES

Brushing whole birds or pieces with a glaze will give poultry an attractive appearance. Similarly, brush with melted butter mixed with herbs or spices. Allow about ½ cup glaze for 4- to 6-pound birds, 1 cup for larger birds. For information on Browning Chicken see pages 180 and 181.

Honey-barbecue Glaze: In 2-cup microwave-safe glass measure, mix *½ cup honey, 1 tablespoon soy sauce*, and *½ teaspoon ground ginger*. Heat on Medium-High (70% power) 1 minute, stirring once. Makes ½ cup.

Wine-jelly Glaze: In 2-cup microwave-safe glass measure, mix *½ cup wine jelly* with *¼ teaspoon salt*. Heat on Medium-High (70% power) 1 minute, stirring once. Makes ½ cup.

DUCKLING WITH OLIVES AND ALMONDS

Color Index page 59. 4 servings. 818 cals per serving. Good source of thiamine, riboflavin, niacin, iron. Begin 1¼ hours ahead.

1 5-pound fresh or frozen (thawed) Long Island duckling, cut into quarters
3 medium onions, cut into ½-inch wedges
2 3-ounce jars green olives stuffed with almonds, or 4 ounces green olives, pitted, and ¼ cup whole blanched almonds

1½ cups Beef Broth (page 125) or canned broth
3 tablespoons dry sherry
2 teaspoons cornstarch dissolved in 1 tablespoon cold water
Salt and pepper to taste
Lemon slices and coriander for garnish

1. Prepare and cook duckling as directed for Duckling with Orange Sauce (page 192) through step 3. Transfer duckling to warmed serving dish and let stand, covered, while preparing sauce.
2. Remove rack from baking dish and pour off all but 3 tablespoons drippings. Add onion wedges and stir. Cook on High (100% power) 3 to 5 minutes, just until onions soften, stirring twice. Add almond-stuffed olives or olives and almonds; stir to coat. Cook on High 1 minute.
3. Into mixture, stir broth. Cook on High 3 to 4 minutes, until boiling, stirring twice. Stir in sherry and dissolved cornstarch. Cook on High 2 to 4 minutes, until sauce thickens, stirring occasionally. Season with salt and pepper. Pour sauce over duckling and garnish.

DUCKLING WITH CHERRY SAUCE

Color Index page 59. 4 servings. 778 cals per serving. Low in sodium. Good source of thiamine, riboflavin, niacin, iron. Begin 1¼ hours ahead.

1 5-pound fresh or frozen (thawed) Long Island duckling, cut in quarters
1 tablespoon all-purpose flour
¼ cup Chicken Broth (page 125) or canned broth

¼ cup dry red wine
½ 16½-ounce can Bing cherries in syrup
½ garlic clove, minced
1 tablespoon lemon juice
Pepper to taste
Watercress sprigs for garnish

1. Prepare and cook duckling as directed for Duckling with Orange Sauce (page 192) through step 3. Transfer duckling to warmed serving dish and let stand, covered, while preparing sauce.
2. Into 4-cup microwave-safe glass measure, pour 2 tablespoons duck drippings; add flour and stir until blended. Cook on High (100% power) 30 seconds.
3. Into flour mixture, stir broth, wine, cherries with their syrup, and garlic. Cook on High 3 to 5 minutes, until sauce thickens, stirring twice.
4. To cherry sauce, add lemon juice, stirring well. Season with freshly ground black pepper. Spoon sauce over duckling and garnish.

When preparing duckling dishes that call for breasts only, it is important to remove skin and fat first. Because of the shortness of microwave cooking time, the fat in the skin does not have enough time to melt out and drain off and skin will not crisp. A browning dish will give the finished meat a more attractive appearance.

DUCK BREASTS WITH APPLE AND GREEN PEPPERCORNS

Color Index page 58. 226 cals per serving. Low in cholesterol, sodium. Good source of thiamine, niacin, iron. Begin 40 minutes ahead.

Ingredients for 4 servings		Microwave cookware
2 whole boneless duck breasts, cut in half 1 tablespoon salad oil 1 dessert apple 1 tablespoon sugar 1 teaspoon green peppercorns packed in brine, drained	½ cup Chicken Broth (page 125) or canned broth ½ teaspoon cornstarch dissolved in 1 teaspoon cold water Salt and pepper to taste Parsley sprigs for garnish	Browning dish

1 Remove skin and fat from duck breasts; discard. Preheat browning dish as manufacturer directs.

2 Meanwhile, core apple and cut into about 20 slices. In small bowl, combine apple slices and sugar. Brush browning dish with oil. Arrange duck breasts on browning dish.

3 Cook duck breasts on High (100% power) 2 to 3 minutes, until rare, turning halfway through cooking. Transfer to warmed plate. Let stand, covered, while preparing sauce.

4 Reheat browning dish. Arrange apple slices in single layer on browning dish. Cook on High 2 minutes. With tongs, remove apple slices to warmed plate; set aside.

5 Reheat browning dish. Add green peppercorns and broth to browning dish. Cook on High 3 minutes, or until bubbling. Add dissolved cornstarch; stir. Cook on High 2 minutes, or until sauce thickens. Season with salt and pepper.

6 To serve: Cut each duck-breast half into slices and arrange on warmed dinner plate with apple slices. Spoon sauce over each serving. Garnish with parsley sprigs and apple slices.

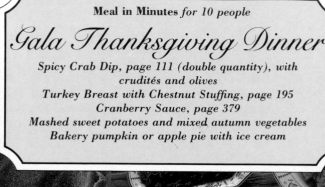

Meal in Minutes *for 10 people*

Gala Thanksgiving Dinner

Spicy Crab Dip, page 111 (double quantity), with crudités and olives
Turkey Breast with Chestnut Stuffing, page 195
Cranberry Sauce, page 379
Mashed sweet potatoes and mixed autumn vegetables
Bakery pumpkin or apple pie with ice cream

PREPARATION TIMETABLE	
1 day ahead:	*Prepare dip, cover and refrigerate. Cut crudités; store in plastic bags in refrigerator. Make Cranberry Sauce, spoon into serving dish; cover and refrigerate.*
1¾ hours ahead:	*Cook turkey and stuffing. Meanwhile, cook sweet potatoes and autumn vegetables conventionally; mash sweet potatoes. Spoon potatoes and vegetables into microwave-safe serving dishes.*
10 minutes ahead:	*While turkey is standing, arrange crudités and olives on platter; spoon dip into bowl. Reheat sweet potatoes and autumn vegetable selection on High (100% power).*
Just before serving:	*Heat pumpkin or apple pie on High 4 to 5 minutes. If frozen, heat pie on High 6 to 8 minutes, until completely thawed. If you like, soften ice cream; for 1 quart, heat on Medium-Low (30% power) 30 to 40 seconds.*

Turkey

TURKEY TORTILLA ROLL-UPS

Color Index page 58. 4 servings. 547 cals per serving. Good source of riboflavin, niacin, vitamin C, calcium, iron. Begin 45 minutes ahead.

1 pound turkey breast, skinned and boned	½ 10-ounce package frozen whole-kernel corn, slightly thawed
1 teaspoon ground cumin	8 8-inch flour tortillas
¼ teaspoon ground cloves	1 8-ounce jar enchilada sauce
1 tablespoon lime juice	½ 14½- to 16- or 17½-ounce can crushed tomatoes
2 tablespoons peanut or salad oil	
1 medium onion, chopped	4 ounces Monterey Jack cheese, shredded (1 cup)
1 medium green pepper, chopped	Coriander sprigs and lime wedges for garnish
2 tomatoes, chopped	
2 tablespoons minced coriander or parsley	Sour cream and guacamole (optional)

1. Cut turkey breast into 1½-inch chunks. In large bowl, combine turkey breast, cumin, cloves, and lime juice. Let mixture stand 5 minutes to blend flavors.

2. Meanwhile, in 10″ microwave-safe quiche dish or pie plate, combine oil, onion, green pepper, and tomatoes. Cook on High (100% power) 3 minutes, stirring twice.

3. To onion mixture, add turkey breast mixture and herbs. Cook on High 6 to 8 minutes, just until turkey turns white, stirring twice. Into turkey mixture, stir corn.

4. Arrange tortillas on work surface. In center of each, place an equal amount of turkey mixture. Roll up each tortilla over filling. Place seam side down in 13″ by 9″ microwave-safe baking dish.

5. In medium bowl, combine enchilada sauce and crushed tomatoes. Pour over roll-ups. Cook on High 8 to 10 minutes, rotating dish halfway through cooking. Sprinkle cheese on top; garnish. If you like, serve with sour cream and guacamole.

Filling and Arranging the Roll-ups

Place turkey mixture in center of each tortilla. Fold over one side of tortilla and roll up jelly-roll fashion over filling.

Place each roll-up seam side down in baking dish. This prevents them from unrolling and the filling from falling out.

A turkey breast is ideal for microwaving, and because cooking time is long enough, the skin will brown if brushed with a mixture of butter or margarine and browning sauce. If you like, try one of our other stuffings, microwaving it separately in a casserole until a thermometer registers 165°F.

TURKEY BREAST WITH CHESTNUT STUFFING

Color Index page 59. 394 cals per serving. Good source of niacin, iron. Begin 1¾ hours ahead.

Ingredients for 16 servings		Microwave cookware
1 6-pound fresh or frozen (thawed) turkey breast, giblets, neck, back and rib bones removed 8 tablespoons butter or margarine (1 stick) ½ teaspoon browning sauce 1 medium onion, chopped 2 celery stalks, chopped 6 cups fresh bread cubes	½ cup golden raisins 2 tablespoons chopped parsley 1 15½-ounce can whole chestnuts, drained, or 2 cups whole, shelled, and roasted chestnuts 1½ teaspoons poultry seasoning ½ teaspoon salt Pepper to taste Parsley sprigs for garnish	13" by 9" baking dish

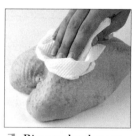

1 Rinse turkey breast; pat dry. In baking dish, place 4 tablespoons butter or margarine. Heat, covered with paper towels, on High (100% power) 45 seconds to 1 minute, until melted. Add browning sauce; stir.

2 Place turkey breast, skin side down, in browning sauce mixture. Cook, covered, on Medium (50% power) 12 to 15 minutes per pound (about 1¼ to 1½ hours).

3 Meanwhile, in 12" skillet over medium heat, melt remaining butter or margarine. Add onion and celery. Cook until tender, stirring occasionally.

STUFFINGS FOR POULTRY

Shorten preparation time for stuffings by microwaving some of the ingredients, then cook stuffed large birds conventionally, or microwave stuffing separately on High (100% power) in a 12" by 8" baking dish until a thermometer inserted in center reaches 165°F. Spinach-ricotta Stuffing takes 10 minutes; Bacon-rice Stuffing 3 minutes.

Spinach-ricotta Stuffing: In a deep, large microwave-safe bowl, place **8 tablespoons diced butter or margarine (1 stick)**. Heat, covered with paper towel, on High (100% power) 1½ (1:30) to 2 minutes, until melted. Stir in **¼ pound thinly sliced mushrooms, 2 diced celery stalks**, and **1 small chopped onion**. Cook, covered, on High 3 to 4 minutes, until vegetables are softened, stirring twice. Stir in **3 cups fresh bread crumbs, ½ 15- to 16-ounce container ricotta cheese (1 cup), 1 egg, 1 tablespoon chopped parsley, 1 teaspoon salt, ½ teaspoon poultry seasoning, ⅛ teaspoon pepper**, and **1 10-ounce package frozen chopped spinach, thawed, drained, and squeezed dry**. Mix well. Makes 3½ cups. 30 cals per tablespoon.

Bacon-rice Stuffing: Cook **1 cup regular long-grain rice** conventionally as label directs. Meanwhile, in 13" by 9" microwave-safe baking dish, place **12 diced bacon slices**. Cook, covered with paper towels, on High (100% power) 4 to 5 minutes, until browned, stirring twice. Remove to paper towels to drain. Discard all but 3 table-spoons drippings; add **1 medium diced onion**. Cook, covered, on High 2 minutes, or until softened. Stir in cooked rice and bacon. Makes 3½ cups. 28 cals per tablespoon.

4 Remove skillet from heat; stir in bread cubes, golden raisins, parsley, chestnuts, poultry seasoning, and salt and pepper. Toss to mix well.

5 About 20 to 30 minutes before end of cooking time, carefully transfer turkey breast to plate. Add chestnut stuffing to turkey drippings in baking dish. Stir well to combine.

6 Place turkey breast, skin side up, on top of chestnut stuffing. Continue cooking, covered, on Medium 20 to 30 minutes, until a meat thermometer inserted in center of turkey breast reaches 160°F., rotating dish twice.

7 On heat-safe surface, let turkey and stuffing stand in dish, tented with foil, 10 minutes. Turkey will continue to cook and will reach 170°F. on meat thermometer.

8 To serve: Place turkey breast on large warmed platter. Spoon stuffing around turkey. Garnish with parsley sprigs.

Turkey

TURKEY ROLLS with CHEESE FILLING

Color Index page 58. 470 cals per serving. Good source of vitamin A, niacin, calcium, iron. Begin 35 minutes ahead.

Ingredients	For 4	For 2	For 1
1 4-ounce package Boursin or soft garlic and herb cheese	1 package	½ package	¼ package
Mozzarella cheese, shredded	¼ cup cheese	2 tablespoons cheese	1 tablespoon cheese
Basil leaves, shredded	4 basil leaves	2 basil leaves	1 basil leaf
Sun-dried tomatoes, drained if packed in oil	4 tomatoes	2 tomatoes	1 tomato
Turkey cutlets (3 to 4 ounces each)	4 cutlets	2 cutlets	1 cutlet
Butter or margarine	2 tablespoons	1 tablespoon	2 teaspoons
Seasoned dried bread crumbs	½ cup bread crumbs	¼ cup bread crumbs	2 tablespoons bread crumbs
Salt	¼ teaspoon	⅛ teaspoon	to taste
Microwave cookware	Small bowl 12″ by 8″ baking dish	Small bowl 12″ by 8″ baking dish	Small bowl 8″ by 8″ baking dish
Time on High (100% power) Butter	45 seconds	30 to 45 seconds	15 to 30 seconds
Turkey	6 to 9 minutes	4 to 6 minutes	2½ (2:30) to 3½ (3:30) minutes
Standing time	4 minutes	3 minutes	2 minutes

1 Chop tomatoes. In bowl, combine cheeses, basil and tomatoes; stir until blended.

2 Spoon an equal amount of filling onto 1 end of each cutlet.

3 Roll up cutlets jelly-roll fashion. Secure with wooden toothpicks.

4 In bowl (see Chart), place butter or margarine. Heat, covered with paper towel, on High for time in Chart, or until melted.

5 In pie plate or on waxed paper, mix bread crumbs and salt. Dip turkey rolls in melted butter or margarine, then coat in bread crumbs.

6 In baking dish, arrange rolls, 1 inch apart. Cook, covered loosely with waxed paper, on High for time in Chart, until fork-tender. Let stand for time in Chart.

TURKEY-NOODLE CASSEROLE

Color Index page 58. 4 servings. 700 cals per serving. Good source of vitamin A, thiamine, riboflavin, niacin, calcium, iron. Begin 55 minutes ahead.

1 8-ounce package tagliatelle	¾ teaspoon salt
3 tablespoons butter or margarine	4 slices Melba toast
3 tablespoons all-purpose flour	3 medium celery stalks, diced
2 cups milk	3 green onions, sliced
1 cup Chicken Broth (page 125) or canned broth	1 10-ounce package frozen peas, thawed
1 teaspoon poultry seasoning	1 pound turkey breast, skinned, boned, and cut into 1½-inch chunks
	½ cup sour cream

1. Cook noodles conventionally as label directs. Drain and keep warm.

2. In 13″ by 9″ microwave-safe baking dish, place butter or margarine. Heat, covered with paper towels, on High (100% power) 45 seconds to 1 minute, until melted. Stir in flour until blended. Gradually stir in milk and broth; add poultry seasoning and salt. Cook on High 8 to 10 minutes, until sauce thickens, stirring twice.

3. Meanwhile, make Melba-toast Crumbs: Place toast in strong bag. With rolling pin, roll until finely crushed.

4. Into sauce, stir celery, green onions, peas, turkey meat, and noodles. Cook, covered, on High 8 minutes, stirring twice. Add sour cream; stir well. Cook, covered, on Medium (50% power) 5 to 8 minutes, ·rotating dish halfway through cooking.

5. Sprinkle with Melba-toast Crumbs. Cook on High 2 minutes. Serve immediately.

Making and Sprinkling the Melba-toast Crumbs

Place toast in strong bag. With rolling pin, go over bag until slices are finely crushed. Or, process toast in food processor with knife blade attached, or in blender.

Just before placing dish in microwave, sprinkle an even coating of crushed Melba-toast Crumbs over the surface. This will give a golden crust to the top.

Meat

**DEFROSTING, COOKING, AND BROWNING MEAT · BEEF
QUICK OUTDOOR COOKING · KIDS' COOKING · PORK
MICROWAVING BACON · HAM · VEAL · LAMB · SAUSAGE
SAUSAGE SNACKS FOR KIDS**

Meat

Meat cooked in the microwave is generally tastier and juicier than if conventionally prepared and, of course, it is ready much sooner. Shrinkage is minimized, especially on large rolled roasts, by shielding ends with foil for part of the cooking time, which prevents overcooking and also ensures that the roast cooks evenly. Thinner ends should be shielded as should bony portions. Smaller cuts cook successfully on High (100% power) but larger cuts, especially roasts, are more tender when cooked at a lower power level.

Meat that is well marbled with fat and contains even layers of fat on the outside will cook more evenly and will be more tender. Drippings, which attract microwave energy away from the meat, should be removed at intervals to prevent spatters and speed cooking.

Roasts with a good, even fat covering will brown due to their longer cooking times. Steaks, which are cooked for a shorter time, can be prepared on a browning dish to sear them attractively while retaining their tenderness. We prepare some of our hamburgers with a coating mixture to make them as flavorful as grilled burgers. Standing time is important for larger cuts as it allows them to complete cooking and the internal temperature of meat to rise to its final desired temperature. Doneness of meat, especially pork, should be based on the temperature guidelines given in our recipes, and also in our Timetable for Cooking Beef (see Box, page 203); appearance is not enough as microwaved meat can look underdone although fully cooked.

Choose evenly shaped cuts: roasts should have a regular diameter; meat for stews and casseroles should be cut to uniform size; steaks, chops, and cutlets should be of the same density throughout. For even cooking, turn roasts and stir or rotate casseroles. Arrange irregular pieces of meat with thicker ends toward edges of dish. Use a rack, if directed, to prevent meat from cooking unevenly in its own juices.

NEW WAYS WITH HAMBURGERS

A simple hamburger quickly cooked in the microwave can be dressed up with a variety of popular accompaniments to create regional variations.

East-coast burger (left) served in a bagel with coleslaw and other typical delicatessen accompaniments.

West-coast cheeseburger (right) with thin slices of goat cheese, served on a toast round with a radish and salad leaves.

Defrosting Meat

Defrosting frozen foods is one of the great uses of a microwave oven. It must be done carefully, however, if quality is to be retained. It is important to defrost meat evenly to prevent some parts from starting to cook before others have completely defrosted. Use a Medium-Low (30% power) or Defrost power level or manually turn your oven on and off, allowing heat to even out during "rest" periods.

DEFROSTING A LARGE ROAST

Remove all wrappings quickly from frozen roast. This speeds defrosting because wrappings insulate bottom of roast.

Place roast on microwave-safe rack in microwave-safe baking dish, so meat does not sit in juices which could cause surface to start cooking.

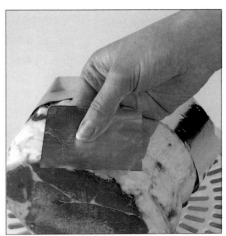

Check for warm areas as roast defrosts and shield these with pieces of smooth foil during defrosting; remove foil before start of cooking.

Using containers to fit
If transferring meat from package to dish, choose one which fits food as closely as possible; this prevents defrosted edges from spreading out and starting to cook.

Separating pieces
As soon as possible, separate frozen hamburgers, steaks, or other pieces which have been stacked; place in a single layer on microwave-safe rack.

Breaking up ground beef
Break up ground beef with a fork as it defrosts; scrape off defrosted parts and set aside.

Covering with waxed paper
Covering meat loosely with waxed paper while defrosting helps retain heat for speedier defrosting.

Separating cubes/strips
As soon as sufficiently defrosted, separate cubes and strips of meat and arrange separately in dish, removing pieces as they defrost.

Testing with skewer
Thick meat cuts are defrosted when a skewer can go through thickest part to center.

Cooking Meat

Careful choice and preparation of meat is essential for successful microwaving, and an understanding of how microwave ovens work helps explain most of the techniques. Microwave energy cooks food quickly but not evenly. Therefore, whenever possible, choose evenly sized pieces or trim meat to make it more uniform in size; at the same time, trim fat so it is evenly distributed over the meat.

Arrange unevenly shaped pieces with thicker parts toward edges of dish where they will cook faster. Thin ends of meat, bone, and cut edges tend to overcook, so shield them with smooth strips of foil.

PREPARING MEAT FOR MICROWAVE COOKING

Removing excess fat from ground meat
Before proceeding with a recipe, place meat in a microwave-safe colander set over a microwave-safe bowl; cook on High (100% power); discard drippings from bowl. For 1 pound beef, cook 4 minutes, stirring twice.

Even fat covering
While a certain amount of fat is desirable to tenderize and add flavor to meat, it should be evenly distributed as well as of uniform thickness; this helps meat cook evenly.

Trimming meat to size
Uniformity of size is important for even cooking in the microwave oven. If meat cubes are required, cut them to a regular size.

Slashing sausages
To prevent sausages and other foods with similar tough coverings from bursting during cooking due to a build-up of steam, slash or pierce casings before cooking in the microwave.

Even diameter
Roasts that are to be rolled should be trimmed and pounded to uniform thickness.

Tenderizing roasts
Roasts, which cook more quickly in a microwave than in a conventional oven, benefit from meat tenderizer. Sprinkle meat with water, rub on tenderizer, then pierce with a fork to get tenderizer beneath meat's surface.

SHIELDING

Ends of meat
To prevent cut ends of roasts from overcooking, shield with smooth, 2-inch-wide strips of foil. Remove or retain these during cooking as necessary. Shield "hot spots" in the same way.

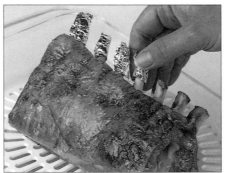

Exposed bones
To prevent overcooking, shield ends of bones or bony areas such as poultry breastbones with smooth strips of foil.

Long, thin sides of steaks
If steaks are irregular in size, shield longer sides with smooth ½-inch-wide strips of foil to prevent them from overcooking. Remove foil halfway through cooking.

BROWNING

Browning conventionally
Meats that will not brown during microwaving – for example, a pot roast cooked in a roasting bag – can be first browned conventionally in a skillet.

Browning agents and coatings
Brush meat before and during cooking with a browning agent or glaze, or coat with beaten egg and a dry topping such as bread crumbs or herbs.

Browning dish
Browning dishes are used to sear and brown meat such as chops, steaks, and hamburgers while they are cooking in the microwave oven.

COOKING TECHNIQUES FOR MEAT

Racks and trivets
Use these to elevate denser meat so microwaves reach bottom of food and it cooks more uniformly. Also, placing meat on rack prevents it from sitting and steaming in cooking juices and fats.

Standing time
It is important to let meats stand to complete cooking after removal from microwave; internal temperatures will rise 10° to 15° during standing.

Roasting bags
Less tender meat cuts are best cooked in liquid, and roasting bags are ideal for this. Use plastic, nylon, or cotton ties and vent to allow steam to escape; do not use metal ties.

Tenting
During standing time, keep meat warm by tenting with foil, shiny side in, or waxed paper.

Using a mold
A ring mold or Bundt pan allows microwaves to penetrate from all sides, ensuring even cooking. This is especially important in dishes that cannot be stirred, such as meat loaves.

Freezer-to-table casseroles
Fit smooth foil onto frozen surface. Place on microwave-safe rack; cook on High (100% power), rotating a quarter turn every 5 minutes until defrosted. Discard foil and continue cooking until hot and bubbling.

Beef Roasts

When choosing beef for cooking in the microwave oven, make sure there is an even marbling of fat throughout, for even cooking and moist, tender results. Be sure to slice our Roast Beef with Herbs (below), as well as other large cuts of meat, across the grain, as meat is always more tender when sliced this way.

ROAST BEEF WITH HERBS

Color Index page 63. 286 cals per serving. Good source of iron. Begin 45 minutes ahead.

Ingredients for 10 servings		Microwave cookware
1 2½-pound beef rib eye roast Water 1¼ teaspoons unseasoned meat tenderizer ⅓ cup mayonnaise 2 tablespoons crumbled fresh thyme or 2 teaspoons dried	2 tablespoons chopped fresh basil or 2 teaspoons dried 1 tablespoon dried bread crumbs ¾ teaspoon cracked black pepper 1 garlic clove, minced Radishes and basil leaves for garnish	12″ by 8″ baking dish with rack 3 wooden toothpicks

1 Moisten roast with water; rub evenly with meat tenderizer. With fork, pierce roast deeply all over.

2 Place roast on rack in baking dish; shield ends of roast with 2-inch-wide strips of smooth foil. Cook, covered loosely with waxed paper, on Medium (50% power) 25 minutes.

3 Meanwhile, in small bowl, mix mayonnaise, thyme, basil, bread crumbs, pepper, and garlic.

4 Remove waxed paper and foil from roast and turn over. Spread mayonnaise mixture evenly over roast.

5 Along top of roast, insert 3 toothpicks, evenly spaced, about 1 inch deep. Cover roast with waxed paper, tenting paper over toothpicks. Cook on Medium 7 minutes, or until a meat thermometer inserted in center of roast reaches 120°F. for medium-rare.

6 On heat-safe surface, let roast stand, covered, 5 to 8 minutes. Temperature will reach 135°F. Cut roast across grain in thin slices. Arrange on warmed serving platter and garnish with radishes and basil leaves. Skim fat from meat juices; pass juices separately in gravy boat.

RIB ROAST

Color Index page 66. 6 servings. 274 cals per serving. Low in sodium. Good source of niacin, iron. Begin 1¼ hours ahead.

1 2-rib beef rib roast (small end), about 3½ pounds, with chine bone removed 1 teaspoon pepper 1 teaspoon thyme leaves 1 teaspoon onion powder	½ teaspoon paprika 1 tablespoon salad oil Salt and pepper to taste Fresh thyme leaves for garnish

1. Trim any large areas of fat from roast.
2. In small bowl, combine pepper, thyme leaves, onion powder, and paprika. Rub seasonings evenly over meat.
3. In 12″ skillet over high heat, heat oil until very hot. Add rib roast and brown on all sides. On microwave-safe rack in 13″ by 9″ microwave-safe baking dish, place roast.
4. Shield ends of bone with smooth strips of foil. Cook on Medium (50% power) 30 to 40 minutes, until a meat thermometer inserted in center of roast reaches 120°F. for medium-rare, removing foil halfway through cooking.
5. Transfer roast to warmed serving platter; tent with foil and let stand 15 to 20 minutes. Temperature will reach 130°F. to 135°F. Season with salt and pepper.
6. Sprinkle roast with thyme leaves and serve with meat juices.

CARVING A RIB ROAST

After cooking, rib roast needs to stand 15 to 20 minutes to complete cooking and allow juices to settle; this makes for easier carving. Transfer meat to a warmed serving platter and tent with foil. Let meat stand while preparing gravy or last-minute vegetables. With practice, and good carving utensils, any roast can be carved on a garnished serving platter.

To be able to carve rib roast on platter at table, have butcher remove chine bone for you. With sharp carving knife, cut ¼-inch-thick slices, using long-tined fork to prevent roast from slipping on platter while carving. Transfer slices to warmed individual dinner plates; continue carving until all guests are served.

Beef Pot Roasts

FREEZER-TO-TABLE POT ROAST

Color Index page 65. 12 servings. 340 cals per serving. Good source of vitamin A, niacin, iron. Begin 2½ hours ahead.

1 cup orange juice	1 16-ounce bag carrots
2 teaspoons salt	1 small rutabaga (about
¼ teaspoon pepper	1 pound)
¼ teaspoon thyme leaves	3 tablespoons all-
2 4" by ½" strips orange	purpose flour
peel	3 tablespoons water
1 4-pound frozen	Parsley for garnish
boneless beef chuck	
shoulder pot roast	

1. In 5-quart microwave-safe casserole, combine orange juice, salt, pepper, thyme leaves, and orange peel. Add frozen chuck roast, turning to coat with orange-juice mixture. Place 2-inch-wide strip of smooth foil over top edge of each end of meat to prevent overcooking. Cook, covered, on Medium (50% power) 1 hour, turning meat over and replacing foil strips halfway through cooking.
2. Meanwhile, cut carrots into 1½-inch pieces. Peel rutabaga and cut into ¼-inch wedges.
3. Turn meat over again and replace foil strips; add vegetables. Cook, covered, on Medium 1 to 1¼ hours longer, until meat and vegetables are tender, turning meat over and removing foil halfway through cooking.
4. Carefully transfer roast to warmed serving platter. Remove vegetables and arrange around meat; let stand, covered, while preparing sauce.
5. With spoon, skim fat from cooking liquid in casserole. In small bowl, combine flour and water until smooth. Gradually stir flour mixture into cooking liquid. Cook on High (100% power) 2 to 3 minutes, until sauce thickens, stirring often.
6. Cut meat into slices. Garnish. Pour sauce into gravy boat and pass separately.

TIMETABLE FOR COOKING BEEF

Beef may look underdone when removed from the microwave, so allow it to stand, tented with foil, to achieve its final temperature. As a general rule, remove it from the microwave when the temperature reaches 10°F. to 15°F. lower than the temperature of doneness you prefer.

Desired doneness	Remove at	Will rise to
Medium-rare	115°F. to 125°F.	125°F. to 140°F.
Medium	130°F. to 140°F.	140°F. to 155°F.
Well done	150°F. to 160°F.	160°F. to 170°F.

OLD-FASHIONED POT ROAST

Color Index page 66. 477 cals per serving. Good source of vitamin A, niacin, vitamin C, iron. Begin 2½ hours ahead.

Ingredients for 6 servings		Microwave cookware
1 tablespoon salad oil	1 teaspoon sugar	Plastic roasting bag
1 3-pound boneless	½ cup Beef Broth (page	with plastic or nylon
chuck roast	125) or canned broth	tie
2 large onions, cut into	1 bay leaf	13" by 9" baking dish
½-inch wedges	1 teaspoon thyme leaves	
4 carrots, cut into 2-inch	¼ teaspoon pepper	
pieces	2 tablespoons butter or	
1 pound small white	margarine (¼ stick),	
potatoes, peeled and	softened	
cut into quarters	2 tablespoons all-	
2 garlic cloves, minced	purpose flour	
½ 14½- to 16-ounce can	Salt and pepper to taste	
tomato puree	Parsley sprigs for	
½ cup dry white wine	garnish	

1 In 12" skillet over high heat, heat oil. Add chuck roast and brown on all sides. Transfer roast to plastic roasting bag and place in baking dish.

2 To roasting bag, add onions, carrots, potatoes, garlic, tomato puree, wine, sugar, broth, bay leaf, thyme leaves, and pepper. Close bag loosely with plastic or nylon tie (do not use metal ties), leaving small opening for venting.

3 Cook meat on High (100% power) 5 minutes. Reduce power level to Medium-Low (30% power) and cook 1½ to 2 hours longer, until meat is fork-tender, turning bag over every 20 minutes during cooking.

4 Carefully open roasting bag and transfer meat to carving board. Tent with foil and let stand 15 to 20 minutes.

5 Meanwhile, empty contents of bag into baking dish. Remove bay leaf. Skim fat from surface. In small bowl, combine butter or margarine and flour to form a soft paste. Stir small pieces into vegetable mixture, a little at a time, until blended. Cook on High 6 to 8 minutes, until thickened, stirring twice. Season with salt and pepper.

6 To serve: Thinly slice roast across grain. Arrange meat on warmed dinner plates and spoon sauce and vegetables over meat. Garnish with parsley sprigs.

Beef Steaks

Try using a browning dish to cook steak in the microwave. It will give the meat a seared look without sacrificing tenderness. Make sure you press the steak lightly with a spatula for even browning, as in our recipe for Steak au Poivre (below). Don't forget to reheat browning dish if cooking steaks in batches.

STEAK AU POIVRE

Color Index page 60. 313 cals per serving. Good source of niacin, iron.
Begin 25 minutes ahead.

Ingredients	For 4	For 2	For 1
Whole peppercorns	*2 tablespoons*	*1 tablespoon*	*2 teaspoons*
Beef tenderloin steaks,	*4 steaks*	*2 steaks*	*1 steak*
cut at least 1 inch			
thick (6 ounces each)			
Dry white wine	*2 tablespoons*	*1 tablespoon*	*2 teaspoons*
Instant beef-flavor	*2 tablespoons*	*1 tablespoon*	*2 teaspoons*
bouillon			
Brandy	*2 tablespoons*	*1 tablespoon*	*1 teaspoon*
Sour cream	*½ cup*	*¼ cup*	*2 tablespoons*
Microwave cookware	Browning dish	Browning dish	Browning dish
Time on High (100% power)			
Steak	4½ (4:30) to 6 minutes	3 to 4½ (4:30) minutes	2 to 3 minutes
Wine mixture	4 minutes	3 to 3½ (3:30) minutes	2 to 2½ (2:30) minutes

1 Place peppercorns in plastic bag, With mallet or rolling pin, crush peppercorns. On waxed paper, evenly spread crushed peppercorns.

2 Press both sides of each steak in crushed peppercorns to coat.

3 Preheat browning dish as manufacturer directs. Arrange steaks on browning dish, pressing lightly with spatula to brown evenly.

4 Cook steaks on High for time in Chart, turning over halfway through cooking. Remove to platter: loosely cover and keep warm while preparing sauce.

5 To browning dish, add wine, bouillon, and brandy. Cook on High for time in Chart, stirring twice. Into sauce, gradually stir sour cream.

6 *To serve*: Arrange steaks on warmed dinner plates. Spoon sauce over steaks; serve immediately.

STEAK FORESTIÈRE

Color Index page 60. 4 servings. 329 cals per serving. Good source of niacin, iron.
Begin 25 minutes ahead.

2 slices bacon, diced
4 beef tenderloin steaks, cut 1 inch thick
1 small onion, diced
4 mushrooms, cut into quarters
2 tomatoes, diced
¼ cup Madeira wine
½ cup Beef Broth (page 125) or canned broth
½ teaspoon cornstarch dissolved in 1 teaspoon cold water
Salt and pepper to taste
Watercress for garnish

1. Preheat browning dish as manufacturer directs. Add bacon. Cook on High (100% power) 2 to 3 minutes, until bacon is browned, stirring halfway through cooking. With slotted spoon, remove bacon to paper towels to drain.
2. Reheat dish with drippings. Place steaks on dish, pressing lightly with spatula. Cook on High 3 to 4½ (4:30) minutes, turning over once. Remove to platter; loosely cover and keep warm while preparing sauce.
3. Discard all but 1 teaspoon drippings. Add vegetables and stir to coat. Cook on High 3 to 4 minutes, until softened, stirring twice. Add Madeira, broth, and cornstarch. Cook on High 3 to 3½ (3:30) minutes, until sauce thickens, stirring halfway through cooking. Season.
4. *To serve*: Into sauce, stir reserved bacon; spoon over steaks. Garnish; serve immediately.

STEAK WITH MUSHROOMS AND ARTICHOKES

Color Index page 60. 4 servings. 374 cals per serving. Good source of riboflavin, niacin, iron.
Begin 25 minutes ahead.

1 9-ounce package frozen artichoke hearts
Water
¾ pound mushrooms
2 green onions, chopped
2 tablespoons butter or margarine (¼ stick)
¾ teaspoon instant beef-flavor bouillon
1 tablespoon dry red wine
4 beef tenderloin steaks, cut 1 inch thick
½ teaspoon browning sauce
½ teaspoon salt
¼ teaspoon pepper
¼ teaspoon marjoram
Parsley for garnish

1. In 1-quart microwave-safe casserole, place artichokes and 2 tablespoons water. Cook, covered, on High (100% power) 6 to 8 minutes, stirring twice. Remove artichokes; drain and cut in half. In same casserole, place mushrooms and next 4 ingredients. Cook, covered, on High 3 minutes, stirring twice. Add artichokes.
2. On microwave-safe rack in microwave-safe baking dish, arrange steaks. In bowl, mix browning sauce with 1 teaspoon water. Brush onto both sides of meat. Season. Cook on Medium-High (70% power) 6 to 8 minutes for medium-rare, rotating dish halfway through cooking.
3. Place steaks on warmed dinner plates. Spoon artichoke mixture around steaks. Garnish.

Less Tender Beef

STEAK AND MUSHROOM PIE

Color Index page 66. 8 servings. 317 cals per serving. Good source of iron. Begin 1¾ hours ahead.

2 tablespoons butter or margarine (¼ stick)
4 small onions, sliced
½ pound mushrooms, cut into quarters
1½ pounds beef for stew, cut into 1-inch chunks
½ cup dry red wine
½ cup Beef Broth (page 125) or canned broth
2 tablespoons steak sauce

1 tablespoon tomato paste
2 tablespoons cornstarch dissolved in ¼ cup cold water
Salt and pepper to taste
Pastry for Baked Piecrust (page 361), or ½ 10- to 11-ounce package piecrust mix
1 egg yolk
Water

1. In deep 9″ microwave-safe quiche dish or pie plate, place butter or margarine. Heat, covered with paper towel, on High (100% power) 45 seconds, or until melted. Add onions and mushrooms. Cook on High 5 to 6 minutes, until onions are tender, stirring twice.
2. To vegetables, add beef, red wine, broth, steak sauce, and tomato paste. Stir until blended. Cook, covered, on Medium (50% power) 40 to 60 minutes, until meat is fork-tender, stirring occasionally. Stir in dissolved cornstarch. Cook on High 2 to 3 minutes, until sauce thickens, stirring halfway through cooking. Season. Let cool.
3. Meanwhile, prepare pastry through step 3. Preheat conventional oven to 400°F.
4. Gently roll pastry onto rolling pin; place loosely over cooled meat mixture. With kitchen scissors, trim edge of pastry, leaving 1-inch overhang. Fold overhang under; then bring up over dish or plate rim; pinch to form high edge on pie, then make Decorative Pie Edge (page 362) of your choice.
6. With tip of knife, cut several slits in pastry top. In 1-cup glass measure, with fork, mix egg yolk with 1 teaspoon water. Brush pastry with egg-yolk mixture. If you like, reroll pastry scraps and, with cookie cutter, cut out shapes; place on top of pie. Brush cut-outs with egg-yolk mixture. Bake pie conventionally 20 minutes, or until crust is golden and filling is hot.

Decorating the Top of Pie

With small sharp knife, slash pastry top to allow steam to escape.

Cut out leaves or other shapes and decorate top of glazed pie.

Cuts of beef, such as flank steak, cook rapidly in the microwave. Our Beef and Asparagus Amandine (below) makes a decorative centerpiece for an elegant yet easy dinner party. Use strips of smooth foil to shield the edges of the meat for a perfect, evenly cooked result.

BEEF AND ASPARAGUS AMANDINE

Color Index page 60. 312 cals per serving. Good source of niacin, vitamin C, iron. Begin 20 minutes ahead.

Ingredients for 4 servings		Microwave cookware
1 pound asparagus, trimmed 3 tablespoons water ½ teaspoon instant beef-flavor bouillon 1 1-pound beef flank steak 4 tablespoons butter or margarine (½ stick) 3 tablespoons dried bread crumbs	2 tablespoons minced parsley 2 tablespoons sliced almonds 2 teaspoons soy sauce 1 teaspoon lemon juice	12″ by 8″ baking dish 2-cup glass measure Small bowl

1 In dish, place asparagus, tips overlapping in center, and water. Cook, covered, on High (100% power) 4½ (4:30) to 6 minutes, until tender-crisp. Remove to warmed serving platter; keep warm.

2 Into glass measure, pour asparagus cooking liquid. Add ¼ teaspoon bouillon. Stir to dissolve; set aside. In same baking dish, place steak. Set aside.

3 In small bowl, place 1 tablespoon butter or margarine. Heat on High 30 to 45 seconds, until melted. Stir in bread crumbs, parsley, and ¼ teaspoon bouillon; pat mixture onto top of steak.

4 Shield long sides of steak with 1½-inch-wide strips of smooth foil. Cook on High 5 to 6 minutes for medium-rare, rotating dish and removing foil halfway through cooking.

5 To reserved asparagus cooking liquid, add almonds, soy sauce, lemon juice, and remaining butter or margarine. Cook on High 1 to 2 minutes, until butter or margarine is melted and sauce is hot, stirring halfway through cooking.

6 *To serve:* Thinly slice steak across grain. Arrange meat on serving platter with asparagus. Pour sauce over steak and asparagus.

Less Tender Beef

BEEF BOURGUIGNON

Color Index page 66. 449 cals per serving. Good source of vitamin A, riboflavin, niacin, iron. Begin 1½ hours ahead.

Ingredients for 4 servings		Microwave cookware
4 slices bacon, diced ½ pound mushrooms, cut into quarters 2 medium carrots, diced 2 medium celery stalks, diced 1 pound beef for stew, cut into 1½-inch chunks 1 cup dry red wine 1 cup Beef Broth (page 125) or canned broth 1 tablespoon tomato paste	1 teaspoon sugar 1 bay leaf ½ teaspoon thyme leaves ½ 16-ounce bag frozen pearl onions, thawed 2 tablespoons butter or margarine (¼ stick), softened 2 tablespoons all-purpose flour Salt and pepper to taste Parsley sprigs for garnish	13″ by 9″ baking dish

1 In baking dish, place bacon. Cook, covered with paper towel, on High (100% power) 4 to 5 minutes, until bacon is browned, stirring twice. With slotted spoon, remove bacon to paper towels to drain.

2 Into bacon drippings, stir mushrooms, carrots, and celery. Cook on High 4 to 6 minutes, until vegetables are softened, stirring twice.

3 To vegetables, add beef; stir to coat with bacon drippings. Add red wine, broth, tomato paste, sugar, bay leaf, and thyme leaves.

4 Cook stew, covered, on Medium (50% power) 45 to 60 minutes, until meat is fork-tender, stirring occasionally. Add pearl onions 5 minutes before end of cooking. With spoon, skim fat from surface. Remove bay leaf.

5 In small bowl, combine butter or margarine and flour to form a soft paste. Stir small pieces into stew, a little at a time, until blended. Cook on High 3 to 4 minutes, until stew bubbles and thickens, stirring twice. Let stand, loosely covered, 10 to 15 minutes.

6 Season stew with salt and pepper. If you like, transfer to warmed serving dish. Sprinkle reserved diced bacon over stew. Garnish with parsley sprigs.

BEEF STROGANOFF

Color Index page 66. 6 servings. 346 cals per serving. Good source of riboflavin, iron. Begin 1½ hours ahead.

2 tablespoons butter or margarine (¼ stick)
2 large onions, chopped
½ pound mushrooms, sliced
1½ pounds beef chuck, cut into 2″ by ½″ strips
1 tablespoon Dijon mustard
1 cup Beef Broth (page 125) or canned broth
1 teaspoon Worcestershire
1 tablespoon cornstarch dissolved in 2 tablespoons cold water
1 cup sour cream
Salt and pepper to taste
Buttered noodles (optional)
Chopped parsley for garnish

1. In 13″ by 9″ microwave-safe baking dish, place butter or margarine. Heat, covered with paper towels, on High (100% power) 45 seconds, or until melted. Add onions and mushrooms; stir. Cook on High 5 to 7 minutes, until vegetables are softened, stirring twice.

2. To vegetables, add beef strips, mustard, broth, and Worcestershire; stir. Cook, covered, on Medium (50% power) 45 to 60 minutes, until meat is fork-tender, stirring occasionally.

3. Into meat mixture, stir dissolved cornstarch. Cook on High 3 to 4 minutes, until mixture thickens, stirring halfway through cooking. Gradually add sour cream, stirring until blended. Let stand, loosely covered, 10 to 15 minutes.

4. Season stroganoff with salt and pepper. If you like, serve with buttered noodles. Garnish with chopped parsley.

BEEF GOULASH

Color Index page 67. 6 servings. 296 cals per serving. Good source of vitamin A, vitamin C, iron. Begin 1½ hours ahead.

2 tablespoons olive or salad oil
2 large onions, sliced
2 green peppers, cut into thin strips
4 garlic cloves, minced
2 tablespoons paprika
1½ pounds beef for stew, cut into 2″ by ½″ strips
1 14½- to 16-ounce can tomato puree
½ cup Beef Broth (page 125) or canned broth
Salt and pepper to taste
Buttered noodles (optional)

1. In 13″ by 9″ microwave-safe baking dish, place oil, onions, green peppers, garlic, and paprika. Cook, covered with paper towels, on High (100% power) 5 to 6 minutes, stirring twice.

2. To vegetables, add beef strips, tomato puree, and broth; stir. Cook, covered, on Medium (50% power) 45 to 60 minutes, until meat is fork-tender, stirring occasionally. Let stand, loosely covered, 10 to 15 minutes.

3. Season goulash with salt and pepper. If you like, serve over buttered noodles.

OLD-FASHIONED BEEF STEW

Color Index page 67. 6 servings. 376 cals per serving. Good source of vitamin A, niacin, vitamin C, iron. Begin 1¾ hours ahead.

2 tablespoons butter or margarine (¼ stick)
2 large onions, cut into wedges
4 medium carrots, cut into 3-inch pieces, then lengthwise into quarters
3 medium celery stalks, cut into 3-inch pieces, then lengthwise into quarters
6 small potatoes, cut in half
3 small turnips, cut into 2-inch chunks
1½ pounds beef for stew, cut into 1½-inch chunks
1½ cups Beef Broth (page 125) or canned broth
½ teaspoon thyme leaves
1 bay leaf
2 tablespoons tomato paste
Salt and pepper to taste

1. In 13″ by 9″ baking dish, place butter or margarine. Heat, covered with paper towels, on High (100% power) 45 seconds, or until melted.
2. To melted butter or margarine, add onions, carrots, celery, potatoes, and turnips. Cook on High 5 to 6 minutes, until softened, stirring twice.
3. To vegetables, add beef, broth, thyme leaves, bay leaf, and tomato paste. Cook, covered, on Medium (50% power) 45 to 60 minutes, or until meat is fork-tender, stirring occasionally. Let stand, loosely covered, 10 to 15 minutes.
4. Discard bay leaf and season stew with salt and pepper before serving.

BEEF CARBONNADE

Color Index page 67. 8 servings. 268 cals per serving. Good source of iron. Begin 1½ hours ahead.

4 slices bacon, diced
3 large onions, thinly sliced
2 pounds beef for stew, cut into 1½-inch chunks
1 12-ounce can beer
1 cup Beef Broth (page 125) or canned broth
1 tablespoon browning sauce
1 bay leaf
1 tablespoon cornstarch dissolved in 2 tablespoons cold water
1 tablespoon red-wine vinegar
Salt and pepper to taste

1. In 13″ by 9″ microwave-safe baking dish, place bacon. Cook, covered with paper towels, on High (100% power) 4 to 5 minutes, until bacon is browned, stirring twice. With slotted spoon, remove bacon to paper towels to drain.
2. Into bacon drippings, stir onions. Cook on High 7 to 10 minutes, until onions are soft and tender, stirring occasionally.
3. Into onions, stir beef and next 4 ingredients. Cook, covered, on Medium (50% power) 45 to 60 minutes, until meat is fork-tender, stirring occasionally. Skim fat. Stir in dissolved cornstarch. Cook on High 3 to 4 minutes, until sauce thickens slightly, stirring twice. Let stand, loosely covered, 10 to 15 minutes.
4. Before serving, discard bay leaf. Into stew, stir vinegar, salt, and pepper.

Meal in Minutes *for 8 people*

Superfast Barbecue

Mexican Dip, page 112 (double quantity) with crudités and potato chips
Chuck Steak Barbecue, page 208
"Barbecued" Chicken, page 188
Corn-on-the-cob with Flavored Butters, page 260
Hot French bread
Vanilla Ice Cream, page 330, and chocolate ice cream (bought)
Strawberries and melon slices
Lemonade

PREPARATION TIMETABLE	
1 day ahead:	*Make Vanilla Ice Cream; store in freezer. Make Mexican Dip; cover and refrigerate.*
2 hours ahead:	*Prepare vegetables for crudités; store in plastic bags in refrigerator. Prepare strawberries and melon, arrange on attractive serving platter, and cover; if you like, store in refrigerator.*
1 hour ahead:	*Prepare outdoor grill for barbecuing. Prepare Chuck Steak Barbecue through step 3 and "Barbecued" Chicken through step 2, to be finished on outdoor grill. Assemble Mexican Dip, crudités, and chips.*
15 minutes before serving:	*Brush chicken with barbecue sauce and complete cooking on grill with chuck steak. Cook Corn-on-the-cob and melt Flavored Butters as recipes direct. Heat French bread in microwave on High (100% power).*

Quick Outdoor Cooking

Use the microwave to make outdoor cooking a snap. Partially cook food in the microwave, then finish on the grill just long enough to brown it and get that delicious outdoor flavor. The food remains moist and tender without charring. Our Chuck Steak Barbecue (shown in the Superfast Barbecue menu on page 207) works perfectly using this tip.

CHUCK STEAK BARBECUE

6 servings. 305 cals per serving. Begin 45 minutes ahead.

1 celery stalk, chopped
1 small green pepper, sliced
1 small onion, thinly sliced
Water
½ cup chili sauce
1 tablespoon all-purpose flour
2 tablespoons dark-brown sugar
1 teaspoon salt
¼ teaspoon garlic powder
⅛ teaspoon ground red pepper
1 1½-pound boneless beef chuck steak
Unseasoned meat tenderizer

1. Prepare outdoor grill for barbecuing.
2. In 12″ by 8″ microwave-safe baking dish, place celery, pepper, and onion. Cook, covered, on High (100% power) 4 to 6 minutes, until tender, stirring twice. Stir in 3 tablespoons water and next six ingredients.
3. Moisten steak with water; rub on tenderizer. With fork, pierce steak deeply all over. Place in dish with vegetables; spoon some sauce over. Cook, covered, on Medium (50% power) 13 minutes, rotating dish and turning steak over halfway through cooking.
4. Scrape off excess sauce from steak. Place steak on preheated grill over high heat. Cook 10 to 12 minutes for medium-rare, or until of desired doneness, turning steak over and brushing with sauce halfway through cooking. Reheat remaining sauce on High 1 minute. Serve with steak.

QUICK BARBECUE SAUCES

Each one of these easy sauces makes enough for a large barbecued steak to serve 6 people, or 6 beef ribs or hamburgers. They taste great on broiled foods as well.

Tex-mex Sauce: In 2-cup microwave-safe glass measure, place *½ cup chili sauce, 2 tablespoons each cider vinegar, brown sugar, finely chopped mild green chilies, 1 teaspoon salt*, and *¼ teaspoon ground cumin (optional).* Cook on High (100% power) 3 to 3½ (3:30) minutes, until bubbling, stirring twice. Makes 1 cup.

Apricot-soy Sauce: In 2-cup microwave-safe glass measure, place *½ cup apricot preserves, 2 thinly sliced green onions, 2 tablespoons soy sauce, 1 teaspoon each cider vinegar and dry mustard*, and *¼ teaspoon ground ginger.* Cook on High (100% power) 1½ (1:30) to 2 minutes, until bubbling, stirring twice. Makes ⅔ cup.

Herb-butter Sauce: In 2-cup microwave-safe glass measure, place *4 tablespoons butter, 1 tablespoon each salad oil* and *lemon juice, ½ teaspoon herbs (such as basil, thyme, rosemary, dill), ¼ teaspoon salt*, and *dash pepper.* Cook on High (100% power) 1 minute, or until butter melts, stirring twice. Makes ⅓ cup.

Beef Brisket

CORNED BEEF AND CABBAGE

Color Index page 65. 6 servings. 520 cals per serving. Good source of vitamin A, niacin, vitamin C, iron. Begin 2 hours ahead.

1 3½-pound corned beef brisket
2 onions, sliced
2 celery stalks, sliced
1 carrot, sliced
8 whole allspice
10 whole cloves
6 peppercorns
2 bay leaves
1 16-ounce bottle ginger ale
2½ cups water
1 small head cabbage, cut into 8 to 10 wedges
Salt and pepper to taste
Horseradish, prepared mustard, and rye bread (optional)

1. In large plastic roasting bag, place brisket, onions, celery, carrot, allspice, cloves, peppercorns, bay leaves, ginger ale, and 1 cup water. Close bag loosely with plastic or nylon tie (do not use metal ties), leaving vent. Place bag in 13″ by 9″ microwave-safe baking dish.
2. Cook meat on High (100% power) 5 minutes. Reduce power level to Medium-Low (30% power) and cook 1 to 1½ hours longer, until meat is fork-tender, turning bag over every 20 minutes during cooking.
3. Carefully open roasting bag and transfer meat to carving board. Tent with foil and let stand 15 to 20 minutes. Set aside bag with vegetables and cooking liquid.
4. Meanwhile, pour remaining water into same baking dish. Add cabbage wedges. Cook, covered, on High 11 to 14 minutes, until tender-crisp, stirring halfway through cooking. To cabbage, add vegetables from bag and ¼ cup cooking liquid. Cook, covered, on High 2 minutes, or until cabbage is tender. Discard bay leaves; season.
5. *To serve:* Thinly slice meat across grain. Arrange on warmed serving platter with vegetables. If you like, serve with horseradish, mustard, and rye bread.

BARBECUE BRISKET

Color Index page 65. 6 servings. 279 cals per serving. Good source of niacin, iron. Begin 1¾ hours ahead.

1 3-pound beef brisket
2 onions, sliced
½ cup barbecue sauce
½ cup apple juice
1 tablespoon brown sugar
1 teaspoon Worcestershire
1 tablespoon grated horseradish
¼ teaspoon ground cloves

1. In large plastic roasting bag, place brisket and all other ingredients. Close bag with plastic or nylon tie (do not use metal ties). Place bag in 13″ by 9″ microwave-safe baking dish.
2. Cook brisket on High (100% power) 5 minutes. Reduce power level to Medium-Low (30% power) and cook 1 to 1¼ hours longer, until meat is fork-tender, turning bag over every 20 minutes. Let meat stand in bag 15 minutes.
3. *To serve:* Thinly slice meat across grain. Serve with cooking sauce spooned over meat.

Ground Beef

CHEESEBURGERS

Color Index page 60. 4 servings. 406 cals per serving. Good source of riboflavin, niacin, calcium, iron. Begin 25 minutes ahead.

1 medium onion, sliced	*2 tablespoons ice water*
¼ pound mushrooms, sliced	*2 teaspoons cornstarch*
2 tablespoons butter or margarine (¼ stick)	*1 teaspoon unseasoned meat tenderizer*
1¼ teaspoons paprika	*½ teaspoon black pepper*
1 pound ground beef	*1 teaspoon browning sauce*
3 ounces Cheddar, fontina, or Muenster cheese, shredded (¾ cup) or 2 ounces blue cheese, crumbled (½ cup)	*4 slices white bread, toasted (optional)*

1. In 10″ round microwave-safe baking dish, place onion, mushrooms, 1 tablespoon butter or margarine, and ¼ teaspoon paprika. Cook, covered, on High (100% power) 5 to 6 minutes, until vegetables are tender, stirring twice. Spoon mixture into small bowl; set aside.

2. In medium bowl, combine ground beef, cheese, and ice water. Shape into 4 patties. On waxed paper, mix cornstarch, tenderizer, pepper, and remaining paprika. In 1-cup microwave-safe glass measure, place remaining butter or margarine. Heat on High 30 seconds, or until melted; stir in browning sauce. Brush on patties and then coat with cornstarch mixture.

3. In same baking dish, place burgers. Cook, covered loosely with waxed paper, on Medium-High (70% power) 5 minutes, rotating dish halfway through cooking. Spoon onion-mushroom mixture over burgers. Cook on Medium-High 1 minute longer, or until hot. If you like, serve on toast.

HEATING HAMBURGER BUNS

Heating hamburger buns in the microwave is fast and easy; the same technique can be used for heating pitas and tortillas. Use paper towels when heating bread, rolls, and other baked goods as they absorb moisture and prevent sogginess.

Wrap 2 hamburger buns in paper towels. Place on paper plate or directly on oven floor. Cook on High (100% power) 12 to 17 seconds, until buns are warm. For 1 bun, heat on High 10 to 15 seconds.

Ground meat of any kind works well for burgers. Eighty to 85 percent lean ("extra-lean ground beef") is best for lower-calorie burgers; the percentage of lean meat to fat is usually listed on the package. When making our Surprise Burgers (below), don't overhandle the meat, as it may result in tough patties.

SURPRISE BURGERS

Color Index page 60. 380 cals per serving. Good source of niacin, iron. Begin 20 minutes ahead.

Ingredients	For 4	For 2	For 1
Ground beef	*1 pound beef*	*½ pound beef*	*¼ pound beef*
Water	*1 tablespoon*	*1½ teaspoons*	*¾ teaspoon*
Salt	*½ teaspoon*	*¼ teaspoon*	*⅛ teaspoon*
Pepper	*⅛ teaspoon*	*to taste*	*to taste*
Roasted pimentos, diced	*¼ cup pimentos*	*2 tablespoons pimentos*	*1 tablespoon pimentos*
Pitted ripe olives, thinly sliced	*4 large olives*	*2 large olives*	*1 large olive*
Chili sauce	*¼ cup*	*2 tablespoons*	*1 tablespoon*
Hamburger buns	*4 buns*	*2 buns*	*1 bun*
Microwave cookware	12″ by 8″ baking dish with rack	9″ by 9″ baking dish with rack	9″ pie plate with rack
Time on High (100% power) Burgers	3 minutes	2 minutes	1 minute
After rotating	1½ (1:30) to 3 minutes	1½ (1:30) to 2 minutes	1½ (1:30) minutes

1 In bowl, mix ground beef, water, salt, and pepper; divide meat mixture into 2 portions per serving.

2 On waxed paper, pat each into a 3½-inch patty; flatten. In small bowl, combine pimentos, olives, and chili sauce.

3 Top half the patties with an equal amount of pimento-olive mixture, leaving a ¼-inch border.

4 Place a plain patty on top of each patty with filling. With fingers, press edges together to seal.

5 On rack in baking dish or pie plate (see Chart), place burgers. Cook on High for time in Chart.

6 With spatula, turn burgers over; rotate dish. Cook on High for time in Chart, or until burgers are of desired doneness. Serve in hamburger buns.

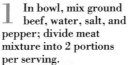

Ground Beef

PARTY BURGERS

Color Index page 67. 106 cals per serving. Low in cholesterol. Begin early in day.

For easy entertaining, dishes such as these Party Burgers can be prepared up to a certain point and frozen, then removed from the freezer and microwaved just before serving.

Ingredients for 12 servings		Microwave cookware
½ pound ground sirloin steak *1 ounce Cheddar cheese, shredded, or blue cheese, crumbled (¼ cup)* *½ teaspoon unseasoned meat tenderizer* *½ teaspoon browning sauce* *¼ teaspoon Worcestershire* *3 tablespoons chopped parsley*	*2 teaspoons cracked black pepper* *½ teaspoon basil* *6 slices white bread* *3 tablespoons butter or margarine, melted* *Garnishes: lettuce, cherry-tomato slices, small white-onion slices, canned sliced mushrooms, or chopped pimento, cheese, or bacon*	Platter 12" by 8" baking dish with rack

1 In small bowl, combine ground sirloin, cheese, meat tenderizer, browning sauce, and Worcestershire. Shape into 6" by 1½" log; wrap in waxed paper. For ease of handling, freeze 1 hour, or until firm.

2 In bowl, combine parsley, pepper, and basil; set aside. Using 2-inch round cookie cutter, cut 2 rounds from each slice of bread. Toast. Dip edges in melted butter or margarine, then coat in parsley mixture. Place in freezer container; cover and freeze.

3 When meat is firm, cut crosswise into twelve ½-inch-thick slices. On waxed-paper-lined cookie sheet, freeze patties until firm. Place in freezer container; cover and freeze.

4 About 15 minutes before serving, on platter, arrange toast rounds in single layer. Heat on High (100% power) 20 seconds, until thawed. Set aside.

5 On rack in baking dish, place burgers. Cook on Medium (50% power) 5 to 5½ (5:30) minutes for medium-rare, rotating dish halfway through cooking.

6 Arrange each burger on a toast round. Garnish with lettuce, cherry-tomato slices, small white-onion slices, canned sliced mushrooms or chopped pimento, cheese or bacon, heating cheese-topped burgers just until cheese melts.

BEST-EVER BURGERS

Color Index page 60. 2 servings. 344 cals per serving. Good source of vitamin A, niacin, calcium, iron. Begin 25 minutes ahead.

1 large carrot
1 small zucchini
3 tablespoons butter or margarine
½ pound ground beef
1 teaspoon cornstarch
½ teaspoon unseasoned meat tenderizer
½ teaspoon paprika
¼ teaspoon pepper
½ teaspoon browning sauce
2 small onions, sliced
2 tablespoons dry red wine

1. With vegetable peeler, shred carrot and zucchini. Place in 1-quart microwave-safe casserole. Add 1 tablespoon butter; cover and set aside.

2. Shape ground beef into two ¾-inch-thick oval patties. On waxed paper, mix cornstarch, meat tenderizer, paprika, and pepper. In 1-cup microwave-safe glass measure, place 1 tablespoon butter or margarine. Heat on High (100% power) 30 seconds, or until melted; stir in browning sauce. Brush on patties and then coat with cornstarch mixture.

3. In 8" by 8" microwave-safe baking dish, place burgers, onions, and remaining butter or margarine. Cook, covered loosely with waxed paper, on Medium-High (70% power) 4 to 5 minutes for medium-rare, rotating dish halfway through cooking. Transfer to platter; set aside and keep warm. Into same baking dish, stir wine. Cook, covered, on High 4 minutes. Keep warm.

4. Cook vegetable mixture, covered, on High 2 to 3 minutes until tender-crisp, stirring halfway through cooking. Spoon onion mixture over burgers and accompany with vegetables.

MEXICAN BEEF CASSEROLE

Color Index page 61. 6 servings. 621 cals per serving. Good source of riboflavin, niacin, calcium, iron. Begin 25 minutes ahead.

1½ pounds ground beef
1 onion, chopped
1 garlic clove, minced
1 6-ounce can pitted ripe olives, drained and sliced (1 cup)
1 10-ounce package frozen whole-kernel corn, thawed
2 10-ounce cans enchilada sauce
6 6-inch corn tortillas, cut into quarters
4 ounces Cheddar cheese, shredded (1 cup)
Coriander sprigs for garnish

1. In microwave-safe colander set over large microwave-safe bowl, place beef, onion, and garlic. Cook on High (100% power) 5 to 6 minutes, until beef is no longer pink, stirring twice. Discard drippings; place meat in bowl. Add ¾ cup olives, corn, and 1 can enchilada sauce.

2. In 13" by 9" microwave-safe baking dish, place alternate layers of remaining enchilada sauce, tortilla pieces, meat mixture, and cheese. Cook, covered, on High 10 to 12 minutes. Garnish with remaining olives and coriander.

CHILI CON CARNE

Color Index page 61. 6 servings. 250 cals per serving. Good source of vitamin A, vitamin C, iron. Begin 25 minutes ahead.

1 pound ground beef	2 teaspoons tomato paste
1 medium onion, chopped	½ cup water
3 garlic cloves, minced	1 16-ounce can red kidney or black beans (optional)
1 green pepper, diced	
2 tablespoons chili powder	Sour cream, shredded Cheddar cheese, and chopped coriander for garnish
1 teaspoon oregano	
1 bay leaf	
2 teaspoons ground cumin (optional)	Tortilla chips and hot-pepper sauce (optional)
1 16-ounce can crushed tomatoes	

1. In microwave-safe colander set over microwave-safe bowl, place ground beef. Cook on High (100% power) 4 minutes, or until beef is no longer pink, stirring twice. Discard all but 3 tablespoons drippings from bowl.

2. In 2-quart microwave-safe casserole, combine drippings, ground beef, onion, garlic, green pepper, chili powder, oregano, and bay leaf. If you like, add cumin. Cook on High 3 minutes, stirring twice.

3. To mixture, add crushed tomatoes, tomato paste, and water. Stir well to combine. Cook, covered with paper towel, on High 5 minutes, stirring twice. Discard bay leaf.

4. If using beans, drain and rinse. Stir into meat mixture. Cook, covered with paper towel, on High 3 minutes, until beans are hot, stirring once.

5. Serve chili in individual bowls garnished with sour cream, Cheddar cheese, and chopped coriander. If you like, serve with tortilla chips and pass hot-pepper sauce separately.

COME-ON-OVER CHILI

Color Index page 61. 8 servings. 385 cals per serving. Good source of niacin, iron. Begin 25 minutes ahead.

1½ pounds ground beef	1 28-ounce can tomatoes
2 medium onions, coarsely chopped	¼ cup tomato paste
2 garlic cloves, minced	1 15¼- to 19-ounce can red kidney beans, drained
1 tablespoon chili powder	
1 medium zucchini, cut into 1-inch chunks	1 10-ounce package frozen whole-kernel corn, thawed

1. In 3-quart microwave-safe casserole, place ground beef, onions, garlic, and chili powder. Cook, covered, on High (100% power) 5 to 7 minutes, just until beef is no longer pink, stirring twice.

2. To meat mixture, add zucchini, tomatoes with their liquid, and tomato paste. Cook, covered, on High 11 to 13 minutes, until zucchini is tender, stirring twice. To mixture, add beans and corn. Cook, covered, on High 3 to 5 minutes, until hot.

INDIVIDUAL MEAT LOAVES

Color Index page 61. 470 cals per serving. Good source of riboflavin, niacin, calcium, iron. Begin 25 minutes ahead.

Ingredients	For 4	For 2	For 1
1 medium cucumber (about 8 ounces), peeled	1 cucumber	½ cucumber	¼ cucumber
Ground beef	1 pound beef	½ pound beef	¼ pound beef
Fresh bread crumbs	¾ cup	⅓ cup	3 tablespoons
Grated onion	1 tablespoon	1½ teaspoons	¾ teaspoon
Salt	¾ teaspoon	½ teaspoon	¼ teaspoon
Pepper	¼ teaspoon	⅛ teaspoon	to taste
Eggs/Water	1 egg	3 tablespoons water	1½ tablespoons water
American cheese slices	8 cheese slices	4 cheese slices	2 cheese slices
Salad and parsley sprigs for garnish	garnish	garnish	garnish
Microwave cookware	12″ by 8″ baking dish	8″ by 8″ baking dish	8″ by 8″ baking dish
Time on Medium-High (70% power)			
Meat loaves	9 minutes	4 minutes	2 minutes
With cheese topping	2 minutes	1 minute	30 seconds
Standing time	3 minutes	2 minutes	2 minutes

1 Cut cucumber lengthwise in half. With spoon, remove seeds. Cut a few slices for garnish; reserve. Coarsely shred remaining cucumber.

2 In medium bowl, combine shredded cucumber and all remaining ingredients except cheese. Divide mixture into required number of servings.

3 Reserve half the cheese slices; fold each remaining slice into 1½″ by ¾″ by ½″ chunk.

4 Shape each portion of meat around a chunk of cheese to make a 4″ by 2″ loaf. In baking dish (see Chart), arrange loaves. Cook, covered loosely with waxed paper, on Medium-High for time in Chart.

5 Remove waxed paper, rotate dish, and top each loaf with a slice of the remaining cheese. Cook on Medium-High for time in Chart.

6 Let meat loaves stand, covered, for time in Chart. Arrange on warmed serving platter. Garnish with salad, parsley, and reserved cucumber slices.

Ground Beef

Ground beef is extremely versatile and can be combined with many other ingredients. Our recipe for Reuben Meat Loaf (below) is based on the ingredients of the famous deli sandwich: substitute seasoned meat for corned beef or pastrami, fill with sauerkraut and Swiss cheese before cooking, then top with dressing.

REUBEN MEAT LOAF

Color Index page 63. 380 cals per serving. Good source of niacin, calcium, iron. Begin 45 minutes ahead.

Ingredients for 6 servings		Microwave cookware
1 8-ounce can sauerkraut, drained 1 tablespoon brown sugar 1 medium celery stalk, finely chopped 2 tablespoons water 1½ pounds ground beef 1½ cups fresh bread crumbs (3 slices)	½ cup milk ⅛ teaspoon pepper 1 egg 2 slices Swiss cheese Thousand Island dressing Radish Flowers (page 116) and parsley for garnish	Medium bowl 12″ by 8″ baking dish

1 In small bowl, combine sauerkraut and sugar; set aside.

2 In medium bowl, place celery and water. Cook, covered, on High (100% power) 3 minutes, or until celery is tender. Add ground beef, bread crumbs, milk, pepper, and egg; mix well.

3 In baking dish, pat half the ground beef mixture into flat 9″ by 6″ oval. Evenly spoon sauerkraut mixture onto meat, leaving a ½-inch border. Top with Swiss cheese slices, folding to fit if necessary.

4 On waxed paper, pat remaining meat mixture into 9½″ by 6½″ oval. Invert over cheese-topped meat in baking dish; remove waxed paper. With fingers, gently press edges together to seal.

5 Cook meat loaf, covered loosely with waxed paper, on Medium-High (70% power) 20 minutes, or until a meat thermometer inserted in center of meat loaf reaches 165°F., rotating dish after 10 minutes. Let stand on heat-safe surface 5 minutes.

6 *To serve:* Spoon ¼ cup Thousand Island dressing over meat loaf. Cut meat loaf crosswise into thick slices. Garnish with Radish Flowers and parsley. If you like, pass extra dressing separately.

MEAT LOAF MILANESE

Color Index page 63. 6 servings. 350 cals per serving. Good source of niacin, vitamin C, iron. Begin 45 minutes ahead.

1 pound small red potatoes, cut in half
1 9-ounce package frozen Italian green beans
¼ cup water
1 small onion, chopped
1 celery stalk, chopped
1 tablespoon lemon juice
1½ pounds ground beef
½ cup dried bread crumbs
1 teaspoon browning sauce
1 egg, slightly beaten
Dry red wine
1 teaspoon basil
1 14½- to 16-ounce can tomatoes, chopped
1 teaspoon sugar

1. In 2-quart microwave-safe casserole, place potatoes, frozen green beans, and water. Cook, covered, on High (100% power) 12 minutes, or until potatoes are tender, stirring twice. Drain; let stand, covered.

2. In 2½-quart microwave-safe bowl, place onion, celery, and lemon juice. Cook, covered, on High 3 minutes. Add beef, bread crumbs, browning sauce, egg, ½ cup wine, and ½ teaspoon basil; mix well. In 12″ by 8″ microwave-safe baking dish, pat meat mixture into 8″ by 4″ loaf.

3. Cook meat, covered loosely with waxed paper, on Medium-High (70% power) 15 minutes, rotating dish a half turn halfway through cooking. Let stand, covered, while preparing sauce.

4. In medium microwave-safe bowl, place tomatoes with their liquid, sugar, 2 tablespoons wine, and remaining basil. Cook, covered, on High 5 minutes, stirring twice.

5. Serve meat loaf with vegetables; pass tomato-basil sauce separately.

MEAT LOAF VARIATIONS
Adapt our Individual Meat Loaves recipe (page 211) by trying one of these variations:

Monterey Meat Loaf: In medium bowl, combine *1 pound ground beef, ¾ cup fresh bread crumbs (1½ slices), 1 tablespoon grated onion, ¼ teaspoon pepper, 1 egg,* and *¼ teaspoon oregano.* In 12″ by 8″ microwave-safe baking dish, pat meat into loaf shape. Cook, covered loosely with waxed paper, on Medium-High (70% power) 10 to 12 minutes, rotating dish once. Remove waxed paper and rotate dish. Top with *4 slices pasteurized process Monterey Jack cheese* and *1 peeled and sliced medium tomato.* Cook on Medium-High 2 minutes. Let stand 3 minutes.

Pineapple Meat Loaf: Prepare Monterey Meat Loaf (above), omitting oregano, cheese, and tomato. Top with slices from *1 8¼-ounce can sliced pineapple.* Cook on Medium-High 2 minutes. Let stand 3 minutes.

MACARONI AND BEEF BOLOGNESE

Color Index page 64. 6 servings. 418 cals per serving. Good source of vitamin A, thiamine, niacin, vitamin C, iron. Begin 55 minutes ahead.

1 pound ground beef	½ 6-ounce can tomato
1 tablespoon olive or	paste
salad oil	½ cup water
2 medium onions,	2 small garlic cloves,
chopped	minced
1 large carrot, chopped	1 8-ounce package large
2 medium celery stalks,	shell macaroni
chopped	Grated Parmesan cheese
1 teaspoon basil	(optional)
1 teaspoon oregano	Parsley for garnish
1 28-ounce can crushed	
tomatoes	

1. In microwave-safe colander set over microwave-safe bowl, place ground beef. Cook on High (100% power) 5 to 6 minutes, until beef is no longer pink, stirring twice. Discard drippings from bowl.
2. In 12″ by 8″ microwave-safe baking dish, combine oil, onions, carrot, celery, basil, and oregano. Cook on High 5 to 6 minutes, until vegetables are softened, stirring twice.
3. Into vegetable mixture, stir cooked beef, crushed tomatoes, tomato paste, and water. Cook on High 10 minutes, or until slightly thickened. Add garlic; stir. Cook on High 5 minutes.
4. Meanwhile, cook macaroni conventionally as label directs; drain.
5. Into beef mixture, stir macaroni; mix well. If you like, sprinkle with Parmesan cheese. Cook, covered loosely with waxed paper, on High 7 to 10 minutes, until hot. Let stand, loosely covered, 10 minutes. Garnish with parsley before serving.

PREPARING GROUND BEEF

Precooking is an ideal way to prepare ground beef for use in casseroles and stews because it reduces the calorie count by getting rid of excess fat, making it healthier for you and your family.

Place ground beef in plastic or other microwave-safe colander set over a microwave-safe bowl.

Cook beef on High (100% power) until no longer pink, stirring twice to break up pieces. Discard drippings from bowl.

You and your microwave oven can produce traditional slow-cooking dishes, like our Stuffed Cabbage (below), in a fraction of the time and without losing that authentic taste. The combination of ground beef, rice, raisins, and seasonings makes for a flavorsome stuffing that can be varied by adding different herbs.

STUFFED CABBAGE

Color Index page 64. 573 cals per serving. Good source of vitamin A, thiamine, niacin, vitamin C, calcium, iron. Begin 55 minutes ahead.

Ingredients for 4 servings		Microwave cookware
1 small cabbage (about 2 pounds)	1 28-ounce can crushed tomatoes	13″ by 9″ baking dish
1 large onion, minced	2 beef-flavor bouillon cubes or envelopes	
1 large carrot, minced	⅛ teaspoon ground cloves	
½ cup regular long-grain rice	1 tablespoon brown sugar	
½ cup raisins	½ teaspoon cider vinegar	
1 pound ground beef	½ 6-ounce can tomato paste	
2 tablespoons steak sauce	Parsley for garnish	
¼ teaspoon ground allspice		
Pepper to taste		

1 Discard tough outer leaves from cabbage. Remove 8 large leaves for cabbage rolls. (Reserve remaining cabbage for use another day.)

2 In baking dish, place cabbage leaves. Cook, covered, on High (100% power) 3 to 4 minutes, until leaves wilt. Remove to paper towels to cool while preparing stuffing.

3 In large bowl, combine onion, carrot, rice, raisins, ground beef, steak sauce, allspice, and pepper.

4 With small, sharp knife, remove rib from each cooled cabbage leaf. On center of each leaf, place an equal amount of beef mixture.

5 Fold 2 sides of cabbage leaf toward center over meat, overlapping edges. From 1 narrow edge, roll jelly-roll fashion. In same baking dish, arrange cabbage rolls, seam side down.

6 In 4-cup glass measure, combine tomatoes, bouillon, cloves, brown sugar, vinegar, and tomato paste. Pour over cabbage rolls. Cook, covered, on Medium (50% power) 30 to 40 minutes, until fork-tender, spooning sauce over and rotating dish halfway through cooking. Arrange cabbage rolls on warmed serving platter, spoon sauce around rolls, and garnish.

Discover how quick and easy cooking for yourself can be using the microwave. In no time at all you can rustle up a number of delicious after-school or anytime snacks. But for safety's sake, pay attention to *Before You Cook* (see Box, page 215) and always make sure an adult is nearby.

TEX-MEX TREATS

Use leftovers from our home-made chili recipes (page 211) or canned chili, to cook up these 2 taste-tempting treats.

Chili Taco: On small microwave-safe plate, place *1 taco shell*. Heat on High (100% power) 45 seconds. Spoon *2 tablespoons chili* into taco shell. Heat on High 30 seconds. Sprinkle *3 tablespoons shredded Cheddar cheese* over, and serve with *lettuce leaves,* and *1 tomato slice.* 1 serving.

Tamale Pie: In microwave-safe soup plate, place *½ cup chili*. Top with *3 tablespoons canned corn, 2 tablespoons shredded Cheddar cheese,* and *2 tablespoons crumbled corn chips.* Cook on High (100% power) 1½ (1:30) to 2 minutes, or until hot. 1 serving.

SUPERQUICK BURGERS

2 servings.
Begin 10 minutes ahead.

½ pound ground beef
2 hamburger buns
2 slices tomato
2 leaves lettuce
Potato chips

1 Shape beef into 2 patties, about 1 inch thick. Line 9″ microwave-safe pie plate with paper towel; place patties on top.

2 Cook, covered with paper towel, on High (100% power) 2 to 3 minutes, turning patties over halfway through cooking. Let stand 2 minutes. Serve in buns with lettuce, tomato, and potato chips.

EASY SLOPPY JOES

4 servings.
Begin 15 minutes ahead.

1 pound ground beef
1 tablespoon dried onion flakes
½ teaspoon garlic salt
¼ teaspoon pepper
½ cup barbecue sauce
2 tablespoons parsley flakes
4 Italian-style rolls or hamburger buns
Lettuce leaves and cherry tomatoes

1 In microwave-safe colander set over large microwave-safe bowl, combine beef and onion. Cook on High (100% power) 4 to 5 minutes, until no longer pink, stirring twice.

2 Discard drippings. Place meat in bowl with garlic salt and next 3 ingredients. Cook on Medium (50% power) 4 to 5 minutes. Spoon onto rolls or buns and serve with lettuce and tomatoes.

EASY PIZZAS

4 servings.
Begin 10 minutes ahead.

1 10½-ounce can pizza sauce
4 English muffins, split and toasted
8 slices mozzarella cheese
Assorted pizza toppings: pepperoni, olives, grated Parmesan or other cheese, sliced mushrooms, red or green pepper strips

1 Spread 1 tablespoon pizza sauce over each muffin half. Top each with 1 slice mozzarella cheese and topping of your choice.

2 Place 4 pizza halves on paper plate. Cook on High (100% power) 1 to 2 minutes, until cheese melts. Repeat with remaining 4 halves.

QUICK BEEF STROGANOFF

4 servings.
Begin 25 minutes ahead.

1 pound ground beef
1 3-ounce can mushroom slices, drained
1 envelope dry onion soup mix
2 tablespoons all-purpose flour
1/4 teaspoon garlic powder
2 tablespoons catchup
1 cup sour cream
Cooked noodles, sour cream, and parsley (optional)

1 Place ground beef in microwave-safe colander set over large microwave-safe bowl. Cook on High (100% power) 4 to 5 minutes, until beef is no longer pink, stirring twice. Discard drippings from bowl. Place meat in bowl.

2 Into beef, stir mushroom slices and onion soup mix. In small bowl, combine flour and next 3 ingredients. Stir into beef mixture. Cook on High 4 to 6 minutes, stirring twice. If you like, serve with noodles, sour cream, and parsley.

BEFORE YOU COOK

While the microwave oven is one of the safest cooking appliances in your home, there are a few things you need to know to keep the cooking fun.

1 Always read the recipe through completely to make certain you understand it and have all the necessary ingredients and cookware.

2 Use only the amounts given in the recipe and cook for the recommended times on the given power.

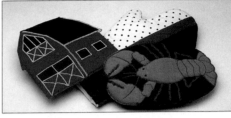

3 Always use potholders. While the oven may feel cool, the dishes will be hot from the heat of the food.

4 Be sure cookware is microwave-safe. Ask an adult to mark microwave-safe items with an "M," using an indelible marker.

5 When using plastic wrap or covers, carefully lift off cooked food so that steam escapes away from your face and fingers.

HAM AND CHEESE MELTS

2 servings.
Begin 20 minutes ahead.

4 slices white bread, toasted
2 teaspoons prepared mustard
2 slices ham
2 slices Swiss cheese
2 gherkins
2 cherry tomatoes

1 Spread 2 slices toast with an equal amount of mustard. Place 1 slice ham on each. Cover each with 1 slice Swiss cheese and remaining toast slice.

2 Place sandwiches on paper plates. Cook on High (100% power) 20 to 30 seconds, just until cheese melts. Cut in half and serve with gherkins and cherry tomatoes.

SOUTH-OF-THE-BORDER BEEF DINNER

4 servings.
Begin 20 minutes ahead.

1 pound ground beef
4 tablespoons tomato sauce
2 teaspoons chili powder
1 tablespoon dried onion flakes
1/2 teaspoon garlic salt
1 8-ounce can refried beans
Assorted accompaniments: sour cream, radishes, coriander, tortilla chips, hot-pepper sauce

1 Place beef in microwave-safe colander set over a large microwave-safe bowl. Cook on High (100% power) 4 to 5 minutes, until beef is no longer pink, stirring twice.

2 Discard drippings. Place meat in bowl. Stir in tomato sauce and next 4 ingredients. Cook on High 4 to 6 minutes, until hot, stirring twice. Serve with accompaniments.

DO NOT
*Turn on microwave with nothing in it.
*Put any metal or foil in microwave.
*Cook an egg in its shell.
*Make microwave popcorn in anything other than manufacturer's container or bag.

Pork Roasts

Choose roasts with uniform diameters. Allow about 22 minutes per pound for a boneless roast and 20 minutes per pound for a bone-in roast. Turn the roast over and rotate the dish halfway through cooking. The roast is done when a thermometer inserted in several places reaches 170°F.

PORK LOIN WITH APRICOT STUFFING

Color Index page 67. 123 cals per serving. Good source of vitamin A, riboflavin, thiamine, niacin, iron. Begin 1½ hours ahead.

Ingredients for 16 servings		Microwave cookware
1 tablespoon butter or margarine	½ teaspoon poultry seasoning	12″ by 8″ baking dish
1 medium onion, chopped	2½ cups fresh bread cubes (about 5 slices)	
1 large celery stalk, chopped	1 2-pound boneless pork loin roast	
1 medium cooking apple, cored and chopped	Pepper to taste	
½ 8-ounce package dried apricots, chopped	1 tablespoon salad oil	
	Parsley sprigs for garnish	

1 In baking dish, place butter or margarine and next 4 ingredients. Cook on High (100% power) 3 minutes, or just until onion is softened, stirring twice. Into mixture, stir poultry seasoning and bread cubes; mix well. Push toward sides of dish.

2 Season pork roast with pepper. In 12″ skillet over high heat, heat oil. Quickly brown roast on all sides.

3 In center of baking dish with stuffing, place pork roast. Cook, covered, on Medium (50% power) 15 minutes.

4 Turn roast over and rotate dish. Cook, covered, on Medium 20 to 30 minutes longer, until a meat thermometer inserted in several places reaches 165°F.

5 On heat-safe surface, let roast stand in dish, tented with foil, 10 to 15 minutes. Temperature will reach 170°F.

6 *To serve*: Thinly slice pork roast. Arrange pork slices and apricot stuffing on warmed serving platter. Garnish with parsley sprigs.

PORK LOIN ROAST WITH GARLIC SAUCE

Color Index page 67. 10 servings. 196 cals per serving. Low in sodium. Good source of thiamine, niacin. Begin 1¼ hours ahead.

20 garlic cloves
1½ cups Chicken Broth (page 125) or canned broth
1 2½-pound boneless pork loin roast
Salt and pepper to taste
Lemon juice to taste
Watercress for garnish

1. In 12″ by 8″ microwave-safe baking dish, place garlic cloves and broth. Cook, covered, on High (100% power) 10 minutes.
2. Season pork. In 12″ skillet over high heat, quickly brown roast on all sides.
3. In center of baking dish with garlic and broth, place pork roast. Cook, covered, on Medium (50% power) 30 to 35 minutes, until a meat thermometer inserted in several places reaches 165°F., turning over and rotating dish after 15 minutes. Let roast stand in dish, tented with foil, on heat-safe surface 10 to 15 minutes. Temperature will reach 170°F. Transfer roast to warmed serving platter; cover and keep warm.
4. In food processor with knife blade attached or in blender, process garlic with broth until smooth. Season with salt, pepper, and lemon juice.
5. *To serve*: Thinly slice pork and arrange on warmed dinner plates; garnish with watercress. Pass garlic sauce separately.

ROAST PORK HASH

Color Index page 62. 4 servings. 366 cals per serving. Good source of thiamine. Begin 20 minutes ahead.

2 cups cubed cooked roast pork
2 cups cubed boiled potatoes
1 large onion, minced
¼ teaspoon thyme leaves
½ teaspoon salt
Pepper to taste
2 eggs
2 tablespoons heavy or whipping cream
2 tablespoons butter or margarine (¼ stick)
Paprika to taste
Parsley for garnish

1. Preheat browning dish as manufacturer directs. Meanwhile, in large bowl, combine pork, potatoes, and onion. Add thyme, salt, and pepper; stir.
2. In small bowl, with fork, combine eggs and cream. Add to pork mixture; stir.
3. Place butter or margarine on browning dish. Add pork mixture, pressing lightly with spatula. Cook on High 7 to 10 minutes, until mixture is set, rotating dish halfway through cooking.
4. If you like, with spatula, slide hash onto broiler-safe serving platter; brown under preheated broiler. Sprinkle with paprika and garnish with parsley.

Pork Loin and Tenderloin

PORK WITH VEGETABLES

Color Index page 62. 4 servings. 440 cals per serving. Good source of vitamin A, thiamine, niacin, vitamin C, iron. Begin 25 minutes ahead.

1 pound pork loin sirloin cutlets, cut ¼ inch thick	*1 pound asparagus, cut into 2-inch pieces*
1 tablespoon butter or margarine	*2 heads Belgian endive, cut lengthwise in half*
1 green onion, minced	*⅓ cup half-and-half*
1 chicken-flavor bouillon cube or envelope	*1 tablespoon all-purpose flour*
½ cup water	*2 tablespoons prepared mustard*
1 12-ounce package baby carrots	*1 tablespoon brandy (optional)*

1. On cutting board, with dull edge of French knife or smooth edge of meat mallet, pound pork cutlets to ⅛-inch thickness. In 12″ by 8″ microwave-safe baking dish, place pork, butter or margarine, green onion, bouillon, and ¼ cup water. Cook, covered, on High (100% power) 8 to 10 minutes, until pork is tender and juices run clear, rearranging cutlets once. Cover and set aside on heat-safe surface.
2. Into shallow 2-quart microwave-safe casserole, pour remaining water; add carrots. Cook, covered, on High 4 minutes. Stir in asparagus. Cook, covered, on High 4 to 5 minutes, until vegetables are tender. To vegetables, add endive; set aside.
3. Remove cutlets to microwave-safe platter. Into mixture in baking dish, whisk half-and-half and flour until blended. Cook on High 2 to 3 minutes, until sauce thickens, stirring once. Stir in mustard and, if you like, brandy.
4. *To serve*: Spoon vegetables around cutlets; pour sauce over cutlets and vegetables. Cook on High 1 to 2 minutes, until hot.

COOKING PORK CHOPS

Choose boneless top loin chops, loin rib chops, or loin chops, ¾ to 1 inch thick.

4 chops, 5 to 7 ounces each	2 chops, 5 to 7 ounces each	1 chop, 5 to 7 ounces
Microwave cookware		
12″ by 8″ baking dish with rack	10″ by 6″ baking dish with rack	9″ pie plate with rack
Time on Medium-Low (30% power)		
20 to 30 minutes	11 to 14 minutes	7 to 9 minutes

On rack in baking dish or pie plate, place chops. Cook, covered, for time in Chart, until meat pulls away from bone and juices run clear, turning chops over and rotating dish halfway through cooking.

Stir-frying is the traditional oriental method of quickly cooking slivers of meat and vegetables in very little oil. Even less oil is necessary when you use a browning dish in a microwave oven, as in our Stir-Fry with Pork (below), so microwave "stir-frying" is delicious *and* nutritious!

STIR-FRY WITH PORK

Color Index page 61. 350 cals per serving. Good source of vitamin A, riboflavin, thiamine, niacin, vitamin C, iron. Begin 25 minutes ahead.

Ingredients for 4 servings		Microwave cookware
2 tablespoons dry sherry *2 tablespoons soy sauce* *1 teaspoon cornstarch* *⅛ teaspoon ground ginger* *1 pork tenderloin (about 1 pound)* *3 green onions, cut into thin strips* *3 large carrots* *1 small yellow squash (about ½ pound)*	*½ pound mushrooms* *2 tablespoons salad oil* *2 tablespoons butter or margarine (¼ stick)* *1 tablespoon lemon juice* *¼ pound Chinese pea pods* *2 tablespoons water* *Spinach leaves for garnish*	Browning dish 1-cup glass measure 2-quart casserole

1 In medium bowl, combine sherry, soy sauce, cornstarch, and ground ginger. With knife held in slanted position, cut pork crosswise into thin slices. To mixture in bowl, add pork slices and green onions.

2 Preheat browning dish as manufacturer directs. Meanwhile, with knife, cut carrots and squash into matchstick-thin strips. Trim and slice mushrooms. Set vegetables aside.

3 Coat surface of browning dish with oil. Add pork-onion mixture; stir quickly to brown. Cook, covered, on High (100% power) 1½ (1:30) to 2 minutes. Transfer to dish and set aside.

4 In glass measure, place butter or margarine and lemon juice. Cook, covered with paper towel, on High 45 seconds, or until butter or margarine is melted.

5 In casserole, place carrots, Chinese pea pods, and water. Cook, covered, on High 5 to 5½ (5:30) minutes, stirring once. Drain. To casserole, add squash, mushrooms, and butter-lemon mixture. Cook, covered, on High 3 to 4 minutes, until vegetables are tender-crisp, stirring once. Place pork-onion mixture on top of vegetables; cook, covered, on High 1 minute, until pork is hot.

6 *To serve*: Arrange pork and vegetable mixture on warmed dinner plates. Garnish with spinach leaves.

PREPARATION TIMETABLE

Early in day:	*Prepare Crab-filled Mushrooms through step 2. Prepare salad ingredients; store in plastic bags in refrigerator. Prepare fruit; sprinkle cut fruit with lemon juice; cover and refrigerate. Prepare Marinated Okra through step 3. Make Crème Brûlée through step 3.*
1½ hours ahead:	*Cook Pork Jambalaya and South-of-the-border Corn Muffins. Complete Crème Brûlée.*
10 minutes before serving:	*While meat is standing, complete Crab-filled Mushrooms. Drain okra; place on platter; garnish. Reheat muffins in 2 batches. Arrange fruit on platter.*

Pork Loin

PORK EMPANADAS

Color Index page 68. 4 servings. 630 cals per serving. Good source of riboflavin, thiamine, niacin, calcium, iron. Begin 2 hours ahead.

1 pound boneless pork loin, trimmed of fat and minced
1 medium onion, minced
2½ teaspoons chili powder
¼ cup seedless raisins
¼ cup slivered almonds
2 tablespoons tomato paste
5 pimento-stuffed olives, chopped

1 cup all-purpose flour
½ cup yellow cornmeal
2 ounces Cheddar cheese, shredded (½ cup)
¼ cup shortening
5 to 6 tablespoons water
Taco sauce and sour cream (optional)
Coriander leaves for garnish

1. In 12″ by 8″ microwave-safe baking dish, place pork and onion. Cook, covered with paper towels, on High (100% power) 5 to 7 minutes, until pork is no longer pink, stirring occasionally.

2. Into pork mixture, stir chili powder, raisins, almonds, tomato paste, and chopped olives. Cook, covered with paper towels, on High 8 to 10 minutes, until raisins are plumped and sauce thickens slightly, stirring occasionally. Set aside to cool while preparing pastry.

3. In medium bowl, place flour and cornmeal; stir. Add cheese and shortening. With 2 knives used scissors fashion or pastry blender, cut in cheese and shortening, until mixture resembles crumbs. Sprinkle water, 1 tablespoon at a time, into mixture, mixing lightly with fork, until pastry just holds together. Shape into ball; flatten slightly. Wrap in waxed paper and refrigerate about 1 hour, until well chilled.

4. On lightly floured surface, with floured rolling pin, roll half the pastry into a round about ⅛ inch thick. Using 5″ round plate as a guide, cut out 4 circles from pastry. Repeat with remaining pastry, rerolling trimmings, to make 8 rounds in all.

5. Preheat conventional oven to 400°F. Onto half of 1 pastry round, spoon an eighth of pork filling. Brush pastry edge lightly with water; fold pastry over filling. With fork, firmly press edges together to seal. Place empanada on ungreased large cookie sheet. Repeat with remaining pastry rounds and pork filling. Bake empanadas conventionally 15 minutes, or until golden brown.

6. *To serve:* Transfer empanadas to warmed serving platter. If you like, serve with taco sauce and sour cream; garnish with coriander.

PORK JAMBALAYA

Color Index page 67. 6 servings. 292 cals per serving. Good source of vitamin A, thiamine, vitamin C, iron. Begin 1½ hours ahead.

3 tablespoons butter or margarine	½ teaspoon filé powder or rubbed sage
3 tablespoons all-purpose flour	⅛ teaspoon ground red pepper
2 large onions, chopped	1 tablespoon tomato paste
2 garlic cloves, minced	
3 medium celery stalks, chopped	1 medium green pepper, diced
1 pound boneless pork loin, cut into 1½-inch cubes	1 medium red pepper, diced
	4 green onions, sliced
2 cups Chicken Broth (page 125) or canned broth	½ cup regular long-grain rice
½ teaspoon poultry seasoning	Salt and pepper to taste

1. In deep 2½-quart microwave-safe casserole, place butter or margarine. Heat, covered with paper towel, on High (100% power) 45 seconds to 1 minute, until melted.
2. Into melted butter or margarine, stir flour until blended. Cook on High 5 to 7 minutes, until golden brown, stirring frequently.
3. Add onions, garlic, celery, and pork cubes; stir until coated with flour mixture. Stir in broth, poultry seasoning, filé powder or rubbed sage, ground red pepper, and tomato paste. Cook, covered, on Medium (50% power) 30 minutes, or until pork is cooked, stirring occasionally.
4. Into mixture, stir peppers, green onions, and rice. Cook, covered, on Medium 15 to 20 minutes, until rice is tender but still firm; season with salt and pepper. Let stand, covered, on heat-safe surface 10 minutes. Transfer to warmed serving plates and serve immediately.

FILÉ Filé powder is derived from ground sassafras leaves. It is used as a thickener and a flavoring in traditional Creole dishes, such as gumbo. It can be added straight to cooking juices or dissolved in water first.

CREAMY AVOCADO SAUCE

Makes 1½ cups. 19 cals per tablespoon. Low in cholesterol, fat, sodium. Begin 10 minutes ahead.

1 ripe avocado, seeded and peeled	1 tablespoon lime juice
2 green onions, sliced	¾ cup plain yogurt
1 teaspoon ground cumin	Salt to taste
	Hot-pepper sauce to taste

1. In food processor with knife blade attached or in blender, process avocado, green onions, cumin, and lime juice until smooth.
2. Add yogurt; process until blended. Season with salt and hot-pepper sauce. Cover and store in refrigerator.

MEXICALI PORK BURRITOS

Color Index page 61. 680 cals per serving (without sauce). Good source of riboflavin, thiamine, niacin, vitamin C, calcium, iron. Begin 25 minutes ahead.

Ingredients	For 4	For 2	For 1
Creamy Avocado Sauce (below left)	1½ cups	¾ cup	½ cup
Boneless pork loin, trimmed of fat and minced	1 pound	½ pound	¼ pound
Onion, chopped	1 large onion	1 small onion	½ small onion
Green pepper, chopped	1 large	1 small	½ small
Taco sauce	½ cup	¼ cup	2 tablespoons
Chili powder	2 teaspoons	1 teaspoon	½ teaspoon
1 16-ounce can refried beans	1 can	½ can	¼ can
Cheddar cheese, shredded	4 ounces (1 cup)	2 ounces (½ cup)	1 ounce (¼ cup)
8" corn tortillas	8 tortillas	4 tortillas	2 tortillas
Microwave cookware	13" by 9" baking dish	12" by 8" baking dish	8" by 8" baking dish
Time on High (100% power) Pork mixture	10 to 12 minutes	6 to 8 minutes	4 to 5 minutes
Tortillas	2 minutes	1 minute	45 seconds
Burritos	3 to 5 minutes	2 to 3 minutes	1½ (1:30) to 2 minutes

1 **Make Creamy Avocado Sauce;** cover and refrigerate. In baking dish (see Chart), mix pork and next 4 ingredients. Cook on High for time in Chart, or until pork is cooked, stirring twice.

2 **On moistened paper** towels, stack tortillas; fold over paper towels. On oven floor, place wrapped tortillas. Heat on High for time in Chart, or until tortillas are softened.

3 **Unwrap tortillas;** place on work surface. Spread an equal amount of refried beans in center of each. Spoon pork mixture over beans; sprinkle with cheese.

4 **Fold right side of** tortilla over mixture; turn bottom edge of tortilla upward. Fold top of tortilla down. Fold left side over to enclose mixture.

5 **Place filled tortillas** (burritos), seam side down, in baking dish used for pork mixture. Cook on High for time in Chart, or until burritos are hot.

6 **To serve:** Place burritos on warmed dinner plates. Top with Creamy Avocado Sauce.

Bacon is best cooked in the microwave; it doesn't curl or shrink as it does when cooked conventionally, and clean-up is easy. Bacon slices vary in thickness, as well as in sugar and fat content. To ensure that your bacon cooks evenly, choose slices of an equal thickness and with a similar fat-to-lean ratio. To separate bacon slices easily, heat package on High 15 to 30 seconds.

Do not let bacon slices overlap or they will not cook properly. When done, bacon will be evenly browned. It should be left to stand for about 5 minutes after which time it will be crisp.

Cooking bacon

Place 2 paper towels, one on top of the other, on plate or paper plate; place 2 slices bacon on towels. Cover with 1 more paper towel. Cook on High 1½ (1:30) to 2 minutes, until bacon is browned; or cook on microwave bacon rack. Let stand 5 minutes.

Cooking bacon in batches

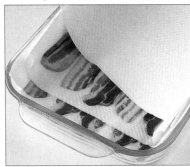

Place 2 paper towels, one on top of the other, in a 12″ by 8″ baking dish; arrange 5 slices of bacon on towels. Cover with 2 more paper towels, 5 more slices of bacon, then 1 more paper towel. Cook on High 7½ (7:30) to 9 minutes, until bacon is browned, rotating dish halfway through cooking. Let stand 5 minutes.

PAPER TOWELS
There is a type of paper towel specially formulated for use in the microwave with all-natural fibers, no artificial colors, and approved by the Food and Drug Administration for contact with food. Brown spots on paper towel are due to sugar content in the bacon, which may also cause the paper towel to stick slightly.

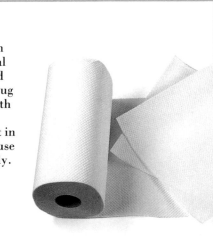

Pork Chops and Ribs

VERMONT PORK AND BEANS

Color Index page 64. 6 servings. 282 cals per serving. Good source of thiamine, calcium, iron. Begin 55 minutes ahead.

1 small onion, thinly sliced	¼ cup cider vinegar
½ cup packed brown sugar	¼ cup tomato paste
2 tablespoons dark molasses	1 16-ounce can navy or pinto beans, drained and rinsed
1 tablespoon dry mustard	1 pound smoked, boneless pork loin chops (about 6 pieces)
1 tablespoon Worcestershire	Parsley for garnish

1. In microwave-safe bean pot or in 2-quart microwave-safe casserole, place onion, brown sugar, molasses, mustard, Worcestershire, vinegar, and tomato paste; stir to combine. Cook, covered, on High (100% power) 5 to 7 minutes, until onion softens slightly and sauce is blended, stirring occasionally.
2. Into mixture, stir beans; mix well. Add pork chops, pushing them down into bean mixture. Cook, covered, on Medium (50% power) 30 to 35 minutes, until flavors are blended and pork chops are hot, stirring occasionally. Serve in pot or casserole; garnish with parsley sprigs.

SAVORY RIBS

Color Index page 64. 4 servings. 473 cals per serving. Good source of vitamin A, thiamine, vitamin C, iron. Begin 55 minutes ahead.

1 large onion, chopped	1 chicken-flavor bouillon cube or envelope
1 large green pepper, cut into thin strips	½ teaspoon caraway seeds, crushed
2 tablespoons salad oil	2 pounds pork loin country-style ribs
2 tablespoons paprika	Sour cream (optional)
1 16-ounce package sauerkraut	
1 8-ounce can tomato sauce	
2 tablespoons brown sugar	

1. In 3-quart microwave-safe casserole, place onion, green pepper, and oil. Cook, covered, on High (100% power) 6 minutes, or until vegetables soften, stirring twice. Add paprika; stir. Cook on High 1 minute.
2. Into mixture, stir undrained sauerkraut, tomato sauce, brown sugar, bouillon, and caraway seeds. Place ribs in casserole and coat with sauce. Cook, covered, on High 35 to 40 minutes, until meat is fork-tender, turning ribs over and rotating casserole after 15 minutes.
3. *To serve*: With spatula, transfer ribs to warmed serving platter. Spoon sauce over. If you like, serve with sour cream.

Ham

GLAZED HAM

Color Index page 64. 8 servings. 258 cals per serving. Good source of thiamine, niacin, vitamin C, iron. Begin 35 minutes ahead.

¼ cup brown sugar	1 3-pound fully cooked
¼ cup Applesauce (page 339)	boneless ham
2 tablespoons prepared mustard	Watercress for garnish

1. In 2-cup microwave-safe glass measure, place brown sugar, applesauce, and mustard; stir until smooth. Cook on High (100% power) 3 to 4 minutes, until glaze is syrupy, stirring twice.
2. With sharp knife, score top of ham in decorative diamond pattern. In 3-quart microwave-safe casserole, place ham; brush with half the glaze. Cook on High 5 minutes. Turn ham over; brush with remaining glaze. Cook on High 5 minutes longer. Turn ham over again and glaze with juices in casserole. Cook on High 5 to 8 minutes more, until a meat thermometer inserted in several places reaches 130°F.
3. On heat-safe surface, let ham stand, tented with foil, 15 minutes. Temperature will reach 140°F. Transfer to warmed serving platter and garnish with watercress.

HAM AND BEAN CASSEROLE

Color Index page 62. 6 servings. 363 cals per serving. Good source of vitamin A, thiamine, niacin, calcium, iron. Begin 25 minutes ahead.

1 medium onion, chopped	1 chicken-flavor bouillon cube or envelope
1 garlic clove, minced	¼ teaspoon rosemary, crushed
1 tablespoon salad oil	¼ teaspoon pepper
3 19-ounce cans white kidney (cannellini) beans	¼ cup water
2 celery stalks, thinly sliced	1 pound fully cooked smoked ham
2 carrots, coarsely shredded	½ bunch escarole

1. In 3-quart microwave-safe casserole, place onion, garlic, and oil. Cook, covered, on High (100% power) 5 minutes, or until onion softens, stirring twice.
2. Drain and rinse 2 cans of beans. To casserole, add drained beans, remaining can of beans with their liquid, celery, carrots, bouillon, rosemary, pepper, and water; stir. Cook, covered, on High 12 to 15 minutes, until hot, stirring twice.
3. Meanwhile, with knife, cut ham into ¾-inch cubes. Tear escarole into bite-sized pieces to make about 3 cups.
4. Into bean mixture, stir ham and escarole. Cook, covered, on High 2 to 3 minutes, until escarole wilts, stirring once. Serve immediately.

Many smoked pork products are available, from large holiday hams to economical, everyday cuts – smoked hocks, spareribs, and bacon. Hams are usually sold fully cooked, although flavor and texture improve by microwaving them to an internal temperature of 130°F. – the temperature will rise to 140°F. during standing.

HAM LOAF

Color Index page 64. 229 cals per serving. Good source of thiamine, niacin, vitamin C, iron. Begin 55 minutes ahead.

Ingredients for 8 servings		Microwave cookware
1½ pounds fully cooked smoked ham	5 pitted ripe olives, sliced	8-cup ring mold or Bundt pan
½ pound ground veal	2 tablespoons dry mustard	
2 green onions, sliced	2 tablespoons steak sauce	
2 eggs	1½ teaspoons celery salt	
1½ cups fresh bread crumbs (3 slices)	Lemon slices and parsley sprigs for garnish	
1 cup tomato juice		
¼ cup diced pimentos		

1 With sharp knife, cut ham into chunks. Place chunks in food processor with knife blade attached or in meat grinder; finely chop.

2 In large bowl, combine chopped ham and veal. To meat, add green onions and remaining ingredients, except garnish. Stir until well combined.

3 With spoon, firmly press mixture into ring mold or Bundt pan; smooth top with back of spoon.

4 Cook loaf, covered loosely with waxed paper, on High (100% power) 5 minutes. Rotate pan. Reduce power level to Medium-Low (30% power) and cook, covered, 15 to 18 minutes longer, until a meat thermometer inserted in center of loaf mixture reaches 150°F.

5 Uncover; rotate pan. Increase power level to High and cook 5 minutes more. On heat-safe surface, let loaf stand, covered loosely with foil, 10 to 15 minutes.

6 To serve: Invert loaf onto warmed serving platter. Garnish with lemon and parsley sprigs.

Veal Roasts

HOLIDAY VEAL ROAST

Color Index page 68. 433 cals per serving. Good source of vitamin A, niacin, calcium, iron. Begin 2 hours ahead.

Ingredients for 12 servings		Microwave cookware
1 4-pound boneless veal breast	2 tablespoons butter or margarine (¼ stick), melted	13″ by 9″ baking dish 2-cup glass measure
1 10-ounce package frozen chopped spinach, thawed	½ teaspoon browning sauce	
4 ounces fontina or Monterey Jack cheese, shredded (1 cup)	1 medium onion, diced	
¼ cup grated Parmesan cheese	¼ cup water	
¾ teaspoon salt	1 16-ounce package orzo (optional)	
1 egg	Sweet-pepper Medley (right, optional)	
1 7-ounce jar roasted pimentos, drained	1 tablespoon all-purpose flour	

SWEET-PEPPER MEDLEY

On cutting board, with sharp knife, cut *10 large peppers (red, green, and yellow)* into 1-inch strips. With same sharp knife, thinly slice *1 large onion.* In 4-quart microwave-safe casserole, place pepper strips, thinly sliced onion, *3 tablespoons salad oil, 1 teaspoon oregano,* and *1 teaspoon salt.* Cook pepper mixture, covered, on High (100% power) 10 to 12 minutes, until vegetables are tender-crisp, stirring occasionally. Serve hot in warmed serving dish as an accompaniment to roasts. 12 servings. 71 cals per serving.

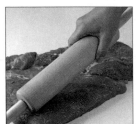

1 On cutting board, spread veal breast flat; trim excess fat. With rolling pin or meat mallet, pound meat to an 18″ by 10″ rectangle, about 1 inch thick.

2 Drain spinach well. In medium bowl, mix spinach, cheeses, salt, and egg; spread evenly over surface of meat.

3 If roasted pimentos are thick, cut each horizontally in half, then into 1½-inch pieces. Arrange pimentos randomly over spinach mixture.

4 Starting from a narrow end, roll up roast tightly; tie with string at 1-inch intervals.

5 In small bowl, mix melted butter or margarine and browning sauce; brush over meat. In baking dish, mix onion and water. Into onion mixture, place roast, seam side up.

6 Cook, covered, on Medium (50% power) 30 minutes. With fork, turn roast seam side down; rotate casserole.

7 Cook roast, covered, on Medium 25 to 30 minutes longer, until a meat thermometer inserted in center of roast reaches 160°F. On heat-safe surface, let roast stand, tented with foil, 15 minutes. Temperature will reach 170°F.

8 If you like, after turning roast, prepare orzo conventionally as package directs, and prepare ingredients for Sweet-pepper Medley. During standing time, cook Sweet-pepper Medley.

9 Into glass measure, strain meat juices from baking dish. With spoon, skim fat from surface. In small bowl, combine flour and 2 tablespoons water until smooth; stir into meat juices. Cook on High (100% power) 4 to 6 minutes, until gravy thickens slightly, stirring halfway through cooking.

10 With sharp knife, cut roast into slices, removing and discarding string as you carve. Arrange slices on warmed serving platter, with orzo and Sweet-pepper Medley if you like. Pass gravy separately.

STUFFED SHOULDER OF VEAL

Color Index page 68. 10 servings. 443 cals per serving. Good source of riboflavin, thiamine, niacin, calcium, iron. Begin 2 hours ahead.

8 ounces fresh (not dried) spinach-filled ravioli, 1- to 1½-inch squares
2 ounces thinly sliced prosciutto, diced
2 ounces Provolone cheese, diced
3 green onions, sliced
½ teaspoon basil
2 tablespoons olive or salad oil
4-pound rolled boneless veal shoulder roast

1 cup dry white wine
1 cup Beef Broth (page 125) or canned broth
1½ tablespoons cornstarch dissolved in 3 tablespoons cold water
Salt and pepper to taste
Parsley sprigs for garnish

1. In medium bowl, combine ravioli, prosciutto, Provolone, green onions, basil, and 1 tablespoon olive or salad oil; set aside.
2. On cutting board, untie veal shoulder roast. Place fat side down. To make veal evenly thick, with sharp knife held parallel to cutting surface, cut off horizontal slices from thick parts of veal. Press cut-off slices where needed along edges of roast to make 12″ by 10″ rectangle. Then, if necessary, pound veal with dull edge of French knife or smooth edge of meat mallet to make about 1 inch thick throughout.
3. Along center of roast, spoon ravioli mixture. Pull meat up and over stuffing. With heavy string, tie roast at 2-inch intervals.
4. In 12″ skillet over medium-high heat, heat remaining oil. Add stuffed shoulder roast and quickly brown on all sides. On microwave-safe rack in 13″ by 9″ microwave-safe baking dish, place meat seam side up.
5. Into skillet, pour wine and broth; stir to loosen any browned bits. Over high heat, bring liquid to a boil; pour over roast in baking dish.
6. Cook roast, covered, on Medium (50% power) 20 minutes. Turn roast seam side down. Cook, covered, on Medium 20 to 30 minutes longer, until a meat thermometer inserted in center of roast reaches 160°F. Remove roast to warmed serving platter and tent with foil. Let stand 10 to 15 minutes. Temperature will reach 170°F.
7. Meanwhile, into 2-cup microwave-safe glass measure, strain meat juices from baking dish. With spoon, skim excess fat. Add dissolved cornstarch and cook on High (100% power) 5 to 6 minutes, until gravy thickens, stirring twice. Season with salt and pepper. With sharp knife, cut roast into slices, removing and discarding string as you carve. Arrange slices on warmed serving platter; serve with gravy and garnish with parsley.

To hold in heat and reduce spatter when cooking a holiday roast, just tent the meat loosely with waxed paper. To prevent the paper sticking to the fat or skin, spray the "food side" of the paper with vegetable cooking spray. Remove waxed paper and tent with foil during standing time, if recipe directs.

ROAST LOIN OF VEAL WITH ACORN SQUASH

Color Index page 68. 357 cals per serving. Good source of riboflavin, niacin, iron. Begin 1¼ hours ahead.

Ingredients for 8 servings		Microwave cookware
1 acorn squash (about 1 pound) *1 small onion, chopped* *2 garlic cloves, minced* *2 tomatoes, chopped* *½ teaspoon ground cumin* *2 tablespoons butter or margarine (¼ stick)*	*1 3-pound rolled boneless veal loin roast* *¼ cup Chicken Broth (page 125) or canned broth* *Salt and pepper to taste* *Watercress sprigs for garnish*	*13″ by 9″ baking dish*

1 To soften squash for cutting, prick all over with fork. In baking dish, place squash. Heat on High (100% power) 1½ (1:30) minutes, or until just warm. Peel squash and cut into 1-inch chunks.

2 In same baking dish, combine squash, onion, garlic, tomatoes, cumin, and butter or margarine. Cook, covered with paper towels, on High 45 seconds to 1 minute, until butter or margarine is melted, stirring halfway through cooking.

3 With spoon, push vegetables to sides of dish. In center of dish, place roast; add broth. Cook, covered, on Medium (50% power) 20 minutes.

4 With fork, turn roast over. Cook, covered, on Medium 20 to 30 minutes longer, until a meat thermometer inserted in center of roast reaches 160°F. Remove roast to warmed serving platter. Let stand, tented with foil, 10 to 15 minutes. Temperature will reach 165°F. to 170°F.

5 Meanwhile, prepare sauce. In food processor with knife blade attached or in blender, process vegetables and cooking juices until smooth. Season with salt and pepper.

6 With sharp knife, cut roast into thin slices, removing and discarding string as you carve. Pour a small amount of sauce onto each of 8 warmed dinner plates. Arrange slices of veal on sauce. Garnish with watercress sprigs and serve immediately.

Veal Cutlets and Shanks

VEAL MARSALA

Color Index page 62. 376 cals per serving. Good source of niacin, iron. Begin 25 minutes ahead.

Ingredients	For 4	For 2	For 1
Veal cutlets, ½ inch thick (about ¼ pound each)	4 cutlets	2 cutlets	1 cutlet
Butter or margarine	4 tablespoons (½ stick)	2 tablespoons (¼ stick)	1 tablespoon
Chicken-flavor bouillon cube	1 cube	½ cube	¼ cube
Dry Marsala wine	½ cup	¼ cup	2 tablespoons
Italian-style dried bread crumbs	¾ cup	½ cup	¼ cup
Chopped parsley for garnish	garnish	garnish	garnish
Microwave cookware	9" pie plate 13" by 9" baking dish	9" pie plate 12" by 8" baking dish	9" pie plate 8" by 8" baking dish
Time on High (100% power) Marsala mixture	3 to 4 minutes	2 to 3 minutes	1½ (1:30) to 2 minutes
Veal cutlets	5 to 8 minutes	3 to 5 minutes	2 to 3 minutes
Reheating Marsala mixture	1 to 2 minutes	1 minute	30 seconds

1 On cutting board, with dull edge of French knife or smooth edge of meat mallet, pound veal cutlets until about ⅛ inch thick.

2 In pie plate (see Chart), place butter or margarine, bouillon, and Marsala. Cook, covered with paper towel, on High for time in Chart, or until butter or margarine is melted, stirring once.

3 On waxed paper, spread bread crumbs. Dip cutlets in Marsala mixture, then in bread crumbs, coating each cutlet on both sides. Reserve remaining Marsala mixture.

4 In baking dish (see Chart), place cutlets, ¼ inch apart. Cook, covered loosely with waxed paper, on High for time in Chart, or until juices run clear.

5 Place cutlets on warmed platter; keep warm. Reheat reserved Marsala mixture on High for time in Chart.

6 Drizzle Marsala mixture over cutlets on platter. Sprinkle with chopped parsley to garnish. Serve immediately.

VEAL WITH SPINACH

Color Index page 62. 4 servings. 430 cals per serving. Good source of vitamin A, riboflavin, niacin, calcium, iron. Begin 25 minutes ahead.

6 tablespoons butter or margarine (¾ stick)
2 tablespoons lemon juice
1 chicken-flavor bouillon cube or envelope
1 garlic clove, minced
¼ cup water
½ teaspoon paprika
¾ cup dried bread crumbs
¼ teaspoon salt
1 pound veal cutlets, each about ¼ inch thick
1 10-ounce bag spinach
1 pint cherry tomatoes

1. In 3-quart microwave-safe casserole, place first 5 ingredients. Cook, covered, on High (100% power) 3½ (3:30) to 4 minutes, stirring once.
2. On waxed paper, mix paprika, bread crumbs, and salt. On cutting board, with smooth edge of meat mallet, pound cutlets until about ⅛ inch thick. Dip cutlets in butter mixture, then in bread crumbs. Toss spinach and tomatoes in remaining butter mixture.
3. In 13" by 9" microwave-safe baking dish, place cutlets. Cook, covered, on High 8 minutes, rearranging cutlets once. Transfer to warmed serving platter. In same dish, place spinach-tomato mixture. Cook, covered, on High 3 to 4 minutes, until spinach wilts. Serve immediately with veal.

OSSO BUCO

Color Index page 68. 4 servings. 495 cals per serving. Good source of riboflavin, thiamine, niacin, iron. Begin 2 hours ahead.

3 tablespoons olive or salad oil
2 onions, chopped
2 large celery stalks, chopped
2 garlic cloves, minced
4 veal shank cross cuts, each 2 inches thick
1 cup dry white wine
1 7½-ounce can crushed tomatoes
½ cup Beef Broth (page 125) or canned broth
¼ ounce dried mushrooms
1 teaspoon basil
1 teaspoon oregano
½ teaspoon rosemary
½ bay leaf
1 cup orzo
Salt and pepper to taste

1. In 13" by 9" microwave-safe baking dish, combine 2 tablespoons oil, onions, celery, and garlic. Cook on High (100% power) 4 to 5 minutes, until vegetables soften, stirring twice.
2. In 12" skillet over high heat, heat 1 tablespoon oil. Add veal shanks and brown on both sides. Arrange veal on top of vegetables in baking dish, at least 1 inch apart.
3. Into skillet, pour wine; stir to loosen brown bits. Over high heat, bring to a boil; pour over veal. Add tomatoes and next six ingredients.
4. Into meat, stir orzo. Cook on High 12 to 15 minutes, until orzo is tender, stirring occasionally. Discard bay leaf and season.

Easter Lunch

Tartlets with Asparagus and Brie Filling, page 117
Glazed Ham, page 221
Mixed Company Vegetables, page 274
Baking-powder biscuits (bakery) and candied sweet potatoes
Hot-pepper Jelly, page 376, Corn Relish, page 377
Light Lemon and Almond Tart, page 370

PREPARATION TIMETABLE

Up to 1 week ahead:	*Make Hot-pepper Jelly and Corn Relish.*
1 day ahead:	*Make Light Lemon and Almond Tart but do not decorate; store in airtight container.*
Early in day:	*Make Tartlets with Asparagus and Brie Filling; cover loosely. Prepare and cook candied sweet potatoes and Mixed Company Vegetables; cover.*
40 minutes ahead:	*Cook Glazed Ham as recipe directs. Decorate tart. Reheat potatoes and vegetables on High (100% power), while meat is standing.*
Just before serving:	*If you like, reheat Tartlets with Asparagus and Brie Filling on High. Heat baking-powder biscuits on High.*

DECORATING A HAM

Scoring the fat on top of a ham gives it an attractive finish for a festive occasion or celebration.

With sharp knife, score top of ham in a decorative, diamond-shaped pattern. Insert 1 whole clove into each diamond shape; glaze and cook as directed.

225

Veal Stews and Meat Glazes

VEAL RAGOUT *

Color Index page 68. 657 cals per serving. Good source of vitamin A, riboflavin, niacin, calcium, iron. Begin 1½ hours ahead.

Ingredients for 4 servings		Microwave cookware
1 pound veal for stew, cut into 1½-inch chunks 2 cups water 2 tablespoons butter or margarine (¼ stick) 1 large carrot, diced 1 large celery stalk, diced 1 garlic clove, chopped 1 teaspoon thyme leaves 1 bay leaf 1 cup Chicken Broth (page 125) or canned broth	½ 16-ounce bag frozen pearl onions 8 medium mushrooms 1 tablespoon all-purpose flour 1 cup heavy cream 2 egg yolks ½ teaspoon salt Pepper to taste 2 cups hot cooked herbed rice (optional)	2-quart soufflé dish or casserole

1 In soufflé dish or casserole, place veal. Add water. Cook, covered, on High (100% power) 8 to 10 minutes, until water boils. With spatula or slotted spoon, remove veal to paper towels to drain. Into medium bowl, pour cooking liquid through cheesecloth-lined strainer. Set aside.

2 In dish or casserole used for veal, place butter or margarine. Heat, covered with paper towel, on High 45 seconds, or until melted. Add carrot, celery, garlic, thyme, and bay leaf. Cook on High 5 to 7 minutes, until vegetables are tender, stirring twice.

3 To vegetables, add veal and broth; stir. Cook, covered, on Medium (50% power) 20 minutes, stirring occasionally. Add pearl onions and mushrooms; stir. Cook, covered, on Medium 15 to 25 minutes longer, until meat is fork-tender.

4 In medium bowl, place flour. Gradually add ½ cup reserved cooking liquid, stirring until smooth. Add flour mixture to ragout. Cook on High 3 to 5 minutes, until sauce thickens slightly, stirring twice.

5 Meanwhile, in same bowl, combine cream and egg yolks. Stir small amount of hot cooking liquid from ragout into cream mixture. Slowly pour cream mixture back into ragout, stirring to prevent lumping.

6 Cook ragout on Medium-Low (30% power) 2 to 3 minutes, until mixture thickens slightly, stirring twice. Discard bay leaf. Season with salt and pepper. If you like, serve with hot cooked herbed rice.

VEAL STEW PROVENÇALE

Color Index page 68. 4 servings. 377 cals per serving. Good source of vitamin A, niacin, vitamin C, iron. Begin 1½ hours ahead.

1 pound veal for stew, cut into 1½-inch chunks
½ cup all-purpose flour
½ teaspoon salt
¼ teaspoon pepper
2 tablespoons olive or salad oil
3 small onions, chopped
1 green pepper, chopped
1 red pepper, chopped
1 cup dry white wine
1 tablespoon tomato paste
1 beef-flavor bouillon cube or envelope
1 teaspoon thyme leaves
1 teaspoon rosemary
1 teaspoon oregano
2 teaspoons browning sauce (optional)
2 garlic cloves, minced
10 pitted ripe olives

1. Trim fat from veal. On waxed paper, combine flour, salt, and pepper. Lightly coat veal chunks in seasoned flour.

2. In 12″ skillet over high heat, heat oil. Add veal chunks and brown on all sides. With slotted spoon, remove veal to 2-quart microwave-safe casserole.

3. In same skillet, over medium-high heat, cook onions and green and red peppers, until softened. Add to veal.

4. In 4-cup glass measure, combine wine, tomato paste, bouillon, thyme, rosemary, oregano, and, if you like, browning sauce. Pour over veal. Cook, covered, on Medium (50% power) 30 minutes, stirring occasionally.

5. Add minced garlic and olives; stir. Cook, covered, on Medium 15 to 20 minutes longer, until veal is fork-tender. Serve immediately.

MEAT GLAZES

These glazes are ideal for dressing up plain cooked pork, lamb, ham, and veal.

Orange-mincemeat Glaze: In blender at low speed, blend *½ cup drained mincemeat* and *¼ cup orange marmalade* until smooth. Makes about ¾ cup.

Curry-orange Glaze: In small bowl, with fork, stir *⅔ cup light corn syrup, 1 tablespoon curry powder*, and *1 tablespoon grated orange peel* until blended. Makes about ⅔ cup.

Tomato-onion Glaze: In 4-cup glass measure, cook *1 tablespoon butter or margarine* and *2 tablespoons minced onion* on High (100% power) 1 minute, until onion softens. Stir in *1 8-ounce can tomato sauce, 2 tablespoons dark-brown sugar* and *1 teaspoon Worcestershire;* mix well to combine. Cook, covered, on High 3 to 5 minutes, until glaze thickens slightly. Makes about 1 cup.

Lamb Roasts

ZESTY LEG OF LAMB

Color Index page 64. 8 servings. 221 cals per serving. Good source of niacin, iron. Begin 55 minutes ahead.

1 3½- to 4-pound leg of lamb, shank half
¼ cup mango chutney
2 tablespoons Dijon mustard
2 garlic cloves, minced
1 tablespoon red-wine vinegar
1 tablespoon Worcestershire
Salt to taste

1. With sharp knife, trim any large pieces of fat from leg of lamb. Place lamb on microwave-safe rack in 13″ by 9″ microwave-safe baking dish.
2. In 2-cup microwave-safe glass measure, combine chutney and next 4 ingredients. Cook on High (100% power) 3 to 4 minutes, until bubbling, stirring once. With brush, coat lamb with half the mixture.
3. Shield thin end of leg with strips of smooth foil. Cook on High 5 minutes. Reduce power level to Medium (50% power) and cook 15 to 20 minutes longer, until a meat thermometer inserted in center of roast reaches 135°F. for medium-rare, removing foil, turning roast over, and brushing with remaining mixture once.
4. Remove roast to platter. Let stand, tented with foil, 10 to 15 minutes. Temperature will reach 150°F. to 155°F. Season with salt before serving.

LAMB PILAF

Color Index page 64. 8 servings. 286 cals per serving. Low in sodium. Good source of calcium, iron. Begin 55 minutes ahead.

2 tablespoons butter or margarine (¼ stick)
1 large onion, minced
1 green pepper, chopped
1½ cups regular long-grain rice
2 tablespoons curry powder
3 cups Chicken Broth (page 125) or canned broth
2 cups roast lamb, cut into 1½-inch cubes
½ 10-ounce package frozen peas, thawed
Salt and pepper to taste
1 cup plain yogurt
2 green onions, thinly sliced
½ small cucumber, diced
Mint for garnish

1. In 13″ by 9″ microwave-safe baking dish, place butter or margarine. Heat, covered with paper towels, on High (100% power) 45 seconds, or until melted. Into melted butter or margarine, stir onion and next 3 ingredients. Cook on High 3 to 4 minutes, until vegetables soften, stirring halfway through cooking.
2. To vegetable mixture, add broth and lamb. Cook on Medium (50% power) 20 to 30 minutes, until rice is tender and liquid is absorbed, stirring occasionally. Into mixture, stir peas. Season with salt and pepper. Let stand, covered, on heat-safe surface 10 minutes.
3. Meanwhile, in small bowl, combine yogurt, green onions, and cucumber. Season.
4. *To serve*: Top each portion of pilaf with yogurt sauce; garnish with mint.

For roast lamb that is medium-rare, remove the meat from the microwave when its temperature registers 130°F. to 140°F. Left to stand, tented with foil, its temperature will rise to 155°F. For a well-done roast, remove the lamb from the microwave when its temperature registers 150°F. to 160°F. Left to stand, its temperature will rise to 175°F.

APRICOT-GLAZED RACK OF LAMB

Color Index page 65. 829 cals per serving. Good source of vitamin A, niacin, iron. Begin 45 minutes ahead.

Ingredients for 4 servings		Microwave cookware
½ teaspoon browning sauce *1 teaspoon water* *1 2½-pound lamb rib roast (ask butcher to cut through backbone for easier carving)* *½ cup apricot preserves* *1 tablespoon lemon juice*	*1 tablespoon prepared mustard* *½ teaspoon salt* *2 16-ounce cans small whole carrots, drained* *Watercress sprigs for garnish*	*12″ by 8″ baking dish with rack* *Large bowl*

1 In small bowl, mix browning sauce with water. Brush on lamb rib roast. Shield bone ends of ribs with smooth strips of foil.

2 On rack in baking dish, place roast, fat side up. Cook, covered loosely with waxed paper, on Medium-High (70% power) 8 minutes.

3 Meanwhile, in small bowl, combine apricot preserves, lemon juice, mustard, and salt. Spoon ¼ cup apricot mixture into large bowl; set aside.

4 Discard foil from roast. Cook on Medium-High 7 to 8 minutes longer for medium-rare, until a meat thermometer inserted in center of roast reaches 140°F. After cooking, brush roast with apricot mixture.

5 On heat-safe surface, let roast stand, tented with foil, 5 to 10 minutes. Temperature will reach 155°F. Meanwhile, into reserved apricot mixture in large bowl, stir carrots. Cook, covered, on High (100% power) 3 to 5 minutes, until hot, stirring twice.

6 *To serve*: Arrange roast on warmed serving platter. Spoon carrots around roast. Garnish with watercress sprigs. If you like, decorate with paper frills.

Lamb Chops

MARINATED LAMB CHOPS WITH HERBED PEAS

Color Index page 69. 217 cals per serving. Good source of niacin.
Begin early in day or 1 day ahead.

Ingredients	For 4	For 2	For 1
Apple jelly	2 tablespoons	1 tablespoon	2 teaspoons
Dijon mustard	2 tablespoons	1 tablespoon	2 teaspoons
Garlic cloves, minced	2 garlic cloves	1 garlic clove	½ garlic clove
Mint leaves, chopped	3 tablespoons	2 tablespoons	2½ teaspoons
Rib lamb chops, each 1 inch thick	8 chops	4 chops	2 chops
1 10-ounce package frozen peas	1 package	½ package	¼ package
Water	2 tablespoons	1 tablespoon	1½ teaspoons
Butter or margarine	1 tablespoon	1½ teaspoons	¾ teaspoon
Mint sprigs for garnish	garnish	garnish	garnish
Microwave cookware	Browning dish	Browning dish	Browning dish
	1½-quart soufflé dish	1½-quart soufflé dish	9″ pie plate
Time on High (100% power)			
Chops	3 to 4½ (4:30) minutes each batch	3 to 4½ (4:30) minutes	2 to 2½ (2:30) minutes
Peas	4 to 5 minutes	2½ (2:30) to 3½ (3:30) minutes	1½ (1:30) to 2 minutes

1 In dish large enough to hold lamb chops in single layer, combine apple jelly, mustard, garlic, and half the mint.

2 To mixture, add lamb chops, turning to coat. Cover dish and refrigerate 2 hours or overnight, turning chops occasionally.

3 Preheat browning dish as manufacturer directs. On browning dish, arrange chops with bones toward center.

4 Cook chops on High for time in Chart, turning halfway through cooking. If cooking for 4, cook in batches, reheating browning dish between batches. Remove chops to platter; keep warm.

5 In soufflé dish or pie plate (see Chart), place peas and water. Cook, covered, on High for time in Chart, or until peas are tender; drain. Toss with butter or margarine and remaining mint.

6 *To serve:* Place 2 chops on each plate. Serve with herbed peas; garnish with mint sprigs.

BACON-WRAPPED LAMB CHOPS

Color Index page 62. 4 servings. 496 cals per serving (with sauce). Good source of niacin, iron.
Begin 25 minutes ahead.

Currant-orange Sauce (below)
4 slices bacon
1 tablespoon butter or margarine
8 pitted prunes
8 dried apricot halves

2 slices white bread, cubed
⅛ teaspoon thyme leaves
⅛ teaspoon basil
4 lamb loin chops, each 1½ inches thick

1. Prepare Currant-orange Sauce. In 9″ microwave-safe pie plate, place bacon. Cook, covered with paper towel, on High (100% power) 1½ (1:30) to 2 minutes, just until bacon begins to curl. Remove bacon to paper towels to drain.
2. To bacon drippings in pie plate, add butter or margarine. Heat, covered with paper towel, on High 30 to 45 seconds, until melted. Add prunes, apricots, bread cubes, thyme, and basil. Stir to coat; set aside.
3. To remove bones from lamb chops, with sharp knife and starting at 1 side of backbone, cut through meat along bone, keeping knife blade against bone. Cut down both sides of bone to separate bone from meat, making sure that the meat remains in 1 piece. Trim off any excess fat from lamb chops.
4. Fill each chop where the bone has been removed with an equal amount of filling. Push meat tightly around filling. To keep filling in place, wrap 1 bacon slice tightly around side of each chop; secure with wooden toothpick.
5. On microwave-safe rack in 12″ by 8″ microwave-safe baking dish, place lamb chops. Cook on High 3 to 5 minutes, until chops are of desired doneness, rotating dish once.
6. *To serve:* Reheat Currant-orange Sauce on High 1 minute. Place lamb chops on warmed serving platter. Pass sauce separately.

CURRANT-ORANGE SAUCE

Makes ½ cup. 27 cals per tablespoon.
Begin 10 minutes ahead.

2 teaspoons grated orange peel
½ cup orange juice

¼ cup red-currant jelly
1 teaspoon honey

1. In 2-cup microwave-safe glass measure, combine orange peel, orange juice, red-currant jelly, and honey; stir until smooth.
2. Cook sauce on High (100% power) 4 to 5 minutes, until boiling and sauce thickens slightly, stirring occasionally.

Lamb Medallions and Kabobs

LAMB MEDALLIONS WITH ORANGE

Color Index page 62. 8 servings. 504 calories per serving. Good source of niacin, iron.
Begin 25 minutes ahead.

5 tablespoons butter	½ teaspoon grated
1 teaspoon browning	orange peel
sauce	¼ teaspoon cider
8 boneless lamb loin	vinegar
chops, each 1 inch	8 3-inch bread rounds,
thick	toasted
½ cup mayonnaise	¼ cup chopped parsley
½ teaspoon rosemary	8 orange slices
½ teaspoon thyme leaves	Rosemary for garnish

1. In small microwave-safe bowl, place 3 tablespoons butter or margarine. Heat, covered with paper towel, on High (100% power) 45 seconds to 1 minute, until melted. Add browning sauce; brush on chops.

2. Arrange chops in 13″ by 9″ microwave-safe baking dish. Cook, covered loosely with waxed paper, on Medium-High (70% power) 9 to 12 minutes for medium-rare, turning chops over occasionally. In small bowl, combine mayonnaise and next 4 ingredients.

3. In small microwave-safe bowl, place remaining butter. Heat, covered with paper towel, on High 45 seconds, or until melted. Dip edges of toast in melted butter and roll in parsley to coat. Arrange toast on warmed serving platter; top each with orange slice and lamb chop. Spoon over mayonnaise mixture; garnish.

LEMON-LIME THAI KABOBS

Color Index page 69. 4 servings. 368 cals per serving. Low in sodium. Good source of vitamin A, niacin, vitamin C, iron.
Begin early in day or 1 day ahead.

3 tablespoons lemon	1 garlic clove, minced
juice	1 pound lamb for stew,
2 tablespoons lime juice	cut into 1½-inch
2 tablespoons chopped	chunks
mint	1 papaya, peeled and
½ teaspoon ground	cut into 2-inch chunks
coriander	1 green pepper, cut into
½ teaspoon ground	1½-inch chunks
cumin	2 cups Hot Cooked Rice
1 tablespoon	(page 293)
Worcestershire	
2 tablespoons olive or	
salad oil	

1. In large bowl, combine first 9 ingredients. Cover and refrigerate 2 hours or overnight.

2. On eight 8″ to 10″ wooden skewers, thread lamb alternately with papaya and green pepper. Arrange on 10″ to 12″ microwave-safe platter. Cook on High (100% power) 5 to 7 minutes, until lamb is fork-tender, turning over once. Spoon rice onto serving platter. Place kabobs on top.

Meal in Minutes *for 4 people*

Mother's Day Lunch

Celebration Shrimp, page 119, for 4
Apricot-glazed Rack of Lamb, page 227
Wild Rice and Mushroom Pilaf, page 292
Mint Jelly, page 376
Dinner rolls
Orange Chiffon Pie, page 368

PREPARATION TIMETABLE

Up to 1 week ahead:	*Make Mint Jelly. Prepare Celebration Shrimp through step 4.*
1 day ahead:	*Make Orange Chiffon Pie but do not decorate; store in airtight container.*
Early in day:	*Prepare and cook Wild Rice and Mushroom Pilaf; cover and set aside.*
45 minutes ahead:	*Cook Apricot-glazed Rack of Lamb; let stand as recipe directs. Decorate pie.*
About 15 minutes before serving:	*Reheat pilaf on High (100% power), until hot. If you like, heat dinner rolls on High. Complete Celebration Shrimp.*

Lamb Stews

Lamb, like any meat that has been cut into uniform cubes, cooks quickly and evenly in the microwave. For the almond garnish in our Lamb Curry (below), place ½ cup blanched almonds in 1-cup microwave-safe glass measure and cook on High (100% power) 2½ (2:30) to 4 minutes, until browned, stirring twice.

LAMB CURRY

Color Index page 69. 402 cals per serving. Good source of vitamin A, thiamine, niacin, vitamin C, calcium, iron. Begin 1½ hours ahead.

Ingredients for 4 servings		Microwave cookware
1 lemon wedge Water 2 cooking apples ½ cup dried apricots 2 tablespoons butter or margarine (¼ stick) 2 tablespoons curry powder 1 large onion, cut into 2-inch chunks 1 green pepper, cut into 2-inch chunks	1 pound lamb for stew, cut into 1½-inch chunks 1 cup Chicken Broth (page 125) or canned broth 1 tablespoon tomato paste 1 10-ounce package frozen peas, thawed ½ cup plain yogurt Hot Cooked Rice (page 293, optional) Toasted almonds and coriander, for garnish	13" by 9" baking dish

1 In medium bowl, place lemon wedge; fill bowl with cold water. Peel, core, and cut apples into 1½-inch chunks; place in lemon water to prevent discoloration. Dice apricots; set aside.

2 In baking dish, place butter or margarine. Heat, covered with paper towels, on High (100% power) 45 seconds, or until melted.

3 Into melted butter or margarine, stir curry powder, onion, green pepper, and apple chunks. Cook on High 3 to 4 minutes, until vegetables are warm, stirring once.

4 Into vegetable mixture, stir lamb chunks, apricots, broth, and tomato paste. Cook, covered, on Medium (50% power) 45 to 60 minutes, until lamb is fork-tender, stirring occasionally.

5 Into lamb mixture, stir peas. Cook on High 3 to 4 minutes, until hot, stirring halfway through cooking.

6 Into lamb mixture, gradually stir yogurt, until blended. If you like, spoon curry over hot cooked rice. Garnish with toasted almonds and coriander leaves.

MOROCCAN LAMB WITH COUSCOUS

Color Index page 69. 6 servings. 337 cals per serving. Good source of vitamin A, niacin, iron. Begin 2 hours ahead.

2 tablespoons olive or salad oil 2 carrots, cut into 3-inch chunks, then lengthwise into quarters 2 large onions, sliced 1 pound lamb for stew, cut into 1½-inch chunks 1½ cups tomato juice 2 tablespoons red-wine vinegar 1 cinnamon stick 1 bay leaf 1 teaspoon ground cumin 1 teaspoon ground coriander	½ teaspoon thyme leaves ⅛ teaspoon ground red pepper ½ 10-ounce package frozen okra, thawed ½ 19-ounce can chick peas, drained and rinsed 1½ cups Chicken Broth (page 125) or canned broth ⅛ teaspoon turmeric 1 cup quick-cooking couscous

1. In 13" by 9" microwave-safe baking dish, place oil. Heat, covered with paper towels, on High (100% power) 45 seconds to 1 minute, until oil is hot.

2. Into oil, stir carrots, onions, and lamb. Cook on High 5 to 6 minutes, until onions soften, stirring twice.

3. Meanwhile, in 4-cup microwave-safe glass measure, combine tomato juice, vinegar, cinnamon stick, bay leaf, cumin, coriander, thyme leaves, and ground red pepper. Stir into lamb mixture. Cook, covered, on Medium (50% power) 30 to 40 minutes, until carrots are tender, stirring occasionally.

4. Into lamb mixture, stir okra and chick peas. Cook, covered, on Medium 15 to 20 minutes, until lamb is fork-tender, stirring occasionally. Discard bay leaf. Let lamb stand, covered, on heat-safe surface while preparing couscous.

5. In same measure, combine broth and turmeric. Cook, covered, on High 4 to 6 minutes, until boiling. Add couscous. Let stand, covered, on heat-safe surface 5 minutes. With fork, fluff couscous.

6. To serve: Spoon couscous onto warmed serving platter. Top with lamb stew.

COUSCOUS Couscous is precooked semolina derived from durum wheat, forming fine, yellow, rice-like pellets. The traditional way to cook couscous involves steaming it over a highly spiced stew. A quick, modern alternative, using the microwave, is to place couscous in boiling broth or water, with spices such as turmeric added to taste, then to leave it to absorb the liquid and fluff up. Its colorful appearance makes it an attractive alternative to rice in many lamb or chicken risottos.

Lamb Stews and Ground Lamb

LAMB STEW WITH LEEKS

Color Index 69. 6 servings. 460 calories per serving.
Good source of vitamin A, niacin, iron.
Begin 1½ hours ahead.

2 medium leeks (about ¾ pound)	1 teaspoon salt
2 tablespoons salad oil	¼ teaspoon pepper
1½ pounds lamb for stew, cut into 1½-inch cubes	Water
	4 medium carrots, cut into 2-inch pieces
1 pound small (new) potatoes	2 tablespoons all-purpose flour

1. Trim root and leaf ends of leeks. Cut each leek lengthwise in half; separate into leaves. Rinse under running cold water to remove sand. Cut leaves crosswise into 2-inch pieces.
2. In 4-quart microwave-safe casserole, place leeks and oil. Cook, covered, on High (100% power) 8 minutes, or until tender, stirring twice.
3. Into leeks, stir lamb, potatoes, salt, pepper, and ¾ cup water. Cook, covered, on High 30 minutes, stirring mixture well after 10 minutes. Stir in carrots. Reduce power level to Medium (50% power) and cook, covered, 20 minutes, or until meat and vegetables are fork-tender, stirring occasionally.
4. In glass measure, combine flour and 3 tablespoons water, stirring until smooth. Into liquid in casserole, stir flour mixture. Cook, covered, on High 2 to 3 minutes, until liquid thickens slightly, stirring halfway through cooking.

LAMB STEW WITH FETA

Color Index page 69. 6 servings. 432 cals per serving. Good source of thiamine, niacin, calcium, iron. Begin 2 hours ahead.

2 tablespoons olive or salad oil	1 pound tomatoes, coarsely chopped
2 large onions, chopped	½ cup dry white wine
2 garlic cloves, minced	2 medium zucchini, cut into 1½-inch chunks
1 pound lamb for stew, cut into 1½-inch cubes	8 ounces elbow macaroni, cooked
1 bay leaf	1 8-ounce package feta cheese, crumbled
1 teaspoon rosemary	
1 teaspoon oregano	2 tablespoons chopped dill
2 tablespoons pitted ripe olives	

1. In 13″ by 9″ microwave-safe baking dish, place oil and next 7 ingredients. Cook on High (100% power) 5 to 6 minutes, until lamb is no longer pink, stirring halfway through cooking.
2. Into mixture, stir tomatoes and wine. Cook, covered, on Medium (50% power) 45 minutes, stirring occasionally. Stir in zucchini. Cook, covered, on Medium 15 to 20 minutes longer, until meat is fork-tender, stirring occasionally.
3. Combine macaroni, feta, and dill. Spoon onto microwave-safe serving platter. Spoon stew over macaroni. Cook, covered, on High 4 to 5 minutes, until hot. Discard bay leaf and serve immediately.

Your microwave can be used not only for cooking hot dishes, but also for taking the chill off cold food. Our Lamb and Eggplant Charlotte (below) can be made ahead, refrigerated, and then reheated to be served at room temperature. Microwave it briefly in its serving dish, then unmold and cut into wedges.

LAMB AND EGGPLANT CHARLOTTE

Color Index page 69. 317 cals per serving. Good source of vitamin A, calcium, iron. Begin 1½ hours ahead.

Ingredients for 8 servings		Microwave cookware
Tomato Sauce (page 380)	⅛ teaspoon ground nutmeg	13″ by 9″ baking dish
1 large eggplant (about 2 pounds)	1 teaspoon salt	2-quart soufflé dish
1 pound ground lamb	¼ teaspoon pepper	
1 large onion, minced	2 tablespoons tomato paste	
2 garlic cloves, minced	¼ cup dry red wine	
1 medium zucchini, diced	1 8-ounce package feta cheese, crumbled	
1 cup dried bread crumbs	2 eggs	
1 teaspoon oregano		

1 Prepare Tomato Sauce. Cut eggplant lengthwise into ¼-inch-thick slices, to make about 10 slices in all.

2 In baking dish, arrange eggplant slices in 2 or 3 layers. Cook, covered, on High (100% power) 5 minutes, or until eggplant softens.

3 Brush soufflé dish with oil. Line with eggplant slices, overlapping slightly. Set aside.

4 In baking dish used for eggplant, place lamb, onion, garlic, and zucchini. Cook on High 10 to 12 minutes, until lamb is no longer pink, stirring twice.

5 Into lamb mixture, stir bread crumbs and next 8 ingredients, until well combined. Into eggplant-lined dish, spoon mixture; pressing lightly. Fold eggplant slices over charlotte mixture. Cook, covered, on Medium (50% power) 15 to 20 minutes, until a meat thermometer inserted in center reaches 160°F.

6 On heat-safe surface, let charlotte stand, covered, 5 to 7 minutes. Meanwhile, reheat Tomato Sauce on High 4 to 5 minutes, stirring occasionally. Unmold charlotte onto warmed serving platter. Cut into wedges to serve. Pass Tomato Sauce separately.

Sausages

KNACKWURST AND POTATO SUPPER

Color Index page 65. 677 cals per serving. Good source of thiamine, niacin, vitamin C, iron. Begin 40 minutes ahead.

Our Knackwurst and Potato Supper adapts easily to many variations. For example, instead of the knackwurst use franks, salami, ham, liverwurst, or even hard-cooked eggs for a different flavor. You can also use any kind of potato, since cooking times are all the same.

Ingredients for 4 servings		Microwave cookware
2 pounds potatoes, unpeeled and well scrubbed, cut into 1½-inch chunks	3 tablespoons cider vinegar	2-quart casserole
Water	1 tablespoon prepared mustard	3-quart casserole
2 slices bacon, diced	½ teaspoon salt	
1 medium onion, chopped	¼ teaspoon pepper	
2 tablespoons brown sugar	1 pound knackwurst	
1 tablespoon all-purpose flour	Chicory leaves	
	Coarsely chopped sweet pickles or sliced beets for garnish	

1 In 2-quart casserole, place potatoes and ½ cup water. Cook, covered, on High (100% power) 10 minutes, stirring once; drain. Cover and set aside.

2 In 3-quart casserole, place diced bacon. Cook, covered with paper towel, on High 2 to 3 minutes, until bacon is browned. Remove bacon to paper towels to drain.

3 To bacon drippings remaining in casserole, add chopped onion. Cook on High 3 to 4 minutes, until onion softens, stirring halfway through cooking.

4 Into onion mixture, stir brown sugar, flour, vinegar, mustard, salt, pepper, and ⅔ cup water, until mixture is well blended. Cook on High 3 minutes, or until flavors blend, stirring halfway through cooking.

5 With small, sharp knife, cut a few diagonal slashes on each knackwurst. To onion mixture, add knackwurst and potatoes. Cook, covered, on High 6 to 8 minutes, until potatoes are tender, stirring twice.

6 To serve: Line serving platter with chicory leaves; spoon knackwurst and potato mixture onto leaves. Sprinkle with bacon and garnish.

KIELBASA AND RED CABBAGE

Color Index page 63. 4 servings. 544 cals per serving. Good source of thiamine, vitamin C, calcium, iron. Begin 25 minutes ahead.

2 tablespoons butter or margarine (¼ stick)	⅓ cup apple juice
2 medium red cooking apples	1 tablespoon sugar
2 medium onions, thinly sliced	3 tablespoons red-wine vinegar
1 small head red cabbage (about 1½ pounds), thinly shredded	1 1-pound kielbasa, cut lengthwise in half, then cut into 2-inch pieces
	Watercress sprigs for garnish

1. In 13″ by 9″ microwave-safe baking dish, place butter or margarine. Heat, covered with paper towels, on High (100% power) 45 seconds, or until melted.
2. Core and dice 1 apple. Into melted butter or margarine, stir onions and diced apple. Cook on High 5 minutes, until onions and apple soften, stirring twice.
3. Into onion-apple mixture, stir shredded cabbage, apple juice, sugar, and vinegar. Cook, covered, on High 7 to 10 minutes, until cabbage is wilted and tender, stirring halfway through cooking.
4. Into cabbage mixture, stir kielbasa. Cut remaining apple into wedges; add to mixture. Cook, covered, on High 5 to 7 minutes, until kielbasa is hot, stirring twice. Garnish and serve.

SAUSAGE AND BISCUIT SUPPER

Color Index page 63. 4 servings. 418 cals per serving. Good source of thiamine, calcium, iron. Begin 25 minutes ahead.

½ pound pork-sausage meat	½ red pepper, cut into matchstick-thin strips
2 tablespoons all-purpose flour	Salt and pepper to taste
2 cups milk	8 buttermilk biscuits
3 tablespoons chopped parsley	Parsley for garnish

1. In 12″ by 8″ microwave-safe baking dish, place sausage meat. Cook on High (100% power) 5 to 7 minutes, until meat is no longer pink, stirring often to break up lumps.
2. Discard all but 2 tablespoons drippings. Into sausagemeat in baking dish, stir flour until blended. Cook on High 1 minute, stirring once.
3. Into sausagemeat, gradually stir milk. Cook on High 4 to 5 minutes, until gravy thickens, stirring twice. Stir in chopped parsley and red pepper. Cook on High 1 minute, or until hot. Season.
4. On oven floor, place paper towels; arrange 4 biscuits on top. Heat on High 2 to 3 minutes, until hot. Repeat with remaining biscuits.
5. To serve: Spoon sausagemeat and gravy onto plates; garnish. Serve with hot biscuits.

Tex-Mex Buffet

Margaritas
Guacamole (below) with fresh vegetables and fruit, olives, and corn chips
Chili con Carne, page 211
Pork Empanadas, page 218 (double quantity)
Turkey Tortilla Roll-ups, page 194
Lime or lemon sorbet (bought)
Mexican Wedding Cookies, page 351 (double quantity)

PREPARATION TIMETABLE

1 day ahead:	*Make Mexican Wedding Cookies; store in airtight container. Cook Chili con Carne; cover and chill. Check bar supplies and ice for Margaritas.*
Early in day:	*Make Pork Empanadas through step 5; arrange on cookie sheet as recipe directs, but do not bake. Prepare Turkey Tortilla Roll-ups through step 4 and make sauce as in step 5, but do not assemble. Cover tortillas and sauce and refrigerate. Prepare fresh vegetables; store in plastic bags in refrigerator.*
2 hours ahead:	*Prepare glasses for Margaritas by dipping rims in lime juice and salt. Make Guacamole; cover and refrigerate.*
15 minutes before serving:	*Complete Pork Empanadas as recipe directs. Reheat Chili con Carne on High (100% power), until bubbling. Pour sauce over tortillas and finish in microwave as recipe directs. Assemble Guacamole, vegetables, fruit, olives, and corn chips. Make Margaritas as guests arrive.*

GUACAMOLE

Set the Mexican mood when your guests arrive by serving spicy hot Guacamole as a first course.

Peel *2 tomatoes* (page 30), then dice. Chop *1 onion*. Mince *2 garlic cloves*. Cut *4 avocados* lengthwise in half; remove seeds and peel. In bowl, mash avocado with *¼ cup lemon juice*. Add tomatoes, onion, garlic, and drained contents of *2 4-ounce cans chopped mild green chilies* and *salt* to taste. Stir. Spoon into serving bowl; garnish with *sliced green chilies*.

Sausages

SAUSAGE AND PEPPERS

Color Index page 65. 6 servings. 445 cals per serving. Good source of thiamine, vitamin C, iron. Begin 45 minutes ahead.

1½ pounds Italian-
sausage links
½ teaspoon browning
sauce
1 teaspoon water
3 large green, yellow,
and/or red peppers,
each cut into ¾-inch
strips
2 medium onions, each
cut into 6 wedges

1 16-ounce can crushed
tomatoes
2 tablespoons tomato
paste
½ teaspoon salt
¼ teaspoon pepper
¼ teaspoon fennel seeds,
crushed

1. With sharp knife, slash sausage links. Place on microwave-safe rack in 13" by 9" microwave-safe baking dish. Mix browning sauce with water; brush on sausage. Cook, covered, on High (100% power) 9 to 10 minutes, until meat is no longer pink, turning sausage over and rotating dish halfway through cooking. Remove sausage and rack; keep warm.
2. To drippings in baking dish, add peppers and onions. Cook, covered, on High 12 to 13 minutes, until softened, stirring twice.
3. Cut sausage into 1-inch pieces. Into pepper-onion mixture, stir sausage, tomatoes, and remaining ingredients. Cook, covered, on High 5 to 6 minutes until flavors blend, stirring halfway through cooking. Serve immediately.

SAUSAGE AND VEGETABLE CASSEROLE

Color Index page 63. 6 servings. 455 cals per serving. Good source of thiamine, vitamin C, iron. Begin 25 minutes ahead.

2 medium onions, each
cut into 8 wedges
1 yellow or green
pepper, cut into pieces
2 garlic cloves, minced
2 tablespoons olive or
salad oil
1 small eggplant (about
1 pound), cut into 2" by
1" pieces
1 zucchini, cut into
1-inch pieces

1 teaspoon oregano
1 1-pound kielbasa, cut
into 1-inch pieces
1 14½- to 16-ounce can
tomatoes
1 14½- to 16-ounce can
garbanzo beans,
drained
½ teaspoon salt
¼ teaspoon pepper

1. In 3-quart microwave-safe casserole, place onions, pepper, garlic, and oil. Cook, covered, on High (100% power) 2 to 3 minutes, until vegetables are slightly softened, stirring once.
2. Into mixture, stir eggplant, zucchini, and oregano. Cook, covered, on High 10 to 12 minutes, until tender-crisp, stirring twice.
3. To vegetable mixture, add kielbasa, tomatoes with their liquid, garbanzo beans, salt, and pepper. Cook, covered, on High 2 to 3 minutes, until vegetables are tender, stirring halfway through cooking. Serve immediately.

Sausage Snacks for Kids

Frankfurters are a snap to cook in the microwave. And if you cook them in their buns, there's no need for washing up. Just remember to slash or pierce the casings with a knife or fork before you put them in the oven.

Hot Dogs in Buns
Place **slashed frankfurter** in **bun** and wrap in paper towel; place on paper plate. Heat on High (100% power) 30 to 40 seconds, until hot. For 2 frankfurters in buns, heat on High 1 to 1¼ (1:15) minutes, until hot.

Hot Dog Melt
Make lengthwise slit in **frankfurter** and fill with **1 slice American cheese**. Place on paper plate. Heat on High (100% power) 30 to 40 seconds, until hot. Serve with **potato chips**.

Mini-franks and Beans
In microwave-safe soup bowl, place contents of **1 14½-ounce can baked beans**. Place in center of microwave-safe dinner plate. Cook, covered loosely with waxed paper, on High (100% power) 2 to 3 minutes, until bubbling. Meanwhile, push wooden toothpicks into **8 cocktail frankfurters**. Arrange in circle around bean-filled bowl. Heat on High 45 seconds to 1 minute, until hot. Serve with **mustard**. 2 servings.

Chili Dogs
In medium microwave-safe bowl, place contents of **1 15-ounce can chili with beans** or **2 cups leftover Chili con Carne**, (page 211). Cook, covered, on High (100% power) 4 to 5 minutes, until bubbling, stirring twice; set aside. Wrap **4 hot dogs** in **buns** in paper towels; place in a circle on oven floor. Heat on High 2 to 3 minutes, until hot. Unwrap; place on platter. Top hot dogs with chili, **sour cream, taco sauce,** and **coriander**. 4 servings.

Vegetables
and Salads

INDIVIDUAL VEGETABLES · MIXED VEGETABLE DISHES

CHICKEN SALADS · MEAT SALADS

WARM SALADS · VEGETABLE SALADS

Vegetables and Salads

Cooking vegetables is one of the things the microwave does best; fresh vegetables cook quickly with a minimum amount of water, so they retain nutrients and have the taste, color, and texture of fresh-from-the-garden produce. A microwave enables you to cook small portions with a minimum of trouble and is ideal for peeling vegetables such as garlic, onions, and tomatoes (see Cook's Tips, page 30), and for precooking vegetables for the barbecue in order to prevent them from charring.

Our charts for cooking vegetables in the microwave (pages 237 to 251) give cooking instructions for a wide variety of fresh vegetables and several popular frozen ones. For best results, remember the following tips: Pierce the skin of whole vegetables; make sure vegetables are uniform in size — small pieces and quantities cook more quickly as do freshly picked young vegetables; slice dense vegetables, such as potatoes and rutabagas; arrange vegetables with tender tops, like asparagus and broccoli, with tops toward center of dish, less tender stems or stalks toward edges. If using salt, add it after cooking or dissolve it in the cooking liquid — sprinkled onto food, it can cause dark spots. Covering is important for most vegetables; we use plastic wrap because it holds in heat and steam. To prevent it from splitting, we recommend "venting" the wrap by turning back a small corner or by puncturing the plastic.

Frozen vegetables are tastier when cooked in the microwave, and they keep more of their nutrients. We use some of them straight from the freezer in our recipes, but we do include cooking charts for portions of some of the most popular frozen vegetables. Many fresh vegetables require blanching before freezing; we give directions on page 259. After patting dry, pack in freezerproof containers, leaving head space, or pack into plastic bags, pressing out all air. Seal, label, and freeze. Smaller vegetables, such as shelled peas, can be tray-frozen; freeze until firm, then pack.

TOMATO GARNISHES WITH FLAIR

The deep red color and year-around availability of the tomato makes it an ideal choice to garnish vegetable dishes and salads you want to set off with style.

Tomato Rose: Cut thin slice from tomato base without cutting completely through (left), then peel continuous strip of skin, keeping it attached.

Tomato Hoops: Hollow out small tomato (right), leaving a ¼-inch ring; discard seeds.

Roll up strip skin side out toward slice cut from base (above). Gently flare rolled strip to resemble rose.

Fill hoops with cooked green beans (right) or matchstick-thin carrot slices.

Cooking Vegetables in the Microwave

These vegetable cooking charts will be an invaluable help as a reference for the basic preparation and cooking of a wide variety of vegetables. You will be able to use your favorite vegetables in other microwave recipes or on their own with a little lemon juice, butter or margarine, salt and pepper, or a sauce.

Because vegetables vary in size, texture, and density, it is important to follow our directions carefully. Remember to rotate the dish a half turn or stir the vegetables during cooking, rearranging larger pieces if necessary. Cover tightly to keep in heat; this helps vegetables cook more quickly and evenly.

Key			
Microwave cookware	Water	Time	Standing time

ARTICHOKES
ALSO CALLED FRENCH OR GLOBE ARTICHOKES

Rinse artichokes under running cold water. Cut off stems and 1 inch of tops. With kitchen shears, trim thorny tips of leaves. Brush cut edges with lemon juice to prevent discoloration. Pull off any loose leaves from around bottoms.

About 67 cals per serving		
For 4	**For 2**	**For 1**
4 artichokes (about ¾ pound each)	2 artichokes (about ¾ pound each)	1 artichoke (about ¾ pound)
Wrap each individually in plastic wrap; *arrange on oven floor in circle*	Wrap each individually in plastic wrap; *arrange on oven floor*	Wrap in plastic wrap; *place on oven floor*
Whatever clings after rinsing	Whatever clings after rinsing	Whatever clings after rinsing
16 minutes; *rotate each artichoke halfway through cooking*	10 minutes; *rotate each artichoke halfway through cooking*	7 minutes; *rotate halfway through cooking*
5 minutes	5 minutes	5 minutes

Cook artichokes, wrapped, on High (100% power) for time in Chart. Let stand, still wrapped, for time in Chart. Artichokes are done when an outer leaf as well as one close to center core can be pulled out without resistance.

ASPARAGUS (SPEARS)

Select asparagus with ½-inch-thick stalks. Hold base of stalk firmly and bend stalk; end will break off at spot where it becomes too tough to eat. Discard ends; trim scales if stalks are gritty.

About 15 cals per serving		
For 4	**For 2**	**For 1**
15 to 16 spears (about 1 pound)	7 to 8 spears (about ½ pound)	3 to 4 spears (about ¼ pound)
12″ by 8″ baking dish; *arrange tips overlapping in center*	8″ by 8″ baking dish; *arrange tips facing in same direction*	8″ plate; *arrange tips facing in same direction*
2 tablespoons	1 tablespoon	2 teaspoons
4½ (4:30) to 6 minutes; *rotate dish halfway through cooking*	2½ (2:30) to 3 minutes; *rotate dish halfway through cooking*	1½ (1:30) to 2 minutes
3 to 5 minutes	3 to 5 minutes	3 to 5 minutes

Cook asparagus and water, covered, on High (100% power) for time in Chart. Let stand, covered, for time in Chart. Asparagus spears are done when tender-crisp. Drain.

ASPARAGUS (PIECES)

Prepare as for Asparagus spears (above). Cut spears crosswise into 1- to 1½-inch pieces.

About 15 cals per serving		
For 4	**For 2**	**For 1**
15 to 16 spears (about 1 pound)	7 to 8 spears (about ½ pound)	3 to 4 spears (about ¼ pound)
1-quart casserole; *add only stems, not tips, at start of cooking*	1-quart casserole; *add only stems, not tips, at start of cooking*	Small bowl; *place tips under stem pieces*
2 tablespoons	1 tablespoon	1 teaspoon
4 to 5 minutes; *stir stems after 2½ (2:30) minutes, then stir in tips*	2 to 2½ (2:30) minutes; *stir stems after 1 minute, then stir in tips*	1 to 1½ (1:30) minutes
3 to 5 minutes	3 to 5 minutes	3 to 5 minutes

Cook only asparagus stems and water, covered, on High (100% power) for time in Chart; when stem pieces are bright green and crisp, stir in tips. Let stand, covered, for time in Chart. Asparagus pieces are done when tender-crisp. Drain.

BEANS, FROZEN BABY LIMA

130 cals per serving		
	For 4	**For 2**	**For 1**
	2 10-ounce packages	1 10-ounce package	1 10-ounce package (use ½ cup plus 1 tablespoon)
	2-quart casserole	1-quart casserole	1-cup glass measure
	½ cup	¼ cup	1 tablespoon
	10 to 12 minutes; *stir every 3 minutes*	7 to 8 minutes; *stir twice during cooking*	2 to 3 minutes; *stir halfway through cooking*
	5 minutes	5 minutes	5 minutes

Cook frozen baby lima beans and water, covered, on High (100% power) for time in Chart. Let stand, covered, for time in Chart. Lima beans are done when tender. Drain.

BEANS, YELLOW WAX

Rinse under running cold water. Cut off stem ends.

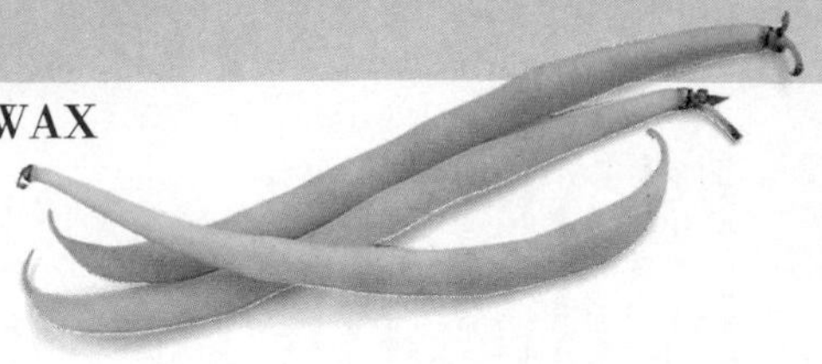

21 cals per serving		
	For 4	**For 2**	**For 1**
	1 pound	½ pound	¼ pound
	8″ by 8″ baking dish	9″ pie plate	Small bowl
	1 cup	½ cup	⅓ cup
	12 to 14 minutes; *stir every 4 minutes*	6 to 7 minutes; *stir halfway through cooking*	3½ (3:30) to 4½ (4:30) minutes; *stir halfway through cooking*
	5 minutes	5 minutes	5 minutes

Cook beans and water, covered, on High (100% power) for time in Chart. Let stand, covered, for time in Chart. Yellow wax beans are done when tender-crisp. Drain.

BEANS, GREEN

Rinse under running cold water. Cut off stem ends.

25 cals per serving		
	For 4	**For 2**	**For 1**
	1 pound	½ pound	¼ pound
	8″ by 8″ baking dish	9″ pie plate	Small bowl
	1 cup	½ cup	⅓ cup
	12 to 14 minutes; *stir every 4 minutes*	6 to 7 minutes; *stir halfway through cooking*	3½ (3:30) to 4½ (4:30) minutes; *stir halfway through cooking*
	5 minutes	5 minutes	5 minutes

Cook beans and water, covered, on High (100% power) for time in Chart. Let stand, covered, for time in Chart. Green beans are done when tender-crisp. Drain.

BEETS

Cut off tops; leave part of stems and roots on beets. Scrub; take care not to damage skins as this will cause beets to "bleed" during cooking. Cut off stems and roots and peel after standing. Skin will peel off easily if it is peeled from bottom to top. If you like, when handling beets, wear rubber gloves to prevent staining hands. Cook beet tops as beet greens (page 244).

27 cals per serving		
	For 4	**For 2**	**For 1**
	8 beets (about ¼ pound each)	4 beets (about ¼ pound each)	2 beets (about ¼ pound each)
	12″ by 8″ baking dish; *arrange along long edges with root ends overlapping in center*	1-quart casserole; *arrange around edge with root ends overlapping in center*	1-quart casserole; *arrange with root ends overlapping in center*
	None	None	None
	20 minutes; *turn beets over, then rotate dish halfway through cooking*	12 minutes; *turn beets over, then rotate dish halfway through cooking*	7½ (7:30) minutes; *turn beets over, then rotate dish halfway through cooking*
	5 minutes	5 minutes	5 minutes

Cook beets, covered, on High (100% power) for time in Chart. Let stand, covered, for time in Chart. Beets are done when tender in center if pierced with sharp knife.

BROCCOLI (SPEARS)

Remove large leaves and cut off woody ends of stalks. Cut through stalks lengthwise 2 or 3 times. Rinse under running cold water.

About 20 cals per serving			
	For 4	**For 2**	**For 1**
	1 large bunch (about 1 pound)	1 small bunch (about ½ pound)	1 small bunch (about ½ pound; use half)
	12" by 8" baking dish; *arrange with flowerets overlapping in center*	9" pie plate; *arrange spears facing in same direction*	8" plate; *arrange spears facing in same direction*
	¼ cup	¼ cup	Whatever clings after rinsing
	5 to 6 minutes; *rotate dish halfway through cooking*	3½ (3:30) to 4 minutes; *rotate dish halfway through cooking*	1½ (1:30) to 1¾ (1:45) minutes
	5 minutes	3 to 4 minutes	3 to 4 minutes

Cook broccoli and water, covered, on High (100% power) for time in Chart. Let stand, covered, for time in Chart. Broccoli spears are done when tender-crisp. Drain.

BROCCOLI (PIECES)

Remove large leaves and cut off woody ends of stalks. Cut stalks and flowerets into bite-sized pieces. Rinse under running cold water.

About 30 cals per serving			
	For 4	**For 2**	**For 1**
	1 large bunch (about 1 pound)	1 small bunch (about ½ pound)	1 small bunch (about ½ pound; use half)
	2-quart casserole	1-quart casserole	Small bowl
	¼ cup	2 tablespoons	1 tablespoon
	6 to 7 minutes; *stir halfway through cooking*	3½ (3:30) to 4 minutes; *stir halfway through cooking*	1½ (1:30) to 2 minutes; *stir halfway through cooking*
	5 minutes	5 minutes	5 minutes

Cook broccoli and water, covered, on High (100% power) for time in Chart. Let stand, covered, for time in Chart. Broccoli pieces are done when tender-crisp. Drain.

BRUSSELS SPROUTS

Look for firm, fresh, bright green sprouts with tight-fitting outer leaves free from black spots. Puffy or soft sprouts are usually poor in quality. Rinse under running cold water.

Remove any yellow leaves and trim stems.

About 43 cals per serving			
	For 4	**For 2**	**For 1**
	2 10-ounce containers	1 10-ounce container	1 10-ounce container (use 1 cup; refrigerate remainder)
	2-quart casserole	9" pie plate	Small bowl
	¼ cup	¼ cup	2 tablespoons
	8 to 9 minutes; *stir halfway through cooking*	6 to 7 minutes; *stir halfway through cooking*	3 to 3½ (3:30) minutes; *stir halfway through cooking*
	5 minutes	5 minutes	5 minutes

Cook Brussels sprouts and water, covered, on High (100% power) for time in Chart. Let stand, covered, for time in Chart. Brussels sprouts are done when centers are tender-crisp if pierced with tip of sharp knife. Drain.

CABBAGE, CHINESE (SLICES)

Trim root end. Rinse leaves under running cold water. Cut crosswise into 1½-inch slices.

About 9 cals per serving			
	For 4	**For 2**	**For 1**
	1 medium head (about 2 pounds, use 8 cups loosely packed; refrigerate remainder)	1 medium head (about 2 pounds, use 4 cups loosely packed; refrigerate remainder)	1 small head (1½ to 2 pounds, use 2 cups loosely packed; refrigerate remainder)
	3-quart casserole	2-quart casserole	1-quart casserole
	¼ cup	2 tablespoons	Whatever clings after rinsing
	4 to 5 minutes; *stir halfway through cooking*	3 to 4 minutes; *stir halfway through cooking*	2 to 3 minutes; *stir halfway through cooking*
	3 to 4 minutes	3 minutes	2 to 3 minutes

Cook cabbage and water, covered, on High (100% power) for time in Chart. Let stand, covered, for time in Chart. Drain. Chinese cabbage slices are done when tender-crisp; the volume will be reduced by about a half. Drain.

239

CABBAGE, GREEN (WEDGES)

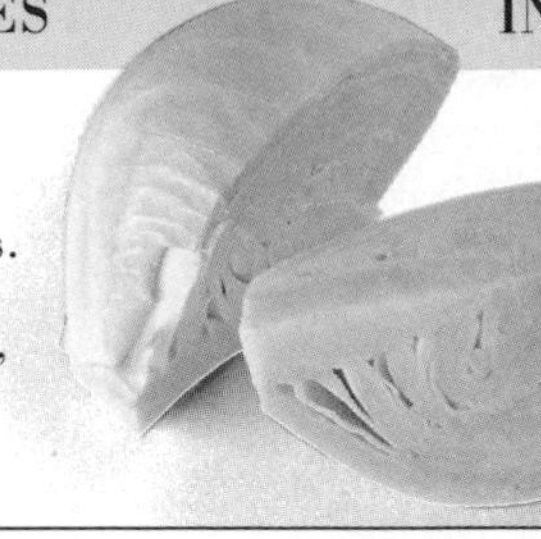

Discard any tough outer leaves. Cut head into half, then into 4 wedges; cut cores from wedges, leaving just enough to retain shapes. Rinse.

About 25 cals per serving		
For 4	**For 2**	**For 1**
1 small head (about 1 pound)	1 small head (about 1 pound, use 2 wedges; refrigerate remainder)	1 small head (about 1 pound, use 1 wedge; refrigerate remainder)
8" by 8" baking dish; *arrange spoke fashion*	8" by 8" baking dish; *arrange 1 inch apart*	9" pie plate
¼ cup	¼ cup	3 tablespoons
12 minutes; *rotate dish halfway through cooking*	6 to 7 minutes; *rotate dish halfway through cooking*	3½ (3:30) to 4 minutes
5 minutes	3 minutes	3 minutes

Cook cabbage and water, covered, on High (100% power) for time in Chart. Let stand, covered, for time in Chart. Green cabbage wedges are done when tender-crisp. Drain.

CABBAGE, RED (SHREDDED)

Prepare as for shredded green cabbage (left).

Red cabbage is usually served shredded. Vinegar is added to the cooking liquid to prevent the cabbage from turning an unappetizing blue.

About 15 cals per serving		
For 4	**For 2**	**For 1**
1 medium head (about 2 pounds; use 4 cups loosely packed)	1 small head (about 1 pound; use 2 cups loosely packed)	1 small head (about 1 pound; use 1 cup loosely packed)
1-quart casserole	Small bowl	Small bowl
¼ cup water *plus* ¼ cup white vinegar; *toss well*	3 tablespoons water *plus* 3 tablespoons white vinegar; *toss well*	2 tablespoons water *plus* 2 tablespoons white vinegar; *toss well*
14 to 16 minutes; *stir halfway through cooking*	10 to 12 minutes; *stir halfway through cooking*	5 to 6 minutes; *stir halfway through cooking*
5 minutes	5 minutes	5 minutes

Cook cabbage, water, and vinegar, covered, on High (100% power) for time in Chart. Let stand, covered, for time in Chart. Red cabbage shreds are done when tender-crisp. Drain.

CABBAGE, GREEN (SHREDDED)

Discard any tough outer leaves. Cut head in half, then cut into wedges; cut cores from wedges. Shred cabbage by hand with a knife or in food processor.

About 25 cals per serving		
For 4	**For 2**	**For 1**
1 medium head (about 2 pounds, use 8 cups loosely packed; refrigerate remainder)	1 small head (about 1 pound; use 4 cups loosely packed; refrigerate remainder)	1 small head (about 1 pound; use 2 cups loosely packed; refrigerate remainder)
2-quart casserole	1-quart casserole	Small bowl
¼ cup	2 tablespoons	1 tablespoon
6 to 7 minutes; *stir every 3 minutes*	4 to 5 minutes; *stir halfway through cooking*	2 to 3 minutes; *stir halfway through cooking*
5 minutes	5 minutes	3 minutes

Cook cabbage and water, covered, on High (100% power) for time in Chart. Let stand, covered, for time in Chart. Green cabbage shreds are done when tender-crisp. Drain.

CARROTS

Peel and rinse under running cold water. Cut off both ends.

About 24 cals per serving		
For 4	**For 2**	**For 1**
1 16-ounce bag	1 16-ounce bag (use half; refrigerate remainder)	1 16-ounce bag (use a quarter; refrigerate remainder)
8" by 8" baking dish; *alternate narrow ends*	9" pie plate; *alternate narrow ends*	8" plate; *alternate narrow ends*
¼ cup	¼ cup	2 tablespoons
7 to 9 minutes; *rearrange carrots halfway through cooking*	5 to 6½ (6:30) minutes; *rearrange carrots halfway through cooking*	2½ (2:30) to 3 minutes; *rotate plate halfway through cooking*
5 minutes	5 minutes	5 minutes

Cook carrots and water, covered, on High (100% power) for time in Chart. Let stand, covered, for time in Chart. Carrots are done when thickest sections are tender-crisp if pierced with tip of sharp knife. Drain.

CARROTS (SLICES)

Peel and rinse under running cold water. Cut off both ends. Cut crosswise into ¼-inch-thick slices.

About 24 cals per serving		
For 4	**For 2**	**For 1**
1 16-ounce bag (about 3 cups)	1 16-ounce bag (use half, about 1½ cups; refrigerate remainder)	1 16-ounce bag (use a quarter, about ¾ cup; refrigerate remainder)
1-quart casserole; *arrange larger slices around edge*	9″ pie plate; *arrange larger slices around edge*	Small bowl
½ cup	¼ cup	2 tablespoons
7 to 9 minutes; *stir twice during cooking*	5 to 6½ (6:30) minutes; *stir halfway through cooking*	2½ (2:30) to 3½ (3:30) minutes; *stir halfway through cooking*
5 minutes	5 minutes	5 minutes

Cook carrots and water, covered, on High (100% power) for time in Chart. Let stand, covered, for time in Chart. Carrot slices are done when larger and smaller pieces are equally tender-crisp. Drain.

CARROTS, BABY

Peel and rinse under running cold water. Cut off root ends.

27 cals per serving		
For 4	**For 2**	**For 1**
2 12-ounce bags	1 12-ounce bag	1 12-ounce bag (use half; refrigerate remainder)
8″ by 8″ baking dish	9″ pie plate	Small bowl
¾ cup	½ cup	¼ cup
10 to 12 minutes; *stir halfway through cooking*	7 to 9 minutes; *stir halfway through cooking*	3½ (3:30) to 4 minutes; *stir halfway through cooking*
5 minutes	5 minutes	5 minutes

Cook carrots and water, covered, on High (100% power) for time in Chart. Let stand, covered, for time in Chart. Baby carrots are done when tender-crisp. Drain.

CAULIFLOWER

Keeping cauliflower whole, remove leaves and cut out core. Rinse under running cold water.

About 25 cals per serving		
For 4	**For 2**	**For 1**
1 medium head (about 2 pounds)	1 small head (about 1 pound)	1 small head (about 1 pound; use half)
9″ pie plate	9″ pie plate	9″ pie plate
¼ cup	3 tablespoons	2 tablespoons
8 to 9 minutes; *rotate plate halfway through cooking*	5 to 6 minutes; *rotate plate halfway through cooking*	3 to 5 minutes; *rotate plate halfway through cooking*
5 minutes	5 minutes	5 minutes

Cook cauliflower and water, covered, on High (100% power) for time in Chart. Let stand, covered, for time in Chart. Cauliflower is done when stem end is fork-tender. Drain.

CAULIFLOWER (FLOWERETS)

Remove outer green leaves and core. Separate into flowerets; large flowerets can be cut in half for more even cooking. Rinse under running cold water.

About 25 cals per serving		
For 4	**For 2**	**For 1**
1 medium head	1 medium head (use half; refrigerate remainder)	1 small head (use half; refrigerate remainder)
2-quart casserole; *arrange larger flowerets around edge*	1-quart casserole; *arrange larger flowerets around edge*	Small bowl
¼ cup	¼ cup	2 tablespoons
8 to 9 minutes; *stir every 3 minutes*	5 to 6 minutes; *stir halfway through cooking*	3 to 4 minutes; *stir halfway through cooking*
5 minutes	5 minutes	3 to 4 minutes

Cook cauliflower and water, covered, on High (100% power) for time in Chart. Let stand, covered, for time in Chart. Cauliflower flowerets are done when tender-crisp. Drain.

CELERIAC (PIECES)
ALSO KNOWN AS CELERY ROOT

Rinse celeriac under running cold water. Cut off roots. Peel and cut out any pitted areas. Cut into ½-inch-thick pieces.

About 40 cals per serving		
For 4	**For 2**	**For 1**
1 large celeriac (about 1½ pounds, 4 cups)	1 medium celeriac (about ¾ pound, 2 cups)	1 small celeriac (about 6 ounces, 1 cup)
2-quart casserole	1-quart casserole	Small bowl
½ cup	¼ cup	2 tablespoons
9 to 10 minutes; *stir every 3 minutes*	4 to 5 minutes; *stir halfway through cooking*	2½ (2:30) to 3 minutes
5 minutes	5 minutes	3 minutes

Cook celeriac and water, covered, on High (100% power) for time in Chart. Let stand, covered, for time in Chart. Celeriac pieces are done when tender-crisp. Drain.

CELERY HEARTS

Rinse under running cold water. Trim tops and bottoms, leaving bunch intact; cut each heart lengthwise in half. Remove any coarse outer stalks and leafy center of each heart.

About 15 cals per serving		
For 4	**For 2**	**For 1**
1-pound bag	1-pound bag (use half; refrigerate remainder)	1-pound bag (use a quarter; refrigerate remainder)
8" by 8" baking dish	8" by 8" baking dish	9" pie plate
¾ cup	½ cup	½ cup
8 to 9 minutes; *turn halves over and rearrange halfway through cooking*	6 to 7 minutes; *turn halves over and rearrange halfway through cooking*	4 to 5 minutes; *turn halves over and rearrange halfway through cooking*
5 minutes	5 minutes	5 minutes

Cook celery hearts and water, covered, on High (100% power) for time in Chart. Let stand, covered, for time in Chart. Celery hearts are done when tender-crisp. Drain.

CELERY (SLICES)

Remove leaves; trim root end. Scrub stalks under running cold water. With vegetable peeler, peel off any coarse strings. Cut stalks crosswise into ¼-inch-thick slices.

CELERY HEARTS
(PIECES)

Prepare as for celery hearts (above), then cut into 1- to 3-inch pieces.

About 14 cals per serving		
For 4	**For 2**	**For 1**
1 medium bunch (about 3½ cups)	1 small bunch (use half, about 1¾ cups; refrigerate remainder)	1 small bunch (use a quarter, about ¾ cup; refrigerate remainder)
1-quart casserole	Small bowl	Small bowl
¼ cup	2 tablespoons	1 tablespoon
6 to 7 minutes; *stir halfway through cooking*	4 to 5 minutes; *stir halfway through cooking*	2 to 3 minutes; *stir halfway through cooking*
5 minutes	5 minutes	5 minutes

Cook celery and water, covered, on High (100% power) for time in Chart. Let stand, covered, for time in Chart. Celery slices are done when tender-crisp. Drain.

About 15 cals per serving		
For 4	**For 2**	**For 1**
1-pound bag (about 4 cups)	1-pound bag (use half, about 2 cups; refrigerate remainder)	1-pound bag (use a quarter, about 1 cup; refrigerate remainder)
1-quart casserole; *arrange larger pieces around edge*	9" pie plate; *arrange larger pieces around edge*	Small bowl
¼ cup	2 tablespoons	1 tablespoon
7 to 8 minutes; *stir halfway through cooking*	4 to 5 minutes; *stir halfway through cooking*	2 to 3 minutes; *stir halfway through cooking*
5 minutes	5 minutes	5 minutes

Cook celery hearts and water, covered, on High (100% power) for time in Chart. Let stand, covered, for time in Chart. Celery heart pieces are done when tender-crisp. Drain.

CHAYOTES
ALSO CALLED MIRLITONS, VEGETABLE PEARS, OR CHRISTOPHINES

These are pear-shaped members of the squash family, 3- to 6-inches long. Select firm, very young ones. Rinse under running cold water; pat dry. With fork, pierce skin of each in several places.

About 48 cals per serving		
For 4	**For 2**	**For 1**
2 chayotes (about ¾ pound each)	1 chayote (about ¾ pound)	1 chayote (about ¾ pound)
Wrap individually in plastic wrap; *arrange in circle on oven floor*	Wrap in plastic wrap; *place in center of oven floor*	Wrap in plastic wrap; *place in center of oven floor*
None	None	None
10 to 12 minutes; *turn and re-arrange halfway through cooking*	7 to 8 minutes; *turn and re-arrange halfway through cooking*	7 to 8 minutes; *turn and re-arrange halfway through cooking*
5 minutes	5 minutes	5 minutes

Cook chayotes, wrapped, on High (100% power) for time in Chart. Let stand, still wrapped, for time in Chart. Chayotes are done when thickest area of flesh can be pierced easily down to seed with tip of sharp knife. Cut in half lengthwise and discard seed. Use pulp as recipe directs. For 1, refrigerate half.

CORN-ON-THE-COB (page 260)

CORN, FROZEN KERNELS

About 80 cals per serving		
For 4	**For 2**	**For 1**
2 10-ounce packages	1 10-ounce package	1 10-ounce package (use ⅔ cup)
1-quart casserole	Small bowl	Small bowl
¼ cup	¼ cup	1 tablespoon
8 to 9 minutes; *stir halfway through cooking*	5 to 7 minutes; *stir halfway through cooking*	1½ (1:30) to 2½ (2:30) minutes; *stir halfway through cooking*
5 minutes	3 to 5 minutes	1 to 2 minutes

Cook frozen corn kernels and water, covered, on High (100% power) for time in Chart. Let stand, covered, for time in Chart. Frozen corn kernels are done when hot. Drain.

EGGPLANT (PIECES)

Prepare just before cooking because flesh turns brown if exposed to air. Rinse under running cold water and pat dry. Trim off the stem end. Cut eggplant into ½-inch pieces.

21 cals per serving		
For 4	**For 2**	**For 1**
1 medium eggplant (about 1½ pounds, 8 cups)	1 small eggplant (about ¾ pound, 4 cups)	1 small eggplant (about ¾ pound, use 2 cups; refrigerate remainder)
3-quart casserole	1½-quart casserole	1-quart casserole
¼ cup	2 tablespoons	1 tablespoon
8 to 9 minutes; *stir halfway through cooking*	6 to 7 minutes; *stir halfway through cooking*	3 to 4 minutes; *stir halfway through cooking*
5 minutes	5 minutes	5 minutes

Cook eggplant and water, covered, on High (100% power) for time in Chart. Let stand, covered, for time in Chart. Eggplant pieces are done when tender. Drain.

ENDIVE, BELGIAN
ALSO KNOWN AS WITLOOF CHICORY

Rinse under running cold water. From each head, remove bruised leaves. Trim root ends without disconnecting leaves; remove core's bitter portion by inserting point of knife about 1 inch into base. You can see a circular outline in the core; follow outline, cutting in circular motion. Pull out cone-shaped core and discard.

About 16 cals per serving		
For 4	**For 2**	**For 1**
8 heads (about 4 ounces each)	4 heads (about 4 ounces each)	2 heads (about 4 ounces each)
12″ by 8″ baking dish; *arrange along narrow ends with tips pointing toward center*	8″ by 8″ baking dish; *alternate tips*	9″ pie plate; *alternate tips*
1 cup	⅔ cup	⅔ cup
16 to 18 minutes; *turn each head over, then rotate dish halfway through cooking*	12 to 14 minutes; *turn each head over, then rotate dish halfway through cooking*	8 to 10 minutes; *turn each head over, then rotate dish halfway through cooking*
5 minutes	5 minutes	5 minutes

Cook endive and water, covered, on High (100% power) for time in Chart. Let stand, covered, for time in Chart. Belgian endive is done when tender. Drain.

FENNEL (SLICES)
ALSO CALLED ANISE OR FINOCCHIO

Rinse under running cold
water. Cut off root ends and
leaves from bulbs. Cut bulbs
lengthwise in half, then slice
crosswise into ¼-inch-
thick slices.

15 cals per serving		
For 4	**For 2**	**For 1**
2 small bulbs (about 8 ounces each)	1 small bulb (about 8 ounces)	1 small bulb (about 8 ounces use half; refrigerate remainder)
8″ by 8″ baking dish	9″ pie plate	Small bowl
1 cup	½ cup	¼ cup
10 to 12 minutes; *stir every 3 to 4 minutes*	7 to 8 minutes; *stir halfway through cooking*	4 to 4½ (4:30) minutes; *stir halfway through cooking*
5 minutes	5 minutes	5 minutes

Cook fennel and water, covered, on High (100% power) for time
in Chart. Drain, then let stand, covered, for time in Chart.
Fennel slices are done when tender-crisp.

GREENS, BEET

Use only tender, green tops.
Discard any damaged, dried, or
yellow leaves and coarse stems.

Wash under running cold
water; drain.

About 26 cals per serving		
For 4	**For 2**	**For 1**
2 pounds (about 8 cups tightly packed)	1 pound (about 4 cups tightly packed)	½ pound (about 2 cups tightly packed)
4-quart casserole	3-quart casserole	1-quart casserole
Whatever clings after washing	Whatever clings after washing	Whatever clings after washing
10 to 12 minutes; *stir every 3 minutes*	6 to 7 minutes; *stir halfway through cooking and after completion*	3 to 4 minutes; *stir halfway through cooking and after completion*
5 minutes	5 minutes	5 minutes

Cook greens, covered, on High (100% power) for time in Chart.
Let stand, covered, for time in Chart. Greens are done when
leaves and stems are tender. Drain.

GREENS, COLLARD, KALE, AND MUSTARD

Prepare as for beet greens
(left).

Collard greens – about 30 cals per serving; kale greens – about 50 cals per serving; mustard greens – about 20 cals per serving		
For 4	**For 2**	**For 1**
2 pounds (about 8 cups tightly packed)	1 pound (about 4 cups tightly packed)	½ pound (about 2 cups tightly packed)
4-quart casserole	3-quart casserole	1-quart casserole
1 cup	¾ cup	½ cup
18 to 20 minutes, *stir every 6 minutes*	10 to 12 minutes, *stir every 3 minutes*	6 to 8 minutes, *stir every 2 minutes*
5 minutes	5 minutes	5 minutes

Cook greens and water, covered, on High (100% power) for time
in Chart. Let stand, covered, for time in Chart. For doneness
test, see beet greens (left).

GREENS, DANDELION

Prepare as for beet greens,
(left).

About 35 cals per serving		
For 4	**For 2**	**For 1**
2 pounds (about 8 cups tightly packed)	1 pound (about 4 cups tightly packed)	½ pound (about 2 cups tightly packed)
4-quart casserole	3-quart casserole	1-quart casserole
Whatever clings after washing	Whatever clings after washing	Whatever clings after washing
6 to 7½ (7:30) minutes; *stir every 3 minutes*	4½ (4:30) to 5½ (5:30) minutes; *stir halfway through cooking and after completion*	3 to 4 minutes; *stir halfway through cooking and after completion*
5 minutes	5 minutes	5 minutes

Cook greens, covered, on High (100% power) for time in Chart.
Let stand, covered, for time in Chart. For doneness test, see beet
greens (left).

GREENS, SWISS CHARD

Prepare as for beet greens (page 244).

About 30 cals per serving		
For 4	**For 2**	**For 1**
2 pounds (about 8 cups tightly packed)	1 pound (about 4 cups tightly packed)	½ pound (about 2 cups tightly packed)
4-quart casserole	3-quart casserole	1-quart casserole
Whatever clings after washing	Whatever clings after washing	Whatever clings after washing
12 to 14 minutes; *stir every 3 minutes*	8 to 9 minutes; *stir halfway through cooking and after completion*	5 to 6 minutes; *stir halfway through cooking and after completion*
5 minutes	5 minutes	5 minutes

Cook greens, covered, on High (100% power) for time in Chart. Let stand, covered, for time in Chart. For doneness test, see beet greens (page 244).

JERUSALEM ARTICHOKES
(PIECES) ALSO CALLED SUN ROOTS AND SUN CHOKES

Scrub under running cold water. Separate larger knobs and tubers for easier peeling; peel. Cut knobs and tubers into ½-inch pieces.

85 cals per serving		
For 4	**For 2**	**For 1**
1½ pounds	¾ pound	6 ounces
2-quart casserole	9″ pie plate	Small bowl
⅓ cup	¼ cup	2 tablespoons
7 to 8 minutes; *stir halfway through cooking*	4 to 5 minutes; *stir halfway through cooking*	2½ (2:30) to 3 minutes; *stir halfway through cooking*
5 minutes	5 minutes	3 minutes

Cook Jerusalem artichokes and water, covered, on High (100% power) for time in Chart. Let stand, covered, for time in Chart. Jerusalem artichoke pieces are done when centers are tender-crisp if pierced with tip of sharp knife. Drain.

KOHLRABI (SLICES)

Cut off tops and discard. Rinse under running cold water. Peel thinly and cut into ¼-inch-thick slices.

About 20 cals per serving		
For 4	**For 2**	**For 1**
1 pound	½ pound	¼ pound
1-quart casserole; *arrange larger slices around edge*	9″ pie plate; *arrange larger slices around edge*	Small bowl
¼ cup	2 tablespoons	1 tablespoon
13 to 14 minutes; *stir halfway through cooking*	9 to 10 minutes; *stir halfway through cooking*	5 to 6 minutes; *stir halfway through cooking*
5 minutes	5 minutes	5 minutes

Cook kohlrabi and water, covered, on High (100% power) for time in Chart. Let stand, covered, for time in Chart. Kohlrabi slices are done when tender. Drain.

LEEKS (HALVES)

Trim off roots and leaf ends, leaving 1 to 2 inches above white parts. Cut each lengthwise in half. Carefully wash under running cold water to remove all sand.

Divide leeks into number of servings. Tie loosely with string into bundles.

About 60 cals per serving		
For 4	**For 2**	**For 1**
8 leeks (about 2 pounds)	4 leeks (about 1 pound)	2 leeks (about ½ pound)
12″ by 8″ baking dish; *arrange bundles along edges with center empty*	8″ by 8″ baking dish	Small bowl
1½ cups	1 cup	½ cup
18 to 20 minutes; *turn leeks over halfway through cooking*	15 to 18 minutes; *turn leeks over halfway through cooking*	10 to 12 minutes; *turn leeks over halfway through cooking*
5 minutes	5 minutes	5 minutes

Cook leeks and water, covered, on High (100% power) for time in Chart. Let stand, covered, for time in Chart. Leeks halves are done when tender. Drain and untie.

MUSHROOMS

Do not peel or soak; soaking will make mushrooms soggy. Instead, rinse under running cold water, then pat dry. Cut off thin slice from base of each stem.

ONIONS

Select onions of uniform size, about 3 inches in diameter.

Cut off tops. Trim root ends just enough to allow onions to stand upright; peel.

34 cals per serving (without butter or margarine)

	For 4	For 2	For 1
	1 pound	½ pound	¼ pound
	2-quart casserole	1-quart casserole	Small bowl
	1 tablespoon water; *or 2 tablespoons melted butter or margarine*	1½ teaspoons water; *or 1 tablespoon melted butter or margarine*	¾ teaspoon water; *or 1½ teaspoons melted butter or margarine*
	5 to 7 minutes; *stir twice during cooking*	4 to 6 minutes; *stir twice during cooking*	1½ (1:30) to 2 minutes; *stir halfway through cooking*
	3 to 4 minutes	3 to 4 minutes	1 to 2 minutes

Cook mushrooms and water or melted butter or margarine, covered, on High (100% power) for time in Chart. Let stand, covered, for time in Chart. Mushrooms are done when tender. Drain if cooked with water.

About 40 cals per serving

	For 4	For 2	For 1
	4 medium onions (about 1½ pounds)	2 medium onions (about ¾ pound)	1 medium onion (about 6 ounces)
	8″ by 8″ baking dish; *arrange in circle*	9″ pie plate; *arrange in center of plate*	Small bowl
	None	None	None
	9 to 10 minutes; *rotate dish halfway through cooking*	6 to 7 minutes; *rotate plate halfway through cooking*	3½ (3:30) to 4 minutes; *rotate bowl halfway through cooking*
	5 minutes	5 minutes	5 minutes

Cook onions, covered, on High (100% power) for time in Chart. Let stand, covered, for time in Chart. Whole onions are done when tender-crisp if pierced with tip of sharp knife.

MUSHROOMS (SLICES)

Prepare as for mushrooms (above). With sharp knife, cut vertically into slices.

ONIONS, SMALL BOILING

For even cooking, select onions of uniform size.

Peel onions, leaving a little of the root ends to help them hold shape during cooking.

34 cals per serving (without butter or margarine)

	For 4	For 2	For 1
	1 pound	½ pound	¼ pound
	2-quart casserole	1-quart casserole	Small bowl
	1 tablespoon water; *or 2 tablespoons melted butter or margarine; stir well to coat*	1½ teaspoons water; *or 1 tablespoon melted butter or margarine; stir well to coat*	¾ teaspoon water; *or 1½ teaspoons melted butter or margarine; stir well to coat*
	5 to 7 minutes; *stir halfway through cooking*	4 to 6 minutes; *stir halfway through cooking*	1½ (1:30) to 2 minutes; *stir halfway through cooking*
	3 to 4 minutes	3 to 4 minutes	1 to 2 minutes

Cook mushrooms and water or melted butter or margarine, covered, on High (100% power) for time in Chart. Let stand, covered, for time in Chart. Mushroom slices are done when tender. Drain if cooked with water.

40 cals per serving

	For 4	For 2	For 1
	1½ pounds	¾ pound	6 ounces
	2-quart casserole	1-quart casserole	Small bowl
	1 tablespoon	1 tablespoon	1 teaspoon
	7 to 8 minutes; *stir halfway through cooking*	4 to 6 minutes; *stir halfway through cooking*	2½ (2:30) to 3 minutes; *stir once*
	5 minutes	5 minutes	5 minutes

Cook onions and water, covered, on High (100% power) for time in Chart. Drain, then let stand, covered, for time in Chart. Small boiling onions are done when centers are tender and outer skins are slightly resistant if pierced with tip of sharp knife.

PARSNIPS

Scrub under running cold water. Cut off tops and root ends.

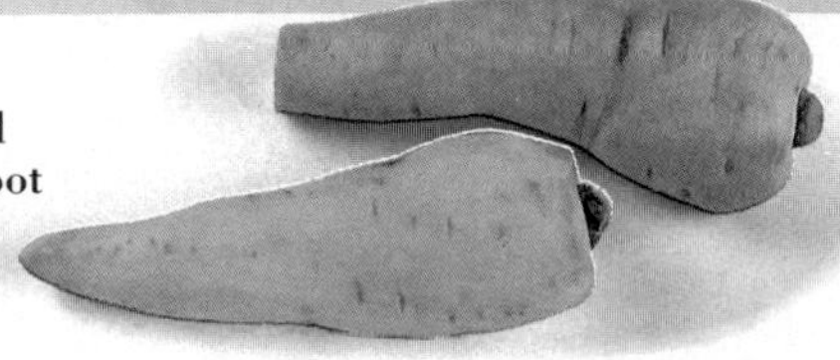

About 75 cals per serving		
For 4	**For 2**	**For 1**
1 pound	½ pound	¼ pound
8″ by 8″ baking dish; *arrange with narrow ends alternating*	8″ by 8″ baking dish; *arrange with narrow ends alternating*	8″ by 8″ baking dish; *arrange with narrow ends alternating*
½ cup	½ cup	½ cup
7 to 9 minutes; *turn parsnips over and rearrange halfway through cooking; do not rearrange if parsnips in center are smaller than those at edges*	5 to 7 minutes; *turn parsnips over and rearrange halfway through cooking; do not rearrange if parsnips in center are smaller than those at edges*	3 to 4 minutes; *turn parsnips over and rearrange halfway through cooking*
5 minutes	5 minutes	5 minutes

Cook parsnips and water, covered, on High (100% power) for time in Chart. Let stand, covered, for time in Chart. Parsnips are done when tender if pierced with tip of sharp knife. Drain.

PARSNIPS (PIECES)

Prepare as for parsnips (above). Cut into 1½-inch-long pieces. If mature parsnips are used, remove woody cores.

About 75 cals per serving		
For 4	**For 2**	**For 1**
1 pound (about 3¼ cups)	½ pound (about 1¾ cups)	¼ pound (about 1 cup)
1-quart casserole; *arrange larger pieces around edge*	9″ pie plate; *arrange larger pieces around edge*	Small bowl
½ cup	¼ cup	2 tablespoons
7 to 9 minutes; *stir every 3 minutes*	5 to 7 minutes; *stir halfway through cooking*	3 to 4 minutes; *stir halfway through cooking*
5 minutes	5 minutes	5 minutes

Cook parsnips and water, covered, on High (100% power) for time in Chart. Let stand, covered, for time in Chart. Parsnip pieces are done when tender. Drain.

PEAS

Shell peas by pressing the pods between your thumb and forefinger to open them.

About 150 cals per serving		
For 4	**For 2**	**For 1**
2 pounds (about 2 cups shelled)	1 pound (about 1 cup shelled)	8 ounces (about ½ cup shelled)
1-quart casserole	Small bowl	Small bowl
¼ cup	2 tablespoons	1 tablespoon
6 to 7 minutes; *stir halfway through cooking*	4 to 5 minutes; *stir halfway through cooking*	2 to 2½ (2:30) minutes; *stir halfway through cooking*
3 to 5 minutes	3 to 5 minutes	3 to 5 minutes

Cook peas and water, covered, on High (100% power) for time in Chart. Let stand, covered, for time in Chart. Shelled peas are done when tender. Drain.

PEA PODS, CHINESE
ALSO CALLED SNOW PEAS

Rinse under running cold water. Remove stems and strings along both sides of pods; do not shell.

24 cals per serving		
For 4	**For 2**	**For 1**
8 ounces	4 ounces	2 ounces
8″ by 8″ baking dish	9″ pie plate	Small bowl
2 tablespoons	1 tablespoon	1½ teaspoons
4 to 5 minutes; *stir halfway through cooking; test for doneness after 4 minutes*	2 to 3 minutes; *stir halfway through cooking; test for doneness after 2½ (2:30) minutes*	1 to 1½ (1:30) minutes; *stir halfway through cooking; test for doneness after 1 minute*
30 seconds to 1 minute	30 seconds to 1 minute	30 seconds to 1 minute

Cook pea pods and water on High for time in Chart. Let stand for time in Chart. Chinese pea pods are done when tender-crisp. Drain.

PEPPERS, SWEET (STRIPS)

Rinse under running cold water. Cut a slice from stem end; remove core, seeds, and white membranes. Cut peppers lengthwise in half, then cut each half lengthwise into ½-inch-wide strips.

About 25 cals per serving		
For 4	**For 2**	**For 1**
4 medium peppers (4 to 5 ounces each)	2 medium peppers (4 to 5 ounces each)	1 medium pepper (4 to 5 ounces)
2-quart casserole	1-quart casserole	Small bowl
3 tablespoons	2 tablespoons	1 tablespoon
5½ (5:30) to 7 minutes; *stir after 3 minutes*	4 to 5 minutes; *stir after 3 minutes*	2 to 3 minutes; *stir halfway through cooking*
5 minutes	5 minutes	5 minutes

Cook peppers and water, covered, on High (100% power) for time in Chart; after stirring, check texture of peppers and stop cooking when slightly less done than desired. Let stand, covered, for time in Chart. Sweet pepper strips are done when tender-crisp. Drain.

POTATOES, ALL-PURPOSE
(CHUNKS)

Scrub potatoes under running cold water. Peel and remove any blemishes or sprouts. Cut into 1-inch chunks.

About 75 cals per serving		
For 4	**For 2**	**For 1**
4 medium potatoes (about 6 ounces each)	2 medium potatoes (about 6 ounces each)	1 medium potato (about 6 ounces)
8″ by 8″ baking dish	9″ pie plate	4-cup glass measure
¾ cup	½ cup	¼ cup
10 to 12 minutes; *stir halfway through cooking*	6 to 8 minutes; *stir halfway through cooking*	5 to 6 minutes; *stir halfway through cooking*
5 minutes	5 minutes	5 minutes

Cook potatoes and water, covered, on High (100% power) for time in Chart. Let stand, covered, for time in Chart. All-purpose potato chunks are done when tender. Drain.

POTATOES, BAKING

Buy oval-shaped baking potatoes of uniform size. Scrub under running cold water. With fork, pierce each several times.

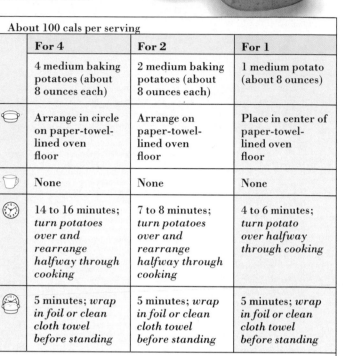

About 100 cals per serving		
For 4	**For 2**	**For 1**
4 medium baking potatoes (about 8 ounces each)	2 medium baking potatoes (about 8 ounces each)	1 medium potato (about 8 ounces)
Arrange in circle on paper-towel-lined oven floor	Arrange on paper-towel-lined oven floor	Place in center of paper-towel-lined oven floor
None	None	None
14 to 16 minutes; *turn potatoes over and rearrange halfway through cooking*	7 to 8 minutes; *turn potatoes over and rearrange halfway through cooking*	4 to 6 minutes; *turn potato over halfway through cooking*
5 minutes; *wrap in foil or clean cloth towel before standing*	5 minutes; *wrap in foil or clean cloth towel before standing*	5 minutes; *wrap in foil or clean cloth towel before standing*

Cook potatoes on High (100% power) for time in Chart. Let stand, wrapped, for time in Chart. Baking potatoes are done when tender.

POTATOES, SMALL RED (NEW)

Scrub potatoes under running cold water. With fork, pierce each potato once. Or, with vegetable peeler, peel strip around center of each.

78 cals per serving		
For 4	**For 2**	**For 1**
1 pound	½ pound	¼ pound
9″ pie plate; *arrange larger potatoes around edge*	Small bowl	Small bowl
¼ cup	2 tablespoons	1 tablespoon
6 to 7 minutes; *turn potatoes over halfway through cooking*	3½ (3:30) to 4 minutes; *turn potatoes over halfway through cooking*	2 to 2½ (2:30) minutes; *turn potatoes over halfway through cooking*
5 minutes	5 minutes	3 to 5 minutes

Cook potatoes and water, covered, on High (100% power) for time in Chart. Drain, then let stand, covered, for time in Chart. Potatoes are done when tender if pierced with tip of sharp knife.

POTATOES, RED (SLICES)

Scrub under running cold water. Potatoes can be cooked with their skins on or peeled. Cut into ¼-inch-thick slices.

About 75 cals per serving		
For 4	**For 2**	**For 1**
4 medium red potatoes (about 4 ounces each, 3 cups)	2 medium red potatoes (about 4 ounces each, 1½ cups)	1 medium red potato (about 4 ounces, 1 cup)
8″ by 8″ baking dish; *arrange larger slices around edges*	9″ pie plate; *arrange larger slices around edge*	9″ pie plate; *arrange larger slices around edge*
½ cup	⅓ cup	3 tablespoons
7 to 9 minutes; *stir halfway through cooking*	4½ (4:30) to 5 minutes; *stir halfway through cooking*	3 to 3½ (3:30) minutes; *stir halfway through cooking*
5 minutes	5 minutes	5 minutes

Cook potatoes and water, covered, on High (100% power) for time in Chart. Let stand, covered, for time in Chart. Red potato slices are done when tender. Drain.

RUTABAGA (CHUNKS)

Cut into quarters. Peel and cut into ¾-inch chunks.

About 60 cals per serving		
For 4	**For 2**	**For 1**
1 medium rutabaga (about 1¼ pounds, use 4 cups; refrigerate remainder)	1 medium rutabaga (about 1¼ pounds, use 2 cups; refrigerate remainder)	1 small rutabaga (about ¾ pound, use 1 cup; refrigerate remainder)
1-quart casserole	1-quart casserole	1-quart casserole
½ cup	¼ cup	¼ cup
17 to 19 minutes; *stir twice during cooking*	12 to 14 minutes; *stir twice during cooking*	7 to 9 minutes; *stir halfway through cooking*
5 minutes	5 minutes	5 minutes

Cook rutabaga and water, covered, on High (100% power) for time in Chart. Let stand, covered, for time in Chart. Rutabaga chunks are done when tender. Drain.

SPINACH

Discard any yellowish and wilted leaves. Remove stems from spinach. Wash leaves under running cold water to remove any sand.

About 20 cals per serving		
For 4	**For 2**	**For 1**
1 10-ounce bag (about 12 cups loosely packed)	1 10-ounce bag (use half, about 6 cups loosely packed; refrigerate remainder)	1 10-ounce bag package (use a quarter, about 3 cups loosely packed; refrigerate remainder)
3-quart casserole	2-quart casserole	Small bowl
Whatever clings after washing	Whatever clings after washing	Whatever clings after washing
5½ (5:30) to 6½ (6:30) minutes; *stir halfway through cooking*	3 to 3½ (3:30) minutes; *stir halfway through cooking*	2 to 2½ (2:30) minutes; *stir halfway through cooking*
3 minutes	3 minutes	2 minutes

Cook spinach, covered, on High (100% power) for time in Chart. Let stand, covered, for time in Chart. Spinach is done when leaves are wilted. Drain.

SQUASH, ACORN (HALVES)

This is a variety of winter squash, also known as hard-skinned squash. Wash under running cold water. To soften slightly for easier cutting, pierce each squash several times; heat on High (100% power) 1 to 1½ (1:30) minutes per squash. Cut lengthwise in half; discard seeds.

About 75 cals per serving		
For 4	**For 2**	**For 1**
2 medium squash (about 1½ pounds each)	1 medium squash (about 1½ pounds)	1 small squash (about 1 pound)
Wrap each half individually in plastic wrap; *arrange in circle on oven floor*	Wrap each half individually in plastic wrap; *arrange on oven floor*	Wrap each half individually in plastic wrap; *arrange on oven floor*
None	None	None
12 to 14 minutes; *rearrange halfway through cooking*	9 minutes; *rearrange halfway through cooking*	7 minutes; *rearrange halfway through cooking*
5 minutes	5 minutes	5 minutes

Cook squash, wrapped, on High (100% power) for time in Chart. Let stand, still wrapped, for time in Chart. Acorn squash halves are done when flesh is tender.

SQUASH, BUTTERNUT (HALVES AND QUARTERS)

Rinse under running cold water and pat dry. Cut lengthwise in half; if squash is heavier than 2 pounds, cut into quarters. With spoon, scoop out seeds.

About 120 cals per serving		
For 4	**For 2**	**For 1**
1 large squash (about 3 pounds)	1 medium squash (about 2 pounds)	1 small squash (about 1¼ pounds)
Wrap individually in plastic wrap; *arrange on oven floor alternating narrow ends*	Wrap individually in plastic wrap; *arrange on oven floor alternating narrow ends*	Wrap in plastic wrap; *arrange on oven floor, alternating narrow ends*
None	None	None
20 to 24 minutes; *rearrange pieces halfway through cooking*	10 to 12 minutes; *rearrange halves halfway through cooking*	7 to 8 minutes; *rearrange halves halfway through cooking*
5 minutes	5 minutes	5 minutes

Cook squash on High (100% power) for time in Chart. Let stand, still wrapped, for time in Chart. Butternut squash is done when flesh is tender and can be scooped easily from the shell; any pale yellow areas will continue to cook during standing. If any area remains pale yellow after standing, continue to cook, rewrapped, 30 seconds at a time until rich yellow-orange.

SQUASH, SPAGHETTI (HALVES)

Rinse under running cold water. Cut squash lengthwise in half. Scrape out seeds and membranes; discard.

About 66 cals per serving		
For 4	**For 2**	**For 1**
1 large squash (4 to 4½ pounds)	1 medium squash (about 2 pounds)	1 small squash (about 1¼ pounds)
Wrap each half individually in plastic wrap; *arrange on oven floor*	Wrap each half individually in plastic wrap; *arrange on oven floor*	Wrap each half individually in plastic wrap; *arrange on oven floor*
None	None	None
22 to 24 minutes; *rearrange halves halfway through cooking*	12 to 14 minutes; *rearrange halves halfway through cooking*	9 to 10 minutes; *rearrange halves halfway through cooking*
5 minutes	5 minutes	5 minutes

Cook squash halves, wrapped, on High (100% power) for time in Chart. Let stand, still wrapped, for time in Chart. Spaghetti squash is done when fork can easily pull and separate squash strands. The texture is crisp compared with other squash.

SQUASH, YELLOW (SLICES)

Select squash which are uniform in size with same diameter top to bottom for even cooking.

Scrub under running cold water. Trim off stem and blossom ends; do not peel. Cut crosswise into ¼-inch-thick slices.

About 21 cals per serving		
For 4	**For 2**	**For 1**
1 pound (about 4 cups)	½ pound (about 2 cups)	¼ pound (about 1 cup)
1-quart casserole; *arrange larger slices around edge*	1-quart casserole; *arrange larger slices around edge*	Small bowl
2 tablespoons	1 tablespoon	1½ teaspoons
6 to 7 minutes; *stir halfway through cooking*	4 to 5 minutes; *stir halfway through cooking*	3 to 4 minutes; *stir halfway through cooking*
5 minutes	5 minutes	3 minutes

Cook squash and water, covered, on High (100% power) for time in Chart. Let stand, covered, for time in Chart. Yellow squash slices are done when tender-crisp. Drain.

SWEET POTATOES AND YAMS

Scrub under cold water; pierce each several times.

Sweet potatoes and yams are not botanically related. What are often sold as fresh and canned yams are, in fact, sweet potatoes; the cooking directions for fresh are the same for both.

Buy oval-shaped sweet potatoes or yams of uniform size. If you can only get ones with tapered ends, these parts will cook more rapidly than the rest of the vegetable; arrange ends pointing toward center. If halfway through cooking, these areas seem to be cooked, shield them with thin strips of foil.

About 161 cals per serving		
For 4	**For 2**	**For 1**
4 sweet potatoes or yams (about 8 ounces each)	2 sweet potatoes or yams (about 8 ounces each)	1 sweet potato or yam (about 8 ounces)
Arrange on paper-towel-lined oven floor	Arrange on paper-towel-lined oven floor	Place on paper-towel-lined oven floor
None	None	None
10 to 11 minutes; *turn potatoes or yams over and rearrange halfway through cooking*	7 to 8 minutes; *turn potatoes or yams over halfway through cooking*	4 to 5 minutes; *turn potato or yam over halfway through cooking*
5 minutes; *wrap in foil or clean cloth towel before standing*	5 minutes; *wrap in foil or clean cloth towel before standing*	5 minutes; *wrap in foil or clean cloth towel before standing*

Cook potatoes or yams on High (100% power) for time in Chart. Let stand, wrapped, for time in Chart. Sweet potatoes or yams are done when tender.

TURNIPS (CHUNKS)

Rinse under running cold water. Peel. Cut into ¾-inch-thick chunks.

18 cals per serving			
	For 4	**For 2**	**For 1**
	2 pounds	1 pound	½ pound
	2-quart casserole	1-quart casserole	Small bowl
	½ cup	¼ cup	2 tablespoons
	8 to 9½ (9:30) minutes; *stir halfway through cooking*	5 to 7 minutes; *stir halfway through cooking*	3½ (3:30) to 4 minutes; *stir halfway through cooking*
	5 minutes	5 minutes	5 minutes

Cook turnips and water, covered, on High (100% power) for time in Chart. Let stand, covered, for time in Chart. Turnip chunks are cooked when tender. Drain.

ZUCCHINI (SLICES)

Prepare as for yellow squash (page 250).

About 16 cals per serving			
	For 4	**For 2**	**For 1**
	1 pound (about 4 cups)	½ pound (about 2 cups)	¼ pound (about 1 cup)
	1-quart casserole; *arrange larger slices around edge*	1-quart casserole; *arrange larger slices around edge*	Small bowl
	2 tablespoons	1 tablespoon	1 teaspoon
	6 to 7 minutes; *stir halfway through cooking*	4 to 5 minutes; *stir halfway through cooking*	2 to 2½ (2:30) minutes; *stir halfway through cooking*
	5 minutes	5 minutes	3 minutes

Cook zucchini and water, covered, on High (100% power) for time in Chart. Let stand, covered, for time in Chart. Zucchini slices are done when tender-crisp. Drain.

SPECIAL TECHNIQUES FOR VEGETABLES

Use the microwave to help cook vegetables in a special way. Purees, ribbons, and rings can make a simple vegetable look really special. Impress your guests by serving a colorful selection of pureed vegetables, or delicate vegetable ribbons or rings following the easy directions below. Use your imagination to create different combinations of colors, flavors, and shapes.

Vegetable purees are particularly good to serve at dinner parties because they can be made in advance and reheated in the microwave; they go well with roast meats and broiled chicken. The ribbons and rings can be served uncooked as a salad with a favorite dressing.

Vegetable purees Root vegetables such as potatoes, carrots, and parsnips cook in a fraction of the time in the microwave; leafy green vegetables such as spinach and broccoli remain bright and green.

Cook vegetable, covered, on High (100% power) 2 minutes longer than chart directs, or until soft, then drain well. In food processor with knife blade attached, process vegetable to a smooth puree. Add 2 tablespoons melted butter or margarine, season with salt and pepper, and process again. If you like, add 1 to 2 tablespoons heavy or whipping cream. Using an ice-cream scoop or spoon, shape puree onto microwave-safe plates. Reheat on High 45 to 60 seconds, until hot.

Ribbon vegetables With vegetable peeler, shred 1 large carrot, 1 medium zucchini, and 1 white radish or 1 medium yellow squash, into long ribbons, about 1-inch wide, pressing lightly with peeler so ribbons will be very thin. In large microwave-safe bowl, toss vegetables with 1 tablespoon melted butter or margarine. Cook, covered, on High (100% power) 30 seconds to 1 minute, until tender-crisp.

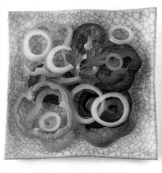

Vegetable rings With sharp knife, cut 3 sweet peppers (green, yellow, and red) and 1 small onion into rings; remove seeds and membranes from peppers. In 13″ by 9″ microwave-safe baking dish, toss vegetables with 1 tablespoon melted butter or margarine, 1 tablespoon salad oil, or 1 tablespoon water. Cook, covered, on High (100% power) 1 to 2 minutes, until tender-crisp. Serve hot, or chill to serve later with a favorite salad dressing.

Asparagus and Beans

ASPARAGUS BUNDLES

Color Index page 70. 68 cals per serving. Low in cholesterol, sodium. Good source of vitamin A. Begin 25 minutes ahead.

Ingredients	For 4	For 2	For 1
Medium asparagus	*1 pound*	*½ pound*	*¼ pound*
Green onions	*2 green onions*	*1 green onion*	*1 green onion*
Water	*2 tablespoons*	*1 tablespoon*	*1½ teaspoons*
Butter or margarine	*2 tablespoons (¼ stick)*	*1 tablespoon*	*1½ teaspoons*
Diced pimento	*2 tablespoons*	*1 tablespoon*	*1½ teaspoons*
Lemon juice	*1 tablespoon*	*1½ teaspoons*	*½ teaspoon*
Microwave cookware	12" by 8" baking dish Small bowl	12" by 8" baking dish Small bowl	12" by 8" baking dish Small bowl
Time on High (100% power) Asparagus	5 to 7 minutes	3 to 5 minutes	1½ (1:30) to 2½ (2:30) minutes
Butter mixture	45 seconds	30 seconds	15 seconds

1 Hold base of each asparagus stalk firmly and bend; the end will break off at the spot where it becomes too tough to eat. Discard tough ends; trim scales if stalks are gritty.

2 With sharp knife, cut green onions where white ends and green starts. Cut green ends lengthwise in half. Thinly slice white ends and reserve.

3 Divide asparagus into bundles, with tips pointing in same direction. Use green ends of onions to tie up asparagus bundles.

4 In baking dish (see Chart), arrange asparagus bundles with tips overlapping in center of dish and tougher, thicker ends pointing toward edges of dish.

5 Sprinkle asparagus bundles with water. Cook, covered, on High for time in Chart, or until asparagus is tender-crisp, rotating dish halfway through cooking. Drain; cover loosely and set aside while preparing sauce.

6 In small bowl (see Chart), place reserved sliced green onions, butter or margarine, and pimento. Cook, covered with paper towel, on High for time in Chart, or until butter or margarine is melted. Stir in lemon juice. Spoon sauce over asparagus bundles and serve.

CALIFORNIA ASPARAGUS WITH CELERY AND PECANS

Color Index page 70. 4 servings. 58 cals per serving. Low in cholesterol, sodium. Begin 25 minutes ahead.

2 teaspoons olive or salad oil
2 tablespoons chopped pecans
3 medium celery stalks
¾ pound medium asparagus
1 garlic clove, minced
Salt to taste

1. In 9" microwave-safe pie plate, combine oil and pecans. Heat on High (100% power) 1 to 3 minutes, until pecans are lightly toasted, stirring once. With slotted spoon, remove pecans to paper towels to drain.
2. Meanwhile, with sharp knife, cut celery stalks diagonally into 2-inch pieces. Discard tough ends and trim scales from asparagus. Cut asparagus diagonally into 2-inch pieces.
3. Into oil remaining in pie plate, stir celery, asparagus, and garlic. Cook on High 6 to 8 minutes, until asparagus is tender-crisp, stirring twice. Season with salt. Add pecans and toss lightly. Arrange on warmed serving platter.

BRAISED GREEN BEANS WITH TOMATOES AND ONIONS

Color Index page 74. 4 servings. 124 cals per serving. Low in cholesterol. Good source of vitamin C, iron. Begin 35 minutes ahead.

2 tablespoons olive or salad oil
2 medium red onions, sliced
1 teaspoon oregano
1 8- to 8¼-ounce can crushed tomatoes
1 pound green beans
½ cup Beef Broth (page 125) or canned broth
Salt to taste
¼ cup grated Parmesan cheese

1. In 2-quart microwave-safe casserole, place oil, onions, and oregano. Cook on High (100% power) 5 to 6 minutes, until onions soften, stirring twice.
2. Into onion mixture, stir tomatoes, green beans, and broth. Cook, covered, on High 20 minutes, or until beans are tender and flavors blend, stirring occasionally. Season with salt.
3. *To serve:* Arrange green beans on warmed serving platter; spoon sauce over. Sprinkle with grated Parmesan cheese.

BABY VEGETABLES
Miniature vegetables are fun to serve whole: their bright colors dress up dinner plates and party platters. In 12" by 8" microwave-safe baking dish, place 8 ounces miniature carrots, zucchini, or yellow or pattypan squash and ¼ cup water. Cook on High (100% power) 4 to 6 minutes, until tender-crisp, stirring halfway through cooking. Drain and serve.

Beans

CHINESE GREEN BEANS WITH PEANUT SAUCE

Color Index page 70. 243 cals per serving. Low in cholesterol. Good source of vitamin A, niacin, vitamin C, iron. Begin 25 minutes ahead.

Ingredients	For 4	For 2	For 1
Garlic cloves	2 garlic cloves	1 garlic clove	½ garlic clove
Red or green pepper	1 pepper	½ pepper	¼ pepper
Chunky peanut butter	½ cup	¼ cup	2 tablespoons
Chicken Broth (page 125) or canned broth	½ cup broth	¼ cup broth	2 tablespoons broth
Soy sauce	1 tablespoon soy sauce	1½ teaspoons soy sauce	¾ teaspoon soy sauce
Cider vinegar	1 tablespoon vinegar	1½ teaspoons vinegar	¾ teaspoon vinegar
Sesame oil	¼ teaspoon	to taste	to taste
Minced peeled gingerroot, or ground ginger	1 tablespoon or 1½ teaspoons	1½ teaspoons or ¾ teaspoon	¾ teaspoon or ¼ teaspoon
Hot-pepper sauce	to taste	to taste	to taste
Green beans	1 pound	½ pound	¼ pound
Water	¼ cup	2 tablespoons	1 tablespoon
Coriander sprigs and red pepper strips for garnish	garnish	garnish	garnish
Microwave cookware	2-cup measure 12" by 8" baking dish	1-cup measure 8" by 8" baking dish	1-cup measure 8" by 8" baking dish
Time on High (100% power)			
Sauce	1 to 1½ (1:30) minutes	45 seconds to 1 minute	30 to 45 seconds
Green beans	7 to 10 minutes	4 to 5 minutes	3 to 4 minutes

1 On cutting board, with sharp knife, mince garlic and red or green pepper. In glass measure (see Chart), place minced garlic and pepper.

2 To same measure, add peanut butter, broth, soy sauce, vinegar, sesame oil, ginger, and hot-pepper sauce. Cook on High for time in Chart, or just until sauce is warm, stirring once. Stir and set aside.

3 In baking dish (see Chart), place beans and water. Cook, covered, on High for time in Chart, or until tender-crisp, stirring once. Drain.

4 To same baking dish, add peanut sauce; toss to coat beans. Transfer to serving platter; garnish. Serve hot or cold.

LIMA BEANS WITH BUTTERED BREAD CRUMBS

Color Index page 70. 153 cals per serving. Low in cholesterol. Begin 20 minutes ahead.

Ingredients	For 4	For 2	For 1
Butter or margarine	2 tablespoons (¼ stick)	1 tablespoon	1½ teaspoons
Fresh bread crumbs	½ cup	¼ cup	2 tablespoons
1 10-ounce package frozen lima beans, thawed	1 package	½ package	¼ package
Water	2 tablespoons	1 tablespoon	1½ teaspoons
Grated Parmesan cheese	2 tablespoons	1 tablespoon	1½ teaspoons
Microwave cookware	9" pie plate Medium bowl	9" pie plate Small bowl	9" pie plate Soup bowl
Time on High (100% power)			
Butter or margarine	45 seconds	30 to 45 seconds	15 seconds
Bread crumbs	2 to 2½ (2:30) minutes	1½ (1:30) to 1¾ (1:45) minutes	1 to 1¼ (1:15) minutes
Lima beans	6 to 8 minutes	4 to 5 minutes	2 to 3 minutes

1 In pie plate (see Chart), place butter or margarine. Heat, covered with paper towel, on High for time in Chart, or until melted.

2 Into melted butter or margarine, stir bread crumbs. Cook on High for time in Chart, or until crumbs are dried and golden, stirring twice. Set aside.

3 In bowl (see Chart), place lima beans and water. Cook, covered, on High for time in Chart, or until tender, stirring once. Drain. Stir in Parmesan. Transfer to warmed serving dish; sprinkle with buttered bread crumbs. Serve immediately.

Beets

Cut tops from fresh medium beets; leave part of stems and roots. Scrub under running cold water, taking care not to damage skins as this will cause "bleeding". Microwave and, after standing time, cut off stems and roots. Peel from bottom to top. The medium beets used in our Fresh Beets with Chicory (below) weigh about 4 to 5 ounces each before they are trimmed, microwaved, and cut into strips. Large beets (6 ounces or more) cook better if individually wrapped in plastic wrap and arranged in a circle in your microwave.

FRESH BEETS WITH CHICORY

Color Index page 74. 143 cals per serving. Low in cholesterol.
Begin 45 minutes ahead.

Ingredients for 6 servings		Microwave cookware
8 medium beets (about 2 pounds without tops) ½ cup water ¼ cup olive or salad oil 1 tablespoon sugar	3 tablespoons red-wine vinegar 1 tablespoon prepared mustard ½ teaspoon salt ¼ teaspoon oregano ½ small head chicory	13″ by 9″ baking dish

1 Wash beets well. In baking dish, place beets and water. Cook, covered, on High (100% power) 14 to 15 minutes, until tender, rotating dish twice.

2 On heat-safe surface, let beets stand, covered, until cool. In large bowl, whisk oil, sugar, vinegar, mustard, salt, and oregano. Set aside.

3 Drain and rinse beets. With rubber glove for protection, peel beets and cut into ¼-inch-thick slices; cut slices into ¼-inch-wide strips.

4 In bowl, place beets. Add dressing and toss to coat. Tear chicory into bite-sized pieces and add to beets.

HARVARD BEETS

Color Index page 70. 62 cals per serving. Low in cholesterol, fat.
Begin 15 minutes ahead.

Ingredients	For 4	For 2	For 1
1 8-ounce can sliced beets	2 cans	1 can	½ can
Liquid from beets	½ cup	¼ cup	2 tablespoons
Cider vinegar	3 tablespoons	4 teaspoons	2 teaspoons
Sugar	2 tablespoons	1 tablespoon	1½ teaspoons
Salt	¼ teaspoon	⅛ teaspoon	to taste
Cornstarch	1½ teaspoons	1 teaspoon	½ teaspoon
Orange Julienne (page 334) for garnish	garnish	garnish	garnish
Microwave cookware	2-quart casserole or bowl	1-quart casserole or bowl	Soup bowl
Time on High (100% power) Sauce	2 to 3 minutes	1½ (1:30) to 2 minutes	1 to 1¼ (1:15) minutes
Beets	3 to 4 minutes	2 to 2½ (2:30) minutes	45 seconds to 1 minute

1 Drain beets, reserving liquid (see Chart). In casserole or bowl (see Chart), combine beet liquid, vinegar, sugar, salt, and cornstarch until blended.

2 Cook mixture on High for time in Chart, or until sauce thickens, stirring twice.

3 To sauce, add sliced beets; stir to coat. Cook on High for time in Chart, or until hot, stirring once.

4 To serve: Spoon beets and sauce into warmed serving dish. Garnish with Orange Julienne.

Broccoli

NEAPOLITAN BROCCOLI

Color Index page 70. 4 servings. 113 cals per serving. Low in cholesterol. Good source of vitamin A, vitamin C. Begin 25 minutes ahead.

2 tablespoons olive or salad oil	2 tablespoons capers
1 red or green pepper, thinly sliced	5 pitted ripe olives
1 garlic clove, finely chopped	2 small bunches broccoli
2 green onions, sliced	1½ teaspoons red-wine vinegar
	Slivered blanched almonds for garnish

1. In 2-quart microwave-safe casserole, place oil, red or green pepper, garlic, green onions, capers, and olives. Cook on High (100% power) 5 to 6 minutes, until pepper softens, stirring twice.
2. Meanwhile, with sharp knife, remove large leaves from broccoli and trim woody stalk ends; separate flowerets from stalks.
3. To vegetable mixture, add broccoli flowerets (refrigerate stalks for use another day); stir to coat. Cook, covered, on High 7 to 10 minutes, until broccoli is tender, stirring twice. Add vinegar; toss. Serve hot or cover and refrigerate to serve chilled later. Garnish before serving.

SAUCES FOR VEGETABLES
Use to add zest to plain cooked fresh or frozen vegetables.

Lemon-butter Sauce: In 2-cup microwave-safe glass measure, place *4 tablespoons butter or margarine (½ stick)*. Heat, covered with paper towel, on High (100% power) 45 seconds to 1 minute, until melted. Stir in *1 tablespoon lemon juice*, *1 tablespoon chopped parsley*, *½ teaspoon salt*, and *dash ground red pepper*. Makes about ⅓ cup. 90 cals per tablespoon.

Fine-herbs Sauce: Prepare Lemon-butter Sauce (above), substituting *3 tablespoons dry white wine* for the lemon juice; add *2 tablespoons chopped chives* and *1 teaspoon chopped fresh dill*. Makes about ⅓ cup. 95 cals per tablespoon.

Mustard-chive Sauce: In 8-cup glass measure, place *4 tablespoons butter or margarine (½ stick)*. Heat, covered with paper towel, on High (100% power) 45 seconds to 1 minute, until melted. Stir in *4 tablespoons all-purpose flour* until blended. Cook on High 1 minute, stirring once. Gradually stir in *2 cups milk*. Cook on High 3 to 5 minutes, until sauce thickens, stirring twice. Stir in *1 tablespoon Dijon mustard* and *1 tablespoon chopped chives*. Makes about 2 cups. 26 cals per tablespoon.

BROCCOLI MORNAY

Color Index page 74. 211 cals per serving. Low in cholesterol. Good source of vitamin A, vitamin C, calcium. Begin 40 minutes ahead.

Ingredients for 4 servings		Microwave cookware
1 small bunch broccoli	2 ounces Cheddar cheese, shredded (½ cup)	4-cup glass measure
3 tablespoons butter or margarine	½ teaspoon salt	8″ by 8″ baking dish
2 tablespoons all-purpose flour	Pepper to taste	Small bowl
1 cup milk	2 tablespoons water	
⅛ teaspoon dry mustard	¼ cup fresh bread crumbs	
	¼ cup minced onion	

1 With sharp knife, remove large leaves from broccoli and trim woody stalk ends. Split stalks lengthwise 2 or 3 times. Rinse well and set aside.

2 In glass measure, place 2 tablespoons butter or margarine. Heat, covered with paper towel, on High (100% power) 45 seconds, or until melted. Stir in flour until smooth and blended. Gradually whisk in milk and dry mustard. Cook on High 3 to 4 minutes, until sauce thickens and is smooth, whisking twice.

3 To sauce, gradually add cheese, whisking until melted and smooth. Season with salt and pepper. Cover and keep warm.

4 In baking dish, arrange broccoli with flowerets pointing toward center of dish and stalks toward edges. Sprinkle with water. Cook, covered, on High 6 to 8 minutes, until tender-crisp, rotating dish halfway through cooking; drain.

5 Rearrange broccoli in attractive pattern in same baking dish or warmed serving dish. Pour reserved cheese sauce over; cover and keep warm. In bowl, place remaining butter or margarine. Heat, covered with paper towel, on High 30 to 45 seconds, until melted.

6 Into melted butter or margarine, stir bread crumbs and onion. Cook on High 2 to 3 minutes, until crumbs are dried and golden, stirring twice. Sprinkle over broccoli. Serve immediately.

Brussels Sprouts and Cabbage

BRUSSELS SPROUTS WITH CHESTNUTS

Color Index page 70. 79 cals per serving. Low in cholesterol, sodium. Good source of vitamin C. Begin 25 minutes ahead.

Ingredients	For 4	For 2	For 1
1 10-ounce container Brussels sprouts	1 container	½ container	¼ container
Chicken Broth (page 125) or canned broth	½ cup	¼ cup	3 tablespoons
Butter or margarine	1 tablespoon	1½ teaspoons	1 teaspoon
Peeled cooked chestnuts (below)	½ cup	¼ cup	4 chestnuts
Salt and pepper	to taste	to taste	to taste
Lemon juice (optional)	½ teaspoon	¼ teaspoon	to taste
Microwave cookware	12″ by 8″ baking dish	8″ by 8″ baking dish	Soup bowl
Time on High (100% power) Brussels sprouts	7 to 9 minutes	5 to 6 minutes	3½ (3:30) to 4½ (4:30) minutes
With chestnuts	5 to 6 minutes	3 to 3½ (3:30) minutes	1½ (1:30) to 2½ (2:30) minutes

1 In baking dish or bowl (see Chart), place Brussels sprouts; add broth. Cook, covered tightly with plastic wrap, on High for time in Chart, or until tender-crisp, stirring twice.

2 To Brussels sprouts, add butter or margarine and peeled cooked chestnuts. Cook on High for time in Chart, or until flavors blend. Season with salt and pepper.

3 If you like, just before serving, sprinkle lemon juice over Brussels sprouts.

PEELING AND COOKING CHESTNUTS

Make horizontal cut through shells of 1 cup chestnuts, cutting across rounded side. Do not cut through meat.

In 4-cup glass measure, place chestnuts and 1 cup water. Heat, covered, on High (100% power) 2½ (2:30) to 4 minutes, until boiling; boil 1 minute longer.

Let nuts stand 7 minutes. Peel off shells and skins; reboil any that do not open. In shallow dish, in single layer, cook nuts on High 1½ (1:30) minutes, or until tender.

PARTY BRUSSELS SPROUTS

Color Index page 71. 6 servings. 108 cals per serving. Low in cholesterol. Good source of vitamin C. Begin 25 minutes ahead.

2 slices bacon, diced
1 pound small white onions, peeled and trimmed
¼ cup water

2 10-ounce packages frozen Brussels sprouts
1 chicken-flavor bouillon cube or envelope
¼ teaspoon salt

1. In 3-quart microwave-safe casserole, place bacon. Cook on High (100% power) 2 to 3 minutes, until browned. With slotted spoon, remove bacon to paper towels to drain.
2. Into bacon drippings in casserole, stir onions and water. Cook, covered, on High 4 minutes, stirring halfway through cooking.
3. To onions, add Brussels sprouts, bouillon, and salt. Cook, covered, on High 10 to 12 minutes, until sprouts are tender-crisp, stirring halfway through cooking.
4. Sprinkle bacon over vegetables. Toss to mix and serve immediately.

SCALLOPED CABBAGE

Color Index page 74. 8 servings. 124 cals per serving. Low in cholesterol, sodium. Good source of vitamin C. Begin 45 minutes ahead.

3 tablespoons butter or margarine
½ cup fresh bread crumbs
2 medium onions, thinly sliced
1 small head green cabbage (about 1½ pounds), shredded

½ cup heavy or whipping cream
Salt and pepper to taste

1. In 3-quart microwave-safe casserole, place 2 tablespoons butter or margarine. Heat, covered with paper towels, on High (100% power) 45 seconds, or until melted. Into melted butter or margarine, stir bread crumbs. Cook on High 3 to 4 minutes, until crumbs are dried and golden, stirring twice. Transfer to small bowl. Set aside.
2. In same casserole, place remaining butter or margarine and onions. Cook, covered with paper towels, on High 5 to 6 minutes, until onions soften, stirring twice.
3. To onion mixture, add cabbage; stir to coat. Cook, covered, on High 10 to 12 minutes, until cabbage is tender, stirring occasionally. Into mixture, stir cream. Season with salt and pepper.
4. Sprinkle cabbage with bread crumbs. Cook on High 3 to 4 minutes, until cabbage is hot and cream bubbles. If you like and if casserole is broiler-safe, brown lightly under preheated broiler.

Cabbage and Carrots

SWEET-AND-SOUR SHREDDED RED CABBAGE

Color Index page 74. 8 servings. 37 cals per serving. Low in cholesterol, fat, sodium. Good source of vitamin C. Begin 35 minutes ahead.

1 small head red cabbage (about 1½ pounds), shredded	1 bay leaf
2 tablespoons brown sugar	Salt and pepper to taste
¼ cup red-wine vinegar	Apple slices and parsley sprig for garnish

1. In 3-quart microwave-safe casserole, combine cabbage, sugar, vinegar, and bay leaf. Cook, covered, on High (100% power) 15 minutes, stirring twice.
2. Uncover; stir. Cook on High 5 to 10 minutes longer, until cabbage is of desired doneness. Discard bay leaf. Season with salt and pepper.
3. Spoon cabbage onto warmed serving platter; garnish with apple slices and parsley. Serve immediately.

GINGER-ORANGE CARROTS

Color Index page 71. 4 servings. 58 cals per serving. Low in cholesterol, fat. Good source of vitamin A. Begin 25 minutes ahead.

1 16-ounce bag carrots, peeled and cut into matchstick-thin strips	4 tablespoons finely shredded peeled gingerroot or 1 teaspoon ground ginger
1 tablespoon orange juice	2 green onions, thinly sliced
2 teaspoons finely grated orange peel	
2 teaspoons soy sauce	

1. In 9″ microwave-safe pie plate, place carrots and orange juice. Cook, covered, on High (100% power) 7 to 9 minutes, until carrots are tender-crisp, stirring occasionally.
2. To carrot mixture, add orange peel, soy sauce, ginger, and green onions. Stir to combine well. Cook on High 1 to 2 minutes, until carrot mixture is hot.
3. Spoon mixture onto serving platter. Serve hot or cover and refrigerate to serve chilled later.

Making "Baby" Carrots

With sharp knife, cut medium carrots into 3-inch pieces. With vegetable peeler, shape each piece until about ½ inch in diameter, tapering to a point at one end. Use trimmings in a salad or refrigerate in plastic bags for use another day.

Carrots may be prepared in a variety of ways. Baby carrots are best microwaved whole if they are a similar size, but larger carrots can be cut into matchstick-thin strips or sliced. For a quick lunch-time snack or vegetable accompaniment, try shredding carrots and combining them with another vegetable as in our Carrot and Potato Pancakes (below).

CARROT AND POTATO PANCAKES

Color Index page 74. 112 cals per serving. Good source of vitamin A. Begin 35 minutes ahead.

Ingredients for 4 servings		Microwave cookware
2 medium carrots 1 baking potato, peeled (about 8 ounces) 2 tablespoons all-purpose flour ½ teaspoon salt ¼ teaspoon baking powder	1 egg 1 small onion, minced Pepper to taste 1 tablespoon butter or margarine Dill sprigs for garnish Applesauce and sour cream (optional)	9″ pie plate Browning dish

1 Into medium bowl, pour 1 cup cold water. Coarsely shred carrots and potato into bowl. In colander, drain carrots and potato.

2 In pie plate, place shredded carrots and potato. Cook, covered, on High (100% power) 5 minutes, or until tender-crisp. In colander, drain carrots and potato. Set aside.

3 Meanwhile, in large bowl, combine flour, salt, and baking powder until blended. Add egg and onion; stir until blended.

4 Stir carrot-potato mixture into egg mixture. Season with pepper. Meanwhile, preheat browning dish as manufacturer directs. Add butter or margarine; stir to coat dish.

5 Drop mounds of carrot-potato mixture onto browning dish; flatten slightly. Cook on High 2½ (2:30) minutes, until set, turning pancakes over halfway through cooking. (If necessary, cook in batches, reheating browning dish between batches.)

6 To serve: Arrange hot pancakes on warmed serving platter. Garnish with dill sprigs. If you like, serve pancakes with applesauce and sour cream.

PREPARATION TIMETABLE

Early in day:	*Prepare all vegetables and store in plastic bags in refrigerator. Slice pork for Stir-fry with Pork; cover and refrigerate. Prepare Szechuan Lobster through step 1; cover and refrigerate. Prepare Szechuan Eggplant through step 4; place on serving platter, cover, and refrigerate to serve chilled later.*
1 hour ahead:	*Prepare Stir-fried Shrimp and Broccoli through step 2. Complete Szechuan Lobster, arrange in warmed serving dish, cover, and keep warm. Prepare rice; keep warm. Arrange cookies in bowls.*
30 minutes ahead:	*Complete Stir-fried Shrimp and Broccoli; keep warm. Prepare and cook Stir-fry with Pork; arrange in warmed serving dishes. Prepare bought dim sum as package directs and arrange in bamboo steamers or bowls. Make Chinese tea.*

Carrots and Cauliflower

GLAZED CARROTS

Color Index page 71. 4 servings. 88 cals per serving. Low in cholesterol, sodium. Good source of vitamin A. Begin 25 minutes ahead.

1 16-ounce bag carrots, cut into 1/4-inch-thick slices	*2 teaspoons sugar*
	1 tablespoon butter or margarine
1/4 cup Chicken Broth (page 125) or canned broth	*Salt and pepper to taste*
	Parsley sprig for garnish

1. In 9" microwave-safe pie plate, combine carrots, broth, and sugar. Cook, covered, on High (100% power) 5 to 7 minutes, until carrots are tender-crisp, stirring twice.
2. Uncover and cook on High 3 to 5 minutes longer, until carrots are fork-tender and liquid has almost evaporated, stirring twice.
3. To carrot mixture, add butter or margarine; stir until carrots are glazed. Season with salt and pepper. Transfer carrots to warmed serving dish; garnish. Serve immediately.

CAULIFLOWER with LEMON and DILL SAUCE

Color Index page 72. 8 servings. 89 cals per serving. Low in cholesterol. Good source of vitamin C. Begin 25 minutes ahead.

1 large cauliflower (about 3 pounds)	*3/4 cup half-and-half*
	2 tablespoons lemon juice
1/4 cup water	
3 tablespoons butter or margarine	*1 tablespoon chopped dill*
1 garlic clove, minced	*Lemon slices and dill sprigs for garnish*
1 tablespoon all-purpose flour	
1 chicken-flavor bouillon cube or envelope	

1. Keeping cauliflower whole, remove large leaves and cut out core. In 3-quart microwave-safe casserole, place cauliflower cored side up; add water. Cook, covered, on High (100% power) 9 to 10 minutes, until cauliflower is tender-crisp, rotating casserole halfway through cooking. Let stand, covered, on heat-safe surface while preparing sauce.
2. In 4-cup microwave-safe glass measure, place butter or margarine and garlic. Heat, covered with paper towel, on High 45 seconds to 1 minute, until butter or margarine is melted. Stir in flour and bouillon until blended. Cook on High 1 minute, stirring once. Into flour mixture, gradually stir half-and-half. Cook on High 2 to 3 minutes, until sauce thickens slightly, stirring twice. Into sauce, stir lemon juice and dill.
3. Drain cauliflower; place on warmed serving platter. Spoon sauce over; garnish.

Cauliflower and Celeriac

CAULIFLOWER WITH MINT-FLAVORED SPINACH

Color Index page 72. 6 servings. 42 cals per serving. Low in cholesterol, fat. Good source of vitamin A, vitamin C, calcium, iron. Begin 25 minutes ahead.

1 10-ounce package frozen spinach, thawed	1 medium cauliflower, trimmed, rinsed, and cut into flowerets
¼ cup fresh mint leaves	¼ cup water
½ 4-ounce can jalapeño peppers, drained	½ cup plain yogurt
1 garlic clove	Salt to taste

1. Squeeze and drain spinach. In food processor with knife blade attached or in blender, process spinach, mint leaves, jalapeño peppers, and garlic until smooth. If necessary, process in batches.
2. In 2-quart microwave-safe casserole, place cauliflower and water. Cook, covered, on High (100% power) 5 minutes, stirring once. Drain.
3. To cauliflower, add spinach mixture; stir well to combine. Cook, covered, on High 5 to 7 minutes, until cauliflower is fork-tender, stirring occasionally.
4. Into vegetable mixture, stir yogurt. Season with salt. Serve hot or cover and refrigerate to serve chilled later.

CELERIAC PUREE

Color Index page 75. 6 servings. 142 cals per serving. Low in cholesterol. Begin 35 minutes ahead.

1 pound celeriac (celery root), peeled and diced	3 tablespoons butter or margarine
½ pound red potatoes, peeled and diced	¼ cup heavy or whipping cream
1 cup Chicken Broth (page 125) or canned broth	Salt and pepper to taste

1. In 2-quart microwave-safe casserole, place celeriac and potatoes; add broth. Cook, covered, on High (100% power) 10 to 15 minutes, until celeriac and potatoes are fork-tender, stirring occasionally.
2. In food processor with knife blade attached or in blender, process celeriac-potato mixture until smooth. To vegetable mixture, add butter or margarine and cream; process until blended. Season with salt and pepper.
3. Return puree to casserole. Cook on High 3 to 5 minutes, until hot, stirring twice. Transfer to warmed serving dish. With metal or rubber spatula, smooth puree, then swirl to make attractive design. Serve immediately.

Blanching Vegetables

Blanching vegetables for the freezer helps preserve their flavors. Prepare each as directed in the charts on pages 237 to 251, then blanch in the microwave for the minimum time below and test for doneness: the vegetable should be bright in color and evenly heated through. Chill in ice water for as long as blanching time. Drain, pat dry, and freeze.

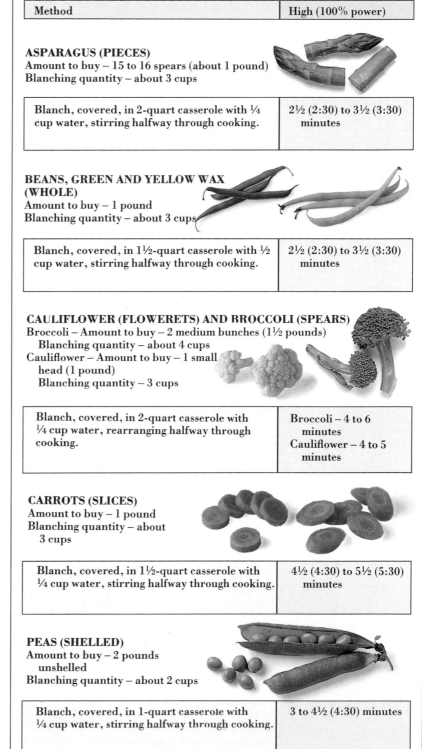

Method	High (100% power)
ASPARAGUS (PIECES) Amount to buy – 15 to 16 spears (about 1 pound) Blanching quantity – about 3 cups	
Blanch, covered, in 2-quart casserole with ¼ cup water, stirring halfway through cooking.	2½ (2:30) to 3½ (3:30) minutes
BEANS, GREEN AND YELLOW WAX (WHOLE) Amount to buy – 1 pound Blanching quantity – about 3 cups	
Blanch, covered, in 1½-quart casserole with ½ cup water, stirring halfway through cooking.	2½ (2:30) to 3½ (3:30) minutes

CAULIFLOWER (FLOWERETS) AND BROCCOLI (SPEARS)
Broccoli – Amount to buy – 2 medium bunches (1½ pounds)
   Blanching quantity – about 4 cups
Cauliflower – Amount to buy – 1 small head (1 pound)
   Blanching quantity – 3 cups	

Blanch, covered, in 2-quart casserole with ¼ cup water, rearranging halfway through cooking.	Broccoli – 4 to 6 minutes Cauliflower – 4 to 5 minutes
CARROTS (SLICES) Amount to buy – 1 pound Blanching quantity – about 3 cups	
Blanch, covered, in 1½-quart casserole with ¼ cup water, stirring halfway through cooking.	4½ (4:30) to 5½ (5:30) minutes
PEAS (SHELLED) Amount to buy – 2 pounds unshelled Blanching quantity – about 2 cups	
Blanch, covered, in 1-quart casserole with ¼ cup water, stirring halfway through cooking.	3 to 4½ (4:30) minutes

Corn-on-the-Cob

Corn-on-the-cob cooks perfectly in the microwave. Simply husk the corn, remove the silk, then rinse and tightly wrap each ear in plastic wrap. Cook 1 ear on High (100% power) 3 to 4 minutes; 2 ears, 5 to 6 minutes; 3 ears, 7 to 8 minutes; 4 ears, 9 to 11 minutes. Halfway through cooking, turn the corn over and rearrange, moving the front ears to the back and vice versa for even, thorough cooking. Serve corn as is, with one of our Flavored Butters (below) or, using a sharp knife, cut cooked kernels from each ear and serve as a vegetable, in salads, or in main dishes.

Preparing the Corn

  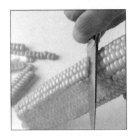

Just before cooking, remove outer husks and silk from cobs.

Rinse under running cold water, and remove any remaining silk with vegetable brush.

After cooking, hold each ear at an angle. With sharp knife, cut down the ear to remove kernels.

FLAVORED BUTTERS

Color Index page 71. Each butter makes enough for 4 ears of corn. 78 cals per tablespoon. Begin 15 minutes ahead.

Golden Spiced Butter: In 2-cup microwave-safe glass measure, place *3 tablespoons butter or margarine, 1 tablespoon lemon juice, ½ teaspoon curry powder,* and *½ teaspoon Dijon mustard.* Stir ingredients until well mixed. Heat, covered, on High (100% power) 45 seconds to 1 minute, until butter or margarine is melted, stirring once.

Three-pepper Butter: In 2-cup microwave-safe glass measure, place *3 tablespoons butter or margarine, 3 tablespoons minced green pepper, ¼ teaspoon cracked pepper, ⅛ teaspoon ground red pepper,* and *⅛ teaspoon salt.* Stir ingredients until well mixed. Heat, covered, on High (100% power) 45 seconds to 1 minute, until butter or margarine is melted, stirring once.

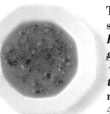

Fresh-snipped-herb Butter: In 2-cup microwave-safe glass measure, place *3 tablespoons butter or margarine* and *2 teaspoons lemon juice.* Stir ingredients until well mixed. Heat, covered, on High (100% power) 45 seconds to 1 minute, until butter or margarine is melted, stirring once. Into melted butter mixture, stir *1 teaspoon snipped fresh herbs*.

Corn

CREAMED CORN WITH PEPPERS

Color Index page 71. 4 servings. 152 cals per serving. Low in cholesterol. Begin 25 minutes ahead.

2 tablespoons butter or margarine (¼ stick)	¼ teaspoon oregano
2 small onions, thinly sliced	¼ cup half-and-half
1 small green pepper, cut into strips	1 small tomato, cut into thin wedges
4 ears corn, husked, or 1 16- to 17-ounce can whole-kernel corn, drained	1 teaspoon salt
	Pepper to taste

1. In 12″ by 8″ microwave-safe baking dish, place butter or margarine. Heat, covered with paper towels, on High (100% power) 45 seconds to 1 minute, until melted.
2. To melted butter or margarine, add onions and green pepper; stir to coat. Cook on High 4 to 5 minutes, until onions are softened, stirring once.
3. Meanwhile, if using fresh corn, with sharp knife, cut kernels from ears.
4. Into onion mixture, stir oregano, corn, and half-and-half. Cook, covered, on High 5 to 7 minutes, until corn is tender, stirring twice. For canned corn, cook, covered, on High 3 to 5 minutes. Add tomato. Cook on High 1 to 2 minutes, until tomato is hot but still firm. Season.

SOUTHERN-STYLE CORN PUDDING

Color Index page 72. 4 servings. 244 cals per serving. Begin 25 minutes ahead.

2 tablespoons all-purpose flour	1 10-ounce package frozen whole-kernel corn, thawed
1 tablespoon sugar	2 tablespoons dried bread crumbs
2 eggs	Paprika to taste
1 cup half-and-half	
1 teaspoon salt	
¼ teaspoon pepper	
1 tablespoon butter or margarine	

1. In 8-cup microwave-safe glass measure, blend flour and sugar. Add eggs; beat until smooth. Into egg mixture, gradually blend half-and-half. Cook on Medium (50% power) 4 to 5 minutes, until mixture thickens, stirring twice. Season with salt and pepper.
2. In 9″ microwave-safe pie plate, place butter and corn. Cook on High (100% power) 2 to 3 minutes, until butter melts, stirring twice. Add bread crumbs; stir until well mixed.
3. To corn, add egg mixture; stir. Cook, covered, on Medium 5 to 7 minutes, until a knife inserted in center comes out clean. Let stand, loosely covered, on heat-safe surface 5 minutes.
4. *To serve:* Sprinkle top of corn pudding with paprika just before serving.

Corn and Eggplant

SUCCOTASH

Color Index page 71. 4 servings. 371 cals per serving. Low in cholesterol. Good source of vitamin C, iron. Begin 25 minutes ahead.

4 slices bacon, diced	1 10-ounce package
1 pound potatoes, peeled and diced	frozen whole-kernel corn, thawed
1 medium onion, diced	1 green pepper, diced
1 10-ounce package frozen baby lima beans, thawed	1 teaspoon sugar
	Salt to taste
1 tomato, chopped	1/8 teaspoon pepper

1. In 2-quart microwave-safe casserole, place bacon. Cook, covered with paper towel, on High (100% power) 4 to 5 minutes, until browned, stirring once. With slotted spoon, remove bacon to paper towels to drain.
2. To drippings, add potatoes and onion; stir to coat. Cook, covered, on High 5 to 7 minutes, until potatoes are almost cooked, stirring once.
3. Into potato-onion mixture, stir beans, tomato, corn, green pepper, and sugar. Cook, covered, on High 5 to 7 minutes, until vegetables are tender, stirring once. Season with salt and pepper. Just before serving, sprinkle bacon over succotash.

SZECHUAN EGGPLANT

Color Index page 72. 4 servings. 73 cals per serving. Low in cholesterol. Begin 25 minutes ahead.

1 small eggplant (about 1 pound)	1/2 teaspoon hot-pepper sauce
1 teaspoon sugar	1 chicken-flavor bouillon cube or envelope
1 teaspoon cornstarch	
1 tablespoon minced peeled gingerroot or	1 tablespoon peanut or salad oil
1 1/4 teaspoons ground ginger	1 green onion, thinly sliced
3/4 cup water	Green-onion Pompoms (page 132) for garnish
1 tablespoon soy sauce	

1. Preheat browning dish as manufacturer directs. Meanwhile, cut eggplant into 4" by 1/2" by 1/2" strips; set aside.
2. In small bowl, combine sugar, cornstarch, and ginger. Gradually stir in water, soy sauce, hot-pepper sauce, and bouillon until blended.
3. Coat browning dish with half the oil. On browning dish, arrange half the eggplant strips. Cook on High (100% power) 3 to 4 minutes, until eggplant softens, stirring once. With spatula, remove eggplant to paper towels to drain. Repeat with remaining oil and eggplant.
4. Return all eggplant to browning dish. Stir in ginger-soy mixture. Cook on High 3 to 4 minutes, until slightly thickened, stirring halfway through cooking. Stir in green onion.
5. *To serve:* Transfer eggplant mixture to serving platter. Garnish; serve hot or cover and refrigerate to serve chilled later.

EGGPLANT STUFFED WITH TABBOULEH

Color Index page 77. 303 cals per serving. Low in cholesterol. Good source of vitamin C, calcium, iron. Begin 1 1/4 hours ahead.

This main dish has a Middle-eastern flavor, with its stuffing of bulgur, vegetables, garlic, raisins, and mint – known as tabbouleh. If you can't find bulgur in your supermarket, substitute the same quantity of packaged "tabbouleh wheat salad mix" and use 1 tablespoon of the flavor mix from the package in place of the herbs.

Ingredients for 4 main-dish servings		Microwave cookware
2 small eggplants (about 3/4 pound each)	2 tablespoons capers, drained	12" by 8" baking dish 12" by 8" platter
Salt	1/2 cup precooked bulgur	
2 medium onions, chopped	1 tablespoon minced mint leaves or 1/2 teaspoon dried mint	
3 celery stalks, chopped		
3 tablespoons olive or salad oil	1/2 teaspoon thyme leaves	
3 garlic cloves, minced	1/3 cup tomato juice	
1 small green pepper, chopped	1 tablespoon lemon juice	
	Salt and pepper to taste	
1/2 cup raisins	Lemon wedges and mint leaves for garnish	
1/2 cup Chicken Broth (page 125) or canned broth		

1 With sharp knife, cut each eggplant lengthwise in half. Cut out center of each eggplant half, leaving a 1/2-inch shell. Finely chop eggplant centers and set aside.

2 Sprinkle hollowed-out halves with salt. On a double thickness of paper towels, place eggplant halves cut side down. Let stand 20 minutes.

3 In baking dish, place onions, celery, and 2 tablespoons oil. Cook on High (100% power) 3 to 4 minutes, until vegetables soften slightly, stirring halfway through cooking.

4 To baking dish, add garlic, green pepper, raisins, broth, and chopped eggplant. Cook on High 10 to 12 minutes, until eggplant is fork-tender, stirring occasionally. Stir in capers and next 5 ingredients. Season.

5 Rinse hollowed-out eggplant halves and pat dry. Lightly brush with remaining oil. Arrange on platter. Cook on High 5 minutes, or until fork-tender (do not cook longer or shells will collapse when filled).

6 Spoon an equal amount of bulgur mixture into each eggplant half. Cook on High 4 to 6 minutes, just until filling is hot. Garnish with lemon wedges and mint and serve immediately.

Belgian Endive and Leeks

Belgian endive is normally used as a salad vegetable, but it is equally delicious braised. Remember to arrange the endive with the delicate, leafy tips pointing toward the center of the dish and the denser stem ends toward the edges; this ensures even cooking.

"BRAISED" BELGIAN ENDIVE

Color Index page 74. 78 cals per serving. Low in cholesterol, sodium.
Begin 35 minutes ahead.

Ingredients	For 4	For 2	For 1
Belgian endive	4 heads	2 heads	1 head
Chicken Broth (page 125) or canned broth	1 cup	½ cup	¼ cup
Green onions, sliced	2 green onions	1 green onion	½ green onion
Thyme leaves	½ teaspoon	¼ teaspoon	to taste
Basil	½ teaspoon	¼ teaspoon	to taste
Butter or margarine	2 tablespoons	1 tablespoon	1½ teaspoons
Sugar	1 teaspoon	½ teaspoon	¼ teaspoon
Lemon juice	1 teaspoon	½ teaspoon	¼ teaspoon
Salt and pepper	to taste	to taste	to taste
Microwave cookware	13" by 9" baking dish	8" by 8" baking dish	8" by 8" baking dish
Time on High (100% power) Endive	12 to 15 minutes	8 to 10 minutes	4 to 6 minutes
Broth mixture	5 minutes	3 to 3½ (3:30) minutes	1½ (1:30) to 2 minutes

1 Trim root ends from heads of endive; cut each endive lengthwise in half. In baking dish (see Chart), arrange endive, cut side down, with stem ends toward edges and leafy tips toward center.

2 Over endive, pour broth; add green onions, thyme leaves, and basil. Cook, covered, on High for time in Chart, or until endive is fork-tender, rearranging endive and rotating dish halfway through cooking.

3 With spatula, remove endive to warmed serving platter, arranging cut side up. Cover and keep warm.

4 To same baking dish, add butter or margarine, sugar, lemon juice, salt, and pepper.

5 Cook mixture on High for time in Chart, or until bubbling, stirring once.

6 To serve: Spoon hot cooking liquid over endive. Serve immediately.

BELGIAN ENDIVE AU GRATIN *

Color Index page 74. 4 servings. 215 cals per serving. Good source of calcium.
Begin 45 minutes ahead.

4 heads Belgian endive
½ cup Chicken Broth (page 125) or canned broth
1 tablespoon lemon juice
½ teaspoon sugar
2 tablespoons butter or margarine (¼ stick)
2 tablespoons all-purpose flour
¾ cup half-and-half
1 garlic clove, minced (optional)
4 ounces Swiss or Cheddar cheese, shredded (1 cup)
1 egg yolk
Salt and pepper to taste
2 tablespoons grated Parmesan cheese (optional)

1. Trim root ends from heads of endive. Cut each endive lengthwise in half. In 13" by 9" microwave-safe baking dish, arrange endive, cut side down, with stem ends toward edges and leafy tips toward center. To dish, add broth, lemon juice, and sugar. Cook, covered, on High (100% power) 7 to 10 minutes, until endive is tender-crisp, rearranging endive and rotating dish halfway through cooking.
2. Drain liquid from dish and reserve. Turn endive cut side up in dish; cover and set aside. In 8-cup microwave-safe glass measure, place butter or margarine. Heat, covered with paper towel, on High 45 seconds, or until melted. Into melted butter or margarine, stir flour until smooth and blended. Cook on High 1 minute, stirring once. Into flour mixture, gradually stir half-and-half, reserved cooking liquid, and, if you like, garlic. Cook on High 3 to 4 minutes, until sauce thickens, stirring twice. Add Swiss or Cheddar cheese. Stir until cheese melts.
3. In small bowl, with fork, lightly beat egg yolk. Stir ¼ cup hot cheese sauce into beaten egg yolk, taking care that yolk does not curdle. Slowly pour egg mixture back into remaining cheese sauce, beating rapidly to prevent lumping. Season with salt and pepper.
4. Over endive, pour cheese sauce. Cook on Medium (50% power) 3 to 5 minutes, until endive is hot. If you like and if dish is broiler-safe, sprinkle Parmesan over endive and sauce and brown lightly under preheated broiler.
5. To serve: With spatula, arrange endive on warmed serving platter. Spoon sauce over endive.

A NO-MESS TRICK FOR STEAMING VEGE-TABLES: To ensure even cooking, use vegetables of similar size or density (such as broccoli and cauliflower flowerets) or cut vegetables into pieces of uniform size (such as sticks of carrot and zucchini). Lightly moisten 1 paper towel; place vegetables on top. Twist corners of paper towel together. Place on oven floor. Cook 8 ounces on High (100% power) 4 to 5 minutes, until tender-crisp.

VEGETABLE PRESENTATION

Simply cooked vegetables make an elegant presentation for a special occasion.

Matchstick Carrots and Parsnips: Cooked matchstick-thin strips of carrot and parsnip in a lattice pattern accentuate the color and pattern of a pretty plate.

Asparagus Parcels: Asparagus spears tied with a strip of cooked leek echo the shape of a long plate. Lemon Twists (page 132) give the finishing touch.

Spinach-filled Tomatoes: Hollowed-out tomatoes filled with Creamed Spinach (page 270) look stunning nestled in a fluted-edged white plate.

New Potatoes in Radicchio Cups: Crisp leaves of colorful radicchio make an ideal shell for small new potatoes garnished with a sprig of fresh dill.

LEEKS WITH HAM IN CHEESE SAUCE

Color Index page 75. 367 cals per serving. Good source of calcium, iron. Begin 50 minutes ahead.

Ingredients	For 4	For 2	For 1
Leeks (1/2 pound each)	*4 leeks*	*2 leeks*	*1 leek*
Chicken Broth (page 125) or canned broth	*1/2 cup*	*1/4 cup*	*3 tablespoons*
Butter or margarine	*2 tablespoons (1/4 stick)*	*1 tablespoon*	*2 teaspoons*
All-purpose flour	*2 tablespoons*	*1 tablespoon*	*2 teaspoons*
Half-and-half	*1 cup*	*1/2 cup*	*1/4 cup*
Swiss or Cheddar cheese, shredded	*4 ounces (1 cup)*	*2 ounces (1/2 cup)*	*1 ounce (1/4 cup)*
Salt and pepper	*to taste*	*to taste*	*to taste*
Cooked ham slices (about 1/2 ounce each)	*8 slices*	*4 slices*	*2 slices*
Parsley for garnish	*garnish*	*garnish*	*garnish*
Microwave cookware	12" by 8" baking dish	8" by 8" baking dish	8" by 8" baking dish
Time on High (100% power) Leeks	5 to 7 minutes	3 to 4 minutes	2 to 2½ (2:30) minutes
Sauce	3 to 3½ (3:30) minutes	2 to 2½ (2:30) minutes	1 to 1½ (1:30) minutes
Leeks with sauce	5 to 6 minutes	3 to 3½ (3:30) minutes	1½ (1:30) to 2 minutes

1 Cut roots from leeks; trim leek tops. Cut leeks lengthwise in half.

2 Carefully rinse leeks under running cold water to remove any sand. In baking dish (see Chart), arrange leeks, cut side down.

3 To leeks, add broth and butter or margarine. Cook, covered, on High for time in Chart, until leeks are tender, rearranging once. Transfer leeks to platter.

4 Into same dish, stir flour until smooth and blended. Gradually stir in half-and-half. Cook on High for time in Chart, or until sauce thickens and is smooth, stirring twice.

5 To sauce, add cheese. Stir until cheese melts. Season with salt and pepper. Wrap each leek half with 1 slice of ham. Place wrapped leeks in cheese sauce.

6 Cook wrapped leeks, covered, on High for time in Chart, or until leeks are hot and cheese sauce is bubbling. Sprinkle with parsley before serving.

Middle Eastern-style Family Supper

Fresh Tomato Soup, page 127
Eggplant Stuffed with Tabbouleh, page 261
Hot pita bread
Tossed green salad
Goat Cheese with dried fruit and nuts

PREPARATION TIMETABLE

Early in day:	*Prepare Fresh Tomato Soup; cover and refrigerate. Prepare salad ingredients; store in plastic bags in refrigerator. Prepare salad dressing of your choice and refrigerate.*
1 hour ahead:	*Cook Eggplant Stuffed with Tabbouleh; cover and set aside. Arrange an assortment of cheese, dried fruit and nuts on serving platter; cover and set aside.*
Just before serving:	*Ladle soup into individual bowls and garnish. Reheat stuffed eggplant on High until hot; garnish. Under preheated broiler, lightly toast pitas; arrange on warmed platter. Place salad ingredients in bowl and toss with dressing.*

Mushrooms

HERBY MUSHROOMS WITH TOMATOES AND GARLIC

Color Index page 72. 6 servings. 199 cals per serving. Low in cholesterol, sodium. Begin 25 minutes ahead.

½ cup olive or salad oil	*½ cup dry white wine*
½ cup Chicken Broth (page 125) or canned broth	*¼ cup tarragon vinegar or white-wine vinegar*
3 garlic cloves, thinly sliced	*2 bay leaves*
	1 teaspoon thyme leaves
2 small onions, cut into ¼-inch wedges	*12 peppercorns*
	12 whole coriander seeds (optional)
2 small tomatoes, cut into chunks	*1 pound button mushrooms, trimmed*

1. In 2-quart microwave-safe casserole, place all ingredients except mushrooms. Cook on High (100% power) 5 to 7 minutes, until bubbling, stirring halfway through cooking.
2. Into tomato mixture, stir whole mushrooms. Cook, covered, on High 10 minutes, or until fork-tender, stirring occasionally. Discard bay leaves.
3. Serve hot or cover and refrigerate to serve chilled later.

ORIENTAL-STYLE MUSHROOMS

Color Index page 75. 4 main-dish servings. 123 cals per serving. Low in cholesterol. Good source of thiamine, iron. Begin 45 minutes ahead.

1 small boneless pork chop (about ¼ pound)	*1 tablespoon soy sauce*
1 teaspoon cornstarch	*1 teaspoon rice-wine or cider vinegar*
½ cup Chicken Broth (page 125) or canned broth	*2 garlic cloves, minced*
	½ pound mushrooms, sliced
2 teaspoons minced peeled gingerroot or 1 teaspoon ground ginger	*¼ pound Chinese pea pods, cut in half*
	1 small tomato, cut into matchstick-thin strips

1. Thinly slice pork. Cut slices into slivers. In small bowl, combine cornstarch, broth, ginger, soy sauce, vinegar, and garlic. Add pork; stir to coat. Cover and marinate 10 minutes.
2. Preheat browning dish as manufacturer directs. With slotted spoon, arrange pork in single layer on browning dish; reserve marinade. Cook on High (100% power) 3 to 4 minutes, until pork is cooked, stirring halfway through cooking. Remove pork to warmed serving platter; cover and keep warm.
3. Reheat browning dish. On dish, place mushrooms. Cook on High 3 to 4 minutes, until softened, stirring halfway through cooking.
4. To mushrooms, add Chinese pea pods, tomato, reserved marinade, and cooked pork. Cook on High 3 to 4 minutes, until sauce bubbles and thickens, stirring twice. Arrange on warmed serving platter with pork. Serve immediately.

Okra and Onions

OKRA, HAM, AND TOMATOES

Color Index page 72. 4 main-dish servings. 63 cals per serving. Low in cholesterol, fat. Good source of vitamin C. Begin 25 minutes ahead.

1 medium onion, diced
1/3 cup diced cooked ham
1 14 1/2- to 16-ounce can crushed tomatoes
1 10-ounce package frozen whole okra, thawed

1/4 teaspoon hot-pepper sauce
1 tablespoon lemon juice
Hot Cooked Rice (page 293) and corn bread (optional)

1. In 13" by 9" microwave-safe baking dish, combine diced onion and ham. Cook on High (100% power) 3 minutes, or until onion softens, stirring mixture halfway through cooking.
2. Into ham mixture, stir tomatoes, okra, and hot-pepper sauce. Cook on High 6 to 9 minutes, until okra is hot and tomatoes are bubbling, stirring twice.
3. Into vegetable-ham mixture, stir lemon juice. Garnish with lemon slices. If you like, serve with Hot Cooked Rice and corn bread.

MARINATED OKRA

Color Index page 77. 4 servings. 145 cals per serving. Low in cholesterol, sodium. Begin 1 day ahead.

1/2 cup olive or salad oil
1/3 cup tarragon vinegar or white-wine vinegar
1/2 teaspoon dry mustard
1/2 teaspoon sugar
1/2 teaspoon thyme leaves
1/4 teaspoon crushed red pepper

1 10-ounce package frozen whole okra, thawed
Parsley for garnish

1. In 1 1/2-quart microwave-safe casserole dish, combine oil, vinegar, mustard, sugar, thyme leaves, and crushed red pepper. Cook on High (100% power) 3 minutes until flavors blend, stirring once.
2. To oil-vinegar mixture, add okra; stir to coat. Cook on High 3 to 5 minutes, until okra is hot, stirring twice.
3. Cover casserole and refrigerate 4 hours or overnight, stirring occasionally.
4. *To serve*: Drain marinade from okra. Arrange okra on serving platter and garnish with parsley. Serve chilled.

STUFFED ONIONS

Color Index page 75. 113 cals per serving. Low in cholesterol. Begin 45 minutes ahead.

Ingredients	For 4	For 2	For 1
Medium onions	4 onions	2 onions	1 onion
Chicken Broth (page 125) or canned broth	1/2 cup	1/4 cup	3 tablespoons
Celery stalks	1 stalk	1/2 stalk	1/4 stalk
Small red pepper	1 pepper	1/2 pepper	1/4 pepper
Butter or margarine	2 tablespoons (1/4 stick)	1 tablespoon	1 1/2 teaspoons
Poultry seasoning	1/2 teaspoon	1/4 teaspoon	to taste
Fresh whole-wheat bread crumbs	1 cup (2 slices)	1/2 cup (1 slice)	1/4 cup (1/2 slice)
Salt	1/2 teaspoon	1/4 teaspoon	to taste
Microwave cookware	2-quart soufflé dish	1-quart soufflé dish	Small bowl
Time on High (100% power)			
Hollowed-out onions	5 to 7 minutes	4 to 6 minutes	2 1/2 (2:30) to 3 minutes
Butter or margarine	45 seconds	30 to 45 seconds	30 seconds
Vegetable mixture	3 to 5 minutes	2 to 3 minutes	1 1/2 (1:30) to 2 minutes
Stuffed onions	4 to 6 minutes	2 to 3 minutes	1 1/2 (1:30) to 2 minutes
Standing time	5 minutes	3 minutes	2 minutes

1 Cut small slice from bottom of each onion so they stand upright. Hollow out centers, leaving 3/4-inch-thick shells. Reserve centers. In dish or bowl (see Chart), place onions.

2 To onions, add broth. Cook, covered, on High for time in Chart, or until tender-crisp, rotating dish once. Remove onions and set aside.

3 To broth, add butter or margarine. Cook on High for time in Chart. Finely chop onion centers, celery, and pepper. Add to broth with seasoning. Cook on High for time in Chart.

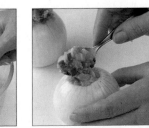

4 Add bread crumbs and salt; stir until stuffing is well mixed.

5 Fill hollowed-out onions with equal amounts of stuffing.

6 Place onions in same dish or bowl. Cook on High for time in Chart, or until hot, rotating dish or bowl halfway through cooking. Let stand, loosely covered, on heat-safe surface, for time in Chart.

Barbecuing Vegetables

Use the microwave to precook vegetables for the barbecue and cut down grilling time. Your vegetables will have that delicious outdoor flavor, and stay tender-crisp without charring. Cook vegetables in ¼ cup water, covered, on High (100% power) for time in Chart, or until almost tender; drain. Skewer and cook on grill over high heat, brushing with salad oil and turning until browned.

Vegetable	Amount	In Microwave	On Grill
Asparagus	1 pound	4 to 6 minutes	2 minutes
Carrots	1 pound	6 to 8 minutes	5 minutes
Cauliflower	1 head, about 1¼ pounds	6 to 8 minutes	5 minutes
Eggplant	1 medium, about 12 ounces, cut into 8 wedges	4 to 6 minutes	3 to 5 minutes
Belgian endive	4 heads, about 4 ounces each	4 to 5 minutes	2 minutes
Fennel	2 bulbs, about 1 pound each, cut lengthwise in half	9 to 11 minutes	5 minutes
Leeks	4 medium, cut lengthwise in half	4 to 5 minutes	5 minutes
Mushrooms	1 pound, medium-size	4 to 6 minutes	5 minutes
Onions	2 large, cut into 1½-inch-thick slices	6 to 8 minutes	5 minutes
Peppers	4 medium, stems, seeds removed	8 to 10 minutes	5 minutes
Yellow summer squash, zucchini	2 medium, cut lengthwise in half	3 to 5 minutes	5 minutes

To prevent the outsides of whole onions or chunks of yellow squash or zucchini from charring before the insides are tender, cook in ¼ cup water, covered, on High (100% power) as follows: 12 whole small white onions, peeled, 6 to 8 minutes; 2 medium yellow squash or zucchini, cut into 1-inch chunks, 3 to 4 minutes. Vegetables should be tender-crisp.

Preparing Vegetables for Kabobs

In microwave-safe baking dish, place onion wedges and chunks of zucchini and red pepper. Add ¼ cup water. Cook, covered, on High for time in Chart, or until almost tender. Drain; set aside until cool enough to handle.

Thread vegetables carefully onto barbecue skewers. Finish cooking on grill over high heat, brushing lightly with salad oil and turning frequently until evenly browned.

Onions

CREAMED ONIONS

Color Index page 72. 8 servings. 82 cals per serving. Low in cholesterol, sodium. Begin 25 minutes ahead.

2 tablespoons butter or margarine (¼ stick)
1 small onion, minced
2 tablespoons all-purpose flour
1½ cups milk
¼ teaspoon salt
⅛ teaspoon pepper
Ground nutmeg to taste
1 16-ounce package frozen pearl onions, thawed
Paprika (optional)

1. In 4-cup microwave-safe glass measure, place butter or margarine. Heat, covered with paper towel, on High (100% power) 45 seconds, or until melted.
2. To melted butter or margarine, add minced onion. Cook on High 2 to 3 minutes, until onion softens, stirring once. Stir in flour until blended. Cook on High 1 minute, stirring halfway through cooking.
3. Into onion mixture, gradually stir milk. Cook on High 3 to 4 minutes, until sauce thickens and is smooth, stirring twice. Season with salt, pepper, and nutmeg.
4. In 9″ round microwave-safe baking dish, combine pearl onions and onion sauce. Cook on High 3 to 5 minutes, until sauce bubbles, stirring once. Just before serving, if you like, sprinkle with paprika.

SWEET-AND-SOUR ONIONS

Color Index page 75. 8 servings. 69 cals per serving. Low in cholesterol, sodium. Begin 40 minutes ahead.

1 pound onions, sliced
3 tablespoons butter or margarine
1 tablespoon sugar
½ cup Beef Broth (page 125) or canned broth
¼ cup dry red wine
1 tablespoon red-wine vinegar
Salt and pepper to taste

1. In 9″ microwave-safe pie plate, combine onions, butter or margarine, sugar, broth, and wine. Cook, covered, on High (100% power) 5 minutes, stirring halfway through cooking.
2. Uncover; stir. Cook on High 15 to 20 minutes longer, until onions brown and cooking liquid evaporates, stirring occasionally.
3. Into onions, stir red-wine vinegar. Cook on High 5 minutes, until vinegar evaporates, stirring halfway through cooking.
4. Season with salt and pepper. Transfer to warmed serving dish. Serve hot.

Onions and Peas

CREAMY ONIONS AND RICE

Color Index page 75. 4 servings. 242 cals per serving. Begin 40 minutes ahead.

2 tablespoons butter or
 margarine (¼ stick)
4 medium onions, sliced
½ cup regular long-
 grain rice
1 cup Chicken Broth
 (page 125) or canned
 broth
¼ cup heavy or
 whipping cream

½ teaspoon salt
⅛ teaspoon pepper
2 ounces Gruyère or
 Swiss cheese, shredded
 (½ cup)
Parsley for garnish

1. In 2-quart microwave-safe casserole, place butter or margarine. Heat, covered with paper towel, on High (100% power) 45 seconds, or until melted.

2. To melted butter or margarine, add onions and rice; stir to coat. Cook on High 3 minutes, stirring halfway through cooking. Add broth; mix well. Cook, covered, on High 15 to 17 minutes, until broth is almost completely absorbed and rice is tender, stirring occasionally.

3. Into onion-rice mixture, stir cream, salt, pepper, and shredded cheese. Spoon mixture into warmed serving dish.

4. If you like and if dish is broiler-safe, brown under preheated broiler; garnish.

GREEN PEAS WITH BACON AND ONIONS

Color Index page 72. 4 servings. 105 cals per serving. Low in cholesterol. Begin 15 minutes ahead.

2 slices bacon, diced
1 10-ounce package
 frozen peas,
 thawed

½ 16-ounce package
 frozen pearl onions,
 thawed
Salt and pepper to taste

1. In 9" microwave-safe pie plate, place bacon. Cook, covered with paper towel, on High (100% power) 2 to 3 minutes, until bacon is browned, stirring occasionally. With slotted spoon, remove bacon to paper towels to drain. Discard all but 1 tablespoon drippings.

2. Into bacon drippings, stir peas and pearl onions. Cook, covered, on High 3 to 5 minutes, until peas and onions are hot, stirring halfway through cooking.

3. *To serve*: Season pea-onion mixture with salt and pepper. Spoon mixture into warmed serving dish; sprinkle with reserved bacon.

LEMON PEAS

Color Index page 73. 81 cals per serving. Low in cholesterol. Begin 15 minutes ahead.

Ingredients	For 4	For 2	For 1
Butter or margarine	1 tablespoon	1½ teaspoons	¾ teaspoon
1 10-ounce package frozen peas, thawed	1 package	½ package	¼ package
Lemon peel, finely grated	2 teaspoons lemon peel	1 teaspoon lemon peel	½ teaspoon lemon peel
Water	1 tablespoon	2 teaspoons	1 teaspoon
Salt	½ teaspoon	¼ teaspoon	to taste
Lemon slices and fresh mint sprigs for garnish	garnish	garnish	garnish
Microwave cookware	2-quart casserole	1-quart casserole	2-cup glass measure
Time on High (100% power) Butter or margarine	30 to 45 seconds	30 seconds	15 to 30 seconds
Peas	4 to 5 minutes	2 to 3 minutes	1½ (1:30) to 2½ (2:30) minutes

1 In casserole or glass measure (see Chart), place butter or margarine. Heat, covered with paper towel, on High for time in Chart, or until melted.

2 Into melted butter or margarine, stir peas, grated lemon peel, water, and salt. Cook peas, covered, on High for time in Chart, or until tender, stirring occasionally.

3 Transfer peas to warmed serving dish; just before serving, garnish with lemon slices and fresh mint sprigs.

CHINESE PEA PODS AND SUGAR SNAP PEAS

Both these edible pea pods are delicious cooked in the microwave. Chinese pea pods, also known as snow peas, have thin, delicate skins and contain peas that are not fully formed. Sugar snap peas, a newer variety, are shorter and rounder than Chinese pea pods and have thicker pods containing fully formed peas. Both can be eaten raw or cooked as a vegetable using any recipe for regular peas. Check page 247 for preparation tips and cooking times. Both are quick-cooking, although sugar snap peas require slightly longer cooking than Chinese pea pods.

Potatoes

NEW POTATOES with BUTTER and CHIVES

Color Index page 73. 215 cals per serving. Low in cholesterol, sodium.
Begin 25 minutes ahead.

Ingredients	For 4	For 2	For 1
New potatoes, unpeeled and well scrubbed	1½ pounds potatoes	¾ pound potatoes	⅓ pound potatoes
Butter or margarine	3 tablespoons	1½ table-spoons	2 teaspoons
Chopped chives	¼ cup	2 tablespoons	1 tablespoon
Salt and pepper	to taste	to taste	to taste
Microwave cookware	12″ by 8″ baking dish	8″ by 8″ baking dish	8″ by 8″ baking dish
Time on High (100% power)	8 to 10 minutes	5 to 7 minutes	3 to 4 minutes

1 With Little Stripper (page 320) or vegetable peeler, remove a spiral of peel from each potato; discard.

2 In baking dish (see Chart), place potatoes and butter or margarine. Cook, covered, on High for time in Chart, or until fork-tender, stirring halfway through cooking.

3 Into potatoes, stir chopped chives. Season with salt and pepper. Serve immediately, spooning chive-butter over potatoes.

QUICK POTATO SNACKS

Use your microwave to cook up a couple of delicious after-school snacks. Serve Potato Nachos (made with potato slices in place of corn or tortilla chips), or our more filling Potato Pizzas.

Potato Nachos: In 13″ by 9″ baking dish, arrange *12 unpeeled potato slices, each 2 inches in diameter and ¼-inch thick.* Sprinkle lightly with *oregano.* Cook, covered, on High (100% power) 3½ (3:30) to 4 minutes. Top each slice with about *2 teaspoons shredded Monterey Jack cheese with jalapeño pepper* ("*Pepper Jack*"). Cook on High 30 seconds, or just until cheese melts. 2 servings. 153 cals per serving.

Potato Pizzas: Wash *1 medium baking potato (about 6 ounces)* under running cold water; don't peel. With fork, pierce potato in several places. On oven floor, place paper towel; place potato on top. Cook on High (100% power) 5 minutes, or until potato feels soft when pierced with tip of sharp knife. Cut potato lengthwise in half. Place halves on paper plate. Top each half with *1 tablespoon pizza sauce, 1 tablespoon shredded mozzarella cheese,* and *2 slices pepperoni.* Cook on High 1 to 1½ (1:30) minutes, until cheese melts. 2 servings. 235 cals per serving.

POTATOES au GRATIN

Color Index page 75. 235 cals per serving. Low in cholesterol. Good source of vitamin C, iron.
Begin 35 minutes ahead.

One of the best ways to cook potatoes is in the microwave, since this retains their full flavor, texture, and nutritional value. When microwaving potatoes, cut slices same thickness to ensure even cooking.

Ingredients for 8 servings		Microwave cookware
4 tablespoons butter or margarine (½ stick)	¼ teaspoon paprika	10″ round baking dish
1 small onion, minced	3 pounds potatoes, peeled or unpeeled	
¼ cup dried bread crumbs	¼ cup water	
¾ teaspoon salt	2 ounces fontina or Cheddar cheese, shredded (½ cup)	
¼ teaspoon pepper		

1 In baking dish, place butter or margarine and onion. Cook, covered, on High (100% power) 2 to 3 minutes, stirring once. Set aside.

2 In small bowl, combine bread crumbs, salt, pepper, and paprika. Stir in cooked onion.

3 With sharp knife, cut potatoes into ⅛-inch-thick slices. In dish used for onion, arrange potatoes in overlapping circles. Add water.

4 Cook, covered, on High 13 to 15 minutes, until fork-tender, rotating dish once. Drain off water, pressing with spatula.

5 Over potatoes, sprinkle cheese, then onion-bread-crumb mixture. Cook on High 1½ (1:30) minutes, or until cheese melts.

MASHED POTATOES

Color Index page 73. 4 servings. 233 cals per serving. Low in cholesterol. Begin 25 minutes ahead.

1½ pounds potatoes, peeled and diced	¼ to ½ cup half-and-half
1 cup water	Chopped chives for garnish
4 tablespoons butter or margarine (½ stick)	Almost Instant Gravy (below, optional)
¾ teaspoon salt	
¼ teaspoon pepper	

1. In 8-cup microwave-safe glass measure, place potatoes and water. Cook, covered, on High (100% power) 10 to 15 minutes, until potatoes are very tender, stirring occasionally. Drain.
2. To potatoes, add butter or margarine, salt, and pepper. With mixer at low speed, beat until ingredients are combined and potato mixture is fluffy. To potato mixture, gradually add half-and-half, beating until smooth. Cook, covered, on High 3 to 5 minutes, until hot, stirring halfway through cooking.
3. Transfer to serving dish; garnish. If you like, pass Almost Instant Gravy separately.

ALMOST INSTANT GRAVY: In 4-cup microwave-safe glass measure, place *1 table-spoon butter or margarine, or chicken or meat drippings*. Heat, covered with paper towel, on High (100% power) 30 to 45 seconds, until melted and hot. Add *1 tablespoon all-purpose flour;* stir until smooth. Gradually blend in *1 cup Chicken or Beef Broth (page 125) or canned broth*. Cook on High 3 to 5 minutes, until gravy boils and thickens, stirring twice. Season with *salt and pepper* to taste. If you like, add *¼ teaspoon browning sauce* for color. Makes 1 cup. 11 cals per tablespoon.

HOME-STYLE POTATOES WITH BACON AND ONIONS

Color Index page 73. 4 servings. 188 cals per serving. Low in cholesterol, sodium. Begin 25 minutes ahead.

3 slices bacon, diced	Salt and pepper to taste
1 large onion, sliced	Chopped parsley for garnish
1½ pounds potatoes, peeled and diced	

1. In 12″ by 8″ microwave-safe baking dish, place bacon. Cook, covered with paper towels, on High (100% power) 3 to 4 minutes, until bacon is browned, stirring halfway through cooking. With slotted spoon, remove bacon to paper towels to drain. Discard all but 2 tablespoons drippings.
2. Into bacon drippings, stir onion and potatoes. Cook on High 12 to 15 minutes, until potatoes are tender, stirring occasionally. Season with salt and pepper. Stir in reserved bacon.
3. *To serve:* Arrange potato mixture on warmed serving platter. Garnish with chopped parsley.

STUFFED POTATOES ORIENTALE

Color Index page 75. 453 cals per serving. Good source of niacin, vitamin C, iron. Begin 45 minutes ahead.

Ingredients	For 4	For 2	For 1
Baking potatoes (about 8 ounces each), well scrubbed	4 potatoes	2 potatoes	1 potato
Chicken breasts, skinned, boned and cut into ¼-inch-thick strips	1 pound chicken	½ pound chicken	¼ pound chicken
Salad oil	1 tablespoon	1½ teaspoons	¾ teaspoon
Cornstarch	2 teaspoons	1 teaspoon	½ teaspoon
Garlic clove, minced	1 garlic clove	½ garlic clove	¼ garlic clove
Ground ginger	½ teaspoon	¼ teaspoon	to taste
1 10-ounce package frozen Japanese-style vegetables with flavor cube	1 package with 1 flavor cube	½ package with ½ flavor cube	¼ 10-ounce package with ¼ flavor cube
Butter or margarine	4 tablespoons (½ stick)	2 tablespoons (¼ stick)	1 tablespoon
Microwave cookware	1-quart baking dish	1-quart baking dish	9″ pie plate
Time on High (100% power) Potatoes	14 to 16 minutes	7 to 8 minutes	4 to 6 minutes
Chicken	4 to 5 minutes	2 to 3 minutes	1 to 2 minutes
With vegetables	4 to 6 minutes	2 to 4 minutes	1 to 2 minutes

1 With fork, pierce potatoes in several places. On oven floor, place paper towels; arrange potatoes on top in circle.

2 Cook on High for time in Chart, turning and rearranging halfway through cooking. Wrap in foil; let stand while preparing filling.

3 In baking dish or pie plate (see Chart), combine chicken, oil, cornstarch, garlic, and ground ginger.

4 Cook chicken mixture, covered, on High for time in Chart, or until chicken is no longer pink, stirring halfway through cooking.

5 Into chicken mixture, stir frozen Japanese-style vegetables with their flavor cube.

6 Cook on High for time in Chart, or until vegetables are tender, stirring once. Stir until sauce is smooth. Remove potatoes from foil. Cut a lengthwise slit on top of each potato. Place an equal amount of butter or margarine in each slit. With fork, fluff potatoes, then top each with chicken-vegetable mixture. Place on warmed serving platter and serve immediately.

Spinach

SPINACH GNOCCHI WITH BUTTER AND PARMESAN

Color Index page 77. 233 cals per serving. Good source of vitamin A, calcium. Begin early in day.

Spinach gnocchi – ricotta and spinach Italian-style "dumplings" spiced with Parmesan for extra flavor – make a light lunch or supper when served with salad and crusty Italian bread, but are equally delicious as an accompaniment to roast veal.

Ingredients for 8 servings		Microwave cookware
1 10-ounce package frozen chopped spinach, thawed 8 tablespoons butter or margarine (1 stick) ¼ 15- to 16-ounce container ricotta cheese (½ cup)	1 small onion, minced 2 eggs 1 cup all-purpose flour ½ cup grated Parmesan cheese ½ teaspoon salt ⅛ teaspoon pepper Ground nutmeg to taste	12" by 8" baking dish 2-cup glass measure

1 Squeeze and drain spinach. In baking dish, place 2 tablespoons butter or margarine. Heat, covered with paper towels, on High (100% power) 45 seconds, or until melted. Into melted butter or margarine, stir spinach, ricotta, and onion. Cook on High 5 minutes.

2 To spinach mixture, add eggs, half the flour, and half the Parmesan; season with salt, pepper and nutmeg. Stir until blended. Refrigerate, loosely covered, until cool enough to handle.

3 Fill 5-quart saucepan halfway with water. On stove, over high heat, heat to boiling. Meanwhile, sprinkle remaining flour on waxed paper. With floured hands, roll 1 tablespoon spinach-ricotta mixture into an oval; coat with flour. Repeat with remaining mixture.

4 To boiling water, carefully add half the spinach-ricotta ovals (gnocchi). Cook about 7 minutes, or until gnocchi are slightly puffed and set.

5 With slotted spoon, remove gnocchi to paper towels to drain. Repeat with remaining gnocchi. Meanwhile, in glass measure, place remaining butter or margarine. Heat, covered with paper towel, on High 1 to 1½ (1:30) minutes, until melted.

6 *To serve:* Arrange gnocchi on warmed serving platter. Pour melted butter or margarine over gnocchi; sprinkle with remaining Parmesan and serve immediately.

CREAMED SPINACH

Color Index page 75. 8 servings. 70 cals per serving. Low in cholesterol. Good source of vitamin A, riboflavin, vitamin C, calcium, iron. Begin 40 minutes ahead.

2 10-ounce bags spinach	1½ cups milk
2 tablespoons butter or margarine (¼ stick)	¾ teaspoon salt
	⅛ teaspoon pepper
2 tablespoons all-purpose flour	Ground nutmeg to taste
	Lemon slices for garnish

1. With sharp knife, remove stems from spinach. Rinse under running cold water to remove any sand; drain lightly. In 3-quart microwave-safe casserole, place spinach with water remaining on leaves. Cook, covered, on High (100% power) 5 to 7 minutes, until leaves are wilted, stirring twice. Drain; set aside.
2. In 4-cup microwave-safe glass measure, place butter or margarine. Heat, covered with paper towel, on High 45 seconds, or until melted. Into melted butter or margarine, stir flour until smooth and blended. Cook on High 1 minute, stirring once.
3. Into flour mixture, gradually stir milk. Cook on High 4 to 6 minutes, until sauce thickens and is smooth, stirring occasionally. Season with salt, pepper, and nutmeg.
4. Into sauce, stir spinach. Cook on High 3 to 5 minutes, until spinach is hot. Spoon into warmed serving dish and garnish with lemon slices.

ALTERNATIVE SERVING IDEAS

For a special occasion, Creamed Spinach can be served in a vegetable shell such as an artichoke bottom or hollowed-out tomato (as on page 263), or in an individual serving dish (below) with Buttered-crumb Topping and dill sprig garnish.

Buttered-crumb Topping: In 2-cup microwave-safe glass measure, heat **2 tablespoons butter or margarine** on High (100% power) 45 seconds, or until melted. Stir in **½ cup fresh bread crumbs** and **⅛ teaspoon thyme or basil**. Cook, covered, on High 2 to 2½ (2:30) minutes, until crumbs are dried and golden.

Squash

HONEY-ORANGE-GLAZED ACORN SQUASH

Color Index page 76. 4 servings. 236 cals per serving. Low in cholesterol, sodium. Begin 40 minutes ahead.

2 acorn squash (about 1½ pounds each)	4 tablespoons butter or margarine (½ stick)
1 teaspoon grated orange peel	Orange slices and parsley sprigs for garnish
4 tablespoons honey	

1. With fork, pierce squash in several places. For easier cutting, heat squash on High (100% power) 2 to 2½ (2:30) minutes until slightly softened. With sharp knife, cut squash lengthwise in half; remove seeds and discard.
2. In 12″ by 8″ microwave-safe baking dish, place squash halves, cut side down, with thicker ends toward edges. Cook, covered, on High 8 to 10 minutes, until tender, rotating dish halfway through cooking.
3. Turn squash cut side up. In each cavity, place a quarter of orange peel, honey, and butter or margarine. Cook on High 5 to 7 minutes, until bubbling, rotating dish halfway through cooking.
4. On heat-safe surface, let stand, covered, 5 minutes. Garnish before serving.

MAPLE BUTTERNUT SQUASH

Color Index page 76. 4 servings. 176 cals per serving. Low in cholesterol, sodium. Good source of vitamin A. Begin 55 minutes ahead.

1 small butternut squash (about 1¼ pounds)	1 small onion, diced
2 tablespoons butter or margarine (¼ stick)	¼ cup maple syrup
1 cooking apple, peeled, cored, and diced	Apple slices and parsley sprigs for garnish

1. With fork, pierce squash in several places. On oven floor, place a double thickness of paper towels; place squash on top. Cook on High (100% power) 10 to 15 minutes, until flesh is tender when pierced with tip of sharp knife, turning squash over halfway through cooking. Set aside until cool enough to handle.
2. In 1-quart microwave-safe casserole, place butter or margarine. Heat, covered with paper towel, on High 45 seconds, or until melted. Into melted butter or margarine, stir apple and onion. Cook on High 3 to 5 minutes, until apple and onion are tender, stirring twice.
3. With sharp knife, cut squash lengthwise in half; discard seeds. With large spoon, scoop out flesh. In food processor with knife blade attached or in blender, process squash, in several batches if necessary. To squash, add apple onion-mixture and maple syrup.
4. Into same casserole, pour blended mixture. Cook on High 10 to 12 minutes, until mixture thickens slightly, stirring often. Garnish.

The many different types of squash available, including butternut, acorn, and Hubbard, lend themselves easily to microwaving. You can microwave them whole (don't forget to pierce the skin) or cut them in half, then serve them with Flavored Butter (page 260). In our Spaghetti Squash with Meat Sauce (below), the cooked squash is pulled up with forks to resemble strands of spaghetti.

SPAGHETTI SQUASH WITH MEAT SAUCE

Color Index page 76. 564 cals per serving. Good source of thiamine, niacin, vitamin C, iron. Begin 55 minutes ahead.

Ingredients for 4 servings		Microwave cookware
1 spaghetti squash (about 2 pounds)	1 14½- to 16-ounce can crushed tomatoes	13″ by 9″ baking dish
1 pound pork-sausage meat	2 tablespoons tomato paste	
1 small onion, diced	1 teaspoon basil	
1 green pepper, diced	Salt to taste	
	Basil leaves for garnish	

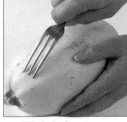

1 With fork, pierce squash in several places. On oven floor, place a double thickness of paper towels; place squash on top.

2 Cook squash on High (100% power) 12 to 15 minutes, until flesh is tender when pierced with tip of sharp knife, turning over halfway through cooking. Wrap in foil; let stand while preparing sauce.

3 In baking dish, place sausage meat and onion. Cook, covered with paper towels, on High 5 to 7 minutes, until meat is no longer pink, stirring often to break up lumps.

4 To sausage mixture, add green pepper, tomatoes, tomato paste, and basil; stir to mix. Cook on High 15 to 18 minutes, until vegetables are tender and sauce thickens slightly, stirring occasionally. Season with salt.

5 Split squash lengthwise in half; discard seeds. With 2 forks, lift up flesh of squash to form spaghetti-like strands and transfer to warmed large serving platter.

6 To serve: Spoon spicy meat sauce over spaghetti squash; garnish with shredded basil leaves.

Sweet Potatoes and Tomatoes

Available all year around but with the best supplies in November in time for Thanksgiving, sweet potatoes make an appetizing change from plain baked potatoes. Cooked in the microwave, they are ready to eat in a matter of minutes.

TWICE-BAKED SWEET POTATOES

Color Index page 77. 147 cals per serving. Low in cholesterol, sodium. Good source of vitamin A. Begin 40 minutes ahead.

Ingredients	For 4	For 2	For 1
Sweet potatoes, well scrubbed	2 large	1 large	1 small
Plain low-fat yogurt	1/4 cup	2 tablespoons	1 tablespoon
Chili powder	1/4 teaspoon	1/8 teaspoon	to taste
Butter or margarine	2 tablespoons (1/4 stick)	1 tablespoon	1 1/2 teaspoons
Salt	to taste	to taste	to taste
Microwave cookware	Baking tray Dinner plate	Baking tray Dinner plate	Baking tray Dinner plate
Time on High (100% power) Sweet potatoes	8 to 10 minutes	5 to 7 minutes	3 to 5 minutes
With stuffing	4 to 5 minutes	2 1/2 (2:30) to 3 minutes	1 to 2 minutes

1 With fork, pierce skin of each sweet potato several times. On baking tray (see Chart), place paper towels; place sweet potatoes on top, with narrow ends pointing toward center.

2 Cook sweet potatoes on High for time in Chart, or until tender, turning over and rearranging halfway through cooking.

3 Wrap sweet potatoes in foil; let stand 5 minutes. Remove foil; on cutting board, with sharp knife, cut each sweet potato lengthwise in half.

4 With spoon, scoop flesh from sweet potatoes into bowl, leaving 1/4-inch-thick shells; reserve shells. On dinner plate (see Chart), arrange sweet-potato shells.

5 In bowl with mixer at low speed, beat sweet-potato flesh, yogurt, chili powder, and butter or margarine until well mixed and fluffy. Season with salt.

6 Spoon mashed sweet-potato mixture into reserved shells. Reheat on High for time in Chart, or until hot. Serve immediately.

SWEET POTATO PUDDING

Color Index page 77. 10 servings. 279 cals per serving. Low in cholesterol, sodium. Good source of vitamin A. Begin 1 1/2 hours ahead.

3 pounds sweet potatoes
6 tablespoons butter or margarine (3/4 stick)
1 cup half-and-half
1/2 teaspoon ground cinnamon
1/2 teaspoon ground nutmeg
1/3 cup brown sugar
1 tablespoon vanilla extract
1/2 cup fresh whole-wheat bread crumbs
1/2 cup pecans, finely chopped

1. With fork, pierce skin of each sweet potato several times. On oven floor, place paper towels. Arrange sweet potatoes spoke-fashion on top. Cook on High (100% power) 20 to 25 minutes until tender, turning over and rearranging half-way through cooking. Wrap sweet potatoes in foil; let stand 5 minutes. Remove foil. With sharp knife, cut each sweet potato lengthwise in half. With spoon, scoop flesh from sweet potatoes into large bowl; reserve. Discard shells.

2. In 9" microwave-safe pie plate, place butter or margarine. Heat, covered with paper towel, on High 1 to 1 1/2 (1:30) minutes, until melted.

3. To sweet potatoes in bowl, add 4 tablespoons melted butter or margarine, add half-and-half and next four ingredients. With mixer at low speed, beat until smooth. Spoon mixture into 9" microwave-safe deep-dish pie plate.

4. Into melted butter or margarine remaining in pie plate, stir bread crumbs and pecans. Cook on High 5 to 6 minutes, until bread crumbs are crisp and pecans are toasted, stirring every minute.

5. Sprinkle bread-crumb-pecan mixture on top of sweet-potato mixture. Cook on High 7 to 10 minutes, until hot. On heat-safe surface, let stand, loosely covered, 5 minutes.

STEWED FRESH TOMATOES

Color Index page 73. 6 servings. 68 cals per serving. Low in cholesterol. Good source of vitamin A. Begin 25 minutes ahead.

2 tablespoons butter or margarine (1/4 stick)
4 green onions, sliced
2 pounds tomatoes, peeled and each cut into 8 wedges
1 1/2 teaspoons sugar
1 1/2 teaspoons garlic salt
1/4 teaspoon pepper

1. In 13" by 9" microwave-safe baking dish, place butter or margarine and green onions. Cook, covered with paper towels, on High (100% power) 45 seconds to 1 minute, until butter or margarine is melted.

2. Into green-onion mixture, stir tomato wedges, sugar, garlic salt, and pepper. Cook, covered, on High 5 minutes, stirring halfway through cooking. Uncover; stir. Cook on High 10 to 15 minutes longer, covered loosely with paper towels, until tomatoes are soft, stirring twice. Serve hot.

Tomatoes and Zucchini

GREEN TOMATO CURRY

Color Index page 73. 4 servings. 121 cals per serving. Low in cholesterol. Good source of vitamin A, vitamin C. Begin 25 minutes ahead.

2 tablespoons butter or margarine (¼ stick)	1 teaspoon curry powder
1 small onion, diced	¼ teaspoon chili powder
1 large cooking apple, peeled, cored, and sliced	¾ teaspoon salt
2 teaspoons sugar	4 medium green tomatoes, cut into wedges

1. In 12″ by 8″ microwave-safe baking dish, place butter or margarine. Heat, covered with paper towels, on High (100% power) 45 seconds, or until melted.
2. Into melted butter or margarine, stir onion. Cook on High 2 to 3 minutes, until onion is softened, stirring twice.
3. Into onion mixture, stir apple slices, sugar, curry powder, chili powder, and salt. Cook on High 3 to 4 minutes, until apple softens slightly, stirring twice.
4. Into onion-apple mixture, stir green tomatoes. Cook on High 5 to 7 minutes, until tomatoes are tender, stirring occasionally.
5. Transfer tomato mixture to warmed serving dish and serve hot.

ZUCCHINI LINGUINE WITH SUN-DRIED TOMATOES AND PINE NUTS

Color Index page 77. 4 servings. 195 cals per serving. Low in cholesterol. Good source of iron. Begin 35 minutes ahead.

4 medium zucchini	1 teaspoon basil
2 tablespoons olive or salad oil	Salt to taste
1 garlic clove, minced	Basil leaves for garnish
¼ cup pine nuts	
⅓ cup chopped sun-dried tomatoes, drained if packed in oil	

1. With sharp knife, cut each zucchini lengthwise into 6 slices. Cut each slice lengthwise into ¼-inch-wide strips. Set aside.
2. In 13″ by 9″ microwave-safe baking dish, place oil, garlic, and pine nuts. Cook on High (100% power) 2 to 3 minutes, until pine nuts are lightly toasted, stirring twice.
3. Into pine-nut mixture, stir zucchini strips, sun-dried tomatoes, and basil. Cook, covered, on High 5 to 7 minutes, until zucchini are tender-crisp, stirring halfway through cooking. Season with salt.
4. Transfer to warmed serving platter. Garnish with basil leaves and serve immediately.

Zucchini and yellow squash – both popular summer squash – make ideal vegetable containers for stuffing. These Stuffed Zucchini (below) are delicious served as an accompaniment to lamb and fish; yellow squash can be substituted using the same ingredients and timings. To save time, they can be prepared ahead through step 4, then cooked at the last minute. If you have extra-large zucchini, use them to make a filling mid-week meal. Look for young squash that feel heavy with smooth skin.

STUFFED ZUCCHINI

Color Index page 77. 87 cals per serving. Low in cholesterol, sodium. Begin 35 minutes ahead.

Ingredients for 2 servings		Microwave cookware
2 medium zucchini	2 tablespoons dried bread crumbs	12″ by 8″ baking dish
1½ teaspoons olive or salad oil	1 tablespoon grated Parmesan cheese	
½ red pepper, diced	Salt to taste	
½ small tomato, diced	Lemon Twists (page 132) and basil leaves for garnish	
1 small garlic clove, minced		
⅛ teaspoon thyme leaves		

1 With sharp knife, cut zucchini lengthwise in half. With spoon, scoop out zucchini leaving ¼-inch-thick shell. Reserve zucchini flesh.

2 In baking dish, arrange zucchini shells, cut side down. Cook, covered, on High (100% power), 2 to 3 minutes, until fork-tender but not soft. With spatula, remove shells to platter. Set aside.

3 Dice reserved zucchini flesh. In same baking dish, place diced zucchini, olive or salad oil, diced red pepper, diced tomato, garlic and thyme leaves; stir well. Cook on High 2 to 3 minutes, until tender, stirring halfway through cooking.

4 Into vegetable mixture, stir bread crumbs and Parmesan. Season with salt. With spoon, mound an equal amount of vegetable mixture in each zucchini shell.

5 In cleaned baking dish, arrange stuffed zucchini with stem ends toward edges. Cook on High 2 to 3 minutes, until hot. On heat-safe surface, let stand, loosely covered, 2 minutes.

6 Arrange stuffed zucchini on warmed serving platter. Garnish with Lemon Twists and basil leaves and serve.

Mixed Vegetable Dishes

Microwaving brings out the best in different vegetables cooked together in the same dish. In the selection in our Mixed Company Vegetables (below), all the vegetables have different densities and water content, so they each microwave at different speeds. To prevent the vegetables from cooking unevenly, they are added to the microwave in stages.

MIXED COMPANY VEGETABLES

Color Index page 76. 107 cals per serving. Low in cholesterol. Good source of vitamin A, vitamin C. Begin 45 minutes ahead.

Ingredients for 8 servings		Microwave cookware
4 green onions	¼ cup water	Medium bowl
1 pound carrots	1 bunch broccoli	4-quart casserole
3 tablespoons salad oil	1 medium red pepper	
¼ teaspoon crushed red pepper	½ pound medium mushrooms	
2 tablespoons soy sauce		

1 On cutting board, with sharp knife, diagonally cut green onions into 1-inch pieces and carrots into ¼-inch-thick slices.

2 In bowl, place green onions, oil, and crushed red pepper. Cook on High (100% power) 3 minutes, until tender-crisp, stirring once. Stir in soy sauce. Cover and set aside.

3 In casserole, place water and carrots. Cook, covered, on High 8 to 10 minutes, until carrots are tender-crisp, stirring halfway through cooking.

4 Meanwhile, with sharp knife, cut broccoli into 2" by 1" pieces. Cut red pepper into matchstick-thin strips. Set aside.

5 To carrots, add broccoli. Cook, covered, on High 5 minutes, stirring once. Add mushrooms. Cook, covered, on High 5 minutes longer, or until vegetables are tender, stirring halfway through cooking.

6 Drain liquid from vegetables. To vegetables, add red-pepper strips and green-onion mixture. Toss to coat well. Arrange vegetables on warmed serving platter and serve immediately.

MASHED HARVEST VEGETABLES

Color Index page 76. 8 servings. 135 cals per serving. Low in cholesterol. Good source of vitamin C. Begin 45 minutes ahead.

1½ pounds winter squash (such as butternut)
1½ pounds rutabaga
½ cup water
4 tablespoons butter or margarine (½ stick)
2 tablespoons dark-brown sugar
1 teaspoon salt

1 tablespoon orange-flavor liqueur
1 teaspoon finely grated orange peel
⅛ teaspoon ground cinnamon
Orange Julienne (page 334), and parsley sprig for garnish

1. With fork, pierce skin of squash several times. For easier cutting, heat squash on High (100% power) 2 to 2½ (2:30) minutes until slightly softened. Peel squash and rutabaga. Cut each into ¾-inch pieces.
2. In 4-quart microwave-safe casserole, place squash, rutabaga, and water. Cook, covered, on High 18 minutes, or until vegetables are very tender, stirring occasionally.
3. To vegetable mixture, add butter or margarine, sugar, salt, liqueur, orange peel, and cinnamon. With potato masher, mash thoroughly.
4. Spoon mixture into microwave-safe serving dish. Reheat on High 2 minutes, or until hot; garnish.

GARDEN MEDLEY

Color Index page 76. 6 servings. 182 cals per serving. Low in cholesterol, sodium. Good source of vitamin A, vitamin C, iron. Begin 45 minutes ahead.

1 pound potatoes, peeled
2 small eggplants (about 8 ounces each)
2 medium onions
4 red or yellow peppers
2 zucchini (about 8 ounces each)
¼ cup water

1 small garlic clove, minced
¼ cup salad oil
2 tablespoons cider vinegar
¼ teaspoon oregano
1 medium tomato

1. Cut potatoes into 1½-inch chunks. Cut each eggplant lengthwise into quarters. Cut each onion into 6 wedges. Cut peppers into 1-inch strips. Cut zucchini diagonally into 1-inch slices.
2. In 13" by 9" microwave-safe baking dish, place potatoes and water. Cook, covered, on High (100% power) 5 minutes, stirring once. Drain.
3. To potato chunks, add eggplant and remaining ingredients except tomato; stir. Cook, covered, on High 15 minutes, stirring twice.
4. Cut tomato into 8 wedges; add to vegetable mixture. Cook, covered, on High 4 to 5 minutes, until vegetables are tender, stirring halfway through cooking. Serve hot or cover and refrigerate to serve chilled later.

RATATOUILLE

Color Index page 76. 8 servings. 115 cals per serving. Low in cholesterol. Begin 45 minutes ahead.

¼ cup olive or salad oil	2 teaspoons salt
1 large onion, diced	2 teaspoons oregano
2 garlic cloves, minced	1 teaspoon sugar
1 red or green pepper, cut into 1-inch pieces	2 large tomatoes, each cut into 8 wedges
1 medium eggplant (about 1½ pounds), cut into 1-inch chunks	2 tablespoons tomato paste
3 medium zucchini, cut into 1-inch chunks	Basil leaves for garnish

1. In 13″ by 9″ microwave-safe baking dish, place oil, onion, and garlic. Cook on High (100% power) 3 to 4 minutes, until onion softens, stirring halfway through cooking.

2. Stir in red or green pepper, eggplant, and zucchini. Cook, covered, on High 10 to 12 minutes, until eggplant and zucchini are slightly softened, stirring twice during cooking.

3. Into eggplant mixture, stir salt, oregano, sugar, tomatoes, and tomato paste. Cook on High 15 to 18 minutes, until vegetables are tender and juices thicken slightly, stirring occasionally.

4. Spoon ratatouille onto serving platter; serve hot or cover and refrigerate to serve chilled later; garnish before serving.

RATATOUILLE-FILLED PEPPERS: Prepare **Ratatouille** (above) through step 3. Cut **4 medium peppers** (**red, green and/or yellow**) lengthwise in half; remove seeds and stems. Brush peppers on all sides with **1 tablespoon salad oil.** Arrange, cut side down, in single layer in 12″ by 8″ microwave-safe baking dish. Cook, covered, on High (100% power) 3 to 4 minutes, just until softened; cool slightly. Spoon equal amounts of Ratatouille into pepper halves and arrange on serving platter. If you like, reheat filled peppers on microwave-safe platter on Medium-High (70% power) 3 to 4 minutes, until hot.

Oiling and Arranging the Peppers

With pastry brush, lightly and evenly brush oil over pepper halves.

Place oiled peppers, cut side down, in single layer in baking dish. Cook, covered, as above.

When cooking a variety of fresh seasonal vegetables in the microwave, be sure to arrange them so that the thicker parts are pointing toward the edges of the dish, where they will receive most microwave energy. If necessary, overlap the pieces slightly as we have done in our recipe for Spring Vegetables with Lemon-chive Butter (below).

SPRING VEGETABLES WITH LEMON-CHIVE BUTTER

Color Index page 73. 141 cals per serving. Low in cholesterol. Good source of vitamin A, vitamin C. Begin 25 minutes ahead.

Ingredients for 6 servings		Microwave cookware
1½ pounds asparagus	2 tablespoons minced chives	12″ by 8″ baking dish
3 small yellow straightneck squash (about 4 ounces each)	1 tablespoon prepared mustard	Small bowl
2 bunches radishes	2 tablespoons lemon juice	
6 medium carrots	1 tablespoon Lemon Julienne (page 334)	
½ cup water	¼ teaspoon salt	
4 tablespoons butter or margarine (½ stick)	Chives for garnish	

1 With sharp knife, trim tough ends from asparagus. Rinse under running cold water to remove any sand. With knife, cut squash lengthwise into quarters. Trim radishes and rinse.

2 With sharp knife, cut carrots lengthwise in half. In baking dish, arrange carrots so that tips are overlapping in center. Add water. Cook, covered, on High (100% power) 4 minutes.

3 Arrange asparagus on top of carrots in baking dish so that tips are overlapping in center.

4 In same dish, arrange squash and radishes in layers on top of carrots and asparagus. Cook, covered, on High 8 to 10 minutes, until vegetables are tender-crisp, rotating dish halfway through cooking.

5 In bowl, combine butter or margarine, chives, mustard, lemon juice, Lemon Julienne, and salt. Cook on High 2½ (2:30) to 3 minutes, until butter is melted.

6 *To serve:* Arrange vegetables on warmed serving platter. Top with lemon-chive butter and garnish with fresh chives.

Main-dish Chicken Salads

OLD-FASHIONED CHICKEN SALAD

Color Index page 78. 399 cals per serving. Good source of niacin. Begin 55 minutes ahead.

Ingredients	For 4	For 2	For 1
Chicken breasts, skinned and boned	2 whole chicken breasts	1 whole chicken breast	1 chicken-breast half
Chicken Broth (page 125) or canned broth	2 tablespoons	1 tablespoon	2 teaspoons
Celery stalk, diced	1 stalk	½ stalk	¼ stalk
Small onion, minced	1 onion	½ onion	¼ onion
Pimento, minced	2 tablespoons	1 tablespoon	1 teaspoon
Mayonnaise	⅔ cup mayonnaise	⅓ cup mayonnaise	3 tablespoons mayonniase
Lemon juice	1 tablespoon	1½ teaspoons	½ teaspoon
Poultry seasoning	½ teaspoon	¼ teaspoon	to taste
Salt	to taste	to taste	to taste
Microwave cookware	9″ pie plate	9″ pie plate	9″ pie plate
Time on High (100% power)	5 to 7 minutes	3½ (3:30) to 5 minutes	2½ (2:30) to 3½ (3:30) minutes

1 In pie plate (see Chart), place chicken breasts and broth. Cook, covered, on High for time in Chart, or until chicken juices run clear, turning pieces over and rotating plate halfway through cooking.

2 Let chicken stand, loosely covered, on heat-safe surface while preparing dressing. In bowl, combine celery, onion, pimento, mayonnaise, lemon juice, and poultry seasoning; mix until well blended.

3 Drain chicken; cut into chunks. Stir into dressing; mix well. Season with salt. For best flavor, cover and refrigerate 30 minutes before serving.

SALAD DRESSINGS

Vinaigrette Dressing: In small bowl, whisk *1 diced small red onion, ¼ cup salad oil, ¼ cup red-wine vinegar, ¼ teaspoon oregano,* and *¼ teaspoon salt* until blended.

Zesty Mayonnaise Dressing: In small bowl, whisk *½ cup mayonnaise, 3 tablespoons milk, 2 tablespoons lemon juice, 1 tablespoon prepared mustard, ½ teaspoon salt, ¼ teaspoon pepper,* and *¼ teaspoon basil* until blended.

CHICKEN CLUB SALAD

Color Index page 78. 2 main-dish servings. 338 cals per serving. Good source of niacin, iron. Begin 40 minutes ahead.

1 whole chicken breast (about 12 ounces), skinned and boned	2 slices bread Lettuce leaves 1 tomato, sliced
⅛ teaspoon thyme leaves	Vinaigrette Dressing (below left)
4 slices bacon	

1. With sharp knife, cut chicken breast in half. In 9″ microwave-safe pie plate, place chicken-breast halves. Sprinkle with thyme. Cook, covered with waxed paper, on High (100% power) 5 to 6 minutes, until chicken juices run clear, turning pieces over and rotating dish halfway through cooking. Discard cooking juices. Cover and refrigerate.

2. Meanwhile, on a double thickness of paper towels, place bacon slices. Cook, covered with paper towel, on High 3½ (3:30) minutes, until browned; set aside.

3. With sharp knife, cut chicken crosswise into ¼-inch-thick slices. Toast bread; cut into quarters. On dinner plates, arrange lettuce leaves, tomato, chicken, and toast points. Chop bacon; sprinkle over salad. Serve with Vinaigrette Dressing.

CHICKEN AND POTATO SALAD WITH ZESTY DRESSING

Color Index page 79. 6 main-dish servings. 414 cals per serving. Good source of niacin, vitamin C, iron. Begin 1¼ hours ahead.

1 3½-pound broiler-fryer, cut up and skinned	10 pitted ripe olives, cut in half
1½ pounds small red (new) potatoes, cut into ½-inch-thick slices	¼ cup milk ⅓ cup mayonnaise ¼ cup sour cream
¼ cup water	2 tablespoons prepared horseradish
1 yellow pepper, sliced	2 tablespoons lemon juice
1 small red onion, sliced	¾ teaspoon salt

1. In 13″ by 9″ microwave-safe baking dish, place chicken legs, thighs, and wings at edges of dish, and breasts in center. Cook, covered, on High (100% power) 22 to 24 minutes, until chicken juices run clear, turning over and rearranging pieces halfway through cooking. Set aside to cool.

2. In 2-quart microwave-safe casserole, place potatoes and water. Cook, covered, on High 8 to 9 minutes, stirring once. Drain; set aside to cool.

3. Cut reserved chicken into bite-sized pieces; discard bones. Place chicken pieces, potatoes, pepper, onion, and olives in large bowl; toss.

4. In small bowl, combine milk and remaining ingredients. Pour dressing over salad, or pass separately.

Main-dish Meat Salads

ANTIPASTO SALAD DINNER

Color Index page 78. 6 main-dish servings. 431 cals per serving. Good source of vitamin A, vitamin C, calcium. Begin 25 minutes ahead.

1 small head cauliflower, cut into flowerets
2 tablespoons water
3 small zucchini, cut into ½-inch slices
Vinaigrette Dressing (page 276)
1 9-ounce package frozen artichoke hearts
Salad greens
3 medium carrots, cut into matchstick-thin strips
8 ounces smoked Gouda, mozzarella, or other cheese, sliced
½ pound salami, cut into chunks
2 medium tomatoes, cut into wedges

1. In 10″ round microwave-safe dish, place cauliflower and water. Cook, covered, on High (100% power) 5 minutes, stirring once. To dish, add zucchini. Cook, covered, 3 to 5 minutes, until vegetables are tender-crisp. With slotted spoon, remove vegetables to small bowl. Pour over half the Vinaigrette Dressing; toss.
2. In same microwave-safe dish, place frozen artichoke hearts. Cook, covered, on High 3 to 5 minutes, until tender, stirring once. Drain.
3. On platter, arrange salad greens, cooked vegetables, carrots, cheese, salami, and tomatoes. Pass remaining dressing separately.

POTATO DELI DINNER

Color Index page 78. 6 main-dish servings. 365 cals per serving. Good source of niacin, calcium, iron. Begin 50 minutes ahead.

2 pounds small red (new) potatoes, peeled and diced
¾ cup Chicken Broth (page 125) or canned broth
¼ teaspoon caraway seeds
¼ teaspoon pepper
4 slices bacon, diced
2 celery stalks, sliced
1 onion, chopped
1 tablespoon all-purpose flour
½ cup cider vinegar
3 tablespoons brown sugar
Salad greens
½ pound deli-sliced meats
4 ounces American or Cheddar cheese, cut into strips

1. In 3-quart microwave-safe casserole, combine potatoes, broth, caraway seeds, and pepper. Cook, covered, on High (100% power) 11 to 13 minutes, until potatoes are tender, stirring halfway through cooking. Drain cooking liquid, reserving ¼ cup. Cover potatoes; set aside.
2. In medium microwave-safe bowl, place bacon. Cook, covered with paper towel, on High 4 to 5 minutes, until browned. Remove to paper towels to drain. Into drippings in bowl, stir celery and onion. Cook on High 3 minutes.
3. To celery-onion mixture, add flour, reserved cooking liquid, vinegar, and sugar; stir. Cook on High 3 to 5 minutes, until mixture thickens, stirring once. Pour over potatoes; add bacon. Let stand 10 minutes. Arrange salad greens on platter with potatoes, meats, and cheese.

Both hot and cold pasta and noodles can be combined with a selection of crisply cooked vegetables and thin slivers of meat to make a hearty salad. In our Thai-style Beef and Noodle Salad (below), we have used crushed red pepper, green onions, mint, and cashews to create an authentic Thai flavor. This dish can be served hot, or prepared well in advance to serve chilled later.

THAI-STYLE BEEF AND NOODLE SALAD

Color Index page 79. 905 cals per serving. Good source of vitamin A, riboflavin, thiamine, vitamin C, iron. Begin 1½ hours ahead or early in day.

Ingredients for 4 main-dish servings		Microwave cookware
1 pound beef tenderloin *½ cup peanut or salad oil* *2 tablespoons lime or lemon juice* *2 tablespoons soy sauce* *2 tablespoons cider vinegar* *2 tablespoons sugar* *¼ teaspoon crushed red pepper*	*3 3-ounce packages ramen noodles, beef or chicken flavor* *⅛ cup shredded mint leaves* *1 small red pepper, diced* *4 green onions, thinly sliced* *¼ cup dry-roasted unsalted cashews*	Large bowl Browning dish

1 On cutting board, with sharp knife, cut beef crosswise into ⅛-inch-thick slices. Cut each slice into thin strips.

2 In medium bowl, combine oil, lime or lemon juice, soy sauce, vinegar, sugar, and crushed red pepper. Add beef; stir to coat. Cover and marinate 30 minutes.

3 Over large bowl, set strainer. Drain beef; reserve marinade. Preheat browning dish as manufacturer directs.

4 Spread half the beef on browning dish. Cook on High (100% power) 1 to 2 minutes, just until beef is of desired doneness, stirring halfway through cooking. Remove beef; set aside and keep warm. Reheat browning dish and cook remaining beef slices.

5 Meanwhile, cook noodles conventionally as label directs. Drain; add to reserved marinade in bowl, and toss well to mix. Heat noodles on High 2 to 3 minutes until hot.

6 Toss noodles with shredded mint, diced red pepper, green onions, and cashews. Place on serving platter. Arrange beef over noodles. Serve hot or cover and refrigerate to serve chilled later.

Warm Salads

Various salad greens such as romaine, arugula, watercress, and radicchio are delicious served wilted with a warm dressing. Escarole, with its pungent flavor, is a particularly good choice.

SPINACH SALAD WITH HOT BACON DRESSING

Color Index page 78. 153 cals per serving. Low in cholesterol. Good source of vitamin A. Begin 20 minutes ahead.

Ingredients	For 4	For 2	For 1
1 10-ounce bag spinach	1 bag	½ bag	¼ bag
Bacon, diced	4 slices	2 slices	1 slice
Cider vinegar	1 tablespoon	1½ teaspoons	¾ teaspoon
Dijon mustard	1 tablespoon	1½ teaspoons	¾ teaspoon
Sugar	1 teaspoon	½ teaspoon	¼ teaspoon
Red onion, sliced	1 medium	1 small	½ small
Microwave cookware	Large bowl 9" pie plate	Medium bowl 9" pie plate	Small bowl 9" pie plate
Time on High (100% power) Bacon	4 to 5 minutes	2 to 3 minutes	1 to 1½ (1:30) minutes
Dressing	1 to 2 minutes	30 seconds to 1 minute	15 to 30 seconds
Salad	2 to 3 minutes	1 to 1½ (1:30) minutes	45 seconds to 1 minute

1 Wash spinach well and cut off any tough stems. Into bowl (see Chart), tear spinach into bite-sized pieces.

2 In pie plate (see Chart), place bacon. Cook, covered with paper towel, on High for time in Chart, or until browned, stirring twice. With spatula, remove bacon to paper towels to drain.

3 Into bacon drippings in pie plate, stir vinegar, mustard, and sugar. Cook, covered with paper towel, on High for time in Chart, or until hot.

4 To spinach, add onion and hot dressing; toss to coat well. Sprinkle reserved bacon over spinach. Cook salad on High for time in Chart, just until spinach wilts.

LEAVES FOR SALAD

While lettuce remains the favorite salad green, there is a wide variety of other leaves available to add interest to your salads. Other popular greens include arugula, Swiss chard, Belgian endive, escarole, red-tipped oak leaf, kale, chicory, and radicchio. Try varying different colors and shapes in your salad bowl, tossing them together with your favorite dressing.

Radicchio: Bitter-flavored, ruby-red leaves; used frequently in Italian salads.

Mâche: A spring and summer salad green, wild or cultivated. Spoon-shaped leaves are tangy; good with other leaves.

Chicory: Somewhat bitter tasting; outer leaves are darker and stronger in flavor than inner ones.

Lollo Rosso: Curly red-tinged leaves; if unavailable, use red-tipped oak leaf.

Escarole: Wide flat leaves, curled at the edges; slightly bitter taste.

WARM SALAD OF ARUGULA, CORN, BLACK BEANS, AND AVOCADO

Color Index page 78. 8 servings. 140 cals per serving. Low in cholesterol. Begin 20 minutes ahead.

3 slices bacon, diced
1 large onion, sliced
2 garlic cloves, minced
1 10-ounce package frozen whole-kernel corn, thawed
1 16-ounce can black beans, drained and rinsed
3 cups shredded arugula
2 tablespoons red-wine vinegar
Salt and pepper to taste
Avocado slices for garnish

1. In 13" by 9" microwave-safe baking dish, place bacon. Cook, covered with paper towels, on High (100% power) 3 to 4 minutes, until bacon is browned, stirring twice. With spatula, remove bacon to paper towels to drain.
2. Into bacon drippings in dish, stir onion, garlic, corn, and black beans. Cook, covered, on High 4 to 5 minutes, until onion softens, stirring once.
3. Into vegetable mixture, stir arugula and vinegar. Cook on High 2 to 4 minutes, until arugula is wilted, stirring once. Season salad with salt and pepper.
4. *To serve*: Spoon salad onto warmed dinner plates; garnish each portion with avocado slices and sprinkle with diced bacon.

PEPPER SALAD

Color Index page 78. 6 servings. 166 cals per serving. Low in cholesterol. Good source of vitamin A, vitamin C, calcium. Begin 25 minutes ahead.

1 large mild sweet onion (about 1 pound)
2 medium red peppers
2 medium green peppers
2 medium yellow peppers
2 tablespoons olive or salad oil
2 tablespoons white-wine vinegar
1 teaspoon sugar
¾ teaspoon salt
½ teaspoon fennel seeds, crushed
1 3.2-ounce can (drained weight) pitted ripe olives, drained and cut in half
½ 8-ounce package feta cheese, crumbled

1. With sharp knife, cut onion into 8 wedges. Separate each wedge to loosen onion layers. Cut red, green, and yellow peppers into ½-inch strips.
2. In 13" by 9" microwave-safe baking dish, place oil and onion. Cook on High (100% power) 3 to 4 minutes, until onion softens slightly, stirring once.
3. To onion mixture, add green, red, and yellow peppers. Cook, covered, on High 7 to 10 minutes, until peppers are tender, stirring occasionally.
4. In large bowl, combine vinegar, sugar, salt, and fennel seeds. Add pepper-onion mixture, olives, and feta cheese. Toss gently to mix well. Serve warm or cover and refrigerate to serve chilled later.

Warm salads make a welcome alternative to plainly cooked green vegetables. They are also delicious served as a first course. An appetizer salad should be light and tangy – to whet the appetite for heartier dishes to come.

WARM SALAD OF ARTICHOKE HEARTS AND CHERRY TOMATOES *

Color Index page 79. 186 cals per serving. Begin 55 minutes ahead.

Ingredients for 6 servings		Microwave cookware
8 tablespoons butter (1 stick)	*1 tablespoon tarragon vinegar*	13" by 9" baking dish
2 9-ounce packages frozen artichoke hearts, thawed	*1 tablespoon dry white wine*	2-cup glass measure
1 pint cherry tomatoes	*¼ teaspoon tarragon*	Medium bowl
½ teaspoon minced onion	*1 egg yolk*	
	Salt and pepper to taste	
	Dill sprigs for garnish (optional)	

1 In baking dish, place 1 tablespoon butter. Heat, covered with paper towel, on High (100% power) 30 seconds, or until melted.

2 Into melted butter, stir artichoke hearts. Cook on High 5 minutes, or until artichokes are hot, stirring twice. Add cherry tomatoes. Cook on High 2 to 3 minutes, until tomatoes are hot, stirring once. Keep warm.

3 In glass measure, place onion, vinegar, wine, and tarragon. Cook on High 2 to 3 minutes, until liquid evaporates. Spoon onion mixture into medium bowl.

4 Into onion mixture in bowl, stir egg yolk. In glass measure used for onion, place remaining butter. Heat, covered with paper towel, on High 1 to 1½ (1:30) minutes, until butter is melted.

5 Beating constantly with whisk, pour hot butter in thin stream into onion mixture until butter is incorporated and mixture thickens. Season with salt and pepper. Cook on Medium (50% power) 30 seconds to 1 minute, stirring every 15 seconds, until hot and slightly thickened.

6 *To serve*: Arrange artichoke hearts in a cirle on warmed serving platter. Spoon cherry tomatoes into center; pour warm sauce over. Garnish with dill sprigs. Serve immediately.

Vegetable Salads

Pasta shapes combine beautifully with a variety of garden vegetables; prepare them in advance and, if you like, reheat them in the microwave. Use the smaller shells, bow ties, and spirals to turn any salad from a light and tasty accompaniment to a satisfying main dish everyone will enjoy.

GARDEN VEGETABLES AND PASTA SALAD

Color Index page 79. 438 cals per serving. Good source of vitamin A, thiamine, riboflavin, vitamin C, calcium, iron. Begin 55 minutes ahead.

Ingredients for 6 main-dish servings		Microwave cookware
1/3 cup cider vinegar	*1 medium yellow straightneck squash, cut into 1/2-inch-thick pieces*	*12" by 8" baking dish*
1/4 cup olive or salad oil		
1 teaspoon oregano		
1 teaspoon salt	*1/2 16-ounce package bow-tie macaroni*	
1/4 teaspoon crushed red pepper	*4 ounces Cheddar cheese, cubed*	
6 green onions, chopped		
1/4 pound green beans	*4 ounces Swiss cheese, cubed*	
3 medium carrots, sliced		
1/4 cup water	*1/2 pint cherry tomatoes*	
1 bunch broccoli, cut into bite-sized pieces		
1 medium zucchini, cut into 1/2-inch-thick slices		

1 In large bowl, mix vinegar, oil, oregano, salt, crushed red pepper, and green onions. In baking dish, place green beans, carrots, and water. Cook on High (100% power) 6 to 8 minutes, until tender-crisp, stirring once.

2 With slotted spoon, transfer green beans and carrots to dressing in bowl; toss to coat. Cover and set aside.

3 To same baking dish, add broccoli. Cook, covered, on High 6 to 7 minutes, until broccoli is tender-crisp, stirring once. Transfer to bowl with vegetables and dressing; toss to mix.

4 Place zucchini and squash in baking dish. Cook, covered, on High 3 to 4 minutes, until tender-crisp, stirring once. Transfer to bowl with vegetables and dressing; toss to mix.

5 Meanwhile, cook bow-tie macaroni conventionally as label directs; drain and set aside.

6 To vegetables in bowl, add macaroni, cheese cubes, and cherry tomatoes. Toss gently and transfer to serving dish. Serve warm or cover and refrigerate to serve chilled later.

LENTILS VINAIGRETTE

Color Index page 79. 8 servings. 183 cals per serving. Low in cholesterol, sodium. Good source of iron. Begin 2 1/2 hours ahead or early in day.

6 tablespoons olive or salad oil	*2 tablespoons red-wine vinegar*
1 medium onion, chopped	*2 tablespoons chopped fresh basil, mint, or parsley*
1 teaspoon thyme leaves	*3 green onions, sliced*
1 bay leaf	*1 green pepper, diced*
1 cup dry lentils	*1 large tomato, diced*
3 cups water	*Salt and pepper to taste*

1. In 12" by 8" microwave-safe baking dish, place 2 tablespoons oil, onion, thyme leaves, and bay leaf. Cook on High (100% power) 3 to 5 minutes, until onion softens, stirring twice.
2. Into onion mixture, stir lentils and water. Cook, covered, on High 15 to 20 minutes, until lentils are tender but not mushy, stirring occasionally. Drain; discard bay leaf.
3. In small bowl, combine remaining oil, vinegar, chopped basil, mint, or parsley, green onions, green pepper, and tomato; add to lentil mixture in baking dish. Toss well. Season salad with salt and pepper.
4. Cover salad and refrigerate at least 2 hours to blend flavors before serving.

THREE BEAN SALAD

Color Index page 79. 8 servings. 247 cals per serving. Low in cholesterol.
Begin 2 1/4 hours ahead or early in day.

1/2 cup sugar	*1 15 1/4- to 19-ounce can red kidney beans*
1/2 cup olive or salad oil	
1/2 cup cider vinegar	*1 onion, chopped*
1 teaspoon salt	*1/4 cup chopped sweet pickle*
1 16-ounce can cut green beans	
1 15 1/2- to 19-ounce can garbanzo beans	*1/2 small green pepper, chopped*

1. In 4-cup microwave-safe glass measure, combine sugar, oil, vinegar, and salt. Heat on High (100% power) 3 to 5 minutes, until mixture boils and sugar dissolves.
2. Meanwhile, drain and rinse green, garbanzo, and kidney beans. In large bowl, place beans, onion, pickle, and green pepper. Pour dressing over salad; mix well.
3. Cover salad and refrigerate at least 2 hours to blend flavors before serving.

WILD RICE SALAD

Color Index page 79. 8 servings. 187 cals per serving. Low in cholesterol, sodium.
Begin 1½ hours ahead.

3 cups water
½ cup wild rice
½ cup regular long-
* grain rice*
¼ cup olive or salad oil
1 tablespoon cider
* vinegar*
1 tablespoon lemon juice
¼ teaspoon ground
* coriander (optional)*

4 green onions, sliced
1 cooking apple, peeled,
* cored, and diced*
2 celery stalks, sliced
¼ cup pine nuts
¼ cup seedless raisins
Salt to taste

1. Into 8-cup microwave-safe glass measure, pour water. Heat on High (100% power) 5 to 7 minutes, until boiling.
2. Into water, stir wild rice. Cook, covered tightly with plastic wrap, on High 20 minutes. Uncover; stir in regular long-grain rice. Cover again and cook on High 15 to 20 minutes longer, until rice is tender. Drain in colander and rinse under running cold water until cooled.
3. Meanwhile, in medium bowl, combine oil, vinegar, lemon juice, and, if you like, coriander. Into dressing, stir green onions, apple, celery, pine nuts, and raisins. Stir in rice. Season with salt.
4. Cover salad and let stand 30 minutes to blend flavors before serving. Serve at room temperature or cover and refrigerate to serve chilled later.

CLASSIC POTATO SALAD

Color Index page 78. 6 servings. 170 cals per serving. Begin 25 minutes ahead.

1½ pounds potatoes, cut
* into ¾-inch chunks*
¼ cup water
⅓ cup mayonnaise
1 tablespoon milk
1 teaspoon vinegar

½ teaspoon salt
¼ teaspoon pepper
1 celery stalk, thinly
* sliced*
1 hard-cooked egg
* (below), finely chopped*

1. In 2-quart microwave-safe casserole, place potatoes and water. Cook, covered, on High (100% power) 7 to 9 minutes, until tender, stirring twice. Drain; allow potatoes to cool slightly.
2. In medium bowl, combine mayonnaise, milk, vinegar, salt, and pepper. Add potatoes, celery, and egg; toss to coat well. Serve immediately or cover and refrigerate to serve chilled later.

HARD-COOKED EGGS: Break *1 egg* into 6-ounce custard cup; prick yolk in several places. Cook, covered, on Medium (50% power) 1½ (1:30) to 2½ (2:30) minutes. Let stand on heat-safe surface 2 minutes, until yolk and white are firmly set. Cook 2 eggs 2½ (2:30) to 3½ (3:30) minutes; 3 eggs, 3 to 4 minutes.

TOMATO ASPIC

Color Index page 79. 38 cals per serving. Low in cholesterol, fat.
Begin early in day.

Ingredients	For 4	For 2	For 1
Water	¾ cup	6 tablespoons	3 tablespoons
Tomato juice	2 cups	1 cup	½ cup
Celery stalk, sliced	1 stalk	½ stalk	¼ stalk
Lemon slices	2 slices	1 slice	½ slice
Hot-pepper sauce	to taste	to taste	to taste
Unflavored gelatin	1 envelope	½ envelope	¼ envelope
Cider vinegar	1½ teaspoons	¾ teaspoon	⅓ teaspoon
Sugar	½ teaspoon	¼ teaspoon	to taste
Salt	½ teaspoon	¼ teaspoon	to taste
Plain low-fat yogurt and chives for garnish	garnish	garnish	garnish
Microwave cookware	8-cup glass measure	4-cup glass measure	2-cup glass measure
Time on High (100% power) Tomato mixture	5 to 7 minutes	3 to 5 minutes	2 to 2½ (2:30) minutes
With gelatin	3 to 4 minutes	2 to 3 minutes	1 to 1½ (1:30) minutes

1 Into glass measure (see Chart), pour water and tomato juice. Add celery, lemon, and hot-pepper sauce; stirring once. Cook, covered, on High for time in Chart.

2 Over bowl, set strainer. Pour mixture through strainer. Discard vegetables and return tomato mixture to measure.

3 Sprinkle gelatin evenly over tomato mixture; let stand 1 minute to soften slightly.

4 Cook mixture, covered, on High for time in Chart, until gelatin completely dissolves, stirring twice. Stir in vinegar, sugar, and salt. Taste and adjust seasoning.

5 Ladle tomato mixture into ½-cup ramekins or individual molds. Cover and refrigerate until firmly set.

6 *To serve:* Dip ramekins or molds in warm water. With knife, loosen aspic from sides. Place small plate upside down over each and invert. Shake gently and remove ramekin or mold. Garnish.

Shrimp Salads

SHRIMP SALAD WITH CHINESE PEA PODS

Color Index page 79. 4 servings. 268 cals per serving. Good source of vitamin A, vitamin C, iron. Begin 2 hours ahead.

1 pound medium shrimp, shelled and deveined	*4 green onions, sliced*
⅓ pound Chinese pea pods, cut crosswise in half	*¼ cup olive or salad oil*
	2 tablespoons dry white wine
1 small red pepper, thinly sliced	*2 tablespoons lemon juice*
1 10-ounce package frozen baby corn, thawed	*1 tablespoon minced dill*
	Salt and pepper to taste

1. In 13″ by 9″ microwave-safe baking dish, place shrimp, Chinese pea pods, red pepper, corn, green onions, oil, and white wine. Cook, covered, on High (100% power) 5 to 7 minutes, until shrimp just turn pink, stirring halfway through cooking.

2. Stir in lemon juice and dill; season with salt and pepper. Transfer to serving dish, cover and refrigerate 1 to 2 hours.

SUPREME SHRIMP SALAD

Color Index page 79. 6 servings. 377 cals per serving. Good source of vitamin C, iron. Begin 45 minutes ahead.

1 pound medium shrimp, shelled and deveined	*1 10½- to 16-ounce can garbanzo beans, drained*
1 tablespoon lemon juice	
1 tablespoon sherry	*1 small red pepper, thinly sliced*
1 pound small red (new) potatoes, unpeeled and cut into quarters	*½ cup pitted ripe olives, cut in half*
2 tablespoons water	*Zesty Mayonnaise Dressing (page 276)*
½ pound green beans	

1. In 10″ round microwave-safe baking dish, arrange shrimp in a circle with tails pointing toward center. Sprinkle with lemon juice and sherry. Cook, covered, on High (100% power) 3 to 4 minutes, just until shrimp turn pink, turning shrimp over and rotating dish halfway through cooking. Drain, cover, and refrigerate.

2. Meanwhile, in 1-quart microwave-safe casserole, place potatoes and water. Cook, covered, on High 7 to 9 minutes, until tender, stirring once. With slotted spoon, remove potatoes to colander. Cool potatoes under running cold water; transfer to large bowl.

3. To water remaining in casserole, add green beans. Cook, covered, on High 4 to 5 minutes, until tender-crisp, stirring once. Remove beans to colander; cool under running cold water. To potatoes in bowl, add green and garbanzo beans, red pepper, olives, and reserved shrimp. Pour dressing over and toss gently. Serve immediately or cover and refrigerate to serve chilled later.

PREPARATION TIMETABLE

Early in day:	*Prepare Shrimp Salad with Chinese Pea Pods. Prepare green salad ingredients; store in plastic bags in refrigerator. Prepare salad dressing of your choice. Arrange fresh fruit assortment on platter; loosely cover. Prepare Banana-coconut Pie through step 5.*
1¼ hours ahead:	*Prepare Potato Deli Dinner and arrange on serving platter. Prepare Warm Salad of Arugula, Corn, Black Beans, and Avocado; spoon into warmed serving dish.*
Just before serving:	*Complete Banana-coconut Pie. Toss Salad ingredients with dressing. Wrap bread in paper towels and heat on High (100% power).*

Pasta, Grains, and Nuts

PASTA SHAPES · MAIN-DISH PASTA

LAYERED PASTA DISHES AND SAUCES

MAIN-DISH RICE · PILAF

BARLEY, BULGUR, AND CORNMEAL · NUTS

Pasta, Grains, and Nuts

Microwaving pasta is usually no faster than conventional cooking. The microwave is best used to cook the delicious sauces we have created to accompany pasta – they are so quick and easy to prepare and cook in the microwave that many can be ready in the same time it takes to boil the pasta. Although we have given specific types of pasta in our recipes, as in Penne with Double-cheese Sauce (page 286), other pastas such as spaghetti, fettuccine, bow ties, or tagliatelle can be substituted.

Layered and filled pasta dishes do cook more quickly in the microwave, however, and our recipes usually call for a single piece of cookware which saves on dishwashing. The microwave is perfect, too, for reheating pasta dishes because tenderness and flavor are retained. Place a single serving on a microwave-safe dinner plate. Cook, covered, on Medium-High (70% power) 2 minutes, or until bottom of plate is warm and food is hot.

Microwave cooking is the preferred cooking method for rice because there is no need to heat the cooking liquid before adding the rice to it. For other grains, such as bulgur and couscous, where cooking liquid should be boiled first, the liquid can be heated in the microwave before it is combined with the other ingredients.

Nourishing breakfasts can be made instantly in the microwave with quick-cooking grains. Try our Breakfast Oatmeal or Farina: For each serving, pour ⅔ cup water into 4-cup microwave-safe glass measure or cereal bowl; heat on High (100% power) 1½ (1:30) to 2 minutes, until boiling. Stir. Add ⅓ cup quick-cooking oatmeal or 3 tablespoons farina, and a dash of salt. Cook 1 to 2 minutes longer, until mixture thickens. If you like, add 2 tablespoons strawberry preserves, or ¼ cup applesauce with a dash of cinnamon and sugar to taste. Stir well and serve immediately.

Nuts can be blanched, peeled, and toasted in the microwave. On page 294 we give easy-to-follow directions for these techniques, plus quick-cooking ideas for a delicious variety of spiced nuts.

ATTRACTIVELY MOLDED RICE

Molded rice always looks attractive and is so easy to prepare. Use large molds or rings for parties, small molds for individual servings. Lightly oil molds and fill with hot cooked rice, gently pressing down. Turn out onto attractive plate or platter. Serve hot or chilled.

Saffron-flavored rice ring (left) filled with chopped cooked ham and cherry tomatoes; garnished with mixed salad greens.

White and wild rice molded together in ramekin (right). Here with poached salmon garnished with mayonnaise and dill, mixed salad greens, and lemon slices.

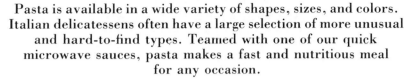

Pasta Shapes

Pasta is available in a wide variety of shapes, sizes, and colors. Italian delicatessens often have a large selection of more unusual and hard-to-find types. Teamed with one of our quick microwave sauces, pasta makes a fast and nutritious meal for any occasion.

Cappelletti: *Small hat-shaped pasta*

Fusilli: *Long spirals or coils of various lengths*

Bow ties or Butterflies: *Crimped in center with frilly edges*

Spaghetti: *Long, thin "strings;"* **spaghettini** *is thinner*

Whole-wheat spaghetti: *Made from whole-wheat flour*

Linguine: *Thin, flat ribbon noodles*

Small Pasta Shapes: *Letters, shells, bows, stars, and animals; for soups and children's dishes*

Orzo: *Small, rice-shaped pasta; for soups and casserole dishes*

Lasagna: *Extra wide noodles, with ruffled edges*

Fettuccine/Tagliatelle: *Flat ribbon noodles, about ¼ inch wide*

Wide Egg Noodles: *Flat, wide noodles, available in white or green*

Manicotti: *Large, ribbed tubes with angled ends for stuffing*

Rigatoni: *Short-cut, straight, ridged tubes*

Cannelloni: *Large, smooth tubes for stuffing*

Shells: *Shell shapes in various sizes; extra-large shells can be stuffed*

Rotelle or Corkscrews: *short spiral, coil, or spring shapes*

Wheels: *Cartwheel or wagon-wheel shapes*

Penne: *Short, tubular "quills" with angled ends*

Main-dish Pasta

SPAGHETTI WITH MEAT AND TOMATO SAUCE

Color Index page 80. 560 cals per serving. Good source of vitamin A, riboflavin, thiamine, niacin, vitamin C, iron. Begin 25 minutes ahead.

Ingredients	For 4	For 2	For 1
Carrot, chopped	1 carrot	½ carrot	¼ carrot
Water	2 tablespoons	1 tablespoon	2 teaspoons
Ground beef	12 ounces	6 ounces	3 ounces
Mushrooms, cut into quarters	4 ounces	2 ounces	1 ounce
Small onion, chopped	1 onion	½ onion	¼ onion
Small zucchini, chopped	1 zucchini	½ zucchini	¼ zucchini
Garlic clove, minced	1 garlic clove	to taste	to taste
1 8-ounce can tomatoes	2 cans	1 can	½ can
1 6-ounce can tomato paste	1 can	½ can	¼ can
Basil	½ teaspoon	¼ teaspoon	⅛ teaspoon
Dry red wine (optional)	2 tablespoons	1 tablespoon	1½ teaspoons
Salt and pepper	to taste	to taste	to taste
1 8-ounce package spaghetti or other pasta	1 package	½ package	¼ package
Parsley for garnish	garnish	garnish	garnish
Microwave cookware	2-quart soufflé dish	1-quart soufflé dish	1-quart soufflé dish
Time on High (100% power)			
Carrot	3 to 5 minutes	2 to 3 minutes	1 to 2 minutes
With ground beef	4 to 6 minutes	3 to 4 minutes	2 to 3 minutes
With tomatoes	8 to 10 minutes	6 to 7 minutes	4 to 5 minutes

1 In soufflé dish (see Chart), place carrot and water. Cook, covered, on High for time in Chart, or until carrot is tender. Drain.

2 To carrot, add ground beef, mushrooms, onion, zucchini, and garlic; stir. Cook, covered, on High for time in Chart, or until meat just loses its pink color, stirring twice.

3 To meat-vegetable mixture, add tomatoes with their liquid, tomato paste, and basil. If you like, add wine. Season with salt and pepper. Stir well.

4 Cook sauce, covered, on High for time in Chart, or until sauce bubbles, stirring often.

5 Meanwhile, cook pasta conventionally as label directs; drain.

6 *To serve:* Place pasta on warmed dinner plates; ladle sauce over Garnish.

PENNE WITH DOUBLE-CHEESE SAUCE

Color Index page 80. 4 servings. 589 cals per serving. Good source of vitamin A, thiamine, vitamin C, calcium, iron. Begin 20 minutes ahead.

2 medium onions, thinly sliced
2 large red peppers, very thinly sliced
¼ cup olive or salad oil
1 8-ounce package penne or other pasta
½ 8-ounce package mozzarella cheese, cut into ¼-inch cubes
4 ounces fontina cheese, shredded (1 cup)
1 3½-ounce can pitted ripe olives, drained and cut in half
½ cup loosely packed shredded parsley or basil leaves
Salt and pepper to taste

1. In 12″ by 8″ microwave-safe baking dish, combine onions, red peppers, and oil. Cook, covered, on High (100% power) 10 to 12 minutes, until vegetables are tender, stirring twice.
2. Meanwhile, cook pasta conventionally as label directs; drain.
3. Toss pasta and vegetable mixture together with cheeses, olives, shredded parsley or basil, salt, and pepper. Serve immediately on warmed dinner plates.

TAGLIATELLE WITH BACON, MUSHROOMS, AND PEAS

Color Index page 80. 4 servings. 581 cals per serving. Good source of vitamin A, riboflavin, thiamine, niacin, calcium, iron. Begin 25 minutes ahead.

4 slices bacon, diced
½ pound mushrooms, cut in half
2 green onions, sliced
2 tablespoons all-purpose flour
1 cup half-and-half
1 cup milk
½ teaspoon salt
¼ teaspoon pepper
1 10-ounce package frozen peas, thawed
1 8-ounce package tagliatelle or other pasta
½ cup grated Parmesan cheese

1. In 3-quart microwave-safe casserole, place bacon. Cook, covered with paper towel, on High (100% power) 4 to 5 minutes, until browned, stirring halfway through cooking. With slotted spoon, remove to paper towels to drain.
2. To bacon drippings, add mushrooms and green onions. Cook on High 2 minutes. Stir in flour until smooth and blended. Gradually stir in half-and-half and milk. Season with salt and pepper. Cook, covered, on High 8 to 10 minutes, until sauce thickens, stirring often. Meanwhile, cook pasta conventionally as label directs.
3. Into sauce, stir peas. Cook, covered, on High 1 to 2 minutes, until hot.
4. Drain pasta. Toss pasta and sauce together. Transfer to warmed serving dish; sprinkle with Parmesan and diced bacon. Serve immediately.

FETTUCCINE PRIMAVERA

Color Index page 81. 4 servings. 726 cals per serving. Good source of vitamin A, riboflavin, thiamine, niacin, vitamin C, calcium, iron. Begin 40 minutes ahead.

3 small leeks, trimmed
2 tablespoons butter or margarine (¼ stick)
1 bunch broccoli
8 mushrooms, sliced
2 medium zucchini, cut into ¼-inch-thick slices
2 medium peppers (green and red), cut into ½-inch chunks
2 carrots, cut into ¼-inch-thick slices

1 8-ounce package fettuccine or other pasta
2 tablespoons all-purpose flour
2 cups half-and-half
2 medium tomatoes, diced
6 ounces Monterey Jack cheese, shredded (1½ cups)
Salt and pepper to taste

1. Cut leeks lengthwise in half; carefully wash under running cold water. Cut into 1-inch pieces.
2. In 3-quart microwave-safe casserole, place butter or margarine and leeks. Cook, covered, on High (100% power) 3 to 4 minutes, until softened, stirring twice.
3. With sharp knife, trim woody stalk ends from broccoli. Separate flowerets from stalks; peel stalks and slice. Stir broccoli and next 4 ingredients into leeks. Cook, covered, on High 8 to 10 minutes, until vegetables are tender-crisp, stirring twice. Meanwhile, cook pasta conventionally as label directs.
4. In medium microwave-safe bowl, place flour. Gradually stir in half-and-half until smooth. Cook on High 5 to 7 minutes, until sauce bubbles and thickens, stirring occasionally.
5. Drain pasta. To vegetables, add pasta, tomatoes, cheese, and sauce; toss. Cook on High 3 to 5 minutes, until hot, stirring twice. Season.

CHEESE TORTELLINI WITH BROCCOLI AND PINE NUTS

Color Index page 80. 8 servings. 307 cals per serving. Low in cholesterol. Good source of vitamin A, riboflavin, thiamine, niacin, vitamin C, calcium, iron. Begin 25 minutes ahead.

2 small bunches broccoli
⅓ cup olive or salad oil
¼ cup pine nuts
2 garlic cloves, minced
¼ teaspoon crushed red pepper (optional)

1 16-ounce package fresh or frozen cheese-filled tortellini
¼ cup grated Parmesan cheese
Salt to taste

1. With sharp knife, trim woody stalk ends from broccoli. Separate flowerets from stalks; peel stalks and slice.
2. In 12″ by 8″ microwave-safe baking dish, combine broccoli and next 4 ingredients. Cook, covered, on High (100% power) 6 to 9 minutes, until broccoli is tender-crisp, stirring mixture occasionally.
3. Meanwhile, cook pasta conventionally as label directs; drain. In warmed large bowl, lightly toss pasta, broccoli, Parmesan and salt.

You can make colorful and delicious combinations of your favorite fresh vegetables and pasta shapes in your microwave. In our recipe for Bow Ties with Chicken and Vegetables (below), try replacing the bow ties with pasta spirals or shells.

BOW TIES WITH CHICKEN AND VEGETABLES

Color Index page 81. 499 cals per serving. Good source of vitamin A, riboflavin, thiamine, niacin, vitamin C, calcium, iron. Begin 35 minutes ahead.

Ingredients for 4 servings		Microwave cookware
1 pound chicken-breast halves, skinned and boned *1 medium bunch broccoli* *⅓ cup soy sauce* *2 tablespoons cornstarch dissolved in 2 tablespoons sherry* *2 tablespoons sesame or salad oil* *1 garlic clove, minced* *½ teaspoon ground ginger*	*¾ cup water* *½ pound mushrooms, cut in half* *4 green onions, cut into 1-inch pieces* *1 8-ounce package bow ties or other pasta* *1 6-ounce package radishes, sliced*	*3-quart casserole*

1. With sharp knife, cut chicken crosswise into thin strips; set aside. Trim woody stalk ends from broccoli. Separate flowerets from stalks; peel stalks and slice. Set aside.

2. In casserole, combine soy sauce, dissolved cornstarch, oil, garlic, ginger, and water. Cook on High (100% power) 5 minutes, or until sauce thickens, stirring halfway through cooking.

3. To sauce, add broccoli, mushrooms, and green onions; stir to coat. Cook, covered, on High 5 to 7 minutes, until vegetables are tender-crisp, stirring halfway through cooking.

4. Into vegetable mixture, stir chicken and radishes. Cook, covered, on High 3 to 4 minutes, until chicken is fork-tender, stirring halfway through cooking.

5. Meanwhile, cook pasta conventionally as label directs; drain and transfer to warmed large bowl.

6. *To serve:* Add chicken and vegetables to pasta and toss to mix. Serve immediately.

Layered Dishes and Sauces

Save on preparation, cooking, and clean-up time by using the microwave for cooking the sauce and the top of the stove for cooking the pasta. In our Lasagna (below), we have created a classic Italian-style dish: a rich, meat-based sauce layered with ricotta, mozzarella and lasagna noodles.

LASAGNA

Color Index page 83. 281 cals per serving. Good source of vitamin A, riboflavin, thiamine, niacin, calcium, iron. Begin 1¾ hours ahead.

Ingredients for 10 servings		Microwave cookware
1 pound ground beef 2 16-ounce jars spaghetti sauce ½ 6-ounce can tomato paste 1 15- to 16-ounce container ricotta cheese (2 cups) 2 eggs	⅔ 16-ounce package lasagna noodles (about 14 noodles) 1 16-ounce package mozzarella cheese, thinly sliced ½ cup grated Parmesan cheese	2-quart soufflé dish 13" by 9" baking dish

1 In soufflé dish, place ground beef. Cook on High (100% power) 5 to 7 minutes, until meat just loses its pink color, stirring occasionally.

2 Into ground beef, stir spaghetti sauce and tomato paste until blended. Cook, covered, on High 5 to 7 minutes, until boiling, stirring occasionally. Uncover and cook on High 5 to 7 minutes longer.

3 Meanwhile, in medium bowl, beat ricotta and eggs until smooth. Cook pasta conventionally as label directs; drain.

4 Cover bottom of baking dish with thin layer of meat sauce. Arrange a third of noodles over sauce, overlapping if necessary. Top with a third of ricotta mixture, then with a third of remaining meat sauce and a third of mozzarella. Repeat layers twice, finishing with mozzarella.

5 Cook lasagna, covered, on Medium (50% power) 25 to 35 minutes, until cheese melts and meat sauce bubbles, rotating dish halfway through cooking. Let lasagna stand, covered loosely with foil, on heat-safe surface 15 to 20 minutes.

6 Uncover lasagna. With spoon, sprinkle top of lasagna evenly with Parmesan. Serve hot on warmed dinner plates.

LASAGNA ROLLS WITH SPINACH AND MUSHROOMS

Color Index page 83. 4 servings. 630 cals per serving. Good source of vitamin A, riboflavin, thiamine, niacin, vitamin C, calcium, iron. Begin 1¼ hours ahead.

2 tablespoons salad oil
2 garlic cloves, minced
⅓ pound mushrooms, sliced
2 10-ounce packages frozen chopped spinach, thawed
1 8-ounce package cream cheese
Salt, ground nutmeg, and ground red pepper to taste

8 lasagna noodles, cooked
2 cups Creamy Tomato Sauce (below) or Basic White Sauce (page 381)
Parsley sprigs for garnish

1. In 13" by 9" microwave-safe baking dish, place oil, garlic, and mushrooms. Cook, covered, on High (100% power) 2 to 3 minutes, until mushrooms are tender, stirring twice.
2. Squeeze spinach to remove excess moisture. Stir into mushroom mixture. Cook on High 5 to 7 minutes, stirring twice. Stir in cream cheese until well blended. Season with salt, nutmeg, and ground red pepper. Transfer spinach mixture to medium bowl.
3. With sharp knife, cut each lasagna noodle crosswise in half. Spread 2 tablespoons of spinach mixture on each noodle half. Roll up noodles jelly-roll fashion.
4. In same baking dish, arrange rolls, seam side down, in single layer. Pour tomato or white sauce over rolls. Cook, covered, on High 5 minutes. Reduce power level to Medium (50% power) and cook 10 to 15 minutes longer, until sauce bubbles, rotating dish halfway through cooking. Let stand, covered loosely, on heat-safe surface 10 minutes. Garnish lasagna rolls with parsley sprigs and serve immediately.

CREAMY TOMATO SAUCE

Color Index page 80. Makes 2 cups. 246 cals per cup. Begin 20 minutes ahead.

¾ 16-ounce can crushed tomatoes
½ cup heavy or whipping cream
½ teaspoon oregano

1 tablespoon shredded fresh basil or 1½ teaspoons dried
2 garlic cloves, minced
Salt and pepper to taste

1. In 8-cup microwave-safe glass measure, combine tomatoes, cream, oregano, basil, and garlic.
2. Cook sauce on High (100% power) 10 to 15 minutes, until sauce thickens slightly and flavors blend, stirring occasionally. Season with salt and pepper. Serve hot over pasta of your choice.

CHEESE-FILLED JUMBO SHELLS

Color Index page 81. 4 servings. 316 cals per serving. Good source of vitamin A, calcium. Begin 55 minutes ahead.

1 16-ounce package jumbo shell macaroni (about 20 shells)	*1 egg*
1 15- to 16-ounce container ricotta cheese (2 cups)	*¼ cup chopped parsley*
	Salt and pepper to taste
	1 16-ounce jar spaghetti sauce
½ 8-ounce package mozzarella cheese, shredded (1 cup)	*Chopped parsley and grated Romano cheese for garnish*
¼ cup grated Romano cheese	

1. Cook pasta conventionally as label directs. Drain immediately under running warm water to stop cooking (cold water causes shells to break); drain again.

2. In large bowl, combine ricotta, mozzarella, Romano, egg, and chopped parsley. Season with salt and pepper.

3. With spoon, fill each shell with an equal amount of cheese mixture. Into 13″ by 9″ microwave-safe baking dish, pour half the spaghetti sauce. Arrange shells, filled side up, in single layer in dish. Pour remaining sauce over shells. Cook, covered, on High (100% power) 5 minutes. Reduce power level to Medium (50% power) and cook 10 to 15 minutes longer, until sauce bubbles, rotating dish halfway through cooking. Let stand, covered loosely, on heat-safe surface 10 minutes before serving.

4. *To serve:* On warmed serving platter, arrange filled shells; spoon sauce over. Garnish with chopped parsley and grated Romano cheese. Serve immediately.

MADE-IN-MINUTES SPAGHETTI SAUCE

Color Index page 80. Makes 6 cups. 410 cals per cup. Begin 25 minutes ahead.

1 pound ground beef	*1 6-ounce can tomato paste*
¼ pound mushrooms, sliced	*¾ teaspoon salt*
1 onion, chopped	*½ teaspoon basil*
1 garlic clove, minced	*½ teaspoon thyme leaves*
1 28-ounce can tomatoes	
1 teaspoon sugar	

1. In large microwave-safe bowl, place ground beef, mushrooms, onion, and garlic. Cook on High (100% power) 5 minutes, or just until meat loses its pink color, stirring occasionally.

2. Into meat mixture, stir tomatoes with liquid, sugar, tomato paste, salt, basil, and thyme leaves. Cook, covered, on High 8 minutes, stirring occasionally. Reduce power level to Medium (50% power) and cook 10 minutes longer, stirring occasionally. Serve hot over pasta of your choice.

Vary the fillings for large pasta shells or tubes. Instead of the usual cheese- or tomato-based fillings, try a stuffing of ground beef or veal, as we have in our Meat-filled Manicotti (below). These can make a substantial evening meal served with a crunchy mixed salad.

MEAT-FILLED MANICOTTI

Color Index page 83. 839 cals per serving. Good source of riboflavin, thiamine, niacin, calcium, iron. Begin 1½ hours ahead.

Ingredients for 4 servings		Microwave cookware
1 tablespoon olive or salad oil	*1 tablespoon tomato paste*	13″ by 9″ baking dish
1 medium onion, chopped	*½ cup dried currants*	
2 celery stalks, chopped	*⅓ cup pine nuts*	
½ pound ground beef	*1 8-ounce package manicotti shells*	
½ pound ground veal	*2 cups Basic White Sauce (page 381) or Creamy Tomato Sauce (page 288)*	
1 teaspoon oregano		
1 teaspoon basil	*½ cup grated Parmesan cheese*	
1 bay leaf		
1 8- to 8¼-ounce can crushed tomatoes	*Basil leaves for garnish*	

1 In baking dish, combine oil, onion, and celery. Cook, covered, on High (100% power) 3 to 4 minutes, until vegetables are soft, stirring halfway through cooking.

2 Into vegetables stir ground beef and veal. Cook on High 8 to 10 minutes, just until meat loses its pink color, stirring occasionally. Stir in oregano, basil, bay, crushed tomatoes, tomato paste, currants, and pine nuts. Cook on High 10 to 15 minutes, stirring occasionally.

3 Meanwhile, cook pasta conventionally as label directs. Drain immediately under running warm water to stop cooking (cold water causes manicotti to break); drain again. Prepare white or tomato sauce. Cover and keep warm.

4 From meat mixture, discard cooking juices. Transfer to large bowl. With spoon, fill each manicotti shell with an equal amount of meat mixture. In same baking dish, arrange shells in single layer.

5 Over shells, pour white or tomato sauce. Cook, covered, on High 5 minutes. Reduce power level to Medium (50% power) and cook 10 to 15 minutes longer, until sauce bubbles, rotating dish once.

6 On heat-safe surface, let manicotti stand in dish, covered loosely, 5 to 10 minutes. Just before serving, sprinkle with Parmesan, and garnish with basil.

Main-dish Rice

ARROZ CON POLLO

Color Index page 82. 644 cals per serving. Good source of thiamine, niacin, vitamin C, iron. Begin 55 minutes ahead.

Ingredients	For 4	For 2	For 1
Olive or salad oil	4 tablespoons	2 tablespoons	1 tablespoon
Onion, chopped	1 large onion	1 small onion	½ small onion
Celery stalks, chopped	2 stalks	1 stalk	½ stalk
Green pepper, chopped	1 large	1 small	½ small
Smoked ham, chopped	4 ounces	2 ounces	1 ounce
Turmeric	½ teaspoon	¼ teaspoon	⅛ teaspoon
Regular long-grain rice	1 cup	½ cup	¼ cup
Chicken Broth (page 125) or canned broth	2 cups	1 cup	½ cup
Bay leaf	1 leaf	½ leaf	to taste
Chicken pieces	1½ pounds	¾ pound	⅓ pound
All-purpose flour	½ cup	½ cup	⅓ cup
Salt	to taste	to taste	to taste
Pimento and parsley for garnish	garnish	garnish	garnish
Microwave cookware	13″ by 9″ baking dish	9″ by 9″ baking dish	8″ by 8″ baking dish
Time on High (100% power) Chicken and rice	5 minutes	4 minutes	2½ (2:30) minutes
Time on Medium (50% power) Chicken and rice	25 to 30 minutes	10 to 15 minutes	7 to 10 minutes
Standing time	5 minutes	5 minutes	3 minutes

1 In skillet, over medium heat, combine half the oil and next 5 ingredients. Stir 2 minutes.

2 In baking dish, place vegetable-ham mixture. Add rice, broth and bay leaf; stir.

3 Pat chicken pieces dry with paper towels. On waxed paper, place flour. Coat chicken in flour.

4 Heat remaining oil in same skillet, over medium heat. Add chicken and cook, in batches if necessary, 5 minutes, or until browned. Transfer to baking dish.

5 Cook, covered tightly with plastic wrap, on High for time in Chart, or until broth boils. Reduce power to Medium and cook for time in Chart, turning chicken once.

6 On heat-safe surface, let stand, covered, for time in Chart, or until liquid is absorbed and rice is tender. Before serving, season with salt; garnish.

ITALIAN SAUSAGE, RICE, AND BEANS

Color Index page 83. 4 servings. 562 cals per serving. Good source of thiamine, niacin, calcium, iron. Begin 35 minutes ahead.

½ pound sweet Italian-sausage links
1 medium onion, sliced
2 garlic cloves, minced
1 15¼- to 19-ounce can red kidney beans, drained and rinsed
1 14½- to 16-ounce can crushed tomatoes

1 beef-flavor bouillon cube or envelope
1 teaspoon oregano
4 cups Hot Cooked Rice (page 293)
¼ cup grated Parmesan cheese
Basil leaves for garnish

1. With sharp knife, cut sausage into 1½-inch pieces; place in 12″ by 8″ microwave-safe baking dish. Cook, covered with paper towels, on High (100% power) 5 minutes, until meat is no longer pink, stirring occasionally. Add onion and garlic. Cook on High 2 to 3 minutes, until onion is hot, stirring halfway through cooking.
2. To sausage mixture, add kidney beans, tomatoes, bouillon, and oregano; stir. Cook, covered, on Medium (50% power) 10 to 15 minutes, until mixture bubbles, stirring occasionally. Stir in rice. Cook on High 3 to 5 minutes, until hot. Just before serving, stir in Parmesan and garnish.

CHINESE-STYLE RICE WITH PORK

Color Index page 82. 4 servings. 393 cals per serving. Good source of thiamine, iron. Begin 35 minutes ahead.

½ pound boneless pork loin cutlets, cut into 1-inch cubes
1 medium onion, chopped
1 celery stalk, sliced
1 medium red pepper, chopped
1 tablespoon peanut or salad oil
1 cup regular long-grain rice

2 cups Beef Broth (page 125) or canned broth
2 tablespoons soy sauce
2 garlic cloves, minced
1 tablespoon minced peeled gingerroot
⅛ teaspoon hot-pepper sauce
¼ cup chopped coriander or parsley

1. In 12″ by 8″ microwave-safe baking dish, combine pork, onion, celery, red pepper, and oil. Cook on High (100% power) 3 to 5 minutes, until meat is no longer pink, stirring twice.
2. Into meat mixture, stir rice and broth. Cook, covered tightly with plastic wrap, on High 5 minutes. Reduce power level to Medium (50% power) and cook 20 to 25 minutes longer, until liquid is absorbed and rice is tender.
3. Meanwhile, in small bowl, combine soy sauce, garlic, gingerroot, hot-pepper sauce, and chopped coriander or parsley. Pour over hot rice, mix well, and serve immediately.

MILANESE-STYLE RISOTTO

Color Index page 81. 4 servings. 333 cals per serving. Low in cholesterol. Good source of calcium, iron. Begin 40 minutes ahead.

2 tablespoons butter or margarine	2 tablespoons lemon juice
1 medium onion, minced	1/8 teaspoon powdered saffron
2 garlic cloves, minced	
1 cup arborio rice (Italian short-grain rice)	1/2 10-ounce package frozen peas, thawed
2 cups Chicken Broth (page 125) or canned broth	1/2 cup grated Parmesan cheese
	Salt and pepper to taste
	Basil leaves for garnish

1. In 12" by 8" microwave-safe baking dish, place butter or margarine, onion, and garlic. Cook on High (100% power) 2 to 3 minutes, until onion softens, stirring twice. Add rice; stir to coat. Cook on High 3 minutes, stirring twice.

2. Into rice mixture, stir broth, lemon juice, and saffron. Cook, covered, on High 15 to 20 minutes, until most of liquid is absorbed and rice is tender, stirring halfway through cooking.

3. Into risotto, stir peas. Cook on High 2 to 3 minutes. Stir in Parmesan; season with salt and pepper. Let stand, covered, on heat-safe surface 5 minutes. Garnish with basil before serving.

RED BEANS AND RICE

Color Index page 82. 4 servings. 534 cals per serving. Low in cholesterol. Good source of thiamine, calcium, iron. Begin 40 minutes ahead.

3 slices bacon, diced	2 15¼- to 19-ounce cans red kidney beans, drained and rinsed
1 medium onion, diced	
1 celery stalk, diced	
1 bay leaf	Hot-pepper sauce to taste
1 teaspoon ground cumin	4 cups Hot Cooked Rice (page 293)
1 teaspoon oregano	
1/4 teaspoon ground red pepper	Parsley sprigs for garnish
2 tablespoons tomato paste	

1. In 12" by 8" microwave-safe baking dish, place bacon. Cook, covered with paper towels, on High (100% power) 3 to 4 minutes, until bacon is browned, stirring twice. With slotted spoon, remove bacon to paper towels to drain.

2. Into drippings, stir onion and next 5 ingredients. Cook on High 3 to 4 minutes, until vegetables soften, stirring twice.

3. Into vegetables, stir tomato paste and kidney beans. Cook on Medium (50% power) 10 to 15 minutes, until mixture thickens slightly, stirring occasionally. Season with hot-pepper sauce.

4. *To serve:* On warmed dinner plates, ladle bean mixture over rice; sprinkle with diced bacon. Garnish with parsley.

SAVORY RICE

Color Index page 81. 398 cals per serving. Good source of vitamin A, calcium, iron. Begin 45 minutes ahead.

Ingredients	For 4	For 2	For 1
Butter or margarine	2 tablespoons	1 tablespoon	2 teaspoons
Onion, chopped	1 medium	1 small	1/2 small
Green pepper, chopped	1 medium	1 small	1/2 small
Regular long-grain rice	1 cup	1/2 cup	1/4 cup
Chicken Broth (page 125) or canned broth	2 cups	1 cup	1/2 cup
Cheddar or fontina cheese, shredded	4 ounces (1 cup)	2 ounces (1/2 cup)	1 ounce (1/4 cup)
Sour cream	1/2 cup	1/4 cup	2 tablespoons
Salt and pepper	to taste	to taste	to taste
Parsley or coriander sprigs for garnish	garnish	garnish	garnish
Microwave cookware	12" by 8" baking dish	8" by 8" baking dish	8" by 8" baking dish
Time on High (100% power)			
Butter or margarine	45 seconds	30 to 45 seconds	30 seconds
With vegetables and rice	3 to 4 minutes	2 to 3 minutes	1 to 2 minutes
With broth	5 minutes	4 minutes	2 minutes
Time on Medium (50% power)			
Vegetables, rice, and broth	15 to 20 minutes	10 to 12 minutes	7 to 10 minutes
With cheese	2 to 3 minutes	2 minutes	1½ (1:30) minutes

1 In baking dish (see Chart), place butter or margarine. Heat, covered, on High for time in Chart, or until melted.

2 To melted butter or margarine, add onion, green pepper, and rice; stir to coat.

3 Cook, covered tightly with plastic wrap, on High for time in Chart, or until vegetables soften, stirring once.

4 Into vegetables and rice, pour broth; stir. Cook, covered tightly with plastic wrap, on High for time in Chart, or until rice mixture boils.

5 Reduce power level to Medium and cook for time in Chart, or until liquid is absorbed and rice is tender.

6 Into rice mixture, stir cheese and sour cream. Season with salt and pepper. Cook, covered, on Medium for time in Chart. Garnish.

After-the-Game Supper

Salami and pepper platter with breadsticks
Spaghetti with Meat and Tomato Sauce, page 286, for 8
Tossed green salad
Garlic Bread, page 308 (double quantity)
Gorgonzola cheese and crackers
Neapolitan ice cream and sugar wafers (bought)

PREPARATION TIMETABLE

Early in day:	*Prepare Spaghetti with Meat and Tomato Sauce, through step 4, in 2 batches. Cover sauce and refrigerate. Prepare salad ingredients: store in plastic bags in refrigerator. Prepare salad dressing of your choice.*
45 minutes ahead:	*Prepare Garlic Bread but do not cook; wrap in paper towels and set aside. Arrange a selection of sliced salami and fresh peppers on a serving platter with breadsticks. Place Gorgonzola on serving platter with crackers and cover until required.*
Just before serving:	*Cook spaghetti conventionally. Meanwhile, reheat meat and tomato sauce on High (100% power) until bubbling. Drain spaghetti: place on warmed dinner plates and ladle sauce over; garnish. Heat Garlic Bread in microwave. Place salad ingredients in bowl and toss with dressing.*

Pilaf

INDIAN PILAF

Color Index page 82. 4 servings. 383 cals per serving. Low in cholesterol, sodium. Good source of iron. Begin 45 minutes ahead.

3 tablespoons butter or margarine	¼ cup seedless raisins
1 medium onion, diced	2 cups Chicken Broth (page 125) or canned broth
2 garlic cloves, minced	
1 teaspoon ground cumin	¼ cup chopped coriander or parsley
1 teaspoon ground coriander	½ 3½-ounce can sliced blanched almonds
1 cup regular long-grain rice	Coriander sprigs for garnish

1. In 12" by 8" microwave-safe baking dish, place 2 tablespoons butter or margarine. Heat, covered with paper towels, on High (100% power) 45 seconds, or until melted.
2. To butter or margarine, add onion, garlic, and ground spices; stir. Cook, covered, on High 3 to 4 minutes, until onion softens, stirring twice. Stir in rice. Cook, covered, on High 2 minutes.
3. Into rice, stir raisins and broth. Cook, covered tightly with plastic wrap, on High 5 minutes. Reduce power level to Medium (50% power) and cook 20 minutes longer, or until liquid is absorbed and rice is tender. Add chopped coriander or parsley; stir. Let stand, covered loosely, on heat-safe surface 5 minutes.
4. Meanwhile, in 8" skillet, over medium heat, melt remaining butter or margarine; add almonds and cook until golden, stirring frequently.
5. *To serve*: Transfer pilaf to warmed serving platter. Top with almonds and garnish.

WILD RICE AND MUSHROOM PILAF

Color Index page 83. 4 servings. 236 cals per serving. Low in cholesterol. Good source of iron. Begin 1¼ hours ahead.

3 cups water	1 medium onion, chopped
1 chicken-flavor bouillon cube or envelope	¼ pound mushrooms, sliced
1 cup wild rice	¼ teaspoon poultry seasoning
3 tablespoons butter or margarine	Salt to taste

1. Into 2-quart microwave-safe casserole, pour water. Heat on High (100% power) 6 to 8 minutes, until boiling. Stir in bouillon and wild rice. Cook, covered tightly with plastic wrap, on High 30 to 40 minutes, until wild rice is tender. Let stand, covered loosely, on heat-safe surface while preparing mushrooms.
2. In 12" by 8" microwave-safe baking dish, place butter. Heat, covered with paper towels, on High 45 seconds, or until melted. Stir in onion, mushrooms and seasonings. Cook, covered, on High 5 to 7 minutes, until vegetables soften, stirring twice. Stir into rice. Cook, covered, on High 3 to 5 minutes, until hot, stirring twice.

Barley, Bulgur, and Cornmeal

BARLEY WITH WILD MUSHROOMS

Color Index page 83. 4 servings. 260 cals per serving. Low in cholesterol, sodium. Begin 40 minutes ahead.

2 tablespoons salad oil	Salt to taste
1 cup pearl barley	Parsley sprigs for
3 cups Beef Broth (page 125) or canned broth	garnish
¼ ounce dried wild mushrooms, broken into ½-inch pieces	

1. In 2-quart microwave-safe casserole, place oil and barley. Cook, covered, on High (100% power) 5 minutes, stirring twice.
2. To barley, add broth and wild mushrooms; stir to mix well. Cook, covered, on High 20 to 30 minutes, until liquid is absorbed and barley is tender, stirring occasionally. Season and garnish.

BULGUR PILAF WITH PEPPERS

Color Index page 82. 8 servings. 139 cals per serving. Low in cholesterol, sodium. Good source of vitamin C, iron. Begin 45 minutes ahead.

3 cups Chicken Broth (page 125) or canned broth	3 medium peppers (green, yellow, red), cut into ½-inch chunks
1 cup bulgur (cracked wheat)	Salt to taste
2 tablespoons olive or salad oil	2 tablespoons shredded basil leaves
2 garlic cloves, minced	
8 mushrooms, sliced	

1. Into 4-cup microwave-safe glass measure, pour broth. Heat on High (100% power) 5 to 7 minutes, until boiling. In medium bowl, place bulgur; pour boiling broth over bulgur. Let stand, covered, on heat-safe surface 30 minutes.
2. Meanwhile, in 12″ by 8″ microwave-safe baking dish, combine oil, garlic, mushrooms, and green, yellow, and red peppers. Cook on High 8 to 10 minutes, until vegetables are tender, stirring occasionally.
3. Drain bulgur well, squeezing out excess moisture. Stir into pepper-mushroom mixture; season with salt. Cook, covered, on High 4 to 5 minutes, until hot. Stir in shredded basil. Serve hot or cover and refrigerate to serve chilled later.

MAKING HOT COOKED RICE
Cook rice conventionally, or in microwave: In large microwave-safe bowl, combine **1 cup regular long-grain rice, 2 cups water**, and **1 teaspoon salt**. Cook, covered, on High (100% power) 5 minutes. Reduce power level to Medium (50% power) and cook 15 to 20 minutes longer, until liquid is absorbed and rice is tender.

Treat your family to a change from pasta or rice with cornmeal, finely ground corn that can be white or yellow—or even blue! We use yellow cornmeal in our recipe for Polenta with Meat Sauce (below). After cooking, present it in a variety of ways by cutting it with crescent-shaped, star-shaped, or heart-shaped cookie cutters, before topping it with our rich Made-in-minutes Spaghetti Sauce.

POLENTA WITH MEAT SAUCE

Color Index page 83. 612 cals per serving. Good source of vitamin A, niacin, calcium, iron. Begin 50 minutes ahead.

Ingredients for 4 servings		Microwave cookware
4 cups Chicken Broth (page 125) or canned broth	Salt and pepper to taste	8-cup glass measure
1½ cups yellow cornmeal	2 cups Made-in-minutes Spaghetti Sauce (page 289) or 16-ounce jar spaghetti sauce with meat	12″ serving platter
4 tablespoons butter or margarine (½ stick)	¼ cup grated Parmesan cheese	
½ 8-ounce package mozzarella cheese, shredded (1 cup)	Basil leaves for garnish	

1 In glass measure, combine broth and cornmeal. Cook on High (100% power) 12 to 15 minutes, until very thick, stirring occasionally.

2 To measure, add butter or margarine, shredded mozzarella, salt, and pepper; stir.

3 Oil a wax-paper-lined 13″ by 9″ jelly-roll pan. Spread polenta mixture in an even layer in pan. Let cool while preparing sauce.

4 With cookie cutter or knife, cut shapes from cooled polenta. Arrange on serving platter.

5 Spoon sauce over polenta. Cook on High 7 to 10 minutes, until both polenta and sauce are hot.

6 To serve: Sprinkle polenta and sauce with Parmesan, and garnish with basil leaves. Serve hot.

Spiced nuts are always a popular appetizer to serve with drinks or at parties. In the microwave oven, they are so quick and easy to make that you can always have some on hand for unexpected guests. Using our Tex-Mex Mixed Nuts (below) as a guide, you can vary the flavors depending on what nuts and spices you have.

TEX-MEX MIXED NUTS

Color Index page 38. Makes 2 cups. 70 cals per tablespoon. Low in cholesterol. Begin 25 minutes ahead.

12 ounces unsalted mixed nuts	*1½ teaspoons ground cumin*
1 tablespoon salad oil	*½ teaspoon ground cinnamon*
1 tablespoon chili powder	*1 teaspoon rock salt*

1. In 9″ by 9″ microwave-safe baking dish, place nuts and oil; stir to coat. Cook on High (100% power) 2 minutes.
2. Combine remaining ingredients; add to nuts and toss well to combine. Cook on High 3 minutes, stirring twice. With slotted spoon, remove nuts to paper towels to drain and cool completely. Store nuts in airtight container; use within 2 weeks.

Hot-pepper Pecans: Prepare as for Tex-Mex Mixed Nuts (left), using *2 6-ounce cans pecan halves* instead of mixed nuts. In step 2, use *4 teaspoons soy sauce and ¼ teaspoon hot-pepper sauce.* Makes 2 cups. 75 cals per tablespoon.

Curried Almonds: Prepare as for Tex-Mex Mixed Nuts (left), using *4 4½-ounce cans blanched whole almonds* instead of mixed nuts. In step 2, use *2 tablespoons curry powder and 2 teaspoons salt.* Makes 3 cups. 66 cals per tablespoon.

Herbed Pistachios: Prepare as for Tex-Mex Mixed Nuts (left), using *2 6-ounce jars pistachios* instead of mixed nuts. In step 2, use *¼ teaspoon thyme leaves and ¼ teaspoon paprika.* Makes 2 cups. 65 cals per tablespoon.

Cashews with Chili: Prepare as for Tex-Mex Mixed Nuts (left), using *1 12-ounce can unsalted cashews* instead of mixed nuts. In step 2, use *1 tablespoon chili powder* and *1 teaspoon salt.* Makes 2 cups. 66 cals per tablespoon.

Toasting Coconut

In 9″ microwave-safe pie plate, spread contents of *1 7-ounce bag shredded coconut.* Heat on High (100% power) 5 to 6 minutes, until toasted, stirring occasionally.

Blanching Almonds

Into 1-quart microwave-safe bowl, pour *1 cup water.* Heat on High (100% power) 3 to 4 minutes, until boiling. Add *1 cup whole shelled almonds.* Heat on High 1 minute; drain. When cool, rub off skins with fingers or between paper towels; dry on paper towels.

Peeling Chestnuts

With sharp knife, slit shells of *1 cup chestnuts.* Place in 4-cup microwave-safe glass measure with *1 cup water.* Heat, covered, on High (100% power) 2½ (2:30) to 4 minutes, until boiling; boil 1 minute longer. Let stand 5 to 10 minutes. Peel shells and inner skins. Reboil any not open.

Toasting Nuts

In 1-cup microwave-safe glass measure, place *½ cup shelled nuts.* Heat on High (100% power) 2½ (2:30) to 4 minutes, until lightly browned, stirring occasionally.

Breads and Sandwiches

QUICK BREADS · MUFFINS · FRUIT-FLAVORED BUTTERS

HOT CHICKEN, TURKEY, PORK, AND BEEF SANDWICHES

CREATIVE SANDWICHES · QUICK CANAPÉS

SIMPLE CHEESE SPREADS · HOT CHEESE SANDWICHES · PIZZA

Breads and Sandwiches

Traditional hard-crusted breads and rolls cannot be cooked successfully in the microwave because of its moist heat, but quick breads and muffins cook up high and delicately textured. Our range of delicious quick breads and muffins are ideal eaten plain or served with a variety of flavorful spreads. We also offer information on cooking and reheating muffins made from a package. Special microwave muffin pans that produce evenly-cooked muffins of a uniform shape are widely available, but 6-ounce custard cups lined with a double thickness of paper liners can be used instead. During cooking, quick breads should be elevated on a rack, trivet, or ramekins turned upside down, and the pans should be rotated frequently. They are done when they spring back if lightly touched with a finger and when a toothpick inserted in the center comes out clean, but they may look paler than if conventionally baked and may be moist to the touch. Any moist spots will dry during standing time in pan.

Our assortment of sandwiches is suitable for almost every meal, from an afternoon snack to a hearty one-dish supper. We have used a wide range of breads as sandwich bases, including sliced white, whole-wheat, French loaves, croissants, pitas, and bagels. Our fillings are guaranteed to cater to all tastes, too.

Most breads reheat successfully in the microwave if they are wrapped in paper towels to absorb moisture. You can also reheat breads and rolls in a straw basket, provided it has no metal parts. A roll, bagel, or hamburger bun can be reheated in 10 to 15 seconds on High (100% power), so also can a Danish pastry, but use caution in handling it; sugar coating will be very hot to the touch. Baked goods should be just warmed through, otherwise they will become tough.

Use your microwave, too, for defrosting and warming frozen breads, pancakes, and muffins, taking from the freezer individual slices or pieces as needed.

SANDWICHES WITH A DIFFERENCE

Use the microwave to soften our Simple Cheese Spreads (page 307) and any other firm fillings to create sandwiches with a difference for a lunch or light supper. Make pretty open-face sandwiches with a variety of thinly sliced meats, fish, shellfish, or vegetables.

Whole-wheat toast triangles (below) topped with Smoked Salmon and Chive Spread and latticed smoked salmon, with herbs for garnish.

Whole-wheat bread rounds (below) spread with cream cheese, then topped with cooked egg slices and tiny shrimp; garnished with chervil.

Tortilla chips (above) topped with refried beans, sour cream, and taco sauce, garnished with coriander and Lime Twists (page 132).

Rye-bread sandwiches (above) filled with cooked ham and Cheddar Cheese Spread, garnished with salad greens.

296

Quick Breads

CRANBERRY-NUT BREAD

Color Index page 86. 12 servings. 182 cals per serving. Low in cholesterol, sodium.
Begin 40 minutes ahead.

½ cup all-purpose flour
¾ cup graham-cracker crumbs
½ teaspoon baking soda
½ teaspoon baking powder
½ cup packed dark-brown sugar
½ cup chopped walnuts

1 cup fresh or frozen cranberries, coarsely chopped
1 tablespoon grated orange peel
1 egg
½ cup milk
⅓ cup salad oil
¼ cup orange juice

1. Line bottom of 9″ by 5″ microwave-safe glass loaf pan with paper towel; set aside.
2. In large bowl, combine flour, graham-cracker crumbs, baking soda, baking powder, and sugar. Add walnuts, cranberries, and orange peel.
3. In 4-cup glass measure, with whisk, beat egg, milk, salad oil, and orange juice until blended. Into flour mixture, pour egg mixture all at once. Stir just until flour is moistened.
4. Into prepared loaf pan, spoon batter. Elevate on trivet, rack, or ramekins turned upside down. Cook, covered loosely with waxed paper, on Medium (50% power) 7 to 10 minutes, until bread springs back when lightly touched with finger, rotating pan a quarter turn every 2 minutes. Let bread stand in pan on heat-safe surface 10 minutes.
5. Invert bread onto rack; carefully remove paper towel. When bread is cool, slice and serve. If you like, wrap in plastic wrap and store in refrigerator up to 1 week.

POLENTA BREAD TOASTS

Color Index page 86. 12 servings. 182 cals per serving. Low in cholesterol, sodium.
Begin 55 minutes ahead.

4 cups Chicken Broth (page 125) or canned broth
1½ cups cornmeal
½ cup golden raisins

4 tablespoons butter or margarine (½ stick)
½ cup pine nuts, toasted
⅓ cup grated Parmesan cheese

1. Lightly oil 9″ by 5″ microwave-safe glass loaf pan; set aside.
2. In 8-cup microwave-safe glass measure, with whisk, beat broth and cornmeal until smooth. Cook on High (100% power) 12 to 15 minutes, until very thick, stirring occasionally. Stir in raisins and remaining ingredients.
3. Into prepared loaf pan, spoon batter. Elevate on trivet, rack or ramekins turned upside down. Cook on High 5 minutes or until firmly set. Let polenta stand in pan until cool.
4. Unmold bread and cut into ¾-inch-thick slices. Place on cookie sheet and toast on both sides under preheated broiler. Serve hot with butter or margarine, on its own or as an accompaniment to soups and salads.

Quick breads are traditionally made without yeast, relying on baking soda and baking powder to rise. The cranberries in our Cranberry-nut Bread (left) make this an attractive snack when served with pats of butter or margarine, and Zucchini Bread (below) is always popular as a snack with tea or coffee, or as an after-school treat.

ZUCCHINI BREAD

Color Index page 86. 158 cals per serving. Begin 35 minutes ahead.

Ingredients for 12 servings		Microwave cookware
1 cup all-purpose flour ⅓ cup corn-flake crumbs ¾ cup sugar 1½ teaspoons baking powder ½ teaspoon salt ½ cup chopped walnuts	2 tablespoons poppy seeds 2 eggs ⅓ cup salad oil 2 small zucchini, shredded (1 cup) 1 teaspoon grated lemon peel	9″ by 5″ glass loaf pan Trivet, rack, or ramekins

1 Line bottom of loaf pan with paper towel. Set aside.

2 In large bowl, combine flour, corn-flake crumbs, sugar, baking powder, salt, chopped walnuts, and poppy seeds.

3 In 4-cup glass measure, with whisk, beat eggs. Stir in oil, zucchini, and lemon peel.

4 Into flour mixture, pour egg-zucchini mixture all at once. Stir just until flour is moistened.

5 Into prepared loaf pan, spoon batter. Elevate on trivet, rack, or ramekins turned upside down. Cook, covered loosely with waxed paper, on Medium (50% power) 7 to 10 minutes, until bread springs back when lightly touched with finger, rotating pan a quarter turn every 2 minutes.

6 On heat-safe surface, let bread stand in pan 10 minutes. Invert bread onto rack; carefully remove paper towel. When bread is cool, slice and serve. If you like, wrap in plastic wrap and store in refrigerator up to 1 week.

Use your microwave to make quick and easy muffins, either from a muffin mix (below), or using our original recipes on page 299. If possible, use a special microwave-safe 6-cup muffin pan.

Line each muffin-pan cup with a double thickness of paper liners and fill only half full. If you do not have one, use 6-ounce custard cups lined with a double thickness of paper liners. For even cooking, arrange cups in a circle, ½ inch apart; rearrange halfway through cooking. If cooking more than 6 muffins, cook in batches. Muffins made in the microwave are best eaten fresh, but they can be frozen and then reheated (see Chart, below).

MUFFINS FROM A MIX

Makes 14 muffins. 188 cals each. Low in cholesterol. Begin 25 minutes ahead.

1 19.1-ounce box muffin mix with topping
1 egg
¼ cup water
½ cup plain or vanilla low-fat yogurt

1. Into large bowl, pour muffin mix, reserving topping; set aside.
2. In 4-cup glass measure, with whisk, beat egg, water, and yogurt. Pour into muffin mix. Stir just until muffin mix is moistened.
3. Line 6 microwave-safe muffin-pan cups with a double thickness of paper liners. Spoon half the batter into muffin-pan cups, filling only half full. Cook on High (100% power) according to Chart (below); sprinkle with half the topping.
4. Lift muffins from muffin-pan cups; remove outer papers. Place muffins on rack to cool.
5. Re-line muffin-pan cups and repeat with remaining batter and topping.

COOKING AND REHEATING MUFFINS IN THE MICROWAVE

You can use your own recipe for muffins, following this Chart for timing. Or, for "just-baked" freshness every morning, reheat frozen muffins in the microwave for time in Chart, wrapping muffins in paper towel. If you are cooking or reheating only 1 muffin, be sure to place in center of the oven floor.

Muffins	Cooking from a mix and homemade on High (100% power)	Defrosting and reheating on High (100% power)
1 muffin	*30 to 45 seconds*	*10 to 15 seconds*
2 muffins	*45 seconds to 1¼ (1:15) minutes*	*20 to 30 seconds*
4 muffins	*1½ (1:30) to 2 minutes*	*45 seconds to 1 minute*
6 muffins	*2½ (2:30) to 3 minutes*	*1 to 1½ (1:30) minutes*

FRUIT-FLAVORED BUTTERS

Follow our easy instructions for Fruit-flavored Butters to turn muffins, tea breads, and other quick breads into something special for a tasty breakfast treat or after-school snack.

To soften butter for Fruit-flavored Butters: In small microwave-safe bowl, place *8 tablespoons butter or margarine (1 stick)*. Heat, covered with paper towel, on Medium-Low (30% power) 30 to 40 seconds, just until softened.

Orange Butter: Into softened butter (above), stir *grated peel of 1 orange* and *2 tablespoons orange juice*. 8 servings. 108 cals per serving.

Strawberry or Raspberry Butter: Into softened butter (above), stir *2 tablespoons strawberry or raspberry jam or preserves*. 8 servings. 116 cals per serving.

Cinnamon-apple Butter: Into softened butter (above), stir *2 tablespoons apple butter or 2 tablespoons applesauce*, and *½ teaspoon ground cinnamon*. 8 servings. 109 cals per serving.

Homemade Muffins

BANANA MUFFINS

Color Index page 84. Makes 12. 82 cals each. Low in cholesterol, sodium. Begin 25 minutes ahead.

⅔ cup all-purpose flour
1 teaspoon baking powder
3 tablespoons sugar
¼ teaspoon salt
½ teaspoon grated orange peel
1 egg yolk
2 tablespoons salad oil

2 tablespoons milk
1 cup mashed bananas (about 2 very ripe medium bananas)
¼ teaspoon ground cinnamon
⅛ teaspoon ground nutmeg

1. In large bowl, combine flour, baking powder, 2 tablespoons sugar, salt, and orange peel.
2. In 4-cup glass measure, with fork, combine egg yolk, oil, milk, and mashed bananas until blended. To flour mixture, add banana mixture all at once. Stir just until flour is moistened.
3. Line 6 microwave-safe muffin-pan cups with a double thickness of paper liners. Spoon half the batter into muffin-pan cups, filling only half full.
4. In bowl, combine remaining sugar, cinnamon, and nutmeg. Sprinkle muffins with half the topping mixture. Cook on High (100% power) for time in Chart (page 298), rotating pan halfway through cooking. Lift muffins from muffin-pan cups; remove outer papers. Place muffins on rack to cool. Re-line muffin-pan cups and repeat with remaining batter and topping.

GINGERBREAD MUFFINS

Color Index page 84. Makes 12. 228 cals each. Begin 20 minutes ahead.

1½ cups all-purpose flour
½ cup packed dark-brown sugar
1 teaspoon baking soda
¼ teaspoon salt
1 teaspoon ground ginger
½ teaspoon ground cinnamon

¼ teaspoon ground cloves
¼ teaspoon ground nutmeg
8 tablespoons butter or margarine (1 stick)
2 eggs
½ cup sour cream
½ cup molasses

1. In large bowl, combine flour and next 7 ingredients. Set aside.
2. In 4-cup microwave-safe glass measure, place butter or margarine. Heat, covered with paper towel, on High (100% power) 1½ (1:30) to 2 minutes, until melted. Let cool slightly. Whisk in eggs, sour cream, and molasses until blended. Into flour mixture, pour egg mixture all at once. Stir just until flour is moistened.
3. Line 6 microwave-safe muffin-pan cups with a double thickness of paper liners. Spoon half the batter into muffin-pan cups, filling only half full. Cook on High for time in Chart (page 298), rotating pan halfway through cooking. Lift muffins from muffin-pan cups; remove outer papers. Place muffins on rack to cool. Re-line muffin-pan cups and repeat with remaining batter.

Muffins are a great favorite for breakfasts and snacks. Serve them warm with butter or margarine, or one of our Fruit-flavored Butters (page 298) as a special treat. You can also make a big batch, store the muffins in the freezer in plastic bags or an airtight container, and reheat in the microwave for piping-hot muffins in seconds.

SOUTH-OF-THE-BORDER CORN MUFFINS

Color Index page 84. 109 cals each. Begin 20 minutes ahead.

Ingredients for 12 muffins		Microwave cookware
3 slices bacon, diced 2 green onions, sliced 2 tablespoons chopped coriander or parsley 1 cup all-purpose flour ½ cup cornmeal 2 teaspoons sugar 1 tablespoon baking powder	2 ounces Monterey Jack cheese with Jalapeño Pepper ("Pepper Jack"), shredded (½ cup) 2 eggs ⅓ cup milk	9" pie plate Muffin pan

1 In pie plate, place bacon. Cook, covered with paper towel, on High (100% power) 3 to 4 minutes, until bacon is browned, stirring twice.

2 Into bacon, stir green onions and coriander or parsley. Cook on High 1 minute. Set aside.

3 In large bowl, combine flour, cornmeal, sugar, baking powder, and cheese. Set aside.

4 In 4-cup glass measure, with fork, beat eggs and milk until blended. Into flour mixture, pour egg mixture all at once. Stir just until flour is moistened. Quickly fold in bacon mixture.

5 Line 6 muffin-pan cups with a double thickness of paper liners. Spoon half the batter into muffin-pan cups, filling only half full. Cook on High for time in Chart (page 298), rotating pan halfway through cooking.

6 Lift muffins from muffin-pan cups; remove outer papers. Place muffins on rack to cool. Reline muffin-pan cups and repeat with remaining batter.

Hot Chicken and Turkey Sandwiches

Remember that several thin slices of meat or poultry microwave more efficiently than 1 thick slice, so slice meat thinly across the grain, or use pounded cutlets or ground meat, as we have done in all our hearty sandwiches. Microwave the sandwiches only for the time given – they're best served warm, not hot. Overcooking can also dry out the fillings.

CHICKEN CLUB SANDWICHES

Color Index page 87. 424 cals per serving. Good source of niacin, iron. Begin 55 minutes ahead.

Ingredients for 4 servings		Microwave cookware

8 slices bacon
1 egg, beaten
1 cup chicken-flavor
  stuffing mix
4 chicken-breast
  halves, skinned and
  boned
	8 slices whole-wheat
	  bread, toasted
	4 large lettuce leaves
	2 tomatoes, sliced
	Mayonnaise (optional)
		13" by 9" baking dish

1 In baking dish, place bacon slices. Cook, covered with a double thickness of paper towels, on High (100% power) 8 to 9 minutes. Remove to paper towels to drain.

2 Discard all but 2 teaspoons bacon drippings; let dish cool slightly. Into drippings, pour beaten egg. With fork, stir until well mixed. Set aside.

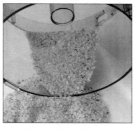

3 In food processor with knife blade attached or in blender, process stuffing mix until fine crumbs form. Place stuffing-mix crumbs on waxed paper; set aside.

4 With dull edge of French knife or smooth edge of meat mallet, pound each chicken-breast half to ¼-inch thickness. Cut each crosswise in half.

5 Dip chicken-breast pieces into egg mixture, then coat in stuffing-mix crumbs. In cleaned baking dish, place coated chicken. Cook, covered loosely with waxed paper, on High 6 to 8 minutes, until juices run clear, rearranging pieces halfway through cooking. Let stand on heat-safe surface 5 minutes.

6 On 4 slices whole-wheat toast, arrange lettuce leaves and tomato slices. Top each slice with 2 pieces of chicken and 2 slices of bacon. If you like, top with mayonnaise. Cover with remaining slices of toast. With serrated knife, cut each sandwich diagonally into quarters; if you like, secure with toothpicks.

OPEN-FACED HOT TURKEY SANDWICHES WITH GRAVY

Color Index page 85. 2 servings. 320 cals per serving. Good source of niacin, iron. Begin 15 minutes ahead.

1 tablespoon butter or margarine
1 tablespoon all-purpose flour
1 cup Chicken Broth (page 125) or canned broth
4 drops browning sauce

Salt and pepper to taste
2 slices whole-wheat bread, toasted
½ pound cooked turkey, thinly sliced

1. In 4-cup microwave-safe glass measure, place butter or margarine. Heat on High (100% power) 30 to 45 seconds, until melted.
2. To melted butter or margarine, add flour. Stir until blended. Gradually stir in broth until smooth. Cook on High 4 to 6 minutes, until gravy boils and thickens, stirring occasionally. Stir in browning sauce. Season with salt and pepper.
3. On 2 microwave-safe dinner plates, arrange toast. Top with equal amounts of turkey and pour gravy over. Cook on High 2 to 3 minutes, until turkey is warm.

SMOKED TURKEY AND SWISS ON CROISSANTS

Color Index page 84. 4 servings. 408 cals per serving. Good source of niacin, calcium. Begin 10 minutes ahead.

4 croissants
½ pound smoked turkey, thinly sliced
4 teaspoons honey-flavored mustard

1 large tomato, thinly sliced
8 ounces Swiss cheese, thinly sliced

1. If you like, preheat conventional oven to 400°F. Heat croissants 5 minutes while preparing filling.
2. On large microwave-safe platter, arrange smoked turkey in 4 portions, leaving at least 1 inch between each portion. Top each with sliced tomato and cheese, cutting cheese to fit. Cook on High (100% power) 2 to 4 minutes, just until cheese melts and turkey is warm.
3. With serrated knife, slice each croissant horizontally in half. Spread bottom halves of croissants with mustard.
4. With spatula, arrange each portion of turkey on bottom half of each croissant. Replace top halves of croissants. Serve immediately.

Hot Pork and Beef Sandwiches

PORK CUTLET SUPPER SANDWICHES

Color Index page 87. 4 servings. 641 cals per serving. Good source of riboflavin, thiamine, niacin, iron. Begin 35 minutes ahead.

4 pork loin cutlets, each ¼ inch thick (about 1 pound)	4 hamburger buns or Kaiser rolls, split
2 egg yolks	1 cup barbecue sauce
¾ cup dried bread crumbs	1 cup coleslaw
Salt and pepper to taste	

1. With dull edge of French knife or smooth edge of meat mallet, pound cutlets to ⅛-inch thickness. In pie plate, with fork, beat egg yolks. Spread bread crumbs on waxed paper.
2. Into egg mixture, dip each pork cutlet, then coat with crumbs.
3. In 13" by 9" microwave-safe baking dish, place cutlets. Cook, covered loosely with waxed paper, on High (100% power) 8 to 9 minutes, until tender, rearranging halfway through cooking. Season with salt and pepper.
4. Meanwhile, lightly toast buns or rolls under preheated broiler. On bottom half of each, place 1 cutlet. Spoon barbecue sauce over, then coleslaw. Replace top halves of buns or rolls.

ROAST BEEF AND BRIE SIZZLER

Color Index page 84. 4 servings. 588 cals per serving. Good source of riboflavin, thiamine, niacin, calcium, iron. Begin 25 minutes ahead.

1 loaf French bread, about 12 inches long	½ pound roast beef, thinly sliced
2 tablespoons butter or margarine (¼ stick)	8 ounces Brie cheese, thinly sliced
¼ teaspoon tarragon	
1 teaspoon Dijon mustard	

1. With serrated knife, diagonally cut French bread into 8 thin slices; set aside.
2. In small microwave-safe bowl, place butter or margarine. Heat, covered with paper towel, on Medium (50% power) 15 to 30 seconds, until softened. Stir in tarragon and mustard. Spread 1 side of each bread slice with butter mixture.
3. Preheat browning dish as manufacturer directs. On waxed paper, place half the bread slices, buttered sides down. Arrange roast beef and Brie on bread. Cover with remaining bread, buttered sides up. Place on browning dish, pressing lightly with spatula. Cook on High (100% power) 3 to 4½ (4:30) minutes, until sandwiches are golden, turning over and pressing lightly with spatula after 2 to 2½ (2:30) minutes. Serve immediately.

STEAK HEROES

Color Index page 86. 692 cals per serving. Good source of riboflavin, thiamine, niacin, calcium, iron. Begin 35 minutes ahead.

Ingredients	For 4	For 2	For 1
Sirloin steak, ¾ inch thick	1 pound	½ pound	¼ pound
Green pepper, sliced	1 green pepper	½ green pepper	¼ green pepper
Red onion, sliced	1 small onion	½ onion	¼ onion
French bread, about 24 inches long, or hero rolls	1 loaf or 4 rolls	½ loaf or 2 rolls	¼ loaf or 1 roll
Dijon mustard	2 tablespoons	1 tablespoon	1½ teaspoons
Swiss or Cheddar cheese, shredded	4 ounces (1 cup)	2 ounces (½ cup)	1 ounce (¼ cup)
Microwave cookware	Browning dish 12" platter	Browning dish 9" plate	Browning dish 7" plate
Time on High (100% power)			
Steak	5 to 7 minutes	3 to 4 minutes	2 to 3 minutes
Pepper-onion mixture	5 to 6 minutes	3 to 4 minutes	2 to 3 minutes
Heroes	2 to 2½ (2:30) minutes	1 to 2 minutes	45 seconds to 1½ (1:30) minutes

1 Preheat browning dish as manufacturer directs. Place steak on browning dish, pressing firmly with spatula.

2 Cook steak on High for time in Chart, or until almost of desired doneness, turning over halfway through cooking. Remove from dish. Set aside and keep warm.

3 Reheat browning dish. Into drippings in browning dish, stir green pepper and red onion.

4 Cook pepper-onion mixture on High for time in Chart, or until vegetables are tender, stirring occasionally.

5 Meanwhile, if using French bread, cut crosswise into 6-inch sections. Split each section or hero roll horizontally in half; toast lightly. On platter or plate (see Chart), arrange bottom halves. Thinly spread with mustard.

6 Thinly slice steak across the grain. Arrange on bottom halves of bread or rolls; top with pepper-onion mixture. Sprinkle cheese over. Cook on High for time in Chart, or just until cheese melts. Cover with top halves of bread or rolls and serve immediately.

Breakfast in a Hurry

Fresh fruit juice of your choice
Chilled grapefruit and orange sections
Scrambled Eggs and Bacon Breakfast, page 139
Toast with jam or jelly of your choice
Café au Lait (below)

Hearty Hot Beef Sandwiches

EASY BEEF TORTILLAS

Color Index page 85. 4 servings. 323 cals per serving. Good source of niacin, iron. Begin 10 minutes ahead.

1 pound ground beef
1 onion, chopped
1 garlic clove, minced
1 8-ounce can tomato sauce
1 teaspoon chili powder
½ teaspoon salt

4 7-inch corn or flour tortillas
4 lettuce leaves
Shredded cheese, sour cream, and salsa (optional)

1. In microwave-safe plastic colander set over large microwave-safe bowl, place ground beef, onion, and garlic. Cook on High (100% power) 5 to 6 minutes, until meat is no longer pink, stirring twice. Discard drippings.
2. In same bowl, combine meat mixture, and next 3 ingredients. Cook, covered, on High 3 minutes, or until hot, stirring once.
3. Place 1 tortilla between lightly moistened paper towels; repeat with remainder. Stack on oven floor. Heat on High 30 seconds, or until hot.
4. *To serve*: Place tortillas on warmed dinner plates. On each tortilla, arrange 1 lettuce leaf and a quarter of meat mixture. If you like, serve with shredded cheese, sour cream, and salsa.

TACO BAR
Our Easy Beef Tortillas are great family fare, but you can turn them into a dish for company by setting out a "taco bar" so guests can add accompaniments like chopped coriander, chopped jalapeño peppers, corn relish, and shredded Cheddar cheese.

Chopped coriander

Chopped Jalapeño Peppers

Corn Relish

Shredded Cheese

PREPARATION TIMETABLE

15 minutes ahead:	*Make Scrambled Eggs and Bacon Breakfast,*
10 minutes ahead:	*Spoon jam or jelly of your choice into small bowl. Mix fruit sections in individual bowls.*
Just before serving:	*Make coffee and heat milk for Café au Lait. Toast bread conventionally. Pour fruit juice into glasses. Complete Café au Lait.*

CAFÉ AU LAIT
This French-style breakfast coffee can be made in minutes in your microwave. Prepare your favorite coffee in the usual way; keep hot.

In 4-cup microwave-safe glass measure, heat **2 cups milk**, covered, on High (100% power) 2 to 3 minutes until almost boiling. Remove from oven and stir in **2 cups hot coffee**. Pour into 4 large cups. Top with **non-dairy cream topping** and sprinkle each with ¼ **teaspoon cocoa**.

SLOPPY JOES

Color Index page 85. 4 servings. 529 cals per serving. Good source of niacin, vitamin C, iron. Begin 20 minutes ahead.

1 onion, chopped	*2 tablespoons water*
1 green pepper, chopped	*Salt and pepper to taste*
1 celery stalk, chopped	*4 hamburger buns, split*
1 pound ground beef	*and toasted*
½ cup catchup	
2 tablespoons chili sauce	

1. In 12″ by 8″ microwave-safe baking dish, place chopped onion, green pepper, celery, and ground beef. Cook on High (100% power) 5 to 6 minutes, until meat is no longer pink, stirring often. Drain off fat.

2. To meat mixture, add catchup, chili sauce, and water; stir. Cook on High 5 to 7 minutes, until flavors blend, stirring occasionally. Season with salt and pepper.

3. Arrange bottom halves of toasted buns on warmed dinner plates and spoon a quarter of ground-beef mixture over each. Replace tops of buns and serve immediately.

MEATBALL SUBS

Color Index page 86. 4 servings. 602 cals per serving. Good source of vitamin A, thiamine, riboflavin, niacin, iron. Begin 35 minutes ahead.

1 small onion, diced	*Salt and pepper to taste*
1 garlic clove, minced	*1 16-ounce jar spaghetti*
2 ounces mushrooms,	*sauce*
finely chopped	*4 large hero rolls or hot-*
1 pound ground beef	*dog buns, split and*
½ cup fresh bread	*toasted*
crumbs (1 slice)	
½ teaspoon basil	

1. In large bowl, mix onion, garlic, mushrooms, ground beef, bread crumbs, and basil until well combined. Season with salt and pepper.

2. Shape ground-beef mixture into 12 meatballs. In 12″ by 8″ microwave-safe baking dish, arrange meatballs, 1 inch apart. Cook, covered with paper towels, on High (100% power) 4 to 5 minutes, until meatballs are no longer pink, rearranging halfway through cooking.

3. Over meatballs, pour spaghetti sauce; stir gently to coat. Cook, covered, on High 5 to 7 minutes, until sauce bubbles and flavors blend, stirring occasionally.

4. Arrange bottom halves of hero rolls or hot-dog buns on warmed dinner plates. Place 3 meatballs on each half and top with any remaining spaghetti sauce. Replace top halves of rolls or buns and serve immediately with knives and forks.

Try toasting bread for a delicious nutty flavor as we have in our recipe for Reubens (below). Toasted and day-old breads, buns, muffins, croissants, and rolls are perfect for making sandwiches. Because they are slightly dry, they absorb enough moisture from the microwaved fillings to refresh them but not make them soggy.

REUBENS

Color Index page 85. 526 cals per serving. Good source of calcium, iron. Begin 20 minutes ahead.

Ingredients	For 4	For 2	For 1
Corned beef, thinly sliced	*8 ounces*	*4 ounces*	*2 ounces*
Sauerkraut, drained	*¾ cup*	*⅓ cup*	*¼ cup*
Swiss cheese slices	*4 slices*	*2 slices*	*1 slice*
Rye-bread slices	*8 slices*	*4 slices*	*2 slices*
Russian dressing	*½ cup*	*¼ cup*	*2 tablespoons*
Dill pickles	*4 pickles*	*2 pickles*	*1 pickle*
Microwave cookware	13″ by 9″ baking dish	12″ by 8″ baking dish	8″ by 8″ baking dish
Time on High (100% power)	5 to 6 minutes	3 to 4 minutes	2 to 3 minutes

1 In baking dish (see Chart), arrange thinly sliced corned beef in 2-ounce portions, leaving at least 1 inch between each portion and shaping them to fit size of rye-bread slices.

2 Spoon sauerkraut over corned beef; cover with cheese slices.

3 Cook fillings on High for time in Chart, or until cheese melts and corned beef is warm, rotating dish halfway through cooking.

4 Meanwhile, lightly toast rye bread conventionally. Spread each slice with Russian dressing.

5 On warmed serving platter, arrange half the toast slices. With spatula, transfer fillings onto rye. Top with remaining toast slices.

6 With serrated knife, cut each sandwich in half; secure with toothpicks. Serve with dill pickles.

Meal in Minutes *for 8 people*

Back Porch Supper

Meatball Subs, page 303 *(double quantity)*
Bakery pizza, or pizza of your choice, page 310 *(double quantity)*
Ice-cream Pie, page 331
Butterscotch Brownies, page 348
Candy apples
Butter Caramels, page 356
Popcorn, peanuts, potato chips, and potato sticks
Fresh fruit juice

PREPARATION TIMETABLE

1 day ahead:	**Early in day:**	**2 hours ahead:**	**15 minutes ahead:**	**Just before serving:**
Make Butterscotch Brownies and Butter Caramels; store in airtight containers. Prepare Ice-cream Pie and freeze; do not garnish.	Prepare Meatball Subs through step 2; cover and refrigerate. Chill fruit juice.	If making pizza, prepare and cook in microwave.	Put out popcorn, peanuts, potato chips and potato sticks. Arrange candy apples on plate. Place Butter Caramels on plate.	Complete Meatball Subs. Reheat bakery or homemade pizza in microwave. Garnish Ice-cream Pie.

Creative Sandwiches

PITA POCKETS WITH SOUVLAKI

Color Index page 84. 4 servings. 486 cals per serving. Good source of riboflavin, thiamine, niacin, calcium, iron. Begin 25 minutes ahead.

1 tablespoon olive or salad oil	2 small tomatoes, each cut into 8 wedges
1 pound boneless lamb steak or beef tenderloin	3 ounces feta cheese, diced
1 small red onion, sliced	Salt and pepper to taste
½ small cucumber, peeled, cut lengthwise in half, seeded, and sliced	4 pitas
	Plain yogurt, lemon wedges, and mint sprigs for garnish
8 large pitted ripe olives, sliced	
2 tablespoons chopped fresh dill or ¾ teaspoon dried	

1. Preheat browning dish as manufacturer directs. Lightly brush dish with 1 teaspoon oil. Place meat on browning dish, pressing firmly with spatula. Cook on High (100% power) 4 to 7 minutes, until of desired doneness, turning meat over and pressing with spatula after 3 to 4 minutes. Let meat stand, covered, on heat-safe surface 5 minutes.

2. Meanwhile, in bowl, place remaining oil, onion, cucumber, olives, dill, tomatoes, and feta cheese; stir to mix. Season with salt and pepper.

3. With sharp knife, thinly slice meat across the grain. To vegetable mixture in bowl, add meat and cooking juices; toss lightly.

4. Lightly toast pitas under preheated broiler until hot and softened. Cut each crosswise in half and separate to form 2 pockets.

5. *To serve*: Into each pita pocket, spoon an equal amount of meat-vegetable mixture. Garnish with yogurt, lemon wedges, and mint sprigs.

Making the Pita Pockets

Lightly toast pitas under preheated broiler until they are hot and softened. With sharp knife, cut each pita crosswise in half and separate to form 2 pockets. Into each pita pocket, spoon an equal amount of filling.

WARM VEGETABLE SALAD WITH CHEESE IN PITA

Color Index page 84. 570 cals per serving. Good source of vitamin A, riboflavin, thiamine, niacin, vitamin C, calcium, iron. Begin 20 minutes ahead.

Ingredients	For 4	For 2	For 1
Carrot, thinly sliced	1 carrot	½ carrot	¼ carrot
Water	3 tablespoons	2 tablespoons	1 tablespoon
Red onion, sliced	1 large onion	1 small onion	½ small onion
Red or green pepper, sliced	1 pepper	½ pepper	¼ pepper
Celery stalk, sliced	1 stalk	½ stalk	¼ stalk
Broccoli, cut into flowerets, and stems peeled and sliced	1 bunch	½ bunch	¼ bunch
Mushrooms, sliced	4 ounces	2 ounces	1 ounce
Italian salad dressing	4 tablespoons	2 tablespoons	1 tablespoon
Tomatoes, diced	2 medium	1 medium	1 small
Monterey Jack cheese, diced	8 ounces	4 ounces	2 ounces
Pitas	4 pitas	2 pitas	1 pita
Microwave cookware	2-quart soufflé dish	1-quart soufflé dish	9″ pie plate
Time on High (100% power) Carrot	2 to 3 minutes	1½ (1:30) to 2 minutes	1 to 1½ (1:30) minutes
With other vegetables	5 to 7 minutes	4 to 5 minutes	2 to 3 minutes

1 In soufflé dish or pie plate (see Chart), place carrot and water. Cook, covered, on High for time in Chart, or until carrot is lightly cooked; drain.

2 Into carrot, stir red onion, red or green pepper, celery, broccoli, and mushrooms.

3 To vegetable mixture, add Italian salad dressing; stir to coat. Cook, covered, on High for time in Chart, or until vegetables are tender-crisp, stirring twice.

4 While vegetables are hot, add tomatoes and cheese; stir gently until cheese begins to melt.

5 Lightly toast pitas under preheated broiler until hot and softened. Cut each crosswise in half and separate to form 2 pockets.

6 *To serve*: Into each pita pocket, spoon an equal amount of vegetable-cheese mixture. Spoon any remaining Italian dressing over filling. Serve immediately.

Quick Canapés

NUTTY GOAT CHEESE TOASTS

Color Index page 86. Makes 24. 82 cals each. Good source of vitamin A, riboflavin, thiamine, niacin, calcium, iron. Begin 35 minutes ahead.

4 tablespoons minced pecans
1 6-ounce package goat cheese
2 ounces sun-dried tomatoes, drained if packed in oil
1 loaf French bread, about 24 inches long
Olive oil
Salad greens for garnish

1. Place minced pecans in shallow dish. Roll goat cheese in pecans until coated. Wrap in plastic wrap; refrigerate 20 minutes, or until firm.
2. Meanwhile, cut sun-dried tomatoes into matchstick-thin slices; set aside.
3. Cut French bread crosswise in half to make two 12-inch pieces; freeze one half for use another day. Cut remaining half into twenty-four ½-inch slices.
4. Toast French bread slices under preheated broiler until golden on both sides.
5. Remove nutty goat cheese from refrigerator and unwrap. Cut into 24 slices; place on toasts. Top each with sun-dried tomatoes.
6. Arrange toasts on microwave-safe serving platter. Heat on Medium (50% power) 1 to 2 minutes, until cheese softens slightly. Cook in batches if necessary. Drizzle each with olive oil. Garnish with salad greens and serve.

PIZZA TARTLETS

Color Index page 86. Makes 16. 145 cals each. Low in cholesterol. Begin 35 minutes ahead.

1 2-ounce can anchovy fillets, well drained
16 2-inch tartlet shells
1 cup pizza sauce
½ 8-ounce package mozzarella cheese, shredded (1 cup)
½ 6-ounce can pitted ripe olives, drained and sliced
Basil leaves for garnish

1. Rinse anchovies under running cold water; pat dry. Cut each anchovy fillet crosswise, then lengthwise to make 4 strips; set aside.
2. Preheat conventional oven to 350°F. Arrange tartlet shells on cookie sheet and place in oven 5 minutes, or until warm. Into small microwave-safe bowl, pour sauce. Heat on High (100% power) 3 to 5 minutes, until hot, stirring twice.
3. On microwave-safe serving platter, arrange tartlet shells. Spoon an equal amount of pizza sauce into each and sprinkle with cheese. Top with anchovy strips and decorate with olives.
4. Heat on Medium (50% power) 1 to 2 minutes, just until cheese begins to melt. Garnish with basil and serve.

SAVORY BREADSTICKS

Color Index page 85. Makes 12. 37 cals each. Low in cholesterol, fat, sodium. Begin 15 minutes ahead.

6 slices lean bacon
12 8-inch breadsticks

1. Line a 13" by 9" microwave-safe baking dish with paper towels. With sharp knife, cut bacon slices lengthwise in half. Wrap 1 bacon piece, spiral-fashion, around each breadstick.
2. Arrange breadsticks in prepared baking dish. Cook, covered with paper towels, on High (100% power) 4½ (4:30) to 6 minutes, until bacon is browned, rotating dish halfway through cooking. Serve hot or cold.

Creative Sandwiches

CHICKEN FAJITAS

Color Index page 86. 4 servings. 377 cals per serving. Good source of thiamine, niacin, calcium, iron. Begin 55 minutes ahead.

2 whole chicken breasts, skinned, boned, and cut in half
1 medium onion, sliced
1 green pepper, sliced
2 tablespoons lime juice
½ teaspoon ground cumin
1 teaspoon sugar
1 teaspoon salad oil
8 8-inch flour tortillas
Guacamole (page 233), sour cream, and shredded Cheddar cheese for garnish
Pico de Gallo (below)

1. With sharp knife, cut chicken-breast halves into 3" by 1" pieces. In large bowl, combine chicken pieces, sliced onion and green pepper, lime juice, cumin, and sugar. Cover and refrigerate 15 minutes, stirring twice.
2. Preheat browning dish as manufacturer directs. Brush with oil. Arrange chicken, onion, and pepper in a single layer on dish. Cook on High (100% power) 7 to 10 minutes, until chicken juices run clear, stirring twice. Transfer to dish and let stand on heat-safe surface 5 minutes.
3. Place 1 tortilla between lightly moistened paper towels; repeat with remaining tortillas. Stack on oven floor. Heat on High 1 to 3 minutes, until hot.
4. *To serve*: Place tortillas on warmed dinner plates. Spoon an equal amount of chicken mixture onto center of each. Top with Guacamole, sour cream, and Cheddar cheese. Fold 1 side of each tortilla over filling, turn bottom up and fold other side over to seal in filling. Serve with Pico de Gallo.

PICO DE GALLO In medium bowl, place **2 diced large tomatoes, 1 diced medium red onion, 1 diced small jalapeño pepper, ⅓ cup chopped coriander, 3 tablespoons lime juice,** and **salt to taste.** Stir well to mix, then cover and leave to stand at room temperature 10 minutes, to allow flavors to blend. Makes 2 cups. 4 cals per tablespoon.

Our delicious homemade spreads, made with a variety of cheeses, can be served on muffins, your favorite bread, or crackers. Serve immediately or refrigerate for use another day. To soften refrigerated spreads, place small quantities in a microwave-safe container. Heat on High (100% power) 5 seconds at a time, until just spreadable.

BASIC YOGURT CHEESE

Makes about 1 cup. 9 cals per tablespoon. Good source of riboflavin, calcium. Begin 1 day ahead.

1 8-ounce container plain yogurt
Salt and ground white pepper to taste

1. Line strainer with a double thickness of cheesecloth or a coffee filter. Set strainer over bowl. In strainer, place yogurt. Let drain, refrigerated overnight.
2. Discard liquid. Spoon yogurt cheese into bowl. Season with salt and white pepper.

APRICOT-CHEESE SPREAD: Prepare Basic Yogurt Cheese (above). Into prepared cheese, stir **2 tablespoons apricot jam** and **½ teaspoon ground ginger.** Makes about 1 cup. 14 cals per tablespoon.

BLUE CHEESE SPREAD

Makes about 1½ cups. 30 cals per tablespoon. Low in sodium. Begin 5 minutes ahead.

1 4-ounce package blue cheese, crumbled
1 3-ounce package cream cheese
2 tablespoons minced green onion
1 tablespoon milk

1. In 4-cup microwave-safe glass measure, place cheeses and green onion. Heat on Medium (50% power) 1 to 2 minutes, until cheeses are softened.
2. To cheese mixture, add milk; stir until smooth. Serve immediately or cover and refrigerate to serve chilled later.

BLUE CHEESE AND WALNUT SPREAD: Prepare Blue Cheese Spread (above). Into prepared spread, stir **¼ cup finely chopped walnuts.** Makes about 1¾ cups. 32 cals per tablespoon.

SMOKED SALMON AND CHIVE SPREAD

Makes about 1½ cups. 22 cals per tablespoon. Begin 5 minutes ahead.

1 3-ounce package cream cheese
1 3-ounce package Neufchâtel cheese
1 tablespoon milk
3 tablespoons chopped chives
2 ounces smoked salmon, chopped
1 teaspoon lemon juice
Ground white pepper to taste

1. In 2-cup microwave-safe glass measure, heat cheeses on Medium (50% power) 1 to 2 minutes, until softened.
2. To cream-cheese mixture, add milk, chopped chives, salmon, and lemon juice, stirring until blended. Season with pepper. Serve immediately or cover and refrigerate to serve chilled later.

CREAM CHEESE AND CHIVE SPREAD: Prepare spread (above), omitting smoked salmon and lemon juice. Makes about 1¼ cups. 23 cals per tablespoon.

CHEDDAR CHEESE SPREAD

Makes about 2¼ cups. 49 cals per tablespoon. Good source of calcium. Begin 5 minutes ahead.

8 tablespoons butter or margarine (1 stick)
8 ounces Cheddar cheese, shredded (2 cups)
3 to 4 tablespoons milk
2 green onions, finely chopped
¼ teaspoon hot-pepper sauce

1. In 4-cup microwave-safe glass measure, place butter or margarine. Heat on Medium (50% power) 30 seconds to 1 minute, until softened.
2. Into butter or margarine, beat cheese. Add milk, stirring until well blended. Stir in green onions and hot-pepper sauce.

TEX-MEX CHEDDAR CHEESE SPREAD: Prepare Cheddar Cheese Spread (above). To prepared spread, add **1 chopped jalapeño pepper, ¼ cup salsa,** and **2 tablespoons chopped coriander,** stirring until blended. Makes about 2½ cups. 55 cals per tablespoon.

Hot Cheese Sandwiches

CROQUE MONSIEUR *

Color Index page 87. 340 cals per serving. Good source of thiamine, calcium, iron. Begin 35 minutes ahead.

Ingredients	For 4	For 2	For 1
Eggs	2 eggs	1 egg	1 egg
Milk	½ cup	¼ cup	¼ cup
White bread slices	8 slices	4 slices	2 slices
Cooked ham slices	4 slices	2 slices	1 slice
Swiss cheese slices	4 slices	2 slices	1 slice
Butter or margarine	2 tablespoons (¼ stick)	1 tablespoon	2 teaspoons
Microwave cookware	Browning dish	Browning dish	Browning dish
Time on High (100% power) Sandwiches	3 to 4 minutes each batch	3 to 4 minutes	1½ (1:30) to 2½ (2:30) minutes
Standing time	2 minutes	1 minute	1 minute

1 In pie plate, with fork, beat eggs and milk until blended.

2 Arrange half the bread slices on cutting board; top each with 1 slice ham and 1 slice cheese, trimming to fit if necessary. Top with remaining bread. Set aside.

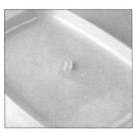

3 Preheat browning dish as manufacturer directs. On browning dish, place butter or margarine.

4 Into egg mixture, dip each sandwich, to coat both sides of bread.

5 On browning dish, place sandwiches, pressing lightly with spatula. Cook on High for time in Chart, until sandwiches are golden, turning sandwiches over halfway through cooking. (If cooking for 4, cook sandwiches in 2 batches, reheating browning dish between batches.)

6 On paper towels, let sandwiches stand for time in Chart. With serrated knife, cut diagonally in half; serve immediately.

GARLIC-CHEESE BREAD

Color Index page 85. 6 pieces. 235 cals each. Low in cholesterol. Begin 10 minutes ahead.

3 tablespoons butter or margarine, softened
1 garlic clove, crushed
¾ teaspoon oregano
1 loaf Italian bread, about 18 inches long
2 ounces mozzarella cheese, shredded (½ cup)

1. In small bowl, combine softened butter or margarine, garlic, and oregano. With serrated knife, cut Italian bread crosswise into three 6-inch sections. Split each section horizontally in half to make 6 halves of bread.
2. Spread cut side of each piece of bread with garlic butter. Sprinkle mozzarella evenly over buttered sides. Arrange bread in a circle on paper towels on oven floor. Cook on High (100% power) 45 seconds, or just until cheese begins to melt. Do not overcook or garlic-cheese bread will become too chewy. Serve immediately.

GARLIC BREAD: Prepare Garlic-cheese Bread (above), omitting mozzarella cheese. Cook on High (100% power) 30 seconds, or just until garlic butter melts.

TUNA MELT

Color Index page 85. 4 servings. 432 cals per serving. Good source of calcium, iron. Begin 15 minutes ahead.

1 3-ounce package cream cheese
1 medium onion, chopped
1 celery stalk, chopped
¼ cup gherkin pickles, chopped
¼ cup pimento-stuffed green olives, chopped
2 tablespoons mayonnaise
Hot-pepper sauce (optional)
1 6½-ounce can white tuna in water, drained
4 English muffins, split
4 slices American cheese

1. In small microwave-safe bowl, place cream cheese. Heat on Medium-Low (30% power) 1½ (1:30) to 2 minutes, until softened.
2. Into cream cheese, stir chopped onion and celery, gherkins, olives, and mayonnaise until blended. If you like, season with hot-pepper sauce. Fold in tuna, stirring to break up.
3. Lightly toast bottom halves of muffins under preheated broiler. On microwave-safe platter, arrange toasted bottom halves of muffins. Spoon an equal amount of tuna mixture onto each half and top with 1 slice American cheese. Cook on High 2 to 3 minutes, until cheese melts and tuna mixture is warm.
4. Meanwhile, toast top halves of muffins. When cheese is melted, replace top halves of toasted muffins and serve immediately.

DESIGNER BAGELS

Color Index page 85. Makes 12 bagel halves. 65 cals each. Begin 25 minutes ahead.

6 2½-inch bagels
2 ounces ricotta cheese, crumbled
¼ cup Smoked Salmon and Chive Spread (page 307)
4 tablespoons Orange Butter (page 298)

Sliced pitted ripe olives; chopped sun-dried tomatoes; shredded basil leaves; red-pepper strips; and Orange Julienne (page 334) for garnish

1. With serrated knife, split bagels. On cutting board, place bagel halves cut side up. Spread 4 bagel halves with ricotta, 4 bagel halves with Smoked Salmon and Chive Spread, and 4 bagel halves with Orange Butter.
2. On microwave-safe serving platter lined with paper towels, place 6 bagel halves. Heat on Medium-Low (30% power) 1½ (1:30) minutes, or just until topping is softened. Repeat with remaining 6 bagel halves.
3. On ricotta-topped bagels, arrange olives, sun-dried tomatoes, and basil. Garnish salmon-and-chive-topped bagels with red-pepper strips, and Orange-butter-topped bagels with Orange Julienne. Serve warm.

MOZZARELLA FRENCH BREAD

Color Index page 86. 8 servings. 296 cals per serving. Low in cholesterol. Good source of calcium. Begin 40 minutes ahead.

1 8-ounce package mozzarella cheese, diced (2 cups)
⅓ cup pimento-stuffed green olives, chopped
4 green onions, sliced
⅓ cup diced prosciutto (about 2 slices)

2 tablespoons olive or salad oil
Salt to taste
1 loaf French bread, about 24 inches long

1. In medium bowl, combine mozzarella, olives, green onions, prosciutto, and oil. Season with salt; set aside.
2. With serrated knife, cut French bread crosswise into four 6-inch sections. With spoon or fingers, scoop out bread leaving a ½-inch-thick crust. (Reserve scooped-out bread for use another day.)
3. Fill each hollowed-out piece with some cheese mixture.
4. Wrap each piece loosely in paper towel. On oven floor, place bread. Heat on Medium (50% power) 45 seconds to 1½ (1:30) minutes, just until cheese begins to soften. Do not overcook or bread will become too chewy. Cut each piece into 12 slices. Serve immediately.

Cheese is one of the most versatile of foods, and your microwave will help transform simple cheese sandwiches into tasty snacks or original main-course dishes. For a change, try using Brie instead of Camembert in the toasted sandwiches below, but be careful in all our cheese-sandwich recipes to microwave only for the time given; if you overcook cheese even slightly in the microwave, it will become rubbery and stringy.

TOASTED SANDWICHES WITH CAMEMBERT AND PEARS

Color Index page 87. 280 cals each. Low in cholesterol. Begin 35 minutes ahead.

Ingredients for 4 servings		Microwave cookware
8 thin slices white bread 2 tablespoons butter or margarine (¼ stick) 1 4½-ounce package Camembert cheese, chilled	1 ripe pear 8 mint leaves Pear slices and mint leaves for garnish	Small bowl Browning dish

1 With serrated knife, remove crusts from bread. In small bowl, place butter or margarine. Heat, covered with paper towel, on Medium (50% power) 15 to 30 seconds, until softened but not melted.

2 Spread 1 side of each slice of bread with softened butter or margarine. Cut chilled Camembert into thin slices; arrange on unbuttered sides of 4 bread slices, cutting cheese to fit.

3 Cut pear lengthwise into quarters, and remove core; do not peel. Cut each quarter lengthwise into 4 slices.

4 Arrange pear slices on top of Camembert. Place 2 mint leaves in center of each sandwich. Top with remaining slices of bread, buttered sides up.

5 Preheat browning dish as manufacturer directs. On browning dish, place 2 sandwiches, pressing lightly with spatula. Cook on High (100% power) 3 to 5 minutes, until sandwiches are golden, turning over and pressing after 2 to 3 minutes. Set aside; keep warm. Reheat browning dish and repeat with remaining sandwiches.

6 *To serve:* Cut each sandwich diagonally into quarters. Garnish with pear slices and mint leaves. Serve warm.

Pizza

CALZONE

Color Index page 87. 504 cals per serving (without extra fillings). Low in cholesterol. Good source of iron. Begin 35 minutes ahead.

Ingredients for 2 servings		Microwave cookware
1½ cups buttermilk-baking mix Water 1 16-ounce jar spaghetti or pizza sauce 1 ounce mozzarella cheese, shredded (¼ cup)	Fillings: Diced green or red pepper, shredded prosciutto, thinly sliced pepperoni, thinly sliced mushrooms, well-drained canned anchovy fillets 1 teaspoon salad oil Basil leaves for garnish	Browning dish 4-cup glass measure

1 In medium bowl, combine buttermilk-baking mix and ⅓ cup water to form soft dough. Divide dough in half. On lightly floured surface, pat each half of dough into 6-inch circle.

2 Onto half of each dough circle, spoon ¼ cup spaghetti or pizza sauce; reserve remaining sauce. Sprinkle with mozzarella. Top with fillings of your choice (above).

3 With pastry brush, moisten edge of each circle with water. Fold each circle in half; press edges together to seal, crimping to decorate.

4 Preheat browning dish as manufacturer directs. Lightly brush with oil. With spatula, place calzone on browning dish.

5 Cook calzone on High (100% power) 5 to 7 minutes, until lightly browned, turning over with spatula after 2 to 3 minutes. Transfer to warmed serving platter; let stand, covered, 3 to 5 minutes.

6 Meanwhile, into glass measure, pour reserved sauce. Heat, covered, on High 2 to 3 minutes, until hot, stirring twice. Garnish calzone with basil and serve with hot spaghetti or pizza sauce.

FOUR SEASONS PIZZA

Color Index page 87. 4 servings. 367 cals per serving. Good source of vitamin A, thiamine, vitamin C, calcium, iron. Low in cholesterol. Begin 35 minutes ahead.

1 10-ounce package refrigerated pizza dough 1 teaspoon salad oil 2 tablespoons prepared pesto or 1 tablespoon basil 1 6-ounce jar marinated artichoke hearts, drained and sliced	1 7-ounce jar roasted sweet red peppers, drained and sliced 2 ounces prosciutto, thinly sliced 2 tomatoes, sliced ¼ cup grated Parmesan cheese

1. On lightly floured surface, pat pizza dough into 10-inch circle. Make a ½-inch rim around edge; crimp rim with fingers.
2. Preheat 9″ round browning dish as manufacturer directs. Lightly brush with oil. Carefully transfer pizza dough to browning dish. With fork, prick dough to prevent puffing. Spread with pesto or sprinkle with dried basil.
3. With knife, lightly mark pizza dough into quarters. Arrange artichoke hearts, red peppers, prosciutto, and tomatoes separately on each quarter. Sprinkle Parmesan evenly over pizza. Cook on High (100% power) 10 minutes, or until crust is firm and vegetables are tender, piercing crust with fork occasionally.
4. If you like, transfer pizza to broiler-safe platter; lightly brown under preheated broiler.

MEDITERRANEAN PIZZA

Color Index page 87. 4 servings. 520 cals per serving. Good source of calcium, iron. Begin 35 minutes ahead.

1 10-ounce package refrigerated pizza dough 2 tablespoons olive or salad oil 1 large red onion, thinly sliced	½ teaspoon rosemary ¼ teaspoon basil ¼ teaspoon thyme leaves Salt and pepper to taste 8 ounces soft goat or feta cheese, crumbled

1. On lightly floured surface, pat pizza dough into 10-inch circle. Make a ½-inch rim around edge; press with fork to make decorative edge.
2. Preheat 9″ round browning dish as manufacturer directs. Lightly brush with 1 teaspoon oil. Carefully transfer pizza dough to browning dish. With fork, prick dough to prevent puffing.
3. In small bowl, combine onion slices, remaining oil, and herbs. Season with salt and pepper.
4. Over pizza dough, spread onion mixture; top with goat cheese. Cook on High (100% power) 10 minutes, or until crust is firm, piercing crust with fork occasionally.
5. If you like, transfer pizza to broiler-safe platter; lightly brown under preheated broiler.

Fruits and Desserts

CHARTS FOR MICROWAVING FRUITS · FRUIT DESSERTS
CREAMY DESSERTS · CHOCOLATE DESSERTS
ICE CREAM AND SORBETS · PUDDINGS · CHEESECAKES

Fruits and Desserts

Fruit cooked in the microwave keeps its shape better and looks more attractive than conventionally cooked fruit. Using our charts (pages 313 to 315), a wide range of fresh and dried fruits, some with added sugar for extra sweetness, can be quickly prepared. Plainly cooked apples, peaches, pears, and plums can be served hot or cold as accompaniments to roast meats and poultry, or served chilled, with their cooking juices, as delicious and nutritious desserts. More elaborate fruit dishes are given among our dessert recipes, such as poached peaches and pears in sweet sauces, apples caramelized with sugar and spices, cherries in a red-wine sauce, creamy soufflés, parfaits, and sorbets.

Many dessert recipes contain delicate ingredients that benefit particularly from microwave cooking. Egg-based creams and mousses that can curdle will be smooth and creamy with only occasional stirring when cooked on Medium (50% power). Better-than-ever cheesecakes can be made in about half of the normal baking time. These delicate mixtures should be elevated on a trivet, then cooked on Medium, and rotated occasionally for even cooking throughout. Remove a cheesecake from the oven while still soft in the center, then allow to stand for about 30 minutes, during which time it will set without cracking.

Our puddings, delicious family favorites, are a particular treat when made in the microwave. They cook quickly, and the milk-based mixtures do not stick or scorch. These, too, need to be elevated and cooked on Medium power.

Chocolate melts perfectly in the microwave without special equipment such as a double boiler. Do not cover it, however, as the moisture that builds up inside a cover can drop onto the chocolate and make it stiff. Remove chocolate from the oven when it changes from dull to shiny, bearing in mind that pieces and squares will retain their shapes until removed from the oven and stirred.

INSTANT DESSERTS
Create an easy, last-minute dessert by combining ice cream or sorbet with canned fruit or fresh bakery goods, then topping with a sweet sauce. Use bottled sweet sauces or make one of our quick microwave sweet sauces (pages 382 to 383).

Peach Melba (left): A canned peach half, filled with vanilla ice cream, set on Melba Sauce and garnished with mint leaves.

Apple Tart à La Mode (right): A small bakery French apple tart and scoop of vanilla ice cream with butterscotch sauce spooned over. Garnished with mint leaves.

Cooking Fruits in the Microwave

Fruit cooked in the microwave keeps its fresh flavor, and retains its shape because it doesn't need constant stirring.

Plastic wrap is the best choice for covering a dish of microwave fruit. "Vent" the wrap a little, turning back a small corner or puncturing to allow steam to escape.

Key				
Microwave cookware	Sugar	Water	Time	Standing time

APPLES

Wash under running cold water and pat dry, then core and peel a third of way down from tops.

About 132 cals per serving		
For 4	**For 2**	**For 1**
4 cooking apples (about 8 ounces each)	2 cooking apples (about 8 ounces each)	1 cooking apple (about 8 ounces)
8″ by 8″ baking dish; *arrange in corners*	8″ by 8″ baking dish	Small bowl
None	None	None
7 to 9 minutes; *rotate apples, then rotate dish halfway through cooking*	4 to 5 minutes; *rotate apples, then rotate dish halfway through cooking*	2 to 3 minutes
5 minutes	5 minutes	5 minutes

Cook apples, standing upright and covered, on High (100% power) for time in Chart. Let stand, covered, for time in Chart. Whole apples are done when tender yet retaining their shapes.

APPLES (SLICES)

Wash under running cold water, then core and, if you like, peel. Cut each apple lengthwise in half; cut each half lengthwise into eighths.

About 108 cals per serving		
For 4	**For 2**	**For 1**
4 cooking apples (about 6 ounces each; 8 cups)	2 cooking apples (about 6 ounces each; 4 cups)	1 cooking apple (about 6 ounces; 2 cups)
2-quart casserole	1-quart casserole	Small bowl
2 teaspoons	1 teaspoon	½ teaspoon
¼ cup water *plus ½ teaspoon lemon juice*	2 tablespoons water *plus ¼ teaspoon lemon juice*	1 tablespoon water *plus ¼ teaspoon lemon juice*
9 to 11 minutes; *stir 3 times during cooking*	5 to 6 minutes; *stir halfway through cooking*	2 to 3 minutes; *stir halfway through cooking*
5 minutes	5 minutes	5 minutes

Stir sugar, water, and lemon juice together. Add apples, stir to coat, then cook, covered, on High (100% power) for time in Chart. Let stand, covered, for time in Chart. Apple slices are done when tender yet retaining their shapes.

CHERRIES, SWEET

Wash under running cold water and drain. Remove stems and pits. Cherries boil vigorously and foam toward end of cooking. Do not allow to boil over.

80 cals per serving		
For 4	**For 2**	**For 1**
1 pound (about 3 cups unpitted)	½ pound (about 1½ cups unpitted)	¼ pound (about ¾ cup unpitted)
2-quart casserole	1-quart casserole	Small bowl
1 tablespoon	2 teaspoons	1 teaspoon
4 to 5 minutes; *stir halfway through cooking*	3 to 4 minutes; *stir halfway through cooking*	1½ (1:30) to 2 minutes; *stir halfway through cooking*
2 to 3 minutes	2 to 3 minutes	2 to 3 minutes

Cook cherries and water, covered, on High (100% power) for time in Chart. Let stand, covered, for time in Chart. Sweet cherries are done when tender.

PEACHES

Rinse under running cold water. To peel, dip whole peaches in rapidly boiling water 15 to 20 seconds, then dip them into pan of cold water; pull off skins.

About 40 cals per serving

	For 4	For 2	For 1
	4 peaches (about 4 ounces each)	2 peaches (about 4 ounces each)	1 peach (about 4 ounces)
	8″ by 8″ baking dish; *arrange in corners*	9″ pie plate	Small bowl
	None	None	None
	3 to 6 minutes; *rotate dish halfway through cooking*	2 to 3½ (3:30) minutes; *rotate plate halfway through cooking*	45 seconds to 2 minutes
	2 minutes	2 minutes	2 minutes

Cook peaches, standing upright and covered, on High (100% power) for time in Chart. Let stand, covered, for time in Chart. Peaches are done when tender yet retaining their shapes.

PEARS (SLICES)

Prepare as Pears (left). If you like, peel. Cut lengthwise into eighths.

About 112 cals per serving

	For 4	For 2	For 1
	4 pears (about 6 ounces each)	2 pears (about 6 ounces each)	1 pear (about 6 ounces)
	2-quart casserole	1-quart casserole	Small bowl
	2 teaspoons	1 teaspoon	½ teaspoon
	¼ cup water *plus* ½ *teaspoon lemon juice*	2 tablespoons water *plus* ¼ *teaspoon lemon juice*	1 tablespoon water *plus* ⅛ *teaspoon lemon juice*
	10 to 12 minutes; *stir 3 times during cooking*	7 to 9 minutes; *stir halfway through cooking*	3 to 5 minutes; *stir halfway through cooking*
	5 minutes	3 to 5 minutes	2 to 3 minutes

Stir sugar, water, and lemon juice together. Add pears, stir to coat, then cook, covered, on High (100% power) for time in Chart. Let stand, covered, for time in Chart. Pear slices are done when tender yet retaining their shapes.

PEARS

Rinse under running cold water. With apple corer, remove cores from bottom of pears but do not remove stems. Peel pears. To prevent turning brown, brush exposed flesh with lemon juice.

About 139 cals per serving

	For 4	For 2	For 1
	4 large pears (about 8 ounces each)	2 large pears (about 8 ounces each)	1 large pear (about 8 ounces)
	8″ by 8″ baking dish; *arrange in corners*	9″ pie plate	Small bowl
	None	None	None
	5 to 7 minutes; *rotate pears, then rotate dish halfway through cooking*	4 to 6 minutes; *rotate pears, then rotate plate halfway through cooking*	2 to 3 minutes
	5 minutes	5 minutes	5 minutes

Cook pears, standing upright and covered, on High (100% power) for time in Chart. Let stand, covered, for time in Chart. Pears are done when tender yet retaining their shapes.

PINEAPPLES (PIECES)

Cut off about 1 inch from top and base of fruit. Cut pineapple lengthwise in half, then into quarters. Cut away fibrous woody cores. Cut off peel, cutting close to fruit. Cut out any remaining eyes. Cut pineapple quarters lengthwise in half, then cut crosswise into ½- to ¾-inch-thick pieces.

About 50 cals per serving

	For 4	For 2	For 1
	1 pineapple (3½ to 4 pounds; about 4 cups)	1 pineapple (3½ to 4 pounds; use 2 cups; refrigerate remainder)	1 pineapple (3½ to 4 pounds; use 1 cup; refrigerate remainder)
	2-quart casserole	1-quart casserole	Small bowl
	None	None	None
	8 to 9 minutes; *stir halfway through cooking*	4 to 5 minutes; *stir halfway through cooking*	2½ (2:30) to 3 minutes; *stir halfway through cooking*
	5 minutes	5 minutes	5 minutes

Cook pineapple, covered, on High (100% power) for time in Chart. Let stand, covered, for time in Chart. Pineapple pieces are done when tender.

PLUMS (HALVES)

Wash plums under running cold water. Pat dry. Cut each plum in half and remove pit.

About 80 cals per serving			
	For 4	**For 2**	**For 1**
	8 plums (about 2 ounces each)	4 plums (about 2 ounces each)	2 plums (about 2 ounces each)
🍲	12″ by 8″ baking dish; *arrange around edges*	9″ pie plate; *arrange around edge*	9″ pie plate; *arrange around edge*
🥤	None	None	None
🕐	3 to 4 minutes; *rotate dish halfway through cooking*	2 to 3 minutes; *rotate plate halfway through cooking*	1 to 2 minutes; *rotate plate halfway through cooking*
🍲	3 to 4 minutes	3 to 4 minutes	2 to 3 minutes

Cook plums, covered, on High (100% power) for time in Chart. Let stand, covered, for time in Chart. Plum halves are done when tender.

RHUBARB (PIECES)

Wash rhubarb and trim any discolored ends; cut off any leaves and discard. Cut rhubarb crosswise into 1-inch pieces.

Rhubarb boils vigorously toward end of cooking. Do not allow it to boil over.

About 140 cals per serving			
	For 4	**For 2**	**For 1**
	1½ pounds (about 4 cups)	12 ounces (about 2 cups)	6 ounces (about 1 cup)
🍲	4-quart casserole	2-quart casserole	1-quart casserole
🥄	⅔ cup	⅓ cup	2½ tablespoons
🥤	¼ cup	2 tablespoons	1 tablespoon
🕐	7 to 8 minutes; *stir halfway through cooking, then stir in sugar before final minute*	4 to 6 minutes; *stir halfway through cooking, then stir in sugar before final minute*	2½ (2:30) to 3 minutes; *stir halfway through cooking, then stir in sugar before final minute*
🍲	10 minutes	10 minutes	10 minutes

Cook rhubarb and water, covered, on High (100% power) for time in Chart, stirring in sugar when indicated. Let stand, covered, for time in Chart. Rhubarb pieces are done when tender.

DRIED FRUIT, APRICOTS, PEACHES, AND PRUNES

About 188 cals per serving for each fruit			
	For 4	**For 2**	**For 1**
	8 ounces (1⅓ cups, tightly packed)	4 ounces (⅔ cup, tightly packed)	2 ounces (⅓ cup, tightly packed)
🍲	1½-quart casserole	1-quart casserole	2-cup glass measure
🥄	¼ cup	2 tablespoons	1 tablespoon
🥤	2 cups	1 cup	½ cup
🕐	10 to 12 minutes; *stir in sugar halfway through cooking*	6 to 7 minutes; *stir in sugar halfway through cooking*	3 to 4 minutes; *stir in sugar at start of cooking*
🍲	30 minutes	30 minutes	30 minutes

Cook dried fruit and water, covered, on High (100% power) for time in Chart, stirring in sugar when indicated. Let stand, covered, for time in Chart. Dried apricots, peaches, and prunes are done when tender; the prunes should remain whole.

DRIED FRUIT, FIGS

210 cals per serving			
	For 4	**For 2**	**For 1**
	12 ounces (1½ cups, tightly packed)	6 ounces (¾ cup, tightly packed)	3 ounces (⅓ cup plus 3 figs, tightly packed)
🍲	1½-quart casserole	1-quart casserole	2-cup glass measure
🥤	2 cups water *plus 2 teaspoons lemon juice*	1 cup water *plus 1 teaspoon lemon juice*	½ cup water *plus ½ teaspoon lemon juice*
🕐	12 to 15 minutes; *stir halfway through cooking*	7 to 8 minutes; *stir halfway through cooking*	3 to 5 minutes; *stir halfway through cooking*
🍲	30 minutes	30 minutes	30 minutes

Cook dried figs, water, and lemon juice, covered, on High (100% power) for time in Chart. Let stand, covered, for time in Chart. Dried figs are done when plump and soft.

Fruits for Garnish

Many new and exciting fruits from exotic places are now widely available. They make ideal garnishes for simple microwave dishes by providing additional color, flavor, texture, and interesting shapes.

Dates: Use whole or chopped as a topping for cakes, cookies, desserts, quick breads, and salads.

Lychees: Peel off skin, remove pit and use halves or quarters on fruit salads and stir-fry dishes.

Pomegranates: The juicy seeds make an unusual garnish for cheesecakes, ice creams, and sorbets.

Kumquats: Cut into slices to garnish fruit salads, stir-fry dishes, and desserts.

Mangoes: Peel and remove large seed, then slice the sweet, juicy flesh. Use to garnish fish and rice dishes, fruit salads, mousses, soufflés, and other desserts.

Cactus Pears: Peel thorny skin as you would peel an apple. Use on salads.

Papayas: Halve and remove seeds; peel and slice. Serve on rice dishes, breakfast cereals, and pies.

Figs: Cut lengthwise in half and serve with cold cuts or on a cheese platter.

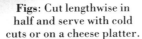

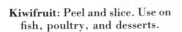

Kiwifruit: Peel and slice. Use on fish, poultry, and desserts.

Passion Fruit: Cut crosswise in half, then spoon out seeds and juice to use as a topping for sorbets and other desserts.

Carambolas: Use this star-shaped, citrus-flavored fruit to garnish fish, vegetable, and dessert dishes.

Apple Desserts

SPICED APPLE SLICES

Color Index page 88. 4 servings. 157 cals per serving. Low in fat, sodium. Good source of vitamin C. Begin 25 minutes ahead.

1½ cups apple juice
¼ cup packed brown sugar
2 teaspoons grated lemon peel
2 3-inch-long cinnamon sticks
3 whole cloves
3 whole allspice
8 cinnamon red-hot candies (optional)
4 small apples
2 tablespoons lemon juice

1. In 12″ by 8″ microwave-safe baking dish, combine apple juice, brown sugar, lemon peel, cinnamon sticks, cloves, and allspice. If you like, add red-hot candies. Cook on High (100% power) 7 to 9 minutes, until sugar dissolves and liquid boils, stirring occasionally.
2. Meanwhile, peel and core apples. Slice crosswise into ¼-inch-thick rings. If you like, cut edges with fluted cookie cutter for a more decorative look. Sprinkle apple rings with lemon juice.
3. To spiced liquid in baking dish, add half the apple rings. Cook on High 3 to 5 minutes, until tender, turning over halfway through cooking. With spatula, transfer rings to warmed serving dish; keep warm. Repeat with remaining apple rings. Strain liquid over apple rings in dish.
4. Serve spiced apple rings warm or cover and refrigerate to serve chilled later.

APPLE VARIETIES
Some apples lose their shape when baked, while others may be too tart for out-of-hand eating. Use this chart to guide your choice, but always choose firm, unblemished fruit.

Variety	E	B	C
Cortland	•	•	•
Golden Delicious	•	•	•
Granny Smith	•	•	•
Gravenstein	•	•	•
Jonathan	•	•	•
McIntosh	•		•
Newton Pippin		•	•
Northern Spy	•	•	•
Red Delicious	•		
Rome Beauty		•	•
Winesap	•	•	•

Key
E Eating
B Baking
C Cooking

NEW ENGLAND BAKED APPLES

Color Index page 89. 360 cals per serving. Low in sodium. Begin 40 minutes ahead.

Ingredients	For 4	For 2	For 1
Large cooking apples	4 apples	2 apples	1 apple
Butter or margarine, softened	2 tablespoons (¼ stick)	1 tablespoon	2 teaspoons
Dark seedless raisins or dried currants	¼ cup	2 tablespoons	1 tablespoon
Finely chopped walnuts	2 tablespoons	1 tablespoon	2 teaspoons
Ground cinnamon	¾ teaspoon	¼ teaspoon	⅛ teaspoon
Apple juice	¼ cup	2 tablespoons	1 tablespoon
Maple or maple-flavor syrup	¾ cup	½ cup	¼ cup
Microwave cookware	8″ by 8″ baking dish	9″ by 5″ loaf pan	Small bowl
Time on High (100% power) Filled apples	7 to 9 minutes	4 to 6 minutes	2 to 2½ (2:30) minutes
Syrup	3 to 5 minutes	2 to 3 minutes	1 to 1½ (1:30) minutes

1 Wash apples well; starting from stem end, core apples, being careful not to go through to the bottom and making opening about 1½ inches in diameter.

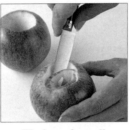
2 Starting from stem end, peel apples one third of the way down. In baking dish, loaf pan, or bowl (see Chart), arrange apples, peeled end up.

3 In small bowl, combine butter or margarine, raisins or currants, walnuts, and cinnamon. Spoon an equal amount of spiced mixture into hollow center of each apple.

4 In glass measure, combine apple juice and maple or maple-flavor syrup; pour over and around filled apples. Cook, covered, on High for time in Chart, until apples are fork-tender, basting with syrup and rearranging apples twice during cooking.

5 With spatula, transfer apples to warmed serving platter. Set aside and keep warm.

6 Cook syrup remaining in dish on High for time in Chart, until slightly thickened. Spoon syrup over apples. Serve hot or cover and refrigerate to serve chilled later.

Apple Desserts

APPLE CARAMEL DESSERT

Color Index page 89. 314 cals per serving. Low in sodium. Begin 40 minutes ahead.

Ingredients for 6 servings		Microwave cookware
¾ cup all-purpose flour	4 tablespoons sugar	9″ broiler-safe pie plate
3 tablespoons dark-brown sugar	3 tablespoons cold water	
¾ teaspoon ground cinnamon	8 small apples, peeled, cored, and thickly sliced	
2 tablespoons shortening	Ice cream or heavy or whipping cream	
5 tablespoons butter or margarine, chilled		
2 to 3 tablespoons ice water		

1 In food processor with knife blade attached, process flour, dark-brown sugar, and cinnamon until blended. Add shortening and 3 tablespoons chilled butter or margarine; process until mixture resembles coarse crumbs. (Or use pastry blender or fingertips.)

2 Into mixture, sprinkle 2 table-spoons ice water. With pulsing motion, process just until mixture begins to hold together. If necessary, add another tablespoon ice water. Do not overprocess or mixture will be tough. Shape into ball; flatten slightly. Wrap in waxed paper and refrigerate 30 minutes.

3 Prepare caramel. In pie plate, place remaining butter or margarine. Heat, covered with paper towel, on High (100% power) 45 seconds, or until melted. Stir in sugar and cold water. Cook on High 6 to 9 minutes, without stirring, just until mixture turns golden, watching carefully since caramel burns easily and continues to cook and darken when removed from the oven.

4 Remove pie plate from oven; stir caramel once to distribute color evenly. In caramel, carefully arrange apple slices in concentric circles. (There will be enough for 2 to 3 layers.)

5 On lightly floured surface, with floured rolling pin, roll dough into 9″ round, ¼ inch thick. Place on top of apples. Cook on High 7 to 10 minutes, until surface looks dry. Lightly brown under preheated broiler. Let stand on heat-safe surface 5 minutes.

6 With knife, loosen dessert from side of pie plate. Invert pie plate onto serving platter. Carefully remove pie plate to unmold dessert. With rubber spatula, loosen any slices sticking to pie plate; place on top of dessert. Serve warm or cover and refrigerate to serve chilled later. If you like, accompany with ice cream or cream.

APPLE BETTY PUDDING

Color Index page 89. 6 servings. 213 cals per serving. Begin 35 minutes ahead.

2 tablespoons butter or margarine (¼ stick)	¼ cup heavy or whipping cream
½ 14½- to 15-ounce jar unsweetened apple-sauce (¾ cup)	1 teaspoon vanilla extract
1 cup whole-wheat bread crumbs	½ teaspoon ground cinnamon
¼ cup all-purpose flour	¼ teaspoon ground ginger
¼ cup packed dark-brown sugar	⅛ teaspoon ground allspice
3 eggs	Crystallized ginger for garnish
½ teaspoon baking powder	

1. Lightly grease 4-cup microwave-safe bowl. Line bottom of bowl with waxed paper; lightly grease paper. Set aside.
2. In food processor with knife blade attached or in blender, process butter or margarine and remaining ingredients, except crystallized ginger until smooth and well blended.
3. Into lined bowl, pour pudding batter. Cook, covered, on Medium (50% power) 12 minutes, or until knife inserted in center comes out clean. Let stand, covered, on heat-safe surface 10 minutes.
4. *To serve:* Invert bowl onto platter. Carefully remove bowl to unmold pudding. Serve warm or cover and refrigerate to serve chilled later. Just before serving, garnish with crystallized ginger.

APPLE-WALNUT CRISP

Color Index page 89. 8 servings. 246 cals per serving. Low in sodium. Begin 35 minutes ahead.

½ cup walnuts, chopped	½ teaspoon ground ginger
½ cup all-purpose flour	
⅓ cup packed dark-brown sugar	4 tablespoons chilled butter or margarine (½ stick), cubed
1 teaspoon ground cinnamon	5 large cooking apples
½ teaspoon ground nutmeg	1 tablespoon lemon juice

1. In food processor with knife blade attached, process walnuts and next 5 ingredients until blended. Add butter or margarine; process until mixture resembles coarse crumbs. (Or use pastry blender or fingertips.) Set aside.
2. Peel, core, and slice apples. In round 1½-quart microwave-safe casserole, place apple slices. Sprinkle with lemon juice.
3. Over apple slices, sprinkle walnut-crumb mixture. Cook on High (100% power) 14 to 16 minutes, until apple slices are tender. If you like, and if casserole is broiler-safe, brown under preheated broiler. Serve warm or cover and refrigerate to serve chilled later.

Banana and Cherry Desserts

GLAZED BANANAS WITH ORANGE

Color Index page 88. 4 servings. 258 cals per serving. Low in sodium. Good source of vitamin C. Begin 15 minutes ahead.

4 medium bananas	1/8 teaspoon ground
2 medium oranges	cinnamon
3 tablespoons butter or	1/3 cup pecan halves
margarine	Orange Julienne (page
3 tablespoons light-brown sugar	334) for garnish

1. Peel bananas and cut into 2-inch pieces. Peel oranges; with sharp knife, separate into sections, removing membranes and any pith. Place fruit in bowl and set aside.
2. In 4-cup microwave-safe glass measure, place butter or margarine. Heat, covered with paper towel, on High (100% power) 45 seconds to 1 minute, until melted. Add brown sugar and cinnamon. Cook on High 2 to 4 minutes, until sugar dissolves and mixture boils, stirring twice.
3. To butter-sugar mixture, add bananas, orange sections, and pecans; stir. Cook on High 2 to 3 minutes, until fruit is hot, stirring twice.
4. Spoon glazed fruit and nuts into warmed serving dish. Garnish and serve warm.

TO FLAMBÉ: Place Glazed Bananas with Orange (above) in heat-safe serving dish. In 1-cup microwave-safe glass measure, heat *1/4 cup dark rum* on High (100% power) 30 to 45 seconds, until hot. Pour over fruit; ignite with long match. Let flames subside before serving.

CHERRIES IN RED WINE

Color Index page 88. 6 servings. 110 cals per serving. Low in cholesterol, fat, sodium. Begin 15 minutes ahead.

2 cups dry red wine	2 teaspoons cornstarch
1/2 8-ounce jar red-currant jelly	dissolved in 2 tablespoons cold water
1 3-inch-long cinnamon stick	Ice cream (optional)
1 pound fresh sweet cherries, pitted, or 1 16 1/2- to 17-ounce can pitted dark sweet cherries, drained	

1. Into 8-cup microwave-safe glass measure, pour red wine; add red-currant jelly and cinnamon stick. Cook on High (100% power) 3 to 4 minutes, until mixture boils. Remove cinnamon stick.
2. Into wine mixture, stir cherries. Cook on High 3 to 4 minutes, stirring halfway through cooking. Stir in dissolved cornstarch. Cook on High 2 to 3 minutes, until mixture thickens, stirring twice.
3. *To serve:* Spoon into dessert dishes and serve warm or cover and refrigerate to serve chilled later. If you like, serve with ice cream.

ZABAGLIONE WITH CHERRIES *

Color Index page 90. 218 cals per serving. Low in sodium. Begin 45 minutes ahead.

Zabaglione is a rich and versatile dessert. It can be served by itself, or with a variety of fruit: strawberries, raspberries, and peaches work well. Or it can be used to create a fruit gratin in a broiler-safe gratin dish: Arrange fruit in a single layer, spoon zabaglione over fruit, brown slightly under preheated broiler, and dust with confectioners' sugar before serving immediately.

Ingredients for 4 servings		Microwave cookware
1 pound fresh sweet cherries, pitted, or 1 16 1/2- to 17-ounce can pitted dark sweet cherries, drained 5 egg yolks	1/4 cup sugar 3 to 4 tablespoons kirsch or dry or sweet Marsala wine Orange Julienne (page 334) for garnish	4-cup glass measure

1 Spoon cherries into wine goblets or dessert dishes; set aside.

2 In glass measure, with mixer at high speed, beat egg yolks and sugar until thick and lemon colored. Cook on Medium (50% power) 1 1/2 (1:30) to 2 minutes, until mixture is thick and fluffy, beating halfway through cooking.

3 To egg mixture, add kirsch or Marsala wine. Beat well.

4 Cook on Medium 30 seconds to 1 1/2 (1:30) minutes, until thickened and hot, beating every 30 seconds. Do not boil or mixture will curdle.

5 With mixer at high speed, beat zabaglione 10 to 15 minutes, until it is fluffy and mounds slightly when dropped from a spoon. Spoon over cherries in goblets.

6 Garnish each serving with Orange Julienne and serve immediately.

Peach and Pear Desserts

All of our attractive fruit dishes make delicious desserts, and the fruits used are naturally sweet so only a minimal amount of sugar is needed. If you like, you can substitute strawberries for the raspberries in the sauce used in our Elegant Poached Peaches (below); or try using different fruits suitable for poaching, such as ripe nectarines instead of peaches.

ELEGANT POACHED PEACHES

Color Index page 92. 276 cals per serving. Low in fat, sodium.
Begin 4 hours ahead or early in day.

Ingredients for 4 servings		Microwave cookware
3 cups water	½ teaspoon almond extract	8-cup glass measure
½ cup sugar	6 amaretti cookies or crisp	
1 tablespoon grenadine	macaroons	
syrup	Raspberries and mint	
4 large peaches, free-	leaves for garnish	
stone if available	Heavy or whipping cream	
1 10-ounce package	(optional)	
frozen raspberries in		
syrup, thawed		

1 In glass measure, combine water, sugar, and grenadine syrup. Cook, covered, on High (100% power) 5 to 6 minutes, until mixture boils, stirring once. Uncover and cook on High 5 minutes longer, stirring twice.

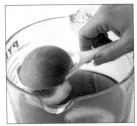

2 Meanwhile, cut each peach in half and twist apart. With small spoon, remove pit from each peach. Into hot syrup, gently place peach halves. Cook on High 4 to 6 minutes, until tender. Cool slightly; remove skin from each peach. Refrigerate peach halves in syrup until cold.

3 Meanwhile, in food processor with knife blade attached or in blender, process raspberries with their syrup until pureed. Over small bowl, set fine sieve. Press puree through sieve to remove seeds. Into puree, stir almond extract and 2 tablespoons syrup from peaches. Cover and refrigerate.

4 When peach halves are cold, remove from measure, reserving syrup. Arrange peach halves, cut side down, in dish to drain.

5 In small bowl, coarsely crumble cookies (to make about ⅓ cup). To crumbs, add 1 to 2 tablespoons reserved peach syrup; stir to moisten. With spoon, fill peach halves with mixture.

6 *To serve*: Onto each of 4 dessert dishes, pour a quarter of raspberry sauce. Place 2 peach halves on top, filled sides up. Serve chilled, garnished with raspberries and mint. If you like, serve with cream.

RASPBERRY-POACHED PEARS WITH CHOCOLATE-RASPBERRY SAUCE

Color Index page 91. 6 servings. 316 cals per serving. Low in sodium.
Begin 4 hours ahead or early in day.

1 10-ounce package frozen raspberries in syrup, thawed
⅓ cup sugar
1 tablespoon lemon juice
6 large pears
1 tablespoon cornstarch dissolved in 2 tablespoons water
1 square semisweet chocolate, chopped
½ cup heavy or whipping cream
1 tablespoon confectioners' sugar
Mint leaves for garnish

1. In food processor with knife blade attached or in blender, process raspberries with their syrup until pureed. Over 3-quart microwave-safe casserole, set fine sieve. Press raspberry puree through sieve to remove seeds. Into puree, stir sugar and lemon juice. Set aside.

2. Peel pears. Starting from bottom end, core pears, being careful not to go through the tops. Do not remove stems.

3. In raspberry puree in casserole, arrange pears spoke-fashion, with wide ends toward edge and stem ends toward center, overlapping stem ends if necessary. Spoon raspberry puree over pears. Cook on High (100% power) 15 to 20 minutes, until pears are nearly tender, turning halfway through cooking.

4. Into casserole, stir dissolved cornstarch until blended. Cook, covered, on High 2 to 5 minutes, until sauce thickens slightly and pears are tender. Cover and refrigerate about 3 hours, until flavors blend, spooning raspberry sauce over pears occasionally.

5. Just before serving, in 2-cup microwave-safe glass measure, place 1 cup raspberry sauce from casserole. Cook on High 2 to 3 minutes, until sauce is very hot. Remove from oven. Add chopped chocolate; stir until chocolate melts.

6. In small bowl, with mixer at medium speed, beat cream and confectioners' sugar until soft peaks form.

7. *To serve*: Onto 6 dessert dishes, pour chocolate-raspberry sauce, reserving some for glaze; place pears on top. Spoon some of reserved sauce over each pear to glaze. Serve with whipped-cream mixture and garnish with mint.

LITTLE STRIPPER
Use this to cut thin strips from peeled or unpeeled fruits such as pears, apples, lemons, or oranges for a decorative effect.

Pear and Pineapple Desserts

POACHED PEARS WITH CHOCOLATE SAUCE

Color Index page 89. 4 servings. 168 cals per serving. Low in sodium. Begin 40 minutes ahead.

2 medium pears	4 teaspoons unsweetened
⅓ cup water	cocoa
5 tablespoons sugar	¼ cup heavy or
½ teaspoon vanilla	whipping cream
extract	Mint leaves for garnish

1. Peel pears; cut pears lengthwise in half. With small spoon, remove cores. On cutting board, place pear halves, cut side down. With sharp knife, starting ½ inch from stem end, slice each pear half lengthwise several times, leaving pear connected at stem end. Press down on each pear half to fan slices slightly. Set aside.
2. In 9″ microwave-safe pie plate, combine water and sugar. Add vanilla extract. Cook on High (100% power) 5 to 7 minutes, until sugar dissolves and syrup boils, stirring occasionally. With spatula, transfer pear fans to pie plate; arrange spoke-fashion, with wide ends toward edge and stem ends toward center. Spoon syrup over each pear fan. Cook, covered, on High 3 to 5 minutes, until tender; reserve syrup.
3. Into 2-cup microwave-safe glass measure, spoon cocoa. With fork or whisk, slowly beat in cream until blended but not whipped. Stir in ⅓ cup reserved syrup. Cook on High 3 to 5 minutes, until sauce thickens slightly, stirring frequently. (If sauce is too thick, stir in more syrup.)
4. *To serve:* Onto each of 4 dessert dishes, pour a quarter of sauce. Arrange pear fans on top. Garnish with mint and serve warm.

SPICED PINEAPPLE

Color Index page 88. 4 servings. 75 cals per serving. Low in fat, sodium. Begin 25 minutes ahead.

1 small pineapple	Lime Julienne (page
2 tablespoons brown	334) and mint leaves
sugar	for garnish
⅛ teaspoon ground	
ginger or cinnamon	

1. With sharp knife, remove leaf and stem end from pineapple. Remove peel and eyes. Cut pineapple lengthwise in half; remove core. Cut each half crosswise into ½-inch-thick slices.
2. In shallow round microwave-safe baking dish, place pineapple slices. Cook, covered, on High (100% power) 3 to 4 minutes.
3. Meanwhile, in small bowl, combine brown sugar and ginger or cinnamon. Over pineapple, evenly sprinkle sugar-spice mixture. Cook on High 1 to 2 minutes, just until sugar melts.
4. *To serve:* Transfer spiced pineapple slices to warmed serving dish. Garnish with Lime Julienne and mint leaves; serve immediately.

CARAMEL PEARS IN STRAWBERRY SAUCE

Color Index page 89. 250 cals per serving. Low in sodium. Begin 45 minutes ahead.

Ingredients	For 4	For 2	For 1
Large pears	4 pears	2 pears	1 pear
Lemon juice	4 teaspoons	2 teaspoons	1 teaspoon
Water	5 tablespoons	4 tablespoons	3 tablespoons
Frozen strawberries in syrup, thawed	1 10-ounce package	½ 10-ounce package	¼ 10-ounce package
Sugar	½ cup	⅓ cup	⅓ cup
Heavy or whipping cream	3 tablespoons	2 tablespoons	2 tablespoons
Microwave cookware	8″ by 8″ baking dish	9″ by 5″ loaf pan	Small bowl
	4-cup glass measure	2-cup glass measure	1-cup glass measure
Time on High (100% power) Pears	10 to 12 minutes	5 to 6 minutes	2 to 3 minutes
Caramel	2 to 4 minutes	2 to 4 minutes	2 to 4 minutes
With cream	1 minute	1 minute	1 minute
Standing time	2 minutes	2 minutes	2 minutes

1 Peel pears. Starting from bottom end, core pears, being careful not to go through the tops. Do not remove stems. If you like, with Little Stripper (page 320) or tines of fork, cut spiral stripes into pears. Brush pears with lemon juice.

2 In baking dish, loaf pan, or small bowl (see Chart), place pears; add water, reserving 1 tablespoon. Cook, covered, on High for time in Chart, until pears are tender, rotating dish halfway through cooking. Set aside.

3 Meanwhile, in food processor with knife blade attached or in blender, process strawberries with their syrup until pureed. Over small bowl, set fine sieve. Press puree through sieve to remove seeds. Set sauce aside.

4 To prepare caramel, in glass measure (see Chart), place sugar; add reserved water. Cook on High for time in Chart, without stirring, just until mixture turns light golden, watching carefully since caramel burns easily and continues to cook and darken when removed from the oven.

5 To caramel, gradually add cream, stirring constantly. Cook on High for time in Chart; stir. Let stand for time in Chart; stir until blended.

6 Onto serving dish or dessert dishes, pour an equal amount of strawberry sauce; place pears on top. Spoon caramel over pears and serve.

Meal in Minutes *for 2 people*

Candlelit Dinner

Chilled Champagne
Shrimp Cocktail (below)
Steak au Poivre, page 204, for 2
Asparagus Bundles, page 252, for 2
Home-fried potatoes
Crème Brûlée, page 325

PREPARATION TIMETABLE

Early in day:	*Make Crème Brûlée; cover and refrigerate. Chill Champagne.*
2 hours ahead:	*Prepare Shrimp Cocktail through step 1; cover and refrigerate. Prepare Asparagus Bundles through step 4; cover and refrigerate.*
45 minutes ahead:	*Make home-fried potatoes conventionally; keep warm. Prepare Steak au Poivre through step 4. Complete Asparagus Bundles; keep warm.*
Just before serving:	*Complete Steak au Poivre. Complete Shrimp Cocktail.*

SHRIMP COCKTAIL
Shrimp cocktail is always an elegant choice for a dinner party.

Line 2 serving bowls with **salad greens**. Arrange *¼ pound shelled and deveined cooked shrimp* in each bowl.

Spoon over **seafood cocktail sauce** to taste. Garnish with **Lemon Twists** (page 132).

Plum and Strawberry Desserts

PLUM KUCHEN

Color Index page 90. 6 servings. 463 cals per serving. Begin 50 minutes ahead.

1½ tablespoons butter or margarine, softened	½ cup Melba-toast Crumbs (page 196)
Brown sugar	8 tablespoons butter or margarine (1 stick), chilled and cubed
2 7½-ounce cans refrigerated buttermilk biscuits	
10 plums	

1. Lightly grease 9″ by 9″ microwave-safe baking dish. Sprinkle with 1 tablespoon brown sugar.
2. In baking dish, press biscuits together to line bottom of dish. Spread with ½ tablespoon softened butter or margarine.
3. With sharp knife, cut plums in half; remove pits. Cut plums into quarters. Press plums, skin side down, into biscuit base, overlapping if necessary.
4. In food processor with knife blade attached, process Melba-toast Crumbs, ½ cup packed brown sugar, and chilled butter or margarine until mixture resembles coarse crumbs. (Or use pastry blender or fingertips.) Sprinkle evenly over plums; press lightly. Cook on High (100% power) 12 to 14 minutes, shielding corners with foil for first 5 minutes and piercing dough with a fork halfway through cooking.
5. If you like and if dish is broiler-safe, brown kuchen under preheated broiler. Let stand on heat-safe surface 5 minutes before serving.

"NOUVELLES" STRAWBERRIES

Color Index page 91. 6 servings. 141 cals per serving. Low in sodium. Good source of vitamin C. Begin 2½ hours ahead or early in day.

1 cup half-and-half	½ teaspoon vanilla extract
2 tablespoons sugar	½ square semisweet chocolate, chopped
⅛ teaspoon salt	
2 egg yolks	2 pints strawberries
1 tablespoon orange-flavor liqueur	Mint leaves for garnish

1. Into medium microwave-safe bowl, pour half-and-half; add sugar and salt. Cook on High (100% power) 3 minutes, or until mixture almost boils, stirring halfway through cooking.
2. In 2-cup glass measure, with whisk, beat egg yolks. Stir small amount of hot mixture into beaten egg yolks. Slowly pour egg mixture back into remaining hot mixture, beating rapidly to prevent lumping. Cook on Medium (50% power) 3 minutes, or until custard sauce thickens slightly, beating twice. Stir in liqueur and vanilla.
3. Reserve half the custard sauce. To remaining sauce, add chopped chocolate, stirring until melted. Refrigerate both sauces until well chilled.
4. *To serve:* Onto dessert plates, spoon an equal amount of each sauce; place strawberries on top and garnish. Serve chilled.

Mixed Fruit Desserts

DRIED FRUIT COMPOTE

Color Index page 89. 8 servings. 171 cals per serving. Low in fat, sodium. Good source of vitamin A. Begin 40 minutes ahead.

1½ cups water	4 whole cloves
¼ cup cider vinegar	Orange Julienne from
½ cup sugar	1 orange (page 334)
1 3-inch-long cinnamon	½ cup dried apricots
stick	½ cup dried pitted
1 vanilla bean, split	prunes
lengthwise or 1	½ cup candied cherries
teaspoon vanilla	(optional)
extract	½ cup dried figs
6 whole allspice	

1. Into 2-quart microwave-safe casserole, pour water and vinegar; add sugar, cinnamon stick, vanilla bean or extract, allspice, cloves, and Orange Julienne, reserving some for garnish. Cook, covered, on High (100% power) 5 to 7 minutes, until mixture boils and sugar dissolves, stirring occasionally.
2. To spiced syrup, add dried fruit. Cook on High 8 to 10 minutes, until fruit plumps, stirring occasionally. With slotted spoon, remove fruit to serving dish.
3. Cook syrup in casserole on High 10 to 15 minutes, until slightly thickened. Over serving dish with fruit, set sieve. Pour hot syrup through sieve to remove spices. Serve compote warm or cover and refrigerate to serve chilled later. Garnish with reserved Orange Julienne before serving.

RED FRUIT COMPOTE

Color Index page 88. 8 servings. 113 cals per serving. Low in fat, sodium. Good source of vitamin C. Begin 20 minutes ahead.

1 16½- to 17-ounce can	¼ cup red-currant jelly
pitted dark sweet	2 tablespoons orange-
cherries	flavor liqueur
1 pint strawberries	1 kiwifruit, peeled and
1 pint raspberries	thinly sliced, for
1 tablespoon cornstarch	garnish

1. Drain cherries, reserving ½ cup syrup; set aside. If strawberries are large, cut them lengthwise in half or into quarters.
2. In 12" by 8" microwave-safe baking dish, combine cherries, strawberries, and raspberries. Cook, covered, on High (100% power) 2½ (2:30) to 3 minutes, until compote is just warm. Spoon compote into warmed serving dish; cover and keep warm.
3. In 2-cup microwave-safe glass measure, dissolve cornstarch in reserved syrup. Stir in red-currant jelly. Cook on High 2½ (2:30) to 4 minutes, until thickened. Stir in orange-flavor liqueur. Pour over compote in serving dish.
4. *To serve:* Serve compote warm or cover and refrigerate to serve chilled later. Garnish with kiwifruit just before serving.

For the busy working woman, the microwave is a great help in preparing some of our delicious desserts ahead. Our Light Cheese Ring with Fruit (below) is ideal for the do-ahead buffet supper table since it is refrigerated until firm and then simply unmolded when ready to serve. Try a combination of any of your favorite fruits for the center and garnish with mint sprigs.

LIGHT CHEESE RING WITH FRUIT

Color Index page 91. 286 cals per serving. Begin 4½ hours ahead or early in day.

Ingredients for 8 servings		Microwave cookware
1 16-ounce container low-fat cottage cheese (2 cups)	1 tablespoon grated orange peel	8-cup glass measure
2 8-ounce packages Neufchâtel cheese	Sliced strawberries, sliced kiwifruit, sliced nectarines, and pineapple chunks	Medium bowl
½ cup sugar	Mint sprigs for garnish	6-cup ring mold
2 tablespoons all-purpose flour		
3 eggs		

1 Over 8-cup glass measure, set strainer. With spoon, press cottage cheese through strainer until smooth.

2 In medium bowl, place Neufchâtel cheese. Heat on Medium (50% power) 2 to 3 minutes, until softened.

3 To cottage cheese in measure, add softened Neufchâtel, sugar, flour, eggs, and grated orange peel. With fork, beat until smooth. Cook on High (100% power) 5 to 8 minutes, until cheese mixture is very hot, beating 3 times during cooking.

4 With pastry brush, lightly oil ring mold. Pour cheese mixture into ring mold. Cook on Medium 6 to 8 minutes, until almost set. Let stand on heat-safe surface 30 minutes. Cover and refrigerate 2 to 3 hours, until well chilled and firm.

5 With knife, loosen cheese ring from side of ring mold. Invert mold onto serving platter. Carefully remove mold.

6 *To serve:* Spoon prepared fruit into center of cheese ring. Garnish with mint sprigs. Serve chilled.

Creamy Desserts

STRAWBERRY CHARLOTTE

Color Index page 91. 313 cals per serving. Low in sodium.
Begin early in day or 1 day ahead.

Ingredients for 12 servings		Microwave cookware
About 20 ladyfingers	*4 eggs, separated*	8-cup glass measure
2 10-ounce packages	*1/2 cup sugar*	
frozen strawberries,	*1/2 teaspoon almond extract*	
thawed	*2 cups heavy or whipping*	
2 cups milk	*cream*	
2 envelopes unflavored	*Strawberries for garnish*	
gelatin		

1 Line bottom of 2-quart soufflé dish with waxed paper. Trim 1 end of ladyfingers to fit dish. Line side of dish with ladyfingers, cut side up. Set aside. In food processor with knife blade attached or in blender, process strawberries until pureed. Set aside.

2 Into glass measure, pour milk. Evenly sprinkle gelatin over milk; let stand 1 minute to soften gelatin slightly. Heat on High (100% power) 4 to 6 minutes, until milk forms small bubbles around edge of measure and gelatin dissolves, stirring twice. In medium bowl, with mixer at high speed, beat egg yolks and half the sugar until thick and lemon colored. Stir small amount of hot milk into egg-yolk mixture.

3 Slowly pour egg mixture back into remaining hot milk, beating rapidly to prevent lumping. Cook on Medium (50% power) 5 to 6 minutes, until mixture thickens slightly and coats back of spoon, stirring twice. Do not boil or custard will curdle. Into large bowl, pour custard. Stir in strawberry puree and almond extract. Cover and refrigerate about 45 minutes, until strawberry mixture mounds slightly when dropped from a spoon, stirring occasionally.

4 In medium bowl, with mixer at high speed, beat egg whites until soft peaks form. Gradually sprinkle in remaining sugar, 2 tablespoons at a time, beating well after each addition, until sugar completely dissolves and whites stand in stiff, glossy peaks. Spoon on top of strawberry mixture. In same bowl, with same beaters, and with mixer at medium speed, beat cream until soft peaks form. Spoon over strawberry mixture, reserving 1/2 cup for garnish.

5 With rubber spatula or whisk, gently fold whipped cream and beaten egg whites into strawberry mixture. Carefully spoon into prepared soufflé dish. Cover and refrigerate about 4 hours, until set.

6 *To serve:* With thin knife, loosen charlotte from side of dish. Invert dish onto chilled serving platter. Carefully remove dish to unmold charlotte; remove waxed paper. Garnish with reserved cream and strawberries.

PASTRY CREAM *

Color Index page 88. Makes 3 cups. 299 cals per cup. Low in sodium. Begin 25 minutes ahead.

2 cups milk
1/4 cup sugar
3 tablespoons all-purpose flour
5 egg yolks
1/2 teaspoon vanilla extract

1. Into 8-cup microwave-safe glass measure, pour milk. Heat on High (100% power) 4 to 6 minutes, until milk forms small bubbles around edge.
2. In medium bowl, with fork or whisk, combine sugar and flour. Add egg yolks, one at a time, beating well after each addition.
3. Stir small amount of hot milk into egg mixture. Slowly pour egg mixture back into remaining hot milk, beating rapidly to prevent lumping. Cook on High 2 to 3 minutes, until mixture thickens, beating every minute. Do not boil. Stir in vanilla.
4. Onto surface of hot pastry cream, press plastic wrap to prevent skin from forming. Refrigerate until chilled.
5. Over bowl, set fine sieve. Press cream through sieve to remove any lumps. Use chilled Pastry Cream plain, or with flavorings (below), in tartlets, pies, and vol-au-vents, and garnish with fresh fruit or other toppings. Pastry cream can also be used as a filling in cakes, cream puffs, and éclairs.

PASTRY CREAM

Our plain Pastry Cream (above) can be varied with different flavors and used to fill these prettily shaped tartlet shells.

Almond Pastry Cream: Prepare Pastry Cream (above), substituting *1/2 teaspoon almond extract* for the vanilla extract.

Orange Pastry Cream: Prepare Pastry Cream (above), substituting *1 tablespoon orange-flavor liqueur* and *1 teaspoon grated orange peel* for the vanilla extract.

Mocha Pastry Cream: Prepare Pastry Cream (above). At end of step 3, stir in *1/4 cup semi-sweet-chocolate pieces* and *1/2 teaspoon instant espresso powder* until chocolate is melted.

CRÈME BRÛLÉE

Color Index page 92. 4 servings. 419 cals per serving. Low in sodium. Good source of vitamin A. Begin early in day or 1 day ahead.

1½ cups heavy or whipping cream
3 egg yolks
3 tablespoons sugar
½ teaspoon vanilla extract

2 tablespoons dark-brown sugar
4 large strawberries for garnish

1. Into 4-cup microwave-safe glass measure, pour cream. Heat on High (100% power) 3 to 5 minutes, until cream forms small bubbles around edge of measure.

2. In small microwave-safe bowl, with whisk, beat egg yolks and sugar. Stir small amount of hot cream into egg mixture. Slowly pour egg mixture back into remaining hot cream, beating rapidly to prevent lumping. Cook on Medium (50% power) 4 to 6 minutes, until mixture thickens, stirring frequently. Do not boil. Stir in vanilla.

3. Into four 4-ounce broiler-safe ramekins, pour hot mixture. Cover and refrigerate about 6 hours, or until well chilled.

4. About 1 hour before serving, preheat broiler. Evenly sprinkle brown sugar over each ramekin so that cream is completely covered; arrange in broiler-safe baking dish. To prevent custard from curdling, place ice cubes between ramekins. Broil 3 to 4 minutes, until sugar melts and makes a shiny crust; refrigerate about 30 minutes, or until crust hardens. Before serving, place ramekins on small plates and garnish.

Sprinkling the Sugar and Adding the Ice Cubes

With spoon, sprinkle sugar evenly over surface of cream mixture to cover completely.

To prevent cream from curdling, place ice cubes between ramekins before broiling.

MAKING CARAMEL

Caramel is easy and quick to prepare in the microwave, but it is essential to watch the mixture carefully, without stirring, and to remove it from the oven as soon as it starts to turn golden, since it continues to cook and darken (even burn) afterward.
To clean glass measure after making caramel: fill with warm water and heat on High (100% power) until water boils.

CRÈME CARAMEL

Color Index page 92. 226 cals per serving. Low in sodium. Good source of calcium. Begin 2½ hours ahead or early in day.

Ingredients for 4 servings		Microwave cookware
½ cup sugar *3 tablespoons water* *1¼ cups milk* *4 eggs*	*1 teaspoon vanilla extract*	4-cup glass measure 4 6-ounce ramekins or custard cups 12" by 8" baking dish

1 In glass measure, place half the sugar; add water. Cook on High (100% power) 4 to 6 minutes, without stirring, just until mixture turns light golden, watching carefully since caramel burns easily and continues to cook and darken when removed from the oven.

2 Into ramekins or custard cups, pour caramel, swirling to coat bottoms of dishes. Set aside to harden. Into same cleaned measure (see Box, below left), pour milk. Heat on High 4 to 6 minutes, until milk forms small bubbles around edge of measure.

3 In medium bowl, with whisk, beat eggs and remaining sugar until blended. Stir small amount of hot milk into egg mixture. Slowly pour egg mixture into remaining hot milk, beating rapidly to prevent lumping. Stir in vanilla. Over 8-cup measure, set fine sieve. Strain custard mixture through sieve to remove any lumps.

4 In baking dish, place ramekins or custard cups. Pour custard mixture into ramekins or cups. Fill baking dish with water to within 1 inch of top of ramekins or cups. Cook on Medium-High (70% power) 10 to 14 minutes, until custards are set but centers are still soft, carefully rotating dish 3 times during cooking.

5 Remove ramekins or cups from baking dish. Let custards stand, covered, on heat-safe surface 5 minutes, or until firmly set. Cover and refrigerate until ready to serve.

6 *To serve:* With thin knife, loosen custards from sides of ramekins or cups. Invert each custard onto a chilled dessert plate. Carefully remove ramekin or cup, allowing caramel syrup to drip onto custard. Serve chilled.

Creamy Desserts

FROSTY LEMON SOUFFLÉS

Color Index page 92. 216 cals per serving. Low in sodium.
Begin early in day or 1 day ahead.

Ingredients for 8 servings		Microwave cookware
2 teaspoons all-purpose flour ¾ cup sugar ¾ cup milk 2 eggs, separated	4 medium lemons 1 cup heavy or whipping cream Lemon slices and mint leaves for garnish	4-cup glass measure

1 In glass measure, with whisk, combine flour and ½ cup sugar until blended. Gradually pour in milk, stirring until smooth. Cook on High (100% power) 4 to 6 minutes, until mixture thickens and boils, stirring occasionally.

2 In small bowl, with whisk, beat egg yolks. Stir small amount of hot milk into egg yolks. Slowly pour egg-yolk mixture back into remaining hot milk mixture, beating rapidly to prevent lumping. Cook on Medium (50% power) 2 to 3 minutes, until custard thickens, stirring often. Do not boil. Pour into large bowl. Onto surface of hot custard, lightly press plastic wrap to prevent skin from forming. Refrigerate 1 hour, until chilled.

3 Grate 1 tablespoon peel from lemons. Squeeze ⅔ cup juice from lemons. Stir lemon peel and juice into chilled custard.

4 In medium bowl, with mixer at high speed, beat egg whites until soft peaks form. Gradually sprinkle in remaining sugar, 1 tablespoon at a time, beating well after each addition, until sugar completely dissolves and whites stand in stiff, glossy peaks. Spoon on top of lemon custard.

5 In same bowl, with same beaters, and with mixer at medium speed, beat cream until soft peaks form. Add to egg whites and lemon custard. With rubber spatula or whisk, gently fold whipped cream and beaten egg whites into custard.

6 Spoon soufflé mixture into 8 freezer-safe glasses or dishes; freeze about 4 hours or overnight. Before serving, let soufflés stand at room temperature about 10 minutes to soften slightly. Garnish with lemon slices and mint leaves. Serve immediately.

RHUBARB TAPIOCA WITH CREAM

Color Index page 93. 8 servings. 167 cals per serving. Low in sodium.
Begin 3½ hours ahead or early in day.

1 cup milk 1 cup water ¾ cup sugar 2 tablespoons quick-cooking tapioca 1½ pounds fresh rhubarb, sliced (about 4 cups)	½ cup heavy or whipping cream 1 tablespoon confectioners' sugar ¼ teaspoon vanilla extract

1. In 4-quart microwave-safe casserole, combine milk and next 3 ingredients. Let stand 5 minutes. Stir in rhubarb. Cook, covered, on High (100% power) 20 to 25 minutes, stirring every 5 minutes. Spoon mixture into dessert dishes; cover and refrigerate 2½ hours, until well chilled.
2. In small bowl, with mixer at medium speed, beat cream, confectioners' sugar, and vanilla until soft peaks form. Top each dessert.

RASPBERRY CREAM PARFAITS

Color Index page 92. 6 servings. 327 cals per serving. Low in sodium.
Begin 3½ hours ahead or early in day.

1 10-ounce package frozen raspberries in syrup, thawed 2 tablespoons water 1 envelope unflavored gelatin	½ teaspoon lemon juice ½ cup sugar 2 egg whites 1½ cups heavy or whipping cream

1. In food processor with knife blade attached or in blender, process raspberries with their syrup until pureed. Over large bowl, set fine sieve. Press raspberry puree through sieve to remove seeds. Into small microwave-safe bowl, pour water. Evenly sprinkle gelatin over; let stand 1 minute to soften. Heat on High (100% power) 1 to 2 minutes, until gelatin dissolves, stirring twice. Do not boil. Stir into raspberry sauce.
2. Into raspberry mixture, stir lemon juice and half the sugar. Cover and refrigerate 15 to 20 minutes, until mixture mounds slightly when dropped from spoon, stirring often.
3. In medium bowl, with mixer at medium speed, beat cream until soft peaks form. Fold half the cream into raspberry mixture. Reserve remainder.
4. In bowl, with mixer at high speed, beat egg whites until soft peaks form. Gradually sprinkle in remaining sugar, 1 tablespoon at a time, beating well after each addition, until sugar dissolves and whites stand in stiff, glossy peaks. Fold into raspberry mixture.
5. Place a spoonful of raspberry mixture in each parfait glass. Top with a spoonful of reserved whipped cream. Repeat layering twice. Cover and refrigerate until set. Serve chilled.

Creamy and Chocolate Desserts

TIRAMISÚ

Color Index page 93. 16 servings. 385 cals per serving. Begin 4 hours ahead or early in day.

1 18.25- to 18.5-ounce package yellow-cake mix	1½ cups heavy or whipping cream
2 eggs	½ cup confectioners' sugar
¼ cup salad oil	⅓ cup dark rum or strong coffee
1 cup water	
½ teaspoon almond extract	1 teaspoon vanilla extract
2 8-ounce packages cream cheese	Cocoa

1. Line bottom of 13" by 9" microwave-safe baking dish with a double thickness of waxed paper.
2. In bowl, with mixer at low speed, beat cake mix, eggs, oil, water, and almond extract until blended, constantly scraping bowl. Increase speed to medium; beat 2 minutes, occasionally scraping bowl. Spoon batter into prepared dish.
3. Elevate dish on microwave-safe trivet, rack, or ramekins turned upside down. Cook on High (100% power) 10 to 12 minutes, until cake springs back when lightly touched with finger, rotating dish twice. Let stand in dish on heat-safe surface 5 minutes. With knife, loosen cake from sides of dish. Invert onto rack; remove paper. Let cool.
4. In 4-cup microwave-safe glass measure, place cream cheese. Heat on High 1 to 2 minutes, until softened. With mixer at low speed, beat cream cheese, cream, confectioners' sugar, half the rum or coffee, and vanilla until blended.
5. Cut cooled cake into 2-inch pieces. Place a third in 2½-quart serving bowl. Pour in a third of cream-cheese mixture. Repeat layers with remaining cake and cream-cheese mixture. Cover and refrigerate until well chilled. Dust surface with cocoa before serving.

CHOCOLATE-DIPPED FRUIT

Color Index page 90. Makes 14 to 30 pieces. Cals per piece: strawberries, 39; grapes, 24; cherries, 24. Begin 35 minutes ahead.

3 squares semisweet chocolate or 3 ounces white chocolate	14 large strawberries; or 24 grapes (about 8 ounces); or 30 cherries (about 10 ounces)
1 teaspoon shortening	

1. Line cookie sheet with waxed paper. In 2-cup microwave-safe glass measure, place chocolate and shortening. Heat on High (100% power) 1½ (1:30) to 2 minutes, until melted, stirring once. Remove from oven; stir until smooth.
2. Dip fruit halfway into melted chocolate. Gently shake off excess chocolate; place dipped fruit on lined cookie sheet.
3. Let chocolate-dipped fruit stand about 10 minutes, until chocolate sets. Do not refrigerate. Serve same day.

CHOCOLATE-CHESTNUT CREAM

Color Index page 93. 430 cals per serving. Low in sodium. Good source of calcium, iron. Begin 4½ hours ahead or early in day.

Ingredients for 12 servings		Microwave cookware
2 cups milk 1 17½-ounce can sweetened chestnut puree 2 squares unsweetened chocolate, chopped 4 eggs, separated	2 envelopes unflavored gelatin ¼ cup sugar 2½ cups heavy or whipping cream Chocolate Curls (page 346) for garnish	8-cup glass measure

1 Prepare collar for 1½-quart soufflé dish: From roll of waxed paper or foil, tear off 24" strip; fold lengthwise into 24" by 6" strip. Wrap strip around outside of dish so collar stands 3 inches above rim. Secure with cellophane tape and set aside.

2 Into glass measure, pour milk; add sweetened chestnut puree. Heat on High (100% power) 6 to 8 minutes, until milk forms small bubbles around edge of measure. Stir chestnut mixture until smooth and well blended. Add chopped chocolate and stir until melted.

3 In large bowl, with whisk, beat egg yolks. Stir small amount of hot chestnut mixture into beaten egg yolks. Slowly pour egg mixture back into remaining hot mixture, beating rapidly to prevent lumping. Evenly sprinkle gelatin over chocolate-chestnut mixture; allow to soften 1 minute. Cook on Medium (50% power) 4 to 6 minutes until mixture thickens and gelatin dissolves, stirring twice. Cover and refrigerate about 45 minutes, until mixture mounds when dropped from spoon, stirring occasionally.

4 In medium bowl, with mixer at high speed, beat egg whites until soft peaks form. Gradually sprinkle in sugar until sugar completely dissolves and whites stand in stiff, glossy peaks. Spoon on top of chocolate-chestnut mixture. In same bowl, with same beaters, and with mixer at medium speed, beat 2 cups cream until soft peaks form. With rubber spatula, fold cream and beaten egg whites into chocolate-chestnut mixture.

5 Into prepared soufflé dish, spoon chocolate-chestnut mixture; cover and refrigerate about 2½ hours until set.

6 To serve: Remove collar from soufflé dish. In small bowl, with mixer at medium speed, beat remaining cream until soft peaks form; spoon into decorating bag fitted with star tube. Pipe top of dessert with whipped cream. If you like, garnish with Chocolate Curls. Serve chilled.

Chocolate Desserts

CHOCOLATE MOUSSE TORTE

Color Index page 92. 297 cals per serving. Low in sodium. Begin 4½ hours ahead or early in day.

Ingredients for 16 servings		Microwave cookware
1½ cups milk *¼ teaspoon salt* *Sugar* *1 envelope unflavored gelatin* *4 eggs, separated* *8 squares semisweet chocolate*	*2 tablespoons butter or margarine (¼ stick)* *1 cup nuts, chopped* *2 cups heavy or whipping cream* *Chocolate Rounds (page 346, optional)*	Large bowl Small bowl

1 In large bowl, combine milk, salt, and ⅓ cup sugar. Evenly sprinkle gelatin over mixture; let stand 1 minute to soften gelatin slightly. Stir. Cook on High (100% power) 3 minutes, until gelatin completely dissolves, stirring halfway through cooking. Do not boil.

2 In small bowl, with whisk, beat egg yolks. Stir small amount of hot milk mixture into egg yolks. Slowly pour egg mixture back into remaining hot milk mixture, beating rapidly to prevent lumping. Cook on Medium (50% power) 4 minutes, or until custard mixture thickens slightly, stirring occasionally. Add 6 squares chocolate to custard; stir until melted. Cover and refrigerate chocolate custard about 20 minutes, to cool slightly. Meanwhile, with pastry brush, lightly oil 9″ by 3″ springform pan.

3 In small bowl, place remaining chocolate and butter or margarine. Heat, covered with paper towel, on High 1½ (1:30) minutes, or until melted. Stir in nuts, reserving 1 tablespoon for garnish. Spread chocolate-nut mixture over bottom of oiled springform pan. Place pan in freezer about 15 minutes, until chocolate-nut mixture sets into a crust.

4 In medium bowl, with mixer at high speed, beat egg whites until soft peaks form. Gradually sprinkle in ¼ cup sugar, beating well after each addition, until sugar completely dissolves and whites stand in stiff, glossy peaks. Spoon on top of cooled chocolate custard. In same bowl, with same beaters, and with mixer at medium speed, beat $1\,^1/_1$ cups cream until soft peaks form.

5 To egg whites and chocolate-custard mixture, add whipped cream. With rubber spatula or whisk, gently fold cream and egg whites into chocolate-custard mixture. Spoon mousse over chocolate-nut crust in pan. Cover and refrigerate about 3 hours, until set.

6 With knife, loosen mousse from side of springform pan. Remove side of pan. In small bowl, with mixer at medium speed, beat remaining cream until soft peaks form; spoon into decorating bag fitted with star tube. Pipe top of torte with whipped cream and sprinkle with reserved nuts. If you like, decorate with Chocolate Rounds. Serve chilled.

CHOCOLATE-CREAM LOAF

Color Index page 93. 16 servings. 299 cals per serving. Low in sodium. Begin early in day.

1 12-ounce bag frozen raspberries, thawed
3 tablespoons sugar
6 egg yolks
1½ cups heavy or whipping cream
3 tablespoons pistachio nuts, finely chopped
12 squares semisweet chocolate
8 tablespoons butter or margarine (1 stick)

1. In food processor with knife blade attached or in blender, process raspberries and sugar until pureed. Press puree through fine sieve to remove seeds. Cover and refrigerate sauce.
2. In medium microwave-safe bowl, with whisk, beat egg yolks and ½ cup cream. Cook on Medium (50% power) 3½ (3:30) to 4 minutes, until egg-yolk mixture coats back of spoon, stirring occasionally. Do not boil. Cover and refrigerate 10 minutes, stirring once.
3. Line 9″ by 5″ loaf pan with foil. Evenly sprinkle bottom with nuts. Set aside.
4. In large microwave-safe bowl, place chocolate and butter or margarine. Heat, covered with paper towel, on High 2 to 3 minutes, until melted. Remove from oven; stir until smooth. In small bowl, with mixer at medium speed, beat remaining cream until soft peaks form. With whisk, beat egg-yolk mixture into melted chocolate mixture. With rubber spatula, fold in whipped cream.
5. Spoon mixture into prepared loaf pan. Refrigerate about 3 hours, until firm. With knife, loosen loaf from sides of pan. Invert loaf onto serving platter. Cut into slices and serve, chilled, with raspberry sauce.

POTS DE CRÈME ÉLÉGANTS

Color Index page 93. 4 servings. 171 cals per serving. Low in sodium. Begin early in day.

½ 6-ounce package semisweet-chocolate pieces
3 eggs, separated
1 teaspoon vanilla extract
Whipped cream (optional)

1. In medium microwave-safe bowl, place chocolate. Heat on High (100% power) 1 to 1½ (1:30) minutes, until melted. Remove from oven; stir until smooth.
2. In small bowl, with fork, beat egg yolks and vanilla. Slowly pour mixture into melted chocolate, beating until blended. Cook on Medium (50% power) 30 seconds, stirring twice.
3. In bowl, with mixer at high speed, beat egg whites until stiff peaks form. With rubber spatula or whisk, gently fold beaten egg whites into chocolate mixture until blended.
4. Into each of 4 pot de crème cups, spoon a quarter of chocolate mixture. Cover and refrigerate at least 4 hours, until firm and well chilled. If you like, serve with whipped cream.

TINY CHOCOLATE CONES

Color Index page 93. Makes 25 cones. 54 cals each. Low in cholesterol, sodium. Begin early in day.

4 squares semisweet
  chocolate, chopped
2 tablespoons butter or
  margarine (¼ stick)
2 tablespoons heavy or
  whipping cream

½ teaspoon vanilla
  extract
½ cup macadamia nuts,
  finely chopped

1. To form cones: If you like, cut twenty-five 3½-inch foil squares. Fold each square diagonally in half to make a triangle. Hold each triangle with long side toward you. Bring lower right point over to meet top point. Roll left side of foil around right side to form a cone with a tight point at the bottom; secure with cellophane tape. Repeat with remaining foil squares.
2. In medium microwave-safe bowl, place chocolate and butter or margarine. Heat, covered with paper towel, on High (100% power) 2 to 2½ (2:30) minutes, until melted. Remove from oven, stir until smooth. Stir in cream and vanilla. Set bowl over ice water. With whisk, beat mixture until fluffy. Fold in nuts, reserving 1 tablespoon.
3. Spoon chocolate mixture into decorating bag fitted with medium star tube. Pipe into foil cones or pipe 1-inch rosettes. Sprinkle with reserved nuts. Refrigerate about 1 hour, until set.

WHITE-CHOCOLATE MOUSSE *

Color Index page 90. 8 servings. 242 cals per serving. Low in sodium. Begin 55 minutes ahead.

6 ounces white chocolate
  or 2 3-ounce bars
  (Töbler, Narcisse or
  Lindt)
3 tablespoons milk
2 eggs

½ teaspoon vanilla
  extract
1 cup heavy or whipping
  cream
Raspberries and mint
  leaves for garnish

1. In medium microwave-safe bowl, place chopped white chocolate. Heat on High (100% power) 2 to 3 minutes, until chocolate is melted, stirring twice. Remove from oven; stir until smooth.
2. In small bowl with fork or whisk, beat milk and eggs. Gradually beat egg mixture into melted chocolate until blended. Cook chocolate mixture on Medium (50% power) 2½ (2:30) to 3 minutes, until thickened slightly, stirring halfway through cooking. Do not boil. Stir in vanilla. Cover and refrigerate about 30 minutes, until well chilled, stirring occasionally.
3. With mixer at medium speed, beat chilled chocolate mixture 1 minute. In bowl, with same beaters, and with mixer at medium speed, beat cream until soft peaks form. With rubber spatula or whisk, gently fold whipped cream into chocolate mixture. Spoon into serving dish or dessert dishes. Serve immediately or cover and refrigerate to serve chilled later. Garnish.

CHOCOLATE-ALMOND DESSERT

Color Index page 93. 616 cals per serving. Good source of iron. Begin 3½ hours ahead or early in day.

Ingredients for 8 servings		Microwave cookware
⅓ cup seedless raisins, chopped 2 tablespoons almond-flavor liqueur 8 squares semisweet chocolate 4 tablespoons butter or margarine (½ stick), softened ½ cup packed light-brown sugar	3 eggs, separated ½ teaspoon baking powder ⅓ cup dried bread crumbs 6 amaretti cookies or crisp macaroons, crushed (about ⅓ cup) 1 tablespoon sugar Chocolate-cream Frosting (page 345) Sliced blanched almonds for garnish	2-quart soufflé dish 2-cup glass measure Trivet, rack, or ramekin

1 Line bottom of soufflé dish with a double thickness of waxed paper. In small bowl, combine chopped raisins and almond-flavor liqueur. Set aside.

2 In glass measure, place chocolate. Heat on High (100% power) 2½ (2:30) to 3 minutes, until melted, stirring once. Remove from oven; stir until smooth. Set aside.

3 In medium bowl, with mixer at low speed, beat butter or margarine and brown sugar until blended. Increase speed to high; beat until light and fluffy. Reduce speed to medium; add egg yolks one at a time, beating well after each addition. With rubber spatula, fold in melted chocolate, baking powder, bread crumbs, and crushed cookies. Add plumped raisins and their liquid.

4 In another medium bowl, with mixer at high speed, beat egg whites until soft peaks form. Add sugar, beating well until sugar completely dissolves and whites stand in stiff, glossy peaks. With rubber spatula, gently fold beaten egg whites into chocolate mixture until blended. Spoon evenly into prepared soufflé dish.

5 Elevate soufflé dish on trivet, rack, or ramekin turned upside down. Cook on High (100% power) 6 to 8 minutes, just until set, rotating dish every 2 minutes. Let stand, covered, on heat-safe surface 10 minutes. With thin knife, loosen dessert from dish. Invert onto serving platter; remove waxed paper. Leave to cool completely.

6 With metal spatula, cover top and side of cake with Chocolate-cream Frosting, making decorative swirls. Garnish with sliced almonds.

Ice Cream and Sorbets

The custard and syrup bases for our ice cream and sorbets are quick to make in the microwave and the resulting desserts are delicious on their own or served with fruit and toppings. Be sure to cool custards and syrups completely before freezing. Our sorbet recipes can also be made in ice-cream freezers as manufacturers direct.

VANILLA ICE CREAM

Color Index page 94. 178 cals per serving. Low in sodium. Begin early in day.

Ingredients for 8 servings or 1½ pints		Microwave cookware
½ cup sugar 4 teaspoons all-purpose flour ¼ teaspoon salt 1½ cups milk 1 egg	1 egg yolk ¾ cup heavy or whipping cream 1 teaspoon vanilla extract	8-cup glass measure

1 In glass measure, combine sugar, flour, and salt. Pour in milk and stir until smooth. Cook on High (100% power) 4 to 6 minutes, until mixture boils and thickens slightly, stirring occasionally.

2 In small bowl, with whisk, beat egg and egg yolk. Stir small amount of hot milk mixture into beaten eggs. Slowly pour egg mixture back into remaining hot milk mixture, beating rapidly to prevent lumping.

3 Cook custard mixture on Medium (50% power) 2 to 3 minutes, until custard thickens, beating frequently. Do not boil or custard will curdle.

4 Onto surface of hot custard, lightly press plastic wrap to prevent skin from forming. Refrigerate about 2 hours, until completely chilled, stirring occasionally.

5 Into 1½- to 2-quart ice-cream freezer container, pour chilled custard, cream, and vanilla extract. Freeze mixture as manufacturer directs. When freezing is finished, ice cream will be soft. Remove dasher. With spoon, scoop ice cream into freezer-safe serving dish. Pack down ice cream, smoothing surface and, if you like, make decorative pattern on top. Cover with plastic wrap.

6 Place dish in freezer at least 2 hours, until ice cream is firm. To soften ice cream slightly before serving, heat on Medium-Low (30% power) 30 seconds to 1 minute. Use ice-cream scoop to serve.

MANGO SORBET

Color Index page 94. 4 servings. 164 cals per serving. Low in fat, sodium. Good source of vitamin A. Begin early in day.

1 cup water
½ cup sugar
1 ripe mango (about 1 pound), peeled and cut into ½-inch chunks

1 tablespoon lime juice
2 tablespoons dark rum
Lime Julienne (page 334) for garnish

1. Into 4-cup microwave-safe glass measure, pour water; add sugar. Cook on High (100% power) 3 to 4 minutes, until sugar dissolves and mixture begins to boil, stirring halfway through cooking. Cook on High 5 minutes longer, stirring occasionally. Cover and refrigerate syrup about 45 minutes, until chilled.

2. In food processor with knife blade attached or in blender, process mango, lime juice, and rum until pureed, scraping side if necessary.

3. Into cooled syrup, stir mango puree. Pour into 9″ by 9″ baking dish. Onto surface, press plastic wrap. Freeze about 3 hours, until sorbet is partially frozen, stirring occasionally.

4. Into chilled large bowl, spoon sorbet. With mixer at medium speed, beat sorbet until smooth but still frozen. Transfer to freezer-safe dish; smooth surface. Cover and freeze again until firm.

5. Let sorbet stand at room temperature 5 to 10 minutes to soften before serving. Garnish.

KIWIFRUIT SORBET

Color Index page 94. 4 servings. 143 cals per serving. Low in cholesterol, fat, sodium. Good source of vitamin C. Begin early in day.

1 cup water
½ cup sugar
4 ripe kiwifruit, peeled, cut into quarters, and cored

1 tablespoon lemon juice
Mint leaves for garnish

1. Into 4-cup microwave-safe glass measure, pour water; add sugar. Cook on High (100% power) 3 to 4 minutes, until sugar dissolves and mixture begins to boil, stirring halfway through cooking. Cook on High 5 minutes longer, stirring occasionally. Cover and refrigerate about 45 minutes, until chilled.

2. In food processor with knife blade attached or in blender, process kiwifruit and lemon juice, until pureed, scraping side if necessary.

3. Into cooled syrup, stir kiwifruit puree. Pour into 9″ by 9″ baking dish. Onto surface, press plastic wrap. Freeze about 3 hours, until sorbet is partially frozen, stirring occasionally.

4. Into chilled large bowl, spoon sorbet. With mixer at medium speed, beat until smooth but still frozen. Transfer to freezer-safe dish; smooth surface. Cover and freeze again until firm.

5. Let sorbet stand at room temperature 5 to 10 minutes to soften before serving. Garnish.

CHOCOLATE-COCONUT DESSERT CUPS

Color Index page 90. 6 servings. 233 cals per serving. Low in sodium. Begin 40 minutes ahead.

½ 6-ounce package semisweet-chocolate pieces	*1 cup flaked coconut*
	1 pint ice cream
2 teaspoons shortening	*Chocolate-dipped Fruit (page 327)*

1. Line six 2½″ muffin-pan cups with a double thickness of paper liners.
2. In small microwave-safe bowl, place chocolate and shortening. Heat on High (100% power) 1½ (1:30) to 2 minutes, until melted and smooth, stirring occasionally. Stir in coconut. Into each muffin-pan cup, place 1 rounded tablespoon chocolate-coconut mixture. Press mixture onto bottom and up edge of each paper liner. Place in freezer about 10 minutes, until firm.
3. Lift out chilled chocolate cups; carefully remove paper liners and discard. Spoon an equal amount of ice cream into each cup. Top with Chocolate-dipped Fruit and serve immediately.

ICE-CREAM PIE

Ice-cream pies are always a popular choice for a party. Use the microwave to create this delicious version by softening peanut butter (page 29) and ice cream (page 31) for easy spreading.

Into *Graham-cracker Crumb Crust* (page 361), evenly spread *1 pint vanilla ice cream, softened*.

In small bowl, combine *½ cup corn syrup* and *⅓ cup peanut butter, softened*; spread evenly over ice cream.

Sprinkle pie with *⅓ cup chopped peanuts or other nuts, chopped*. Top with *1 pint chocolate ice cream, softened*.

Freeze Ice-cream Pie about 4 hours, or until firm. Garnish with *whipped cream* and *chopped nuts*.

CHOCOLATE CREAM PUFFS

Color Index page 94. 179 cals each. Begin 1½ hours ahead.

Ingredients for 12 cream puffs		Microwave cookware
1 cup water *8 tablespoons butter or margarine (1 stick)* *¼ teaspoon salt* *1 cup all-purpose flour* *4 eggs*	*Chocolate Glaze (below)* *Vanilla Ice Cream (page 330), bought ice cream, or Pastry Cream (page 324), chilled*	8-cup glass measure

1 Preheat conventional oven to 400°F. Lightly brush 1 large cookie sheet with oil.

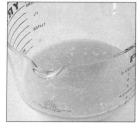

2 Into glass measure, pour water; add butter or margarine and salt. Heat on High (100% power) 5 to 7 minutes, until water boils.

3 To mixture, add flour all at once. With wooden spoon, vigorously beat until mixture forms a ball and leaves side of measure.

4 To flour mixture, add eggs, one at a time, beating well after each addition, until mixture is smooth and satiny. Let mixture stand until slightly cooled.

5 Onto greased cookie sheet, using large spoon and rubber spatula, drop batter into 12 mounds, about 2 inches apart. Bake conventionally 40 minutes, or until golden.

6 Turn off oven; let puffs remain in oven 10 minutes to dry. Remove puffs from oven and place on racks to cool.

7 Make Chocolate Glaze: In 4-cup microwave-safe measure, place *3 ounces semisweet-chocolate pieces, 1 table-spoon butter, 1 ½ tea-spoons milk, and 1 ½ teaspoons light corn syrup*.

8 Cook chocolate mixture on High 2 to 3 minutes, until chocolate melts, stirring halfway through cooking. Remove from oven. Stir until smooth.

9 *To serve*: When puffs are cool, slice tops off. Fill shells with ice cream or chilled Pastry Cream. Replace tops and drizzle with warm Chocolate Glaze. Serve immediately.

Puddings

All milk-based desserts or those with a high milk content turn out particularly well when cooked in the microwave because they don't stick or scorch as they tend to do when cooked conventionally. Our Nutty Chocolate Pudding (below) is a favorite all-American dessert especially popular with children. Easy to make in the microwave, it is irresistible garnished with whipped cream.

NUTTY CHOCOLATE PUDDING

Color Index page 93. 438 cals per serving. Good source of calcium. Begin 2½ hours ahead or early in day.

Ingredients for 6 servings		Microwave cookware
⅔ cup sugar	1 egg	8-cup glass measure
¼ cup all-purpose flour	1 teaspoon vanilla extract	
¼ teaspoon salt	½ cup pecans, chopped	
¼ teaspoon ground cinnamon	½ cup heavy or whipping cream	
2 cups milk	Ground cinnamon for garnish	
4 tablespoons butter or margarine (½ stick)		
3 squares unsweetened chocolate		

1 In glass measure, combine sugar, flour, salt, and cinnamon. Stir in milk until blended. Add butter or margarine and chocolate. Cook on High (100% power) 5 to 7 minutes, until mixture bubbles and thickens slightly, stirring occasionally.

2 Meanwhile, in small bowl, with whisk, beat egg. Stir small amount of hot chocolate mixture into beaten egg. Slowly pour egg mixture back into remaining hot chocolate mixture, beating rapidly to prevent lumping.

3 Cook mixture on Medium (50% power) 2 to 3 minutes, until pudding thickens, stirring frequently. Do not boil or pudding will curdle. Stir in vanilla extract and chopped pecans.

4 Into each of 6 dessert bowls, pour an equal amount of pudding. Onto surface of hot puddings, lightly press plastic wrap to prevent skin from forming. Refrigerate about 2 hours, until well chilled and set.

5 Just before serving, in small bowl, with mixer at medium speed, beat cream until soft peaks form.

6 *To serve:* Remove plastic wrap from puddings. Top each serving with whipped cream. Lightly sprinkle with cinnamon. Serve chilled.

BROWNIE PUDDING

Color Index page 91. 8 servings. 274 cals per serving. Begin 45 minutes ahead.

4 tablespoons butter or margarine (½ stick)
1 cup all-purpose flour
½ teaspoon instant espresso powder (optional)
2 teaspoons baking powder
¾ cup sugar
6 tablespoons cocoa
½ cup half-and-half
1 teaspoon vanilla extract
⅓ cup packed light-brown sugar
¼ cup walnuts, chopped
1 cup water
Confectioners' sugar

1. In 2-cup microwave-safe glass measure, place butter or margarine. Heat, covered with paper towel, on High (100% power) 45 seconds to 1 minute, until melted. Set aside.
2. In medium bowl, combine flour, espresso powder, if using, baking powder, ½ cup sugar, and 3 tablespoons cocoa. Into melted butter or margarine, stir half-and-half and vanilla. Stir half-and-half mixture into flour mixture until smooth. Pour batter into a 9″ microwave-safe deep-dish pie plate.
3. In small bowl, combine brown sugar, walnuts, and remaining sugar and cocoa. Evenly sprinkle over batter. Carefully pour water over top. Elevate pie plate on microwave-safe trivet, rack or ramekin turned upside down. Cook on Medium (50% power) 12 to 15 minutes, until pudding rises and is almost set, rotating every 3 minutes. Let stand on heat-safe surface 15 minutes. Dust with confectioners' sugar; serve warm.

CREAMY RICE PUDDING

Color Index page 90. 6 servings. 283 cals per serving. Low in sodium. Good source of calcium. Begin 50 minutes ahead.

3 cups milk
½ cup regular long-grain rice
1 teaspoon vanilla extract
2 egg yolks
3 tablespoons sugar
½ cup heavy or whipping cream
¼ teaspoon ground cinnamon
¼ teaspoon ground allspice
½ cup raisins

1. In 2-quart microwave-safe casserole, combine milk, rice, and vanilla. Cook on High (100% power) 5 minutes, or until boiling. Reduce power level to Medium-High (70% power) and cook 20 to 30 minutes longer, until tender, stirring often.
2. In small bowl, with whisk, beat egg yolks and next 4 ingredients until blended. Stir small amount of rice mixture into egg mixture. Pour egg mixture back into remaining rice mixture, stirring rapidly to prevent lumping. Stir in raisins. Cook on Medium (50% power) 3 to 4 minutes, until slightly thickened, stirring every minute.
3. On heat-safe surface, let pudding stand, covered, 5 minutes. Serve warm or cover and refrigerate to serve chilled later. Garnish.

Meal in Minutes *for 12 people*

Valentine's Dessert Party

Strawberry Charlotte, page 324
Tartlets filled with Pastry Cream, page 324, and fruit
Caramel Pears in Strawberry Sauce, page 321, for 4 (double quantity)
Black Forest Cake, page 343
Pink Champagne

PREPARATION TIMETABLE

Early in day:	**4 hours ahead:**	**3 hours ahead:**	**30 minutes ahead:**	**Just before serving:**
Chill Champagne. Prepare Strawberry Charlotte through step 5.	*Prepare Caramel Pears in Strawberry Sauce through step 5, in 2 batches. Make Black Forest Cake; cover loosely and refrigerate.*	*Make Pastry Cream in flavors of your choice; cover with plastic wrap and refrigerate. Prepare fruit for tartlets; cover and refrigerate. Complete Strawberry Charlotte as in step 6. Refrigerate until ready to serve.*	*If you like, reheat tartlet shells to crisp; set aside to cool. Fill tartlet shells with Pastry Cream and decorate with fruit; arrange on serving platter.*	*Complete Caramel Pears in Strawberry Sauce as in step 6.*

333

Puddings

Use your microwave to make traditional bread-based desserts. These puddings are a delicious and economical way to use up any day-old bread you may have left over, as we have done in our Old-Fashioned Bread and Butter Pudding (below), in which the crusts are removed for an attractive presentation. For a nutritious change, substitute whole-wheat bread for the white bread.

OLD-FASHIONED BREAD AND BUTTER PUDDING

Color Index page 90. 290 cals per serving. Good source of calcium. Begin 45 minutes ahead.

Ingredients for 10 servings		Microwave cookware
12 slices day-old white bread	¾ cup sugar	Shallow 2-quart baking dish
4 tablespoons butter or margarine (½ stick), softened	½ teaspoon ground cinnamon	4-cup glass measure
2 cups half-and-half	⅛ teaspoon ground nutmeg	Trivet, rack, or ramekins
1 cup milk	⅛ teaspoon ground cloves	
4 eggs	1 teaspoon vanilla extract	
	Confectioners' sugar	

1 Remove crusts from bread. Cut slices diagonally in half to form triangles. Arrange slices on cookie sheet; toast lightly. Spread each triangle with softened butter or margarine.

2 In baking dish, working from outer edge toward center, arrange toast triangles in overlapping circles.

3 Into glass measure, pour half-and-half and milk. Heat on High (100% power) 4 to 6 minutes, until mixture forms small bubbles around edge of measure.

4 In medium bowl, with mixer at medium speed, beat eggs, sugar, spices, and vanilla until blended. Stir small amount of hot milk mixture into egg mixture. Slowly pour egg mixture back into remaining hot milk mixture, beating rapidly to prevent lumping.

5 Over toast in baking dish, carefully ladle custard.

6 Elevate baking dish on trivet, rack, or ramekins turned upside down. Cook on Medium (50% power) 14 to 16 minutes, until knife inserted 1 inch from edge comes out clean, rotating dish twice. Let stand on heat-safe surface until slightly cooled. Just before serving, dust with confectioners' sugar. Serve warm.

ORANGE CHALLAH PUDDING

Color Index page 91. 10 servings. 270 cals per serving. Begin 45 minutes ahead.

1 loaf challah or French bread	¼ teaspoon ground nutmeg
1½ cups half-and-half	Confectioners' sugar
1½ cups orange juice	Orange Julienne (below) for garnish
4 eggs	Maple syrup (optional)
½ cup sugar	
1 teaspoon vanilla extract	

1. Lightly grease 2-quart microwave-safe baking dish. With serrated knife, cut bread into 1-inch-thick slices. Arrange bread in baking dish.

2. Into 4-cup microwave-safe glass measure, pour half-and-half. Heat on High (100% power) 3 to 4 minutes, until half-and-half forms small bubbles around edge of measure.

3. In 2-cup glass measure, with whisk, beat orange juice, eggs, sugar, vanilla, and nutmeg. Stir small amount of hot half-and-half into egg mixture. Slowly pour egg mixture back into remaining hot half-and-half, beating rapidly to prevent lumping. Carefully ladle custard over bread in baking dish.

4. Elevate baking dish on microwave-safe trivet, rack, or ramekins turned upside down. Cook on Medium (50% power) 14 to 16 minutes, until knife inserted 1 inch from edge comes out clean, rotating dish twice. If you like, and if dish is broiler-safe, brown under preheated broiler.

5. Just before serving, dust pudding with confectioners' sugar and garnish with Orange Julienne. Serve warm. If you like, pass maple syrup separately.

ORANGE, LEMON, AND LIME JULIENNE

Julienne garnish can intensify the flavors of a dish, as in our Orange Challah Pudding (above), or provide a zesty contrast, as in our Harvard Beets (page 254).

With vegetable peeler, remove peel from orange, lemon, or lime, leaving bitter white pith behind. Stack peel and cut into fine strips.

Or use zester to remove fine strips of peel as shown. Zester is best for the thinner skin of limes.

Puddings and Cheesecakes

CHOCOLATE-CINNAMON BREAD PUDDING

Color Index page 90. 10 servings. 280 cals per serving. Begin 45 minutes ahead.

12 slices cinnamon bread	4 eggs
3 squares semisweet chocolate, melted	¾ cup sugar
2 cups half-and-half	1½ teaspoons vanilla extract
1 cup milk	

1. Remove crusts from bread. With serrated knife, cut slices diagonally in half to form triangles. In shallow 2-quart microwave-safe baking dish, arrange half the triangles in a single layer, overlapping if necessary. Drizzle half the melted chocolate over triangles. Arrange remaining triangles in single layer on top. Set aside.
2. Into 4-cup microwave-safe glass measure, pour half-and-half and milk. Heat, covered, on High (100% power) 4 to 6 minutes, until mixture forms small bubbles around edge of measure.
3. In medium bowl, with whisk, beat eggs, sugar, and vanilla. Stir small amount of hot cream mixture into egg mixture. Slowly pour egg mixture back into remaining hot cream mixture, beating rapidly to prevent lumping. Ladle custard over bread. Drizzle with remaining melted chocolate.
4. Elevate baking dish on microwave-safe trivet, rack, or ramekins turned upside down. Cook on Medium (50% power) 14 to 16 minutes, until knife inserted 1 inch from edge comes out clean, rotating dish twice. Let stand on heat-safe surface until slightly cooled. Serve warm or cover and refrigerate to serve chilled later.

RICH NOODLE PUDDING

Color Index page 91. 8 servings. 319 cals per serving. Begin 45 minutes ahead.

1 8-ounce package ribbon egg noodles	¾ cup sour cream
6 tablespoons butter or margarine, (¾ stick), melted	1 egg, beaten
	2 tablespoons sugar
	¼ cup golden raisins
1 cup fresh bread crumbs	¼ cup dried apricots, diced
1 cup cottage cheese	1 teaspoon ground cinnamon

1. Lightly grease 12" by 8" microwave- and broiler-safe baking dish. Cook noodles conventionally as label directs. Drain and keep warm.
2. In small bowl, mix half the melted butter or margarine with bread crumbs; set aside.
3. In large bowl, combine cottage cheese, sour cream, beaten egg, and sugar until blended. Stir in noodles, raisins, apricots, and cinnamon. Add remaining melted butter or margarine; stir. Pour mixture into baking dish. Cook, covered, on Medium (50% power) 10 to 12 minutes, until set.
4. Sprinkle pudding with crumb mixture. Brown under preheated broiler. Let stand on heat-safe surface 5 minutes before serving.

CREAMY CHEESECAKE

Color Index page 94. 420 cals per serving. Begin early in day or 1 day ahead.

Ingredients for 12 servings		Microwave cookware
6 tablespoons butter or margarine (¾ stick)	¼ cup milk	1-cup glass measure
1½ cups graham-cracker crumbs	2 tablespoons grated lemon peel	9" by 2" round baking dish
1¼ cups sugar	1 teaspoon vanilla extract	Large bowl
3 8-ounce packages cream cheese	Sour cream, canned cherry-pie filling, or fresh berries and melted jelly for topping (optional)	Trivet, rack, or ramekin
3 tablespoons all-purpose flour		
3 eggs		

1 In glass measure, place butter or margarine. Heat, covered, with paper towel, on High (100% power) 1 to 1½ (1:30) minutes, until melted. In medium bowl, with fork, place graham-cracker crumbs and ¼ cup sugar. Pour in melted butter or margarine; stir with fork until well blended.

2 With pastry brush, lightly oil bottom and side of baking dish. Line bottom with a double thickness of waxed paper. With spoon, press a third of crumb mixture onto side of dish to form side of crust. Set aside with remaining crumb mixture.

3 In large bowl, place cream cheese. Heat on Medium (50% power) 2 to 3 minutes, until softened. With mixer at medium speed, beat cream cheese until smooth. Gradually beat in remaining sugar. With mixer at low speed, add flour, eggs, milk, lemon peel, and vanilla extract; beat 5 minutes, occasionally scraping bowl.

4 Cook cream-cheese mixture on High 5 to 8 minutes, until hot, beating 3 times. Spoon into prepared baking dish, smoothing surface. With spoon, lightly press remaining crumb mixture evenly onto surface to form a crust. Elevate dish on trivet, rack, or ramekin turned upside down.

5 Cook cheesecake on Medium 6 to 10 minutes, until softly set, rotating dish twice. Do not overcook or cheesecake will not be creamy. Let stand in dish on heat-safe surface about 30 minutes, until set. Cover and refrigerate at least 4 hours, until well chilled.

6 To serve: With thin knife, loosen cheesecake from side of dish. Invert dish onto serving platter to unmold cheesecake; remove waxed paper. If you like, spread top of cheesecake with sour cream, canned cherry-pie filling, or fresh berries brushed with melted jelly.

Cheesecakes

For cheesecakes such as our lighter-than-traditional Individual Raspberry Cheesecakes (below), attractive microwave-safe cookware can double as serving dishes. This easy way of cooking and serving in individual ramekins makes a nice presentation and eliminates having to unmold the desserts. Microwave-safe custard cups can be used if you do not have individual ramekins.

INDIVIDUAL RASPBERRY CHEESECAKES

Color Index page 94. 437 cals per serving. Begin 3½ hours ahead or early in day.

Ingredients for 8 servings		Microwave cookware
4 tablespoons butter or margarine (½ stick)	2 8-ounce packages cream cheese	2-cup glass measure
1 cup vanilla-wafer crumbs	¾ cup sugar	Large bowl
1 10-ounce package frozen raspberries, thawed	2 eggs	8 4-ounce ramekins
	1 teaspoon vanilla extract	
	Confectioners' sugar to taste	

1 In glass measure, place butter or margarine. Heat, covered with paper towel, on High (100% power) 45 seconds to 1 minute, until melted. Stir in vanilla-wafer crumbs. Set aside.

2 In food processor with knife blade attached or in blender, process raspberries until pureed. Over medium bowl, set fine sieve. Press puree through sieve to remove seeds. Set aside.

3 In large bowl, place cream cheese. Heat on Medium (50% power) 2 to 3 minutes, until softened. With mixer at low speed, beat cream cheese, sugar, eggs, vanilla, and ½ cup raspberry puree until smooth and well blended, occasionally scraping bowl. Cook on High 4 to 6 minutes, until very hot, beating 3 times during cooking. Remove from oven; beat until smooth.

4 Into ramekins, spoon crumb mixture. With spoon, lightly press crumb mixture onto bottoms to form crust. Spoon cream-cheese mixture on top of crust, smoothing surface. On oven floor, arrange ramekins in a circle, at least 1 inch apart. Cook on Medium 3 to 4 minutes, until almost set, rearranging ramekins twice.

5 On heat-safe surface, let cheesecakes stand in ramekins 15 minutes until set. Sweeten remaining raspberry puree with confectioners' sugar. Refrigerate cheesecakes and raspberry puree until well chilled.

6 *To serve*: Decorate each cheesecake with a swirl of raspberry puree. Place ramekins on dessert dishes and serve chilled. Pass any remaining puree separately.

CHOCOLATE-AMARETTI CHEESECAKE

Color Index page 94. 12 servings. 542 cals per serving. Good source of vitamin A. Begin early in day or 1 day ahead.

1½ cups crushed amaretti cookies (about 40 cookies) or crisp macaroons	3 8-ounce packages cream cheese
6 tablespoons butter or margarine (¾ stick), melted	1 cup sugar
	3 eggs
	¼ cup milk
½ 6-ounce package semisweet-chocolate pieces (½ cup)	¼ teaspoon almond extract
	1 cup heavy or whipping cream, whipped

1. In medium bowl, with fork, combine cookie crumbs and melted butter or margarine until well blended. Line 9″ by 2″ round microwave-safe baking dish with a double thickness of waxed paper. With spoon, press a third of crumb mixture onto side of dish to form side of crust. Set aside with remaining crumb mixture.

2. In large microwave-safe bowl, place chocolate and cream cheese. Heat on Medium (50% power) 2 to 3 minutes, until cream cheese softens and chocolate melts, stirring halfway through cooking. With mixer at medium speed, beat until smooth. Add sugar, eggs, milk, and almond extract; beat until blended, occasionally scraping bowl. Cook on High (100% power) 5 to 8 minutes, until very hot, beating 3 times.

3. Pour cheesecake mixture into prepared dish. With spoon, lightly press remaining crumbs evenly onto surface to form a crust. Elevate dish on microwave-safe trivet, rack, or ramekin turned upside down. Cook on Medium (50% power) 6 to 8 minutes, until softly set. Let stand in dish on heat-safe surface 30 minutes, until set. Cover and refrigerate 4 to 5 hours, or overnight.

4. *To serve*: With thin knife, loosen cheesecake from side of dish. Invert dish onto platter. Carefully remove dish to unmold cheesecake; remove waxed paper. Garnish cheesecake with whipped cream. Pass remaining whipped cream separately.

CHEESECAKE TOPPINGS

Dress up a basic cheesecake with a mouth-watering topping. Spread with *sour cream* and top with fresh fruit, such as *hulled and sliced strawberries, whole blueberries,* or *kiwifruit slices.* Or brush with *melted jelly* for an elegant glazed finish. Or use canned fruit filling such as *cherry-pie filling* with *1 tablespoon grated lemon peel* and *½ teaspoon lemon juice* added for extra zest. Or pipe *whipped cream* in decorative rosettes and garnish with *Chocolate Curls (page 346)* or *whole berries.*

Cakes, Cookies, and Candies

SIMPLE CAKES · LAYER CAKES · CHOCOLATE GARNISHES

SPECIAL CAKES · BROWNIES · SHORTBREAD · CREATIVE COOKIES

CAKE DECORATIONS · CHOCOLATE COOKIES

HARD AND SOFT CANDIES · CHOCOLATE AND CHEWY CANDIES

Cakes, Cookies, and Candies

Microwaved cakes are light textured and delicious. In keeping with the time-saving qualities of microwave cooking, we have developed a range of cakes all based on packaged cake mixes used in conventional baking. You can produce family-pleasing cakes each time by following a few simple tips. Elevate the pans on trivets, racks, or ramekins, and rotate the pans halfway through cooking for even cooking. Cakes should be removed from the microwave when they spring back if lightly touched with a finger. Any moist spots on the top of a cake will dry during standing time in the pan, and the cake will begin to pull away from the sides of the pan by end of standing time. The cake is done when a toothpick inserted in the center comes out clean. To cool a cake completely after standing time, invert it onto a rack and remove the waxed paper. To keep moist, wrap cake layers when completely cool. A wide range of tasty brownies plus everyday and elegant cookies can be made in the microwave. When done the cookies are soft; let them stand as directed, then remove to a rack to cool completely and become firm. Cookies and cakes can be tailored to special occasions with the decorations featured on pages 352 and 353.

Candies cook easily in the microwave, and cleaning up afterwards is much easier. A microwave candy thermometer is a useful tool for cooking mixtures to exactly the right temperature. Choose one with a clip; a dry wooden spoon, pushed through the clip, then placed across the top of the bowl, will keep the thermometer resting in the mixture. To test the thermometer for accuracy, fill a 1-cup microwave-safe glass measure with water; place thermometer in water. Heat on High (100% power) 2 to 3 minutes until water boils. The thermometer should read 212°F. (at sea level). If it reads higher or lower than this, adjust the cooking time accordingly. If you do not have a microwave candy thermometer, follow our Cold-water Test (page 355) which provides an accurate and simple way of judging when the right temperature has been reached.

PRETTY GIFTS

Use your microwave oven to make Christmas baking more fun than ever. Make any of our delicious cookies and candies, then pack them in pretty tins and boxes lined with colorful paper. These gifts will be as much fun to give as receive.

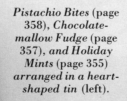

Pistachio Bites (page 358), Chocolate-mallow Fudge (page 357), and Holiday Mints (page 355) arranged in a heart-shaped tin (left).

Holiday Mints (page 355) and Tiny Chocolate Cones (page 329) are packed together to make an attractive gift (right) for someone with a sweet tooth.

Simple Cakes

APPLESAUCE SPICE CAKE

Color Index page 96. 6 servings. 424 cals per serving. Good source of iron. Begin 1¼ hours ahead.

½ 18.25- to 18.5-ounce package yellow-cake mix	1 apple, peeled, cored, and sliced
1 teaspoon ground cinnamon	¼ cup all-purpose flour
⅛ teaspoon ground cloves	¼ cup packed brown sugar
⅛ teaspoon ground nutmeg	2 tablespoons butter or margarine (¼ stick), cubed
½ cup Applesauce (below) or ¼ 16-ounce jar applesauce	½ cup chopped walnuts
2 tablespoons salad oil	Confectioners' Icing (below)
1 egg	

1. Lightly grease bottom of 9″ by 2″ round microwave-safe baking dish.
2. In large bowl, with mixer at low speed, beat dry cake mix, ½ teaspoon cinnamon, cloves, nutmeg, applesauce, oil, and egg until blended, constantly scraping bowl. Increase speed to high; beat 2 minutes, occasionally scraping bowl.
3. Pour batter into prepared baking dish, smoothing surface. Arrange apple slices on top of batter.
4. In food processor with knife blade attached or in blender, process flour, brown sugar, and remaining cinnamon. Add butter or margarine; process until mixture resembles coarse crumbs. (Or use pastry blender or fingertips.) Stir in walnuts. Sprinkle topping over apples in baking dish. Elevate on microwave-safe trivet, rack, or ramekin turned upside down.
5. Cook on High (100% power) 6 to 8 minutes, until cake springs back when lightly touched with finger, rotating dish halfway through cooking. On heat-safe surface, let cake stand in dish 5 minutes. Prepare Confectioners' Icing. Drizzle over top of cake. Serve warm or cover loosely and refrigerate to serve chilled later.

CONFECTIONERS' ICING: In small bowl, combine ¾ *cup confectioners' sugar* and *1 tablespoon milk*. Use immediately. Makes ¾ cup. 25 cals per tablespoon.

APPLESAUCE: Cut *6 medium cooking apples* into quarters; do not peel or core. In 2-quart microwave-safe casserole, place apples and ¼ *cup water*. Cook, covered, on High (100% power) 10 to 15 minutes, until apples are very tender. Over large bowl, set strainer. Press apple mixture through strainer to remove skin and seeds; discard. To apple puree, add ⅓ *cup sugar* and *1 teaspoon lemon juice*; stir. Cover and refrigerate. Makes 4 cups. 180 cals per cup.

PINEAPPLE UPSIDE-DOWN CAKE

Color Index page 96. 427 cals per serving. Good source of iron. Begin 1¼ hours ahead.

Our Pineapple Upside-down Cake is a real old-time favorite as well as one of the most popular choices for novice bakers. It is quick and easy to make in the microwave oven, and it rises just as well as when conventionally baked. Whipped cream or vanilla ice cream is the perfect accompaniment.

Ingredients for 12 servings		Microwave cookware
1¼ cups packed brown sugar 8 tablespoons butter or margarine (1 stick) 1 15½-ounce can pineapple rings, drained	Maraschino cherries 1 18.25- to 18.5-ounce package yellow-cake mix 1 cup water ¼ cup salad oil 3 eggs	13″ by 9″ baking dish Trivet, rack, or ramekins

1 In baking dish, place brown sugar and butter or margarine. Cook on High (100% power) 3 to 5 minutes, until butter or margarine melts, stirring twice.

2 In sugar mixture, arrange pineapple rings. Place 1 maraschino cherry in center of each ring and, if you like, place extra cherries between rings. Set aside.

3 In large bowl, with mixer at low speed, beat dry cake mix, water, oil, and eggs until blended, constantly scraping bowl. Increase speed to medium; beat 2 minutes, occasionally scraping bowl. Carefully pour batter over pineapple arrangement in baking dish. Smooth surface.

4 Elevate baking dish on trivet, rack, or ramekins turned upside down. Cook on High 10 to 12 minutes, until cake springs back when lightly touched with finger, rotating dish halfway through cooking.

5 On heat-safe surface, let cake stand in dish 10 minutes. With knife, loosen cake from sides of dish. Invert dish onto serving tray. Carefully remove dish to unmold cake. With rubber spatula, loosen any pineapple rings sticking to baking dish and replace on cake.

6 *To serve:* Cut cake into 12 portions. Serve warm or cover and refrigerate to serve chilled later.

Simple and Layer Cakes

Chocolate and peanut butter are two of the most popular ingredients in America, so a combination of the two is irresistible. We use a scrumptious mixture of semisweet chocolate and peanut butter, melted with ease and no mess in the microwave, to frost our Peanut-butter Cupcakes (below). For extra texture in this super-rich frosting, you can use chunky instead of smooth peanut butter.

PEANUT-BUTTER CUPCAKES

Color Index page 96. 310 cals each. Begin 1¼ hours ahead or early in day.

Ingredients for 12 cupcakes		Microwave cookware
½ 18.25- to 18.5-ounce package yellow-cake mix 1 egg ½ cup peanut butter	¾ cup milk Peanut-butter-chocolate Frosting (below)	Muffin pan

1 In large bowl, with mixer at low speed, beat dry cake mix, egg, peanut butter, and milk until blended, constantly scraping bowl. Increase speed to medium; beat 2 minutes, occasionally scraping bowl.

2 Line 6 muffin-pan cups with a double thickness of paper liners. Spoon half the batter into cups, filling them only half full.

3 Cook cupcakes on Medium (50% power) 4 to 5½ (5:30) minutes, until they spring back when lightly touched with finger, rotating pan halfway through cooking.

4 Lift cupcakes from muffin-pan cups; remove outer papers. Place cupcakes on rack to cool. Meanwhile, reline muffin-pan cups and repeat with remaining batter. Let cupcakes cool completely.

5 Prepare Peanut-butter-chocolate Frosting: In small microwave-safe bowl, place **1 cup semisweet-chocolate pieces**. Heat on High (100% power) 1 to 2 minutes, until melted. Stir in **½ cup peanut butter** until smooth and well blended.

6 With metal spatula, spread top of cupcakes immediately with Peanut-butter-chocolate Frosting.

SUNNY ORANGE LAYER CAKE

Color Index page 95. 10 servings. 506 cals per serving. Good source of vitamin C, calcium. Begin early in day.

Lemon-curd Filling (below, half quantity) *1 18.25- to 18.5-ounce package yellow-cake mix* *1 6-ounce container frozen orange juice concentrate, thawed*	*3 eggs* *¼ cup salad oil* *1 teaspoon grated orange peel* *Orange Whipped Cream (page 367) for frosting* *Mandarin orange sections for garnish*

1. Prepare Lemon-curd Filling. Line bottom of 9″ by 2″ round microwave-safe baking dish with waxed paper. In large bowl, with mixer at low speed, beat dry cake mix, orange juice concentrate, eggs, oil, and orange peel until well blended, constantly scraping bowl. Increase speed to medium; beat 2 minutes, occasionally scraping bowl.

2. Spoon half the batter into prepared baking dish, smoothing surface. Elevate on microwave-safe trivet, rack, or ramekin turned upside down. Cook on High (100% power) 6 to 8 minutes, until cake springs back when lightly touched with finger, rotating dish halfway through cooking.

3. On heat-safe surface, let cake stand in dish 5 minutes. Invert cake onto rack, remove waxed paper, and let cool completely.

4. Meanwhile, reline baking dish with waxed paper and repeat steps 2 and 3 with remaining batter.

5. Prepare Orange Whipped Cream. On serving platter, place 1 cake layer, rounded side down; spread with Lemon-curd Filling. Top with remaining layer, rounded side up. Frost top and side of cake with Orange Whipped Cream; chill 15 minutes. Garnish with mandarin orange sections before serving.

LEMON-CURD FILLING: In 4-cup microwave-safe glass measure, combine **1 tablespoon grated lemon peel, 3 tablespoons lemon juice, 12 tablespoons butter or margarine (1½ sticks), and 1 cup sugar.** Cook on High (100% power) 1 to 2 minutes, until butter or margarine melts, stirring once. In small bowl, with whisk, beat **3 eggs.** Stir small amount of hot butter mixture into beaten eggs. Slowly pour egg mixture back into remaining hot butter mixture, beating rapidly to prevent lumping. Cook on Medium (50% power) 2 to 3 minutes, until mixture is very thick, stirring occasionally. Do not boil or mixture will curdle. Onto surface of hot filling, lightly press plastic wrap to prevent skin from forming. Refrigerate about 3 hours, until well chilled. Makes enough to fill two 2-layer cakes. 2,245 cals.

CARROT CAKE

Color Index page 96. 10 servings. 603 cals per serving (without frosting). Good source of vitamin A, calcium, iron. Begin 2½ hours ahead or early in day.

1 18.25- to 18.5 ounce package yellow-cake mix	*¼ cup golden raisins*
	¼ cup chopped walnuts
1 cup plain low-fat yogurt	*3 medium carrots, peeled and shredded (1½ cups)*
¼ cup wheat germ	
¼ cup salad oil	*Cream-cheese Frosting (below)*
1 teaspoon ground cinnamon	*Walnut halves for garnish*
½ teaspoon ground allspice	
¼ teaspoon ground nutmeg	
3 eggs	

1. Line bottom of 9″ by 2″ round microwave-safe baking dish with waxed paper.

2. In large bowl, with mixer at low speed, beat dry cake mix, yogurt, wheat germ, oil, cinnamon, allspice, nutmeg, and eggs until well blended, constantly scraping bowl. Increase speed to medium; beat 2 minutes, occasionally scraping bowl. Stir in golden raisins, walnuts, and shredded carrots.

3. Spoon half the batter into prepared baking dish, smoothing surface. Elevate on microwave-safe trivet, rack, or ramekin turned upside down. Cook on High (100% power) 6 to 8 minutes, until cake springs back when lightly touched with finger, rotating dish halfway through cooking.

4. On heat-safe surface, let cake stand in dish 5 minutes. Invert cake onto rack, remove waxed paper, and let cool completely.

5. Meanwhile, reline baking dish with waxed paper and repeat steps 3 and 4 with remaining batter.

6. Prepare Cream-cheese Frosting. On serving platter, place 1 cake layer, rounded side down; spread with frosting. Top with remaining layer, rounded side up. Frost top and side of cake with remaining frosting. Garnish with walnut halves.

CREAM-CHEESE FROSTING: Unwrap *2 3-ounce packages cream cheese;* place cheese in medium microwave-safe bowl. Heat on Medium (50% power) 1 to 2 minutes, until softened. With mixer at low speed, beat in *2 tablespoons milk* until smooth. Gradually add *contents of 1 16-ounce package confectioners' sugar,* and *1 teaspoon vanilla extract;* beat until smooth. Makes enough to fill and frost one 2-layer cake. 2,374 cals.

TWO-TONED LAYER CAKE

Color Index page 96. 474 cals per serving. Good source of calcium, iron. Begin 3 hours ahead or early in day.

Ingredients for 12 servings		Microwave cookware
1 18.25- to 18.5-ounce package marble-cake mix	*3 eggs*	9″ by 2″ round baking dish
	1 3.5- to 5.9-ounce package chocolate mousse mix	Trivet, rack, or ramekin
1 cup water	*Chocolate-cream Frosting (page 345)*	
¼ cup salad oil		

1 Line bottom of baking dish with waxed paper. In large bowl, with mixer at low speed, beat dry yellow-cake mix, water, oil, and eggs until blended, constantly scraping bowl. Increase speed to high; beat 2 minutes, occasionally scraping bowl. Spoon half the batter into prepared baking dish, smoothing surface.

2 Elevate baking dish on trivet, rack, or ramekin turned upside down. Cook on High (100% power) 6 to 8 minutes, until cake springs back when lightly touched with finger, rotating dish halfway through cooking.

3 On heat-safe surface, let cake stand in dish 5 minutes. Invert cake onto rack; remove waxed paper, and let cool completely.

4 Meanwhile, reline baking dish with waxed paper. To batter remaining in bowl, add dry chocolate-flavor mix; stir until blended. Spoon into relined dish, smoothing surface. Repeat steps 2 and 3.

5 Meanwhile, prepare chocolate mousse as label directs; cover and refrigerate until chilled. Prepare Chocolate-cream Frosting.

6 With serrated knife, cut each cake layer horizontally in half. On serving platter, place 1 yellow cake layer, rounded side down. Spread with a third of chocolate mousse. Top with 1 chocolate cake layer, rounded side up; spread with a third of chocolate mousse. Repeat layering, ending with chocolate cake layer. Frost top and side of cake with Chocolate-cream Frosting. Cover loosely with waxed paper and refrigerate to serve chilled.

Layer Cakes

STRAWBERRY SHORTCAKE

Color Index page 95. 399 cals per serving. Begin 3 hours ahead.

Ingredients for 8 servings		Microwave cookware
½ 18.25- to 18.5-ounce package yellow-cake mix ½ cup water 2 tablespoons salad oil 1 egg 1 egg yolk 1 pint strawberries	2 tablespoons sugar 1½ cups heavy or whipping cream 3 tablespoons confectioners' sugar 1 teaspoon vanilla extract	9″ by 2″ round baking dish Trivet, rack, or ramekin

1 Line bottom of baking dish with waxed paper. In large bowl, with mixer at low speed, beat dry cake mix, water, salad oil, egg, and egg yolk until blended, constantly scraping bowl. Increase speed to medium; beat 2 minutes, occasionally scraping bowl.

2 Spoon batter into prepared baking dish, smoothing surface. Elevate on trivet, rack, or ramekin turned upside down. Cook on High (100% power) 6 to 8 minutes, until cake springs back when lightly touched with finger, rotating dish halfway through cooking. On heat-safe surface, let cake stand in dish 5 minutes.

3 Invert cake onto rack, remove waxed paper, and let cool completely. With serrated knife, cut cake horizontally into 3 layers. Set aside.

4 Hull strawberries; cut into quarters, reserving a few whole berries for garnish. In small bowl, gently mix cut-up strawberries and sugar until sugar dissolves; set aside. In another small bowl, with mixer at medium speed, beat cream, confectioners' sugar, and vanilla until soft peaks form.

5 On serving platter, place bottom cake layer, cut side up. Spread with a third of whipped cream; top with half the strawberry mixture. Place middle cake layer on top of strawberry mixture. Spread with a third of whipped cream and top with remaining strawberry mixture. Cover with last cake layer, cut side down.

6 On top of cake, spread remaining whipped cream. Garnish with reserved strawberries just before serving.

WHITE CHOCOLATE AND STRAWBERRY GÂTEAU *

Color Index page 95. 12 servings. 579 cals per serving. Good source of calcium. Begin early in day.

White-chocolate Mousse (page 329, double quantity) 1 18.25- to 18.5-ounce package yellow-cake mix 1 cup water	2 eggs ¼ cup salad oil 1½ pints strawberries Strawberry Fans (below) for garnish

1. Prepare White-chocolate Mousse. Cover with plastic wrap and and refrigerate until mousse is well chilled.
2. Line bottom of 9″ by 2″ round microwave-safe baking dish with waxed paper.
3. In large bowl, with mixer at low speed, beat dry cake mix, water, oil, and eggs until blended, constantly scraping bowl. Increase speed to medium; beat 2 minutes, occasionally scraping bowl.
4. Spoon half the batter into prepared baking dish, smoothing surface. Elevate on microwave-safe trivet, rack, or ramekin turned upside down. Cook on High (100% power) 6 to 8 minutes, until cake springs back when lightly touched with finger, rotating dish halfway through cooking.
5. On heat-safe surface, let cake stand in dish 5 minutes. Invert cake onto rack, remove waxed paper, and let cool completely.
6. Meanwhile, reline bottom of baking dish with waxed paper and repeat steps 4 and 5 with remaining batter. Hull and slice strawberries.
7. On serving platter, place 1 cake layer, rounded side down. Spread with a third of White-chocolate Mousse. Cover with sliced strawberries. Top with remaining cake layer, rounded side up. Frost top and side of cake with remaining White-chocolate Mousse. Decoratively garnish with Strawberry Fans. Chill until ready to serve.

Making the Strawberry Fans

Select firm whole strawberries with stems. Starting just below stem end, thinly slice each strawberry lengthwise several times, leaving strawberry connected at stem end.

With fingertips, gently press down on each strawberry to fan slices slightly.

BLACK FOREST CAKE

Color Index page 95. 441 cals per serving. Begin early in day.

Ingredients for 12 servings		Microwave cookware
1 18.25- to 18.5-ounce package devil's-food-cake mix *1 cup water* *¼ cup salad oil* *3 eggs* *1 16-ounce can pitted dark sweet cherries in light syrup*	*4 tablespoons kirsch* *4 squares semisweet chocolate* *1½ cups heavy or whipping cream* *1 tablespoon sugar* *Maraschino cherries and Chocolate Curls (page 346) for garnish*	*9" by 2" round baking dish* *Trivet, rack, or ramekin*

1 Line baking dish with waxed paper. In large bowl, with mixer at low speed, beat dry cake mix, water, oil, and eggs until blended, constantly scraping bowl. Increase speed to medium; beat 2 minutes, occasionally scraping bowl.

2 Spoon half the batter into prepared baking dish, smoothing surface. Elevate on trivet, rack, or ramekin turned upside down. Cook on High (100% power) 6 to 8 minutes, until cake springs back when lightly touched with finger, rotating dish halfway through cooking.

3 On heat-safe surface, let cake stand in dish 5 minutes. Invert cake onto rack, remove waxed paper, and let cool completely.

DECORATING THE CAKE

A simple microwave cake can be turned into something special with a garnishing of cream, chocolate, and maraschino cherries.

With spoon, gently press grated chocolate onto side of frosted cake until evenly coated.

Spoon remaining whipped cream into decorating bag fitted with star tube.

Pipe decorative border around top edge of cake.

Garnish top of cake with maraschino cherries and Chocolate Curls.

4 Meanwhile, reline baking dish with waxed paper and repeat steps 2 and 3 with remaining batter. Drain cherries, reserving 2 tablespoons syrup. Cut each cherry in half; set aside. In medium bowl, combine reserved syrup and 3 tablespoons kirsch; set aside.

5 With cheese grater or in food processor with grating disc attached, coarsely grate chocolate squares; set aside.

6 On serving platter, place 1 cake layer, rounded side down. With fork, prick cake layer. Evenly spoon half the cherry-kirsch syrup over. In small bowl, with mixer at medium speed, beat cream, sugar, and remaining kirsch until soft peaks form.

7 Onto cake layer on platter, evenly spread a quarter of whipped cream. Spoon cherries onto cream. Top with remaining cake layer, rounded side up. With fork, prick top; spoon remaining syrup over.

8 Frost top and side of cake with two thirds of remaining whipped cream. Decorate cake with reserved grated chocolate, remaining whipped cream, maraschino cherries, and Chocolate Curls (see Box, above). Cover loosely and refrigerate until ready to serve.

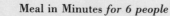

Meal in Minutes *for 6 people*

Easy English Tea Party

Strawberry Shortcake, page 342
Lemon Tuiles, page 350
Assorted tea sandwiches of your choice
Hot tea with milk or lemon

PREPARATION TIMETABLE

Early in day:	*Make Lemon Tuiles; store in airtight container. Make cake for Strawberry Shortcake; cool and wrap in plastic wrap.*
2 hours ahead:	*Prepare a selection of sandwiches with white and whole-wheat bread and fillings of your choice, such as smoked salmon, thinly sliced cucumber, egg salad, and thinly sliced cooked ham. With serrated knife, cut off crusts, then cut diagonally into quarters to make triangles; wrap in plastic wrap and refrigerate.*
30 minutes ahead:	*Fill small pitchers with milk and cut lemon slices for tea; cover and refrigerate. Complete Strawberry Shortcake.*
Just before serving:	*Arrange Lemon Tuiles and tea sandwiches on attractive serving platters. Make hot tea.*

Layer Cakes

BOSTON CREAM PIE

Color Index page 95. 12 servings. 224 cals per serving. Begin 2 hours ahead or early in day.

½ 18.25- to 18.5-ounce package yellow-cake mix
1 cup water
¼ cup salad oil
1 egg
1 egg yolk

1 package vanilla-flavor instant pudding and pie filling for 4 servings
Chocolate Glaze (below)
Confectioners' Icing (page 339)

1. Line bottom of 9″ by 2″ round microwave-safe baking dish with waxed paper.
2. In large bowl, with mixer at low speed, beat dry cake mix, water, oil, egg, and egg yolk until blended, constantly scraping bowl. Increase speed to medium; beat 2 minutes, occasionally scraping bowl.
3. Spoon batter into prepared baking dish, smoothing surface. Elevate baking dish on microwave-safe trivet, rack, or ramekin turned upside down. Cook on High (100% power) 6 to 8 minutes, until cake springs back when lightly touched with finger, rotating dish once.
4. On heat-safe surface, let cake stand in dish 5 to 10 minutes, until bottom of dish is almost cool. Invert cake onto rack, remove waxed paper, and let cool completely. Meanwhile, prepare vanilla pudding as label directs.
5. Make Chocolate Glaze and Confectioners' Icing. With serrated knife, cut cake horizontally in half. On platter, place 1 cake layer, rounded side down. Evenly spread with vanilla-flavor pudding. Top with second cake layer, rounded side up. Frost top of cake with Chocolate Glaze; feather with Confectioners' Icing. Refrigerate at least 15 minutes.

CHOCOLATE GLAZE: In 4-cup microwave-safe glass measure, place **3 ounces semisweet-chocolate pieces (½ cup), 1 tablespoon butter, 1½ teaspoons milk,** and **1½ teaspoons light corn syrup.** Cook on High 2 to 3 minutes, until chocolate melts, stirring once. Remove from oven; stir until smooth.

Feathering with the Confectioners' Icing

Spoon Confectioners' Icing into decorating bag fitted with small round tube and pipe parallel horizontal lines at regular intervals over top of cake.

Hold skewer or knife at right angle to piped lines and, starting at edge, draw lines at same regular intervals over top of cake, alternating direction of lines.

Special Cakes

Use your microwave to make the different stages of cake-making quick and easy, as we have done in this version of the classic French Christmas cake, Bûche de Noël (below).

BÛCHE DE NOËL

Color Index page 95. 410 cals per serving. Good source of iron.
Begin 3½ hours ahead or early in day.

Ingredients for 14 servings		Microwave cookware
1 18.25- to 18.5-ounce package chocolate-fudge-cake mix 1 cup water ¼ cup salad oil 3 eggs, separated ¼ cup sugar ⅓ cup cocoa	1 package chocolate pudding and pie filling for 4 servings Chocolate-cream Frosting (see Box, right) Cinnamon red-hot candies (optional)	14″ by 11″ baking dish or tray Trivet, rack, or ramekins

1 Line bottom of baking dish or tray with waxed paper. In large bowl, with mixer at low speed, beat dry cake mix, water, oil, and egg yolks until blended, constantly scraping bowl. Increase speed to medium; beat 2 minutes, occasionally scraping bowl.

2 In medium bowl, with mixer at high speed, beat egg whites until soft peaks form. Gradually sprinkle in sugar, 2 tablespoons at a time, beating well after each addition, until sugar completely dissolves and whites stand in stiff, glossy peaks.

3 With rubber spatula or whisk, gently fold beaten egg whites into cake batter until blended. Spoon batter into prepared dish or tray.

4 With metal spatula, evenly spread batter in dish or tray, smoothing surface. Elevate on trivet, rack, or ramekins turned upside down. Cook on High (100% power) 6 to 9 minutes, until cake springs back when lightly touched with finger, rotating dish or tray halfway through cooking.

5 Meanwhile, evenly sift cocoa onto clean cloth towel. When cake is done, immediately invert onto towel; remove waxed paper. Starting from a long end, roll cake with towel, jelly-roll fashion. Cool completely, seam side down, on rack. Meanwhile, prepare chocolate pudding as label directs; cover and refrigerate until chilled.

6 Carefully unroll cooled cake; spread evenly with chilled chocolate pudding. Starting at same long end, roll up cake without towel. Place cake, seam side down, on serving platter. Prepare Chocolate-cream Frosting.

7 With serrated knife, diagonally cut a 3-inch-wide slice from one end of cake. Onto diagonal side of slice, spread a small amount of Chocolate-cream Frosting. Firmly press frosted side of slice to cake about halfway down side of "log" to form a "branch."

8 Frost cake with remaining Chocolate-cream Frosting. With small knife or fork, mark frosting to resemble bark. If you like, decorate cake with cinnamon red-hot candies.

CHOCOLATE-CREAM FROSTING
Using this luscious frosting or its variations is an easy way to dress up any cake.

Into medium microwave-safe bowl, pour ¾ cup **heavy or whipping cream**. Heat on High (100% power) 2 to 4 minutes, until small bubbles form around edge. Add **12 ounces chopped bittersweet chocolate**; stir until melted; add 1 **teaspoon vanilla extract**. Cover and chill.

With mixer at medium speed, beat chocolate mixture until fluffy and thick enough to spread. Makes enough to frost one 2-layer cake. 2,254 cals.

Orange-chocolate-cream Frosting: Prepare frosting (above), adding **1 tablespoon grated orange peel** with the vanilla.

Almond-chocolate-cream Frosting: Prepare frosting (above), substituting **1 teaspoon almond extract** for the vanilla.

Rum-chocolate-cream Frosting: Prepare frosting (above), substituting **1 teaspoon rum extract** for the vanilla.

Chocolate Garnishes

CHOCOLATE LEAVES

Makes about 20 leaves. 431 cals. Low in sodium. Good source of iron.
Begin 40 minutes ahead.

½ 6-ounce package
semisweet-chocolate
pieces (½ cup)

1. You will need about 20 real leaves to use as forms (be sure to use only nontoxic leaves, like rose, lemon, ivy, or geranium). Rinse leaves and pat dry.
2. In 2-cup microwave-safe glass measure, place chocolate. Heat on High (100% power) 1½ (1:30) to 2 minutes, until melted, stirring once. Remove from oven; stir until smooth. With small pastry brush, brush melted chocolate onto underside of leaves. Refrigerate about 15 minutes, until set. With cool hands, carefully peel leaves from set chocolate.

CHOCOLATE ROUNDS

Makes about twelve 2-inch rounds. 33 cals each. Low in sodium.
Begin 25 minutes ahead.

2 squares semisweet
chocolate
1 tablespoon shortening

1. In 2-cup microwave-safe glass measure, place chocolate and shortening. Heat on High (100% power) 1½ (1:30) minutes, or until melted, stirring once. Remove from oven; stir until smooth.
2. Onto waxed-paper-lined cookie sheet, drop teaspoonfuls of hot chocolate mixture. Spread out slightly with back of spoon. Refrigerate about 15 minutes, until set. Lift off with metal spatula.

CHOCOLATE CURLS

Makes enough curls to decorate top of 9″ cake. 144 cals. Low in sodium.
Begin 15 minutes ahead.

1 square semisweet
chocolate

1. In small microwave-safe bowl, place chocolate. Heat on High (100% power) 15 seconds at a time, just until beginning to soften.
2. Using a vegetable peeler or cheese plane, draw along smooth surface of chocolate to form large curls. For short curls, draw along sides of square. To avoid breaking, use toothpick to place curls on cakes and desserts.

Special Cakes

APRICOT PARTY ROULADE

Color Index page 97. 14 servings. 417 cals per serving. Begin 3 hours ahead or early in day.

1 18.25- to 18.5-ounce
package yellow-cake
mix
1 cup water
¼ cup salad oil
3 eggs, separated
¼ cup sugar
Confectioners' sugar

1 10- to 12-ounce jar
apricot preserves
2 cups heavy or
whipping cream
¼ teaspoon almond
extract

1. Line bottom of 14″ by 11″ microwave-safe baking dish or tray with waxed paper. In large bowl, with mixer at low speed, beat dry cake mix, water, oil, and egg yolks until blended, constantly scraping bowl. Increase speed to medium; beat 2 minutes, occasionally scraping bowl.
2. In medium bowl, with mixer at high speed, beat egg whites until soft peaks form. Gradually sprinkle in sugar, 2 tablespoons at a time, beating well after each addition, until sugar completely dissolves and whites stand in stiff, glossy peaks.
3. With rubber spatula or whisk, gently fold beaten egg whites into cake batter until blended. Spoon batter into prepared dish or tray.
4. With spatula, gently and evenly spread batter in dish or tray. Elevate on microwave-safe trivet, rack, or ramekins turned upside down. Cook on High (100% power) 6 to 9 minutes, until cake springs back when lightly touched with finger, rotating dish or tray halfway through cooking.
5. Meanwhile, evenly sift ⅓ cup confectioners' sugar onto clean cloth towel. When cake is done, immediately invert onto towel; remove waxed paper. Starting at a short end, roll cake with towel, jelly-roll fashion. Cool completely, seam side down, on rack.
6. Over bowl, set fine sieve; press apricot preserves through.
7. Carefully unroll cooled cake; spread evenly with preserves. Starting at same short end, roll up cake without towel. Place cake, seam side down, on serving platter.
8. In large bowl, with mixer at medium speed, beat cream and ¼ cup confectioners' sugar until soft peaks form. Fold in almond extract.
9. Spoon whipped cream into decorating bag fitted with medium star tube. Pipe onto cake in decorative fashion. Cover loosely and keep refrigerated until ready to serve.

CHOCOLATE FUDGE BOMBE

Color Index page 97. 10 servings. 601 cals per serving. Good source of calcium, iron. Begin early in day.

1 18.25- to 18.5-ounce package chocolate-fudge-cake mix	1 3.5- to 5.9-ounce package chocolate mousse mix
1 cup water	¼ cup confectioners' sugar
¼ cup salad oil	Cocoa
3 eggs	
3 cups heavy or whipping cream	

1. Grease 2-quart microwave-safe bowl. Line bottom of bowl with 3-inch circle of waxed paper.
2. In large bowl, with mixer at low speed, beat dry cake mix, water, oil, and eggs until blended, constantly scraping bowl. Increase speed to medium; beat 2 minutes, occasionally scraping bowl. Spoon into bowl, smoothing surface.
3. Elevate bowl on microwave-safe trivet, rack, or ramekin turned upside down. Cook on High (100% power) 9 to 12 minutes, until cake springs back when lightly touched with finger, rotating bowl once.
4. On heat-safe surface, let cake stand in bowl 10 minutes. Cover and let cool completely on rack. Meanwhile, use 2 cups cream in place of 1 cup milk to prepare chocolate mousse as label directs.
5. With serrated knife, cut out center of cake, leaving a 1½-inch shell. Reserve removed cake center. Spoon chocolate mousse into center of shell. Cut reserved cake into small chunks and press onto surface of mousse. Invert onto serving platter. Carefully remove bowl to unmold cake. Cover and refrigerate until chilled.
6. In medium bowl, with mixer at medium speed, beat remaining cream and confectioners' sugar until soft peaks form. Spoon into decorating bag fitted with medium star tube. Pipe in rosettes over surface of cake. Dust with cocoa. Cover loosely and keep refrigerated until ready to serve.

Decorating the Bombe

With star tube, pipe rows of rosettes to cover surface of cake.

With fine sieve, lightly dust cocoa over cream-covered cake.

CHOCOLATE SWIRL BUNDT CAKE

Color Index page 97. 16 servings. 294 cals per serving. Begin early in day.

This rich cake has a delicious cream-cheese filling. If you like, for a special decorative effect, dust finished cake with confectioners' sugar and pipe whipped cream around bottom.

Ingredients for 16 servings		Microwave cookware
1 8-ounce package cream cheese, softened ⅓ cup sugar 4 eggs ½ teaspoon vanilla extract 1 18.25- to 18.5-ounce package devil's-food-cake mix	1 cup water ¼ cup salad oil Chocolate Glaze (page 344)	12-cup Bundt or tube pan Trivet, rack, or ramekins

1 Grease Bundt or tube pan. In small bowl, with mixer at low speed, beat cream cheese until smooth. Add sugar, 1 egg, and vanilla; beat until well blended.

2 In large bowl, with mixer at low speed, beat dry cake mix, water, oil, and remaining eggs until blended, constantly scraping bowl. Increase speed to medium; beat 2 minutes, occasionally scraping bowl.

3 Spoon a third of batter into prepared pan. With tablespoon, drop spoonfuls of cream-cheese mixture in a ring onto batter, being careful not to let cream-cheese mixture touch side of pan. Carefully cover cream-cheese mixture with remaining batter.

4 Elevate pan on trivet, rack, or ramekins turned upside down. Cook on High (100% power) 10 to 15 minutes, until cake springs back when lightly touched with finger, rotating pan halfway through cooking.

5 On heat-safe surface, let cake stand in pan 15 minutes, or until bottom of pan is almost cool. With knife, loosen cake from side of pan. Invert pan onto serving platter. Carefully remove pan to unmold cake. Let cake cool completely.

6 Meanwhile, make Chocolate Glaze. Transfer cake to serving platter. With spoon, drizzle glaze over cooled cake.

Brownies

It's easy to see why brownies – which take their name from the dark-brown chocolate traditionally used in making them – are one of America's favorite sweet snacks. They adapt beautifully to microwave cooking, coming up moist, chewy, and tempting. Some of our brownie recipes are made with traditional chocolate and some with fudge-brownie mix, but you can top all of them with chopped walnuts or pecans as a special treat.

FUDGE BROWNIES

Color Index page 97. 191 cals each. Low in sodium. Begin early in day.

Ingredients for 24 brownies		Microwave cookware
8 tablespoons butter or margarine (1 stick) 4 squares unsweetened chocolate 2 cups sugar 4 eggs ⅔ cup all-purpose flour	1 teaspoon vanilla extract ½ teaspoon salt ¾ cup semisweet-chocolate pieces ½ cup walnuts, chopped	12″ by 8″ baking dish 8-cup glass measure Trivet, rack, or ramekins

1 Line bottom of baking dish with waxed paper.

2 In glass measure, place butter or margarine and chocolate. Heat on High (100% power) 1½ (1:30) to 2 minutes, until melted, stirring once. Remove from oven; stir until smooth.

3 To chocolate mixture, add sugar and eggs. Beat until well blended. Stir in flour, vanilla extract, and salt until blended and smooth. Spoon batter evenly into prepared baking dish.

4 Over top of batter, sprinkle chocolate pieces and walnuts.

5 Elevate baking dish on trivet, rack, or ramekins turned upside down. Cook on High (100% power) 5 to 6 minutes, just until beginning to set (do not overbake), rotating dish halfway through cooking.

6 On heat-safe surface, let brownie mixture stand in dish 5 minutes. Cover and refrigerate until well chilled. Cut into 24 squares and store in airtight container.

BUTTERSCOTCH BROWNIES

Color Index page 97. Makes 24. 134 cals each. Low in sodium. Begin early in day.

8 tablespoons butter or margarine (1 stick), softened ¾ cup packed light-brown sugar 1 cup all-purpose flour 1 teaspoon baking powder ¼ teaspoon salt	1 teaspoon vanilla extract 1 egg ¾ cup flaked coconut ¾ cup pecans, chopped ½ 6-ounce package semisweet-chocolate pieces (½ cup)

1. Line bottom of 12″ by 8″ microwave-safe baking dish with waxed paper.

2. In large bowl, with mixer at low speed, beat butter or margarine and sugar until blended. Add flour, baking powder, salt, vanilla extract, egg, ½ cup coconut, and ¼ cup pecans; beat until well blended, constantly scraping bowl. Spoon batter evenly into prepared baking dish, smoothing surface. Over top of batter, sprinkle remaining coconut, pecans, and chocolate pieces.

3. Elevate baking dish on microwave-safe trivet, rack, or ramekins turned upside down. Cook on High (100% power) 5 to 6 minutes, just until beginning to set (do not overbake), rotating dish halfway through cooking. On heat-safe surface, let brownie mixture stand in dish 5 minutes. Cover and refrigerate until well chilled.

4. Cut into 24 squares; store in airtight container.

NO-BAKE MINT BROWNIES

Color Index page 97. Makes 24. 233 cals each. Low in sodium. Begin 2½ hours ahead.

6 ounces solid chocolate mint patties (not cream-filled) 1 6-ounce package semisweet-chocolate pieces (1 cup) 4 tablespoons butter or margarine (½ stick) 2½ cups graham-cracker crumbs	1½ cups walnuts, chopped 1 14-ounce can sweetened condensed milk 1 teaspoon vanilla extract

1. Grease and flour 12″ by 8″ baking dish.

2. In 4-cup microwave-safe glass measure, place mint patties, chocolate pieces, and butter or margarine. Heat on High (100% power) 2 to 3 minutes, until melted, stirring once. Stir until smooth.

3. In large bowl, combine graham-cracker crumbs and walnuts. Stir in condensed milk and vanilla extract until crumbs are moistened. Stir in chocolate mixture until blended. Spoon brownie mixture evenly into prepared baking dish, smoothing surface. Leave at room temperature about 2 hours until firm.

4. Cut into 24 squares and store in airtight container.

Brownies and Shortbread

ROCKY ROAD BROWNIES

Color Index page 98. Makes 16. 344 cals each. Good source of iron. Begin 2½ hours ahead.

1 20.5- to 23.6-ounce package fudge-brownie mix	1 cup walnuts, chopped
⅓ cup water	2 ounces miniature marshmallows (1 cup)
⅓ cup salad oil	1 6-ounce package semisweet-chocolate pieces (1 cup)
2 eggs, slightly beaten	

1. Line bottoms of two 9″ microwave-safe pie plates with waxed paper. In large bowl, beat dry fudge-brownie mix, water, oil, and eggs until blended. Spoon batter evenly into prepared pie plates, smoothing surface.
2. In medium bowl, combine walnuts, marshmallows, and chocolate pieces. Sprinkle mixture evenly over batter.
3. Elevate 1 pie plate on microwave-safe trivet, rack, or ramekin turned upside down. Cook on High (100% power) 5 to 7 minutes, until top puffs slightly and marshmallows begin to melt, rotating pie plate halfway through cooking. Let cool completely in pie plate on rack. Meanwhile, repeat with remaining batter in second pie plate; cool completely.
4. When both rounds are cool, cut each into 8 wedges and store in airtight container.

CREAM-CHEESE BROWNIES

Color Index page 98. Makes 16. 296 cals each. Begin 2½ hours ahead.

1 8-ounce package cream cheese	1 20.5- to 23.6-ounce package fudge-brownie mix
3 tablespoons sugar	⅓ cup water
½ teaspoon almond extract	⅓ cup salad oil
3 eggs	

1. Line bottoms of two 9″ microwave-safe pie plates with waxed paper. In medium microwave-safe bowl, place cream cheese. Heat on Medium (50% power) 1 to 2 minutes, until softened. Add sugar, almond extract, and 1 egg; stir until smooth. Set aside.
2. In large bowl, beat dry fudge-brownie mix, water, oil, and remaining eggs until blended. Spoon batter evenly into prepared pie plates. Drop cream-cheese mixture by spoonfuls on top of batter. With knife, cut through batter and cream-cheese mixture to obtain a marbled effect.
3. Elevate 1 pie plate on microwave-safe trivet, rack, or ramekin turned upside down. Cook on High (100% power) 5 to 7 minutes, until top puffs slightly and is almost dry, rotating pie plate halfway through cooking. Let cool completely in pie plate on rack. Meanwhile, repeat with remaining batter in second pie plate; cool completely.
4. When both rounds are cool, cut each into 8 wedges and store in airtight container.

ALMOND SHORTBREAD

Color Index page 98. 177 cals each. Begin 1½ hours ahead or early in day.

Our Almond Shortbread is a classic made special by the addition of toasted sliced almonds. Shortbread dough can be very delicate and somewhat difficult to handle, but cooking it in the microwave makes the finished cookie beautifully light. As an alternative to the almond flavoring, substitute ¼ teaspoon ground ginger for the ½ teaspoon almond extract, and decorate the top of the shortbread with thin slivers of crystallized ginger to emphasize the flavor.

Ingredients for 8 wedges		Microwave cookware
8 tablespoons butter or margarine (1 stick), softened	½ teaspoon vanilla extract	9″ pie plate
⅓ cup confectioners' sugar, sifted	½ teaspoon almond extract	Trivet, rack, or ramekin
1 cup all-purpose flour	¼ teaspoon salt	
½ teaspoon baking powder	Sliced almonds, toasted, for garnish	

1 Line bottom of pie plate with waxed paper.

2 In large bowl, with mixer at low speed, beat butter or margarine and sugar until blended. Add flour, baking powder, vanilla and almond extracts, and salt; beat until blended, constantly scraping bowl.

3 Pat dough evenly into prepared pie plate. With fork, prick dough all over in decorative pattern. With knife, mark dough into 8 wedges.

4 Press toasted sliced almonds into dough in decorative pattern.

5 Elevate pie plate on trivet, rack, or ramekin turned upside down. Cook on Medium (50% power) 7 to 8 minutes, until puffed and set, rotating pie plate halfway through cooking.

6 On heat-safe surface, let shortbread stand in pie plate 5 minutes. Cut shortbread into wedges along knife marks; let cool completely in pie plate. Remove and store in airtight container.

Creative Cookies

Our delicate cookies are perfect when served with after-dinner coffee. For a zesty change, substitute the same quantity of grated lemon peel for the grated orange peel in our recipe for Coconut Rounds (below). Store soft and crisp cookies in separate containers with tight fitting covers for maximum freshness.

COCONUT ROUNDS

Color Index page 98. 44 cals each. Low in sodium. Begin 1½ hours ahead.

Ingredients for 30 cookies		Microwave cookware
½ cup flaked coconut 2 tablespoons all-purpose flour ¼ cup sugar 1 tablespoon grated orange peel	¼ teaspoon vanilla extract 2 egg whites 4 tablespoons butter or margarine (½ stick) 3 squares semisweet chocolate	9″ pie plate 2-cup glass measure 12″ flat round platter Trivet, rack, or ramekins Small bowl

1 In pie plate, place coconut. Heat on High (100% power) 3 to 4 minutes, until coconut is lightly toasted, stirring occasionally.

2 In food processor with knife blade attached or in blender, process toasted coconut until finely ground. Add flour, sugar, orange peel, vanilla, and egg whites. Process until blended.

3 In glass measure, place butter or margarine. Heat, covered with paper towel, on High 45 seconds to 1 minute, until melted. Into coconut mixture in food processor or blender, with motor running, pour hot butter or margarine in thin, steady stream. Process until blended.

4 Lightly grease platter. Drop 6 teaspoonfuls batter onto platter in a ring, at least 2 inches apart. Elevate on trivet, rack, or ramekins turned upside down. Cook on Medium-High (70% power) 3 to 4 minutes, until cookies begin to brown lightly, rotating platter halfway through cooking. Let stand 1 to 2 minutes.

5 With spatula, transfer cookies to rack. Let cool completely. Meanwhile, repeat with remaining batter. (If you like, only use some of the batter, then cover and refrigerate remaining batter up to 5 days.)

6 In bowl, place chocolate. Heat on High 2 to 3 minutes, until melted, stirring once. Remove from oven; stir until smooth. Drizzle melted chocolate over each cooled cookie. Let cool completely. Store in airtight container.

LEMON TUILES

Color Index page 98. Makes 30. 43 cals each. Low in sodium. Begin 1½ hours ahead.

½ cup sugar
¼ cup all-purpose flour
2 tablespoons cornstarch
½ teaspoon grated lemon peel
½ teaspoon almond extract

2 egg whites
4 tablespoons butter or margarine (½ stick)
½ cup sliced almonds

1. Grease 12″ flat round microwave-safe platter. In food processor with knife blade attached or in blender, process sugar and next 5 ingredients until blended.
2. In 2-cup microwave-safe glass measure, place butter or margarine. Heat, covered with paper towel, on High (100% power) 45 seconds to 1 minute, until melted. Into batter in food processor or blender, with motor running, pour hot butter or margarine in thin, steady stream. Process until blended.
3. Drop 6 teaspoonfuls batter on platter in a ring, at least 2 inches apart. Sprinkle with almonds. Elevate on microwave-safe trivet, rack, or ramekins turned upside down. Cook on Medium-High (70% power) 3 to 4 minutes, until cookies begin to brown lightly, rotating platter halfway through cooking. Let stand 2 minutes.
4. With spatula, transfer cookies to rack. Or, if you like, quickly remove each cookie and roll around rolling pin for characteristic shape. Let cool completely. Meanwhile, repeat with remaining batter. Let cool completely and store in airtight container.

VIENNESE MELTAWAYS

Color Index page 99. Makes 36. 51 cals each. Low in sodium. Begin 1½ hours ahead.

8 tablespoons butter or margarine (1 stick)
1 cup all-purpose flour
½ cup slivered blanched almonds, ground

1 teaspoon almond extract
Confectioners' sugar

1. Line 12″ round microwave-safe platter with waxed paper. In medium microwave-safe bowl, place butter or margarine. Heat, covered with paper towel, on Medium (50% power) 45 seconds, or just until softened; do not melt. Add ¼ cup confectioners' sugar, flour, ground almonds, and almond extract; stir until blended.
2. Shape dough, 1 teaspoonful at a time, into 1-inch balls. Place on platter in a ring, 1 inch apart. Elevate on microwave-safe trivet, rack, or ramekins turned upside down. Cook on Medium 4 to 5 minutes, until dry and firm, rotating platter once. Let stand 2 minutes.
3. With spatula, transfer cookies to rack. Let cool completely. Meanwhile, repeat with remaining dough. Store in airtight container. Just before serving, dust with confectioners' sugar.

FLORENTINES

Color Index page 98. Makes 24. 111 cals each. Low in sodium. Begin 2½ hours ahead.

4 tablespoons butter or
  margarine (½ stick)
½ cup sugar
½ cup heavy or
  whipping cream
2 tablespoons honey

⅓ cup all-purpose flour
½ cup candied fruit,
  finely chopped
¼ cup sliced almonds
4 squares semisweet
  chocolate

1. Grease 12″ flat round microwave-safe platter. In 4-cup microwave-safe glass measure, place butter or margarine, sugar, cream, and honey. Heat on High (100% power) 4 minutes, or until butter or margarine is melted, stirring once. Stir in flour until blended. Fold in candied fruit and almonds.

2. Drop 6 teaspoonfuls batter on platter in a ring, at least 2 inches apart. Elevate on microwave-safe trivet, rack, or ramekins turned upside down. Cook on Medium-High (70% power) 2 to 4 minutes, until cookies begin to brown lightly, rotating platter halfway through cooking.

3. With 2½″ round cookie cutter, trim uneven edges off cookies. Let stand 1 to 2 minutes, until slightly firm. With spatula, transfer cookies to rack. Let cool completely. Meanwhile, repeat with remaining batter; cool completely.

4. In small microwave-safe bowl, place chocolate. Heat on High 2 to 3 minutes, until melted, stirring once. Remove from oven; stir until smooth. Spread smooth side of cooled cookies with melted chocolate. If you like, with fork, make a design in chocolate. Let cool completely and store in airtight container.

MAPLE SNAPS

Color Index page 99. Makes 24. 49 cals each. Low in sodium. Begin 1½ hours ahead.

4 tablespoons butter or
  margarine (½ stick)
¼ cup maple or maple-
  flavor syrup
¼ cup light corn syrup

⅓ cup all-purpose flour
¼ cup walnuts, finely
  chopped
¼ teaspoon maple
  extract

1. Grease 12″ round microwave-safe platter. In 4-cup microwave-safe glass measure, place butter or margarine, maple or maple-flavor syrup, and corn syrup. Heat on High (100% power) 4 minutes, or until butter or margarine is melted, stirring once. Fold in remaining ingredients.

2. Drop 6 teaspoonfuls batter on platter in a ring, at least 2 inches apart. Elevate on microwave-safe trivet, rack, or ramekins turned upside down. Cook on Medium-High (70% power) 2 to 4 minutes, until cookies begin to brown lightly, rotating platter halfway through cooking.

3. Let cookies stand 1 to 2 minutes until slightly firm. With spatula, transfer cookies to rack. Let cool completely. Meanwhile, repeat with remaining batter. Let cool completely and store in airtight container.

MEXICAN WEDDING COOKIES

Color Index page 98. 80 cals each. Low in sodium. Begin early in day.

Make a traditional and attractive addition to your holiday cooking with our Mexican Wedding Cookies, made light and delicate in the microwave. Chilling helps make dough easier to handle. For an alternative, striking effect, decorate half the cookies with confectioners' sugar and half with cocoa powder.

Ingredients for 24 cookies		Microwave cookware
8 tablespoons butter or margarine (1 stick) ⅓ cup walnuts 1¼ cups all-purpose flour	¾ cup confectioners' sugar ½ teaspoon vanilla extract	12″ flat round platter Medium bowl Trivet, rack, or ramekins

1 Line platter with waxed paper. Finely chop walnuts; set aside. In bowl, place butter or margarine. Heat on Medium (50% power) 45 seconds, or until softened; do not melt.

2 To softened butter or margarine, add flour, ¼ cup confectioners' sugar, vanilla extract, and chopped walnuts; stir until blended. Shape dough into ball; flatten slightly. Wrap in plastic wrap and refrigerate about 1 hour, until dough is firm.

3 On lightly floured surface, with floured rolling pin, roll out chilled dough ¼ inch thick. With crescent cookie cutter, cut out as many cookies as possible. Reroll trimmings and cut again. Place cookies on platter in a ring and in center, at least ¼ inch apart.

4 Elevate platter on trivet, rack, or ramekins turned upside down. Cook on Medium (50% power) 4 to 5 minutes, until cookies are firm and look dry, rotating platter halfway through cooking. Let stand 2 minutes.

5 With slotted pancakes turner, transfer cookies to rack. Let cool completely. Meanwhile, repeat with remaining cut-out cookies; cool completely.

6 Sift remaining confectioners' sugar over cooled cookies to coat completely. Store in airtight container.

Cake Decorations

There are many cake decorations, confections, and colorings available to make microwave cakes, cookies, and pies, tarts, and desserts, look even prettier. Choose from hard and soft candies, as well as candied fruits and chocolate decorations.

These hard candies (above) are commercial products made of boiled hard sugar tinted with food colorings. They range from tiny crystal sprinkles to larger shapes such as teddy bears and clowns, which can be used as instant decorations

Gum-drop Diamonds: Soft and chewy sugar decorations

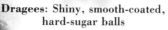

Marzipan Fruits: Tinted almond paste shaped to resemble fruits

Dragees: Shiny, smooth-coated, hard-sugar balls

Candied Cherries: Cherries coated with sugar glaze

Candied fruits and other sugar-based decorations make ideal finishing touches for cakes and cookies. Candied fruits can also be used as ingredients in cakes and candies

Candy Oranges and Lemons: "Fruit slices" made of sugar and gelatin

Angelica: Stalk of the herb coated in sugar

Rock Candy Crystals: Small refined-sugar crystals colored with vegetable dyes

Candles: Small decorative candles with a variety of patterns; used for celebration cakes

Cinnamon red-hot Candies: Cinnamon-flavored hard-candy decorations

Chocolate Sprinkles: Tiny tube-shaped decorations

Chocolate Flakes: Semi-sweet chocolate and milk-chocolate pieces

Chocolate Curls: Homemade Chocolate Curls (page 346)

Chocolate is one of the most versatile forms of decoration for cakes, cookies, pies, and all kinds of desserts, as the taste goes well with most other flavors. Chocolate can be bought in a variety of shapes such as these above, or made into Chocolate Rounds and Chocolate Leaves (page 346)

Chocolate Leaves: Small, commercially made chocolate decorations

Chocolate Cookies

CARAMEL-PECAN BARS

Color Index page 99. 168 cals per bar. Low in sodium. Begin 2 hours ahead.

Ingredients for 24 bars		Microwave cookware
8 tablespoons butter or margarine (1 stick)	1 cup pecan halves	4-cup glass measure
1 cup packed brown sugar	6 tablespoons heavy or whipping cream	1-cup glass measure
¾ cup all-purpose flour	6 tablespoons light corn syrup	Candy thermometer (optional)
¼ teaspoon salt	¾ cup semisweet-chocolate pieces	
1 teaspoon vanilla extract		

1 Preheat conventional oven to 350°F. Grease bottom and sides of 8″ by 8″ baking dish.

2 In large bowl, with mixer at medium speed, beat 4 tablespoons butter or margarine until creamy. Add ⅓ cup brown sugar, flour, salt, and ½ teaspoon vanilla extract; beat until smooth, constantly scraping bowl.

3 Pat dough evenly into prepared baking dish. Evenly arrange pecans over dough. Bake conventionally 20 to 25 minutes, until pecans are toasted and dough is golden.

4 Meanwhile, in 4-cup glass measure, combine remaining brown sugar, butter or margarine, and vanilla. Stir in cream and corn syrup. With candy thermometer in place, if using, cook on High (100% power) 6 to 8 minutes, until temperature reaches 234°F. to 240°F. or Soft-ball Stage (see Cold-water Test, page 355), stirring twice.

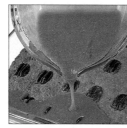

5 Pour caramel mixture over baked layer in baking dish. Let caramel cool completely in dish on rack.

6 In 1-cup glass measure, place semisweet-chocolate pieces. Heat on High 2 to 3 minutes, until melted, stirring once. Remove from oven; stir until smooth. Drizzle melted chocolate over cooled caramel layer. When set, cut into 24 bars. Store in airtight container.

FRUIT and NUT BARS

Color Index page 98. Makes 16. 226 cals each. Low in sodium. Begin 1¼ hours ahead.

1 cup blanched almonds	1 cup pitted prunes
1 cup walnuts	1 6-ounce package
1 cup dried apricots	semisweet-chocolate
1 cup seedless raisins	pieces (1 cup)

1. Line bottom of 8″ by 8″ baking dish with foil. In food processor with knife blade attached or in blender, process almonds and walnuts until finely chopped; spoon into medium bowl. Process apricots, raisins, and prunes into very small pieces (do not puree). In medium bowl, add chopped fruit to nuts. Press evenly into prepared baking dish.
2. In small microwave-safe bowl, place chocolate pieces. Heat on High (100% power) 2 to 3 minutes, until melted, stirring once. Remove from oven; stir until smooth. With rubber spatula, spread melted chocolate over fruit-nut mixture. Cover and refrigerate until firm.
3. Cut fruit-nut mixture into 16 bars. Store in airtight container.

CHOCOLATE-CHIP CRISPS

Color Index page 99. Makes 30. 69 cals each. Low in sodium. Begin 1½ hours ahead.

1 cup walnuts	4 tablespoons butter or
½ cup packed brown sugar	margarine (½ stick)
⅛ teaspoon ground cinnamon	½ cup miniature semisweet-chocolate pieces
2 egg whites	
½ teaspoon vanilla extract	

1. Grease 12″ round microwave-safe platter.
2. In food processor with knife blade attached or in blender, process ½ cup walnuts until coarsely chopped; remove. Process remaining walnuts until ground. Add brown sugar, cinnamon, egg whites, and vanilla; process until smooth.
3. In 2-cup microwave-safe glass measure, place butter or margarine. Heat, covered with paper towel, on High (100% power) 45 seconds to 1 minute, until melted. Into walnut mixture in food processor or blender, with motor running, pour hot butter or margarine in thin, steady stream. Process until blended.
4. Drop 6 teaspoonfuls batter on platter in a ring, at least 2 inches apart. Sprinkle each cookie with chocolate pieces and chopped walnuts. Elevate on microwave-safe trivet, rack, or ramekins turned upside down. Cook on Medium-High (70% power) 3 to 4 minutes, until cookies begin to brown lightly, rotating platter halfway through cooking. Let stand 1 to 2 minutes.
5. Transfer cookies to rack. Let cool completely. Meanwhile, repeat with remaining batter. Let cool completely and store in airtight container.

Hard Candies

MAPLE-WALNUT DROPS

Color Index page 100. Makes 42. 64 cals each. Low in sodium. Begin 1½ hours ahead.

*1 cup packed brown
  sugar
1 cup sugar
¼ cup light corn syrup
¼ cup water
1 cup walnuts, chopped*

*1 tablespoon butter or
  margarine
1 teaspoon maple-flavor
  extract*

1. Lightly grease cookie sheets; line with waxed paper.
2. In large microwave-safe bowl, combine brown sugar, sugar, corn syrup, and water. With microwave-safe candy thermometer in place, if using, cook on High (100% power) 7½ (7:30) to 8 minutes, without stirring, until temperature reaches 234°F. to 240°F. or Soft-ball Stage (see Cold-water Test, below).
3. To syrup, add chopped walnuts, butter or margarine, and maple-flavor extract; stir until well combined. Let stand 2 minutes.
4. Onto prepared cookie sheets, drop teaspoonfuls mixture. Let cool on rack about 1 hour, until set. Store in airtight container.

COLD-WATER TEST

If you do not own a microwave-safe candy thermometer, use this Cold-water Test. Fill a glass measure with very cold water. With clean spoon, drop ½ teaspoon hot candy mixture into water. Let stand 1 minute, then test firmness with your fingers.

Soft-ball Stage

Small amount of syrup dropped into cold water forms soft ball that flattens between forefinger and thumb when removed.

Hard-crack Stage

Small amount of syrup dropped into cold water separates into hard, brittle threads.

HOLIDAY MINTS

Color Index page 99. 70 cals each. Low in sodium. Begin early in day.

Cleaning up is so much easier when you cook the sugar syrup for our Holiday Mints in the microwave. Use different food colors for a pretty effect.

Ingredients for 36 candies		Microwave cookware
3 cups sugar *3 tablespoons light corn syrup* *Water* *1 teaspoon peppermint extract*	*Food color (optional)* *Melted chocolate (optional)*	Large bowl Candy thermometer

1 In large bowl, place sugar, corn syrup, and ¾ cup water. Cook on High (100% power) 7 to 8 minutes, until sugar completely dissolves, stirring twice.

2 With candy thermometer in place, cook fondant on High 5 to 6 minutes, until temperature reaches 234°F. to 240°F. or Soft-ball Stage (see Cold-water Test, left). Do not stir.

3 Without scraping side of bowl, pour fondant into 15½" by 10½" jelly-roll pan. Place pan on rack and let fondant mixture cool until temperature is 120°F.

4 With wide, stiff metal spatula, pastry scraper, or clean, wide putty knife, push mixture to one end of pan, fold over, then spread out to ¼-inch thickness. Repeat pushing, folding, and spreading until fondant turns white and clay-like. Knead mixture to form a ball. Store in airtight container up to 1 week, until ready to use.

5 When ready to use, lightly grease cookie sheets; line with waxed paper. Crumble fondant into large bowl; add peppermint extract, 2 drops food color, if using, and 2 teaspoons water. Heat on High 1½ (1:30) minutes, until softened, stirring once. Remove from oven; stir until smooth.

6 Working quickly, drop teaspoonfuls mixture onto prepared cookie sheets. (If fondant becomes too hard and thick, add a few drops of water and heat on High 20 to 30 seconds.) If you like, dip into melted chocolate when candies are firm. Store in airtight container.

Hard and Soft Candies

PEANUT BRITTLE

Color Index page 99. 142 cals per 1-ounce serving. Low in sodium. Begin 1¼ hours ahead.

Peanut Brittle is one of the simplest and most popular candies to make conventionally because of the all-in-one preparation and cooking process. Using your microwave oven makes it even quicker and easier! Be sure to grease your cookie sheet well before pouring the peanut-caramel mixture onto it; this will help lifting and breaking it into pieces for serving.

Ingredients for 1 pound brittle		Microwave cookware
1 cup sugar *½ cup light corn syrup* *¼ cup water* *¼ teaspoon salt* *1 cup shelled roasted peanuts*	*2 tablespoons butter or margarine (¼ stick)* *1 teaspoon baking soda*	8-cup glass measure Candy thermometer (optional)

1 With pastry brush, generously oil large cookie sheet.

2 In glass measure, place sugar; add light corn syrup, water, and salt. Stir until well blended.

3 With candy thermometer in place, if using, cook syrup mixture on High (100% power) 12 to 15 minutes, without stirring, until temperature reaches 300°F. or Hard-crack Stage (see Cold-water Test, page 355), just until caramel begins to turn light golden. Watch carefully since caramel burns easily and continues to cook and darken when removed from the oven.

4 To caramel mixture in measure, add peanuts, butter or margarine, and baking soda. Stir well until peanuts are evenly coated. Immediately pour peanut mixture onto prepared cookie sheet.

5 With 2 forks, quickly lift and stretch peanut mixture into 14" by 12" rectangle. Let cool on rack until firm.

6 With hands, break cold brittle into small pieces. Store in airtight container.

BUTTER CARAMELS

Color Index page 100. Makes 64. 45 cals each. Low in sodium. Begin 1½ hours ahead.

1½ cups heavy or whipping cream
1 cup sugar
½ cup light corn syrup
4 tablespoons butter (½ stick)
1 teaspoon vanilla extract

1. Lightly grease 8" by 8" baking dish.
2. In 8-cup microwave-safe glass measure, combine cream, sugar, and light corn syrup. With microwave-safe candy thermometer, if using, in place, cook syrup mixture on High (100% power) 15 to 20 minutes, without stirring, until temperature reaches 234°F. to 240°F. or Soft-ball Stage (see Cold-water Test, page 355).
3. Into mixture, stir butter and vanilla extract. Pour caramel mixture immediately into prepared baking dish, smoothing surface. Let cool completely in baking dish on rack until firm.
4. Invert baking dish onto cutting board. Remove baking dish to unmold. With sharp knife, cut caramel into 1-inch squares. Wrap each square in cellophane or plastic wrap. Store in airtight container.

CHOCOLATE-CHERRY CUPS

Color Index page 100. Makes 36. 68 cals each. Low in sodium. Begin 1½ hours ahead.

1 6-ounce package semi-sweet-chocolate pieces
2 tablespoons shortening
1¼ cups confectioners' sugar
2 tablespoons orange-flavor liqueur
2 teaspoons light corn syrup
2 10-ounce jars maraschino cherries with stems, well drained

1. On cookie sheet, arrange 36 fluted paper bonbon cups. In medium microwave-safe bowl, place chocolate and shortening. Heat on High (100% power) 1½ (1:30) minutes, or until melted, stirring once. Remove from oven; stir until smooth.
2. With small pastry brush, coat inside of each bonbon cup with chocolate mixture. Refrigerate about 30 minutes, until set.
3. When chocolate is set, carefully remove paper bonbon cups, handling them as little as possible so that chocolate cups keep their shape.
4. In small bowl, combine confectioners' sugar, orange-flavor liqueur, and light corn syrup until smooth. Spoon 1 teaspoonful filling into each chocolate cup; top with a cherry. Cover and refrigerate until ready to serve.

Chocolate Candies

SUPER-EASY TRUFFLES

Color Index page 100. Makes 30. 59 cals each. Low in sodium. Begin 1½ hours ahead.

8 squares semisweet chocolate
4 tablespoons butter or margarine (½ stick)
¼ cup heavy or whipping cream
¼ teaspoon almond extract

1. Arrange 30 foil bonbon cups on cookie sheet. In medium microwave-safe bowl, place chocolate and butter or margarine. Heat on High (100% power) 1½ (1:30) to 2 minutes, until melted, stirring once. Remove from oven; stir until smooth.
2. Into melted chocolate mixture, stir cream and almond extract until evenly blended. Set bowl over pan of iced water. With whisk, beat mixture until soft peaks form.
3. Spoon truffle mixture into decorating bag fitted with medium star tube; pipe into bonbon cups. Refrigerate about 1 hour, until truffles are set.

CHOCOLATE-MALLOW FUDGE

Color Index page 99. Makes 36. 111 cals each. Low in sodium. Begin 1¼ hours ahead.

1½ cups sugar
1 4-ounce can evaporated milk
4 tablespoons butter or margarine (½ stick)
4 ounces miniature marshmallows (2 cups)
1 cup walnuts, chopped
1 6-ounce package semisweet-chocolate pieces
2 squares bittersweet chocolate, chopped

1. Lightly grease 8″ by 8″ baking dish.
2. In 8-cup microwave-safe glass measure, combine sugar, evaporated milk, and butter or margarine. With microwave-safe candy thermometer in place, if using, cook sugar mixture on High (100% power) 8 to 9 minutes, stirring after 3 minutes, until thermometer reaches 234°F. to 240°F. or Soft-ball Stage (see Cold-water Test, page 355).
3. To mixture, add marshmallows, walnuts, semisweet-chocolate pieces, and chopped bittersweet chocolate. Stir until marshmallows and chocolate melt. Spread fudge into prepared baking dish, smoothing surface.
4. On rack, let fudge cool completely in dish until firm. Cut fudge into 36 pieces. Store in airtight container.

Our decadent chocolate-based candies cook easily in the microwave and can be stored in the refrigerator as long as you like. Adding water to the caramel in our Fudge Slices (below) makes it much easier to handle and spread, while the sweetened condensed milk added to the chocolate makes the fudge rich and creamy.

FUDGE SLICES

Color Index page 100. 97 cals each. Low in sodium. Begin 3 hours ahead or early in day.

Ingredients for 36 slices		Microwave cookware
1 6-ounce package semi-sweet-chocolate pieces	1 10-ounce jar maraschino cherries, drained	Medium bowl
½ cup sweetened condensed milk	½ 14-ounce package caramels (1 cup)	9″ pie plate
½ cup confectioners' sugar	1 tablespoon water	
1½ teaspoons vanilla extract	1 cup walnuts, chopped	

1 In bowl, combine chocolate pieces and sweetened condensed milk. Heat on High (100% power) 1½ (1:30) minutes, or until chocolate melts, stirring halfway through cooking. Add confectioners' sugar and vanilla; stir until smooth and well blended.

2 On square piece of foil, with metal spatula, spread half the fudge mixture to make a 6-inch square. On another piece of foil, repeat with remaining mixture. Freeze fudge about 5 minutes, or until easy to handle.

3 With paper towels, pat cherries dry. On each fudge square, arrange cherries in a single line about ½ inch from one edge.

4 Starting at edge with cherries, loosen fudge from foil and roll up jelly-roll fashion. Press to seal seam. Wrap roll in waxed paper; refrigerate 1 hour, until well chilled and set.

5 In pie plate, place caramels and water. Heat on High 1½ (1:30) to 2 minutes, stirring halfway through cooking. Remove from oven; stir until smooth. Working quickly, with metal spatula, spread half the caramel mixture over 1 fudge roll, then coat with half the chopped walnuts.

6 Reheat caramel mixture remaining in pie plate on High 30 seconds. Spread remaining fudge roll with caramel mixture and coat with remaining walnuts. Refrigerate both rolls about 1 hour, until set. Cut each roll into 18 slices.

It's so quick and easy to make popcorn in the microwave! Bagged microwave popcorn is readily available and there are a number of microwave popcorn poppers on the market. Follow the directions on the bag or those given with your popcorn maker; never pop corn in your microwave using any brown paper bag other than the one provided – it could catch fire. You can also use your microwave to refresh stale popcorn. Place 4 to 5 cups in a large microwave-safe bowl and heat on High (100% power) 45 seconds to 1 minute, until warm, tossing after 30 seconds.

POPCORN BALLS

6 servings. 248 cals per serving. Low in sodium. Good source of iron.

Begin 25 minutes ahead.

6 cups popped corn
4 ounces candied cherries, cut in half
1 cup light corn syrup
1½ teaspoons white vinegar
1 teaspoon vanilla extract
Salt (optional)

1. With pastry brush, oil large microwave-safe bowl. Mix popped corn with cherries.
2. In 8-cup microwave-safe glass measure, with microwave candy thermometer in place, heat corn syrup and vinegar on High (100% power) 10 to 12 minutes, without stirring, until temperature reaches 250°F. or a small amount of syrup mixture dropped into very cold water forms a hard but pliable ball. Stir in vanilla extract. If you like, season with salt.
3. Quickly pour hot syrup over popcorn mixture, tossing kernels. With greased hands, shape mixture into 3-inch balls, using as little pressure as possible, so balls will not be too compact.

Making the Popcorn Balls

With pastry brush, lightly brush inside of large bowl with oil.

Pour hot syrup over popcorn mixture, tossing to coat kernels.

With greased hands, scoop up handfuls of popcorn mixture; shape into balls.

MAKING POPCORN CHRISTMAS ORNAMENTS

Let Popcorn Balls harden overnight. Wrap a length of ribbon around each ball; tie bow on top. Fold 8-inch lengths of very narrow ribbon in half; gently thread folded end under knot of bow. Take loose ends through loop to close. Attach balls to Christmas tree by tying narrow ribbon around branches.

Chewy Candies

COCONUT HAYSTACKS

Color Index page 100. Makes 20. 72 cals each. Begin 1¼ hours ahead.

1 cup shredded coconut
8 ounces bittersweet chocolate

1. Line cookie sheets with waxed paper. In 9″ microwave-safe pie plate, place coconut. Heat on High (100% power) 3 to 4 minutes, until lightly toasted, stirring occasionally.
2. In medium microwave-safe bowl, place bittersweet chocolate. Heat on High (100% power) 2 to 4 minutes, until chocolate melts, stirring once. To melted chocolate, add toasted coconut; stir until smooth.
3. Onto prepared cookie sheet, drop teaspoonfuls of coconut mixture, mounding them slightly to resemble haystacks.
4. Let candies cool completely until firm. Store in airtight container.

PISTACHIO BITES

Color Index page 100. Makes 32. 73 cals each. Low in sodium. Begin 3 hours ahead.

12 ounces white chocolate, chopped
⅓ cup heavy or whipping cream
1 tablespoon butter or margarine
¾ teaspoon vanilla extract
Green food color
2 tablespoons finely chopped pistachios

1. Line bottom and sides of 9″ by 5″ loaf pan with foil. In medium microwave-safe bowl, place white chocolate. Heat on High (100% power) 3 to 4 minutes, until melted, stirring once. Remove from oven; stir until smooth.
2. To melted white chocolate, add cream and butter or margarine; stir until smooth. Transfer half the white-chocolate mixture to another medium bowl; set aside.
3. To white-chocolate mixture remaining in bowl, add vanilla extract and a few drops of green food color. Evenly spread green mixture in prepared loaf pan. Refrigerate.
4. To reserved white mixture, add chopped pistachios; stir until blended. Evenly spread pistachio mixture over green layer in loaf pan. Refrigerate about 2 hours, until set.
5. Invert pan onto cutting board. Remove loaf pan to unmold; remove foil. Cut layered chocolate mixture lengthwise in half, then cut each strip into 16 pieces. Cover and refrigerate candies until ready to serve.

Pies and Tarts

TART SHELLS, CRUMB CRUSTS, AND PIECRUSTS
DECORATIVE PIE EDGES · FRUIT PIES AND TARTS
CUSTARD PIES · CREAM PIES · CHIFFON PIES
NUT PIES, TARTS, AND TARTLETS

Pies and Tarts

A combination of microwave and conventional cooking is ideal for producing quick-to-prepare, mouth-watering pies and tarts. Although pastry piecrusts cooked in the microwave turn out crisp and flaky, they look better when cooked in a conventional oven; while your piecrust is baking, you can use the microwave to prepare a delicious fruit, custard, cream, chiffon, or nutty filling.

To create a shiny top on a two-crust pie, brush it with slightly beaten egg white before baking; for a golden-brown glaze, use beaten whole egg or, for an even richer color, apply beaten egg yolk. To add a bit of sparkle to a piecrust, sprinkle it lightly with granulated sugar.

As an alternative to conventional piecrusts, our crumb crusts made with graham crackers, gingersnaps, and chocolate or vanilla wafers can be cooked in the microwave. When making a crumb crust, press the crumbs firmly and evenly onto the bottom and up the side of the pie plate, then, after microwaving, let the crust cool on a rack before filling. When filled with ice cream, instant pudding, mousse, or canned pie filling, they make almost-instant desserts.

The egg-enriched fillings of our custard and cream pies work particularly well in the microwave. Cooked on Medium (50% power), these fillings are creamy and smooth. If you press plastic wrap directly onto the surface of the warm custard it will prevent a skin from forming while the custard chills (page 366). Chiffon pies depend upon both gelatin and beaten egg whites for their lightness and height; some also have whipped cream folded into their fillings. Cooking the filling on Medium results in a smooth mixture that blends well with beaten egg whites.

Your microwave can also help provide the finishing touches to your cooked pie or tart. Use it to toast almonds or coconut, to soften chocolate for making Chocolate Curls, or make a delicious glaze from fruit jelly or preserves to set off a fruit filling (see Glazes for Pies and Tarts, page 368).

PRETTY PIES AND TARTLETS

Our conventionally baked tart shells or bakery tartlet shells make ideal bases for last-minute pastry treats. You can create instant desserts and special-occasion snacks using a variety of fillings such as jams, jellies, puddings, or mousses, topped with berries or tropical fruit.

Chocolate-pudding-filled bakery tartlet shells (left) topped with piped whipped cream and candied cake decorations.

Bakery tartlet shells (right) filled with mango, nectarine, and kumquat slices, garnished with whipped cream and mint leaves.

Tart Shells, Crumb Crusts, and Piecrusts

PASTRY FOR TART SHELL

Color Index page 101. Makes 9″ to 10″ tart shell. 1,478 cals. Good source of vitamin A, riboflavin, thiamine, niacin, iron. Begin 2½ hours ahead.

1¼ cups all-purpose flour	4 tablespoons butter or margarine (½ stick), chilled
1 tablespoon sugar	
¼ teaspoon salt	3 to 4 tablespoons water
¼ cup shortening	

1. In medium bowl, combine flour, sugar, and salt. With 2 knives used scissors fashion or pastry blender, cut in shortening and butter or margarine until mixture resembles crumbs.
2. Into mixture, sprinkle water, 1 tablespoon at a time, mixing lightly with fork until pastry just holds together. Shape into ball; flatten slightly. Wrap in waxed paper and refrigerate about 1 hour, until well chilled.
3. Preheat conventional oven to 425°F. On lightly floured surface, with floured rolling pin, roll pastry into round about 1 inch larger than 9″ or 10″ tart pan with removable bottom. Roll pastry onto rolling pin; transfer to tart pan and unroll, pressing pastry onto bottom and up side of pan.
4. Trim edge of pastry even with top of pan. With fork, prick bottom and side in many places; line with foil; add beans, lentils, or rice (Baking the Pastry Blind, page 363), and bake conventionally 10 minutes. Remove beans, lentils, or rice and foil; prick pastry again. Bake 15 minutes longer, or until golden. Let cool on rack.

GRAHAM-CRACKER CRUMB CRUST

Color Index page 101. Makes 9″ crumb crust. 1,524 cals. Good source of vitamin A, riboflavin, iron. Begin 1¼ hours ahead.

6 tablespoons butter or margarine (¾ stick)	1½ cups graham-cracker crumbs
¼ cup sugar	

1. In 9″ microwave-safe pie plate, place butter or margarine. Heat, covered with paper towel, on High (100% power) 1 to 1½ (1:30) minutes, until melted. Stir in sugar and graham-cracker crumbs. Press mixture onto bottom and up side of pie plate.
2. Elevate pie plate on microwave-safe trivet, rack, or ramekin turned upside down. Cook on High 1 to 2 minutes, until warm. Let cool on rack.

GINGERSNAP-CRUMB CRUST: Prepare crumb crust (above), substituting **gingersnap crumbs** for the graham-cracker crumbs. 1,434 cals.

VANILLA- OR CHOCOLATE-WAFER CRUMB CRUST: Prepare crumb crust (above), substituting **vanilla- or chocolate-wafer crumbs** for the graham-cracker crumbs. 1,497 cals.

When making pastry handle it as little as possible. If pastry becomes too soft to handle, shape it into a ball, then flatten it slightly with floured rolling pin and wrap in waxed paper; refrigerate 30 minutes or until firm. When rolling pastry into a round, flour rolling pin and roll from center to edge. Add more flour if pastry begins to stick to countertop.

BAKED PIECRUST

Color Index page 101. 1,136 cals. Good source of riboflavin, thiamine, niacin, iron. Begin 2½ hours ahead.

When making a Baked Piecrust in a conventional oven, check the pie recipe to see if the filling is to be microwaved in the piecrust. If so, bake the piecrust in a conventional-oven- and microwave-safe pie plate.

Ingredients for 9″ piecrust

1 cup all-purpose flour	2 to 3 tablespoons water
½ teaspoon salt	
6 tablespoons shortening	

1 In medium bowl, combine flour and salt. With 2 knives used scissors fashion or pastry blender, cut in shortening until mixture resembles crumbs.

2 Into mixture, sprinkle water, 1 tablespoon at a time, mixing lightly with fork until pastry just holds together. Shape pastry into ball, then flatten slightly, and wrap it in waxed paper; refrigerate about 1 hour, until firm and well chilled.

3 On lightly floured surface, with floured rolling pin, roll pastry into round about 2 inches larger than pie plate.

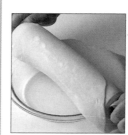  

4 Gently roll pastry onto rolling pin; transfer to 9″ pie plate and unroll, pressing pastry onto bottom and up side of pie plate.

5 Trim edge of pastry, leaving 1-inch overhang. Fold overhang under, then bring up over pie-plate rim; make Decorative Pie Edge (page 362) of your choice.

6 Preheat conventional oven to 425°F. With fork, prick bottom and side of pastry. Bake conventionally 15 minutes, or until golden. (If pastry puffs up, gently press into pie plate with spoon.)

361

Decorative Pie Edges

Piecrusts

PASTRY FOR 2-CRUST PIE

Makes 9″ 2-crust pie.
2,270 cals. Good source of riboflavin, thiamine, niacin, iron. Begin 2½ hours ahead.

2 cups all-purpose flour	¾ cup shortening
1 teaspoon salt	5 to 6 tablespoons water

1. In medium bowl, combine flour and salt. With 2 knives used scissors fashion or pastry blender, cut in shortening until mixture resembles crumbs.
2. Into mixture, sprinkle water, 1 tablespoon at a time, mixing lightly with fork until pastry just holds together. Shape into 2 balls, 1 slightly larger; flatten slightly. Wrap both in waxed paper and refrigerate about 1 hour, until well chilled.
3. On lightly floured surface, with floured rolling pin, roll larger ball into round 2 inches larger than 9″ pie plate. Roll pastry onto rolling pin; transfer to pie plate and unroll, pressing pastry onto bottom and up side of pie plate.
4. Fill piecrust as recipe directs. For top crust, roll smaller ball as for bottom crust. Moisten edge of bottom crust with water. Center top crust over filling. Trim pastry edges, leaving 1-inch overhang. Fold overhang under, then bring up over pie-plate rim; make Sharp Fluted Edge (left). Cut slashes or design in center. Brush with Milk or Egg Glaze (page 368). If you like, decorate top of pie with cut-outs from remaining pastry and brush with glaze. Bake conventionally as recipe directs.

Fluted Edge: Pinch to form stand-up edge. Place 1 index finger on inside edge of pastry, and, with index finger and thumb of other hand, pinch pastry to make a flute. Repeat around edge, leaving ¼-inch space between each flute.

Sharp Fluted Edge: Pinch to form stand-up edge. Vary the Fluted Edge by using the pointed edge of a cookie cutter or the back of a knife to make deeper indentations in the pastry.

Leaf Edge: With sharp knife or leaf-shaped cutter, cut out leaves from remaining rolled-out pastry. Press each leaf onto lightly moistened piecrust edge, overlapping leaves slightly to cover edge.

Pinched Edge: Pinch to form stand-up edge. Pinch pastry edge at an angle between thumb and knuckle of index finger. Repeat around edge, rotating pie plate clockwise.

Decorating the 2-crust Pie

With small sharp knife, slash pastry top to allow steam to escape. Brush with Milk or Egg Glaze (page 368).

With remaining rolled-out pastry, cut out leaves or other shapes and arrange on top of glazed pie. Brush cut-outs with same glaze.

Fork-scalloped Edge: Pinch to form stand-up edge. Place thumb against outside pastry edge and press toward center while pressing down next to it with 4-tined fork. Repeat around edge, leaving alternate fork marks and ruffle effect.

Braided Edge: Prepare double quantity of pastry for Baked Piecrust (page 361), using half to line pie plate. Roll out remaining pastry ¼ inch thick and cut into ¼-inch-wide strips. Gently braid strips together and press onto lightly moistened piecrust edge. Join ends of braid together to cover edge completely.

Fruit Pies and Tarts

APPLE, PEAR, AND CRANBERRY TART

Color Index page 104. 10 servings. 326 cals per serving. Begin 2½ hours ahead.

Pastry for 2-crust Pie (page 362)	½ teaspoon ground cinnamon
3 medium cooking apples, peeled, cored, and thinly sliced	¼ teaspoon ground ginger
2 pears, peeled, cored, and thinly sliced	¼ teaspoon ground cloves
1 cup cranberries	1 tablespoon grated orange peel
½ cup sugar	1 egg yolk
2 tablespoons all-purpose flour	1 tablespoon water

1. Preheat conventional oven to 425°F. Prepare pastry through step 3, using 10″ tart pan with removable bottom.

2. Trim edge of pastry even with top of pan. With fork, prick bottom and side of pastry in many places; line with foil, add beans, lentils, or rice and bake conventionally 10 minutes. Remove beans, lentils, or rice, and foil; prick pastry again. Bake 5 minutes longer, or until golden. Leave oven control at 425°F.

3. Meanwhile, in large microwave-safe bowl, combine apples, pears, cranberries, sugar, flour, cinnamon, ginger, cloves, and orange peel. Cook, covered, on High (100% power) 10 to 12 minutes, until apples are tender and juices thicken, stirring twice. Let cool slightly.

4. On lightly floured surface, with floured rolling pin, roll remaining pastry ¼ inch thick. With floured cookie cutters, cut out decorative shapes. Spoon fruit mixture into prepared tart shell. Place pastry cut-outs on top of filling.

5. In small bowl, with fork, beat egg yolk and water until blended. Lightly brush pastry cut-outs with egg mixture. Bake conventionally 10 to 15 minutes, until pastry is golden. Serve warm.

Baking the Pastry Blind

Line pastry with piece of foil cut slightly larger than tart pan. Press foil onto bottom and up side of pastry shell.

Fill foil-lined pastry shell with beans, lentils, or rice to prevent shell from puffing during baking. After baking, remove beans, lentils, or rice, and foil; prick pastry again and return to oven, until golden.

DELUXE APPLE PIE

Color Index page 102. 290 cals per serving. Begin 3½ hours ahead.

Unlike the traditional 2-crust apple pie, our microwave Deluxe Apple Pie has an unusual oat-based crumble topping that is both quick and nourishing.

Ingredients for 10 servings		Microwave cookware
Baked Piecrust (page 361)	½ cup packed brown sugar	9″ pie plate
6 medium cooking apples, peeled, cored, and cut into 1½-inch chunks	¼ cup quick-cooking or old-fashioned oats, uncooked	Large bowl
⅓ cup sugar	4 tablespoons butter or margarine (¼ stick), chilled	Trivet, rack, or ramekin
All-purpose flour	Cheddar cheese, ice cream, or whipped cream (optional)	
2 teaspoons lemon juice		
½ teaspoon ground cinnamon		
¼ teaspoon ground nutmeg		
½ teaspoon grated lemon peel		

1 Prepare Baked Piecrust, using microwave- and conventional-oven-safe 9″ pie plate; cool. In large bowl, combine apple chunks, sugar, 2 tablespoons flour, lemon juice, cinnamon, nutmeg, and lemon peel.

2 Cook apple mixture, covered, on High (100% power) 5 minutes. Uncover; stir. Cook on High 5 to 7 minutes longer, until apples are tender and juice thickens, stirring twice. Spoon into piecrust; set aside.

3 In small bowl, combine brown sugar, oats, butter or margarine, and ¼ cup flour. With 2 knives used scissors fashion or pastry blender, cut in butter or margarine until mixture resembles coarse crumbs.

4 Over apple filling, sprinkle crumb mixture. Elevate pie plate on trivet, rack, or ramekin turned upside down.

5 Cook pie on High 7 to 10 minutes, until topping is crisp, rotating pie plate halfway through cooking.

6 Serve pie warm or cover and refrigerate to serve chilled later. If you like, serve with Cheddar cheese, ice cream, or whipped cream.

Fruit Pies and Tarts

SUMMER FRUIT TART

Color Index page 102. 310 cals per serving. Good source of vitamin C, calcium. Begin 2½ hours ahead.

For a seasonal treat, try our Summer Fruit Tart – a crumb crust filled with vanilla custard and topped with a mixture of juicy strawberries, raspberries, blueberries, and sliced kiwifruit.

Ingredients for 10 servings		Microwave cookware
6 tablespoons butter or margarine (¾ stick)	1½ teaspoons vanilla extract	9″ pie plate
3 tablespoons brown sugar	¼ cup apple jelly	Trivet, rack, or ramekin
1¼ cups vanilla-wafer crumbs	1 tablespoon water	Medium bowl
½ cup sugar	1 pint strawberries	Small bowl
2 tablespoons cornstarch	½ pint raspberries	
2 cups half-and-half	½ pint blueberries	
3 egg yolks	1 kiwifruit, peeled and sliced	

1 In pie plate, place butter or margarine and brown sugar. Heat, covered with paper towel, on High (100% power) 1 to 1½ (1:30) minutes, until butter or margarine melts and sugar dissolves, stirring halfway through cooking. Stir in crumbs until blended.

2 With back of spoon, press crumb mixture onto bottom and up side of pie plate. Elevate on trivet, rack, or ramekin turned upside down. Cook on High 1 minute. Let cool on rack.

3 In medium bowl, combine sugar and cornstarch. With whisk, beat in half-and-half and egg yolks until well blended. Cook on High 5 to 6 minutes, until custard thickens slightly and coats back of spoon, stirring often. Stir in vanilla extract.

4 Pour custard into cooled crumb crust. Onto surface of hot custard, lightly press plastic wrap to prevent skin from forming. Refrigerate about 2 hours, until set.

5 In small bowl, combine apple jelly and water. Heat on High 1½ (1:30) to 2 minutes, until jelly is melted and smooth, stirring often. Hull strawberries and cut in half. If you like, reserve 1 whole berry for garnish.

6 When custard is set, remove plastic wrap. Carefully arrange strawberries, raspberries, blueberries, and sliced kiwifruit on top of custard. If you like, garnish with whole strawberry. With pastry brush, coat fruit with apple-jelly glaze. Refrigerate 15 minutes or until glaze is set.

APRICOT-CUSTARD TART

Color Index page 104. 10 servings. 260 cals per serving. Good source of vitamin A. Begin early in day.

Pastry for Tart Shell (page 361)	*½ teaspoon almond extract*
½ cup heavy cream	*2 17-ounce cans apricot halves, drained*
2 egg yolks	*¼ cup sliced almonds, toasted*
3 tablespoons sugar	
1 tablespoon all-purpose flour	

1. Prepare Pastry for Tart Shell through step 4, using 9″ by 2″ microwave- and conventional-oven-safe tart pan or baking dish. Into 4-cup microwave-safe glass measure, pour cream. Heat on High (100% power) 2 to 3 minutes, until cream bubbles around edge.
2. In small bowl, with whisk, beat egg yolks, sugar, flour, and almond extract. Stir small amount of hot cream into egg mixture. Slowly pour egg mixture back into remaining hot cream, beating rapidly to prevent lumping. Cook on Medium (50% power) 3 to 5 minutes, until custard thickens slightly and coats back of spoon, stirring often.
3. In cooled tart shell, arrange apricots. Pour custard over apricots. Elevate pan on microwave-safe trivet, rack, or ramekin turned upside down. Cook on Medium 7 to 10 minutes, until custard is softly set, rotating pan halfway through cooking. Sprinkle almonds over surface. Let stand on heat-safe surface 10 minutes. Cover and refrigerate about 2 hours, until well chilled.

RASPBERRY CHESS PIE

Color Index page 104. 10 servings. 318 cals per serving. Begin 3 hours ahead.

Baked Piecrust (page 361)	*1¼ cups sugar*
5 tablespoons butter or margarine	*½ cup milk*
2 tablespoons all-purpose flour	*3 eggs, beaten*
2 tablespoons yellow cornmeal	*1 teaspoon vanilla extract*
	¼ teaspoon ground nutmeg
	1 pint raspberries

1. Prepare Baked Piecrust, using 9″ broiler-safe pie plate; do not cool. In 8-cup microwave-safe glass measure, place butter or margarine. Heat, covered with paper towel, on High (100% power) 1 to 1½ (1:30) minutes, until melted.
2. In medium bowl, combine flour, cornmeal, and sugar. With whisk, beat in milk and eggs until blended. Gradually add melted butter or margarine, stirring constantly. Pour mixture into glass measure. Cook on Medium (50% power) 8 to 10 minutes, until thick, stirring often. Stir in vanilla and nutmeg. Pour into piecrust.
3. Lightly brown pie under preheated broiler. Top with raspberries. Serve warm or cover and refrigerate to serve chilled later.

Custard and Cream Pies

PILGRIM PUMPKIN PIE

Color Index page 102. 10 servings. 289 cals per serving. Good source of vitamin A, calcium, iron. Begin early in day.

Baked Piecrust (page 361)
1 16-ounce can pumpkin or 2 cups mashed cooked pumpkin
1 12-ounce can evaporated milk
3/4 cup packed brown sugar
1 1/2 teaspoons ground cinnamon

1/2 teaspoon ground ginger
1/2 teaspoon ground nutmeg
2 eggs
1/4 cup heavy or whipping cream (optional)

1. Prepare Baked Piecrust, using 9″ microwave-safe pie plate; cool on rack. In 2-quart microwave-safe casserole, place pumpkin, evaporated milk, brown sugar, cinnamon, ginger, nutmeg, and eggs. With mixer at medium speed, beat until smooth. Cook on Medium (50% power) 6 to 8 minutes, until custard thickens slightly and coats back of spoon, stirring often.
2. Spoon pumpkin mixture into cooled piecrust. Elevate pie plate on microwave-safe trivet, rack, or ramekin turned upside down. Cook on Medium 15 to 20 minutes, until set, rotating pie plate halfway through cooking. Let stand on heat-safe surface 10 minutes. Cover and refrigerate about 3 hours, until well chilled.
3. To serve: If you like, in small bowl, with mixer at medium speed, beat cream until soft peaks form. Spoon into decorating bag fitted with medium star tube; pipe garnish onto pie.

PEACHES AND CREAM PIE

Color Index page 102. 10 servings. 334 cals per serving. Begin 2 hours ahead.

Graham-cracker Crumb Crust (page 361)
6 peaches, peeled, pitted, and sliced
1/2 cup sugar
1 tablespoon all-purpose flour
1/2 teaspoon vanilla extract

1 cup heavy or whipping cream
1/2 package vanilla-flavor instant pudding and pie filling for 4 servings
1 tablespoon peach preserves

1. Prepare Graham-cracker Crumb Crust. In large microwave-safe bowl, place peach slices, sugar, flour, and vanilla; toss to coat. Cook, covered, on High (100% power) 8 to 10 minutes, until peaches are tender and juices thicken, stirring twice. Set aside.
2. Into medium bowl, pour cream; add vanilla pudding mix. With mixer at low speed, beat until smooth and thickened. Beat in peach preserves.
3. Pour pudding mixture into cooled crumb crust. Arrange peach slices on top. Cover and refrigerate about 30 minutes, until well chilled.

Custard makes a perfect base for fruit such as the peaches in our Peaches and Cream Pie (below left). In our Lemon Meringue Pie (below), the creamy texture of custard contrasts delightfully with the fluffy meringue and the crunchy, crisp piecrust.

LEMON MERINGUE PIE

Color Index page 102. 270 cals per serving. Begin 3 1/2 hours ahead.

Ingredients for 10 servings		Microwave cookware
Baked Piecrust (page 361) 1/3 cup cornstarch 1 1/4 cups sugar 1 1/2 cups water 4 eggs, separated 1/2 cup lemon juice	1 tablespoon butter or margarine 1 teaspoon grated lemon peel 1/4 teaspoon cream of tartar	4-cup glass measure

1 Prepare Baked Piecrust; cool on rack. In glass measure, combine cornstarch and 3/4 cup sugar. Gradually add water, stirring until smooth. Cook on High (100% power) 3 to 5 minutes, until mixture thickens, stirring often.

2 In small bowl, with whisk, beat egg yolks. Stir small amount of hot cornstarch mixture into egg yolks. Slowly pour egg-yolk mixture back into remaining hot cornstarch mixture, beating rapidly to prevent lumping.

3 Cook custard on Medium (50% power) 2 to 3 minutes, until custard thickens slightly and coats back of spoon, stirring often. Do not boil or custard will curdle.

4 To hot custard, add lemon juice, butter or margarine, and lemon peel, stirring until butter or margarine melts. Pour into piecrust. Onto surface of hot custard, lightly press plastic wrap to prevent skin from forming. Refrigerate about 30 minutes, until set.

5 Preheat conventional oven to 400°F. In large bowl, with mixer at high speed, beat egg whites and cream of tartar until soft peaks form. Gradually sprinkle in remaining sugar, beating until sugar completely dissolves and whites stand in stiff, glossy peaks.

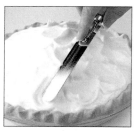

6 When custard is set, remove plastic wrap. With spatula, spread beaten egg whites over custard to edge of piecrust. Swirl to make attractive design. Bake conventionally 10 minutes, or until golden. Serve warm or refrigerate to cool slightly.

Cream Pies

BANANA-COCONUT PIE

Color Index page 101. 318 cals per serving. Begin early in day.

Use the microwave for an old-time favorite such as our Banana-coconut Pie. When the pie is assembled, refrigerate until ready to serve, sprinkling the coconut over just before serving.

Ingredients for 10 servings		Microwave cookware
Baked Piecrust (page 361) *1⅓ cups milk* *4 eggs, separated* *¾ cup sugar* *¼ teaspoon salt*	*2 envelopes unflavored gelatin* *1 cup heavy cream* *1½ teaspoons vanilla extract* *1 large banana, sliced* *½ cup flaked coconut*	4-cup glass measure 9″ pie plate

1 Prepare Baked Piecrust; cool. Into glass measure, pour milk. Add egg yolks, ½ cup sugar, and salt. Whisk until blended. Evenly sprinkle gelatin over mixture; let stand 1 minute to soften slightly. Cook on High (100% power) 4 to 6 minutes, until custard thickens slightly and coats back of spoon, stirring often. Do not boil or custard will curdle.

2 Into large bowl, pour custard. Cover and refrigerate 30 to 40 minutes, until custard mounds slightly when dropped from a spoon, stirring often.

3 Meanwhile, in large bowl, with mixer at high speed, beat egg whites until soft peaks form. Gradually sprinkle in remaining sugar, beating until sugar completely dissolves and whites stand in stiff, glossy peaks. Spoon on top of chilled custard.

4 In same bowl, with same beaters and mixer at medium speed, beat cream and vanilla until soft peaks form. Spoon over custard. With rubber spatula or whisk, gently fold whipped cream and beaten egg whites into custard.

5 Cover bottom of prepared piecrust with banana slices. Carefully spoon custard mixture over banana slices in piecrust. Cover and refrigerate about 3 hours, until set.

6 In pie plate, spread coconut. Heat on High 3 to 4 minutes, until toasted, stirring often. Just before serving, sprinkle toasted coconut over pie.

CHOCOLATE-CREAM PIE

Color Index page 104. 10 servings. 395 cals per serving. Begin early in day.

Vanilla- or Chocolate-wafer Crumb Crust (page 361) *2 cups milk* *½ cup sugar* *⅓ cup all-purpose flour* *3 egg yolks* *3 tablespoons butter or margarine*	*2 squares unsweetened chocolate, chopped* *1 teaspoon vanilla extract* *1 cup heavy or whipping cream*

1. Prepare Vanilla- or Chocolate-wafer Crumb Crust. Into 8-cup microwave-safe glass measure, pour milk. Heat on High (100% power) 3 to 5 minutes, until milk forms small bubbles around edge.

2. In 4-cup glass measure, combine sugar and flour. Gradually pour in hot milk, stirring until smooth. Pour milk mixture back into 8-cup measure. Cook on High 6 to 8 minutes, until thick and smooth, stirring occasionally.

3. In same 4-cup measure, with whisk, beat egg yolks. Stir small amount of hot milk mixture into egg yolks. Slowly pour egg mixture back into remaining hot milk mixture, beating rapidly to prevent lumping. Cook on Medium (50% power) 2 to 3 minutes, until custard is very thick, stirring often. Do not boil or custard will curdle.

4. Into custard, stir butter or margarine and chocolate until melted and smooth. Stir in vanilla. Pour chocolate custard into cooled crumb crust. Onto surface of chocolate custard, lightly press plastic wrap to prevent skin from forming. Refrigerate pie about 3 hours, until set.

5. Just before serving, remove plastic wrap from filling. In small bowl, with mixer at medium speed, beat cream until soft peaks form. With rubber spatula, swirl whipped cream over filling to edge of crumb crust. Spoon remaining cream into decorating bag fitted with medium star tube; pipe garnish around edge of pie.

Covering the Custard with Plastic Wrap

Lightly press plastic wrap onto surface of hot custard to prevent skin from forming during cooling and setting.

When custard is set, carefully remove plastic wrap from surface.

Chiffon Pies

GRASSHOPPER PIE

Color Index page 101. 10 servings. 321 cals per serving. Begin 4½ hours ahead or early in day.

Chocolate-wafer Crumb Crust (page 361)
1 envelope unflavored gelatin
½ cup sugar
½ cup water
3 eggs, separated
¼ cup crème de menthe
½ cup cold coffee
1 cup heavy or whipping cream
Chocolate Curls for garnish (page 346)

1. Prepare Chocolate-wafer Crumb Crust. In 4-cup microwave-safe glass measure, combine gelatin and ¼ cup sugar. In 2-cup glass measure, with fork, beat water and egg yolks. Gradually stir egg-yolk mixture into gelatin mixture until blended. Cook on Medium (50% power) 1 to 2 minutes, until mixture thickens slightly and coats back of spoon, stirring often. Do not boil. Pour into large bowl and stir in crème de menthe and coffee. Cover and refrigerate about 20 minutes, until custard mounds slightly when dropped from a spoon, stirring often.

2. In medium bowl, with mixer at high speed, beat egg whites until soft peaks form. Gradually sprinkle in remaining sugar, beating until sugar completely dissolves and whites stand in stiff, glossy peaks. Spoon on top of chilled custard.

3. In same bowl, with same beaters and mixer at medium speed, beat cream until soft peaks form. Spoon over custard. With rubber spatula or whisk, gently fold beaten egg whites and whipped cream into custard. Spoon into cooled crumb crust. Cover and refrigerate about 3 hours, until set. Garnish with Chocolate Curls.

FLAVORED WHIPPED CREAM

Whipped cream is an ideal garnish for pies of all kinds, as well as cakes and desserts.

Basic Whipped Cream: In small bowl, with mixer at medium speed, beat *1½ cups heavy or whipping cream* and *¼ cup confectioners' sugar* until peaks form. Fold in *½ teaspoon vanilla extract*. Makes 3 cups. 56 cals per tablespoon.

Chocolate Whipped Cream: Prepare Basic Whipped Cream. Fold in *melted and cooled contents of 1 8-ounce package semisweet-chocolate pieces*. 104 cals per tablespoon.

Coffee Whipped Cream: Prepare Basic Whipped Cream, folding in *1 teaspoon instant coffee powder* with the confectioners' sugar. 57 cals per tablespoon.

Orange Whipped Cream: Prepare Basic Whipped Cream, folding in *1 teaspoon grated orange peel* and *⅛ teaspoon orange extract* with vanilla. 57 cals per tablespoon.

BLACK-BOTTOM PIE

Color Index page 102. 367 cals per serving. Begin 3½ hours ahead.

Ingredients for 10 servings		Microwave cookware
Gingersnap-crumb Crust (page 361) 1¼ cups milk 3 eggs, separated ¾ cup sugar 2¼ teaspoons cornstarch 1 envelope unflavored gelatin	1 teaspoon vanilla extract 1 tablespoon dark rum 2 squares unsweetened chocolate, chopped ½ cup heavy or whipping cream	4-cup glass measure

1 Prepare Gingersnap-crumb Crust. In glass measure, heat milk on High (100% power) 3 to 4 minutes, until milk forms small bubbles around edge. In medium bowl, with whisk, beat egg yolks, ½ cup sugar, and cornstarch. Whisk small amount of hot milk into egg-yolk mixture. Slowly pour egg-yolk mixture back into remaining hot milk, beating rapidly to prevent lumping.

2 Evenly sprinkle gelatin over custard mixture; let stand 1 minute to soften slightly. Cook on Medium (50% power) 2 to 3 minutes, until custard thickens slightly and coats back of spoon, stirring often. Stir in vanilla.

3 Into small bowl, pour half the custard; stir in rum. Cover and refrigerate about 30 minutes, until custard mounds slightly when dropped from a spoon, stirring often. Meanwhile, into remaining custard, stir chocolate until melted. Spread chocolate custard evenly in cooled crumb crust; cover and refrigerate.

4 In medium bowl, with mixer at high speed, beat egg whites until soft peaks form. Gradually sprinkle in remaining sugar, beating until sugar completely dissolves and whites stand in stiff, glossy peaks. Spoon on top of chilled rum custard.

5 With rubber spatula or whisk, gently fold beaten egg whites into rum custard. Spoon onto chocolate custard in crust, being careful not to overfill. Cover and refrigerate 10 minutes. Spoon any remaining rum custard on top. Cover and refrigerate about 20 minutes, until set.

6 In small bowl, with mixer at medium speed, beat cream until soft peaks form. Spoon whipped cream into decorating bag fitted with medium star tube and pipe garnish around edge of pie; or, with spatula, spread whipped cream over pie in attractive design.

Chiffon Pies

STRAWBERRY CHIFFON PIE

Color Index page 103. 298 cals per serving. Good source of vitamin C. Begin 3 hours ahead.

Ingredients for 10 servings		Microwave cookware
Graham-cracker Crumb Crust (page 361)	*1 cup water*	4-cup glass measure
2 pints strawberries	*2 eggs, separated*	Small bowl
¾ cup sugar	*⅓ cup heavy or whipping cream*	
1 tablespoon lemon juice	*Fruit Glaze for Pies and Tarts (below right)*	
1 teaspoon cornstarch		
1 envelope unflavored gelatin		

1 Prepare Graham-cracker Crumb Crust. Reserve 1 whole strawberry. Hull and slice remaining berries. Cover and refrigerate half the sliced berries. In small bowl, combine remaining sliced berries, ¼ cup sugar, and lemon juice; toss lightly. With fork, crush berries slightly. Set aside.

2 In glass measure, combine ¼ cup sugar, cornstarch, and gelatin. Stir in 1 cup water. Cook on High (100% power) 3 to 4 minutes, until mixture thickens slightly and coats back of spoon, stirring often. In small bowl, with whisk, beat egg yolks. Into egg yolks, stir small amount of hot gelatin mixture. Slowly pour egg-yolk mixture back into remaining hot gelatin mixture, beating rapidly.

3 Cook custard on Medium (50% power) 2 to 3 minutes, until custard thickens slightly and coats back of spoon, stirring often. Stir in crushed strawberry mixture. Cover and refrigerate about 45 minutes, until custard mounds slightly when dropped from a spoon, stirring often.

4 After custard has chilled, in large bowl, with mixer at high speed, beat egg whites until soft peaks form. Gradually sprinkle in remaining sugar, beating until sugar completely dissolves and whites stand in stiff, glossy peaks. Spoon over chilled custard. In same bowl, with same beaters and mixer at medium speed, beat cream until soft peaks form. Spoon over custard.

5 With rubber spatula or whisk, gently fold whipped cream and beaten egg whites into custard. Spoon into cooled crumb crust. Cover and refrigerate about 30 minutes, until set.

6 Cover top of pie with reserved sliced berries. Place whole berry in center. Brush glaze over top of pie. Refrigerate 15 minutes, or until glaze is set.

ORANGE CHIFFON PIE

Color Index page 101. 10 servings. 381 cals per serving. Begin 3 hours ahead.

Graham-cracker Crumb Crust (page 361)
¾ cup sugar
1 envelope unflavored gelatin
1 teaspoon grated orange peel
1 cup orange juice
2 tablespoons lemon juice
3 eggs, separated
1½ cups heavy cream
Orange Julienne (page 334) for garnish

1. Prepare Graham-cracker Crumb Crust. In 4-cup microwave-safe glass measure, combine ½ cup sugar, gelatin, peel, and orange and lemon juice. Cook on High (100% power) 3 to 4 minutes, until small bubbles form around edge, stirring twice.

2. In small bowl, with whisk, beat egg yolks. Stir small amount of hot juice into beaten egg yolks. Slowly pour egg-yolk mixture back into remaining hot juice, beating rapidly to prevent lumping. Cook on Medium (50% power) 3 to 5 minutes, until custard thickens slightly, stirring often. Pour into large bowl. Cover and refrigerate about 45 minutes, until custard mounds slightly when dropped from a spoon, stirring often.

3. After custard is chilled, in large bowl, with mixer at high speed, beat egg whites until soft peaks form. Gradually sprinkle in remaining sugar, beating until sugar completely dissolves and whites stand in stiff, glossy peaks. Spoon over chilled custard. In same bowl, with same beaters and mixer at medium speed, beat ½ cup cream until soft peaks form. Spoon over custard.

4. Gently fold whipped cream and beaten egg whites into custard. Spoon into cooled crumb crust. Cover; refrigerate pie about 30 minutes until set. Beat remaining cream until peaks form. Pipe decorative edge onto pie. Garnish.

GLAZE FOR PIES AND TARTS

Milk or Egg Glaze: Before baking a 2-crust pie conventionally, brush top lightly with milk, half-and-half, or undiluted evaporated milk to enhance browning. For a shiny top, brush with beaten egg white; for a richer, golden-brown color, brush with beaten egg yolk.

Fruit glazes are the ideal way to set off the colors of fresh fruit tarts. Use apricot jelly or preserves to complement pale or yellow fruit, and red-currant or strawberry jelly or preserves for berries or plums.

Fruit Glaze: In 1-cup microwave-safe glass measure, combine ¼ **cup jelly or preserves** and **1 tablespoon water**. Heat on High (100% power) 1½ (1:30) to 2 minutes, until glaze coats back of spoon, stirring often. If necessary, press glaze through fine sieve until smooth. Lightly brush over fruit.

BAVARIAN CREAM PIE

Color Index page 104. 10 servings. 281 cals per serving. Begin 4 hours ahead.

Baked Piecrust
  (page 361)
1¼ cups milk
½ cup sugar
1 envelope unflavored
  gelatin
3 eggs, separated
1 teaspoon vanilla
  extract

1 cup heavy or whipping
  cream
¼ teaspoon ground
  nutmeg
Chocolate Curls (page
  346) for garnish

1. Prepare Baked Piecrust; cool. Into 4-cup microwave-safe glass measure, pour milk. Heat on High (100% power) 3 to 4 minutes, until milk forms small bubbles around edge.
2. In small bowl, combine ¼ cup sugar and gelatin. With whisk, beat in egg yolks and vanilla. Stir small amount of hot milk into egg-yolk mixture. Slowly pour egg-yolk mixture back into remaining hot milk, beating rapidly to prevent lumping. Cook on Medium (50% power) 2 to 3 minutes, until custard thickens slightly and coats back of spoon, stirring often. Pour into large bowl. Cover and refrigerate about 45 minutes, until custard mounds slightly when dropped from a spoon, stirring often.
3. After custard has chilled, in another large bowl, with mixer at high speed, beat egg whites until soft peaks form. Gradually sprinkle in remaining sugar, beating until sugar completely dissolves and whites stand in stiff, glossy peaks. Spoon over chilled custard. In same bowl, with same beaters and mixer at medium speed, beat cream until soft peaks form. Spoon over custard.
4. With rubber spatula or whisk, gently fold whipped cream and beaten egg whites into custard. Spoon into piecrust; sprinkle top with ground nutmeg. Refrigerate pie about 3 hours, until set.
5. To serve: Garnish pie with Chocolate Curls.

Grating Chocolate

With grater, coarsely grate semisweet-chocolate squares. Or, grate chocolate squares in food processor with grating disc attached. Sprinkle over any dessert or cake for a special effect, or use to cover uneven surfaces on the sides of frosted cakes. Store any leftover grated chocolate in airtight container in refrigerator.

Our chiffon recipes are ideal for use in a variety of crusts. Try pastry, crumb, or coconut crusts to give subtle variations in taste.

COCONUT BAVARIAN CREAM PIE

Color Index page 104. 270 cals per serving. Begin 4 hours ahead.

Ingredients for 10 servings		Microwave cookware

1¾ cups flaked coconut
¼ cup confectioners'
  sugar
3 tablespoons butter or
  margarine, softened
1¼ cups milk
½ cup sugar
1 envelope unflavored
  gelatin
	3 eggs, separated
	¼ teaspoon almond extract
	1 cup heavy or whipping
	  cream
	Whipped cream and
	  toasted coconut for
	  garnish
		12″ by 8″ baking dish
		4-cup glass measure
		Small bowl

1 In baking dish, place coconut. Heat on High (100% power) 5 to 6 minutes, until toasted, stirring often. Reserve ½ cup toasted coconut.

2 In medium bowl, with fork, combine remaining toasted coconut, confectioners' sugar, and butter or margarine. With back of spoon, press mixture onto bottom and up side of 9″ pie plate. Refrigerate.

3 Into glass measure, pour milk. Heat on High (100% power) 3 to 4 minutes until milk forms small bubbles around edge.

4 In small bowl, combine sugar and gelatin. With whisk, beat in egg yolks and almond extract. Stir small amount of hot milk into egg-yolk mixture. Slowly pour egg-yolk mixture back into remaining hot milk, beating rapidly to prevent lumping. Cook on Medium (50% power) 2 to 3 minutes, until custard thickens slightly and coats back of spoon, stirring often. Pour into large bowl. Cover and refrigerate about 45 minutes, until custard mounds slightly when dropped from a spoon, stirring often.

5 After custard has chilled, in large bowl, with mixer at high speed, beat egg whites until soft peaks form. Gradually sprinkle in remaining sugar, beating until sugar completely dissolves and whites stand in stiff, glossy peaks. Spoon over chilled custard. In same bowl, with same beaters and mixer at medium speed, beat cream until soft peaks form. Spoon over custard.

6 With rubber spatula or whisk, gently fold reserved toasted coconut, whipped cream, and beaten egg whites into custard. Spoon into chilled coconut crust. Cover and refrigerate pie about 3 hours, until set. Just before serving, garnish pie with whipped cream and toasted coconut.

Nut Pies and Tarts

AMARETTO PIE

Color Index page 103. 266 cals per serving. Begin early in day.

Our light yet full-flavored Amaretto Pie, in its crushed-amaretti-cookie crumb crust, is flavored with amaretto. Create a special look with a Lattice Design cream decoration, then garnish with toasted sliced almonds.

Ingredients for 10 servings		Microwave cookware
6 tablespoons butter or margarine (¾ stick) About 30 amaretti cookies or crisp macaroons, crushed (about 1¼ cups) ¼ cup sugar 1 envelope unflavored gelatin	3 eggs, separated Water ⅓ cup amaretto (almond-flavor liqueur) 1 cup heavy or whipping cream Whipped cream and toasted sliced almonds for garnish	9″ pie plate Trivet, rack, or ramekin 4-cup glass measure

1 In pie plate, place butter or margarine. Heat, covered with paper towel, on High (100% power) 1 to 1½ (1:30) minutes, until melted. Stir in amaretti cookie crumbs. With back of spoon, press mixture firmly onto bottom and up side of pie plate. Elevate pie plate on trivet, rack, or ramekin turned upside down. Cook on High 1 minute. Let cool on rack.

2 In glass measure, combine sugar and gelatin. In small bowl, with whisk, beat egg yolks and ½ cup water. Gradually stir egg-yolk mixture into gelatin mixture until blended. Cook on Medium (50% power) 1 to 2 minutes, until custard thickens slightly and coats back of spoon, stirring often. Do not boil or custard will curdle. Stir in amaretto.

3 Pour custard into large bowl. Cover and refrigerate about 45 minutes, until custard mounds slightly when dropped from a spoon, stirring often.

4 In large bowl, with mixer at high speed, beat egg whites until soft peaks form. Spoon over custard. In same bowl, with same beaters and mixer at medium speed, beat cream until soft peaks form. Spoon over custard.

5 With rubber spatula or whisk, gently fold whipped cream and beaten egg whites into custard. Spoon into cooled amaretti crust.

6 Cover and refrigerate about 3 hours, until set. Just before serving pipe whipped cream in Lattice Design on top of pie (see Decorating with Whipped Cream, right). Garnish with toasted sliced almonds.

LIGHT LEMON AND ALMOND TART

Color Index page 102. 10 servings. 444 cals per serving. Low in sodium. Begin 3½ hours ahead.

Pastry for Tart Shell (page 361) 2 cups heavy or whipping cream 1½ cups sugar 1 teaspoon vanilla extract ¼ teaspoon almond extract	1 tablespoon grated lemon peel 1 tablespoon lemon juice 1 cup slivered almonds ¼ cup sliced almonds Lemon Julienne (page 334) for garnish

1. Prepare Tart Shell through step 4, using 10″ tart pan with removable bottom. Reduce conventional oven control to 350°F. Into 8-cup microwave-safe glass measure, pour 1½ cups cream; add sugar. Cook on High (100% power) 10 minutes, or until sugar completely dissolves, stirring occasionally. Stir in vanilla and almond extracts, lemon peel, lemon juice, and slivered almonds. Pour mixture into cooled tart shell. Bake conventionally 10 to 15 minutes, until golden; cool on rack.

2. In 9″ microwave-safe pie plate, place sliced almonds. Heat on High 3½ (3:30) to 4½ (4:30) minutes, until almonds are toasted, stirring occasionally. Set aside.

3. In medium bowl, with mixer at medium speed, beat remaining cream until peaks form. Spoon whipped cream into decorating bag fitted with medium star tube and pipe around edge of pie. Sprinkle toasted sliced almonds over pie. Garnish with Lemon Julienne.

DECORATING WITH WHIPPED CREAM

Whipped cream is a delicious and attractive garnish for pies. It complements a custard or chiffon filling or it can be used as a contrast on rich or nutty pies. Be careful not to overwhip cream; it should just hold its shape. Spoon whipped cream into decorating bag fitted with medium star tube.

Zig-Zag Edge: Pipe a continuous border around edge of pie where filling meets edge. As you pipe, move tube to the left and right.

Lattice Design: Pipe 4 lines of cream, 2 inches apart, over pie. Pipe 4 more lines diagonally across first lines to create a lattice effect.

Nut Pies and Tartlets

PECAN PIE

Color Index page 103. 10 servings. 351 cals per serving. Good source of iron. Begin 3½ hours ahead.

Baked Piecrust, (page 361)
4 tablespoons butter or margarine (½ stick)
1 cup dark corn syrup
¼ cup sugar
1 teaspoon vanilla extract
3 eggs
1 3-ounce can pecan halves (1 cup)

1. Prepare Baked Piecrust using 10″ pie plate; cool on rack. Reduce conventional oven control to 350°F. In 8-cup microwave-safe glass measure, place butter or margarine. Heat, covered with paper towel, on High (100% power) 45 seconds to 1 minute, until melted.
2. Into melted butter or margarine, with whisk, beat corn syrup, sugar, vanilla, and eggs until blended. Cook on Medium (50% power) 6 to 8 minutes, until mixture thickens slightly and coats back of spoon, stirring often. Pour into piecrust. Sprinkle pecans over.
3. Bake pie conventionally 10 to 15 minutes, until knife inserted 1 inch from edge comes out clean. Let pie cool on rack.

CHOCOLATE-BROWNIE PIE

Color Index page 103. 10 servings. 404 cals per serving. Begin early in day.

Baked Piecrust (page 361)
4 tablespoons butter or margarine (½ stick)
2 squares unsweetened chocolate, chopped
½ cup sugar
½ cup milk
¼ cup all-purpose flour
2 tablespoons corn syrup
1 teaspoon vanilla extract
3 eggs
1 cup walnuts, chopped
Whipped cream and walnut halves for garnish
1 pint vanilla ice cream (optional)

1. Prepare Baked Piecrust, using 9″ microwave-safe pie plate; cool on rack. In 8-cup microwave-safe glass measure, place butter or margarine and chocolate. Heat, covered with paper towel, on High (100% power) 45 seconds to 1 minute, until melted, stirring twice.
2. Into chocolate mixture, with whisk, beat sugar, milk, flour, corn syrup, vanilla, and eggs until blended. Stir in walnuts. Cook on Medium (50% power) 5 to 6 minutes, until mixture thickens slightly and coats back of spoon, stirring often.
3. Spoon chocolate mixture into piecrust. Elevate pie plate on microwave-safe trivet, rack, or ramekin turned upside down. Cook on Medium 10 to 12 minutes, until mixture is puffed and set, rotating pie plate halfway through cooking. Let pie cool completely on rack. Garnish with whipped cream and walnut halves or if you like, serve with ice cream.

You can use nuts as a main ingredient, as in our Pecan Pie (left), or to add texture and flavor to other ingredients such as the mincemeat filling in our Mince and Apple Tartlets (below).

MINCE AND APPLE TARTLETS

Color Index page 103. 596 cals each. Low in cholesterol. Good source of iron. Begin 2½ hours ahead.

Ingredients for 10 tartlets		Microwave cookware
Pastry for Tart Shell (page 361, double quantity)	*1 cup walnuts, coarsely chopped*	8-cup glass measure
Milk	*½ cup packed light-brown sugar*	
1 28-ounce jar prepared mincemeat	*1 tablespoon lemon juice*	
1 large cooking apple, peeled, cored, and diced	*¼ cup brandy or rum (optional)*	
	Hard Sauce (page 382, optional)	

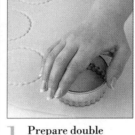

1 Prepare double quantity of Pastry for Tart Shell through step 2. Preheat conventional oven to 425°F. On lightly floured surface, with floured rolling pin, roll pastry ⅛ inch thick. With floured 4″ round cookie cutter, cut out 10 rounds. Cover and reserve pastry trimmings.

2 Gently press each round onto bottom and up side of 3″ fluted tartlet pan. With fork, prick pastry in many places. Arrange tartlet pans in 2 jelly-roll pans for ease of handling.

3 Bake conventionally 20 to 25 minutes, until pastry is golden. Let cool on rack 10 minutes. With knife, loosen tartlet shells from pans. Carefully remove tartlet shells and place on rack. Let cool completely. Leave oven control at 425°F.

4 Meanwhile, reroll pastry trimmings. With small decorative cutters, cut out shapes and place on cookie sheet. Brush with milk. Bake conventionally 15 to 20 minutes, until golden. Let cool on rack.

5 In glass measure, combine mincemeat, apple, walnuts, brown sugar, and lemon juice. If you like, stir in brandy or rum. Cook, covered, on High (100% power) 5 minutes, stirring twice. Uncover; stir. Cook on High 5 to 7 minutes longer, until apple is tender and flavors are blended, stirring halfway through cooking.

6 *To serve:* Spoon warm mincemeat mixture into tartlet shells; decorate with pastry cut-outs. If you like, serve with Hard Sauce.

Summer Pie Party

Iced tea with lemon and mint
Grasshopper Pie, page 367
Strawberry Chiffon Pie, page 368
Lemon Meringue Pie, page 365
Summer Fruit Tart, page 364
Peaches and Cream Pie, page 365
Raspberry Chess Pie, page 364
Summer berry selection

PREPARATION TIMETABLE

1 day ahead:	**Early in day:**	**About 2 hours ahead:**	**Just before serving:**
Make Grasshopper Pie, but do not garnish; cover and refrigerate. Prepare Strawberry Chiffon Pie through step 5; cover and refrigerate. Prepare piecrusts and crumb crusts for remaining pies and tart; cover and refrigerate. Prepare pitchers of iced tea; cover and refrigerate.	*Make custard and cream fillings for Lemon Meringue Pie, Summer Fruit Tart, and Peaches and Cream Pie; fill, cover and refrigerate.*	*Make custard filling for Raspberry Chess Pie; fill, cover and refrigerate. Complete Strawberry Chiffon Pie, Lemon Meringue Pie, Summer Fruit Tart, and Peaches and Cream Pie. Arrange a selection of summer berries in bowls; cover and refrigerate.*	*Garnish Grasshopper Pie. Top Raspberry Chess Pie with raspberries. Remove summer berries from refrigerator. Place ice cubes, lemon slices, and mint sprigs in glasses for iced tea.*

Preserves
and Sauces

PRESERVES · JELLIES · CONDIMENTS · CHUTNEYS · SAUCES
GRAVIES · SWEET DESSERT SAUCES

Preserves and Sauces

Small amounts of preserves and relishes to keep on hand at home or to give as presents can be quickly cooked in the microwave. It is therefore possible to take advantage of seasonal bounty from the garden or farmers' markets without spending long hours over a hot stove. Quantities up to 2 pints are easy to prepare, requiring little stirring, and with no danger of scorching. However, it is important to stir as directed in order to redistribute the sugar in the mixture so that it cooks evenly.

Half-pint jars are a convenient size for storing your preserves in the refrigerator. They must be sterilized first. This cannot be done in the microwave; jars and lids must be covered in water, boiled on top of the stove for at least 10 minutes, and kept hot. Add the preserves and relishes directly to the hot, sterilized jars and, if directed, remember to leave a ¼-inch space between the jam, jelly, or relish and the top of the jar. You can store preserves and relishes in the refrigerator for up to 3 weeks if you keep them tightly covered.

This chapter also contains a wide variety of savory and sweet sauces. Always use a large enough measure or casserole to prevent sauces from boiling over; ideally, the cookware should hold twice the volume of the sauce. Also, be certain to stir when indicated to prevent lumping, especially when the sauces are flour-based. Most sauces cook well on High (100% power) but delicate egg-based sauces such as Hollandaise, Béarnaise, and custard turn out more smooth and even when cooked on Medium (50% power); the lower temperature prevents boiling which would result in curdling.

Our dessert sauces are especially quick and easy and make delicious toppings for ice cream and desserts. As well as traditional chocolate, fudge, Melba, and butterscotch, we offer popular and simple fruit-based sauces, such as orange and blueberry.

FRESH FRUIT FLAVORS

Preserves are quick and easy to make in the microwave so, if you put up a few jars as fruits ripen, you will always have a selection of favorite flavors on hand.

Accompany a croissant or breakfast roll with a fruit preserve, such as (left to right) Fresh Strawberry Jam (page 375), Blackberry Spread (page 376), and Apricot-pineapple Butter (page 375).

Preserves

FRESH STRAWBERRY JAM

Color Index page 108. Makes about 4 half-pints. 45 cals per tablespoon. Low in cholesterol, fat, sodium. Begin 1 day ahead.

2 pints strawberries	*½ 6-ounce package*
3½ cups sugar	*(1 3-ounce pouch)*
2 tablespoons lemon	*liquid fruit pectin*
juice	

1. Sterilize four ½-pint jars and lids conventionally by placing in enough water to cover, and boiling 10 minutes; keep hot.
2. In 8-cup microwave-safe glass measure, with potato masher or slotted spoon, thoroughly crush enough strawberries to make about 2 cups.
3. Into crushed strawberries, stir sugar and lemon juice. Cook, covered, on High (100% power) 7 to 10 minutes, until mixture boils and thickens slightly, stirring occasionally. With spoon, skim foam from surface of strawberry mixture.
4. Into strawberry mixture, stir pectin. Immediately ladle hot strawberry mixture into hot sterilized jars to ¼ inch from top. Cover with lids. Store Fresh Strawberry Jam in refrigerator up to 3 weeks.

APRICOT-PINEAPPLE BUTTER

Color Index page 107. Makes about 2 half-pints. 36 cals per tablespoon. Low in cholesterol, fat, sodium. Begin 55 minutes ahead.

1½ cups water	*1 8-ounce can crushed*
1 8-ounce package dried	*pineapple in*
apricot halves	*unsweetened juice*
¼ cup sugar	

1. Sterilize two ½-pint jars and lids conventionally by placing in enough water to cover, and boiling 10 minutes; keep hot.
2. Into 8-cup microwave-safe glass measure, pour water; add apricots, sugar, and crushed pineapple with juice. Cook on High (100% power) 15 to 20 minutes, until apricots are very tender, stirring occasionally.
3. Into large bowl, press fruit mixture through mill or strainer to make smooth.
4. Immediately ladle hot fruit mixture into hot sterilized jars to ¼ inch from top. Cover with lids. Store Apricot-pineapple Butter in refrigerator up to 3 weeks.

PEACH BUTTER: Prepare Apricot-pineapple Butter (above), substituting *1 8-ounce package dried peach halves* for the dried apricots and *¾ cup orange juice* for the crushed pineapple and juice. Makes about 2 half-pints. 30 cals per tablespoon.

The microwave is ideal for making small amounts of jams and preserves to share with family and friends when fruits are in season. It is much quicker and easier than the bulk jam-making of days gone by. Pick fruit when it is just ripe, then, using the microwave, put up 2 or 3 pints. If necessary, use fruit that is slightly under-, rather than overripe, because the early fruit contains more of the pectin necessary for the jam or preserve to set.

PEACH PRESERVES

Color Index page 108. 37 cals per tablespoon. Low in cholesterol, fat, sodium. Begin 1 day ahead.

Ingredients for 4 half-pints	Microwave cookware
6 large peaches (about 3 pounds) *2½ cups sugar* *¼ cup lemon juice*	8-cup glass measure

1 Sterilize four ½-pint jars and lids conventionally by placing in enough water to cover, and boiling 10 minutes; keep hot. With small, sharp knife, peel peaches. Cut each peach lengthwise in half and twist apart. With small spoon, remove pits; discard.

2 Thinly slice peaches. In glass measure, combine peach slices, sugar, and lemon juice.

3 Cook peach mixture, covered, on High (100% power) 5 minutes, or until mixture boils. Uncover; stir. Cook on High 20 to 30 minutes longer, stirring occasionally, until syrup thickens and fruit is translucent.

4 Remove measure from microwave. On heat-safe surface, with spoon, carefully skim foam from surface of hot peach mixture.

5 Immediately ladle hot peach mixture into hot sterilized jars to ¼ inch from top.

6 Cover jars with lids. Store Peach Preserves in refrigerator up to 3 weeks.

Preserves and Jellies

HOT-PEPPER JELLY

Color Index page 108. 38 cals per tablespoon. Low in cholesterol, fat, sodium. Begin 1 day ahead.

Our Hot-pepper Jelly is an old Southern favorite and makes a great accompaniment to a Southern ham or any cold roast meat. It is also popular in the Southwest. In our recipe, we use sweet red peppers with the added zest of a red-hot jalapeño pepper to create a clear jelly with a jewel-like color. If you like, use sweet green peppers and flavor them with green-chili peppers.

Ingredients for 2 half-pints		Microwave cookware

2 large red peppers
1 large hot red or
  jalapeño pepper
1/3 cup white vinegar
1 1/2 cups sugar
1/2 6-ounce package
  (1 3-ounce pouch)
  liquid fruit pectin
	1 to 2 drops red food color
	(optional)
		8-cup glass measure

1 Sterilize two 1/2-pint jars and lids conventionally by placing in enough water to cover, and boiling 10 minutes; keep hot.

2 On cutting board, with sharp knife, finely chop red peppers and hot red or jalapeño pepper. Over glass measure, set fine sieve. Transfer pepper mixture to sieve.

3 With spoon, press chopped pepper mixture in sieve until liquid drains into glass measure, making about 1/2 cup juice. Discard chopped pepper mixture.

4 To pepper juice in glass measure, add white vinegar and sugar; stir. Cook, covered, on High (100% power) 8 to 10 minutes, until mixture boils, stirring twice.

5 Into pepper-juice mixture, stir pectin. If you like, add red food color. Cook on High 5 minutes, stirring halfway through cooking. With spoon, skim foam from surface of pepper-juice mixture.

6 Immediately ladle hot pepper-juice mixture into hot sterilized jars to 1/4 inch from top. Cover with lids. Store Hot-pepper Jelly in refrigerator up to 3 weeks.

BLACKBERRY SPREAD

Color Index page 108. Makes 4 half-pints. 38 cals per tablespoon. Low in cholesterol, fat, sodium. Begin 1 day ahead.

2 pints blackberries
2 cooking apples, peeled,
  cored, and cut into
  quarters
2 1/2 cups sugar

1/2 6-ounce package
  (1 3-ounce pouch)
  liquid fruit pectin
2 tablespoons lemon
  juice

1. Sterilize four 1/2-pint jars and lids conventionally by placing in enough water to cover, and boiling 10 minutes; keep hot.
2. In 8-cup microwave-safe glass measure, combine blackberries, apples, and sugar. Cook on High (100% power) 10 to 12 minutes, until apples are softened and sugar dissolves, stirring twice.
3. Into medium bowl, press fruit mixture through food mill or strainer to make smooth. Pour mixture back into measure. Cook on High 8 to 10 minutes, until mixture thickens slightly, stirring occasionally. With spoon, skim foam from surface of blackberry mixture.
4. Into blackberry mixture, stir pectin. Immediately ladle the hot mixture into hot sterilized jars to 1/4-inch from top. Cover with lids. Store Blackberry Spread in refrigerator up to 3 weeks.

MINT JELLY

Color Index page 107. Makes 4 half-pints. 45 cals per tablespoon. Low in cholesterol, fat, sodium. Begin 1 day ahead.

1 1/2 cups apple juice
1/2 cup cider vinegar
1 cup packed mint
  leaves, chopped
Water
3 1/2 cups sugar

1/2 6-ounce package
  (1 3-ounce pouch)
  liquid fruit pectin
1 to 2 drops green food
  color (optional)

1. Sterilize four 1/2-pint jars and lids conventionally by placing in enough water to cover, and boiling 10 minutes; keep hot.
2. Into 8-cup microwave-safe glass measure, pour apple juice and vinegar; add chopped mint. Cook, covered, on High (100% power) 8 to 10 minutes, until mixture boils, stirring twice.
2. Over medium bowl, set strainer. Pour mint mixture through strainer; discard chopped mint. Pour liquid back into measure. If necessary, add enough water to make 1 3/4 cups liquid. Stir in sugar. Cook, covered, on High 8 to 10 minutes, until mixture boils, stirring twice.
3. Into mint-flavored mixture, stir pectin. If you like, add green food color. Cook on High 4 minutes, stirring halfway through cooking. With spoon, skim foam from surface of mixture.
4. Immediately ladle hot mint-flavored mixture into hot sterilized jars to 1/4 inch from top. Cover with lids. Store Mint Jelly in refrigerator up to 3 weeks.

Condiments

CRANBERRY-CHESTNUT RELISH

Color Index page 108. Makes 4 half-pints. 48 cals per tablespoon. Begin 1 day ahead.

1 12-ounce package frozen cranberries, thawed (about 3 cups)	½ cup water
	⅓ cup cider vinegar
	1 teaspoon dry mustard
¾ pound pearl onions, peeled	¼ teaspoon ground cinnamon
½ cup golden seedless raisins	1 10-ounce jar marrons (chestnuts) in syrup, drained
2 cups packed light-brown sugar	

1. Sterilize four ½-pint jars and lids conventionally by placing in enough water to cover, and boiling 10 minutes; keep hot.
2. In 3-quart microwave-safe casserole, combine cranberries, onions, raisins, brown sugar, water, vinegar, mustard, and cinnamon. Cook, covered, on High (100% power) 10 minutes. Uncover; stir. Cook on High 15 minutes longer, or until mixture thickens, stirring occasionally. Stir in marrons.
3. Immediately ladle hot cranberry mixture into hot sterilized jars to ¼ inch from top. Cover with lids. Store Cranberry-chestnut Relish in refrigerator up to 3 weeks.

CORN RELISH

Color Index page 107. Makes about 4 half-pints. 13 cals per tablespoon. Low in cholesterol, fat, sodium. Begin 1 day ahead.

4 ears corn, husked, or 1 16- to 17-ounce can whole-kernel corn, drained	1 small tomato, diced
	1 small onion, diced
	1 cup cider vinegar
	½ cup sugar
1 small green pepper, diced	¼ teaspoon celery seeds
	¼ teaspoon dry mustard
1 small red pepper, diced	¼ teaspoon turmeric

1. Sterilize four ½-pint jars and lids conventionally by placing in enough water to cover, and boiling 10 minutes; keep hot.
2. If using fresh corn, with sharp knife, cut kernels from ears of corn to make about 2½ cups.
3. In 2-quart microwave-safe casserole, combine corn, diced green and red peppers, tomato, onion, vinegar, sugar, celery seeds, mustard, and turmeric. Cook, covered, on High (100% power) 5 to 7 minutes, until mixture boils. Uncover; stir. Cook on High 10 to 15 minutes longer, until vegetables are tender-crisp, stirring occasionally.
4. Immediately ladle hot corn mixture into hot sterilized jars to ¼ inch from top. Cover with lids. Store Corn Relish in refrigerator up to 3 weeks.

The microwave is ideal for making small, easily stored quantities of relish in a fraction of the time it takes to make them conventionally. Combine cranberries and chestnuts for an unusual accompaniment to Thanksgiving dinner, or serve your hamburgers with relish made from summer corn. Or, try our spicy homemade Tomato Catchup (below) – it's easier than you think!

TOMATO CATCHUP

Color Index page 107. 29 cals per tablespoon. Low in cholesterol, fat, sodium. Begin 1 day ahead.

Ingredients for 3 half-pints		Microwave cookware
2 pounds ripe tomatoes, cut into quarters (about 8 cups)	¼ teaspoon ground cloves	2 large bowls
	⅛ teaspoon ground red pepper	
1½ cups sugar	1 tablespoon cornstarch dissolved in 2 tablespoons cold water	
1 cup cider vinegar		
1 teaspoon dry mustard		
½ teaspoon ground cinnamon		
¼ teaspoon celery seeds		

1 Sterilize three ½-pint jars and lids conventionally by placing in enough water to cover, and boiling 10 minutes; keep hot.

2 In 1 large bowl, place tomato quarters, sugar, cider vinegar, dry mustard, ground cinnamon, celery seeds, ground cloves, and ground red pepper. Stir to combine.

3 Cook tomato mixture, covered, on High (100% power) 20 minutes, or until mixture thickens slightly, stirring occasionally.

4 In food processor with knife blade attached or in blender, process tomato mixture until smooth, in batches if necessary. Over another large bowl, set fine sieve. Press tomato mixture through sieve to remove seeds; discard.

5 Into tomato mixture in bowl, stir dissolved cornstarch until blended. Cook on High 8 to 10 minutes, until catchup boils and thickens, stirring occasionally.

6 Immediately ladle hot catchup into hot sterilized jars to ¼ inch from top. Cover with lids. Store Tomato Catchup in refrigerator up to 3 weeks.

Chutneys

Cooking chutneys in the microwave makes quick work of a job that used to take hours – and it won't leave strong smells in your kitchen! Try a delicious, traditional chutney such as Heirloom Chutney (right), or an unusual combination of fruit as in our Cantaloupe Chutney (below right). Both add contrast and texture to cold meats, cheese, rice dishes, and to Indian food.

PICCALILLI

Color Index page 108. 21 cals per tablespoon. Low in cholesterol, sodium. Good source of vitamin C. Begin 1 day ahead.

Ingredients for 4 half-pints		Microwave cookware
1 pound green tomatoes, cut into quarters (about 2 cups)	1¼ cups sugar	Large bowl
2 cups cider vinegar	1 tablespoon mustard seeds	
2 green peppers, cut into quarters	1 tablespoon celery seeds	
2 red peppers, cut into quarters	¾ teaspoon ground allspice	
1 large onion	¼ teaspoon ground cinnamon	

1 Sterilize four ½-pint jars and lids conventionally by placing in enough water to cover, and boiling 10 minutes; keep hot.

2 In food processor with knife blade attached or in blender, process tomatoes and 1 cup vinegar until tomatoes are roughly chopped. Transfer tomato mixture to bowl.

3 In food processor with knife blade attached or in blender, process green and red peppers and onion until roughly chopped. Stir into tomato mixture in bowl. Cook, covered, on High (100% power) 10 minutes, or until softened; stir once. Uncover; drain liquid and discard.

4 To vegetable mixture, add sugar, mustard and celery seeds, ground allspice, and ground cinnamon. Stir to combine.

5 Cook vegetable mixture, covered, on High 10 to 15 minutes, until sugar dissolves and vegetables are tender, stirring twice.

6 Immediately ladle hot vegetable mixture into hot sterilized jars to ¼ inch from top. Cover with lids. Store Piccalilli in refrigerator up to 3 weeks.

HEIRLOOM CHUTNEY

Color Index page 108. Makes about 4 half-pints. 27 cals per tablespoon. Low in cholesterol, fat, sodium. Begin 1 day ahead.

2 large cooking apples, peeled, cored, and diced
2 medium onions, diced
1 medium green or red pepper, diced
1 garlic clove, crushed
¾ cup sugar
¾ cup white vinegar
½ cup water
1 12-ounce package pitted prunes, cut into quarters
1 tablespoon minced peeled gingerroot
2 tablespoons mustard seeds
½ teaspoon crushed red pepper

1. Sterilize four ½-pint jars and lids conventionally by placing in enough water to cover, and boiling 10 minutes; keep hot.
2. In large microwave-safe bowl, place apples and next 6 ingredients. Cook, covered, on High (100% power) 10 minutes, or until mixture boils. Uncover; stir. Cook on High 10 minutes longer, or until vegetables are tender, stirring occasionally.
3. Into chutney mixture, stir prunes, gingerroot, mustard seeds, and crushed red pepper. Cook on High 10 to 15 minutes, until mixture thickens and becomes slightly syrupy, stirring often.
4. Immediately ladle hot chutney into hot sterilized jars to ¼ inch from top. Cover with lids. Store in refrigerator up to 3 weeks.

CANTALOUPE CHUTNEY

Color Index page 108. Makes about 4 half-pints. 30 cals per tablespoon. Low in cholesterol, fat. Begin 1 day ahead.

4 garlic cloves, minced
3 medium onions, cut into 1-inch chunks
2 medium tomatoes, cut into 1-inch chunks
1 small cantaloupe, peeled, seeded, and cut into 1-inch chunks
1½ cups packed light-brown sugar
¾ cup cider vinegar
½ cup golden raisins
1 tablespoon curry powder
1 tablespoon mustard seeds
2 tablespoons cornstarch dissolved in 3 table-spoons cold water

1. Sterilize four ½-pint jars and lids conventionally by placing in enough water to cover, and boiling 10 minutes; keep hot.
2. In large microwave-safe bowl, combine garlic and next 8 ingredients. Cook, covered, on High (100% power) 10 minutes, stirring twice. Uncover; stir. Cook on High 10 to 15 minutes longer, until vegetables are tender, stirring occasionally.
3. Into vegetable mixture, stir dissolved cornstarch until blended. Cook on High 3 to 5 minutes, until mixture thickens, stirring twice.
4. Immediately spoon hot chutney into hot sterilized jars to ¼ inch from top. Cover with lids. Store in refrigerator up to 3 weeks.

Sauces

BARBECUE SAUCE

Color Index page 106. Makes about 1 cup. 32 cals per tablespoon. Low in cholesterol, fat. Begin 25 minutes ahead.

1 medium onion, diced	*⅔ cup catchup*
1 garlic clove, minced	*2 tablespoons cider*
2 tablespoons olive or	*vinegar*
salad oil	*¼ teaspoon dry mustard*
1 medium jalapeño	
pepper, diced (2	
tablespoons)	

1. In 4-cup microwave-safe glass measure, combine onion, garlic, and olive or salad oil. Cook, covered with paper towel, on High (100% power) 2 to 3 minutes, until onion softens slightly, stirring twice.

2. Into onion mixture, stir diced jalapeño pepper, catchup, vinegar, and mustard until well blended. Cook, covered, on High 3 to 5 minutes, until sauce thickens, stirring occasionally. Let stand, covered, on heat-safe surface 10 minutes until flavors blend. Spoon sauce into serving bowl. Serve hot.

CHILI SAUCE: Prepare Barbecue Sauce (above) adding *1 tablespoon chili powder* and *1 tablespoon Worcestershire* with the mustard in step 2.

SATAY SAUCE

Color Index page 106. Makes about ⅓ cup. 40 cals per tablespoon. Low in cholesterol, sodium. Begin 10 minutes ahead.

2 garlic cloves, minced	*1 tablespoon cider*
1 red pepper, diced	*vinegar*
½ cup chunky peanut	*¼ teaspoon sesame oil*
butter	*(optional)*
Chicken Broth (page	*Coriander sprigs for*
125) or canned broth	*garnish*
1 tablespoon minced	
peeled gingerroot	
1 tablespoon soy sauce	

1. In 2-cup microwave-safe glass measure, combine garlic, red pepper, peanut butter, ½ cup broth, gingerroot, vinegar, and soy sauce. If you like, stir in sesame oil. Cook on High (100% power) 1 to 2 minutes, until hot, stirring halfway through cooking.

2. If necessary, add a few additional drops of broth to thin sauce to desired consistency. Spoon sauce into serving bowl and garnish with coriander sprigs. Serve warm.

Our sauces are all based on traditional recipes, but are much quicker to prepare, some taking only 5 minutes! Microwaving these sauces also cuts down on dishwashing, since most, like our Cranberry Sauce (below), require only a single microwave-safe glass measure. Use a measure with a handle for easy and safe pouring and remember to use a pot holder if necessary.

CRANBERRY SAUCE

Color Index page 107. 25 cals per tablespoon. Low in cholesterol, fat, sodium. Begin 35 minutes ahead.

Ingredients for 1¾ cups		Microwave cookware
½ 12-ounce package cranberries (about 1½ cups) *⅔ cup sugar*	*½ cup orange juice* *⅓ cup red-port wine*	8-cup glass measure

1 Inspect cranberries; remove any stems and discard any shriveled, soft, or imperfect fruit. In colander, rinse fruit under running cold water.

2 In glass measure, combine cranberries, sugar, orange juice, and red-port wine. Stir to mix. Cook, covered, on High (100% power) 5 to 7 minutes, until cranberries pop and sugar dissolves, stirring occasionally.

3 Uncover sauce; stir. Cook on High 3 to 5 minutes longer, until sauce coats back of spoon, stirring occasionally.

4 Pour Cranberry Sauce into serving bowl and serve warm.

5 If you like, make Molded Cranberry Sauce: Rinse 2-cup loaf pan or mold. Pour warm sauce into pan or mold. Cover and refrigerate 2 to 3 hours or overnight, until firm and well chilled.

6 With knife, loosen mixture from sides of pan or mold. Invert pan onto serving platter. Carefully remove pan. Cut Molded Cranberry Sauce into slices and serve chilled.

Sauces and Gravies

Making the gravy can sometimes create a last-minute rush in the kitchen, but with the microwave you can prepare perfect Giblet Gravy (below) hours ahead with little fuss or clean-up. Cook, cover, and refrigerate it in a microwave-safe container. Reheat to serve with roast turkey or chicken. Brown Gravy (below right) is perfect with those creamy mashed potatoes the family loves.

GIBLET GRAVY

Color Index page 107. 8 cals per tablespoon. Good source of vitamin A, riboflavin, niacin, iron. Begin 40 minutes ahead.

Ingredients for 4 cups		Microwave cookware
2 cups Chicken Broth (page 125) or canned broth Giblets and neck of 1 chicken or turkey 2 garlic cloves 1 small onion, sliced 1 carrot, sliced	1 celery stalk, sliced ½ bay leaf 2 tablespoons butter or margarine (¼ stick) 2 tablespoons all-purpose flour 1 teaspoon browning sauce Salt and pepper to taste	8-cup glass measure Medium bowl

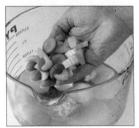

1 Into glass measure, pour broth; add giblets and neck of chicken or turkey, garlic, onion, carrot, celery and bay leaf.

2 Cook giblet mixture, covered, on High (100% power) 15 to 20 minutes, until giblets are tender, stirring occasionally. With slotted spoon, remove giblets and neck from stock. Transfer to cutting board.

3 Over bowl, set strainer. Pour stock through strainer to remove vegetables and seasonings; discard.

4 On cutting board, with sharp knife, finely chop giblets. Cut off meat from neck. Set chopped giblets and meat aside.

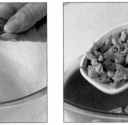

5 In medium bowl, place butter or margarine. Heat, covered with paper towel, on High 45 seconds, or until melted. Stir in flour until smooth and well blended. Cook on High 45 seconds, stirring once.

6 Into flour mixture, gradually stir strained stock. Cook on High 3 to 5 minutes, until gravy thickens and is smooth, stirring twice. Stir in browning sauce and reserved giblets and meat. Heat on High 1 minute, or until giblets and meat are hot. Season with salt and pepper; serve hot.

TOMATO SAUCE

Color Index page 107. Makes about 2½ cups. 11 cals per tablespoon. Low in cholesterol. Begin 45 minutes ahead.

2 garlic cloves, minced 1 green onion, sliced 2 tablespoons olive or salad oil 6 ripe tomatoes, cut into quarters ¼ cup chopped parsley	1 teaspoon red-wine vinegar ¾ teaspoon sugar ½ teaspoon basil ⅛ teaspoon pepper 2 tablespoons tomato paste

1. In 8-cup microwave-safe glass measure, combine garlic, green onion, and oil. Cook on High (100% power) 1 to 2 minutes, until green onion softens. Into green-onion mixture, stir tomatoes, parsley, vinegar, sugar, basil, and pepper. Cook, covered, on High 10 to 12 minutes, until mixture thickens, stirring occasionally.
2. In food processor with knife blade attached or in blender, process tomato mixture until smooth. Over large bowl, set strainer. Press tomato mixture through strainer to remove seeds and skins; discard.
3. Return tomato mixture to glass measure. Stir in tomato paste. Cook on High 10 to 12 minutes, until flavors blend and sauce thickens slightly, stirring occasionally. Serve warm or cover and refrigerate to serve chilled later.

BROWN GRAVY

Color Index page 106. Makes about 2 cups. 13 cals per tablespoon. Low in cholesterol, fat, sodium. Begin 20 minutes ahead.

2 tablespoons meat drippings, or butter or margarine, melted ½ small carrot, minced ½ celery stalk, minced ½ small onion, minced 2 tablespoons all-purpose flour	2 cups Chicken or Beef Broth (page 125) or canned broth ½ bay leaf Salt and pepper to taste ½ teaspoon browning sauce (optional)

1. In 8-cup microwave-safe glass measure, place drippings, or butter or margarine. Stir in minced carrot, celery, and onion. Cook on High 2½ (2:30) to 3 minutes, until vegetables are tender-crisp, stirring twice.
2. Into vegetable mixture, stir flour until blended. Gradually stir in broth. Add bay leaf. Cook on High 6 to 8 minutes, until gravy boils and thickens, stirring occasionally.
3. Over medium microwave-safe bowl, set strainer. Pour gravy through strainer to remove vegetables and bay leaf; discard. Season with salt and pepper. If you like, add browning sauce. Heat on High 2 minutes, or until gravy is hot. Serve immediately.

HOLLANDAISE SAUCE *

Color Index page 106. Makes about 1 cup. 59 cals per tablespoon. Low in sodium.
Begin 20 minutes ahead.

8 tablespoons butter or margarine (1 stick)
2 egg yolks
1 tablespoon lemon or lime juice
Salt and ground red pepper to taste

1. In 2-cup microwave-safe glass measure, place butter or margarine. Heat, covered with paper towel, on High (100% power) 1½ to 2 minutes, until melted.
2. In small microwave-safe bowl, with whisk, beat egg yolks, lemon or lime juice, salt, and ground red pepper until smooth.
3. Into egg-yolk mixture in bowl, gradually pour hot butter or margarine in a thin, steady stream, beating constantly, until butter or margarine is completely incorporated.
4. Cook sauce on Medium (50% power) 30 seconds to 1 minute, until slightly thickened, beating every 15 seconds. Do not boil or sauce will curdle. Keep warm over hot, not boiling, water or in thermos until ready to serve.

BÉARNAISE SAUCE *

Color Index page 106. Makes about 1 cup. 85 cals per tablespoon. Low in sodium. Begin 20 minutes ahead.

¼ cup white-wine vinegar
½ green onion, minced (1 tablespoon)
1½ teaspoons tarragon
¼ teaspoon pepper
12 tablespoons butter or margarine (1½ sticks)
2 egg yolks
1 tablespoon chopped parsley

1. Into small microwave-safe bowl, pour vinegar; add green onion, tarragon, and pepper. Cook on High (100% power) 2 to 4 minutes, until vinegar is reduced to about 1 tablespoon. Set aside.
2. In 2-cup microwave-safe glass measure, place butter or margarine. Heat, covered with paper towel, on High 2¼ (2:15) minutes, or until melted.
3. In medium microwave-safe bowl, with whisk, beat egg yolks until smooth. Into beaten egg yolks, gradually pour hot butter or margarine in a thin, steady stream, beating constantly, until butter or margarine is completely incorporated.
4. Cook sauce on Medium (50% power) 30 seconds to 1 minute, until slightly thickened, beating every 15 seconds. Do not boil or sauce will curdle. Into sauce, stir green-onion mixture and chopped parsley. Keep warm over hot, not boiling, water or in thermos until ready to serve.

BASIC WHITE SAUCE

Makes 2 cups. 17 cals per tablespoon. Low in cholesterol, fat, sodium.
Begin 15 minutes ahead.

4 tablespoons butter or margarine (½ stick)
4 tablespoons all-purpose flour
2 cups milk
Salt, pepper, and ground nutmeg to taste

1. In 8-cup microwave-safe glass measure, place butter or margarine. Heat, covered with paper towel, on High (100% power) 45 seconds to 1 minute, until melted.
2. Into melted butter or margarine, stir flour until smooth and blended. Cook on High 45 seconds to 1 minute, stirring once. Into flour mixture, gradually stir milk. Cook on High 3 to 5 minutes, until sauce thickens and is smooth, stirring twice.
3. Season sauce with salt, pepper, and nutmeg. Serve immediately.

PARSLEY-LEMON SAUCE: Prepare Basic White Sauce (above). Stir in *1 teaspoon grated lemon peel, 2 tablespoons lemon juice*, and *1 tablespoon parsley*. 17 cals per tablespoon.

CHEESE SAUCE: Prepare Basic White Sauce (above). Stir in *1 ounce grated cheese (¼ cup)* until melted. 54 cals per tablespoon.

MUSHROOM SAUCE
In this variation of a white sauce, the sliced mushrooms are lightly sautéed in butter or margarine before the sauce is thickened and enriched with half-and-half, sherry, and sour cream. It is delicious with broiled steaks and hamburgers.

Makes 2 cups. 23 cals per tablespoon. Low in cholesterol, fat, sodium. Begin 25 minutes ahead.

2 tablespoons butter or margarine (¼ stick)
½ pound mushrooms, thinly sliced
1 tablespoon all-purpose flour
1¼ cups half-and-half
1 tablespoon dry sherry
2 tablespoons sour cream
Salt and pepper to taste
2 tablespoons chopped parsley

1. In 8-cup microwave-safe glass measure, place butter or margarine. Heat, covered with paper towel, on High (100% power) 45 seconds, or until melted.
2. To melted butter or margarine, add sliced mushrooms; stir to coat. Cook on High 5 to 6 minutes, until mushrooms soften, stirring occasionally. Stir in flour until blended.
3. Into mushroom mixture, gradually stir half-and-half and sherry until blended. Cook on High 5 to 7 minutes, until mixture thickens, stirring occasionally.
4. Into mushroom mixture, stir sour cream until well blended. Season with salt and pepper. Stir in chopped parsley.

Sweet Sauces

Brandied
Strawberry
Sauce

Custard
Sauce

Peach
Sauce

Hot
Fruit Sauce

Chocolate
Sauce

Butterscotch
Sauce

HOT FRUIT SAUCE

Color Index page 105. Makes 4 cups. 13 cals per tablespoon. Begin 10 minutes ahead.

3 large nectarines, chopped
3 large plums, chopped
½ cup sugar
½ cup orange juice
2 tablespoons brandy (optional)

1. In 8-cup microwave-safe glass measure, combine chopped nectarines and plums, sugar, and orange juice.
2. Cook on High (100% power) 3 to 5 minutes, until fruit is tender, stirring twice. If you like, stir in brandy. Serve warm over vanilla ice cream.

BRANDIED STRAWBERRY SAUCE

Color Index page 105. Makes 2½ cups. 35 cals per tablespoon. Low in fat, sodium. Begin 10 minutes ahead.

3 10-ounce packages frozen sliced strawberries, thawed
1 tablespoon cornstarch dissolved in 1 tablespoon cold water
½ cup red-currant jelly
¼ cup brandy

1. Drain strawberries, and set aside, reserving ½ cup juice. Into juice, stir dissolved cornstarch.
2. In 8-cup microwave-safe glass measure, place red-currant jelly. Heat on High (100% power) 30 seconds to 1 minute, until melted; stir once. Stir in dissolved cornstarch; cook on High 1 to 2 minutes, until slightly thickened.
3. Into red-currant mixture, stir reserved strawberries and brandy. Serve warm with pancakes or chilled over ice cream, or tapioca pudding.

CHOCOLATE SAUCE

Color Index page 105. Makes about 3 cups. 54 cals per tablespoon. Good source of vitamin A, riboflavin, calcium, iron. Begin 10 minutes ahead.

1 cup heavy or whipping cream
1¼ cups sugar
4 squares unsweetened chocolate, chopped
2 tablespoons butter or margarine
1 teaspoon vanilla extract

1. Into 8-cup microwave-safe glass measure, pour cream; add sugar, chocolate, and butter or margarine. Cook on High (100% power) 8 to 9 minutes, until chocolate melts and mixture boils, stirring occasionally.
2. Into chocolate mixture, stir vanilla until smooth. Serve warm over banana splits or sundaes.

BUTTERSCOTCH SAUCE

Color Index page 106. Makes 1 cup. 76 cals per tablespoon. Low in cholesterol, fat, sodium. Begin 10 minutes ahead.

1 cup packed light-brown sugar
¼ cup half-and-half
2 tablespoons light corn syrup
2 tablespoons butter or margarine (¼ stick)

1. In 8-cup microwave-safe glass measure, combine all ingredients.
2. Cook butterscotch mixture on High (100% power) 5 minutes, or until sugar dissolves and sauce boils, stirring twice. Serve warm over ice cream, apple pie, or bread pudding.

CUSTARD SAUCE *

Color Index page 105. Makes about 1¼ cups. 27 cals per tablespoon. Low in fat, sodium. Begin 15 minutes ahead.

1 cup half-and-half
2 tablespoons sugar
2 egg yolks
½ teaspoon vanilla extract

1. Into 4-cup microwave-safe glass measure, pour half-and-half; add sugar. Cook on High (100% power) 3 minutes, or until mixture boils, stirring twice.
2. In small bowl, with whisk, beat egg yolks slightly. Stir small amount of half-and-half mixture into beaten egg yolks. Slowly pour egg mixture back into remaining half-and-half mixture, beating rapidly to prevent lumping.
3. Cook mixture on Medium (50% power) 3 to 4 minutes, until sauce thickens slightly, beating twice. Do not boil or sauce will curdle. Stir in vanilla. Serve warm over fruit salad, fruit cake, or apple pie.

PEACH SAUCE

Color Index page 105. Makes 1 cup. 17 cals per tablespoon. Begin 10 minutes ahead.

1 10-ounce package frozen peaches, thawed
¼ teaspoon almond extract
⅛ teaspon ground nutmeg

1. In food processor with knife blade attached, process peaches, almond extract, and nutmeg until smooth.
2. Transfer peach mixture to 4-cup microwave-safe glass measure. Heat on High (100% power) 1 to 2 minutes, until hot, stirring twice. Serve warm over ice cream, or with fruit or cake.

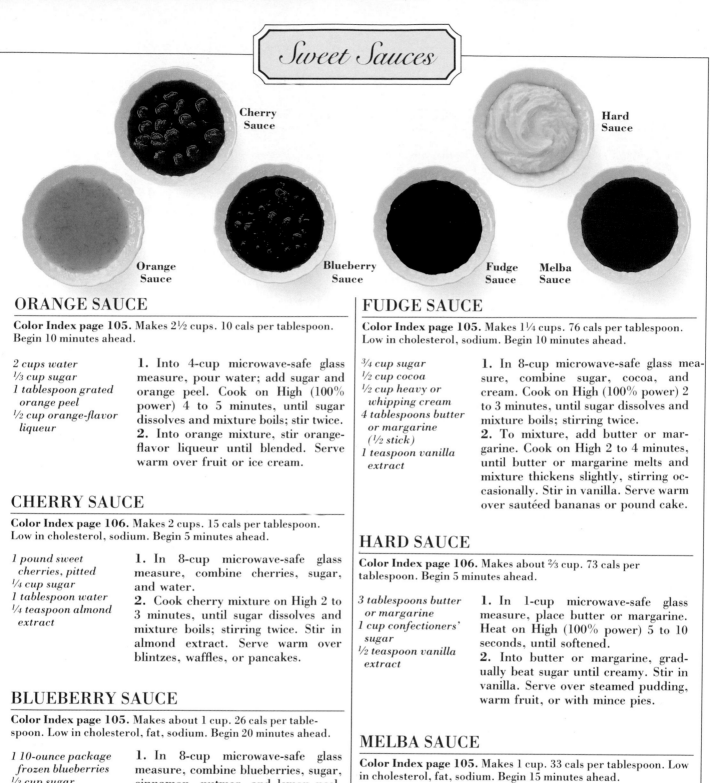

Cherry
Sauce

Hard
Sauce

Orange
Sauce

Blueberry
Sauce

Fudge
Sauce

Melba
Sauce

ORANGE SAUCE

Color Index page 105. Makes 2½ cups. 10 cals per tablespoon.
Begin 10 minutes ahead.

2 cups water
⅓ cup sugar
1 tablespoon grated
  orange peel
½ cup orange-flavor
  liqueur

1. Into 4-cup microwave-safe glass measure, pour water; add sugar and orange peel. Cook on High (100% power) 4 to 5 minutes, until sugar dissolves and mixture boils; stir twice.
2. Into orange mixture, stir orange-flavor liqueur until blended. Serve warm over fruit or ice cream.

CHERRY SAUCE

Color Index page 106. Makes 2 cups. 15 cals per tablespoon.
Low in cholesterol, sodium. Begin 5 minutes ahead.

1 pound sweet
  cherries, pitted
¼ cup sugar
1 tablespoon water
¼ teaspoon almond
  extract

1. In 8-cup microwave-safe glass measure, combine cherries, sugar, and water.
2. Cook cherry mixture on High 2 to 3 minutes, until sugar dissolves and mixture boils; stirring twice. Stir in almond extract. Serve warm over blintzes, waffles, or pancakes.

BLUEBERRY SAUCE

Color Index page 105. Makes about 1 cup. 26 cals per tablespoon. Low in cholesterol, fat, sodium. Begin 20 minutes ahead.

1 10-ounce package
  frozen blueberries
⅓ cup sugar
¼ teaspoon ground
  cinnamon
⅛ teaspoon ground
  nutmeg
⅛ teaspoon grated
  lemon peel
1 teaspoon lemon
  juice

1. In 8-cup microwave-safe glass measure, combine blueberries, sugar, cinnamon, nutmeg, and lemon peel. Cook, covered, on High (100% power) 5 minutes, or until sugar dissolves and blueberries are thawed. Uncover; stir. Cook on High 3 to 4 minutes longer, until blueberries pop and sauce thickens slightly.
2. Into blueberry mixture, stir lemon juice. Serve warm over poached peaches, fresh fruit, or ice cream.

FUDGE SAUCE

Color Index page 105. Makes 1¼ cups. 76 cals per tablespoon.
Low in cholesterol, sodium. Begin 10 minutes ahead.

¾ cup sugar
½ cup cocoa
½ cup heavy or
  whipping cream
4 tablespoons butter
  or margarine
  (½ stick)
1 teaspoon vanilla
  extract

1. In 8-cup microwave-safe glass measure, combine sugar, cocoa, and cream. Cook on High (100% power) 2 to 3 minutes, until sugar dissolves and mixture boils; stirring twice.
2. To mixture, add butter or margarine. Cook on High 2 to 4 minutes, until butter or margarine melts and mixture thickens slightly, stirring occasionally. Stir in vanilla. Serve warm over sautéed bananas or pound cake.

HARD SAUCE

Color Index page 106. Makes about ⅔ cup. 73 cals per tablespoon. Begin 5 minutes ahead.

3 tablespoons butter
  or margarine
1 cup confectioners'
  sugar
½ teaspoon vanilla
  extract

1. In 1-cup microwave-safe glass measure, place butter or margarine. Heat on High (100% power) 5 to 10 seconds, until softened.
2. Into butter or margarine, gradually beat sugar until creamy. Stir in vanilla. Serve over steamed pudding, warm fruit, or with mince pies.

MELBA SAUCE

Color Index page 105. Makes 1 cup. 33 cals per tablespoon. Low in cholesterol, fat, sodium. Begin 15 minutes ahead.

1 10-ounce package
  frozen raspberries
  in syrup
¼ cup red-currant
  jelly
4 teaspoons corn-
  starch dissolved in
  1 tablespoon cold
  water

1. In 8-cup microwave-safe glass measure, place raspberries and red-currant jelly. Heat on High (100% power) 5 to 6 minutes, until jelly melts and raspberries are thawed.
2. Into raspberry mixture, stir dissolved cornstarch. Cook on High (100% power) 3 to 4 minutes, until mixture boils and thickens; stir twice. Press mixture through fine sieve to remove seeds; discard. Serve warm over poached pears, or with peaches or ice cream.

COOKWARE

What can I use to keep butter or margarine and bacon from spattering when I cook them in my microwave?

Foods that tend to spatter during microwaving should be covered with absorbent paper towels, which soak up any fat but also allow the microwaves to penetrate and cook the food. Lightly moisten paper towels to cook food such as poultry, fish, and vegetables; wrap in the towel and then "steam" in the microwave.

I have been told that some paper towels are unsafe for microwave use. Is this true and, if so, which ones are they?

It is true that towels made of recycled paper are unsuitable for use in the microwave because they contain impurities, such as small amounts of metal, that may cause blue sparks (arcing).

There are now paper towels available on the market that are specially formulated for use in the microwave. These contain all-natural fibers and no artificial colors and they have been approved by the Food and Drug Administration for contact with food.

How can I be sure that my china bowl will not break during cooking before I actually use it for cooking in the microwave?

Place the bowl in the microwave beside a glass measure containing 1 cup cold water. Heat on High (100% power) 1 minute. If the bowl remains cool and the water in the measure is warm, the bowl is microwave-safe. If the bowl is hot, it has absorbed too much microwave energy for efficient cooking and should not be used.

Can I use plastic containers, measures, and bowls in the microwave?

Avoid using plastic containers, measures, bowls, and so on to microwave anything with a high fat or sugar content. For other foods, the safest plastic cookware to use is the specially formulated type labeled "microwave-safe."

Dishwasher-safe plastic containers can be used for brief reheating in the microwave. Plastic containers that hold ready-to-serve food from the store are generally considered to be unsafe because they may break or melt.

Which cookware is best used for microwaving desserts?

Desserts that have a high sugar or fat content reach very high temperatures during the cooking process and they should always, therefore, be cooked in microwave-safe glass measures or bowls, not plastic cookware.

Which cookware is recommended for microwaving sauces and gravies?

A microwave-safe glass measure is ideal for convenience and easy clean-up. Always use a measure that is able to hold twice the volume of the sauce or gravy to be cooked in it.

TECHNIQUES

How can I prevent chocolate from overcooking when I melt it in the microwave?

Melting chocolate in the microwave is almost risk-free. However, when chocolate is melted in the microwave, it retains its shape and you may not realize it is ready. When the chocolate loses its dull look and becomes shiny, that's your clue it is done; remove from oven and stir until smooth.

Why do my cakes overcook when done in the microwave?

If you remove cakes from the microwave when they *look* done, they will be overcooked and will become hard on standing. Cakes should look moist when removed from the microwave; they will spring back when lightly touched with a finger.

Standing time is necessary to complete the cooking process; after standing time, the cake will pull away from sides of pan and a toothpick inserted into the center will come out clean.

Why do my vegetables sometimes have dark spots on them when cooked in the microwave?

Salt may be the culprit. If you use salt, add it to vegetables after cooking, or dissolve it in the cooking liquid or sauce.

Q When I microwave eggs, I find the yolks are always tougher than they should be. How can I prevent this?

A Egg yolks contain more fat than egg whites, therefore they attract more microwave energy and cook faster. To avoid overcooking the yolk while waiting for the white to be done, you must remove the eggs before the whites are completely set and let stand for the time recommended in the recipe; this allows the white to finish cooking outside the microwave. Don't forget to gently prick yolks with a toothpick before cooking. This permits the steam to escape and prevents the egg from exploding during cooking.

Q When I scramble eggs in the microwave, I find the edges too set and hard while the center is still liquid. Why does this happen and how can I prevent it?

A Microwaves penetrate food to a depth of 1½ inches, thereby cooking the food nearest the edges of the dish first. To prevent this, push the cooked part at the edges toward the center of the dish before it is set completely, allowing the uncooked eggs to flow to the edges. Remove from oven while still moist. Eggs will complete cooking during standing time.

Q I find that after heating water in the microwave, it boils over when I add instant coffee, tea, or dry soup mix. How can I prevent this?

A Be sure to stir the water *before* heating it. This incorporates air into the liquid, which will prevent boil-ups from happening once cooking has started.

Q How can I keep my gravy from being lumpy, and the edge of the gravy from becoming too thick?

A Stir gravies and sauces frequently with a whisk or fork to obtain a smooth consistency throughout.

Q Why am I advised not to deep-fry food in the microwave?

A This potentially hazardous procedure is not recommended because the temperature of the cooking oil can climb rapidly in the microwave and the oil can suddenly burst into flames. In addition, microwave-safe cookware may not be able to withstand the intense heat and has been known to crack or explode.

Q My food seems to cool more quickly when it has been cooked in the microwave. Why?

A In the microwave, only the food gets hot from the cooking process — any warmth you feel in the dish has been transferred from the food. This is the opposite of what happens in a conventional oven, where the cooking heats up the dish first, then the food, and the hot dish keeps food warmer longer after it is removed from the oven.

To help keep microwaved foods warm, heat food that has been stored in the refrigerator an extra minute or so to give the cooking vessel time to warm. Cover foods while reheating or cooking to hold in warmth. At the table, wrap a covered dish in a pretty towel or quilted casserole holder, or keep warm on a warming tray.

Q How can I keep microwaved foods warm without retaining steam? I find crumb-coated chicken dishes get soggy if I use a cover.

A Casserole lids or plastic wraps hold in steam, which may make certain foods limp, such as breads, cakes, or anything with a crumb coating. To prevent this, cover these foods with waxed paper or paper towel, which holds in heat but not steam.

Q How can I make poultry, meat, and fish look as if it has been conventionally cooked?

A Make a sauce to rub on food before the start of cooking: In a glass measure, place enough butter or margarine to coat the food. Heat, covered with paper towel, on High (100% power) until butter or margarine melts. Stir in browning, teriyaki, soy, or Worcestershire sauce or a dash of bitters. For a zestier flavor, mix in mustard, taco sauce, or catchup.

To glaze poultry and give it a lovely golden color, brush with marmalade, apple jelly, or apricot preserves during cooking.

You can also brush meat, poultry, or fish with butter or margarine or beaten egg, milk, or water then coat with bread or corn-flake crumbs, herbs, shredded cheese, or onion-soup mix. There are also available specially formulated coating mixes with seasonings to complement the taste of meat, poultry, or fish.

How can I make breads, cakes, cookies, and piecrusts baked in my microwave look as if they were conventionally baked?

A For a baked appearance, choose recipes that call for molasses or brown sugar; alternatively, you can add ground allspice, cinnamon, or nutmeg to cake batter, or add a few drops of yellow food coloring or browning sauce to pastry for piecrusts. Try substituting whole-grain flour for part of the all-purpose flour in quick breads and muffins. For an attractive coating to conceal an underdone appearance, evenly sprinkle minced or chopped nuts or wheat germ on greased cake or loaf pan before adding batter or dough.

Toppings that add texture and flavor to confections include sugar, chopped nuts, ground cinnamon, frosting, and toasted coconut.

Q **When I make caramel in the microwave, I frequently find it burns. How can I prevent this?**

A Microwave the mixture just until the sugar is golden; it will continue to cook during its standing time outside the oven, and a deeper color will develop. A microwave-safe glass measure should always be used. Its handle makes pouring easier, and the special glass can withstand the high cooking temperature of sugar.

Q **How do you convert conventional recipes for use in the microwave?**

A Not all recipes can be converted for microwave cooking, but in general the following rules should be applied: Keep serving numbers small – up to eight at the most; reduce liquids, fat, and seasonings; use microwave-safe cookware; cut cooking time back to a quarter or a half of the conventional recipe time.

 What foods should be pierced before being cooked in the microwave, and why?

A Any food enclosed in a skin or membrane should be pierced to release steam and prevent the food from bursting during cooking. Pierce with a fork whole vegetables with skins, such as potatoes, tomatoes, squash, and peppers. Use a toothpick for anything with a delicate membrane, such as egg yolks or liver. Sausage casings should also be pierced with a fork or slashed diagonally with a knife.

 Why do cookbooks give a range of timings for microwave recipes?

A Good Housekeeping recipes are developed for 600- to 700-watt microwave ovens. The longer cooking time is for the 600-watt oven, the shorter for the 700-watt oven.

 My microwave has a different wattage from those used in most microwave recipes. How do I adjust the timing to give good results?

A If a recipe has been developed in a 600-watt oven, reduce the timing by 10 seconds per minute if you have a 700-watt oven and increase it by 15 seconds per minute if you have a 500-watt oven. This is a very general guide, so check the food frequently to prevent it from overcooking.

 I am instructed to rotate certain foods in the microwave. Why is this?

A In general, rotate foods that cannot be stirred such as lasagna, bread pudding, and so on. Get to know your oven's personality (cooking pattern) by observing how food cooks – for example, food may cook more quickly on one side than the other; if that happens, rotate the dish for more even cooking. Other foods that must be rotated in their dishes include fish that may be too delicate to move and cake batter that has to set. Rotate the dish in one direction only and keep track by marking the cookware with a dot. Place the dish in the microwave with the dot at the oven back. When a quarter turn is specified in the recipe, turn the dish so that the dot is at oven side; for a half turn, rotate the dish so that dot is at the oven front.

 How can I be sure that the microwave has cooked eggs thoroughly?

A An instant-read thermometer, available at cookware and hardware stores, will enable you to test the temperature of dishes that call for softly cooked eggs, and to make sure that the ingredients reach the temperature of 140°F. recommended by the FDA. In this book, all recipes containing softly cooked eggs are marked with an asterisk; see also USE AND CARE GUIDELINES FOR EGGS (page 137).

Q My microwave retains the smell of any strongly spiced dishes I cook, such as curry or chili con carne. How can I counter this?

A Be certain to wipe oven clean after each use with a damp cloth. Use a mild detergent when needed. For a quick oven refresher, pour ½ cup water into a 4-cup microwave-safe glass measure or bowl. Add one of the following fresheners: 2 slices fresh lemon, orange or lime, 1 tablespoon lemon juice, ¼ teaspoon ground cinnamon, 8 whole cloves with 8 whole allspice, or 1 teaspoon baking soda. Heat on High (100% power) 1 to 2 minutes, or until water boils. Your oven (and kitchen!) will smell fresh and clean.

To make the kitchen smell as though you have been cooking up a storm, try this oven pot-pourri: Into 1-quart microwave-safe glass measure, pour 1 cup warm water; add 2 teaspoons pumpkin-pie spice, or a few thyme sprigs. Heat on High (100% power) 3 minutes.

DEFROSTING AND REHEATING

 Q Since the microwave is so useful for reheating food, why am I advised not to reheat egg dishes?

A Most leftovers, such as meat and pasta dishes, reheat very well in the microwave, but delicate egg dishes will overcook if reheated.

The same principle applies when trying to reheat cheese dishes in the microwave; the cheese toughens and becomes stringy.

Q Is it a good idea to use the microwave for defrosting food from my freezer?

A Yes. Follow the directions in the guide that comes with your oven. In general, most small items can be defrosted by placing them in the microwave for a few seconds on High (100% power). Larger items are best defrosted, covered, on Medium-Low (30% power) or Defrost power level for several minutes at a time, then allowed to stand. They are briefly microwaved again, allowed to stand, and so on until defrosted. This standing time is very important when defrosting larger items because it allows the temperature to equalize throughout the food. Do not microwave until the center defrosts because the outer edges will start to cook; delicate parts of chicken and fish may have to be shielded with strips of smooth foil. Melted ice should be drained off at intervals. Food should be cooked immediately after defrosting in the microwave.

 Q How can I tell when an individual dinner reheated in the microwave is ready to serve?

A Allow about 2 minutes for 1 dinner plate of food. Heat, covered, on Medium-High (70% power). Remove from the microwave and feel the center bottom of plate. If it is warm, the food is ready to serve; if cool, cook, covered, 1 minute longer.

 Q When I reheat dinners, the center sometimes stays cold. How can I ensure even reheating?

A If food at edge of plate is hot while food at the center is not, cut out a doughnut-shaped piece of foil to place over the food, making sure that the foil is smooth and at least 1 inch away from oven walls. The center will then become hot while the edges will be shielded from microwaves.

Another solution, especially when reheating different types of food, is to arrange the denser foods, such as potatoes which take longer to heat through, at the edge of the plate, while leaving the more delicate foods, such as fish, in the center.

 Q What size container should I use for defrosting and cooking frozen food?

A Always use a dish that fits the food as closely as possible so the edges of the food do not melt, spread out over the bottom of a large dish, and burn before the center of the food is hot. Cover while defrosting to retain the heat.

 Q My family loves hamburgers, so I often make them up in bulk and freeze them. How can I use my microwave for speedier defrosting?

A Freeze the hamburgers with sheets of waxed paper between them. Defrost on Medium-Low or Defrost (30% power); discard the waxed paper as soon as possible, separate the still partially frozen hamburgers, and place in a single layer on a microwave-safe rack set in a baking dish. Using a rack prevents the hamburgers from stewing in their own juices, which could cause the surfaces to start cooking.

 Q When I reheat such baked goods as rolls or hamburger buns, they become dry. Am I doing something wrong?

A You are overcooking them. Baked goods should be *just* warmed through; otherwise they become dry and tough. Most breads reheat successfully in the microwave if they are wrapped in paper towels to absorb moisture. Heat rolls, hamburger buns, and bagels on High (100% power) 10 to 15 seconds.

The Index

Italic numbers indicate recipes with step-by-step illustrations

ACKNOWLEDGMENTS

Dorling Kindersley would like to offer a special thank you to Laurie
Orseck of William Morrow and Company for her professionalism and
good humor.

R. E. Schiffmann Associates, Inc. developed our fruit and vegetable
cooking charts. We are particularly grateful to Marthajean White for her
assistance in answering many queries. We would also like to give thanks to
Whirlpool Corporation for their assistance with the Blanching Vegetables
Chart on page 259.

Recipe nutrient analysis by Hill Nutrition Associates, Inc.

Photographers   Clive Streeter
    Karl Adamson

Home Economists   Lyn Rutherford
    Elizabeth Wolf Cohen

With thanks also to Karen Cochrane, Margaret Little, Eunice Paterson
and Sandra Schneider.